NEW ZEALAND

JAMIE CHRISTIAN DESPLACES

Albatross Point
Lake Rotorua
Whakatane
East Cape
Raukumara Forest Park
Raukumara Range
Opotiki
Rotorua
Tasman Sea
North Taranaki Bight
Hauhungaroa Range
Te Urewera National Park
Taupo
Lake Taupo
Whirinaki Forest Park
New Plymouth
Gisborne
Huiarau Range
Turangi
Cape Egmont
Egmont National Park
Kaweka Range
Tongariro National Park
Whanganui National Park
Wairoa
Morere
Opunake
Kaimanawa Ranges
Table Cape
Ohakune
Hawera
Hawke Bay
Ahuriri Point
South Taranaki Bight
Napier
Hastings
Wanganui
Ruahine Range
Ruahine Forest Park
Palmerston North
Golden Bay
Cape Turnagain
Abel Tasman NP
South Island
Tararua Range
Tararua Forest Park
Tasman Bay
Cook Strait
0
50 mi
Masterton
Upper Hutt
Picton
0
50 km
Nelson
Lower Hutt
Wellington
Mount Richmond Forest Park
Haurangi Forest Park
Cook Strait Ferry
Palliser Bay
Blenheim
3
4
5
1
2
6
32
35
38
45
57
60
63
© AVALON TRAVEL

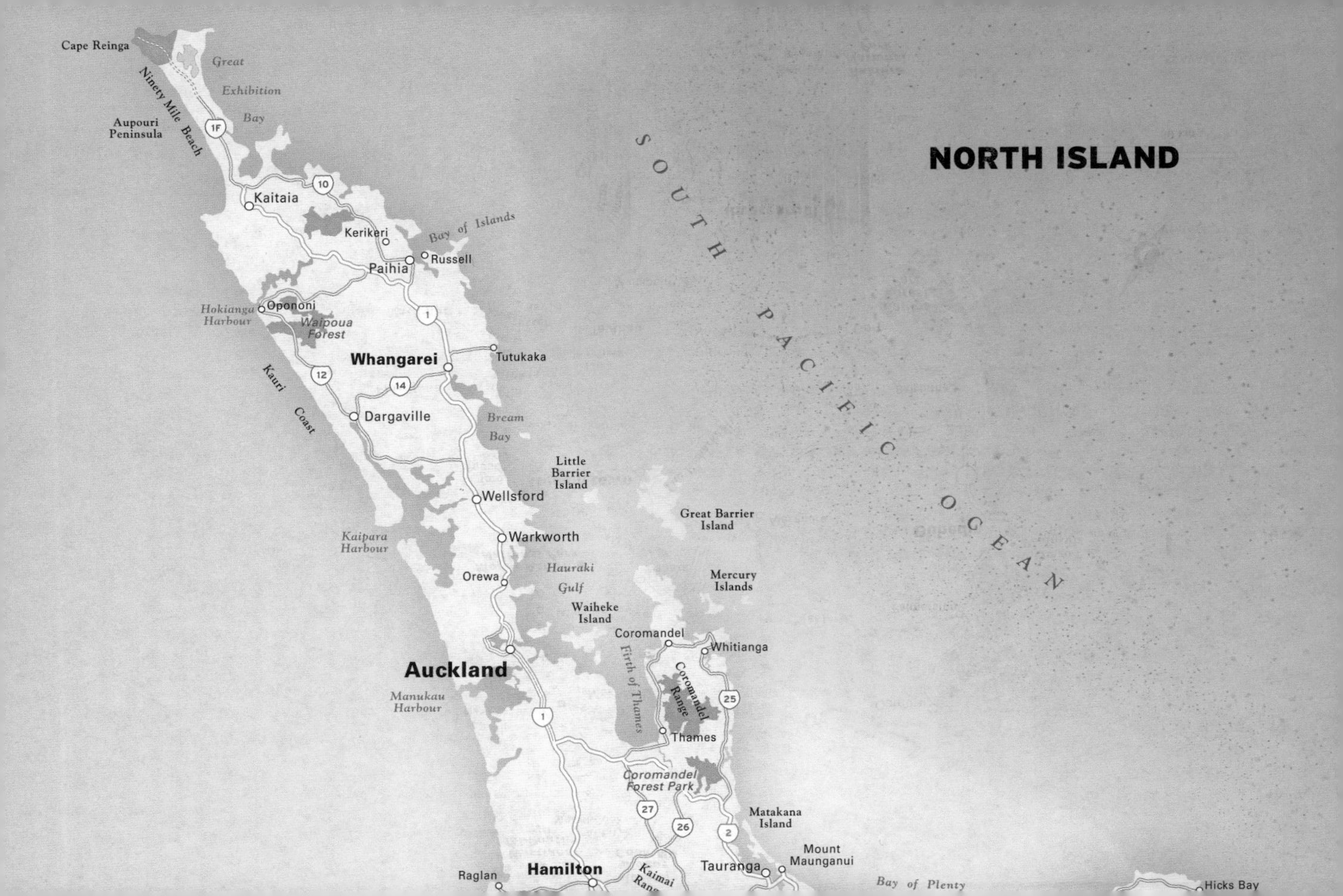

NORTH ISLAND

SOUTH PACIFIC OCEAN

Cape Reinga
Great Exhibition Bay
Ninety Mile Beach
Aupouri Peninsula
1F
10
Kaitaia
Kerikeri
Bay of Islands
Russell
Paihia
Hokianga Harbour
Opononi
Waipoua Forest
1
Whangarei
Tutukaka
Kauri Coast
12
14
Dargaville
Bream Bay
Little Barrier Island
Wellsford
Great Barrier Island
Warkworth
Kaipara Harbour
Hauraki Gulf
Orewa
Mercury Islands
Waiheke Island
Coromandel
Whitianga
Firth of Thames
Coromandel Range
Auckland
Manukau Harbour
25
1
Thames
Coromandel Forest Park
27
26
Matakana Island
2
Mount Maunganui
Raglan
Hamilton
Kaimai Range
Tauranga
Bay of Plenty
Hicks Bay

Tasman Sea
Fox Village
Westland Tai Poutini NP
Aoraki/ Mount Cook NP
Aoraki Mount Cook
Timaru
Southern Alps
Haast
Makarora
Lake Pukaki
Lake Ohau
Lake Benmore
Waitaki River
Omarama
Oamaru
Lake Hawea
Lake Wanaka
Wanaka
Palmerston
Mount Aspiring National Park
Harris Mtns
Alexandra
Otago Peninsula
Dunedin
Milford Sound
Queenstown
The Remarkables
Lake Wakatipu
Fiordland National Park
Franklin Mtns
Stuart Mtns
Murchison Mtns
Lake Te Anau
Te Anau
Balclutha
Gore
Catlins Forest Park
The Catlins
Manapouri
Lake Manapouri
Hunter Mtns
Cameron Mtns
Tuatapere
Invercargill
Riverton
Bluff
Te Waewae Bay
Foveaux Strait
Oban
Stewart Island
Rakiura National Park
0
50 mi
0
50 km
6
80
70
8
83
85
1
90
94

SOUTH ISLAND

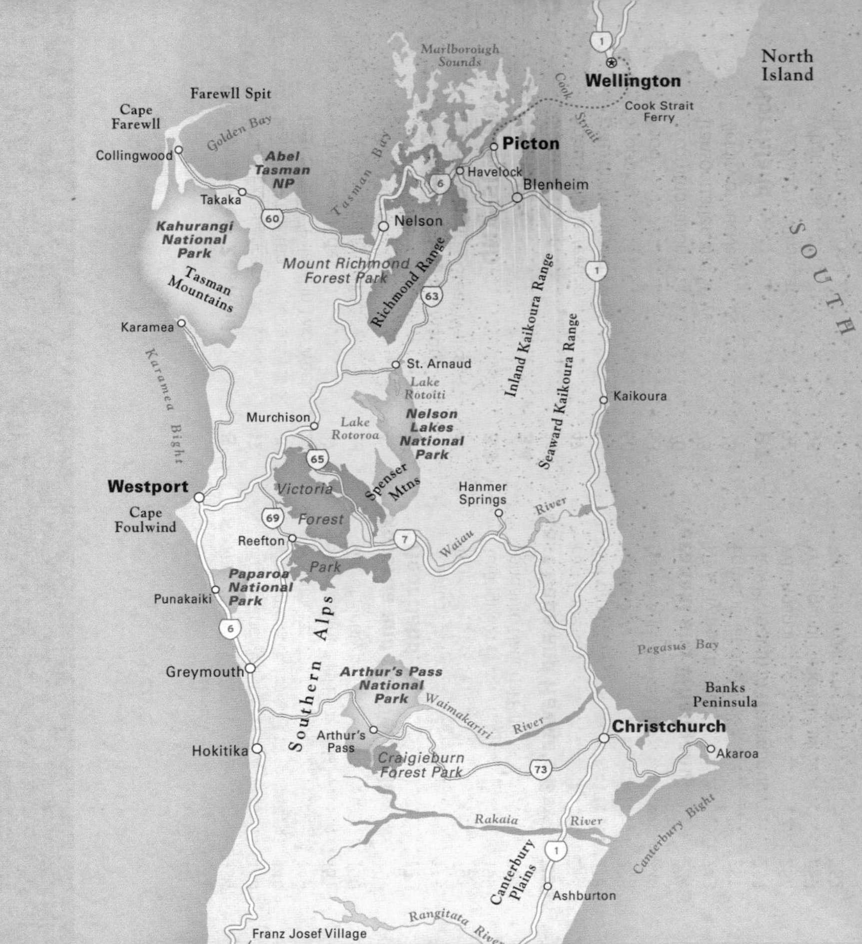

Contents

Discover New Zealand **8**
- 10 Top Experiences 12
- Planning Your Trip 20
- Best of New Zealand in Two Weeks... 24
- • The Great Rides................ 27
- Get Your Adrenaline Fix............ 28
- • Best Hikes 29
- Explore Middle-Earth 30
- • *Kia Ora:* Meeting the Maori....... 31
- • New Zealand's Great Walks 32

NORTH ISLAND................ **33**

Auckland **34**
- Sights 38
- Sports and Recreation............. 47
- Entertainment and Events.......... 53
- Shopping 60
- Food 63
- Accommodations 70
- Transportation and Services 75
- Vicinity of Auckland.............. 78

Northland **87**
- Auckland to Whangarei............ 92
- Whangarei....................... 95
- The Tutukaka Coast.............. 100
- Bay of Islands................... 103
- The Far North and Cape Reinga 116
- The Kauri Coast 124

Waikato, Bay of Plenty, and The Coromandel............ **129**
- Hamilton 134
- Raglan and Vicinity 140
- Waitomo 144
- Matamata 149
- The Coromandel Peninsula......... 151
- Bay of Plenty 160

Rotorua and the Volcanic Heartland.................. **171**
- Rotorua 175
- Taupo 191
- Turangi 199
- Tongariro National Park............ 202

East Cape and Hawke's Bay ... **210**
- East Cape 213
- Gisborne 218
- Te Urewera 223
- Napier and Hawke's Bay 226

Taranaki and Whanganui **238**
- New Plymouth 243
- Egmont National Park............. 251
- New Plymouth to Whanganui....... 254
- Whanganui 256
- Whanganui National Park 259
- Palmerston North 262

Wellington and Wairarapa **265**
- Wellington...................... 270
- The Kapiti Coast 289
- The Hutt Valley 293
- Wairarapa 295

SOUTH ISLAND ... **301**

Marlborough and Nelson ... **302**
- Picton ... 307
- Marlborough Sounds ... 310
- Marlborough Wine Region ... 315
- Kaikoura ... 319
- Nelson and Vicinity ... 324
- Abel Tasman National Park ... 331
- Golden Bay ... 335
- Nelson to the West Coast ... 340

Christchurch and Canterbury ... **344**
- Christchurch ... 349
- Akaroa and the Banks Peninsula ... 364
- Arthur's Pass National Park ... 367
- Lake Tekapo and the McKenzie District ... 372
- Aoraki/Mount Cook National Park ... 376
- Timaru ... 380

West Coast ... **383**
- Westport and Vicinity ... 386
- Paparoa National Park ... 392
- Greymouth ... 395
- Hokitika and Vicinity ... 398
- Westland Tai Poutini National Park ... 403
- Haast and Vicinity ... 411

Queenstown and Otago ... **414**
- Queenstown ... 419
- Wanaka ... 434
- Mount Aspiring National Park ... 440
- Central Otago ... 443
- Oamaru ... 446
- Dunedin ... 449

Fiordland and Southland ... **460**
- Te Anau and Vicinity ... 465
- Fiordland National Park ... 470
- Southern Scenic Route ... 477
- Invercargill ... 480
- The Catlins Coast ... 486
- Stewart Island ... 488

Background ... **492**
- The Landscape ... 493
- Plants and Animals ... 495
- History ... 498
- Economy and Government ... 502
- People and Culture ... 503

Essentials ... **506**
- Transportation ... 507
- Visas and Officialdom ... 511
- Recreation ... 512
- Accommodations ... 513
- Health and Safety ... 515
- Travel Tips ... 516

Resources ... **518**
- Glossary ... 518
- Suggested Reading ... 520
- Internet Resources ... 522

Index ... **524**

List of Maps ... **534**

DISCOVER

New Zealand

Legend has it that a Polynesian demigod by the name of Maui fished New Zealand's North Island from the depths of the Tasman Sea. Maui, it is said, sat battling his catch from the cocoon of his mighty South Island canoe, anchored beneath by Stewart Island.

This isolated nation, shrouded in mist and mystery and balancing precariously at the bottom of the globe, lends itself beautifully to such a romantic myth. The truth is that New Zealand's moody, mountainous islands are the summits of a submerged continent. And so New Zealand, known in Maori as Aotearoa ("the land of the long white cloud") straddles a pair of shifting tectonic plates. Subterranean activity forms its legendary landscape, from the highly volcanic zones in the north to South Island's alpine spine.

In this compact country, adventure awaits around every bend. The scenery morphs from brilliant green forest to blackened basalt in the blink of an eye. Snow-topped mountains stand guard over golden beaches brilliant with blue surf. And bubbling hot mud pools give way to the world's clearest lake. It's a land so dramatic and imposing, and yet so welcoming, it will make a lasting impression.

Clockwise from top left: Dunedin Railway Station; tui bird; Maori Marae decoration; Cathedral Cove; surfing in Tawharanui Regional Park; Hooker Valley Track.

Thanks in part to *The Hobbit* and *The Lord of the Rings* movies, the world is getting wise to what was once one of its best kept secrets. Part of you will wish it could stay that way, while another part realizes that such magic should not remain caged.

So *kia ora,* welcome to Middle-earth. Enjoy your journey. You'll never quite be the same again.

Clockwise from top left: New Zealand seafood; bungee jump above the Waikato River in Taupo; cycling near Queenstown; Auckland's Sky Tower.

SKYCITY

10 TOP EXPERIENCES

1 **Milford Sound:** This fabled fiord is home to sweeping glacial landscapes that give way to glassy black waters (page 473).

2 **Explore Waitomo Caves:** A sprawling network of underground caverns is lit by twinkling glowworms (page 144).

3 **Maori Culture:** Rich and vibrant Maori culture is evident throughout New Zealand (page 31).

4 **Watch Wildlife: Wild dolphins** (page 109) swim along the Bay of Islands, **little blue penguins** (page 446) waddle ashore in Oamaru, and **kiwis** (page 177) roam wild in national parks and wildlife reserves.

5 Hauraki Gulf: These glistening islands include the vineyard-stitched Waiheke Island, the wildlife sanctuary of Tiritiri Matangi, and the striking Rangitoto volcano (page 78).

6 Thrills and Spills in Queenstown: The birthplace of bungee jumping boasts world-class biking and hiking trails, ski slopes, paragliding, rock climbing, and jet-boating (page 419).

7 **Wai-O-Tapu:** This vibrant, volcanic landscape verges on the psychedelic (page 180).

8 Ride the rails on the *TranzAlpine*: This regal railway journey traverses South Island, taking in Christchurch, the Canterbury Plains, the Southern Alps, Arthur's Pass National Park, and the Otira rail tunnel (page 360).

9 Wineries and Breweries: The top wine-producing regions are **Marlborough** (page 315) and **Hawke's Bay** (page 229), while **Wellington** (page 280) bills itself as the craft beer capital.

10 **Great Walks:** These popular multiday treks showcase the nation's landscapes—ancient native bush, rugged coasts, glacial valleys, fiords, and volcanoes (page 32).

Planning Your Trip

Where to Go

North Island

AUCKLAND

Auckland is New Zealand's largest and most diverse city. Admire the world's largest collection of Maori artifacts at the **Auckland Museum** or bungee-jump off the 328m **Sky Tower.** The town hosts fun festivals, such as **Music in Parks** and **Taste of Auckland,** and is rife with sailing events like the weekly **Rum Races.** To get outdoors, you're never far from a beach, a park, or even a volcano.

NORTHLAND

There's plenty to enjoy in New Zealand's farthest northern region. Drive across the scenic sands of **Ninety Mile Beach** and explore forests of enormous 2,000-year-old kauri trees. There's swimming with dolphins in the **Bay of Islands,** not to mention visiting the site of the signing of the **Treaty of Waitangi,** New Zealand's founding document.

WAIKATO, BAY OF PLENTY, AND THE COROMANDEL

The Coromandel, North Island's sunny peninsula, harbors magnificent beaches beneath a majestic mountain spine. Here you can find caves lit by **glowworms,** beaches where you can dig your own **hot-spring spa** in the sand, a real-life hobbit village outside **Matamata,** and surf the beckoning waves at the hip town of **Raglan.**

ROTORUA AND THE VOLCANIC HEARTLAND

Many of New Zealand's best bits lie within this area. The country's geothermal heartland is the

Cape Reinga Lighthouse

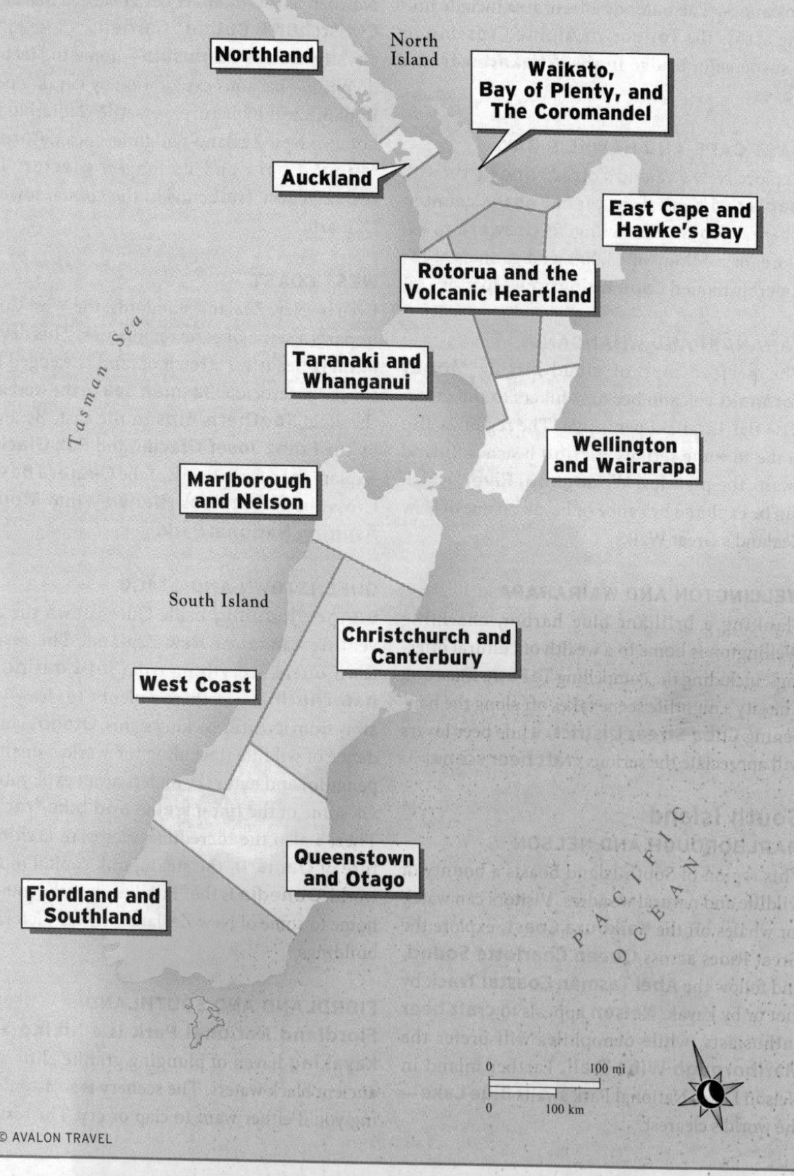
North Island
Northland
Waikato, Bay of Plenty, and The Coromandel
Auckland
East Cape and Hawke's Bay
Rotorua and the Volcanic Heartland
Taranaki and Whanganui
Tasman Sea
Wellington and Wairarapa
Marlborough and Nelson
South Island
Christchurch and Canterbury
West Coast
Queenstown and Otago
Fiordland and Southland
PACIFIC OCEAN
0
100 mi
0
100 km
© AVALON TRAVEL

result of some of the most highly tectonic activity on Earth. **Polynesian spas** and the volcanic sites of **Wai-O-Tapu** take advantage of the area's colorful sulfur springs, steaming mud pools, and volcanoes. The outdoor adventures include hiking across the **Tongariro Alpine Crossing** or a suspension bridge in the **Whakarewarewa Forest.**

EAST CAPE AND HAWKE'S BAY

Explore New Zealand's oldest **vineyards** with **Napier,** the art deco capital of the country. There's also the sprawling **Te Urewera** to explore, or a colony of 13,000 wild gannets at the superbly named **Cape Kidnappers** to visit.

TARANAKI AND WHANGANUI

The perfect cone of cloud-kissing **Mount Taranaki** volcano beckons hikers to the otherwise flat Taranaki peninsula. The region is also home to some serious **surfing** beaches. Inland awaits the mythical **Whanganui River,** which can be explored by canoe or kayak on one of New Zealand's Great Walks.

WELLINGTON AND WAIRARAPA

Flanking a brilliant blue harbor, charming Wellington is home to a wealth of cultural offerings, including the compelling **Te Papa** museum. The city's nightlife scene takes off along the happening **Cuba Street District,** while beer lovers will appreciate the serious **craft beer scene.**

South Island

MARLBOROUGH AND NELSON

This region of South Island boasts a bounty of wildlife and natural wonders. Visitors can watch for whales off the **Kaikoura Coast,** explore the Great Rides across **Queen Charlotte Sound,** and follow the **Abel Tasman Coastal Track** by foot or by kayak. **Nelson** appeals to **craft beer** enthusiasts, while oenophiles will prefer the **Marlborough Wine Trail.** Farther inland in Nelson Lakes National Park awaits **Blue Lake**—the world's clearest.

CHRISTCHURCH AND CANTERBURY

Still recovering from the enormous earthquakes of 2010 and 2011, Christchurch remains South Island's cultural capital and "Garden City." Nowhere is this moniker better earned that at the **Christchurch Botanic Gardens.** Close to the city, the **Banks Peninsula**—home to Hector's dolphins—beckons exploration by kayak. Poetic in name and by nature, versatile Canterbury is home to New Zealand's mightiest peak, **Aoraki/Mount Cook,** and its longest **glacier.** The **Alps2Ocean Trail** ends in the coastal town of Oamaru.

WEST COAST

Even by New Zealand standards, the West Coast imparts a sense of eerie remoteness. This devastatingly beautiful stretch of land is wedged between the ferocious **Tasman Sea** to the west and the stoic **Southern Alps** to the east. Be awed by the **Franz Josef Glacier** and **Fox Glacier.** Explore the cave network of the **Oparara Basin.** Cross the **Haast Pass Highway** into **Mount Aspiring National Park.**

QUEENSTOWN AND OTAGO

Bungee jumping made Queenstown the adventure capital of New Zealand. The resort town offers everything from **jet-boating** to **parachuting,** yet there's plenty to draw you away from its thrill-seeking sights. **Otago**'s abundance of wildlife (including the world's smallest penguin) and natural wonders await exploration via some of the finest **walks and bike tracks.** There's also the incredible Victorian architecture of **Oamaru,** the steampunk capital of the world. **Dunedin** is the "Edinburgh of the south," home to some of New Zealand's finest Victorian buildings.

FIORDLAND AND SOUTHLAND

Fiordland National Park is a **hiking** and **kayaking** haven of plunging granite cliffs and ancient black waters. The scenery is so astonishing you'll either want to clap or cry. The rest of

Southland is bordered by spectacular **beaches** so battered by Antarctic blasts that the trees grow bent over. But what draws everyone to this magnificent region are the fiords of **Milford Sound.**

When to Go

New Zealand lies in the southern hemisphere, and the seasons are reversed from those in the northern hemisphere.

HIGH SEASON

December-February is New Zealand's **summer** and its **peak season.** This is the time to come in order to make the most of **outdoor activities.** Tour operators, bars, and restaurants are open **extended hours** and **accommodations fill fast**—especially between Christmas and mid-January, when most Kiwis holiday.

SHOULDER SEASONS

September-November and **March-May,** destinations are quieter and the temperatures a little cooler, though there are still plenty of scorching hot days, depending where you visit. You'll have a greater chance of scoring some **great deals** on tours, attractions, and lodgings.

LOW SEASON

June-August is New Zealand's **winter** and is the **coldest** and **wettest** time of the year (except for parts of South Island). A visit is best avoided, unless you're into **snow sports.** There are **world-class ski hills** around Ruapehu on North Island and throughout the Southern Alps. Parts of the country, especially small hubs and coastal regions, go into hibernation and many attractions and services have **limited hours** (and some even close). However, hotels in winter sports hot spots such as **Queenstown** may charge high rates.

Know Before You Go

Passport and Visas

New Zealand has a visitor visa waiver agreement with the United States and Canada, as well as Australia and many European nations. **Passports** are required and must be valid for at least three months. Visitors must have an **onward ticket** and **funds** equivalent to $1,000 per month of stay.

Transportation

The only way of reaching New Zealand is to fly here. The majority of visitors fly into **Auckland International Airport** via **Air New Zealand.** Though New Zealand is a relatively small nation, its sights are spread out and isolated. Domestic flights and an excellent nationwide bus service offers a means to reach the main cities and attractions, but you'll need a shuttle bus to visit more remote sights—which is both inconvenient and expensive. Rail service is limited. Your best option is to **rent a car** or a **camper van**—you won't regret it. This country was designed for road trips.

Best of New Zealand in Two Weeks

Visitors should plan at least two weeks just to explore the highlights on North and South Island, with one week on each island. Fly into Auckland and begin your journey there. Consider renting a campervan to tour the country; holiday parks and campgrounds are cheap and plentiful. However, most highways are long, two-lane roads and driving distances are far. It's possible to cover greater distance in less time by taking domestic flights from Auckland to Wellington, or from Wellington to destinations on South Island.

North Island

Day 1: Auckland

Fly into **Auckland** and recover after your long flight. Check in to your hotel and then walk along **Queen Street,** stopping at **Aotea Square** to admire its carved *waharoa,* finishing your stroll at the water's edge. In town, dine alfresco on fresh seafood at **Soul Bar & Bistro** near the Viaduct while admiring the harbor yachts. At night, get your energy going at **Britomart,** home to the trendiest bars and eateries.

Day 2: Excursion to Waiheke Island

Take a ferry over to **Waiheke Island** for a half-day tour of the vineyards before heading back into town. If you're feeling brave, take the plunge

Aotea Square

Wellington's magnificent harbor

from atop of the **Sky Tower,** or simply soak up the views with a cocktail in the tower's **Sugar Club.** In the evening, head to **Ponsonby** and nearby Karangahape Road **(K' Road),** where swanky shops, ethnic eateries, and a smattering of LGBT-friendly venues await.

Day 3: Bay of Islands

Head north to the **Bay of Islands,** stopping in one of a collection of sleepy seaside settlements such as **Paihia,** where you can **swim with wild dolphins.** Don't leave without checking out the **Waitangi Treaty Grounds** and **Te Kongahu Museum**—the site where the Treaty of Waitangi was signed between Maori chiefs and the British Crown.

Day 4: Waitomo Caves

Stop in at the **Waitomo Caves,** a mind-blowing underground wonderland beneath the lush rolling farmlands of Waikato. The caves are adorned with **glowworms** and offer further adventures like **rappelling.** Surfers should spend the night in the hip surf town of **Raglan,** 90km northwest, and hit the waves in the morning.

Day 5: Rotorua

Two hours east of Waitomo, **Rotorua** literally fizzes thanks to volcanic activity, resulting in bubbling mud, steaming springs, and erupting geysers. Visit **Wai-O-Tapu** to experience the geothermal heartland, then soak in the waters of a Polynesian spa. When you're done exploring the volcanic wonders, check out a Maori cultural show at the **Tamaki Maori Village** and feast on a *hangi* for traditional Maori cooking.

Day 6: Tongariro National Park

Less than 2.5 hours southwest of Rotorua awaits the **Tongariro Alpine Crossing** in **Tongariro National Park.** One of the world's great day hikes, the spectacular route winds past three active volcanoes, including *The Lord of the Rings*'s "Mount Doom." If hiking is not your thing, head to **Lake Taupo** instead, where an extraordinary Maori artwork sits carved into the sheer rock above **Mine Bay.**

Day 7: Wellington

South of Rotorua, it's a long drive to **Wellington.** (Another option is to return your car rental and take a domestic flight from Auckland instead.) It would be easy to spend the day at the extraordinary **Te Papa** museum, but then you'd miss the **Zealandia** wildlife reserve, the **Wellington Cable Car,** and the **Botanic Garden.** Head to **Mount Victoria** for a spectacular sunset view. Once you've built up a thirst, quench it in the city's numerous **craft beer** joints. Tomorrow, you'll take the ferry from Wellington to Picton to begin exploration of South Island.

South Island

Day 1: Marlborough Sounds

Take the ferry from Wellington to **Picton** and start the morning with a coffee in the pretty seaside town, then take a walk or bike ride along the coastal **Queen Charlotte Track** to marvel at the **Marlborough Sounds.** As you head back, watch for dolphins. After your exercise, explore the abundance of first-class **wineries.**

Day 2: Abel Tasman Coast Track

Rent a kayak or book a tour to explore the **Abel Tasman Coast Track,** a Great Walk that can be explored by paddling ashore to numerous mainland beach landings. Head into the tiny port of **Mapua** to savor some craft beers.

Day 3: Kaikoura

A New Zealand must-do, the rich waters off **Kaikoura** are home to resident **sperm whales,** as well as a few other migratory species, dolphins, fur seals, and albatross. Book a cruise to see these majestic beasts up close.

Day 4: Christchurch

South of Kaikoura, **Christchurch** remains on the mend following two major earthquakes. It's still

kayaking along the coastline of Abel Tasman National Park

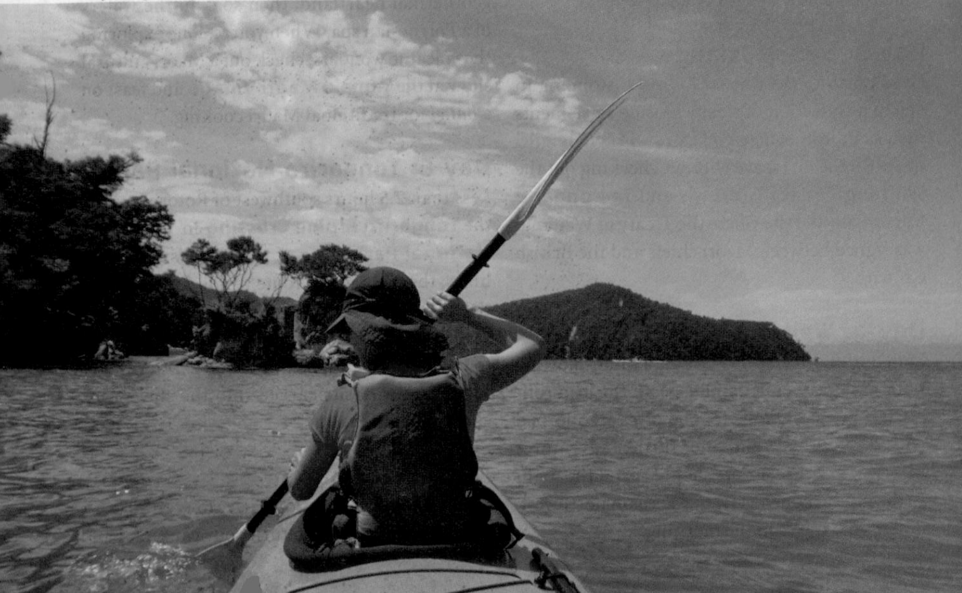

The Great Rides

New Zealand's iconic Great Rides are a nationwide network of predominantly off-road cycle trails.

Collectively called **The New Zealand Cycle Trail** (www.nzcycletrail.com), or Nga Haerenga ("the journeys"), the more than 20 tracks total 2,500km. They often follow old mining routes or disused railway lines that occasionally pass over viaducts and through pitch-black tunnels (bring a flashlight). There are grades for all levels of riders: Choose rides that last anywhere from a few hours to several days.

- **Alps2Ocean:** This 4-6-day ride begins at Aoraki and works its way from the Southern Alps across the Canterbury Plains to the coastal town of Oamaru (page 379).
- **Otago Central Rail Trail:** New Zealand's original Great Ride, this track runs for 150km through gorges and high-country sheep stations with the Southern Alps never far from view (page 445).
- **Queen Charlotte Track:** This 70km trail in the heart of the Marlborough Sounds can be combined with a scenic cruise (page 311).
- **Tasman's Great Taste Trail:** Set aside at least a day to tackle this 38-175km route that takes in Nelson's scenic landscape, plus several eateries, wineries, and breweries (page 328).

the Queen Charlotte Track

a cultural paradise, with wonderful **museums, art galleries,** and the **Christchurch Botanic Garden.** Squeeze in a drive to the scenic **Banks Peninsula,** where secluded beaches await—and you may spot dolphins or penguins. The historic French village of **Akaroa** is the perfect place to relax and refuel.

Day 5: Aoraki/Mount Cook National Park

On the way to **Aoraki** (Mount Cook), New Zealand's tallest peak, call in for breakfast at the **Astro Café** atop **Mount John** and enjoy 360-degree views over the **McKenzie District**—including the impossibly blue **Lake Tekapo.** The drive into **Mount Cook Village** alongside Lake Pukaki is mesmerizing, with Aoraki rarely out of view. Book a scenic helicopter flight over to **Franz Josef or Fox Glaciers,** where you can land on the ice. Explore some of **Aoraki/Mount Cook National Park** on foot via several short walks.

Day 6: Queenstown

There's enough fun in **Queenstown** to spend the entire two weeks here. The top of your list should be **bungee jumping** or **jet-boating** the Shotover River. Afterward, ride the **gondola** to Bob's Peak for views of Queenstown, Lake Wakatipu, and the Remarkables mountain range—it's one of New Zealand's most memorable vistas.

Day 7: Milford Sound

Save **Milford Sound,** New Zealand's most iconic sight, for last. Take a flight from Queenstown for an aerial view of **Fiordland National Park** before cruising or kayaking (or both) through Milford Sound. It's a long day, but cheaper, to travel by road—allow at least four hours to drive each way, or consider taking this lengthy winding journey by coach. Break it up with a night at **Te Anau,** 120km south of Milford Sound.

Get Your Adrenaline Fix

New Zealand bills itself as the adventure capital of the world. The nation that gave us commercial bungee jumping, the zorb, and the jet-boat is stitched together by thousands of kilometers of world-class hiking and biking trails, pounded by ferocious surf, and sliced by raging rivers. It is one big playground.

Bungee Jumping

Commercial bungee jumping began at Kawarau Bridge in **Queenstown,** home of the nation's highest bungee jump: the **Nevis** at a knee-trembling 134m. On North Island, the 47m **Lake Taupo** bungee is the country's highest water-touch jump.

Zip-Lining

There's no more joyous way to explore the forest canopy than dangling from a zip line. Discover the country's best in **Queenstown** and **Rotorua**.

Skydiving

New Zealand's wildly varied landscape makes for some stunning vistas from above. Choose from views over subtropical **Northland**, above

skydiving above Kaipara Harbour

Best Hikes

You don't have to undertake a multiday backpacking trip to get a taste of the country's fantastic hikes. Here's a selection of top treks than can be completed in a day or less.

- **The Pinnacles** (6 hours round-trip): Follow a pioneer gold-mining route to a 759m lookout from a collection of craggy fingerlike outcrops over the Coromandel Peninsula. If you time it to spend the night at Pinnacles Hut, you can watch the sun rise over the formations in the morning (page 152).
- **Tasman Glacier Lake Walk** (1 hour round-trip): At 27km, the Tasman Glacier is New Zealand's longest glacier. Check it out via the adjoining Blue Lakes and Tasman Glacier Lake Walk in Aoraki/Mount Cook National Park. Blue Lakes make for a refreshing dip in the summer (page 377).
- **Rob Roy Glacier** (3-4 hours round-trip): This hike in Mount Aspiring National Park is a fantastic. The trail rises through native bush for a couple of hours, then passes some impressive waterfalls before emerging in a clearing staggeringly close to the glacier—so abruptly that it seems to appear from nowhere (page 440).
- **Roy's Peak Track** (5-6 hours round-trip): Positioned near Wanaka, this iconic Kiwi trail has a mile-high summit that affords mesmeric views of Lake Wanaka and the Southern Alps including Mount Aspiring (page 436).
- **Tongariro Alpine Crossing** (6-8 hours round-trip): If you get a chance to do only one day hike, make sure it's this one (page 202).

Rob Roy Glacier

North Island **volcanoes**, or across the mountains and glaciers along **South Island**.

Caving and Canyoneering

Get your adrenaline pumping underground: Scramble over rocks and rappel down waterfalls in **Wanaka** or raft in the dark through the **Waitomo Caves**.

Surfing, Rafting, and Jet-Boating

There's plenty of decent surf around the Coromandel, Canterbury, and Bay of Plenty regions, but the west coast—especially **Raglan** and **Taranaki**—has the best waves. Whitewater rafting hot spots include the **West Coast**, **Lake Taupo**, and **Queenstown**—which all boast the best of jet-boating, too.

Hit the Slopes

It's called **zorbing** and it involves being inside a giant inflatable ball and slung down a hillside. **Rotorua** is the best place to test your mettle as a human bowling ball. Come winter, North Island's **Ruapehu** region and the slopes of the Southern Alps in **Canterbury** and **Otago** are transformed into premier ski fields.

Explore Middle-Earth

Tolkien aficionados might consider dedicating a few days to explore the numerous Middle-earth attractions. Most of the more accessible (and obvious) ones are clustered around the center of North Island. Movie locations on South Island are generally less-developed scenic landscapes scattered over a wide region and are often more difficult to reach.

If you'd rather leave the planning to others, **Great Sights** (www.greatsights.co.nz) offers a range of Middle-earth tours across both islands. **Moa Trek** (www.moatrek.com) visits a greater range of movie locations via hike or helicopter ride.

Hobbiton (the Shire)

The rolling green meadows of **Waikato** served as the Shire backdrop for *The Hobbit* and *The Lord of the Rings* movies. You can explore the original movie set by guided tour at **Hobbiton**, on the outskirts of Matamata. The tour ends with a cup of specially brewed cider at the Green Dragon.

Tongariro National Park (Mount Doom)

In **Tongariro National Park** stands Mount Ngauruhoe—otherwise known as "Mount Doom." It's easily viewable from the roads around the park; better still, hike past it along the **Tongariro Alpine Crossing**, a 6-8-hour hike that winds right under the peak. Even hiking an hour or so from Mangatepopo car park brings the volcano into view.

Wellington

Wellington is filled with Tolkien goodies. If you fly into **Wellington Airport,** you'll be greeted by Gollum as he catches a fish, along with an array of enormous movie props. The woods around **Mount Victoria** are where the hobbits ran from the Ringwraiths. **Kaitoke**

The Lord of the Rings' Mount Doom

Kia Ora: Meeting the Maori

Modern Maori trace their ancestry to the Polynesian population that arrived in New Zealand AD 1200-1300. Today, Maori culture, traditions, and language suffuse the country, offering visitors numerous opportunities to learn and engage. As you travel across New Zealand, use these sights and stops to enhance your knowledge and respect.

Visitors are most likely to arrive first in Auckland, so check out **Auckland Museum** (page 41) to marvel at the world's largest collection of Maori artifacts, including cloaks, weaponry, and carvings.

Don't miss the Bay of Islands' **Waitangi Treaty Grounds** (page 107), where Maori chiefs and the British Crown signed the Treaty of Waitangi in 1840. It's the founding document of modern New Zealand.

Rotorua is a lakeside city steeped in indigenous culture. Visit the **Tamaki Maori Village** (page 177), where you can witness cultural performances and sample a *hangi*—a traditional meal cooked in the earth.

The intricately carved ancestral house **Mataatua Wharenui** (page 167) in Whakatane marks one of the first Polynesian landing points.

The **Te Ana Maori Rock Art Centre** (page 380) in Timaru is home to a significant collection of Maori rock art. From here you can embark on a tour to nearby limestone cliffs adorned with ancient drawings.

For something more contemporary, check out the **Maori Rock Carvings** (page 191) at Mine Bay on Lake Taupo. These fantastic artworks rise 14m above the water and were chiseled by a master carver in 1970s. It is only viewable by boat.

Maori rock carving at Mine Bay

Regional Park, otherwise known as Rivendell, is lined with handy information boards around its trails detailing its cinematic history.

Fans should not miss a visit to **The Weta Cave and Workshop**, where most of the special effects used in the films were created.

One Ring to Rule Them All

In **Nelson,** visit the jewelers **Jens Hansen**, where the One Ring was made. (There were actually 40 rings made for the film, not just one.) Original rings are on display and replicas are available for sale.

New Zealand's Great Walks

Routeburn Track

Great Walks (DoC, www.doc.govt.nz, free) are premier, self-guided, multi-day trails that traverse some of New Zealand's most dramatic backcountry.

Great Walks range from 2-6 days, with 4-8 hours spent trekking per day. The season runs mid-October-April. Some walks can be completed year-round; however, walks through alpine environments—such as the Kepler and Milford Tracks—become impassible May-September due to adverse weather conditions and avalanche risk. Some of the treks, such as the Abel Tasman or Milford, may require a water taxi, while the Whanganui River journey takes place almost entirely on water.

Accommodations are usually in backcountry huts ($24-70 per night) or basic campsites ($6-20) and must be booked in advance through DoC (www.doc.govt.nz). Huts have bunks with mattresses, but no bedding, and include a water supply, a wood burner, and toilets. Some huts are also equipped with solar lighting and cook tops, and may have a DoC warden present.

A handful of operators offer guided tours along a selection of the Great Walks. Guests stay in high-end private lodgings that have private rooms with bedding, hot showers, and meals included—greatly reducing the amount of supplies to carry. Prices vary depending on the length of the walk, but generally begin around $1,500 per trek.

There are nine official New Zealand Great Walks, with a tenth (West Coast's Paparoa Track) due to open in 2019. From north to south, they are:

- **Tongariro Northern Circuit,** Tongariro National Park (page 203)
- **Lake Waikaremoana,** Te Urewera (page 224)
- **Whanganui Journey,** Whanganui National Park (page 259)
- **Abel Tasman Coast Track,** Abel Tasman National Park (page 331)
- **Heaphy Track,** Kahurangi National Park (page 339)
- **Routeburn Track,** Mount Aspiring and Fiordland National Parks (page 432)
- **Milford Track,** Fiordland National Park (page 470)
- **Kepler Track,** Te Anau (page 466)
- **Rakiura Track,** Steward Island (page 489)

North Island

Auckland

Sights 38
Sports and Recreation 47
Entertainment and Events 53
Shopping. 60
Food 63
Accommodations. 70
Transportation and Services 75
Vicinity of Auckland 78

Auckland boasts all of the trappings of a major city while overlooking a stunning harbor hemmed in by verdant, volcanic scenery. Nowhere else in New Zealand will you find such a colorful and cosmopolitan urban landscape.

For most visitors, Auckland will be the first stop. Attracted by New Zealand's legendary landscape, many afford the city only a cursory visit, taking in attractions such as the Sky Tower, the museums and art galleries, a few meals, and perhaps a hike up the majestic Rangitoto volcano. However, they miss the funky suburban streets where fine-dining eateries share space with craft breweries; the wild west coast of the Waitakere Ranges, where native rainforest gives way to black sand beaches; and the Hauraki Gulf islands, with world-class wineries and sanctuaries where endangered endemic species roam free.

This isthmus city stands stubbornly between the might of the Tasman Sea on the west and the Pacific Ocean to the east. Maori first named the settlement Tamaki Makaurau, a comment on the land's desirability. It's now more commonly referred to as the "City of Sails" thanks to its residents' love of those seas. There is simply no other metropolis quite like Auckland.

PLANNING YOUR TIME

Auckland is home to some of North Island's most jaw-dropping sights. Spend a **couple of days** acclimatizing and take in the central attractions of the **Sky Tower** and **waterfront** while sampling an array of exquisite eateries and bohemian bars. For a day trip, head across the harbor to picturesque **Devonport,** a seaside suburb on the North Shore. Even if you're only in town for a weekend or a day, visiting a volcanic island of the **Hauraki Gulf** is a must.

Previous: Auckland Museum; Auckland from the North Shore. **Above:** a colony of gannets at Murawai Beach.

Look for ★ to find recommended sights, activities, dining, and lodging.

Highlights

★ **Sky Tower:** The southern hemisphere's tallest structure boasts the best views as well as the highest dining and base-jumping in town (page 38).

★ **Auckland Museum:** The world's largest collection of Maori and Pacific artifacts is set on the ridge of a former volcano, now a sprawling city park (page 41).

★ **Sailing:** The City of Sails offers a raft of oceangoing adventures for novices or sea captains (page 48).

★ **Auckland Bridge Climb and Bungy:** Walk across—or leap from—Auckland's "coat-hanger" bridge (page 50).

★ **Waiheke Island:** The jewel of the sparkling Hauraki Gulf is a former bohemian haven where some of New Zealand's finest wines are made (page 79).

★ **Rangitoto Island:** Trek to the summit of this picture-perfect volcano, home to an array of native plantlife and birdlife (page 80).

★ **Waitakere Ranges:** The *Jurassic Park*-like forest reserve surrenders to beaches of volcanic black sand and ferocious Tasman waves (page 82).

★ **Waiti Bay:** Visit secluded, white-sand Tawhitokino Beach, which is only accessible at low tide (page 84).

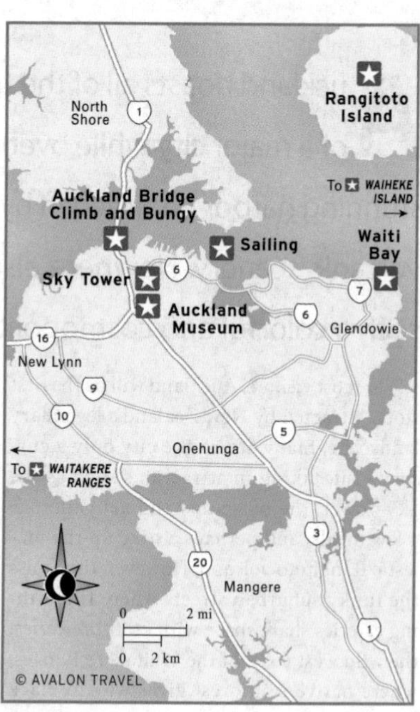

Auckland

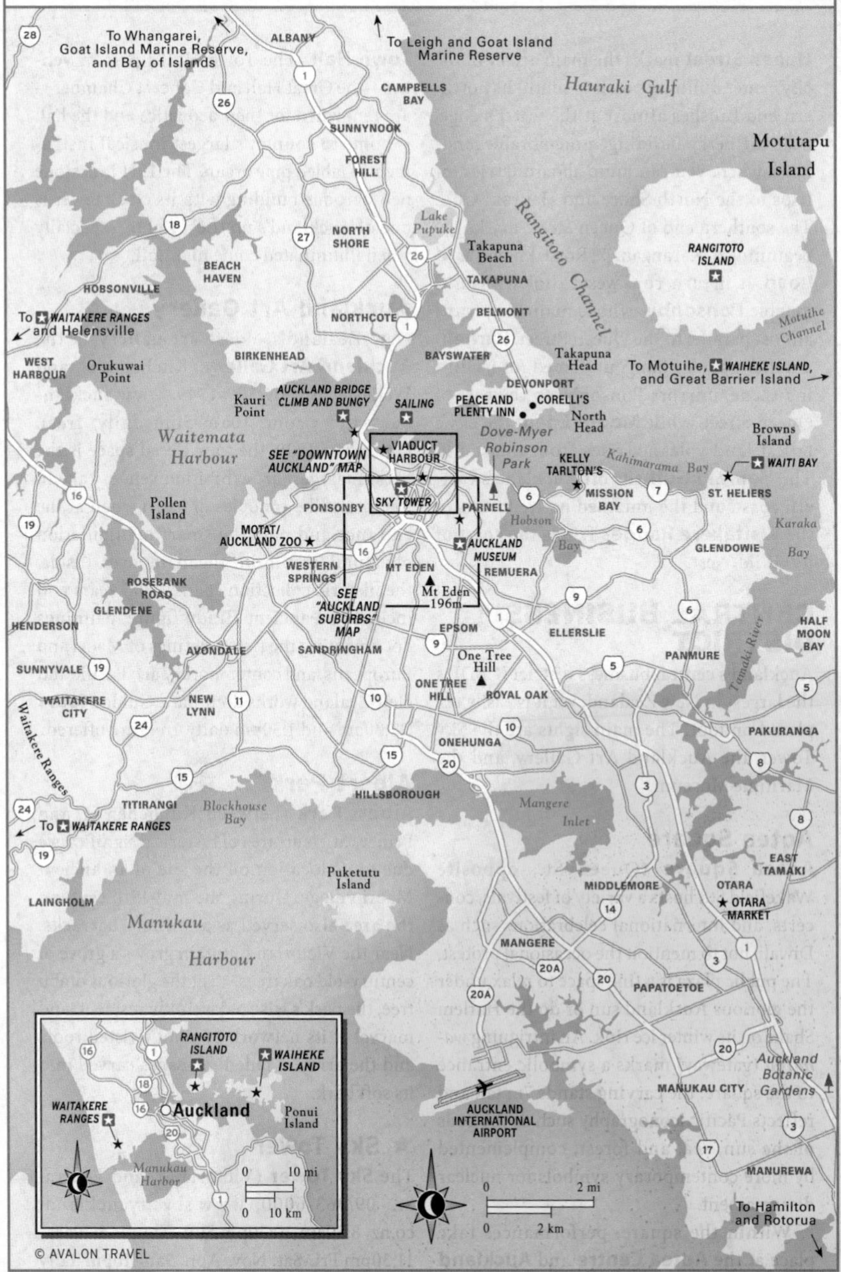
To Whangarei, Goat Island Marine Reserve, and Bay of Islands
ALBANY
To Leigh and Goat Island Marine Reserve
Hauraki Gulf
CAMPBELLS BAY
SUNNYNOOK
FOREST HILL
Motutapu Island
Lake Pupuke
NORTH SHORE
Takapuna Beach
Rangitoto Channel
RANGITOTO ISLAND
BEACH HAVEN
TAKAPUNA
HOBSONVILLE
To WAITAKERE RANGES and Helensville
NORTHCOTE
BELMONT
Motuihe Channel
WEST HARBOUR
Orukuwai Point
BIRKENHEAD
BAYSWATER
Takapuna Head
To Motuihe, WAIHEKE ISLAND, and Great Barrier Island
DEVONPORT
Kauri Point
AUCKLAND BRIDGE CLIMB AND BUNGY
SAILING
PEACE AND PLENTY INN
CORELLI'S
North Head
Waitemata Harbour
SEE "DOWNTOWN AUCKLAND" MAP
VIADUCT HARBOUR
Dove-Myer Robinson Park
KELLY TARLTON'S
Kahimarama Bay
Browns Island
WAITI BAY
SKY TOWER
MISSION BAY
ST. HELIERS
Pollen Island
PONSONBY
PARNELL
Hobson Bay
Karaka Bay
MOTAT/ AUCKLAND ZOO
AUCKLAND MUSEUM
GLENDOWIE
WESTERN SPRINGS
MT EDEN
REMUERA
ROSEBANK ROAD
SEE "AUCKLAND SUBURBS" MAP
Mt Eden 196m
GLENDENE
HENDERSON
EPSOM
ELLERSLIE
HALF MOON BAY
AVONDALE
SANDRINGHAM
One Tree Hill
PANMURE
Tamaki River
SUNNYVALE
ONE TREE HILL
ROYAL OAK
WAITAKERE CITY
NEW LYNN
PAKURANGA
Waitakere Ranges
ONEHUNGA
HILLSBOROUGH
TITIRANGI
Blockhouse Bay
Mangere Inlet
To WAITAKERE RANGES
EAST TAMAKI
Puketutu Island
MIDDLEMORE
OTARA
OTARA MARKET
LAINGHOLM
Manukau Harbour
MANGERE
PAPATOETOE
Auckland Botanic Gardens
MANUKAU CITY
AUCKLAND INTERNATIONAL AIRPORT
MANUREWA
To Hamilton and Rotorua
0 2 mi
0 2 km
RANGITOTO ISLAND
WAIHEKE ISLAND
WAITAKERE RANGES
Auckland
Ponui Island
Manukau Harbor
0 10 mi
0 10 km
© AVALON TRAVEL

Sights

Queen Street marks the main artery of the city center, running north to south. Its northern end finishes almost at the water's edge, near the Ferry Building, a memorable landmark where you can jump aboard ferries for trips to the North Shore and Hauraki Gulf. The southern end of Queen Street marks the beginning of Karangahape Road, known as **K' Road.** It, in turn, runs west to link with fashionable **Ponsonby,** whose main strip runs almost parallel to the Queen Street. **Parnell,** another popular hangout, famed for its dining scene, mirrors Ponsonby to the east of Queen Street, while **Mount Eden,** the city's tallest land volcano, rises from the south. The **Hauraki Gulf** sits off Auckland's eastern coast, and the untamed native forests of the **Waitakere Ranges** fringe the coast of its "Wild West."

CENTRAL BUSINESS DISTRICT

Auckland's central business district (CBD) is the largest in New Zealand, yet it is easily explored on foot. The main sights are the Sky Tower, the Auckland Art Gallery, and the Maritime Museum.

Aotea Square

Aotea Square (Queen St., opposite Wakefield St.) hosts a variety of festivals, concerts, and international celebrations such as Diwali, not to mention the occasional protest. The public plaza is a fine space to relax under the glorious Auckland sun or do the Harlem Shake on its winter ice rink. An intriguing *waharoa* (gateway) marks a symbolic entrance to the square; the carving stands 7m tall and reflects Pacific iconography such as the gods of the sun, sea, and forest, complemented by more contemporary symbols for nuclear disarmament.

Within the square, performances take place at the **Aotea Centre** and **Auckland Town Hall.** The Town Hall's pair of venues—the Great Hall and Concert Chamber—are renowned for their acoustics and the hall is home to country's largest musical instrument, a fabled pipe organ. The 1911 limestone neo-baroque building with its clock tower is one of Auckland's prettiest sights, especially when illuminated come nightfall.

Auckland Art Gallery

New Zealand's oldest art gallery is the **Auckland Art Gallery** (Kitchener St. and Wellesley St., 09/379-1349, www.aucklandartgallery.com, 10am-5pm daily, free). Opened in 1888, the four-tiered space is the nation's largest art exhibition venue. Take in the forest-like canopies of kauri wood at the entrance and note the smart manipulation of natural light inside the main foyer. Inside, the historic collection spans 1,000 years and includes an ancient Hindu figure, paintings documenting the first meetings of Maori and Europeans, and contemporary art; Pacific and New Zealand works dominate. Guided **tours** (11:30am and 1:30pm daily, free) are offered.

Albert Park

Albert Park (between Kitchener St. and Princes St.) is an area of historical significance due to its location on the site of an ancient Maori village. During the mid-19th century, the area also served as a military barracks. Near the Victorian fountain grows a grove of century-old oak trees. Visit the glorious ombu tree, the park's wise old wrinkly resident, and marvel at its network of giant twisted roots and the array of faded messages carved into its soft bark.

★ Sky Tower

The **Sky Tower** (Victoria St. and Federal St., 09/363-6000, www.skycityauckland.co.nz, 8:30am-10:30pm Sun.-Thurs., 8:30am-11:30pm Fri.-Sat. Nov.-Apr., 9am-10pm daily

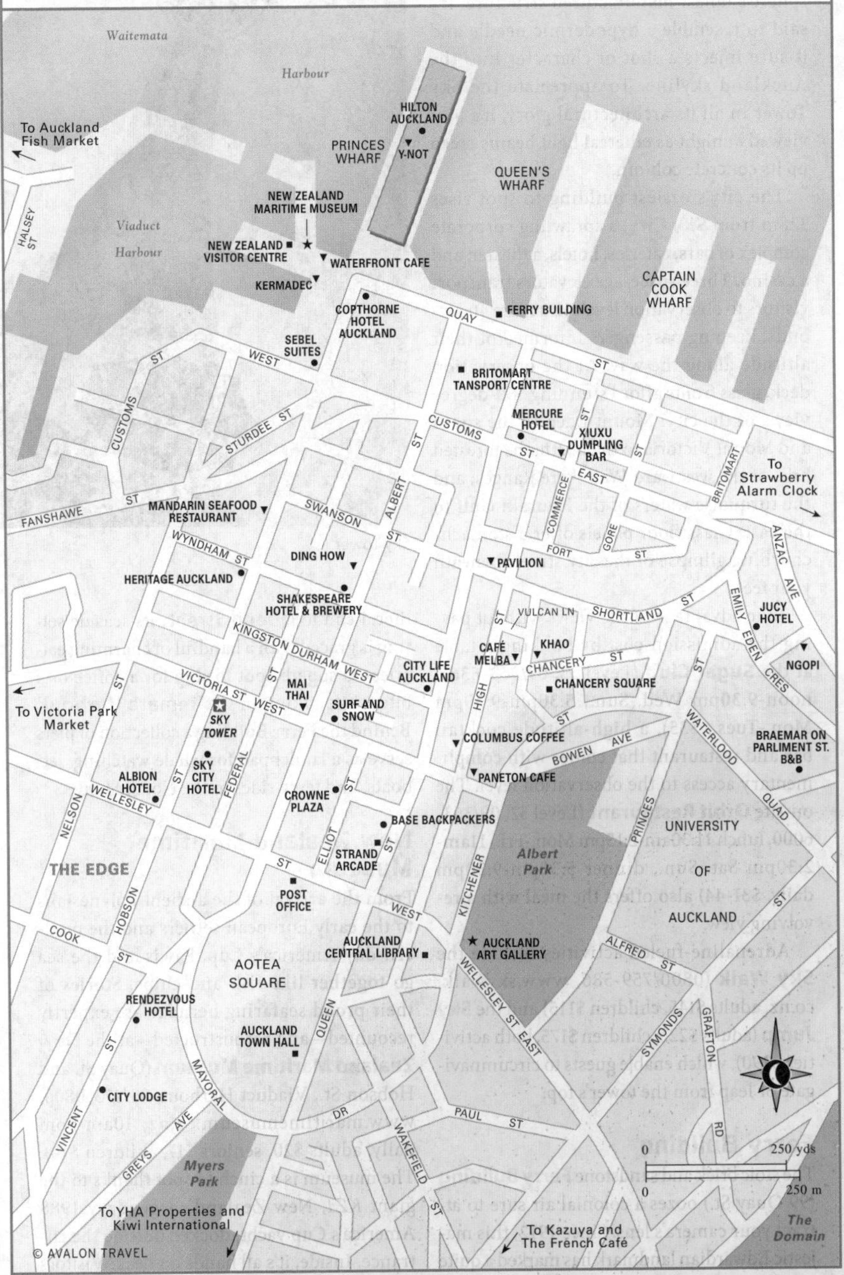
Downtown Auckland
Waitemata
Harbour
To Auckland Fish Market
HILTON AUCKLAND
PRINCES WHARF
Y-NOT
QUEEN'S WHARF
NEW ZEALAND MARITIME MUSEUM
Viaduct
Harbour
NEW ZEALAND VISITOR CENTRE
WATERFRONT CAFE
KERMADEC
CAPTAIN COOK WHARF
COPTHORNE HOTEL AUCKLAND
FERRY BUILDING
QUAY
SEBEL SUITES
WEST
BRITOMART TANSPORT CENTRE
CUSTOMS
STURDEE ST
MERCURE HOTEL
XIUXU DUMPLING BAR
EAST
COMMERCE
BRITOMART
To Strawberry Alarm Clock
FANSHAWE
MANDARIN SEAFOOD RESTAURANT
SWANSON
ALBERT
WYNDHAM ST
DING HOW
FORT
GORE
PAVILION
ANZAC AVE
HERITAGE AUCKLAND
SHAKESPEARE HOTEL & BREWERY
VULCAN LN
SHORTLAND
EMILY
JUCY HOTEL
KINGSTON DURHAM WEST
CAFÉ MELBA
KHAO
CHANCERY
EDEN CRES
NGOPI
VICTORIA ST WEST
CITY LIFE AUCKLAND
MAI THAI
CHANCERY SQUARE
To Victoria Park Market
SKY TOWER
SURF AND SNOW
HIGH
WATERLOO
COLUMBUS COFFEE
BRAEMAR ON PARLIMENT ST. B&B
SKY CITY HOTEL
FEDERAL
BOWEN AVE
PANETON CAFE
ALBION HOTEL
WELLESLEY
NELSON
CROWNE PLAZA
QUAD
BASE BACKPACKERS
PRINCES
UNIVERSITY OF AUCKLAND
THE EDGE
ELLIOT
STRAND ARCADE
Albert Park
KITCHENER
POST OFFICE
HOBSON
COOK
AUCKLAND ART GALLERY
AUCKLAND CENTRAL LIBRARY
AOTEA SQUARE
ALFRED ST
WELLESLEY ST EAST
RENDEZVOUS HOTEL
QUEEN
SYMONDS
GRAFTON
AUCKLAND TOWN HALL
MAYORAL
CITY LODGE
DR
PAUL ST
RD
VINCENT
GREYS AVE
WAKEFIELD
Myers Park
0 250 yds
0 250 m
To YHA Properties and Kiwi International
To Kazuya and The French Café
The Domain
© AVALON TRAVEL

May-Oct., adults $28, seniors $22, children $11, under age 5 free) is the southern hemisphere's tallest manufactured structure. It's said to resemble a hypodermic needle and it sure injects a shot of character into the Auckland skyline. To appreciate the Sky Tower in all its architectural glory, it's best viewed at night as ethereal light beams creep up its concrete column.

The city's easiest building to spot rises 328m from **Sky City,** a sprawling corporate complex of bars, eateries, hotels, a theater, and a casino. Three space-age elevators transport visitors to observation levels in a mere 40 seconds, keeping passengers informed of their altitude along the way. At the observation deck, glass fronts afford stunning 360-degree views of the city: Mount Eden to the south and Mount Victoria to the north; the forested hills of the westward Waitakere Ranges; and the turquoise waters of the Hauraki Gulf to the east. Glass floor panels offer a stomach-churning glimpse of the city streets beneath your feet.

Sky Tower

Take advantage of the views without paying the admission cost by booking a table at the **Sugar Club** (Level 53, 09/363-6365, noon-9:30pm Wed.-Sun., 5:30pm-9:30pm Mon.-Tues., $35), a high-altitude cocktail bar and restaurant that comes with complimentary access to the observation level. The on-site **Orbit Restaurant** (Level 52, 09/363-6000, lunch 11:30am-2:15pm Mon.-Fri., 11am-2:30pm Sat.-Sun., dinner 5:30pm-9:30pm daily, $31-44) also offers the meal with a revolving view.

Adrenaline-fueled activities include the **Sky Walk** (0800/759-586, www.skywalk.co.nz, adults $145, children $115) and the **Sky Jump** (adults $225, children $175, both activities $290), which enable guests to circumnavigate or leap from the tower's top.

Ferry Building

The stoic brick and sandstone **Ferry Building** (99 Quay St.) oozes a colonial air sure to attract your camera's lens. Since 1912, this majestic Edwardian landmark has marked a quite literal end to **Queen Street.** Its seaside setting is graced with a handful of charming eateries—a superb spot to stop for a coffee or a bite while taking in **Waitemata Harbour.** Behind the Ferry Building a collection of piers serve as a launchpad for whale watching, jetboats, and ferry rides to the North Shore.

New Zealand Maritime Museum

From the arrival of the ancient Polynesians to the early European settlers and the modern-day America's Cup, Kiwis and the sea go together like fish-and-chips. Stories of their proud seafaring heritage are expertly recounted—and reconstructed—at the **New Zealand Maritime Museum** (Quay St. and Hobson St., Viaduct Harbour, 09/373-0800, www.maritimemuseum.co.nz, 10am-5pm daily, adults $20, seniors $17, children $10). The museum is a cinch to spot thanks to the giant *KZ1*, New Zealand's legendary 1988 America's Cup yacht, docked outside the entrance. Inside, it's all hands on deck: Visitors

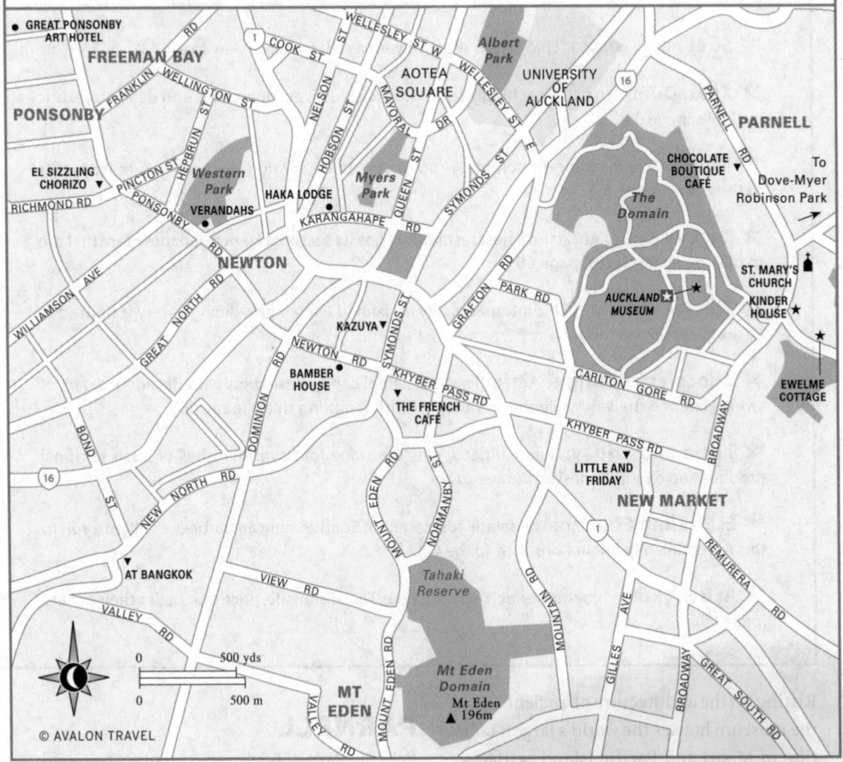

are able to design a yacht, hoist some sails, and test out their sea legs in the rocking steerage cabin of a Victorian ship. Free guided tours (10:30am and 1pm Mon.-Fri.) are given, or hop aboard a fully restored heritage scow for an authentic tour of Auckland from the sea (adults $50, seniors $40, children $25, includes museum entry).

THE DOMAIN

The Domain (Domain Dr., entrance off Park Rd., Grafton) was the city's first park. The Domain sprouts from the fertile soils of one of Auckland's oldest volcanoes, the 100,000-year-old Pukekawa (Maori for "hill of bitter memories," in reference to historic intertribal battles). The park sprawls more than 75ha, with multiple access points. The entrance on Domain Drive guides you past the tranquil lair of the **Wintergarden** (9am-4:30pm daily Apr.-Oct., 9am-5:30pm Mon.-Sat., 9am-7:30pm Sun. Nov.-Mar., free), an idyllic Victorian oasis of greenhouses and hot-houses with fascinating native flora and tropical plants. Outside, friendly ducks float amid a sizable pond. Relax and watch the show with ice cream from the adjacent **Wintergarden Café** (09/354-3360, www.wintergardenpavilion.co.nz, 8am-4pm daily).

★ Auckland Museum

Nestled on the rim of the crater at the Domain's highest point is the graceful **Auckland Museum** (Auckland Domain, 09/309-0443, www.aucklandmuseum.com, 10am-5pm daily, adults $25, children $10).

Best Food

★ **Soul Bar & Bistro:** Enjoy fresh seafood with a sunny harbor view (page 63).

★ **XuXu Dumpling:** This achingly cool Asian oasis delivers dumplings and delicious exotic cocktails (page 63).

★ **Ngopi:** This magnificent volunteer-run Malaysian eatery donates a portion of its profits to the needy (page 63).

★ **Kazuya:** One of Auckland's best restaurants boasts seasonal French-Japanese fare that are to plated masterpieces (page 66).

★ **The French Café:** This internationally acclaimed French fine-dining eatery is housed in an art gallerylike setting (page 66).

★ **Chocolate Boutique Café:** This old-school candy store drips with decadence. Jars of sweets line the shelves, while the menu brims with tempting treats (page 66).

★ **Little and Friday:** Minimal decor sets the stage for flavorful dishes of fresh seasonal produce and exquisite desserts (page 67).

★ **El Sizzling Chorizo:** The scintillating scent of South American barbecue will lead you to this Argentinian haunt in Ponsonby (page 68).

★ **At Bangkok:** Enjoy authentic, unpretentious Thai dishes at a price that belies their quality (page 69).

Riffing on the architecture of ancient Greece, the museum houses the world's largest collection of Maori and Pacific Island artifacts as well as sobering memorials honoring fallen soldiers of both world wars. Exhibits include fossil displays and a simulated eruption of Rangitoto as viewed from a mock seaside home that shakes and shudders at the "blast," causing kids to shriek and parents to adopt an air of sometimes unconvincing nonchalance.

Bookings are essential for the hour-long museum-wide **Highlights Tour** (09/306-7048, 10:45am, 12:45pm, and 2:15pm daily, adults $40, children $20) and recommended for the **Maori Cultural Performance** (11am, noon, and 1:30pm daily Apr.-Oct., 11am, noon, 1:30pm, and 2:30pm daily Nov.-Mar., adults $45, children $20), which affords a fine familiarization with Maori traditions, culminating in a performance of the legendary *haka* dance (adults $55, children $25).

PARNELL

Pristine Parnell is a wonderful place to spend a lazy afternoon sauntering along its fashionable establishments. Among its white timber constructions sits an array of beautifully preserved heritage buildings befitting its "city village" vibe, where it's easy to forget a bustling CBD hums just a few kilometers away. But it wasn't always this way for Auckland's oldest suburb. By the mid-20th century, it had fallen into a state of such disrepair and was earmarked for major redevelopment. Les Harvey, a well-known and much loved local character, bought a great swathe of the buildings and reinvented them as the heart of Parnell Village, attracting similarly sentimental proprietors hell-bent on preservation. In 2014, a **bronze statue** was unveiled in Harvey's honor beside Antoine's Restaurant (333 Parnell Rd.).

Best Accommodations

★ **Haka Lodge:** The new kid on Auckland's hostel block has raised the bar for city-center budget boarding (page 70).

★ **Braemar on Parliament:** Ever wondered how the colonial rich lived? Find out at this B&B, set in the central business district's last Edwardian townhouse (page 71).

★ **Nautical Nook:** All aboard for a mid-price marine stay near the beach. Weather permitting, you'll even get a free sailing trip on your host-cum-skipper's yacht (page 72).

★ **Verandahs:** Auckland's best backpacker hostel is set in stylish Victorian wooden villas a short stroll from Auckland's trendiest bars and eateries (page 72).

★ **Great Ponsonby Art Hotel:** Bursting with color and drenched in happy vibes, the hotel is a stone's throw from the swankiest strip in the city (page 73).

★ **Bamber House:** This spacious, sociable setup in underrated Mount Eden is just minutes from the mighty volcanic lookout (page 73).

★ **Peace and Plenty Inn:** A resplendent lodging crafted from iconic native kauri wood, everything about Peace and Plenty whispers class (page 74).

★ **Takapuna Beach Holiday Park:** Pitch a tent for one of the best views in town, right on the shoreline of the Hauraki Gulf (page 74).

St. Mary's Church

The imposing Holy Trinity Cathedral may physically overshadow **St. Mary's Church** (St. Stephens Ave. and Parnell Rd., 09/303-9500, www.holy-trinity.org.nz), but aesthetically it can't compete with its Gothic neighbor, which is one of the largest wooden churches in the world. The timber theme continues inside, where guests can marvel at beams of native kauri along with pews and a pulpit of English oak, all of which serve to enrich a sense of history. The religious house once resided on the other side of the road, and a collection of photos show its big move across the street in 1982.

Kinder House

The **Kinder House** (2 Ayr St., 09/379-4008, www.kinder.org.nz, noon-3pm Wed.-Sun., donation) was commissioned by legendary New Zealand bishop George Selwyn. Constructed in 1857, the striking gray stone exterior comes courtesy of Rangitoto's volcanic rock and is surrounded by original oak, totara, and bay trees. Inside the heritage dwelling, a gallery exhibits works of 19th-century artist John Kinder, including watercolors and photographs.

Ewelme Cottage

Travel back in time at **Ewelme Cottage** (14 Ayr St., 09/524-5729, www.heritage.org.nz, 10:30am-4:30pm Sun., adults $8.50, children free). Constructed in 1864 from native kauri wood, this historic house is a freeze-frame of Victorian life thanks to seemingly untouched furnishings and everyday items such as knitting needles. Original artworks and thousands of 19th-century books and sheets of music are all encircled by well-preserved colonial gardens.

Dove-Myer Robinson Park

At the northern end of Parnell, **Dove-Myer Robinson Park** (85-87 Gladstone Rd.)

Sitting on a Volcanic Field

New Zealand is nicknamed "Shaky Isles" due to its regular tremors and the odd major earthquake, but in Auckland, it's all about the volcanoes. A number of the city's historic buildings were constructed using volcanic rock; this volcanic rock also accounts for the great swaths of black-sand beaches along its west coast.

The Auckland Volcanic Field comprises approximately 50 cones covering 360sq-km, the first of which erupted 250,000 years ago. A number of major lava flows stretched for 10km. The last eruption occurred 600 years ago, relatively recent by geological standards, thrusting the spectacular Rangitoto Island from the sea. Human footprints found in its ash are believed to belong to Maori living on the adjoining island of Motutapu, one of Auckland's oldest cones.

Visitors need not worry about getting caught in any ash clouds, but scientists estimate there to be a 1 in 1,000 chance of an eruption in any given year, and an 8 percent probability of one over an average human lifetime. If a volcano were to blow its top, we'd likely have plenty of warning.

cradles the iconic **Parnell Rose Gardens** (24 hours daily, free) where 5,000 roses bloom boldest October-April. North of the park, the grassy slopes tumble down into **Judges Bay,** a secluded sandy beach out of place on the city-center fringe.

ORAKEI

Kelly Tarlton's Sea Life Aquarium

The well-regarded **Kelly Tarlton's Sea Life Aquarium** (23 Tamaki Dr., 09/531-5065, www.kellytarltons.co.nz, 9:30am-5pm daily, adults $39, seniors $30, children $22, under age 2 free) has been a tourist hot spot since 1985. The aquarium is home to the world's largest sub-Antarctic penguin colony display, which includes a spectacular view of their underwater antics. Discover a superb replica of Captain Scott's Antarctic Hut adorned with authentic memorabilia, watch stingray feed, and admire an impressive collection of seahorses. Walk through the underwater tunnel, where you can get even closer to the sharks and their marine mates with a **cage snorkel** (1pm and 2:30pm Thurs.-Tues., $99).

While a great option on a rainy afternoon, the aquarium is no substitute for the wealth of wildlife you'll encounter in the country. A free shuttle bus—shaped like a great white shark—departs opposite the **Ferry Building** (172 Quay St., hourly 9:30am-3:30pm daily, free) for the 6km ride west to Orakei. Book aquarium tickets online to avoid the lengthy queue.

PONSONBY

Storied Ponsonby, widely touted as the hippest hangout in Auckland, is one of its earliest inner-city suburbs. The main strip is awash with galleries, cafés, bars, trendy stores, and top-notch eateries. Resplendent **Ponsonby Central** (136/138 Ponsonby Rd., 09/376-8300, 7am-10:30pm Sun.-Wed., 7am-midnight Thurs.-Sat.), a food marketplace with a few boutiques, serves as a microcosm of the suburb's best bits. Stalls of inviting organic produce and cured meats sit alongside barrels of craft beer. A few blocks south is **Western Park** (5-7 Ponsonby Rd.), where local artist John Radford's sculptures of semi-buried structures set a postapocalyptic scene.

WESTERN SPRINGS

Western Springs Park

Charming **Western Springs Park** (731 Great North Rd., Grey Lynn) surrounds a natural spring-fed lake that served as one of the city's first water supplies. It was originally noted by Maori for its fertile resources and abundance of eels, a traditional food. Fittingly, a free-to-enter open wildlife sanctuary now thrives throughout the reserve; famous residents include black swans, rabbits, koi carp, and eels.

Three Days in Auckland

DAY 1

Fill your stomach with a wholesome breakfast at **Federal Delicatessen** before heading out to **Waiheke Island** for the half-day **Taste of Waiheke Tour** to take in vineyards, a craft brewery, and an olive grove, with complimentary tastings and a light lunch. Back on the mainland, head to **Sky Tower** for spectacular views and a sunset cocktail at the sky-high **Sugar Club,** then continue the evening with a seafood dinner at **Soul Bar and Bistro** overlooking the **Viaduct.** If there's still time, finish off the night in a **Waterfront** bar or head to the fashionable establishments of **Britomart.**

DAY 2

Begin the day with breakfast at the picturesque **Wintergarden Café** in **Auckland Domain** before wandering through the **Wintergarden.** Spend a few hours strolling **Auckland Museum,** home to the world's biggest collection of Maori and Pacific artifacts, before lunch at **Parnell 149.** Then get out on the water for the afternoon on an **America's Cup Sailing Experience, Auckland Sea Kayaks tour,** or hop on a ferry to historic **Devonport.** Close the day in **Ponsonby** with its endless choice of bars, clubs, and eateries. **Ponsonby Central** is a good place to start.

DAY 3

Forget the hangover, get up early to catch a sunrise from **Mount Eden** before heading to the delightful **La Cigale French Market** for breakfast and consider grabbing some French bread and cheese for a picnic lunch on the black sands of **Piha Beach** in the **Waitakere Ranges.** Alternatively, if you'd rather stay closer to home, make for the happy-go-lucky seaside suburb of **Mission Bay.** Later, grab a casual dinner at any of **Kingsland**'s fantastic eateries before craft beers and live music at the **Portland Public House** or **Flight 605** for Sunday night gigs.

A kids play area sits among an array of native trees, plants, and winding paths—an ideal environment in which to put some hide-and-seek skills to the test. The park is 5km from the center of Auckland.

Auckland Zoo

Adjacent to Western Springs Park, **Auckland Zoo** (Motions Rd., Western Springs, 09/360-3805, www.aucklandzoo.co.nz, 9:30am-5.30pm daily Sept.-Apr., 9:30am-5pm daily May-Aug., adults $28, seniors $23, children $12, under age 4 free) houses exotic species such as African lions, orangutans, and Asian elephants alongside homegrown talent like kiwis, tuatara, and lesser short-tailed bats. The hundreds of animals on-site are kept in precincts cultivated to mirror their natural habitats, such as the Pridelands, the African savanna (viewed from an elevated boardwalk), and the muddy waters of the Elephant Clearing. The zoo is renowned for its high standards of animal care and conservation programs.

Museum of Transport and Technology

At the **Museum of Transport and Technology** (MOTAT, 805 Great North Rd., 09/815-5800, www.motat.org.nz, 10am-5pm daily, adults $16, children $8, under age 5 free), visitors can hitch a ride on a working tram to explore the country's largest collection of antique land, sea, and air vehicles. An incredible permanent display of World War II airplanes includes one of the last Lancaster bombers in existence.

MOUNT EDEN

Known as **Maungawhau** (250 Mt. Eden Rd., 7am-8:30pm daily summer, 7am-7pm daily winter, pedestrians 24-hour access, vehicle parking available), Auckland's tallest city volcano rises to 196m, providing a panoramic view of the CBD skyline and the Hauraki Gulf. Make your way to the eastern side of the volcanic cone via a short well-trodden trail for a bird's-eye view of the Domain and to appreciate Auckland Museum in all its majesty. The volcano once served as a fortified Maori village, or *pa*, and sheltered many hundred people on its slopes.

You'll find water features, rock formations, and merrily chirping native birds in the aptly named **Eden Garden** (24 Omana Ave., Epsom, 09/638-8395, www.edengarden.co.nz, 9am-4pm daily, adults $8, under age 12 free), a sanctuary in the remnants of a quarry on the volcano's east flank. While flora blooms year-round, visit in spring when the tulips make for a sensory treat. The scenic oasis affords splendid city views. There's a café on-site.

One Tree Hill

Auckland is full of surprises. The extinct volcano of **One Tree Hill** (670 Manukau Rd., Royal Oak, 7am-8:30pm daily summer, 7am-7pm daily winter, 24-hour pedestrian access) is one of the best. This 182m monolith was formerly New Zealand's mightiest *pa*, serving populations thousands-strong.

Maori named the peak Te Totara-i-ahua, after the single totara tree that once sprung from its soil. In 1852 the tree was cut down by settlers and replaced by imported pine that became the subject of attacks by Maori activists. In June 2016, a grove of native trees, including totara, were planted in its place.

From the summit protrudes an **obelisk** (named Maungakieie) to honor the Maori people. Sir John Logan Campbell, a Scottish immigrant known as the "Father of Auckland," lies buried nearby. In 1901, Sir John donated the sprawling farmland that surrounds the volcano to the city. Upon the vast verdant slopes of **Cornwall Park,** herds of free-roaming livestock still graze, just 8km from the city center.

STARDOME OBSERVATORY AND PLANETARIUM

Stardome Observatory and Planetarium (09/624-1246, www.stardome.org.nz, 10am-5pm Mon-Fri., 11am-11pm Sat., 11am-10pm Sun.) has a small gallery and exhibit that complements the wonderful planetarium shows (6pm-9:30pm Tues.-Thurs., 6pm-9:30pm Fri., hours vary Sat.-Sun., adults $12-15, children and seniors $10-12). After the celestial screening, you may be invited to view some powerful

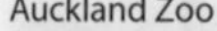

Auckland Zoo

telescopes. Tuesday nights are reserved for guests over age 18 and feature cheese and wine with laser shows set to the music of Led Zeppelin or Pink Floyd.

Auckland Botanic Gardens

The award-winning **Auckland Botanic Gardens** (102 Hill Rd., Manurewa, 09/267-1457, www.aucklandbotanicgardens.co.nz, 8am-8pm daily Oct.-Mar., 8am-6pm daily Apr.-Sept., free) is worth the 20-minute drive from the city. An abundance of native plants share the soil with exotic imports at the African Plants Garden, while the Edible Plants Garden is sure to impart plenty of culinary inspiration. Bountiful bird life, sculptures, and walks round off the soothing setting.

DEVONPORT

Just a 15-minute ferry ride from downtown is the sleepy Victorian suburb of Devonport, the jewel of the North Shore. One of the city's best-preserved and prettiest regions, it also affords a knockout view of the city skyline over the harbor. **Cheltenham Beach,** on the eastern end of the headland, offers white sands and tranquility and an uninterrupted view across the Hauraki Gulf to Rangitoto.

Maori first recognized Devonport's potential in the 14th century, using the cone of Takarunga—or Mount Victoria—as a *pa*, as they did with Maungauika, its sister volcano to the east. Today, it's home to the **North Head Historic Military Site** (Takarunga Rd., Cheltenham Beach, www.doct.govt.nz, vehicle access 6am-8pm daily, pedestrians 10pm-close daily, free). Once the nation's greatest historical coastal defense site, this interactive museum now serves as an example of its military past. Long abandoned guns and fortifications can easily be explored and even clambered over. An array of signage and images, along with a video presentation, offer in-depth insight. There have been whispered rumors of secret passageways, buried airplanes, and lost ammunition stashes, but it's unlikely you'll stumble across any. The views more than make up for that.

Sports and Recreation

BEACHES

The vibrant seaside suburb of Mission Bay hosts Auckland's most popular beach—**Mission Bay Beach** (Tamaki Dr.). Just 15 minutes from downtown, it feels like another universe thanks to a long white sandy stretch that surrenders to the calmest of waters from which the island of **Rangitoto** rises in the distance. To the back of the sands is a palm-lined boulevard of bars and eateries from fine dining to fish-and-chips.

A couple of kilometers closer to town is **Kohimaramara** (Tamaki Dr.), a relatively uninhabited beach that offers a similarly spectacular scenic view. Though there are few shops nearby, there are toilets and barbecues and plenty of shady, grassy areas. Just a couple of kilometers on from the other side of Mission Bay sits **St. Heliers,** a lovely seaside suburb on a much smaller and quieter scale. Around the city are a handful of sandy retreats. Parnell's **Judges Bay** (Judges Bay Rd.) is a wonderful secluded cove with a safe swimming spot complete with pontoons. **Sentinel Beach** (Sentinel Rd.) in Herne Bay is unknown even to many Aucklanders.

On the North Shore, **Takapuna** is the biggest summertime draw. The coastal suburb sports a long white sandy stretch and plenty of socializing options post-sunbathing. Devonport's quieter **Cheltenham Beach** slopes to soothing currents ideal for swimming and has a cinematic view of Rangitoto.

BOATING AND WATER SPORTS

★ Sailing

Aucklanders love to boast that they have the highest rate of boat ownership per capita in the world. While that's difficult to prove, just a brief stroll past the jungles of masts at the marinas demonstrates that Auckland is well deserving of its "City of Sails" moniker. Visitors should not leave without partaking in this great national pastime at least once. The **America's Cup Sailing Experience** on an authentic America's Cup yacht is just one of a handful of oceangoing expeditions offered by the **Explore Group** (09/359-5987, www.exploregroup.co.nz, 11am or 2pm daily Nov.-Mar., 1pm daily Apr.-Oct., adults $170, children $120). Novices are welcome on the two-hour voyage, though children must be over age 10. Would-be sailors learn to take the helm and hoist the mainsail, all under the watchful eye of a professional sailing crew. Alternatively, simply sit back with the wind on your face and enjoy the salty spray and city skyline from Waitemata Harbour.

There's no such optional idling on the smaller vessels of Auckland's legendary **Rum Races** (Westhaven Marina, 09/360-5870, www.westhaven.co.nz). Skippers from Auckland's yacht clubs seek a volunteer crew for weekly semi-competitive regattas that traverse the length of Waitemata Harbour and back. Duties include racing from one side of the boat to the other to counter-balance the yacht when it leans into a turn, and maybe manning some ropes. It's all heaps of fun and yes, there is rum. The trade-off for your toil is a free voyage—though turning up with a few cold beers for your crewmates will certainly stand you in good stead. Spaces fill fast, especially in summer. Races are held Thursday and Friday afternoon.

Cruises

Fullers (09/367-9111, www.fullers.co.nz) is the main point of call for sight-seeing trips around the Hauraki Gulf—the 90-minute **Auckland Harbour Cruise** (10:30am and 1:30pm daily, adults $42, children $21) is the best option for those pushed for time.

The **Auckland Whale and Dolphin Safari** (09/357-6032, www.awads.co.nz, adults $160, children $105) is a 4.5-hour eco-cruise through the Hauraki Gulf Marine Park aboard a 20m luxury boat with a fully licensed bar. The sighting of bottlenose and common dolphins is a given, while orcas and other whales are spotted in spring and summer.

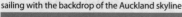

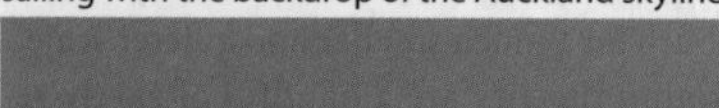
sailing with the backdrop of the Auckland skyline

Auckland and the America's Cup

The America's Cup is the most glamorous competition of what is the most glamorous of sports, and also the oldest sporting competition on earth. The sailing event is, rather confusingly, named after the first yacht to have won it, rather than the country where the yacht was built (the competition was born in Britain anyway), while the actual trophy is known as Auld Mug.

In 1995, led by legendary yachtsman Sir Peter Blake, the little island nation of New Zealand stunned the sailing world by securing an America's Cup victory over the Americans in their own backyard. Five years later the Kiwis became only the second team ever to retain the sea-faring crown (the USA was the other).

Winners of the cup win the right to host their defense in their own nation, and so it was that Team New Zealand's victories led to some major redevelopment in and around Auckland's Waitemata Harbour, most significantly at the Viaduct, in preparation to welcome the world's yachting elite.

New Zealand's 1988 America's Cup boat, *KZ1*, is on display outside the Maritime Museum. It was nicknamed the "Aircraft Hanger" due to its enormous size.

Kayaking and Jet-Boating

The greatest way to savor the splendor of the Hauraki Gulf is with **Auckland Sea Kayaks** (09/213-4545, www.aucklandseakayaks.co.nz, from $135). Kayaks can more easily reach the islands that are less frequented by the ferries. A plethora of guided and self-guided tours range from half-day to multiday, with equipment (camping gear and gourmet food) included. The **Rangitoto Sunset Tour** concludes by kayaking back from Rangitoto Island under the stars.

For those wanting something a lot faster, let **Auckland Adventure Jet** (Pier 3A, Quay St., 021/37-9155, www.aucklandadventurejet.co.nz, hourly 9am-5pm daily, adults $98, children $58) turn the city into a blur at speeds of more than 50 knots in the country where the jet-boat was invented. Plastic ponchos are provided to protect you from the inevitable.

Fishing

Your best bet to bring back a decent catch is to book with **Megabites Fishing Charter** (09/444-7710, www.megabitesfishing.co.nz, 7am-2pm $120 pp, 4pm-8pm $95 pp, bait $20, rods $20). These guided fishing tours have half-day, full-day, and extended full-day options, and can ferry you as far as the outer Hauraki Gulf Islands. Snag some snapper and kahawai, then call ahead at **Billfish Café** (3/31 Westhaven Dr., St. Mary, 09/379-9875, www.billfishcafe.co.nz, 7:30am-5pm Mon.-Tues., 7:30am-8:30pm Wed.-Sun., 7:30am-4pm Sun.). If they're not too busy, the chef will fillet and serve your fish (for a fee) while you kick back in contemplation with an ice-cold brew.

Contact Westhaven's **Pier Z** (Westhaven Marina, 09/360-5870, www.westhaven.co.nz) for a variety of budget water excursions, including skippered tours, stand-up paddleboarding, kitesurfing, and fishing.

Surfing

Auckland's "Wild West" coast is an iconic surf location with a handful of surf schools with boards for hire. For novices, **Elements Surf** (108 Piha Rd., Piha, 0800/000-985, www.elementssurf.com, Thurs.-Mon. $200, Tues.-Wed. $160) provides three-hour lessons and a chance to explore the coastal region. Return transport to Auckland is included.

Swimming

Parnell Baths (Judges Bay Rd., Parnell, 09/373-3561, 6am-8pm Mon.-Fri., 8am-8pm Sat.-Sun., adults $6.40, seniors $4.90, under age 16 free) offers a splendid saltwater pool.

While away an afternoon in pleasant surroundings, complete with a café, spa, and aqua playground.

AIR SPORTS

Experience the highest tandem jump in the North Island (up to 16,500 feet) with **Skydive Auckland** (0800/921-650, www.skydiveauckland.com, $295-425). An ultimate view follows the ultimate rush thanks to a 75-second freefall at more than 200km/h. Once the chute pops and the screaming stops, you can savor views of the Pacific Ocean and Tasman Sea of Auckland's east and west coasts, along with the rainforests, volcanoes, and downtown. Splurge for photo and video ($129-189) of your jump, or pay for a separate camera operator to jump with you ($299). A free shuttle ferries guests to the take-off point in Parakai, 45 minutes from the city. Jumps are available all year, weather permitting.

Auckland Bridge Climb and Bungy

★ Auckland Bridge Climb and Bungy

Thrill-seekers can get within touching distance of the Auckland Harbour Bridge via the **Auckland Bridge Climb and Bungy** (09/360-7748, www.bungy.co.nz, climb $125, bungee $165). The climb is not as terrifying as it sounds—there's no climbing, for a start. Instead, clipped-on visitors have the chance to traverse the arch of the bridge and take in (but not take photos of) the mesmeric sea- and cityscapes. Alternatively, you can head straight for the waves via the 40m bungee jump from the bridge. Both activities are organized by AJ Hackett, the company that created commercial bungee.

Sky Tower

A higher walk and a jump (albeit a controlled one) await around two-thirds of the way up the Sky Tower. Don a fetching jumpsuit then try to stop your knees from knocking as you walk around the outer ledge of the Sky Tower for the **Sky Walk** (0800/759-586, www.skywalk.co.nz, adults $145, children $115).

Visitors can go one step farther—literally—from the edge of the ledge for the 192m plunge of the **Sky Jump** (adults $225, children $175, combined Sky Jump and Sky Walk $290), which blends bungee and base jumping. You'll be strapped up then strapped on to a fixed vertical wire that runs down the outside of the tower before being ushered to lean over the city skyline and place your trust in that line. Next comes the 11-second fall at a speed of 85km/h. Don't be fooled by the controlled element of the plunge; it still takes guts to step off the southern hemisphere's tallest building.

If taking a step into thin air is too much, hand over the controls to a stranger instead. Be propelled 60m upward at speeds of 200km/h encased within the slingshot-like **Sky Screamer** (Victoria St. and Albert St., 09/377-1328, www.skyscreamer.co.nz, 9am-10pm Mon.-Thurs., 10am-2am Fri.-Sat., 10am-10pm Sun., 2-3 people $100-120). Ever wondered what it's like to experience 5 gs of force? Your stomach will tell you about it later.

City Walks

The **Auckland Free Walking Tours** (89 Quay St., www.aucklandfreewalkingtours.co.nz, 10am daily, free) presents well-established urban strolls. The three-hour walks take in all the major highlights. No bookings are necessary, but donations are welcome. The following walks are self-guided.

HERITAGE HIKE

Beginning at the historic **Ewelme Cottage** on Ayr Street, Parnell, head north past **Kinder House** before taking a right onto **Parnell Road.** You'll soon pass the imposing **Holy Trinity Cathedral,** next to which sits the Gothic structure of **St. Mary's Church,** one of the world's largest wooden churches. Continuing downhill on Parnell Road, stop to take a snap of the bronze statue of **Les Harvey,** creator of the "City Village," before browsing the charming collection of Kiwi arts and crafts in the **Elephant House.** From here continue north then take the first left onto Gibraltar Crescent then right onto Ngahere Terrace, which will lead you into **Auckland Domain.** Make for the botanical wonderland of the **Wintergarden** before grabbing an ice cream from **Wintergarden Café** and settling by the lake. If you still have the energy, you're practically on the doorstep of **Auckland Museum.** This 2km walk will take around 35 minutes without stops.

CENTRAL STROLL

Head to the back of St. Kevin's Arcade on **K' Road** for a Narnia-esque descent into **Myer's Park** beyond, and from here follow the signs north for **Aotea Square.** You'll pass by the **Basement Theatre** and **Town Hall** before reaching the public plaza, from where you'll link up with **Queen Street.** Head north, downhill until you reach the art deco architecture of **The Civic.** Turn right onto Wellesley Street East, where you'll discover **Auckland Art Gallery** on the corner of Kitchener Street. Behind the gallery, exit **Albert Park** onto Courthouse Lane, which becomes O'Connell Street, where you can browse the preloved tomes of **Jason Books.** Take a left onto Shortland Street, then the first right for the funky **Fort Lane,** which terminates in the fashionable **Britomart** for refreshments. Once you reach the waterfront, take a left to pass the **Ferry Building** and reach the **Maritime Museum** in the **Viaduct.** The walk is 3.5km; allow an hour or more with stops.

BIKING

Cycle Auckland (Shop 6, Devonport Wharf, 09/445-1189, www.cycleauckland.co.nz) rents all manner of rides, including tandems, and offers guided and self-guided tours. There are two bike-hire stations at Wynyard Quarter ($4 registration fee, first 2 hours free). Take a ride along **The Promenade,** a harborside boardwalk that connects Wynyard Quarter to Westhaven. In the opposite direction, the **Waterfront Cycle Path** stretches 7km from Britomart to Mission Bay along the flat and scenic Tamakai Drive.

Visitors who prefer to travel light should make a note of centrally located **Adventure Capital** (23 Commerce St., www.adventure-capital.co.nz, 9am-5pm daily). Their rental packages include camping equipment (tents and sleeping bags), hiking gear (packs, poles, and jackets), and bikes with safety equipment. Packages can be combined with car and 4WD rentals for anywhere from a few hours to a month.

Much-needed ongoing investment has made Auckland a much more cycle-friendly city. **Auckland Transport** (www.aucklandcouncil.govt.nz) has detailed routes and information, as does the **Auckland Cycle Touring Association** (www.acta.org.nz).

YOGA

The secret sanctuary of the **Loft Yoga Lounge** (103 Beach Rd., 1st Fl., 09/379-7301, www.theloft.org.nz, 6pm Mon.-Thurs., $15-19) may be the best 90 minutes you can spend in Auckland. Newbies are welcome, and everyone's rewarded with a sumptuous vegetarian dinner to conclude.

THEME PARKS

Take part in a hyperrealistic zombie apocalypse at **Spookers** (833 Kingseat Rd., Karaka, 09/291-9002, www.spookers.co.nz, 8pm-10:30pm Fri.-Sat., $40-55), a ghost train ride on steroids. But instead of riding the gauntlet of ghosts and ghouls in the safety of a carriage, visitors make the journey on foot. The attraction is made all the more petrifying due to its setting at a former psychiatric institute located out in the sticks. Much effort has gone into ensuring this is an real horror experience; guests are forced to navigate haunted corridors and cornfields prowled by chainsaw-wielding ghouls. Family-friendly events are held during the safety of daylight. For nighttime events, guests must be over age 16.

For thrills of a different kind, head on over to New Zealand's largest theme park, **Rainbow's End** (2 Clist Crescent, Manukau, 09/262-2030, www.rainbowsend.co.nz, 10am-5pm daily, adults $59, seniors $30, children $48, family pass available). Not to be missed is the superbly named Stratosfear, essentially a giant spinning top affixed to the end of a 360-degree pendulum, which is sure to raise your heart rate, and possibly your lunch.

SPECTATOR SPORTS

Eden Park (Reimers Ave., Kingsland, 09/815-5551, www.edenpark.co.nz), plays host to regular rugby and cricket matches.

Rugby

Rugby is followed with an almost religious fervor by a significant proportion of Kiwis. The sport can be split into two categories: rugby league and rugby union. Each have slightly different rules. **Rugby union** is by far the most popular and is the version played by legendary national team, the **All Blacks** (www.allblacks.com). Most visitors will be interested in catching an atmospheric All Blacks match, which are held in winter and split between a handful of stadiums around the country.

Tickets for local Auckland rugby teams the **Blues** (www.blues.co.nz) and **Auckland Rugby** (www.aucklandrugby.co.nz) are available online; locations vary.

Cricket

In summer, Eden Park plays host to national and international cricket matches. The national team is the **Black Caps** (www.blackcaps.co.nz); the local team is the **Auckland Cricket Club** (www.aucklandcricket.co.nz). The rules of cricket are complicated and the pace is slow; only hard-core fans need attend.

Motor Sports

Western Springs Speedway (Western Springs, 09/588-4050, www.springsspeedway.com, adults $26-35, children free or $5) has hosted motor-sporting events since 1929. Today the live racing events mainly take the form of speedway races.

Entertainment and Events

NIGHTLIFE

Central Business District

Many of the best bars, restaurants, and theaters are in the city center, some of which are open late, though visitors from other major international cities will likely be surprised at the number of establishments that close relatively early—it's not uncommon for eateries to shut their kitchens at 9pm.

BARS AND CLUBS

City Works Depot springs from the site of former council workshops and wears its industrial heritage with pride. The space houses boutiques, bars, and eateries all worth checking out, but **Brothers Beer** (City Works Depot, 90 Wellesley St. W., 09/366-6100, www.brothersbeer.co.nz, noon-10pm daily) is the star act, boasting a collection of craft beers hundreds strong—some brewed in-house—poured by passionate staff. The bare iron exterior may not be the most visually appealing of surroundings, but is a fine sun trap best enjoyed in the afternoon through early evening. Try the tasting paddle ($20) if you're not sure which brew to choose.

With its low-slung roof of timber beams above brick fireplaces and creaking leather couches, the welcoming **Bluestone Room** (9-11 Durham Lane, 09/302-0930, www.thebluestoneroom.co.nz, 11:30am-11pm Mon.-Fri., 3:30pm-11pm Sat.-Sun.) resembles an archetypal backdrop of a classic beer ad, further enriched in character thanks to its heritage building structure of stone walls set down a secret street. A generous happy hour (5pm-6pm Sun.-Fri., 8pm-10pm Sat.) is accompanied by free bowls of fresh warm popcorn. This place is popular with office workers and fills fast, especially on weekends.

The atmospheric **Vulcan Lane** is home to a collection of European-inspired bars. A favorite with locals come nightfall, this sophisticated thoroughfare presents a rather stark contrast to the garish Queen Street. Craft beer lovers should head to **Vultures' Lane** (10 Vulcan Lane, 09/300-7117, www.vultureslane.co.nz, noon-late daily), a funky bar with 22 rotating taps backed by dozens of bottles of

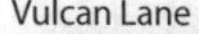
Vulcan Lane

hard-to-find brews. The wood-lined interior sure is welcoming, but grab a table outside for people-watching.

In shadowy **Fort Lane** (adjacent to Vulcan Lane) establishments are neatly slotted within fashionable brick facades. **The Jefferson** (7 Fort Lane, www.thejefferson.co.nz, 4pm-1am Mon.-Thurs., 4pm-3am Fri.-Sat.) is an achingly stylish underground lair with a collection of more than 500 whiskeys. Reached via a meandering corridor, The Jefferson gives the impression you've stumbled upon an exclusive guest-list-only venue, but the obliging staff are more than happy to discuss their extensive (and expensive) drinks list. Cocktails are named after Hollywood icons—the Dean Martin is exceptional.

For guaranteed partying early into the hours, head to **Forte Bar and Nightclub** (2 Fort Lane, 09/354-4422, 10pm-5am daily) a dimly lit drinking den with great drinks deals, live DJs, and dancing.

Britomart (an area northeast of the CBD) is a vibrant hangout for creatives and city workers, and home to some of the trendiest bars and eateries in town. Enjoy live jazz, blues, and soul food at the sultry **Orleans** (48 Customs St. E., 09/309-5854, www.orleans.co.nz, noon-close Mon.-Fri., 4pm-close Sat.-Sun.), a New Zealand take on great Southern hospitality. Tap beers, wines, and classic liquors are served alongside classic Southern snacks. This bar's buzz is emboldened thanks to an intimate alleyway location. Drink outside on a balmy evening, and you'll really know your holiday has begun.

Next door, the cellar-like **Racket Bar** (44 Customs St. E., 09/309-5854, www.racketbar.co.nz, 4pm-4am Tues.-Sat.) mirrors a clandestine speakeasy, with a fireplace, antique furnishings, and an extensive selection of rums. There's usually a pithy chalk musing or two on the blackboard or brick wall, sure to raise a smile.

Mo's (5 Federal St., 09/366-6066, www.mosbar.co.nz, 3pm-4am Mon.-Fri., 6pm-4am Sat.) is a lonely looking little corner venue with a whole lot of heart. The tucked-away treasure doesn't disappoint on its "friendliest bar in town" tagline. Inside, you'll be serenaded by soul legends from the speakers as cigar-wielding Latin American revolutionaries peer from picture frames on the walls. Indeed, it's the kind of cozy, romantic venue that feels as though it should be filled with a haze of smoke.

On the waterfront is an interesting blend of bars and restaurants to that cater to all tastes and budgets, but be warned, the Viaduct area especially is a tourist trap. For those on a shoestring, **Provedor** (131 Quay St., 09/377-1114, www.provedor.nz, 3pm-2am Sun.-Thurs., 3pm-4am Fri.-Sat.) is superb, with happy-hour drinks as low as $4 and a million-dollar harbor view from the deck. The happy hours are often accompanied by free bar snacks and barbecue, set to a soundtrack of classic pop and rock.

Continue jiving well into the night just around the corner at **Danny Doolans** (204 Quay St., 09/358-2554, www.dannydoolans.co.nz, 11am-2am Sun.-Thurs., 11am-4am Fri.-Sat.), a no-nonsense Irish-inspired disco with live bands backed by some clichéd but fun-filled playlists. Expect a certain level of boisterousness once the early hours arrive—there's an often-cramped outdoor smoking area should the noise inside become too much.

The Caribbean-themed **Bungalow 8** (48 Market Pl., 09/307-1500, www.bungalow8.co.nz, 4pm-10pm Mon.-Tues., 4pm-3am Wed., 4pm-1am Thurs., 4pm-4am Fri.-Sat.) generally doesn't get going until late, and is probably best avoided if fine wines and Chopin are more your vibe—think sticky bar, neon lights, and tropical fish tanks—but drinks can cost as little as three bucks. The comfortable balcony area overlooks a collection of superyachts and is a fine space to make new friends.

BACKPACKER BARS

Weekly bar crawls (four drinks and four bars for $10) are just one of the many legendary inhibition-obliterating social events organized by **Fat Camel Bar** (38 Fort St., 09/307-0181, 4pm-1am daily), a backpacker-friendly watering hole hosted by Nomads, a hostel in the heart of downtown. Solo travelers will soon find new mates here among the party-loving international crowds.

Partying and parsimony rarely mix well in Auckland, so hordes of local and foreign students along with globe-trotting travelers gather at the gyrating **Habana Joes** (4 Darby St., 09/357-3980, 8pm-4am daily), part of Base hostel. Daily happenings include pool competitions, quiz nights, and frat parties in a dark and fashionable industrial-inspired setting.

COCKTAIL LOUNGES

There's a complimentary side serving of nostalgia with each drink at the **Gin Room** (Queen's Ferry Hotel Bldg., 12 Vulcan Lane, 1st Fl., 09/377-1821, 5pm-midnight Tues.-Wed., 5pm-2am Thurs., 4pm-4am Fri., 6pm-4am Sat.), a beautiful, jazz-age-furnished second-level hangout with premium drinks that are actually rather reasonably priced for Auckland. A hip crowd heads here for the legendary cocktails—the bathtub gin sour should top your list.

A couple of hundred or so whiskeys grace the handsome bar of **Coley & Punch** (Shed 22, Princes Wharf, 09/320-4375, www.coleyandpunch.co.nz, 4pm-close daily), a sophisticated drinking den with a spirited harbor-side setting. Classy highlights include cognac-infused The Emblem, and the Montenegro Mule, which swaps the vodka for *amaro,* muddled with ginger and served over ice with fresh lime.

Better views are found upstairs at the Sky Tower's **Sugar Club** (Level 53, Sky Tower, 09/363-6365, www.skycityauckland.co.nz, noon-9:30pm Wed.-Sun., 5:30pm-9:30pm Mon.-Tues., $35), a cocktail bar and restaurant best enjoyed as the sun sets behind the city. A faultless cocktail list incorporates the classic and the contemporary; the bourbon-based Fig Old Fashioned neatly complements the orange sky. You'll have complementary access to the Sky Tower viewing deck ($28), so reserve ahead.

Karangahape Road

BARS AND CLUBS

Karangahape Road (K' Rd.) links the south end of Queen Street to Ponsonby. The street evolved from an ancient Maori thoroughfare into a swanky shopping street in Auckland. Today, K' Road teems with galleries, tattoo parlors, thrift stores, and ethnic eateries. There's a large LGBT presence on its west end, with a colorful collection of adult-only stores and strip clubs scatted among a smattering of gay bars. The topless young woman perched above the Las Vegas Club, at number 339, is somewhat of a contentious icon—she's certainly difficult to miss.

Take your pick of nighttime venues. **The Wine Cellar** (183 Karangahape Rd., 09/377-8293, 5pm-close daily) is a favorite Auckland haunt. The brooding and badly lit bohemian affair links underground to the equally grungy **Whammy Bar** and hosts regular gigs. Enter through St. Kevin's Arcade.

If hip-hop and drum and bass are more your thing, head to **Neck of the Woods** (155B Karangahape Rd., 027/733-9325, www.neckofthewoods.co.nz, 5pm-4am Tues.-Fri., 8pm-4am Sat.) and dance into the early hours with a fashionable clientele.

Few Auckland bars boast as legendary status as the louche **Shanghai Lil's** (335 Karangahape Rd., 09/309-0213, 5pm-3am Wed.-Sat.), a timeless watering hole furnished in the manner of a luxurious opium den. It was originally opened as a gay bar, but everyone is welcome and everyone goes. If the owner, Russell, happens to be around (he usually is), ask about the time he danced with his Hollywood guests.

Ponsonby

BARS AND CLUBS

There are three certainties in life: death, taxes, and a well-dressed crowd spilling onto the street from the **Chapel Bar** (147 Ponsonby Rd., 09/360-4528, www.chapel.co.nz, 3pm-midnight Mon.-Wed., noon-1am Thurs.-Sat., noon-11pm Sun.). It's not the most imaginative selection of tap beers in town, but the

Auckland's LGBT Community

Though New Zealand could be considered relatively conservative in some social and cultural matters, in others it is a bastion of progressive politics. The first country in the world where women could vote (1893) was also one of the earliest to legalize same-sex marriage (2013). LGBT visitors will feel particularly welcome in Auckland. Come in February for **Rainbow Month,** when the Pride Festival comes to town. Most LGBT bars and clubs can be found on **K' Road,** and **Ponsonby** is another favorite community 'hood. **Shanghai Lil's** is the most famous (but by no means exclusively gay) gay bar. For more listings and events, pick up *Gay Express,* a free magazine. It's found at a variety of public places, including cafés and supermarkets.

lively atmosphere more than makes up for it, along with a menu of lip-smacking bar snacks.

The Ponsonby Social Club (152 Ponsonby Rd., 09/361-2320, www.ponsonbysocialclub.co.nz, 5pm-11pm Sun.-Wed., 5pm-3am Thurs.-Sat.) is an elegant, understated affair with minimal decor and maximum cool. The hippest hangout on the hip Ponsonby strip sports an inventive roofless indoor-outdoor area and friendly staff and live bands and DJs set the tone. Take the chance to build your own burger over a cocktail.

COCKTAIL LOUNGES

New York-inspired **Mea Culpa** (3/175 Ponsonby Rd., 09/376-4460, 5pm-2am Mon.-Sat.) is staffed by some of the most cluedup bartenders in town. Classic and tailored cocktails are concocted in an intimate environment with drinkers at stools along the bar. It's made all the more cozy thanks to some seriously sumptuous snacks.

As the night progresses, many of the cool kids head to the hard-to-find **Deadshot** (45 Ponsonby Rd., www.deadshot.co.nz, 5pm-2am daily), a riff on an old-school speakeasy. Behind a discreet doorway lies a brooding bar replete with booth seating and vintage mirrors imported from Prague. The staff take great pride in the craft cocktails.

Kingsland

This neighborhood is home to a swag of the city's coolest bars.

BARS AND CLUBS

Kingsland has experienced a gentrification boom but retains more of an alternative edge. If Ponsonby is the city's slickest suburb, then Kingsland is the nonchalant, leather jacket-wearing little brother. **Neighbourhood Brewbar** (498 New North Rd., 09/846-3773, www.neighbourhood.co.nz, 11:30am-close daily). The airy, contemporary space features fluffy suspended clouds, cut-out artwork, and an outdoor wood-fired pizza oven.

You'll find thrift store furniture and beer served in jam jars at **The Portland Public House** (463 New North Rd., www.theportlandpublichouse.co.nz, noon-midnight Sun., 4pm-midnight Mon.-Wed., 4pm-3am Thurs., noon-3am Fri.-Sat.), one of Auckland's best bars and also one of its best-kept secrets. Free to enter, the standard of the nightly live acts is astonishing and though this small space can become cramped, especially at weekends, it's never rowdy, and a warm friendly vibe remains.

Just past Kingsland's main hub is the quirky **Flight 605** (605 New North Rd., www.flight605bar.co.nz, 4pm-1am Tues.-Sat., 2pm-close Sun.), an aeronautical-themed place (the owners are former flight attendants) with various flying paraphernalia on the walls and even some airplane seating. Discover a superb collection of craft brews served by bartenders who love nothing more than telling you the story behind the booze. Drinks arrive with warm buttery

the Portland Public House

popcorn. Get there on a Sunday to reward your ears with a seriously cool live set.

THE ARTS

Theater

Opened in 2016, the **ASB Waterfront Theatre** (138 Halsey St., Wynyard Quarter, 09/309-3395, www.asbwaterfronttheatre.co.nz) is the home of the **Auckland Theatre Company** (09/309-3395, www.atc.co.nz). Performances range from musicals to dramas and everything in between, including overseas productions. Even if you don't manage to catch a show, the sustainable design—which architect Gordon Moller describes as "a timber crucible within a glass box"—is well worth a snap.

For shows a little more left-field, **Q Theatre** (305 Queen St., 09/309-9771, www.qtheatre.co.nz) is renowned for hosting off-beat productions. Tiny **Basement Theatre** (Lower Greys Ave., behind Queen St., 09/309-7433, www.basementtheatre.co.nz, $5-25) is a big favorite, with audience seats right in the actors' faces for a raw and immersive experience. This is highly affordable entertainment and a chance to support emerging talent.

Classical Music and Ballet

The Royal New Zealand Ballet (04/381-9000, www.rnzb.org.nz), **New Zealand Opera** (09/379-4020, www.nzopera.com), **New Zealand Symphony Orchestra** (09/358-0952, www.nzso.co.nz), and **Auckland Philharmonia Orchestra** (09/623-1052, www.apo.co.nz) spread their performances between Auckland's Town Hall (Aotea Square, Queen St.), the Aotea Centre (Aotea Square, Queen St.), and the Civic Theater. Aotea Centre, with its 2,000-seat three-tiered contemporary auditorium, is Auckland's premier performance hub.

Opened in 1929, nearly demolished in 1988, then restored in 2000, the wonderful **Civic Theater** (269-287 Queen St., 09/309-2677) is famed for its opulent East Asian-inspired interior. The venue opens 90 minutes prior to performances, so make the most of it.

For show and venue information, contact **Auckland Live** (09/309-2677, www.aucklandlive.co.nz). For tickets, contact **Ticketmaster** (09/970-9700 or 0800/111-999, www.ticketmaster.co.nz).

Live Music

Not many Aucklanders have heard of **The Bunker** (Mount Victoria, off Kerr St., Devonport, 09/445-2227 www.devonport-folkmusic.co.nz, performance times vary, $5-20), a half-century-old live folk venue hosted on the slopes of a volcano in a former military stronghold. Be serenaded on balmy evenings by local and overseas folk artists to views over a star-speckled Hauraki Gulf, or in front of a cozy log fire in the colder months. This is a great place to mix with the locals.

COMEDY

The **Classic Comedy Club** (321 Queen St., 09/373-4321, www.comedy.co.nz, shows daily, $5-25) is a super intimate venue. Laughs can be had for a bargain each Sunday when **Little Easy** (198 Ponsonby Rd., 09/360-0098, www.littleeasy.co.nz, $10) hosts its weekly comedy night. The acts begin at 7:30pm, but arrive between 4pm-7pm for happy hour drinks and delicious $10 burgers (these two deals are daily).

CINEMA

Film-lovers must set aside at least an afternoon or evening to visit **The Vic** (48-56 Victoria Rd., Devonport, 09/446-0100, www.thevic.co.nz), the oldest purpose-built cinema in New Zealand. Inside, not much seems to have changed since its 1912 opening. A selection of new releases are screened, so indulge in a glass of local wine or craft beer as you take in this magical moviegoing experience. From downtown, snag a bargain return ferry and cinema ticket deal with Fullers (adults $17, children $10).

Slotted into the basement of Auckland's main library, **Academy Cinema** (Central Library Bldg., 44 Lorne St., 09/373-2761, www.academycinemas.co.nz) is a chic art-house hideaway with a charming little bar and snack shop. Wednesday tickets are $5.

FESTIVALS AND EVENTS

Auckland's council, along with an array of arts and community groups, organize a variety of happenings in and around the city throughout the year, many of which are free. **Eventfinder** (www.eventfinder.co.nz) or **Auckland NZ** (www.aucklandnz.com) list what's on in Auckland. While some of the events and performances may change from year to year, an abundance of regular festivals prop up Auckland's cultural calendar.

January-March

The year gets off to a sterling start with free live concerts and outdoor cinemas thanks to **Music in Parks** (www.musicinparks.co.nz) and **Movies in Parks** (www.moviesinparks.co.nz), which take place in selected green spaces across the city January-March. Also in January, the three-day **Tamaki Herenga Waka Festival** (www.aucklandnz.com, free) is one of Auckland's youngest, created to celebrate and promote Maori culture.

For four days in February, the ethereal **Lantern Festival** (www.asianz.org.

Lantern Festival

nz, free), in honor of the Chinese New Year, transforms a section of the Domain into a Far East wonderland, climaxing in a spectacular fireworks display. Continuing with the colorful, **February** is also rainbow month in Auckland, as the **Pride Festival** (www.aucklandpridefestival.org.nz) comes to town for two weeks.

The world's two largest Maori and Pacific Island parties take place in March. At the four-day **Polyfest** (www.asbpolyfest.co.nz, free), tens of thousands of visitors descend on the south Auckland suburb of Manukau to watch traditional Pacific Island dances by performers from local schools with a decidedly community atmosphere. The weekend-long **Pasifika Festival** (www.aucklandnz.com, $5 per day) showcases and celebrates Pacific culture with food stalls and authentic performances from the likes of the Cook Islands and Samoa.

For three weeks of March, the **Auckland Arts Festival** (www.aucklandfestival.co.nz, cost varies) sees weird and wonderful shows and exhibits spring up throughout the city. An eclectic list includes art displays, light shows, circus performances, plays, and contemporary dance from around the world.

April-August

In April, the monthlong **NZ International Comedy Festival** (www.comedyfestival.co.nz, prices vary) showcases the best of Kiwi comics at various theaters in the city. May hosts the highly regarded **Writers' Festival** (www.writersfestival.co.nz), which attracts international talent from the publishing world. Events include writing workshops and Q&As with acclaimed authors.

Celebrations are written in the stars come June. The wondrous four-week **Matarki Festival** (www.matarikifestival.org.nz) marks the beginning of the Maori New Year; dates change depending on celestial alignment. Traditionally seen as a period of reflection, remembrance, and thanks for the land, it's manifested through dozens of citywide events that incorporate storytelling, kite-flying, and dance. Most events are free.

Spanning three weeks of July-August, the **New Zealand International Film Festival** (www.nziff.co.nz, prices vary) showcases the best new movies from local and international filmmakers, directors, and actors at cinemas and theaters throughout the city.

September-October

For two weeks in September, Auckland throws a party with the **Heritage Festival** (www.heritagefestival.co.nz), which takes a look at the history of the city and promotes all the things that make it great. Expect happenings like historical art and photography exhibitions, high tea, and arts and crafts at locations across Auckland. Many of the events are free.

For one weekend in October, Eastern sounds and colors fill Aotea Square with the arrival of the **Diwali Festival** (www.asianz.org.nz). Queen Street blooms with wonderful stalls selling spicy treats.

November-December

Taste buds are teased in November courtesy of **Taste of Auckland** (Western Springs Park, www.tasteofauckland.co.nz, from $25), the city's legendary four-day food fair.

Get in the festive spirit on the second Saturday of December at **Coca-Cola Christmas in the Park** (The Domina, www.coke.co.nz, free), a family-friendly event that includes a music concert of Christmas songs, firework displays, and Christmas tree lighting by a local celebrity.

The New Year's Eve party **Wondergarden** (Silo Park, www.wondergarden.co.nz, adults $93, children $46, under age 5 free) celebrates with live music, art installations, bars, and street food.

Shopping

SHOPPING DISTRICTS

Central Business District

QUEEN STREET

The downtown end of **Queen Street** is a good start for practical and conventional vacation needs such as camera and electronics equipment, souvenirs, and currency exchanges. Greenstone (a type of jade) is a big deal in New Zealand thanks to its use in Maori iconography. The **Jade Centre** (HSBC Bldg., 1 Queen St., ground fl., www.jadecentre.co.nz, 09/369-5898, 10am-6pm daily) specializes in traditional handcrafted designs such as fish hooks and whale tails in the form of jewelry, figurines, and charms.

An Auckland institution, **Real Groovy** (369 Queen St., www.realgroovy.co.nz, 09/302-3940, 9am-7pm Sat.-Wed., 9am-9pm Thurs.-Fri.) stocks a famed array of new and used books, clothing, and records.

You'll find all manner of weird and wonderful souvenirs at **From N to Z** (Shop 2, 75 Queen St., 09/302-1447, www.fromntoz.co.nz, 9:30am-8pm Mon.-Fri., 9:30am-7:30pm Sat., 9:30am-7pm Sun.), a Kiwi gift shop with a twist. Classic items like merino clothing, manuka honey, and hand-carved wood shares space with chocolate-coated raisins—called Kiwi Poo.

BRITOMART

Britomart boasts an interesting blend of contemporary and heritage buildings home to a bounty of high-end fashion boutiques and sports and outdoor stores.

The flagship store of the experimental designer fashion brand **World** (60 Tyler St., 09/373-3034, www.worldbrand.co.nz, 10am-6pm Mon.-Fri., 10am-5pm Sat.-Sun.) it's worth exploring for taxidermy, art, and furniture alongside their clothes.

Zambesi (56 Tyler St., 09/303-1701, www.zambesistore.com, 10am-6pm Mon.-Fri., 10am-5pm Sat.-Sun.) is one of the country's most bankable clothing labels. Style-conscious men and women love the moody hues sold at the flagship store in Britomart.

HIGH STREET

There's much browsing potential on High Street and its tributary lanes. **Jason Books** (16 O'Connell St., www.jasonbooks.co.nz, 09/379-0266, 9am-5pm Mon.-Sat.) is a literary lair teeming with rare and secondhand prints and a fine collection of Maori and Pacific tomes.

Intimate **Pauanesia** (35 High St., 09/366-7282, www.pauanesia.co.nz, 10am-5pm Mon. and Sat., 9:30am-6:30pm Tues.-Thurs., 9:30am-7pm Fri., 10:30am-4.30pm Sun.) stocks classic textiles, jewelry, and merino. It's all locally crafted with a strong Kiwi slant.

Untouched World (20 High St., 09/303-1382, www.untouchedworld.com, 10am-6pm Mon.-Thurs., 10am-6:30pm Fri., 10am-5pm Sat., 11am-4pm Sun.) crafts ethical clothes from merino and possum wool for men and women. The company has been recognized by the United Nations for its eco-credentials.

K' Road

Lovers of antiques and vintage clothes will be spoiled for choice on K' Road. Make the Old World shopping mall of **St. Kevin's Arcade** (183 Karangahape Rd., www.stkevinsarcade.co.nz) your first stop.

The Green Dolphin Book Shop (shop 10, St. Kevins Arcade, 10am-5pm Sat.-Wed., 10am-10pm Thurs.-Fri.) is one of the best secondhand bookshops in town. The fascinating selection sits alongside a decent collection of used DVDs and games.

Wonderfully fragrant boutique **The Bread and Butter Letter** (225 Karangahape Rd., www.breadandbutterletter.co.nz, 09/940-5065, 10am-6pm Mon.-Fri., 10am-5pm Sat., 11am-5pm Sun.) stocks a collection of locally sourced scents and goodies such as art, crafts, and teas. Only the best of vintage clothing makes it to the store's modest rail.

More retro-fashion and accessories can be found at the **Vixen Vintage Boutique** (191-193 Karangahape Rd., 09/309-8884, 10am-6pm Mon.-Sat., 11am-5pm Sun.), where many of the men's and women's wares have a decidedly American slant.

Newmarket

Newmarket is widely touted as the fashion capital of New Zealand. The suburb is home not just to a local and international labels but also a sizable collection of electronic goods suppliers. Camping and outdoor stores include the flagship **Kathmandu** (151-153 Broadway, 09/520-6041, www.kathmandu.co.nz, 9am-5:30pm Mon.-Fri., 10am-5:30pm Sat.-Sun.), a Kiwi icon that stocks packs, clothing, tents, and adventure accessories at reasonable prices.

The shelves of **Texan Art Schools** (366 Broadway, www.texanartschools.co.nz, 09/529-1021, 9:30am-5:30pm Mon.-Sat., 10am-5pm Sun.) are filled with handmade prints, jewelry, and ceramics by more than 100 Kiwi artists.

A favorite fashion label of many Hollywood celebrities, **Karen Walker** (6 Balm St., www.karenwalker.com, 09/522-4286, 10am-6pm Mon.-Fri., 10am-5:30pm Sat., 11am-5pm Sun.), sells a collection of accessories, jewelry, perfume, and women's clothing.

An international A-listers' darling, **Deadly Ponies** (16 Osborne St., 09/522-5228, www.deadlyponies.com, 10am-5:30pm Mon.-Fri., 10am-5pm Sat., 10am-4pm Sun.) offers a range of purses and bags for women and men. All of it is crafted by hand from deer leather (as opposed to what the name implies).

Trade Aid (370 Broadway, 09/523-2605, www.tradeaid.org.nz, 9:30am-5:30pm Mon.-Fri., 9:30am-5pm Sat., 10am-4pm Sun.) is worth a visit for their extensive collection of fair trade art, crafts, textiles, coffees, and chocolates made by people in Africa, Asia, and Latin America. This admirable volunteer-run nonprofit has stores in other New Zealand cities, too.

Parnell

You'll find plenty of authentic New Zealand wares, such as Maori wood carvings, hand-woven goods, wool, and greenstone, at the legendary **Elephant House** (237 Parnell Rd., www.nzcrafts.co.nz, 09/309-8740, 9:30am-6pm Mon.-Fri., 10am-5pm Sat.-Sun.). Unfortunately, the friendly little labradoodle is not for sale.

shopping on K' Road

Guys looking for new headwear should head straight for **Hatitude** (2/235 Parnell Rd., www.hattitude.co.nz, 09/215-8955, 10am-5pm Mon.-Fri., 10am-4pm Sat., 11am-3pm Sun.), makers of everything from flat caps to fedoras and top hats. It's the country's only traditional hat shop for men.

If you don't have enough room in your suitcase for your souvenirs, **Woolly For You** (237 Parnell Rd., www.woollyforyou.com, 09/377-5437, 10am-5:30pm Mon.-Fri., 10am-4:30pm Sat., 10am-4pm Sun.) ships their products overseas, tax-free. They specialize in all manner of woolen goods such as slippers and knitwear, including possum wool.

Art lovers must stop by the gorgeous **Black Door Gallery** (251 Parnell Rd., www.blackdoorgallery.co.nz, 09/368-4554, 10am-5pm Mon.-Fri., 10am-4pm Sat., 11am-3pm Sun.), set in a historic villa. Check out the selection of paintings, sculptures, ceramics, and more, all created by Kiwis.

Ponsonby

Ponsonby is not far behind Newmarket on the pricey fashion boutique front. You're sure to snag a bargain at **Tatty's** (159 Ponsonby Rd., www.tattys.co.nz, 09/376-2761, 10am-6pm Mon.-Thurs., 10am-7pm Fri., 10am-5pm Sat., 11am-5pm Sun.), where rails are filled with high-quality secondhand designer clothing brands for men and women, including New Zealand names like Karen Walker and Moochi.

Head to **Clothesline** (132 Ponsonby Rd., www.clothesline.co.nz, 09/376-6747, 10am-5:30pm Mon.-Sat., 10am-4pm Sun.) for creative New Zealand-designed print T-shirts.

You'll discover something a little different at **The Garden Party** (71 Ponsonby Rd., www.thegardenparty.co.nz, 09/378-7799, 10am-6pm Mon.-Fri., 10am-5pm Sat.-Sun.), where shelves bulge with countless uniquely Kiwi-designed items such as cushion covers, wrapping paper, and kitchenware. There's a big emphasis on supporting small-scale arts and crafts setups.

Kingsland

There's a generous range of hand-carved greenstone items at the **Greenstone Factory** (453 New North Rd., 09/849-5519, 9am-3pm Mon.-Fri., 9am-1pm Sat.) along with carvings of other precious stones, wood, and bone. It's the best store of its kind in Auckland.

The Royal Jewellery Studio (486 New North Rd., www.royaljewellerystudio.com, 09/846-0200, 10am-6pm Mon.-Fri., 10am-4pm Sat.-Sun.) is a family-run affair with a wide range of New Zealand-designed jewelry, such as rings, wrist-wear, and brooches, using local stones and gems.

An array of fluffy rugs, slippers, boots, and bedding awaits at **The Woolskin Company** (322 New North Rd., www.woolskin.co.nz, 09/379-2422, 8am-4:30pm Mon.-Fri.). All goods are crafted using sheepskin, calfskin, or possum wool.

MARKETS

Enjoy a thoroughly Gallic vibe at **La Cigale French Market** (69 St. Georges Bay Rd., Parnell, 09/366-9361, www.lacigale.co.nz, 8am-1:30pm Sat., 9am-1:30pm Sun.) where you can wander stalls of fresh produce, coffee, and crepes. A smaller version of this market is in the CBD (Te Ara Tahuhu Walkway, Britomart, 8am-1pm Sat., 9am-1pm Sun.).

Do visit **Auckland Fish Market** (22 Jellicoe St., Wynyard Quarter, 09/303-0262, www.afm.co.nz, 7:30am-6pm daily) while at the waterfront. You don't need to buy anything to cook, as there are a handful of eateries that will do it for you.

Otara Flea Market

Auckland is home to the world's largest Maori and Polynesian market, the **Otara Flea Market** (Otara Leisure Centre Carpark, Newbury St., 09/274-0830, www.otarafleamarket.co.nz, 5am-noon Sat.). It's a fun environment with a colorful vibe thanks to an array of live performers and steel bands that will have you bopping away between the stalls of Pacific fabrics and produce, Maori carvings, and fresh fruit, vegetables, and fish.

Food

Auckland's culinary scene boasts an abundance of fine eateries, with a superb selection of ethnic offerings along Dominion Road.

CENTRAL BUSINESS DISTRICT

Cafés

You have to travel a long way from central Auckland and its surrounding suburbs to find a café that doesn't grind its own java beans and serve freshly prepared fare. Many even bake in-house. **Federal Delicatessen** (86 Federal St., 09/363-7184, www.thefed.co.nz, 7am-close daily), a funky U.S.-diner-inspired establishment, is the brainchild of Kiwi celebrity chef Al Brown. The coffee is bottomless and the blueberry buttermilk pancakes the most indulgent way to begin the day—you are on vacation, after all. It's also open for lunch, dinner, and late-night snacks at the weekend.

Remedy Coffee (1 Wellesley St. W., 09/377-1030 6:30am-3:30pm Mon.-Fri., 8am-3pm Sat.-Sun.) has a cozy atmosphere, a collection of board games, a book swap, and a super-friendly staff.

Discover a tantalizing range of gourmet dairy products at **Kapiti Store** (19 Shortland St., 09/358-3835, www.kapitistore.co.nz, 9am-5:30pm Mon.-Fri., 11:30am-4pm Sat.) where fragrant *fromages* and imaginatively flavored ice cream, like lemongrass or blood orange and cranberry, stimulate the senses. The grilled cheese sandwich is the best $5.50 you'll spend in Auckland.

Seafood

The Viaduct (western end of Quay St.) is a waterfront area and former dilapidated fishing dock converted into a collection of yacht berths flanked by high-end bars and eateries. ★ **Soul Bar & Bistro** (Viaduct Harbour, 09/356-7249, www.soulbar.co.nz, 11am-close daily, $29-39) is all about seafood straight from the sea, served as you sit sipping sauvignon blanc in the shadow of the harbor and its superyachts. Book ahead for a waterside view.

Founded by a real-life pirate on a former ship graveyard, **Swashbucklers** (23 Westhaven Dr., Westhaven, 09/307-5979, www.swashbucklers.co.nz, 11am-close daily, $23-44) has attained an almost mythical status on the Auckland social scene. But, pirates or no pirates, there are no free passes from the city's ever-demanding foodies, so don't be fooled by the laid-back beach-hut vibe; "Swashies" sure knows how to cook their fish.

Set among a vibrant gathering of trendy hangouts with the Sky Tower looming overhead, **Depot Eatery and Oyster Bar** (86 Federal St., 09/363-7048, www.eatatdepot.co.nz, 7am-close Mon.-Fri., 11am-close Sat.-Sun., $17-34) serves sophisticated seasonal dishes in a no-nonsense industrial setting, mostly cooked the old-school way over charcoal or hard wood.

Asian

Peek out from the protection of baby bamboo shoots in the outdoor area at ★ **XuXu Dumpling Bar** (Galway St. and Commerce St., Britomart, 09/309-5529, www.xuxu.co.nz, 4pm-close Mon.-Tues., noon-close Wed.-Fri., 5pm-close Sat., $7-10), one of the coolest hangouts in the CBD. Tucked into a quiet corner of vibrant Britomart, the intriguing Far East decor tastefully sets the tone for a menu of airy handcrafted dumplings and exotic cocktails. What better way to spend an Auckland afternoon?

Known for its ethical, authentic, international eating, ★ **Ngopi** (79 Anzac Ave., 09/303-4172, www.ngopi.co.nz, 11am-3pm Mon.-Fri., 4pm-8pm Mon.-Thurs., $12-14) is a nonprofit establishment staffed by volunteers serving curries and other Malaysian delights of such a high standard as to put many of its pricier competitors to shame. It's a great vibe

"BYO"

In 2016, Deutsche Bank's annual "Sin Index" placed Auckland as the third most expensive city in the world for alcohol and cigarettes, above the likes of London and New York. Perversely, Kiwi wine is often more expensive to buy in New Zealand than it is abroad (blame the tax department), so drinking and dining can turn into a costly night out. Thankfully many restaurants, even at the high end, offer a **bring-your-own service**: Guests can bring their own bottles of wine (and occasionally beer, but not spirits) for a per-bottle or per-head "corkage" fee. Corkage is usually only a couple of bucks, but can sometimes reach double digits, so make sure you check before booking.

Some Auckland BYO restaurants include:

- At Bangkok
- Barilla Dumpling
- Bona Pizzeria
- Cinta Malaysian
- Covo
- Everest Dine
- The Java Room
- Parnell 149
- Sri Pinang
- Wooden Board Kitchen

created by great people doing great things; this place satisfies both the stomach and the soul.

It's all about sharing—the plates, the tables, the experience—at **Indochine Kitchen** (42 Fort St., 09/974-2895, www.indochinekitchen.co.nz, 12:30pm-2:30pm Mon.-Fri., 5:30pm-close daily, $6-24), a mouth-watering collection of fresh Hanoi street food set in an übercool contemporary space. The Vietnamese tapas bar is perfect either for a quick bite or a sit-down dinner—the three-course set menu ($30) is an excellent value.

The indecisive diner's dream destination, **Food Alley** (9 Albert St., 09/373-4917, 10:30am-10pm daily, $10-15) boasts a delicious gathering of inexpensive, unpretentious Asian plates in a bustling food-court setting.

European

Covo (44 Fort St., 09/377-9290, www.covo.co.nz, noon-2pm Tues.-Fri., 5:30pm-close Mon.-Sat., $19-35) is a cozy Italian eatery that prides itself on its homemade pasta and gnocchi. Here, fresh daily produce complements the best of imported Italian ingredients, and it's one of the few BYOs in the city center with outdoor seating, but corkage ($15) is pricey.

It's all about degustation at **The Grove** (33 St. Patrick Square, Wyndham St., 09/368-4129, www.thegroverestaurant.co.nz, noon-3pm Thurs.-Fri., 6pm-close Mon.-Sat., $89-145), an eatery famed for its fine-dining flare. The revolving contemporary menu has bagged an array of awards.

Ensure you secure an outdoor seat at **Jack Tar** (34-47 Jellicoe St., Wynyard Quarter, 09/303-1002, www.jacktar.co.nz, 8am-close daily, $15-34), set in a former boat shed with great vibes and splendid sea views. Best enjoyed under the scorching sun, there's something for everyone at this lively but casual gastropub, including heaps of vegetarian options—but the thin-crust pizzas and juicy homemade burgers are especially tasty.

At the top end of Queen Street, reasonably priced **Wooden Board Kitchen** (2/4 Upper Queen St., 09/309-2775, www.woodenboardkitchen.co.nz, 5:30pm-11pm Thurs.-Sat., 5:30pm-9:30pm Tues.-Wed. and Sun., $22-26) affords an intimate dining experience with a rich and wholesome menu—think glazed roast chicken and shoulders of lamb—all beautifully presented and generously portioned. It's BYO.

International

Billed as an "Epicurean Village"—essentially a very posh food court—**Elliott Stables** (39-41 Elliot St., 021/104-4386, www.elliottstables.co.nz, 7am-close Mon.-Fri., 8am-close Sat.-Sun.) collects the best of world cuisine under one roof. Pick a food venue and then order drinks from somewhere else if you so please. The international fare includes Spanish tapas, sushi, and French crepes. A fun, warm, and sociable scene, there's live entertainment each Thursday.

There is no entry fee for the Sky Tower when you reserve a table at **Orbit Restaurant** (Level 52, Sky Tower, 09/363-6000, 11:30am-2:15pm Mon.-Fri., 11am-2:30pm Sat.-Sun., 5:30pm-9:30pm daily, $31-44), where the three-course set menus ($75-85) with a view are a superb value. A popular daytime option is **High Tea** (2:30pm-4:30pm Sat.-Sun.). When making a reservation, be sure to request window seats.

Latin American

Sate your Latin yearnings at the bustling **Mexico** (23 Britomart Place, 09/366-1759, www.mexico.net.nz, noon-close daily, $7-18) an atmospheric hangout with vibrant furnishings, colorful cocktails, and a massive selection of small plates to mix and match.

Mediterranean and Middle Eastern

For a charming Turkish and Mediterranean experience, **Café Midnight Express** (59 Victoria St. W., 09/303-0312, www.cafemidnightexpress.co.nz, noon-2pm Mon.-Fri., 5pm-10pm daily, $19-26) has delighted diners since 1989. Situated in the shadow of the Sky Tower, the restaurant's extensive menu is where modern meets traditional—think moussaka, falafel, kebabs, steak, and burgers. The comfortable setting is decorated in sepia tones.

Quick Eats

The White Lady (Commerce St. and Fort St., 027/706-8782, www.thewhitelady.co.nz, 7pm-4am Mon.-Thurs., 24 hours Fri.-Sun., $5-22) food truck has been serving weary late-night souls since 1948. Though everything's yummy when you're a little worse for wear in the wee hours, the burgers here truly cut the mustard, even when you're sober. Other offerings include fries, toasted sandwiches, and heavenly indulgent milk shakes.

The **Food Truck Garage** (City Works Depot, 09/973-2305, www.foodtruckgarage.co.nz, noon-8pm Mon.-Thurs., noon-close Fri., 11am-close Sat., 11am-3pm Sun., $15-20) was spawned from an award-winning TV show that sent a food truck to travel the country, proving that fast food doesn't have to be poor quality. The simple nourishing fare incorporates burgers made from high-quality meat, fresh fish, salads, and hand-cut fries, all organic and locally sourced. The truck now takes pride of place next to the permanent eatery and is a much-photographed mascot.

Dessert

It's worth wandering into **Milse** (31 Tyler St., Britomart, 09/215-8996, www.milse.co.nz, 10am-close daily, $2.50-15) simply to admire the astonishingly intricate detailing, which goes into creating indulgent sugary cupcakes and cookies. A desert-cum-art bar like no other, prepare to wait for a table or takeout.

K' ROAD

Asian

Situated on the fringe of the CBD, K' Road and Symonds Street are famed for their international eateries. **Mukunda's** (268 K' Rd., 09/300-7585, www.mukundas.co.nz, 11am-7pm Mon.-Fri., 11am-3pm Sat., $8-15), offers a unique and inexpensive dining experience in the form of a Hare Krishna vegetarian and vegan menu. The combos ($9) may just well be the best value meal deal in Auckland, while the masala teas and the mango *lassi* are the best this side of New Delhi.

Book well in advance (especially on weekends) to secure seats at **Sri Pinang** (356 K' Rd., 09/358-3886, 11am-2:30pm Tues.-Fri., 5:30pm-10pm daily, $15-30), an authentic family-run Malaysian BYO establishment where corkage is just $1.

At **Krung Thep Thai Street Food** (305 K' Rd., 012/94-8575, www.krungthepthai.co.nz, 11am-10pm daily, $11-14), if you order rice, the main dishes are substantial enough for two. You may as well be curbside in Bangkok, as the traditional Thai food is prepared in an audibly sizzling kitchen. The fresh chili chicken stir-fry is superb.

★ **Kazuya** (193 Symonds St., 09/377-8537, www.kazuya.co.nz, 6pm-close Tues.-Sat. and noon-4pm Fri., lunch set menu $45, degustation $80-165) may be easy to miss, but it's impossible to forget. The windowless entrance is hidden among a run-down row of dairies and dry cleaners, but the slick interior is striking. Space is at a premium, adding further exclusivity to one of Auckland's finest restaurants. The French-Japanese fusion menu changes according to season, with dishes such as Ora King Salmon Confit presented like works of art.

French

Auckland's most famous eatery, ★ **The French Café** (210 Symonds St., 09/377-1911, www.thefrenchcafe.co.nz, noon-2:30pm Fri., 6pm-midnight Tues.-Sat., $35-48) is an airy understated space befitting its contemporary seasonal Gallic offerings. Order market fish served with leeks, scallops, and seaweed in oyster cream accompanied by a staggering selection of wines, all overseen by the most professional waiters around. The eatery has bagged a host of local and international awards and is considered among the world's best restaurants.

PARNELL

Asian

For those who've not had the pleasure of experiencing Nepalese hospitality or cuisine, the family-run **Everest Dine** (279 Parnell Rd., 1st fl., 09/303-2468, www.everestdine.co.nz, 11am-3pm and 5pm-11pm daily, $16-24) affords a taste of both. You must scale a staircase to get here, but the reward is inexpensive BYO fine-dining. The *mo-mos* are a must.

Book a table out back at **The Java Room** (7/317 Parnell Rd., 09/366-1606, www.thejavaroom.co.nz, 5:30pm-close Mon.-Sat., $19-33) where a fashionable restaurant gives way to a romantic outdoor seating area with an unexpected Sky Tower view. The contemporary Asian menu focuses on curry, stir-fry, and perfectly prepared fish. It's BYO.

European

Considering both cost and quality, lunch at **Parnell 149** (149 Parnell Rd., 09/309-3878, www.parnell149.co.nz, noon-3pm and 6pm-close Tues.-Sun., $29-33) is peerless. Tuck in to garlic bread, a side salad, and mains such as braised lamb shank, and enjoy it with a beer or glass of wine. Dinners include grass-fed fillet steak and crispy duck drizzled in caramelized orange sauce. It's BYO.

Dessert

Beat that 3pm energy slump with a trip to ★ **Chocolate Boutique Café** (323 Parnell Rd., 09/377-8550, www.chocolateboutique.co.nz, 11am-10pm daily), an old-world candy store and café that's a treasure trove for the little kid inside you. The molasses-thick chili hot chocolate and the lighter-than-air mousse are recommended.

NEWMARKET

Due to its unparalleled assortment of shopping venues, Newmarket has long been considered a daytime destination, but much effort has gone into promoting an ever-burgeoning hospitality scene. Day or night, it's definitely worth taking a stroll down **Nuffield Street,** where designer stores, fashionable bars, and European-style restaurants spill onto the street.

Café

A respite from the bustle, ★ **Little and Friday** (11 McColl St., 09/489-8527, www.littleandfriday.com, 8am-3pm daily) is framed by bright-white walls and giant windows that capture oodles of soothing natural light. The decor may be minimalist, but the rich seasonal food (buffalo mozzarella on Turkish bread) is complemented by a superb offering of sandwiches, quiches, and cakes, not to mention Auckland's most revered doughnuts. Give the raspberry custard a go.

American

Galleries, boutiques, and eateries are squeezed into the former industrial space of **Osborne Lane,** now all green leaves and bare brick. Devour old-fashioned shakes, beer, and the obvious at **Burger Burger** (3B York St., Osborne Lane, 09/524-2859, www.burgerburger.co.nz, 11:30am-close daily, $12-14), where you can not only create your own main course but even build your own ice-cream tower.

Spanish

Tasca (25 Nuffield St., 09/522-4443, www.tasca.co.nz, 9:30am-close Mon.-Fri., 9am-close Sat.-Sun., $22-35), with its tapas-heavy menu, Estrella Damm beer on tap, and matador and flamenco dancer-adorned walls, affords a real taste of Spain, where, over the din of lunchtime traffic, you can just make out the sparrows merrily chirping in the timber beams above.

Dessert

Petal Cupcakes (8 Teed St., 09/524-0934, www.petal.kiwi, 9am-5pm Mon.-Fri., 9:30am-5pm Sat., 9:30am-4pm Sun., $5) bakes cupcakes from the classic and the quirky, with offerings such as Hawke's Bay Peach and Lavender Honey. It's impossible to smell this place and not step inside.

MISSION BAY

Seafood

Head to **Sea Cow on the Bay** (2/33 Tamaki Dr., 09/521-5891, 11:30am-8pm Tues.-Sun., $10-21) for fish-and-chips and a range of

fish and chips, a classic Kiwi dish

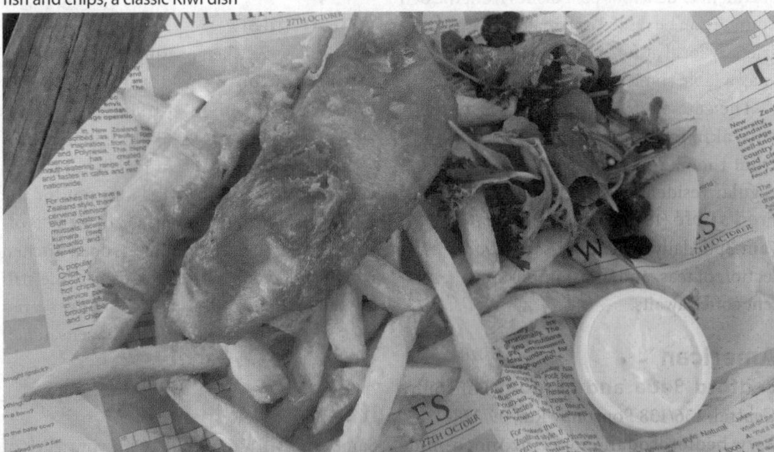

fresh seafood, such as mussels and calamari. Everything is served in a delightful coastal setting.

European

No visit to this humming seaside suburb is complete without a bite at the legendary **Mission Bay Café** (85 Tamaki Dr., 09/528-0017, www.missionbaycafe.co.nz, 7am-close daily, $20-31). The menu includes breakfast, an all-day brunch, Kiwi classics, and seafood. It's located just across the street from the sand.

PONSONBY

Eateries in Ponsonby and the adjacent Herne Bay are among the city's most reputable—and most expensive—but there are still plenty to satisfy the taste buds without straining the wallet. **Ponsonby Central** (136/138 Ponsonby Rd., 09/376-8300, www.ponsonby-central.co.nz, 7am-10:30pm Sun.-Wed., 7am-midnight Thurs.-Sat.) is awash with inviting eateries, and it's well worth taking the delightful stroll through the complex before settling on one.

Cafés

Dida's Foodstore (54 Jervois Rd., 09/361-6157, 6am-6pm Mon.-Fri., 7am-6pm Sat.-Sun.) serves fresh hot food, while an assortment of delicious cold dishes from the deli counter can be mixed and matched. Enjoy the friendly local atmosphere, but get in quick to snag a table come lunchtime.

The cutest café in Ponsonby is an experience akin to sitting in your quirky friend's front room. You even have to go through a regular residential-style front door to enter **Fred's Café** (181 Ponsonby Rd., 09/360-1551, 7am-3pm daily), where old-school sodas, a selection of teas, and, most importantly, excellent coffee awaits.

American

Bedford Soda and Liquor (Ponsonby Central, 136/138 Ponsonby Rd., 09/378-7362, www.bedfordsodaliquor.co.nz, noon-midnight daily, $14-25), a vibrant NYC-inspired industrial space with a fascinating drinks list and cocktails served from copper kettles. Create your own sliders, subs, and meatball dishes courtesy of a fun menu, which you mark with a pen. Non-meat eaters won't go hungry here, either.

Ponsonby Central

Argentinian

Vegans beware when passing ★ **El Sizzling Chorizo** (Ponsonby Central, 136/138 Ponsonby Rd., 09/378-0119, www.elsizzlingchorizo.co.nz, 11:30am-9:30pm Sun.-Thurs., 11:30am-10:30pm Fri.-Sat., $22-35), an Argentinian barbecue haunt not for the faint of heart (though a vegetarian menu is offered). A bar area surrounds an open kitchen where enormous hunks of meat—some still affixed to limbs and racks of ribs—are seared over open flames. You'll notice the sensational smell long before you arrive.

Italian

Sample a real slice of Italy with your slice of pizza at the family-run **Bona Pizzeria** (286

Ponsonby Rd., 09/360-8866, www.bonapizzeria.co.nz, 12:30pm-9pm daily, $17-28). An extensive menu includes delicious vegetarian and pasta options, all superb value, and corkage is free when you BYO. This intimate establishment is on the small—and popular—side, so call ahead.

Seafood

For an entirely different dining experience, head to the city's finest fish-and-chips shop, **Fish Smith** (200 Jervois Rd., 09/376-3763, www.fishsmith.co.nz, noon-8:30pm Sun.-Thurs., noon-9pm Fri.-Sat., $6-16) and give the sweet potato, or *kumara,* fries a try. Rather than wait for a table in the tiny seating area, take the five-minute stroll to Sentinel Beach (take Sentinel Rd., opposite) to enjoy your spread with sand between your toes and a mesmeric ocean view.

KINGSLAND

You'll discover a vibrant café culture by day, but it's when the sun sets that Kingsland truly shines. Dine at any of the high-quality and highly affordable eateries that serve cuisine from across the globe.

Café

Coffee aficionados must stop by **Atomic Coffee Roasters** (420c New North Rd., 0800/286-642 7am-3pm Mon.-Fri., 8am-3pm Sat.-Sun.), where their collection of single-origin coffees are prepared in vintage roasters and then served in a variety of contraptions akin to a school chemistry experiment.

American

Springing from an old motorbike workshop (check out the old signage on the brickwork outside), there's a definite U.S. feel to **Citizen Park** (424 New North Rd., 09/846-4964, www.citizenpark.co.nz, 8:30am-close daily, $14-34), but the menu stretches to Mexican classics. The outside bar area is a highlight, flooded with sun during the daytime and cloaked beneath twinkling fairy lights at night.

Thai

Auckland's best Thai restaurant, ★ **At Bangkok** (438 New North Rd., 09/849-6436, 5pm-10pm Tues.-Sun., $14-25), is also one of its most affordable. The duck red curry and sizzling plates are beautiful, and the ever-smiling staff wonderful. It's also BYO. Reservations are essential on weekends.

Vegan and Vegetarian

Healthy, sweet, and savory treats grace **Mondays** (503B New North Rd., 09/849-7693, www.mondayswholefoods.com, 8:30am-3pm Mon.-Fri., 8am-3:30pm Sat.-Sun., $12-19), a secret space down a secret alley and behind its own secret garden. The whole-food menu comprises all manner of vegan, dairy-free, and gluten-free goodies, and the smoothies alone are worth the trip.

MOUNT EDEN AND VICINITY

The suburb in the shadow of Auckland's highest volcano is peppered with an array of charming eateries befitting its village vibe.

Café

The café-cum-library **Chapter Book and Tea Shop** (442 Mt. Eden Rd., 09/551-8981, www.chapter.co.nz, 9am-5pm Tues.-Fri., 9am-4pm Sat.-Sun.) is the ultimate reading room, a comfortable colorful space to enjoy some tea leaves—more than 200 flavors to choose from—as you leaf through a good book.

Asian

Dominion Road is noted for its affordable international dining establishments, many of which are BYO.

Queues often equal quality. They also equal anticipation at **Eden Noodles** (105 Dominion Rd., 09/887-8272, 11am-9:30pm Tues.-Sun., $5-16) as the spicy scents waft by from one of Auckland's hottest kitchens. Go for the *dan-dan* noodles, which are well worth the wait. At **Barilla Dumpling** (571 Dominion Rd., 09/638-8032, 11:30am-11:30pm Thurs.-Tues.,

$10-30), you'll find an extensive selection of the legendary Hong Kong dumplings (20 for $12-14) along with plenty of other Chinese treats. It's BYO.

Wraparound corner windows and a smiling proprietor make for the most welcoming of spaces at **Cinta Malaysian** (454 Dominion Rd., 09/623-2808, www.cinta-malaysian.co.nz, 11am-2:30pm and 5:30pm-10:30pm daily, $13-28). Huge portions must be shared and are accompanied by affordable beer and wine. It's BYO.

European

Rustic feasts such as Harvest Soup and slow-cooked lamb are served in leafy surroundings at the beautiful **Garden Shed** (470 Mt. Eden Rd., 09/630-3393, www.thegardenshed.kiwi, 11am-11pm Mon.-Fri., 9am-11pm Sat.-Sun., $23-40), with a choice of 30 craft tap beers to wash them down with. Stay past dusk and see the garden glow beneath a web of fairy lights.

DEVONPORT

Café

All knickknacks and mismatched furniture, the decidedly boho ★ **Corelli's** (46 Victoria Rd., 09/445-4151, www.corelliscafe.co.nz, 7am-close daily, $10-25) is atypical of Devonport's quaintly colonial feel. Inside, bask in the airy atmosphere thick with the scent of freshly baked treats, while out front, the greenery creates a street-side garden. Breakfast, lunch, or dinner, you won't be disappointed.

Accommodations

Mid-range and high-end accommodations are plentiful in Auckland and of superb standards. For budget lodgings, your dollar will go a lot further if you head for suburban hostels; all are close to their own vibrant hubs and just a few kilometers from the city center. Beds fill fast in summer; when visiting out of season, you may get some good discounts.

CENTRAL BUSINES DISTRICT

Under $100

One of Auckland's youngest accommodations, ★ **Haka Lodge** (373 Karangahape Rd., 09/379-4559, www.hakalodge.com, dorm $27-36, $95-110 s or d) is also its best inner-city hostel. Perversely, the 20-bunk dorm offers more privacy than most smaller dorms in other hostels thanks to some seriously cozy pod-type bunks, complete with a curtain, personal power points, and a storage locker (opt for a bunk rather than a single bed when booking a dorm). The decor is fashionable, the Wi-Fi unlimited, and there's even a mini cinema room. The K' Road location is close to Ponsonby and the south end of Queen Street, but it's a 20-minute walk to the waterfront. As with many inner-city hostels, street noise can be an issue in some rooms—ask for the free ear plugs.

Enjoy the freedom of apartment-like living right in the city, along with a free evening snack, at **Nomads Fat Camel** (38 Fort St., 09/307-0181, www.nomadsworld.com, dorm $21-30, $70-80 s or d). Its collection of clean twins and doubles are accompanied by small dorms—including women-only ones—and the staff will organize tours and excursions. You won't find a better party place—or cheaper dorms—in Auckland. Its sister hostel, **Nomads Auckland** (16-20 Fort St., 09/300-9999, www.nomadsworld.com, dorm $23-40, $79-126 s or d), just a few blocks away, is a similar set up, with the slight increase in price reflecting slightly superior amenities like free Wi-Fi, en suite double rooms, and a rooftop spa and sauna.

You'll never be forced to share your space with strangers at **Jucy Snooze Hostel** (62 Emily Place, 09/379-6633, www.jucyhotel.

com, $69 s, $99 d) where room sizes range from single to four-bed "quads" for $139. Social butterflies won't be impressed with the quiet and clinical communal areas, but for those who'd rather nurse their hangovers in private, or for the business traveler on a budget, it's excellent. If you're visiting outside peak summer season, ask about a deal in the adjoining hotel.

A collection of some of the most comfortable budget CBD beds await at **YHA Auckland International** (5 Turner St., 09/302-8200, www.yha.co.nz, dorm $30-35, $92-105 s or d). The well-located, well-stocked lodgings boast a splendid natural-light-filled dining area, free Wi-Fi, and billiards.

The chilled-out vibe of **YHA Auckland City** (18 Liverpool St., 09/309-2802, www.yha.co.nz, dorm $28-38, $98-105 s or d) is just a short stroll from K' Road, sports a generously equipped kitchen, and is spotlessly clean—just what you'd expect from a former hotel building. Secure a room on an upper level for some stunning views.

The staff are great and the rooms tidy at **Kiwi International Hotel** (411 Queen St., 09/379-6487, www.kiwihotel.co.nz, $79 s, $99-119 d), superb value-for-money accommodations on south Queen Street, with family apartments also available. Wi-Fi is free in public areas, and there's parking and a restaurant.

Right on the fringe of the CBD, **Freeman's Backpacker Lodge** (65 Wellington St., Freemans Bay, 09/376-5046, www.freemansbackpackers.co.nz, dorm $31, $69 s, $80 d) offers a more suburban-style stay, in a converted villa just a 15-minute walk from central Queen Street. There's a free airport shuttle and free Wi-Fi..

$100-200

The conveniently located **City Lodge** (150 Vincent St., 09/379-6183, www.citylodge.co.nz, $99 s, $145-169 d) is mere minutes from most of central Auckland's major attractions. Hotel facilities are offered at backpacker-friendly rates, each room has an en suite bathrooms and is equipped with a TV and refreshments, while the spacious communal kitchen is faultless. Triple and quad rooms ($179-195) are excellent value. You'll sleep well here.

Since 1898, the **Shakespeare Hotel & Brewery** (61 Albert St. 09/373-5396, www.shakespearehotel.co.nz, $119-129 s or d) has been providing weary Auckland travelers with a place to hang their hats. The 10 boutique rooms each have an en suite bath with a TV, a mini fridge, and tea- and coffee-making facilities; some rooms have balconies. There is no elevator in this historic lodging. It's a great value in a great location with a great bar downstairs. The triple room ($149) is a steal.

$200-300

Those in town to take in some of the cultural delights might want to head straight for **Scenic Hotel** (380 Queen St., 09/374-1741, www.scenichotelgroup.co.nz, $219-329 s or d). Positioned across from Aotea Square, and just a stone's throw from the main art gallery, it's equipped with its own gym and café. Economy rooms come equipped with free Wi-Fi, a kitchenette, air-conditioning, and Sky TV. More spacious Superior Rooms are available. Book on a higher floor for city views and to escape the Queen Street din.

It's more about the experience than the amenities at the romantic ★ **Braemar on Parliament St. B&B** (7 Parliament St., 09/377-5463, www.aucklandbedandbreakfast.com, $250-400 s or d), the CBD's last Edwardian townhouse. Inside awaits creaking timber floors and opulent marble arches, a scene that owner John describes as "stuck in a time before the world went mad." Four uniquely furnished rooms are draped in elegant fabrics and house antique furniture; some rooms have a claw-foot bath. Most have the trappings of the 21st century, such as Wi-Fi. The 1901 boutique B&B is capped at 10 guests.

Over $300

The splendid **Heritage Hotel** (35 Hobson

St., 09/379-8553, www.heritagehotels.co.nz, $396-819 s or d) is a uniquely Auckland experience set in a former department store once frequented by the city's elite. Immaculate spacious lodgings sport high ceilings; rooms include a writing desk and soft beds. Some rooms have kitchenettes, and all come with Sky TV. In keeping with its privileged heritage, the colonial hotel offers harbor views, a floodlit tennis court, and a swimming pool on the roof. The palm-lined restaurant is noted for its vegetarian and vegan fare.

From the city's classiest hotel to its trendiest, **Sofitel** (21 Viaduct Harbour Ave., 09/909-9000, www.sofitel.com, $408-700 s or d), is so at one with its harborside setting that you can actually arrive by boat. Yacht-less souls are still afforded a Hollywood entrance to this French-themed establishment, which drips with sophistication—from its pebble ponds to the floor-to-ceiling glass panels that have panoramic marina views. Modern rooms sport balconies and enormous baths; specify a harbor view when booking or risk views of an office block. Luxury amenities include a spa, a cocktail bar, and Lava Dining, a top-drawer Auckland restaurant.

PARNELL

Under $100

Set on a quiet suburban street in leafy Parnell, the homey **City Garden Lodge** (25 St. Georges Bay Rd., Parnell, 09/302-0880, www.citygardenlodge.co.nz, dorm $29-33, $60 s, $79-88 d) is a hostel set in the former residence of the Queen of Tonga and it has lost little of its majestic charm. A first-floor chill-out deck overlooks a spacious garden area with a yoga room, while the deceptively roomy interior harbors immaculate sleeping quarters. Dorm rooms are on the small side, but the bunks are comfortable, the kitchen is cozy, and the communal area has couches of the utmost comfort.

$100-200

A sterling—if somewhat generic—mid-range lodging, the majority of the 105 airy modern rooms at **Quality Hotel Parnell** (10-20 Gladstone Rd., Parnell, 09/303-3789, www.theparnell.co.nz rooms from $171 s or d) have balconies affording varied views of the harbor and city skyline. More than half of the contemporary pristine lodgings have full kitchens; all come with air-conditioning and free Wi-Fi. Room service is available, and there's a 24-hour reception.

ORAKEI

$100-200

Hosts Keith and Trish will soon put you at ease at ★ **Nautical Nook** (23b Watene Crescent, Okahu Bay, 09/521-2544, www.nauticalnook.co.nz, $108 s, $151-162 d). Comfortable, cozy, and unpretentious rooms in soft warm hues add a homey feel. Your stay will include parking, free Wi-Fi, a continental or cooked breakfast, and a complimentary sailing trip around the harbor and Hauraki Gulf aboard Keith's yacht, weather permitting. The marine-themed premise is nestled on a hillside 5km from downtown and just minutes from the beach.

PONSONBY

Under $100

Happen upon the rickety **Brown Kiwi** (7 Prosford St., 09/378-0191, www.brownkiwi.co.nz, dorm $31-34, $60 s, $80 d) on a stormy night and you could well imagine Uncle Fester answering its front door, but it's more Waltons than Addams Family inside. The rooms are bright and spotless, the rustic kitchen is well-equipped, and the gorgeous garden looks lifted straight from the set of *The Hobbit*. The obliging staff will book tours, and there is free Wi-Fi throughout. You'll be hard-pressed to find a cozier and friendlier hostel environment in the whole of Auckland, located minutes from Ponsonby's thriving cafés.

It's almost worth booking your stay around any dates you can to secure a bed at ★ **Verandahs** (4-6 Hopetoun St., 09/360-4180, www.verandahs.co.nz, dorm $32-36, $60 s, $82 d). Located in magnificently restored turn-of-the-20th-century villas overlooking

Western Park, the dorms are decked out with plush single beds, while many of the amenities are hotel standard. The timber-clad kitchen, in particular, is exceptional. The family-run setup offers free tea, coffee, and Wi-Fi.

Framed certificates of excellence adorn the wall behind the reception desk of **Ponsonby Backpackers** (2 Franklin Rd., 09/360-1311, www.ponsonby-backpackers.co.nz, dorm $30-33, $55 s, $78 d), and you soon discover why. The laid-back lodging sports an array of comfortable communal areas and is within touching distance of the Ponsonby strip. High-ceilinged rooms are of a high standard, modern and with plenty of natural light. The largest dorm sleeps seven, and there is a women-only room.

$100-200

Slightly away from the hustle and bustle of Ponsonby Road, **Abaco on Jervois** (57 Jervois Rd., 09/360-6850, www.abaco.co.nz, $155-225 s or d) is an immaculate motel with oodles of off-street parking. Slick contemporary decor is enhanced by the likes of stainless-steel worktops and large flat-screen TVs. Some rooms come equipped with a kitchenette, and all are flooded with natural light courtesy of well-proportioned windows. The executive suite ($218) has a pullout sofa bed that can accommodate a couple of extra guests.

Officially, guests must book a week minimum at **Ponsonby Manor Guesthouse** (229 Ponsonby Rd., 09/360-7977, www.ponsonbymanor.co.nz, $140-195 s or d), but short-term reservations are taken if space is available, and this charming retreat is well worth inquiring. The gleaming white Victorian villa gives way to a rich green garden with a banana tree and herbs section where guests can help themselves. The eight bright rooms are immaculate, with French doors and a harbor view from the penthouse, and a single room that opens straight onto the garden. The kitchen is well equipped. Other amenities include a TV room, laundry, and free Wi-Fi.

$200-300

Something of an Auckland icon, the ★ **Great Ponsonby Art Hotel** (30 Ponsonby Terrace, 09/376-5989, www.greatpons.co.nz, $260-290 s or d), set in a quiet cul-de-sac, prides itself on its sustainable philosophies. The 19th-century structure is adorned with handmade local timber furnishings and boasts its own vegetable garden and worm farm. Choose from villa rooms, courtyard studios, or luxurious suites, all adorned with stained glass and colorful original Pacific art.

MOUNT EDEN AND VICINITY

Under $100

There's a family feel to ★ **Bamber House** (22 View Rd., Mount Eden, 09/623-4267, www.bamberhouse.co.nz, dorm $32-36, $88 s or d), an enormous colonial villa where guests are invited to take part in regular poker, pizza, and quiz nights. Dorm rooms are small, with singles and doubles; some have balconies and some share baths. En suite private rooms are available, separate from the main house. The wraparound deck affords a sterling view of Mount Eden volcano while the extensive surrounding garden plays host to numerous soccer games and to Mars, the chocolate Labrador—who's always keen for a walk.

Just around the corner, and closer to Mount Eden's hub, **Oaklands Lodge** (5a Oaklands Rd., Mount Eden, 09/638-6545, www.oaklandslodge.co.nz, dorm $29-35, $50-55 s, $80-85 d) is a smaller and more intimate affair. Three-bed dorms have all single beds; the 4-11 dorms have bunks (the 11-bed dorm is very spacious). Super facilities include handy USB power points and free unlimited Wi-Fi. Throughout the summer months, barbecues are organized for a small charge.

$200-300

So classy is **Eden Park B&B** (20 Bellwood Ave., Mount Eden, 09/630-5721, www.bedandbreakfastnz.com, $145-165 s, $235-250 d) that there are even chandeliers in the bathrooms. Claw-foot bathtubs, glass sinks, and gold-leaf mirrors are among the decorative indulgences to grace these pristine lodgings. Four uniquely lavish boutique bedrooms are equipped with fresh flowers, Egyptian cotton bedsheets, and floor heating. There's a shady palm oasis out back.

REMUERA

$200-300

Tucked away in a sizable though well-disguised villa, the stylish **Remuera B&B** (38 Pukeora Ave., Remuera, 027/329-3328, www.rembb.co.nz, $200 s or d) is befitting of its location in one of Auckland's most desirable suburbs. The private two-bedroom retreat comes equipped with cable TV and Wi-Fi and is just a few minutes stroll from the quaint village center of Remuera.

DEVONPORT

$100-200

Local yogis David and Gillian play host at **Accommodation Devonport** (33 Clarence St., Devonport 09/445-3757, www.accommodationdevonport.co.nz, $150 s or d, subsequent nights $100 s or d), a welcoming apartment overlooking a garden of organic fruit and vegetables. The en suite unit is peaceful and well-equipped, sporting a small kitchenette with tea- and coffee-making facilities, a toaster, a microwave, and a fridge. The rate is for two guests, but two additional guests can be accommodated on the sofa bed ($15 pp per night). It's just a few minutes' walk to Devonport's main drag. Guests get a 10 percent discount at Corelli's Café. Ask your hosts about their wellness class deals, and the onsite massage and yoga studio.

Over $300

A stunning colonial villa seconds from the seafront, each of the seven rooms at the ★ **Peace and Plenty Inn** (6 Flagstaff Terrace, Devonport, 09/445-2925, www.peaceandplenty.co.nz, $325-415 s or d) are furnished in a manner befitting their individual royal names, such as the Windsor Room. Kauri wood floors, high ceilings, and high tea set the tone at this storied establishment. There's complimentary tea, coffee, cookies, port, and sherry. Check out the sprawling collections of sterling-silver tea pots and fine bone china, not to mention the accompanying period dress hats, as you enjoy a gourmet breakfast.

CAMPING AND MOTOR LODGES

The leafy **Remuera Motor Lodge and Campground** (16 Minto Rd., Remuera, 09/524-5126, www.remueramotorlodge.co.nz, RV and tent sites $20-30 s, $40-48 d) comes equipped with its own swimming pool. Motel units ($130 s or d) are available, while other units accommodate up to five guests (additional $20 pp adults, $15 pp children). It's 6km east of the city.

The cream of the outdoor crop is undoubtedly ★ **Takapuna Beach Holiday Park** (22 The Promenade, Takapuna, 09/489-7909, www.takapunabeachholidaypark.co.nz, RV and tent sites $30 s, $42-47 d, trailers $72-90 s or d, small cabins $72 s or d, large cabins $135 s or d). You don't need to take too many steps before your feet are touching sand at this prime coastal Rangitoto Island-facing location. The large cabins (up to 5 guests), with bunk beds and a kitchen, are a superb value for groups, while the small cabins sport their own bath, kitchenette, and outdoor deck, ideal for a solo or pair of travelers.

Westhaven Z Pier (Westhaven Dr., Westhaven, www.zpier.co.nz, $20 for self-contained RV or trailer overnight parking) is a rare and relatively unknown central spot on the waterside, a couple of kilometers from the CBD and with stunning harbor views. Guests can park their self-contained vehicle for up to four consecutive days. There is a dump station to dispose of sewage, but no water or power supply.

AIRPORT ACCOMMODATIONS

One of the closest accommodations to the airport, **Ibis Budget Auckland Airport** (2

Leonard Isitt Dr., 09/255-5152, www.ibis.com, $113-139 s or d) is just a 15-minute stroll from the international terminal. Rooms are clean and come equipped with TVs, so it's an ideal chill-out choice during a stopover.

Airport Skyway Lodge (30 Kirkbride Rd., Mangere, 09/275-4443, www.skyway-lodge.co.nz, dorm $59, $119 s, $129-199 d) offers a useful range of accommodations for various budgets, along with a pool, a kitchen, and free Wi-Fi. It costs $7 for the 4km shuttle to the airport.

For those looking for something a little more luxurious to alleviate the jet-lag, **Sudima Hotel** (18 Airpark Dr., Mangere, 0800/783-462, www.sudimahotels.com, $299-339 s or d), 2km from the airport, offers whirlpool baths, air-conditioned rooms and an indoor pool and gym. Extra fees are required to get fed and connected.

Transportation and Services

GETTING THERE

Air

Auckland Airport (AKL, Ray Emery Dr., 09/275-0789, www.aucklandairport.co.nz) has an international and a domestic terminal. A free terminal transfer bus operates every 15 minutes 5am-10:30pm daily. **Air New Zealand** (09/357-3000, www.airnewzealand.co.nz) is the nation's flagship carrier, with local and international routes. Check out Air New Zealand's **Grab A Seat** (www.grabaseat.co.nz) for regular discounts on domestic journeys. Low-priced domestic flights can be consistently secured with **Jetstar** (09/975-9426, www.jetstar.com). Most cities and towns can be reached from Auckland.

AIRPORT TRANSPORTATION

SkyBus (09/222-0084, www.skybus.co.nz, $18 one-way, $32 round-trip) is the cheapest option. Buses operate 24 hours daily with pick ups every 10-15 minutes. The bus ride terminates at 396 Queen Street, with a complimentary shuttle to downtown. **Super Shuttle** (09/522-5100 www.supershuttle.co.nz, $35 for 1 passenger, $8 each additional person) is a door-to-door operation. Book online or call in advance. **Cheap Cabs** (09/621-0505, www.cheaptaxi.co.nz, $35) offers a fixed rate from the airport to central Auckland (avoid other taxis, as the rates for this route are extortionate). There is no train service to the Auckland Airport.

Train

New Zealand's long-distance trains terminate at the **Strand Station** (Ngaoho Place, Parnell, 09/366-6400, www.at.govt.nz). Trains in and out of Auckland are operated by national provider **KiwiRail** (04/495-0775 www.kiwirailscenic.co.nz).

The first of three magnificent scenic routes, the ***Northern Explorer*** (7:45am Mon., Thurs., and Sat., adults $179, children $125) departs Auckland for Wellington with stops at Otorohanga near Waitomo Caves and Tongariro National Park. The other two routes take in South Island. When booking, you can opt to terminate the trip at any of the stops along the way.

Bus

Bus travel is the most flexible form of public transport within New Zealand. The reliable **Intercity** (www.intercity.co.nz) operates the largest bus network. Buses depart from the Sky City bus terminal (102 Hobson St.) opposite the Sky Tower.

Mana Bus (www.manabus.com) is an inexpensive option for exploring North Island. Buses pick up from downtown Auckland (115 Mayoral Dr.) for transportation to Whangarei, Hamilton, Rotorua, Taupo, and Wellington.

The hop-on, hop-off backpacker buses, **Kiwi Experience** (09/336-4286, www.kiwiexperience.com) and **Stray Travel** (09/526-2140, www.straytravel.com), offer a selection of touring routes that take in major highlights. Kiwi Experiences picks up in downtown Auckland (99 Queen St.) near Nomad Backpackers. Purchase passes for Stray Travel routes at their Stray Shop (50 Fort St., 9:30am-5pm Tues.-Fri., 10am-4pm Sat.).

GETTING AROUND

Transport throughout central Auckland is convenient, but the vicinity is not well serviced. Plan routes easily at **Auckland Transport Journey Planner** (www.at.govt.nz). If you are staying longer than a few days, get an **AT HOP Card** (www.at.govt.nz, $10), a prepaid smart card for travel on most buses, trains, and ferries. You'll save 20 percent on fares, and even more on the Link Buses. The **AT Hop Day Pass** ($18) can be loaded onto an existing AT HOP Card; the pass expires at midnight.

Britomart Transport Centre (8-10 Queen St.) is Auckland's main transportation hub, used for both bus and train travel. Find the staffed **Auckland Transport Information Kiosks** (7:30am-8pm Mon.-Sat., 8:30am-5pm Sun.) on the ground level of the transport center for travel inquiries, information, and to purchase rail tickets. Train tickets can be purchased from automated ticket machines at train stations before travel. Tickets cannot be bought on trains.

Bus fares are paid to the driver when boarding, so have your money ready. The exact amount is appreciated, but change can be given up to small notes.

Bus

The easiest way to make your way around the city is by the three color-coded **Link Bus** (www.at.govt.nz). The red **CityLink** bus (every 7 minutes 6:25am-11:25pm Mon.-Fri., every 10 minutes 7am-11:20pm Sun., $1) runs between Wynyard Quarter and K' Road via Queen Street. The green **InnerLink** bus (every 10-15 minutes 6:30am-11pm Mon.-Sat., every 10-15 minutes 7am-11pm Sun., $3) runs a circular route via Britomart, Sky City, Ponsonby, K' Road, Newmarket, Auckland Museum, and Parnell. The orange **OuterLink** bus (every 15 minutes 6:30am-11pm Mon.-Sat., every 15 minutes 7am-11pm Sun., $3-5) runs through the city center and outer suburbs. The three routes interconnect. Drivers have change for cash, or use your AT HOP Card.

Rail

Britomart Transport Centre (8-10 Queen St., www.at.govt.nz) is the main rail hub. Western and southern suburbs are best served from the city center. The main routes run from Britomart Transport Centre west to Swanson via Newmarket, Mount Eden, and Kingsland; and south to Pukekohe via Newmarket and Remuera. The eastern line travels via eastern suburbs, including Orakei, before terminating south in Manakau.

Trains run every 20-30 minutes approximately 5am-11pm daily, and every 10 minutes 7am-9am and 4pm-6pm Monday-Friday. Some lines provide later weekend services. Tickets ($3 per stage) must be purchased from machines at the station.

Ferry

Fullers (Quay St., 09/367-9111, www.fullers.co.nz) operates ferry service to the North Shore, Coromandel, and Hauraki Gulf Islands. All ferries depart the Ferry Building downtown. Depending on the destination, ferries run as often as every 15 minutes up to once a week. Eight North Shore suburbs are served, with journeys taking around 15 minutes. Most visitors will likely head for Devonport, where ferries run every 15-30 minutes throughout the day. Return tickets to Devonport are $12. Tickets do not need to be booked in advance.

The two-hour ferry ride to Coromandel Town ($55 one-way, $90 round-trip) leaves Auckland at 8:45am Tuesday, Thursday, and Saturday-Sunday, returning at 3pm Tuesday and Thursday, 4:30pm Saturday-Sunday. Book in advance to secure a seat, especially in summer.

Taxis

Taxis can be ordered from **Auckland Co-op Taxis** (09/300-300). Auckland is also an **Uber** (www.uber.com) city.

Car

Parking in central Auckland is expensive. Roadside meters can be found for as little as $2 per hour on the outer fringes of the city center, but similar spots downtown and in multilevel car parks can quickly reach double figures. Opt for the excellent Link Bus or train instead of driving. Streets in the suburbs provide ample parking, but parking in suburban shopping areas is usually limited.

Congestion in Auckland is a problem. During peak times, avoid crossing the Harbour Bridge to or from the North Shore, or driving along Tamaki Drive east along the waterfront from downtown to Mission Bay.

CAR RENTAL

Auckland car rental companies are abundant, both in the city and at the airport, but some charge an airport fee. Competitive prices can be found at **Budget** (09/976-2270, www.budget.co.nz), **Thrifty** (09/309-0111, www.thrifty.co.nz), and **Hertz** (09/367-6350, www.hertz.co.nz). You'll save a few extra bucks with **Rent a Dent** (09/309-0066, www.rentadent.co.nz) and **Go Rentals** (09/525-7321, www.gorentals.co.nz). Reputable campervan and motorhome rental companies include **Spaceships** (09/526-2137, www.spaceshipsrentals.co.nz), **Escape** (09/302-4139, www.escaperentals.co.nz), and **Maui** (09/255-3910, www.maui.co.nz).

SERVICES

Visitor Information

Auckland Airport's **i-SITE Visitor Centre** (arrivals hall, international terminal, 09/365-9925, 6am-10pm daily) is part of New Zealand's official nationwide visitor information network. There are more than 80 dotted around the country, and they're an invaluable source of local wisdom. Be sure to grab some free visitor guides and maps. They also offer a free booking service for tours, vehicle rentals, and accommodations, and sell travel SIM cards for your cell phone. Two other i-SITEs are conveniently located in central Auckland at **Princes Wharf** (137 Quay St., 09/365-9914, 9am-5pm daily) and **SkyCity** (Victoria St. and Federal St., 09/365-9918, 9am-5pm daily).

Make the **Department of Conservation (DoC) Auckland Visitor Centre** (137 Quay St., Princes Wharf, 09/379-6476, 9am-5pm daily, closed every 2nd and 4th Wed. of the month) your main point of call for information on walks, campsites, regional parks, and visiting the Hauraki Gulf islands.

Banks are generally open 9am-4:30pm Monday-Friday, and a handful of branches are open weekends. Banks offer the most competitive **currency exchange** rates. There are nonbank currency exchange counters at the airport and many more on Queen Street.

Baggage storage is available at Pier 1 behind the Ferry Building at the bottom of Queen St. It's $5 per bag per day, and luggage can be left overnight for multiple days, but only dropped off and picked up 9am-5pm daily. Call Harbor Information (09/357-0550) for details.

Media and Communication

Auckland **Central City Library** (44/46 Lorne St., 09/377-0209, www.aucklandlibraries.govt.nz, 9am-8pm Mon.-Fri., 10am-4pm Sat.-Sun.) is a large multilevel library with an abundance of information leaflets. More libraries can be found in most of the surrounding suburbs; check the website for addresses. All New Zealand public libraries have free Wi-Fi, but some have a daily limit of 1GB.

Free public **Wi-Fi** hot spots are limited and generally only found in the city. Most accommodations have free Wi-Fi, sometimes limited, with a charge for more. Most coffee shops and eateries will hook you up for free.

Post offices (0800/081-190, www.nzpost.co.nz)—Kiwis call them "post shops"—are generally open 9am-5pm Monday-Friday, and some are open 9am-1pm Saturday.

Emergencies

For all emergency services, call 111. **Auckland City Hospital** (Park Rd., Grafton, 09/367-0000) is the most central hospital and has 24-hour emergency care.

Vicinity of Auckland

While the immensity of Auckland makes for great diversity, it's difficult for visitors to fit everything in. But it would be a tragedy to not see the "Wild West" coast and at least a couple of the Hauraki Gulf Islands (namely Waiheke and Rangitoto). The area north of Auckland can be explored on the way to Northland; heading south, take the picturesque Pohutukawa Coast route down the east flank.

TOP EXPERIENCE

HAURAKI GULF ISLANDS

Beside the eastern fringe of New Zealand's largest city rests the nation's largest marine reserve, in the Hauraki Gulf. Stretching from Auckland to the Coromandel Peninsula, more than 50 islands protrude from an area of more than 1.2 million hectares graced by marinelife that includes dolphins, orcas, and whales. Most islands are managed by DoC, and a handful are home to endangered endemic species such as the tuatara—one of the world's oldest reptiles—and the fabled kiwi bird.

Getting There

The majority of the islands are served by ferries operated by **Fullers** (09/367-9111, www.fullers.co.nz). Eco-friendly **Auckland Sea Kayaks** (09/213-4545, www.aucklandseakayaks.co.nz, from $135) offers a unique gulf experience and reaches some places that ferries cannot. For a bird's-eye view of the archipelago, book a trip with **Auckland Seaplanes** (09/390-1121, www.aucklandseaplanes.com); their array of sightseeing packages and tours include the Waiheke vineyards.

the Hauraki Gulf from Waiheke Island

★ Waiheke Island

Once a hippie haven, Waiheke Island is the Tuscany of the Hauraki Gulf, brimming with more jet-setters than gypsies—yet it retains its über-laid-back bohemian charm. A clutch of lovely white sandy beaches—Oneroa, Onetangi, and Palm Beach—frame Waiheke Island, and its unique microclimate allows an array of boutique wineries, olive groves, craft breweries, galleries, and eateries to flourish. Hiking is also popular on the island; pick up trail maps at the ferry terminal.

Most people head to Waiheke (which means "cascading waters" in Maori) for the wine, and it's easy to navigate the island's growers independently or on a tour. The **Taste of Waiheke Tour** (09/367-9111, www.fullers.co.nz, departs Auckland 11am daily, $140) visits three vineyards, one craft brewery, and an olive grove. All tastings are included and are spread over 5.5 hours. Rates include a light lunch, the return ferry to Auckland, and an all-day bus pass.

Kayak Waiheke (09/372-5550, www.kayakwaiheke.co.nz, $30) rents kayaks and offers a range of guided tours. **EcoZip Adventures** (150 Trig Hill Rd., Onetangi, 09/372-5646, www.ecozipadventures.co.nz, adults $119, children $79) affords some thrilling Waiheke views from a zip line.

FOOD AND ACCOMMODATIONS

Enjoy relaxing views at majestic **Mudbrick Vineyard and Restaurant** (126 Church Bay Rd., 09/372-9050, www.mudbrick.co.nz, 10am-5pm daily), where you can taste up to five wines ($10-20) and gorge on fine seafood, steaks, and lamb at the alfresco **Archive Bar and Bistro** (9am-close daily, $15-42) or inside the luxury **Mudbrick Restaurant** (6pm-8pm daily, $83-100 pp). Luxurious accommodations ($950-3,000) include a selection of fully self-contained two-bedroom cottages and a three-bedroom lodge with antique furnishings and views of Rangitoto Island.

Stonyridge (80 Onetangi Rd., 09/372-8822, www.stonyridge.co.nz) boasts a spectacular setting and is famed for its award-winning blends. Take the 40-minute tour with two tastings (11:30am Sat.-Sun., $10) or make reservations for lunch at the vineyard's **Verandah Cafe** (11:30am-5pm daily, $32-42).

The Oyster Inn (124 Oceanview Rd., Oneroa, 09/372-2222, www.theoysterinn.co.nz, noon-close daily, $24-35) serves produce from the island and seafood from its waters. It is very popular, so book early to snag a seat on the balcony. Spend the night in one of three boutique hotel rooms ($375-450) with skylights, en suite baths, bathrobes, Sky TV, mini bars, music docking stations, Wi-Fi, and hot drink-making facilities. Two of the rooms have private verandas.

The sociable **Hekerua Lodge** (11 Hekerua Rd., Oneroa, 09/372-8990, www.hekerualodge.co.nz, 2-night minimum, dorm $31-33, $55 s, $90 d) is set amid 0.6ha of native forest a short stroll from the beach. It boasts a spa, a pool, and group activities such as volleyball and yoga.

Fossil Bay Lodge (58 Korora Rd., Oneroa, 09/372-8371, www.fossilbay.net, $60 s, $90-130 d) is set in an idyllic bush environment with affordable lodgings in cottages, apartments, and luxurious en suite tents.

Family-run **Palm Beach Bungalows** (77 Hill Rd., Palm Beach, 027/372-6649, www.palmbeachbungalows.com, $225-305 s or d) offers three individual character-filled dwellings in a shady oasis minutes from the sea. Treat yourself to a massage and a dip in the outdoor French tub.

You'll find few places more inspired to pitch a tent than **Poukaraka Flats Campground** (339 Gordons Rd., 09/366-2000, adults $15, children $6, under age 6 free) in Whakanewha Regional Park. Set at the end of Rocky Bay with life-affirming ocean views, there are handy on-site free barbecues and showers (brace yourself, they're cold).

GETTING THERE

Fullers (09/367-9111, www.fullers.co.nz, 6am-12:30am Tues.-Sat., 6am-11:15pm Sun.-Mon., adults $36, children $18) operates ferries every half hour daily. They also offer a selection of tour packages and occasional "Hot Seats" ($10 one-way). The ferry ride to Waiheke Island takes about 35 minutes from downtown Auckland.

Sealink (09/300-5900, www.sealink.co.nz) passenger fares are comparable to Fullers; they can also ferry your vehicle ($170). For a Hollywood-style Waiheke entrance, fly in by helicopter with **Heletranz** (09/415-3550, www.heletranz.co.nz, one-way from $700 for up to 3 people, $900 for 4-5 people).

Operated by Fullers, the **Waiheke Bus Company** (www.fullers.co.nz, all-day pass adults $10, children $6, or one-way $2 to Oneroa) covers all locations. A timetable and a route map are available on the website.

Two wheels is a fun way to crisscross the island. **Waiheke Bike Hire** (7 Oceanview Rd., Oneroa, 09/372-7937, www.waihekebike-hire.co.nz, $35 per day) advises about bike routes and provides maps. Or get an electric bike from **Onya Bikes** (124 Oceanview Rd., 09/372-4428, www.ecyclesnz.com, $60 per day) or a scooter from **Rent Me Waiheke** (14 Oceanview Rd., 09/372-3339, www.rent-mewaiheke.co.nz, $59 per day).

Rent a car from **Waiheke Rental Cars** (09/372-8635, www.waihekerentalcars.co.nz) or call a cab from **Waiheke Express Taxis** (0800/700-789).

★ Rangitoto Island

The youngest volcano in the Hauraki Gulf is also its largest and most recognizable thanks to a nearly symmetrical cone whose gentle slopes, formed just six centuries ago, belie the violence of its eruptions. Today, **Rangitoto** (which means "bloody sky" in Maori) nurtures native birds and more than 200 species of endemic plants. There are no accommodations on Rangitoto. Camping is available on adjoining Motutapu Island.

WALKS AND TOURS

The stroll to the 259m **summit** takes one hour through forests and over lava fields; wear sturdy footwear and bring refreshments to enjoy the 360-degree views. Bring a flashlight and check out the lava caves on the way back down.

The 4.5km **coastal track** (2.5 hours one-way) heads east from Rangitoto Wharf, passing a number of boatsheds and secluded beaches ideal for a lunchtime picnic and cooling off in the ocean.

Learn all about the geology of the island and the flora and fauna that inhabit it on 3.5-hour **guided tours** (www.rangitoto.co.nz, $68), which include a round-trip ferry ride via Fullers to the island and a 4WD tram to the summit followed by a 900-meter boardwalk to the top.

Auckland Sea Kayaks (09/213-4545, www.aucklandseakayaks.co.nz, from $135) operates guided paddles to Rangitoto.

GETTING THERE

It takes 25 minutes to reach Rangitoto by boat. **Fullers** (09/367-9111, www.fullers.co.nz, 9:15am Mon.-Fri., 7:30am Sat.-Sun., adults $20, children $10) ferries leave daily from the Auckland Ferry Building. Early-bird prices are available for 7:30am trips. There are also services from Devonport.

Motutapu Island

Motutapu (meaning "sacred hill") has more than 300 Maori archaeological sites, such as *pa*, along with World War II bunkers. Motutapu cradles all manner of endemic flora and fauna, including the kiwi.

WALKS AND CAMPING

A number of walks are accessible from the ferry at Islington Bay causeway or from the **Rangitoto Coastal Track,** which connects the islands via the causeway. Walks are well-signed and provide access to beaches and views across the Hauraki Gulf.

The **Home Bay campsite** (09/379-6476, www.doc.govt.nz, adults $8, children $4) provides overnight stays for campers.

GETTING THERE

Ferry services to Motutapu are infrequent. **Fullers** (09/367-9111, www.fullers.co.nz) runs a service every second Sunday (sometimes every fourth Sun., check the website to be sure). Alternately, you can hop on the ferry to Rangitoto and take the three-hour walking track to Motutapu from Rangitoto Wharf via the Rangitoto Coastal Track.

Tiritiri Matangi Island

Tiritiri Matangi (www.tiritirimatangi.org.nz) is a pest-free island paradise 30km north of Auckland. This open sanctuary houses endemic species such as the tui, fantail, takahe, and red-crowned parakeet.

WALKS AND ACCOMMODATIONS

Stay overnight at the dorms-only **Tiritiri Matangi Island Bunkhouse** (09/379-6476, www.doc.govt.nz, adults $30, children $20) for an excellent chance of spotting kiwi, the ancient reptile tuatara, and the blue penguin. The island's jagged coastline gives way to secluded nooks easily explored via a navigable network of trails from the wharf and the bunkhouse. A few steps from the bunkhouse is New Zealand's oldest lighthouse.

Fullers (09/367-9111, www.fullers.co.nz) organizes 90-minute guided walks (Wed.-Sun., adults $10, children $2.50, plus ferry fare) where visitors can learn about the history of the island and its birds.

GETTING THERE

Fullers ferries (09/367-9111, www.fullers.co.nz, adults $70, children $40) leave Auckland at 9am Wednesday-Sunday, departing from the island at 3:30pm. Book a superb guided tour ($10) when purchasing your ferry ticket.

Great Barrier Island

Great Barrier Island (Aotea Rd., 09/429-0848, www.thebarrier.co.nz) is a sprawling wilderness on the outer-edge of the Hauraki Gulf that crams a heap of Kiwi classics into one rugged space: mountainous bushland, hot springs, and windswept beaches screaming to be surfed. The island is partly cut-off from civilization, just the way the 1,000 or so residents like it—there are no banks, ATMs, or public transportation. Its six **campsites** (09/379-6476, www.doc.govt.nz, adults $13, children $6.50) can be booked through DoC.

Tiritiri Matangi Island

Kauri Dieback: A Slayer of Giants

Since being identified in 2008, kauri dieback has felled thousands of kauri trees across New Zealand. The disease affects kauri of any age and size with microscopic spores migrating through the soil to attack the roots and prevent the trees from absorbing nutrients. Symptoms include loss of leaves, yellowing of the foliage, and decaying branches, with nearly all infected trees dying. The spores are easily spread, and there is currently no known kauri dieback treatment. Paths into New Zealand's kauri forests have cleaning stations with a detergent spray and brush for the soles of your shoes. Be sure to use them, and upon entering a forest, always keep to the trails.

GETTING THERE

Sealink (09/300-5900, www.sealink.co.nz, 8am Tues.-Fri. and Sun., adults $102, children $81, vehicles $347) sails from Auckland Wynyard Wharf one-way for the 4.5-hour trip. Get there faster with **Barrier Air** (09/275-9120 www.barrierair.kiwi, $178). The first of six daily flights depart Auckland International Airport at 8am daily; the 30-minute flight makes a day trip possible. For shuttles, accommodations, or to rent a car, contact **Go Great Barrier Island** (0800/997-222, www.greatbarrierislandtourism.co.nz, shuttles from $20, car hire from $60 per day).

Motuihe Island

You may want to spend longer on **Motuihe Island,** where crystal seas lap white-sand beaches in the shadow of glorious native greenery, home to kiwi birds and the tuatara. An array of walks navigates idyllic beaches, pastures, and, at low tide, rock pools.

TOURS AND CAMPING

Guided **tours** (2.5 hours, www.motuihe.org.nz, $5 pp, plus ferry fare) are available in summer. You can also book a spot at the DoC-run **campsite** (09/379-6476, www.doc.govt.nz, adults $8, children $4) to relish your visit.

GETTING THERE

Fullers (09/367-9111, www.fullers.co.nz) offers sporadic Sunday service; call to confirm dates, times, and fares. **Auckland Sea Kayaks** (09/213-4545, www.aucklandseakayaks.co.nz, from $135) offers a more leisurely transport.

Rotoroa Island

Rotoroa is a conservation island awash with birdlife. Snaking trails lead to white beaches and fascinating restored heritage sites such as a **jail** and **chapel** along with a **museum** and **exhibition center** (all buildings 10am-5pm daily, free).

ACCOMMODATIONS

Modern **dorms** (www.rotora.org.nz, $40) come with a well-equipped kitchen, free tea and coffee, a stereo, and outdoor shower. Fully self-contained cottages ($490) include barbecues, free Wi-Fi, and TVs with DVD players. All lodgings are surrounded by expansive serene landscapes of trees and lawns, some with sea views.

GETTING THERE

Fullers (09/367-9111, www.fullers.co.nz, adults $52, adults $30) runs ferry service once daily. The trip takes 1 hour and 15 minutes.

★ WAITAKERE RANGES

West of Auckland, you're entering real Kiwi country and they don't call it the "Wild West" coast for nothing. The evocative **Waitakere Ranges** are 16,000ha of densely forested hills laced with waterfalls and 250km of walking trails. Fringing the tree-clad coastline are dramatic cliffs and black sand beaches pounded by year-round surf.

While large proportion of the tracks and forests throughout the Waitakere Ranges may close to prevent the spread of kauri dieback disease, beaches, pasturelands, and some bush walks remain accessible. Contact the Auckland Council (www.regionalparks.aucklandcouncil.govt.nz/waitakereranges) for status updates.

Piha

The tiny surf town of **Piha** sits over a black sand beach. Make sure to scale **Lion Rock** (you can't miss it); this neck of an ancient volcano has eroded into a shape resembling that of a big cat. Protruding from the middle of Piha Beach, it once served as a *pa*. A short track (30 minutes round-trip) scales the steep sections of the "neck" with hypnotic views of the windswept coast.

Kitekite Falls is a popular swimming hole; the 45-minute bush walk starts from the car park at the end of Glen Esk Road. To the north, steep sand dunes surround **Lake Wainamu** near **Bethells Beach,** a popular surf spot home to a sizable cave. This area provides some serious sandboarding opportunities. Follow the 90-minute loop track around Lake Wainamu for a romantic stroll, crossing a lovely waterfall and swimming hole.

Among the Waitakere Ranges' 250km of walking tracks is the relatively unknown **Hillary Trail.** Plotted with the help of late legendary mountaineer Sir Edmund Hillary, the gnarly 76km multiday hike easily stands up to some of New Zealand's more famous walks. The walk begins at the **Aritaki Visitor Centre** (300 Scenic Dr., Titirangi, 09/817-0077, 9am-5pm daily) and ends at **Murawai Beach,** the most dramatic on Auckland's west coast and the nesting site of a colony of gannets (Aug.-Mar.) thousands-strong. Sections of the track can be tackled separately.

Food and Accommodations

Bethells Cafe (Bethells Rd., 5:30pm-9:30pm Fri., 10am-6pm Sat.-Sun. Nov.-May, 10am-5pm Sat.-Sun. June-Oct., $15) is a food truck positioned at Bethells Beach. This local icon has been around for 40 years, renowned in the community for its high-quality fast food, especially its incredible burgers and pizza. There is a smattering of seats in the sand under and around the awning, or take your slice down to the crashing waves. Fridays, there're usually live bands.

The dishes at **The Piha Cafe** (20 Seaview

a water crossing along the Hillary Trail

Rd., 09/812-8808, 8am-3pm Wed. and Sun.-Mon., 8am-9:30pm Thurs.-Sat., $19-30) are handmade using seasonal free-range and organic ingredients; the pizza is particularly good. This is a popular hangout for laid-back locals.

Black Sands Lodge (9 Sylvan Glade, 021/777-219, www.pihabeach.co.nz, $160-330) offers accommodations surrounded by dense shrub close to the beach. Three soothing units are equipped with full kitchens and living areas with TVs and Wi-Fi; the two cottages are fully self-contained, while the cabin shares a bath with the owners. Ask about surf lessons and massage service.

Experience Auckland's rugged west coast of dramatic black sand dunes and wild surf from the comfortable base of **Wainamu Luxury Tents** (022/384-0500, tehenga2004@hotmail.com, Oct.-May, $250), on privately owned land near Bethalls Beach. Tents come fully equipped with linens, a gas barbecue, a hot outdoor bath, showers, and flush toilets.

Transportation

Piha is 40km (45 minutes) west of Auckland via State Highway 16, Route 13, and Piha Road. Bethells Beach is 37km (45 minutes) north of Piha via Piha Road and Scenic Drive.

The west coast is not served by public transport, and private shuttles are expensive. **Surf Shuttle** (0800/952-526, www.surfshuttle.co.nz, $45 one-way) provides door-to-door service.

POHUTUKAWA COAST

Auckland's eastern region is fringed with many white-sand beaches caressed by glassy waters sheltered by the dozens of Hauraki Gulf monoliths.

Leaving Auckland, head south along Highway 1. Take exit 448 west onto Redoubt Road, then take Murphys Road and Ormiston Road toward the Pacific Coast Highway. Follow signs for Whitford and Maraetai at the northern end of the Pohutukawa Coast (www.pohutukawacoast.co.nz).

Maraetai

Maraetai ("meeting place by the sea") is 44km (40 minutes) west of Auckland. The small seaside settlement overlooks the Hauraki Gulf islands and an ocean so still you'll think it's a lake. A handful of beachside eateries include **Bach 'n Café** (249 Maraetai Dr., 09/536-7182, 9am-4pm Sun.-Fri., 9am-6pm Sat., $17-22) with premium breakfasts like banoffee crumpets, salmon and eggs, and freshly prepared lunchtime delights such as Thai beef salad or seafood. Massive windows and a deck area afford unobstructed ocean views.

Clevedon Village

Twenty minutes (16km) South of Maraetai via the Pacific Coast Highway and Whitford-Maraetai Road is quaint **Clevedon Village.** Every Sunday, the village hosts Auckland's best **farmers market** (107 Monument Rd., www.clevedonfarmersmarket.co.nz, 8:30am-1pm Sun.) The food stalls are superb, and the market is renowned for its whitebait fritters (a Kiwi staple) and buffalo mozzarella. Take a seat on a hay bale to enjoy the live folk tunes.

★ Waiti Bay

From Clevedon, drive 20km (25 minutes) east along Clevedon-Kawakawa Road to the end of Kawakawa Bay Coast Road and the car park for the beach at **Waiti Bay.** A stepped path (1.5 hours round-trip) winds over the headland to **Tawhitokino Beach,** a pristine stretch of sand that can only be accessed at low tide.

At the far end sits a small basic **campsite** (Auckland Council, 09/366-2000, www.aucklandcouncil.govt.nz, adults $8, children $4) with a cooking shelter, a toilet, and running water. It's not uncommon to have the coastal spot to yourself, except for the odd weka.

NORTH OF AUCKLAND

The drive north out of Auckland isn't the most scenic of routes, but a few detours will allow you to discover an abundance of treasures along the way.

Army Bay

Shakespear Regional Park (1468 Whangaparaoa Rd., www.aucklandcouncil.govt.nz, 6am-9pm daily summer, 6am-7pm daily winter, free) is home to three beautiful golden beaches framed by dunes with bright-blue water and verdant bush and farmland. Take a dip in the ocean and wander paths that wind through a fenced predator-free haven for native birds like the tui and the red-crowned parakeet.

Stay the night at scenic **Te Haruhi Bay Campground** (adults $15, children $6), located within the protected sanctuary about 250m along the park access road. The campground can only be entered during park hours; sites book up to six months in advance. There are sites for up to 160 people. Facilities include toilets, cold showers, and drinking water.

The park is 50km (50 minutes) northeast of Auckland via Highway 1.

Orewa

The sleepy coastal village of **Orewa** is a fine spot for lunch or an ice cream while strolling expansive golden sands that are popular with swimmers, surfers, kayakers, and kitesurfers. Its 3km coastline is one of Auckland's safest beaches.

Just across from the beach, popular **Oliver's Café** (340 Hibiscus Coast Hwy., 09/421-1156, 7am-4pm daily) is strewn with ocean artwork, including a surfboard on the wall. Enjoy top-drawer java, scones, and a wonderful chocolate milk amid a super-chilled vibe.

Orewa is 19km (25 minutes) northwest of Shakespear Regional Park via Whangaparaoa Road and the Hibiscus Coast Highway. Heading straight from Auckland, take Highway 1 to the Hibiscus Coast Highway and continue 37km (30 minutes) from there.

Warkworth

Warkworth, 58km (40 minutes) north of Auckland via Highway 1, is a languid hub that sprouted around the Mahurangi River in the mid-19th century. The **Warkworth District Museum** (Tudor Collins Dr., 09/425-7093, www.warkworthmuseum.co.nz, 10am-4pm daily summer, 10am-3pm daily winter, adults $7, children $3, under age 6 free) affords a glimpse into the town's provincial past life by way of recreated historic homes and workshops. Adjacent is the **Parry Kauri Park,** home to magnificent kauri specimens explored via a 20-minute boardwalk stroll.

The Honey Centre (7 Perry Rd., 09/425-8003, www.honeycentre.com, 8:30am-5pm daily) sells all manner of unusual blends of honey made from native flowers such as pohutukawa, rewarewa, and tawari. Ask for a tasting session to choose which honey you like best.

The **Warkworth i-SITE Visitor Centre** (1 Baxter St., 09/425-9081, www.matakana-coast.co.nz, 9am-5pm Mon.-Fri., 10am-3pm Sat.-Sun.) offers travel advice for the region, including maps, tours, and accommodations info. There's also a gift shop.

Matakana

Pretty Matakana is a village brimming with cafés, boutiques, and a **farmers market** (2 Matakana Valley Rd., www.visitmatakana.co.nz, 8am-1pm Sat.) with a big emphasis on locally crafted organic food like pies, cheese, and mussel fritters. Enjoy it all while listening to live local musicians.

Stop for lunch and wine-tasting at **Plume** (49 Sharp Rd., 09/422-7915, www.plumerestaurant.co.nz, 11am-2pm Wed.-Fri., 11am-3pm Sat.-Sun., 6pm-close Fri.-Sat., $29-42), a restaurant with valley and vine views. Its tipples are crafted at its boutique winery, Rubber Duck. The menu melds Kiwi and Asian fare with a modern twist on classics like Peking duck or pork belly with stir-fried soba noodles.

If craft beer is your thing, head to **Sawmill Brewery** (1004 Leigh Rd., 09/422-6555, www.sawmillbrewery.co.nz, noon-10pm daily summer, noon-10pm Wed.-Sun. winter), an überhip establishment in an old timber mill. Imaginative gastropub-grub like smoked mullet wrapped in banana leaf or spicy venison ribs accompanies 14 in-house beers on tap.

Matakana is 9km (10 minutes) northeast of Warkworth via Highway 1, Sandspit Road, and Matakana Road.

Leigh

There is little to occupy the traveler in this tiny harbor town that services Goat Island. One exception is the legendary **Leigh Sawmill Cafe** (142 Pakiri Rd., 09/422-6019, www.sawmillcafe.co.nz, 10am-close daily Dec. 27-Feb. 15, 10am-3pm Mon.-Wed., 10am-close Thurs.-Sun. Feb. 15-Mar. 27, 10am-close Thurs.-Sun. Mar. 28-Dec., $25-32). Enjoy a pizza, burger, or fish in its sunny garden. The small venue attracts big names for nighttime gigs that keep diners entertained. The site also offers superb **accommodations:** bunk rooms ($40) share baths and a fully equipped kitchen; suites ($125) include private baths with toiletries as well as TVs, fridges, tea and coffee, and private decks; and fully self-contained apartments and cottages ($200) come with private kitchens, lounge areas, and private courtyards.

Leigh lies 13km (15 minutes) northeast of Matakana via Leigh Road.

Goat Island Marine Reserve

Goat Island is the common name for the **Cape Rodney-Okakari Point Marine Reserve,** New Zealand's original marine reserve. The actual island is 300m offshore. Its shimmering waters contain an abundance of kelp and coral that are patrolled by plentiful fish, rays, and rock lobsters. It's a snorkeling, scuba diving, and kayaking haven.

View the underwater reserve from the comfort and relative warmth of a **Glass Bottom Boat** (Goat Island Rd., 09/422-6334, www.glassbottomboat.co.nz). The 45-minute cruises (adults $30, senior $25, children $15) enable guests to catch sight of the region's marine birds while navigating the jagged cliffs and caves of Goat Island. The company also offers kayak rentals.

Goat Island Dive and Snorkel (142a Pakiri Rd., Leigh, 09/422-6925, www.goatislanddive.co.nz) rents snorkel equipment ($15-38) and leads guided scuba dives ($175).

It's worth spending at least one night here. **Goat Island Camping and Accommodation** (123 Goat Island Rd., 09/422-6185 www.goatislandcamping.co.nz) offers reasonably priced accommodations with incredible views. Choose from camping (adults $25, children $10) to quirky trailers, cabins, and bungalows ($80-160 s or d for 4-5 people, $10-20 per extra adult). The site has a prime position on the mainland, right next to the reserve.

The marine reserve is 3km north of Leigh, along Pakiri Road and Goat Island Road. It is 83km north of Auckland.

Northland

Auckland to Whangarei......... 92
Whangarei...................... 95
The Tutukaka Coast............ 100
Bay of Islands..................... 103
The Far North and Cape Reinga... 116
The Kauri Coast.................. 124

Look for ★ to find recommended sights, activities, dining, and lodging.

Highlights

★ **Waipu Caves:** These limestone caves, adorned with stalactites and stalagmites, twinkle with the light of glowworms (page 93).

★ **Diving off Poor Knights Islands:** Jacques Cousteau rated this small volcanic archipelago one of the top-10 dive sites in the world (page 101).

★ **Twin Coast Cycle Trail:** This easy Great Ride merges Maori and European cultural highlights with spectacular scenery (page 105).

★ **Dolphin Encounters:** The Bay of Islands gets you up close and personal with wild dolphins (page 109).

★ **Coca Cola Lake:** This cola-colored lake looks good enough to drink and makes for a refreshing place to swim (page 117).

★ **Sand boarding on Ninety Mile Beach:** New Zealand's drivable beach boasts 140m-high sand dunes that beg to be surfed (page 120).

★ **Cape Reinga:** At the tip of Northland stands a historic lighthouse and an 800-year-old pohutukawa tree of Maori legend (page 121).

★ **Waipoua Forest:** This isolated forest of giant ancient kauri trees is home to some 2,000-year-old specimens (page 126).

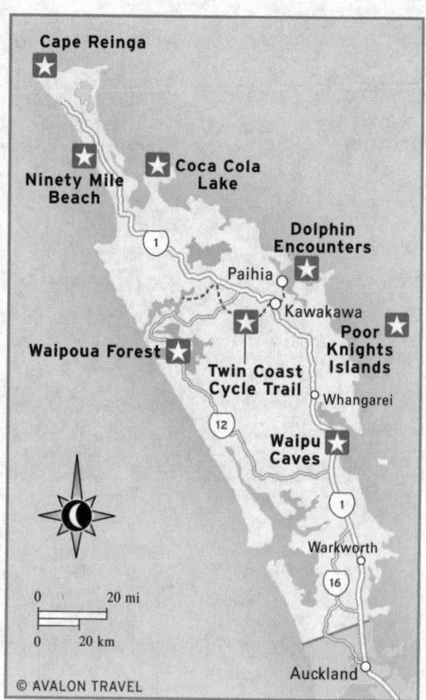

Northland stretches from Auckland to Cape Reinga at the tip of the Aupouri Peninsula, where the Pacific Ocean dramatically clashes with the Tasman Sea.

On its headlands stands a pohutukawa tree said by Maori to be the spot where the spirits of the deceased voyage to their final resting place.

The Bay of Islands, on the Northland's jagged east coast, is where Maori chiefs and the British Crown signed the Treaty of Waitangi in 1840, the founding document of modern New Zealand. Today, the Bay of Islands provides an excellent base for oceangoing adventures, such as swimming with dolphins. South of the Bay of Islands, the marine reserve around Poor Knights Islands afford some of the world's finest scuba diving.

Northland's west coast boasts the drivable Ninety Mile Beach as well as monolithic sand dunes that can be surfed like waves. Don't miss hidden gems like glowworm caves, a "cola"-filled lake, and an ancient forest of kauri trees so old that some specimens were around when the Greek empire fell to Rome.

PLANNING YOUR TIME

Use **Paihia** as a base to explore the **Bay of Islands;** spend at least one night and a full day here. Spreading your trip over a few more days leaves time to take in other attractions such as **Ninety Mile Beach, Cape Reinga,** and the **Karikari Peninsula.** Much of the east coast—the Bay of Islands to Ninety Mile Beach and Cape Reinga—is served by public transport, but you'll need a vehicle to explore the west coast south of Hokianga Harbour to the **Kauri Coast.**

Previous: the waters around Karikari Peninsula; Opua's harbor. **Above:** kayaks at Paihia.

Northland

Coast
Kai-Iwi Lakes
Maropiu
14
Tangihua Forest
WAIPU CAVES
Ruakaka
Bream
Bay
Hen and Chickens Islands
Dargaville
Ripiro Beach
Wairoa River
12
Waipu
Ruawai
Matakohe
Brynderwyn
Mangawhai Heads
Mangawhai
Goat Island Marine Reserve
Tasman
Sea
Kaipara
Kellys Bay
TE HANA TE AO MARAMA CULTURAL CENTRE
Te Hana
Wellsford
Pakiri Beach
Leigh
Cape Rodney
1
Pouto
North Head
South Head
South Head
Warkworth
Sandspit
Kawau Island
Harbour
16
Wenderholm Regional Park
Mahurangi
Waioneke
Waiwera
Orewa
Red Beach
Whangaparaoa Peninsula
Shakespear Regional Park
Parakai
Helensville
16
Hauraki Gulf
Muriwai Beach
Waiheke Island
AUCKLAND
Piha
Papatoetoe
Manukau
Harbour
Papakura
Awhitu
Paerata
0
20 mi
0
20 km
© AVALON TRAVEL

CAPE REINGA
Spirits Bay
North Cape
Te Piki Recreation Reserve
Cape Maria Van Dieman
Te Paki Stream
Waitiki Landing
Aupouri Peninsula
Great Exhibition Bay
Te Kao
The Bluff
1
Houhora Harbour
NINETY MILE BEACH
Pukenui
Ninety Mile Beach
Houhora Heads
Rangaunu Bay
Maitai Bay
Karikari Peninsula
COCO COLA LAKE
Doubtless Bay
SOUTH PACIFIC OCEAN
Taipa
Mangonui
Coopers Beach
Whangaroa Harbour
Whangaroa
Matauri Bay
Motukawanui (Big Cavalli Island)
Waipapakauri Beach
Awanui
Kaitaia
Mangamuka Gorge
Takou Bay
Kaeo
10
DOLPHIN ENCOUNTERS
Ahipara
Puketutu 420m
Tauroa Point
Raetea Forest
Mangamuka
Puketi Forest
Kerikeri
Bay of Islands
Cape Brett
Mangamuka Bridge
Russel
Waitangi
Paihia
Opua
Kohukohu
Horeke
Lake Omapere
Kawakawa
Rawene
Kaikohe
Moerewa
KAWITI CAVES
POOR KNIGHTS ISLANDS
TWIN COAST CYCLE TRAIL
Opononi
Omapere
Hokianga Harbour
Whananaki
Matapouri
12
WAIPOUA FOREST
Hikurangi
Tutukaka
Trounson Kauri Park
Whangarei Falls
Whangarei
MOUNT PARIHAKA
ABBEY CAVES
Kauri
Maungatapere
Kaihu

Auckland to Whangarei

The drive from Auckland north to Whangarei takes about two hours along Highway 1. The Northern Gateway Toll Road (www.nzta.govt.nz, $2.30) is an uninspiring stretch along Highway 1 that begins at Silverdale, 31km north of Auckland.

Take the scenic route instead by turning east onto the **Hibiscus Coast Highway** (Hwy. 17). With the ocean at your side, this detour passes through Orewa before rejoining Highway 1. Continue east by turning off at Mangawhai Road, past Te Hana to see the breathtaking coastal formations at Mangawhai Heads. Follow Cove Road to Waipu, then head inland to the Waipu glowworm caves. Whangarei is a 30-minute drive north.

TE HANA

Te Hana Te Ao Marama Cultural Centre

The tiny town of Te Hana marks the symbolic merging of Auckland into Northland. The region's rich Maori heritage is well represented at the **Te Hana Te Ao Marama Cultural Centre** (311 Hwy. 1, 09/423-8701, www.tehana.co.nz, 9am-4pm Wed.-Sun. Sept.-Apr., 9am-4pm Wed.-Sat. May-Aug., adults $28.50, children $18.50), which boasts a fastidiously fashioned replica of a 17th-century Maori village. The cultural experience includes a fortified defensive site *(pa)*, a meeting house *(marae)*, and seeing "villagers" going about their everyday lives fishing, weaving, and performing ceremonial dances in authentic dress. It's a worthwhile introduction for your Northland adventures ahead.

Te Hana is 80km north of Auckland on Highway 1.

MANGAWHAI

Mangawhai Heads

About 5km north of the sleepy village of Mangawhai is the cliff walk along **Mangawhai Heads** (2-3 hours). It's a fine way to savor the splendor of the coastline and Hauraki Gulf from up high. Begin from the Mangawhai Surf Life Saving car park (Wintle Rd.). Time your walk so that you begin or return at mid- to low tide, and you can turn the trail into a loop. Nearby sprawling dunes, maintained by the Department of Conservation (DoC), are home to terns, oystercatchers, and dotterels.

Mangawhai is located about 20km northeast of Te Hana. From Highway 1, take Mangawhai Road east for 17km. Continue north on Tomarata Road as it becomes Insley Street into Mangawhai village.

Accommodations

Positioned next to the estuary and near the dunes, **Mangawhai Heads Holiday Park** (2 Mangawhai Heads Rd., 09/431-4675, www.mangawhaiheadsholidaypark.co.nz) is an especially scenic spot to camp. An array of campsites ($18-20 pp) includes beachfront options, along with cabins and motel rooms ($65-135); some are en suite, with cooking facilities, TVs, and private outdoor areas. Kayak and paddleboard rentals are available.

WAIPU

This unusual settlement was the destination of one of history's most fascinating migrations. Between 1819 and 1853, a group of hardy Scots led by the Reverend Norman McLeod built their own ships and made arduous globe-spanning journeys to Nova Scotia, then southern Australia, before finally sailing to Waipu.

Waipu is 26km northwest of Mangawhai, about a 30-minute drive from Mangawhai. Take Molesworth Drive north for 5km to Mangawhai Heads Road and continue 18km to Cove Road, then turn east.

Best Food

★ **Tonic:** Enjoy fine dining and creative menus in an intimate setting (page 99).

★ **Charlotte's Kitchen:** Positioned on a pier jutting out over the water, this relaxing establishment focuses on seafood, grass-fed free-range meat, and wood-fired pizzas (page 112).

★ **Pear Tree Restaurant and Bar:** Stellar dishes complement the setting in a stately villa on the banks of the Kerikeri River (page 115).

★ **Mangonui Fish Shop:** You must try the "World Famous" fish-and-chips (page 117).

★ **North Drift Café:** This laid-back beach hut serves innovative burgers (page 119).

★ **Boatshed Café:** Freshly prepared dishes are served in a historic boat shed with an ocean setting (page 125).

Sights and Events

The story of the 940 Scots who made it to these shores is told at the lovely **Waipu Museum** (36 The Centre, 09/432-0746, www.waipumuseum.com, 9:30am-4:30pm daily, adults $10, children $5, students and seniors $8). Inside, visitors browse historical photos and genealogy information, watch short films, and peruse naval artifacts and bagpipes. Pick up a trail map to follow the nearby heritage trail, which takes in historic sights built by the Scots, such as the reverend's house and church. The museum's gorgeous gift shop museum sells Celtic souvenirs, including tartan textiles, knitwear, and ceramics, along with traditional Kiwi wood carvings and *pounamu* jewelry.

If you're here on New Year's Day, don't miss the **Waipu Highland Games** (Caledonian Park, The Centre, www.waipugames.co.nz, Jan.). Held since 1871, this significant event incorporates Celtic traditions like caber tossing, bagpipes, and traditional dance.

Accommodations

A short stroll from the white sands of Bream Bay, **Waipu Cove Resort** (891 Cove Rd., 09/432-0348, www.waipucoveresort.co.nz, $150-350) is equipped with a swimming pool, a heated spa, and barbecue areas. Its 12 units range from studios to three bedrooms and are equipped with Sky TV, DVD players, free Wi-Fi, and private palm-lined patios. All rooms have en suite baths with kitchens or kitchenettes.

★ Waipu Caves

Shaded by dense bush, the magical **Waipu Caves** (Waipu Caves Rd.) punch their way 200m through limestone rock adorned with intricate stalactites and stalagmites. A 90-minute round-trip walking track snakes through karst formations then climbs through forest to a farmland ridgeline with views across Whangarei Harbour. Return is via the same trail. (Although it's called the Waipu Caves Track, there are no more caves along the trail.)

From the car park, enter the cave and cross a small stream as you navigate a winding passageway whose ceiling is awash with a galaxy of twinkling turquoise glowworms. There are more water crossings if you venture deeper into the cave; bring a flashlight.

This is an unguided trail, and though the water is usually only ankle- to knee-deep, surfaces can be slippery and unstable, so tread with care. Avoid entering the water during or

Best Accommodations

★ **Lodge Bordeaux:** Tasteful, spacious suites impart a sophisticated air to this impressive motel (page 99).

★ **Lodge 9:** Reclaimed timbers, fashionable decor, and original art create a soothing feel while plentiful amenities pamper guests (page 101).

★ **Helena Bay Lodge:** The world's best luxury hotel includes four private beaches along 3km of unspoiled coastline (page 102).

★ **Duke of Marlborough Hotel:** New Zealand's oldest licensed premises has been a favorite with travelers since 1827 (page 107).

★ **Haka Lodge:** This well-designed lodge features great touches and sprawling views overlooking the bay (page 112).

★ **Bay Cabinz Motel:** Nestled within a bird-filled forest, this budget-friendly motel boasts private patios with sea or garden views (page 112).

★ **Decks of Paihia:** One of the Bay of Islands' best B&Bs is a 10-minute walk from the beach (page 113).

★ **Takou River Lodge:** This idyllic slice of eco-luxury offers cozy cottages and lodges with river or bush views (page 116).

★ **Kahoe Farms Hostel:** Immaculate rooms and friendly hosts elevate this hostel to the superb level of a B&B (page 117).

★ **Old Oak:** An exquisitely kept boutique motel, this rambling colonial villa is surrounded by gardens and a wraparound balcony (page 117).

following heavy rainfall. Wear sturdy footwear that you don't mind getting wet, and bring a change of clothes; there is a free cold shower in the car park.

Waipu Caves are well signed off Waipu Caves Road, 13km northwest of Waipu. From Waipu, take Shoemaker Road north to Mountfield Road and head west. The main cave is a short stroll from the car park on Waipu Caves Road.

Whangarei

Whangarei, the northernmost city in New Zealand, spills onto a majestic harbor and dramatic coastline of volcanic headlands and white and golden sand beaches (the Whangarei district has more than 100—and you're never more than 40km from one), buffered by bush-clad hills to the back. The hub is mostly flat, compact, and easily walkable, boasting a pedestrian mall and a renovated Town Basin that overlooks a sparkling, mast-filled marina lined with cosmopolitan cafés, galleries, boutiques, bars, and a pair of museums.

SIGHTS

Whangarei Art Museum

The **Whangarei Art Museum—Te Manawa Toi** (91 Dent St., 09/430-4240, www.whangareiartmuseum.co.nz, 10am-4pm daily, free) is in the Hub in the Town Basin. The permanent space houses the region's civic art collection and hosts tours. Historic photography vies for space with contemporary and traditional pieces, such as cloth and canvas paintings and Pacific island warrior masks.

Clapham's National Clock Museum

A quirky collection, **Clapham's National Clock Museum** (Dent St., 09/438-3993, www.claphamsclocks.com, 9am-5pm daily, adults $10, children $4, seniors and students $8) exhibits every time-telling artifact imaginable, gathering cuckoo and grandfather clocks, sundials, watches, and more from across the globe. Free 40-minute guided tours can be booked in advance, where you'll learn more about the history of time and the mechanics behind the objects that keep it.

Botanica Whangarei

Witness bountiful New Zealand bush alongside tropical plants and stoic desert-dwelling specimens at **Botanica Whangarei** (1st Ave., 09/430-4200, www.wdc.govt.nz, 9am-4pm daily, free). This unlikely urban oasis includes the nation's greatest gathering of ferns, an impressive cactus house, and an intimate Japanese garden. Cross the stream to Cafler Park for horticultural treats like a fragrant rose garden.

Whangarei Quarry Gardens

Community-led, volunteer-run **Whangarei Quarry Gardens** (37a Russell Rd., 09/437-7210, www.whangarei.org.nz, 9am-5pm daily, free), in the suburb of Kensington, northwest of the city, blooms across 24ha in a former quarry. Thousands of specimens thrive in swaths of native forest; the subtropical climate is regulated in part by the quarry stones' trapped heat. The gardens are complemented by a pair of waterfalls, streams, and a sizeable lake. Plentiful birdlife—wood pigeons, tui, and fantails—are rarely far away. This is a much-loved labor of love; donations are deserved and welcome.

Kiwi North

Historical and natural attractions alike await 6km southwest of Whangarei at **Kiwi North** (500 Hwy. 14, Gate 1, 09/438-9630, www.kiwinorth.co.nz, 10am-4pm daily, adults $20, children $5, students and seniors $15). Spread across 25ha of farmland, forest, and volcanic hills, this indoor-outdoor museum of natural and human history honors early Maori. Exhibits tell the story of European arrival through a 40,000-piece collection that includes wonderful Maori cloaks, bone and stone carvings, a canoe, muskets, cannon balls, and early-20th-century photography. The dimly lit kiwi houses the legendary birds as they look for food in a nearly natural environment (it's the only place in Northland you're guaranteed to spot one). Other endemic critters include the tuatara and a collection of geckos. The surrounding grounds are

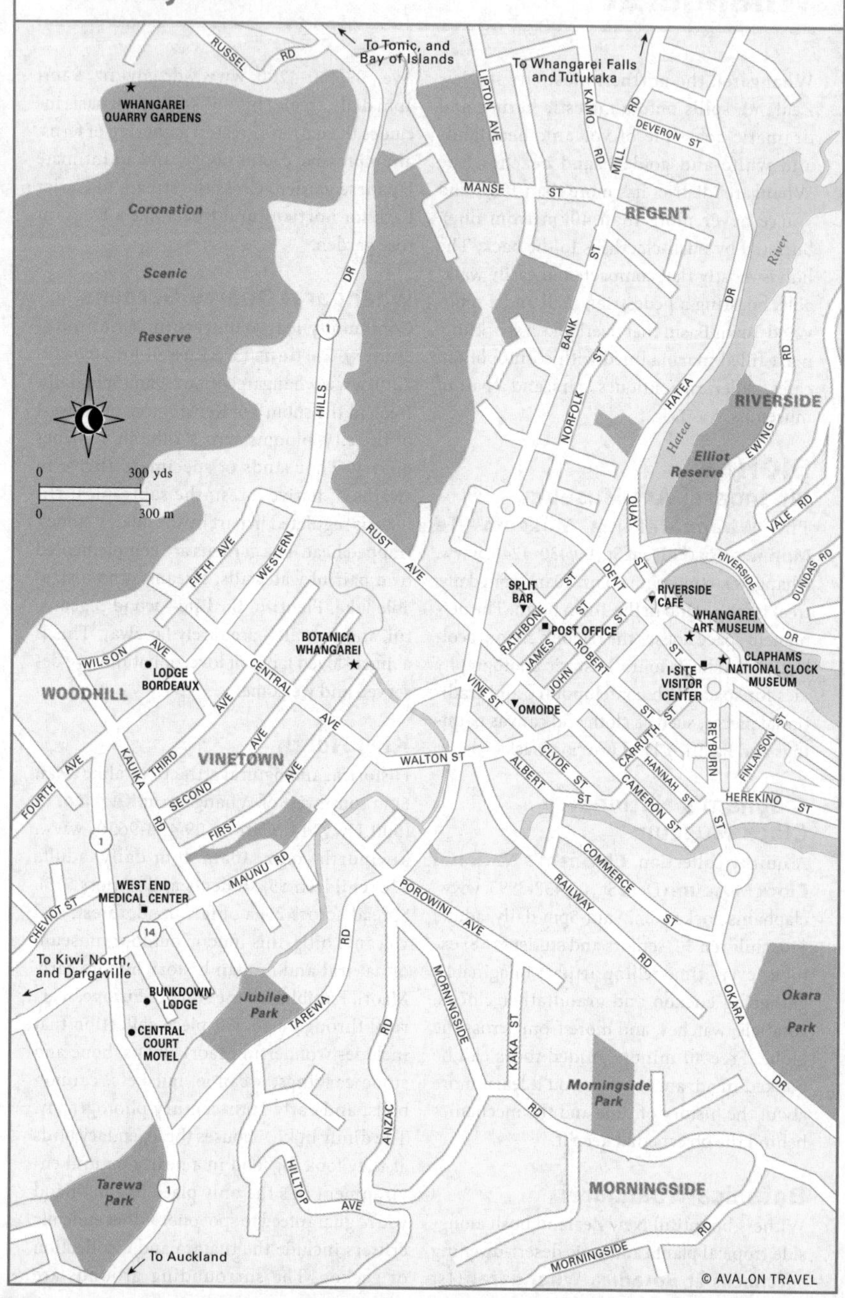
Whangarei
To Tonic, and Bay of Islands
To Whangarei Falls and Tutukaka
WHANGAREI QUARRY GARDENS
Coronation
Scenic
Reserve
REGENT
RIVERSIDE
Elliot Reserve
Hatea River
WOODHILL
VINETOWN
SPLIT BAR
POST OFFICE
RIVERSIDE CAFÉ
WHANGAREI ART MUSEUM
CLAPHAMS NATIONAL CLOCK MUSEUM
I-SITE VISITOR CENTER
OMOIDE
BOTANICA WHANGAREI
LODGE BORDEAUX
WEST END MEDICAL CENTER
BUNKDOWN LODGE
CENTRAL COURT MOTEL
To Kiwi North, and Dargaville
Jubilee Park
Tarewa Park
Morningside Park
Okara Park
MORNINGSIDE
To Auckland
0 300 yds
0 300 m
© AVALON TRAVEL

dotted with historic buildings from the mid-19th century onward: New Zealand's smallest octagonal chapel, a kauri homestead, and Whangarei's former women's jail.

RECREATION

Walks

Hatea Loop Walk (1 hour) is a pleasant city stroll. It begins at the waterside walkway in the Town Basin and makes its way past cultural sights and sculptures, such as the Waka and Wave and the lauded Te Matau a Pohe (Fishhook of Pohe) bridge, built in 2013 in honor of Northland's significant Maori heritage. The bridge incorporates fishhook and war canoe shapes into its design. Heritage panels offer history lessons along the way, and the route is bike-friendly.

Ah Reed Memorial Park (5km north of the Whangarei marina) is an example of what's left of the original Northland kauri forests. Explore it via a boardwalk across the treetop canopy. The main access point is from two car parks on Whareora Road.

MOUNT PARIHAKA

Northeast of Whangarei is **Mount Parihaka**, an ancient volcanic cone now clad in a verdant scenic reserve. The mount rises to 241m, its peak accessible via three well-marked tracks (40-50 minutes) that follow the Hatea River. The best is the Ross Track (end of Dundas Rd.), which leads though bush and past an old gold mine. The mount was home to one of the nation's largest *pa* (a Maori fortified village). A carved rock at the top honors Parihaka's *mauri* (life essence), along with a viewing deck overlooking the district.

WHANGAREI FALLS

Considered the most-photographed waterfall in the country, **Whangarei Falls** (off Ngunguru Rd.) plunges 26m from a basalt cliff. The water was said to have healing powers, and the base of the fall, once considered *tapu* (sacred) by Maori, who fished the area extensively, now serves as a popular swimming hole. Two scenic loop walks (30-90 minutes) leave from the car park.

Whangarei Falls is 6km northwest of downtown. Take Mill Road north as it becomes Waiatawa Road, then Kiripaka Road.

ABBEY CAVES

Pack a flashlight and wear decent footwear for **Abbey Caves** (Abbey Caves Rd.), a cluster of untouched caverns alive with glowworms. These fascinating rock formations

Whangarei Falls

stretch for around 200m. Mild scrambling is required, and you'll get your feet wet in the stream; watch the weather and don't head in during or following heavy rain. For more information, visit the Whangarei i-SITE Visitor Centre, or download a map (www.wdc.govt.nz). The caves are 6km east of Whangarei off Whareora Road.

WHANGAREI HEADS

Clawing their way into the Pacific Ocean, the **Whangarei Heads** (www.discoverwhangareiheads.nz) are a cluster of volcanic peaks 20 million years in the making. The scenic rocky outcrops are home to a wildlife sanctuary and historic Maori and World War II defensive sites. Explore them via a well-marked beach, woodland, and clifftop tracks.

The **Patuaua South Track** (20 minutes-1 hour) is a cinch. From the car park (Mahanga Rd.), follow the edge of the estuary and cross a rickety yet photogenic footbridge to Pataua North beach. There are plenty of swimming spots en route. **Mount Manaia** (1.5 hours round-trip) is one of the best tracks. From the lower car park (Whangarei Heads Rd.), the route weaves through bush and peaks before rising to the 420m lookout over Whangarei Harbour and the Hen and Chicken Islands opposite.

Whangarei Heads are 30km southeast of Whangarei. Follow Riverside Drive east for almost 5km to Onerahi, where it becomes Onerahi Road. Continue 14.5km to Whangarei Heads Road.

BREAM HEAD SCENIC RESERVE

The **Bream Head Scenic Reserve** (www.breamheadtrust.org.nz) is home to a coastal pohutukawa forest filled with feathered wildlife like the brown kiwi. Well-signed walks take anywhere from 30 minutes to two days. The reserve is 10km east of Whangarei Heads; access it off Urquhart or Ocean Beach Roads.

SHOPPING

Northland is famed for its artists, with an especially strong showing of Maori craftsmanship, and there are several fine examples in Whangarei. Perusing the handmade offerings, and sometimes the creative process, is time well spent.

The Quarry Arts Centre (21 Selwyn Ave., 09/438-1215, www.quarryarts.org, 9:30am-4:40pm Mon.-Sat.) is a community space where local artists create while others can view and buy the work. The ceramics collection is of real note.

Burning Issues Gallery (8 Quayside, 09/438-3108, www.burningissuesgallery.co.nz, 10am-5pm daily) showcases a stunning range of contemporary crafts—sculptures, ceramics, and jewelry. You can also watch glass-blowing.

Grab the ultimate historical souvenir from **Kauri Creations** (3 Nell Place, 09/438-8884, www.kauri.net, 8:30am-5pm Mon.-Fri., 9:30am-4pm Sat., 10am-2pm Sun.), a working factory whose wares—furniture, key rings, clocks, and mirrors—are carved from kauri wood tens of thousands of years old. It's worth a visit regardless of whether you buy something, though international shipping is offered.

FOOD

There are worse ways to begin the day than sipping coffee overlooking the Town Basin marina at **Riverside Café** (14 Quayside, 09/430-0467, www.riversidecafe.co.nz, 8am-5pm daily, $17-20). Serving a selection of organic and free trade produce, the display cabinet brims with fresh cakes and sandwiches. Put the French toast or grilled Moroccan lamb skewers at the top of your list.

Welcoming **Split Bar** (15a Rathbone St., 09/438-0999, www.splitrestaurant.co.nz, 11am-close Mon.-Sat., $25-36) is just the place to kick back with a cold beer or a chilled Kiwi pinot gris. The casual gastropub has an indoor-outdoor vibe, all-day menus, big screen TVs, an outdoor bar, and regular live music. The menu emphasizes locally caught fish and succulent New Zealand red meat. The braised beef short rib with sticky glaze is excellent.

Omoide (45 Vine St., 09/430-3005, www.omoidenz.wixsite.com, lunch 11am-3pm Mon. and Wed.-Sat., dinner 5pm-close Mon.-Sat., $5-23) is a relaxing establishment equipped with paper lanterns and bamboo furnishings that impart an authentic Eastern air. It's complemented by a well-priced menu brimming with delicious Japanese classics like sushi, tempura, and *donburi*.

A leading Northland eatery, ★ **Tonic** (239 Kamo Rd. 09/437-5558, www.tonicrestaurant.co.nz, lunch 11:30am-2pm Thurs.-Fri., dinner 6pm-close Tues.-Sun., $30-40) is an intimate affair with low lighting and high-backed leather chairs. The creative fine-dining menu includes five-spice braised pork belly with pickled red cabbage and pan-roasted chicken thighs in red-pepper sauce. Save space for the vanilla *panna cotta* with blood orange.

ACCOMMODATIONS

What **Bunkdown Lodge** (23 Otaika Rd., 09/438-8886, www.bunkdownlodge.co.nz, dorm $29-31, $64 s, $67-75 d) lacks in modern conveniences, it makes up for in character. This elegant, clean, and cozy BBH hostel is set in a white Edwardian kauri villa with hospitable owners and beautiful gardens. Guests enjoy a log fire and an abundance of games and DVDs and can play the piano or strum a guitar. There's plenty of outdoor seating, with a barbecue and two well-stocked kitchens with free tea and coffee. Bedding rental is $3 (double rooms excluded), plus there's space for camping ($20 pp).

Basic rooms are a good value at **Central Court Motel** (54 Otaika Rd., 09/438-4574, www.centralcourt.co.nz, $95-115), a few minutes' drive from the city center. Studio, one-bedroom, and two-bedroom units all have en suite baths and free Wi-Fi, Sky TV, and cooking facilities. Communal facilities include a spa, a sauna, a swimming pool, and a barbecue area. A three-bedroom family unit ($220) is also available.

Whangarei's most impressive motel, ★ **Lodge Bordeaux** (361 Western Hills Dr., 09/438-0404, www.lodgebordeaux.co.nz, $195-270) imparts a sophisticated air thanks to its tasteful, spacious suites with modern baths, cooking facilities, and Sky TV. Some rooms have private decks; most have a spa bath. Expend some energy in the heated swimming pool, then restore it in the super comfy beds. The lodge is a few kilometers from the Town Basin.

★ **Historic Lupton Lodge** (555 Ngunguru Rd., 09/437-2989, www.luptonlodge.co.nz, $135-350 s, $190-410 d) is in a stellar Victorian villa surrounded by plush pastures with fruit orchards (help yourself) and its own swimming pool. Accommodations range from suites to apartments to a self-contained studio in a converted barn. All of the unique rooms have en suite baths, with bathrobes, private decks, free Wi-Fi, and satellite TV. À la carte breakfasts include bagels, bacon, and omelets. The lodge is a 10-minute drive from downtown.

Whangarei Falls Holiday Park & YHA Backpackers (12 Ngunguru Rd., 09/437-0609, www.whangareifalls.co.nz) is nestled on idyllic grounds that feature a swimming pool, a hot tub, and a barbecue area. Communal areas are well-equipped, if dated, with a stocked kitchen, a TV, and a reading room. Campsites ($25 pp) are accompanied by backpacker dorms ($32-34). Budget cabins ($72) come with a double bed, single bunk, and a small desk. Standard cabins ($86) sleep up to six and are equipped with small private kitchens with breakfasts bars, but they don't have en suite baths. The BBH-affiliated park is 5km from downtown Whangarei.

Overnight accommodations near Bream Head are courtesy of the DoC-maintained **Peach Cove Hut** (09/470-3300, www.doc.govt.nz, adults $15, children $7.50, under age 11 free). The basic lodging has eight beds and no cooking facilities; it must be booked in advance.

TRANSPORTATION AND SERVICES

Whangarei is 158km north of Auckland and 40km north of Waipu via Highway 1.

Air

Whangarei Airport (WRE, Handforth St., 09/436-0047, www.whangareiairport.co.nz) is 7.4km southeast of the downtown area, with daily flights to Auckland via **Air New Zealand** (www.airnewzealand.co.nz). **Sunair** (www.sunair.co.nz) operates flights to Hamilton, Tauranga, Rotorua, and Great Barrier Island. Car rentals at the airport include **Hertz** (www.hertz.co.nz), **Avis** (www.avis.co.nz), and **Budget** (www.budget.co.nz). **Whangarei Passenger Service** (09/438-6005, www.whangareibus.co.nz) operates a shuttle bus from the airport to downtown.

Bus

Whangarei is served by national bus operators **Intercity** (09/583-578, www.intercity.co.nz) and **Naked Bus** (09/979-1616, www.nakedbus.com) as well as North Island-wide operator **Mana Bus** (09/367-9140, www.manabus.com). The city of Whangarei is served by public bus operator **City Link** (www.citylinkwhangarei.co.nz). **Whangarei Coastal Commuter** (09/435-2532, www.coastalcommuter.co.nz) is a minibus service that runs to Auckland, the airport, the Tutukaka Coast, and a handful of regional destinations.

Rental Cars and Taxis

In town, **Rent a Dent** (12 Albert. St., 09/459-6504, www.rentadent.co.nz) has a decent selection of rental cars and vans at great prices. **Loop de Loop** (Reyburn House Lane, 022/060-6799, www.loopdeloop.co.nz, 10am-4pm Tues.-Sun.) rents bikes and kayaks. For cabs, call **Kiwi Cabs** (09/438-4444) or **A1 Cabs** (09438-3377).

Services

The **Whangarei i-SITE Visitor Centre** (91 Dent St., 09/430-1188, www.whangareinz.com, 9am-5pm Mon.-Fri., 9am-4:30pm Sat.-Sun.) offers booking services and advice, as well as accommodations options. **The Hub** (91 Dent St., 09/430-1188) is an arm of the visitors center in the Town Basin.

The **Whangarei Central Library** (5 Rust Ave., 09/430-4206, www.whangarei-libraries.com, 9am-6pm Mon.-Fri., 9am-1pm Sat., 10am-1pm Sun.) has 10 carved poles *(pou)* outside, half of which represent Maori heritage (the rest are from other cultures).

The Tutukaka Coast

East of Whangarei, the Tutukaka Coast unravels north toward the Bay of Islands. A detour here rewards with expanses of virgin white sand, punctuated with the occasionally rocky bay, and fringed by green forest. It all overlooks sapphire seas fed by a handful of sparkling estuaries. There are heaps of walking tracks; pick up the "Tutukaka Coast Tracks and Walks" leaflet (www.tutukakacoastnz.com) from **Whangarei i-SITE** (91 Dent St., 09/430-1188, www.whangareinz.com, 9am-5pm Mon.-Fri., 9am-4:30pm Sat.-Sun.).

TUTUKAKA

Positioned around a scenic harbor, the port of Tutukaka, 30km northeast of Whangarei via Ngunguru Road, serves as a launchpad for the world-renowned scuba-diving destination: Poor Knights Islands Marine Reserve.

The **Tutukaka Headland Walkway** (1 hour round-trip) is a pleasurable stroll from the car park on Landowners Lane (0.5km past the marina). Enjoy wonderful views to Poor Knights Islands from the headland before descending to the beach and crossing over to the Kukutauwhao Island lighthouse. (It's easier to cross at low tide, but should be possible at other times, providing the weather is good.)

Food and Accommodations

After you've worked up a thirst or an appetite diving and hiking, head to **Schnappa**

Rock (1 Marina Rd., 09/434-3774, www.schnapparock.co.nz, 7am-close daily, Mon.-Sat. only June-Sept., $25-36). There's plenty of feel-good Pacific vibes at this palm-fringed marina-side haunt. Tuck into a hearty meat dish or seafood entrée using produce straight from the garden. The green shell mussels, washed down with a chilled sauvignon blanc, are especially good.

The shady grounds of **The Sands Motel** (48 Whangaumu St., 09/434-3747, www.sandsmotel.co.nz, $180) spill out on to the beach of Whangaumu Bay. The airy self-contained two-bedroom units boast private decks with sea views, separate lounge areas, Sky TV, and free Wi-Fi. Don't leave without enjoying a barbecue to the sound of the lapping waves.

Adorned with reclaimed timbers, fashionable decor, original art, and plentiful plants, the ★ **Lodge 9** (9 Rona Place, 09/434-3687, www.lodge9.co.nz, $250-375) has a soothing feel. Six en suite boutique rooms boast king beds, espresso machines, and eco-toiletries; two upstairs rooms have balconies. Communal amenities include a saltwater pool, a spa, and a barbecue area where you can enjoy free wine and tapas each evening. Straw-topped canopies in the shadow of the rainforest-clad valley lend a tropical air.

★ POOR KNIGHTS ISLANDS

Jacques Cousteau was such a fan of this small ancient volcanic archipelago, 25km off the Tutukaka coast, that he rated it one of the top-10 dive sites in the world. Its network of submarine caves and arches punctuates 100m underwater cliffs, a protected marine reserve populated with colorful exotic fish, rays, coral, and kelp forests. With visibility stretching to 30m, the water is so clear you'll have memorable views. Maori call the island chain (and the largest island) Tawhiti Rahi; it is of great spiritual significance, and landing on the island is forbidden.

The islands are home to wildlife, notably rare birds such as the Buller's shearwater, which travels to nest here from North America. The islands are their only nesting place, along with New Zealand's endemic reptile, the tuatara.

Dive Tutukaka (Poor Knights Dive Centre, Marina Rd., 09/434-3897, www.diving.co.nz) is the region's oldest dive company. They offer both guided scuba diving ($319) and snorkeling (adults $189, children $95) in the reserve, with all equipment included, along with hot drinks and soup ($10 for lunch). Kayaks are also available. Groups meet

Poor Knights Islands

at the dive center at 8am and return around 4pm. The day includes scenic cruises around the islands and passing through Rikoriko Cave, the largest sea cave in the world.

Perfect Day Ocean Cruise (Poor Knights Dive Centre, Marina Rd., 09/434-3867, www.aperfectday.co.nz, adults $189, children $95) is a dive-free, leisurely voyage around the islands that departs at 11am and returns at 4:15pm. You'll pass caves and arches, admire wildlife, and enjoy the opportunity to swim, snorkel, or kayak. Drinks and antipasto platters are included; there are hot showers onboard.

MATAPOURI

North of Tutukaka, the sleepy seaside settlement of Matapouri gives way to its eponymous sugar-sanded sheltered bay. At low tide, enticing crystal saltwater rock pools, known as **Mermaid Pools,** are revealed. At high tide, join the locals as they jump from the bridge over the estuary. Matapouri is 7km north of Tutukaka along Matapouri Road.

Whale Bay

Whale Bay is one of the most scenic nooks on the coast. The intimate sheltered white-sand cove is framed by turquoise water and the overhanging red and green of the pohutukawa tree. Get here via a 10-minute track from Matapouri Road; there's also a 20-minute walkway that links across the headland to Matapouri Bay. Don't forget your snorkel.

Recreation

Look for signs for the **Te Araroa Walkway** (Clements Rd., 4 hours round-trip). The track travels through bird-filled bush to Tane Moana, the largest kauri tree on the east coast. Measuring more than 11m in circumference, the majestic giant rises above the ridgeline in a shady forest, home to flying feathered friends.

Don't worry if you've never straddled a steed before. **Sandy Bay Horse Trekking** (5 McAuslin Rd., 09/434-4480, www.sandybayhorses.co.nz, $70-200) obliges all riding levels with tours that last from an hour to a half day. Tours cross bush and farmland and the occasional stream, from ridgelines also affording some wonderful views of the white-sand coastline. Some of the tours include riding on the beach.

WHANANAKI AND VICINITY

Whananaki is home to the longest footbridge in the southern hemisphere. The nearly 400m structure is just a few feet wide, linking North and South Whananaki across the Te Wairahi Stream estuary. It's not uncommon to see marinelife swimming beneath.

Whananaki is an hour's drive north of Matapouri. Unfortunately, no coastal road links the two towns. From Matapouri, follow Matapouri Road 15km north to Whananaki Road. Turn east and continue 8.5km to Hailes Road. Turn west and drive 6km to Whananaki North Road, where you'll head east again to the town.

Ruapekapeka Pa

Ruapekapeka Pa (Ruapekapeka Rd.) is one of the nation's best-preserved and most historically significant former Maori defensive sites, with rows of trenches and bunkers still visible in the hilltop. This was the site of the final 1846 battle of the War of the North, which erupted following Maori frustration with the Treaty of Waitangi. The wildly outnumbered warriors held fast against heavy British artillery. Although an uneasy truce was made, other uprisings around the country soon followed. The site is less than an hour northwest of Whananaki. From Highway 1, drive 4km north along Ruapekapeka Road.

Accommodations

Voted the world's best luxury hotel in 2016 by *Luxury Travel Intelligence*, the ★ **Helena Bay Lodge** (1948 Russell Rd., 09/433-6006, www.helenabay.com, $2,000-3,800 s, $2,350-4,150 d), 30km northwest of Whananaki in Helena Bay, is on a bush-clad 320ha site that includes four private beaches and 3km of unspoiled coastline. Make the most of the kayaking, fishing (there's a specially designated pontoon), and biking equipment, along with the gym, Russian bathhouse-inspired spa, and lap pool before retiring to resplendent suites with enormous beds draped in handmade linens. Amenities include TVs with movie channels, robes, mosaic-tile baths, and balconies overlooking Helena Bay. Rates include meals and pre-dinner drinks.

Bay of Islands

A wildly popular tourist destination, the Bay of Islands is a cluster of well-connected coastal towns that overlook luminous waters peppered with approximately 150 isles. Captain Cook first anchored here in 1769. In the decades that followed, a stream of European missionaries set about converting Maori—who had long been lured by the fertile land, plentiful fishing and whaling, and sheltered natural harbors—to Christianity. However, sporadic uprisings and battles between Maori and Pakeha (the Maori term for New Zealanders of European—usually British—descent) soon followed, until the signing of the Treaty of Waitangi in 1840. The agreement between local chiefs and the British Crown sought to establish a peaceful cultural and political coexistence; controversies linger still.

Today the islands are blossoming as sanctuaries for native birds, and their waters are inhabited by dolphins and frequented by an array of marine mammals, including whales. Most of the islands are unoccupied and under the joint protection of *iwi* (local Maori tribes) and DoC.

Most visitors use the sleepy towns of Kerikeri, Russell, and Paihia as a base for wildlife-watching cruises through the islands. Many of the popular dolphin-encounter cruises stop at some of the islands or sail through "The Hole in the Rock," an enormous archway that punctures Motukokako Island (also referred to as Piercy Island).

KAWAKAWA AND VICINITY

There's little in the tiny town of Kawakawa to keep you away from the rest of the bay for too long, but don't leave without checking out the iconic **Hundertwasser public toilets** (Gilles St.) designed in 1997 by reclusive Austrian artist Friedensreich Hundertwasser. Hundertwasser lived in Kawakawa from 1975 until his death in 2000 at age 71. His "toilet block" is adorned with a wonderful mishmash of colorful tiles, copper handwork, and bottle-glass windows. It was the artist's final work and the only one he completed in the southern hemisphere, Today it attracts hordes of camera-wielding fans from across the world.

Bay of Islands Vintage Railway

Kawakawa is the only Kiwi town with a rail line running along its main street. The old steam and diesel engine trains are operated by **Bay of Islands Vintage Railway** (09/404-0684, www.bayofislandsvintagerailway.org.nz, adults $20, children $5, under age 5 free). Visitors can hop aboard the vintage carriages for a round-trip jaunt between Kawakawa Station and Tauarere (1 hour, 10:45am, noon, 1:15pm, and 2:30pm Fri.-Sun.).

Kawiti Caves

The **Kawiti Caves** (49 Waiomio Rd., 09/404-0583, www.kawiticaves.co.nz, 9am-4pm daily, adults $20, children $10) are home to galaxies of glowworms and intriguing underground formations. The guided 30-minute tour takes in the snaking system by way of a boardwalk followed by a bush walk among karst rock formations and rainforest. To get here, follow Highway 1 south for 5km and turn east on Waiomio Road.

Getting There

Kawakawa is 55km (45 minutes) north of

Bay of Islands

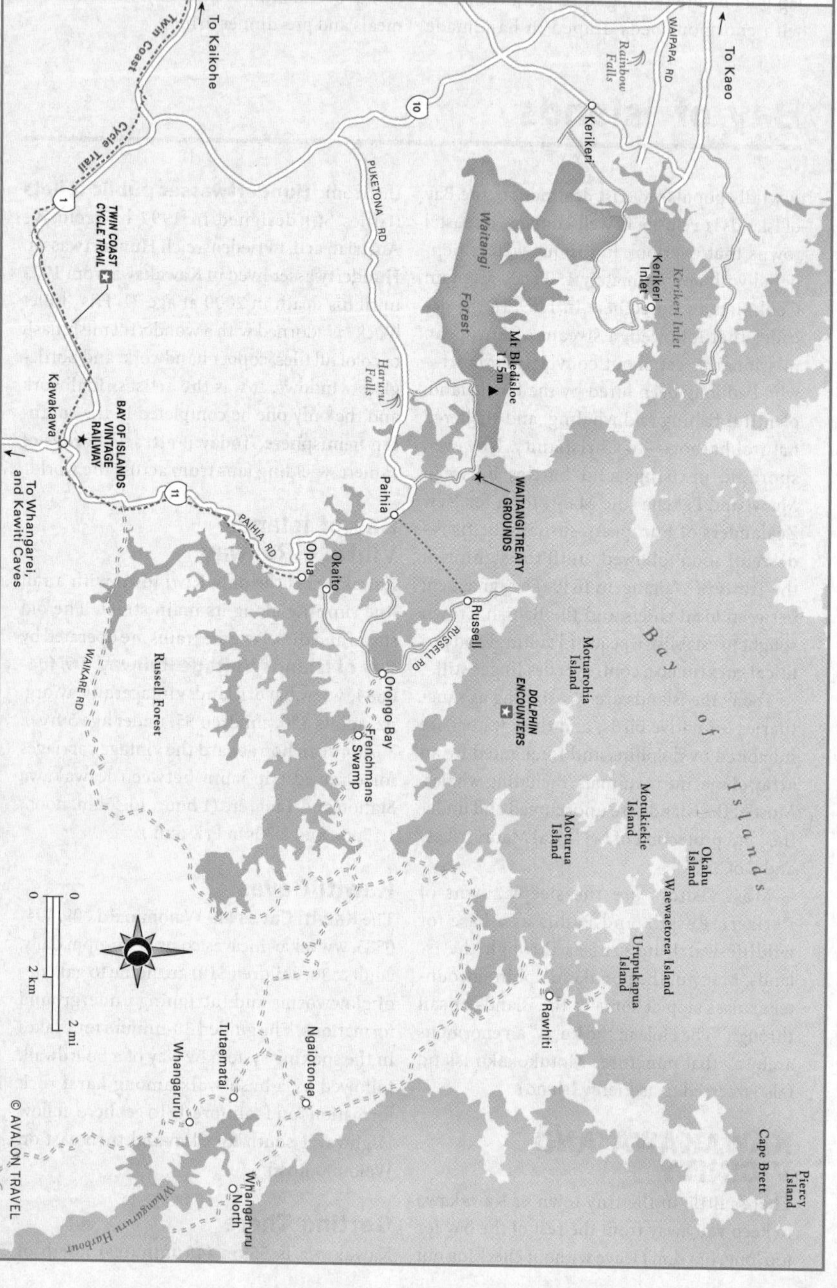

To Kaikohe
Twin Coast Cycle Trail
To Kaeo
Rainbow Falls
WAIPAPA RD
Kerikeri
10
PUKETONA RD
Waitangi Forest
Kerikeri Inlet
Kerikeri Inlet
1
TWIN COAST CYCLE TRAIL
Mt Bledisloe 115m
Haruru Falls
Kawakawa
BAY OF ISLANDS VINTAGE RAILWAY
WAITANGI TREATY GROUNDS
To Whangarei, and Kawiti Caves
11
Paihia
PAIHIA RD
Opua
Okaito
Russell
RUSSELL RD
Bay of Islands
Motuarohia Island
DOLPHIN ENCOUNTERS
WAIKARE RD
Russell Forest
Orongo Bay
Frenchmans Swamp
Motukiekie Island
Moturua Island
Okahu Island
Waewaetorea Island
Urupukapua Island
Rawhiti
0
0
2 km
2 mi
Tutaematai
Ngaiotonga
Whangaruru
Whangaruru North
Whangaruru Harbour
Cape Brett
Piercy Island

Whangarei via Highway 1, and 55km (50 minutes) northwest of Whananaki. Kawakawa is served by national bus operators **Intercity** (09/583-578, www.intercity.co.nz) and **Naked Bus** (09/979-1616, www.nakedbus.com) as well as North Island-wide operator **Mana Bus** (09/367-9140, www.manabus.com).

OPUA

Opua is 12km northeast of Kawakawa via Highway 11. The port serves as the vehicle ferry to Russell and offers one of New Zealand's Great Rides.

★ Twin Coast Cycle Trail

The port of Opua marks the beginning of the **Twin Coast Cycle Trail** (www.twincoastcycletrail.kiwi.nz), an easy Great Ride. The trail merges Northland's Maori and European cultural highlights with spectacular scenery and some good old-fashioned two-wheeled action.

The 84km route links the Bay of Islands to Hokianga Harbour and takes two days to complete. Along the way, you'll follow a former railway corridor through tunnels and historic townships, over farms, and past wetlands, rivers, and an estuary. The sections are manageable, but if you don't have time to do the entire ride, try the popular 12km stretch from the boat yard (Baffin St.) in Opua to Kawakawa's railway station (Gillies St.).

Twin Coast Cycle Transport (2 Baffin St., 0800/891-340, www.twincoastcycletransport.co.nz) offers advice, bike rentals, and shuttle services.

RUSSELL

One of New Zealand's most photogenic towns, Russell retains a sense of idyllic isolation. Its cluster of bright white historic buildings is scattered along the seafront and up a hillside. It's hard to imagine that these shimmering Victorian streets were once prowled by hordes of drunken sailors and whalers so lawless that the town, then called Kororareka, became known as the "Hellhole of the Pacific." Nearby Okiato served as New Zealand's first capital, in 1840-1841.

Sights

RUSSELL MUSEUM

Russell Museum (2 York St., 09/403-7701, www.russellmuseum.org.nz, 10am-4pm daily, adults $10, children $3) houses a one-fifth scale model of Captain Cook's ship, the *Endeavour,* which anchored in the bay in 1769. Other exhibits include Maori and whaling artifacts such as tools, weapons, oars, carvings,

Russell

and a canoe, along with a 10-minute documentary about the history of Russell.

POMPALLIER MISSION

New Zealand's only remaining printer and tannery resides at **Pompallier Mission** (The Strand, 09/403-9015, www.pompallier.co.nz, 10am-5pm daily Nov.-Apr., 10am-4pm daily May-Oct., adults $10, children free). The building's rammed-earth construction was completed in 1842 to host the Roman Catholic mission's printing press. It later became the church's western Pacific headquarters. In its first three decades, the mission produced 40,000 religious books in Maori (one of the world's first Maori texts). Today the original printing press has been restored, and visitors can experience the printing and binding process up close—or even try their hand.

CHRIST CHURCH

Built in 1836 and modified in 1871, **Christ Church** (Robertson Rd.) is one of New Zealand's first churches. It still bears battle scars in the form of musket fire and cannonball holes from the New Zealand Wars. Stop here to wander around the cemetery, home to prominent historical figures such as the Ngapuhi chief Tamati Waka Nene, one of the earliest Maori leaders to support better relations with the Europeans.

FLAGSTAFF HILL

North of the town center, **Flagstaff (Maiki) Hill** not only offers splendid views of Russell and the Bay of Islands beyond, but marks Maori defiance of—then reconciliation with—the British Crown. Several flagstaffs were raised atop the hill under orders of the Crown during the 1840s, only to be chopped down by Ngapuhi warriors under the orders of their leader, Hone Heke. A monument now marks the 1857 end of hostilities. A flag is flown on the pole only on certain days of the year—such as the anniversary of Hone Heke's death.

Access is via Flagstaff Road from the east, or take the 4km Flagstaff Loop Track from the north end of The Strand.

TAPEKA POINT RESERVE

About 1km north of Flagstaff Hill, **Tapeka Point Historic Reserve** (Tapeka Rd.) marks the site of a former *pa*. At the tip of a steep-faced headland, the site harbors some of Northland's most impressive earthworks, including defensive trenches and terraces. The area was once known as Lovers Leap; according to an old Maori tale, a young couple threw themselves into the sea here after their elders forbade them from marrying. Explore the reserve via the **Tapeka Point Track** (1km round-trip).

Sports and Recreation

Harness your inner Captain Jack Sparrow with **R Tucker Thompson Tall Ship** (Maritime Bldg., Marsden Rd., 09/402-8431, www.tucker.co.nz), a sailing experience straight out of Hollywood. The legendary Northland-built schooner operates full-day (10am-4pm, adults $149, children $74.50) or afternoon (4pm-5:45pm, adults $65, children $32.50) trips around the bay with the opportunity to climb some rigging and ride the bowsprit—or simply lie back and savor the trip. Excursions include morning tea, an island stop for lunch, and a shared antipasto platter on the afternoon jaunt. Free ferry transfers to Russell are provided, and you can feel good about your fun—the company is a charitable trust that supports youth-development sailing schemes.

Experience some of New Zealand's highest parasailing on a 366m towline with **Flying Kiwi Parasail** (0800/359-691, www.parasailnz.com). Departing either from Russell or Paihia, parasailers can choose to glide solo ($115), in tandem ($95), or in triple ($95) formation for breathtaking views of the bay. Children ($65) must be accompanied by an adult.

Food and Accommodations

Most of Russell is positioned along the seafront and offers some of the region's most romantic dining and sleeping spots (though they tend to come at slightly inflated prices).

Enjoy your morning coffee to the sound of

lapping waves at **Waterfront Café** (23 The Strand, 09/403-7589, 8am-4pm daily). The top-notch traditional breakfast menu is accompanied by a smattering of home-baked treats, fresh wraps, and pies.

Sally's Restaurant (25 The Strand, 09/403-7652, 10:30am-9pm daily, $15-32) is a decades-old Russell stalwart with plenty of small-town charm. The seafood-leaning menu includes fish-and-chips, seafood pasta, and a seafood chowder that is quite good. It's located literally at the water's edge; try to secure a spot there.

The historic ★ **Duke of Marlborough Hotel** (35 The Strand, 09/403-7829, www.theduke.co.nz, $170-395) is New Zealand's oldest licensed premises, serving travelers since 1827. Framed by pristine white decorative timbers and adorned with chandeliers, an open fire, antique furnishings, and plush carpets, you'll receive the warmest of welcomes. The rooms have a contemporary feel; all have en suite baths with free Wi-Fi, Sky TV, hot drink facilities, and comfortable beds. Some rooms come with balconies sporting sea views. The on-site **restaurant** (11:30am-9pm daily, $25-42) serves delectable dishes with plenty of seafood and tender meats (try the lamb), all crafted with local produce and paired with a plentiful and well-picked wine list.

Hananui Lodge (4 York St., 09/403-7875, www.hananui.co.nz, $155-250) is surrounded by well-loved gardens. Some rooms have sea views, but all come with TVs, private patios or decks, and cooking facilities. Amenities include free Wi-Fi, communal barbecues, a hot tub, and free kayak rentals. The sea is but a short stroll away.

Campers make their way to **Orongo Bay Holiday Park** (5960 Russell Rd., 09/403-7704, www.russellaccommodation.co.nz, $44-48) for the pool, barbecue, and campfire areas. Accommodations range from basic cabins to self-contained lodges ($95-289), with open fires, TVs, and separate lounge and dining areas. Glamping options ($99-110) include cool tepee tents on private patches of land with sea views. Come nightfall, go kiwi spotting in the surrounding bush; weka are also regular visitors.

Transportation and Services

Reach Russell via ferry from Opua or Paihia. The Russell **passenger ferry** (09/403-7866, www.dolphincruises.co.nz, round-trip adults $12, children $6) connects Russell with Paihia's wharf. The first ferry departs Russell at 7am daily, then runs hourly 9am-9pm for the 15-minute trip to Paihia. Return ferries depart Paihia at 7:20am daily, then hourly 8:30am-9:30pm.

The **vehicle ferry** (6:50am-10pm daily, one-way $12.50 with driver, extra passengers adults $1, children $0.50) departs Opua 5.5km southeast of Paihia via Highway 11. Arriving at Okiato, it is then a 10-minute drive south along Russell Whakapara and Aucks Roads. The return ferry runs every 10 minutes 6:40am-9:50am daily. Buy tickets onboard.

Fullers (09/402-7421, www.dolphincruises.co.nz, adults $30, children $15) runs a **Russell Mini Tour** (1 hour). Knowledgeable bus driver-tour guides whisk visitors around sites such as Christ Church and Pompallier House and up to Flagstaff Hill for a scenic photo opportunity.

The **Russell Booking and Information Centre** (The Wharf, 09/403-8020, www.russellinfo.co.nz, 8am-6pm daily) can advise on tours, transport, and accommodations.

PAIHIA

The seaside settlement of Paihia is the perfect balance of lively and laid-back. Bars, eateries, and lodgings lie along its 2km seafront strip within a scenic enclave of bush-clad headlands and golden sand. The town serves as a launching pad for the Bay of Islands' ocean-going excursions and is a gateway to the Waitangi Treaty Grounds.

Waitangi Treaty Grounds

Across the Waitangi River, the **Waitangi Treaty Grounds** (Tau Henare Dr., 09/402-7437, www.waitangi.org.nz, 9am-6pm daily

The Treaty of Waitangi

A contract between Maori chiefs and the British Crown, signed on February 6, 1840, the Treaty of Waitangi is the nation's most important text—essentially the founding document of modern New Zealand. But disputes over its implementation, meaning, and translation continue to this day. Most confusion stems from the fact that the Maori and British texts were not direct translations of each other and so were interpreted slightly differently when presented to the various chiefs from around the country. Maori believed they were to be bestowed equal rights as British citizens, and that the land and its resources would only be leased to the Crown, whereas the British government claimed they were gifted full sovereignty.

Later governments then passed additional laws that gave greater land rights to the ever-expanding number of British settlers, and often land was outright confiscated from the indigenous people. Tensions boiled into conflict around the country with the eruption of a series of extremely bloody battles, known as the New Zealand Wars, in the 1860s. It wasn't until 1973 that Waitangi Day was recognized by the government as an official public holiday.

Dec. 26-Feb., 9am-5pm daily Mar.-Dec. 24, adults $40, under age 18 free) guards the most historically significant site in New Zealand—the spot where the Treaty of Waitangi was signed between Maori and the British Crown.

Set aside at least a half day to explore the 1830s **Treaty House,** one of the nation's oldest. Its immaculate grounds are where the treaty was signed in 1840, and where the Declaration of Independence was signed in 1835. Just opposite is the **Whare Runanga** (House of Assembly), a carved meeting house that opened in 1940 to celebrate the partnership between Maori chiefs and the British Crown. Across the grounds is the 35m ceremonial *waka*, Ngatokimatawhaorua, the world's largest war canoe. It was named after Kupe's original vessel and is launched every Waitangi Day (Feb. 6).

The **Te Kongahu Museum of Waitangi** covers two floors. The ground-level **Ko Waitangi Tenei** is a fixed exhibition of the area's Maori and European heritage. Browse state-of-the-art interactive displays, historical texts and images, artifacts, jewels, and weaponry. The upstairs level plays host to visiting artworks.

VISITOR SERVICES

Stop at the visitors center, where you can catch a superb 20-minute historical film, watch a live **Maori cultural performance** (11am, 1pm, and 3pm daily Mar.-Dec. 24, 10am, 11am, noon, 1:30pm, 2:30pm, and 3:30pm daily Dec. 26-Feb.), or take a **guided tour** (50 minutes, every half-hour 10am-4:30pm daily Dec. 26-Feb., hourly 10am-4pm daily Mar.-Dec. 24).

EVENTS

The ***Hangi* and Concert** (6pm-8:30pm Tues., Thurs., and Sun. Dec.-Mar., adults $110, children $50, includes entry) delves deeper into New Zealand's ancient culture. Guests can savor the traditional Maori feast, the *hangi,* and learn about the preparation process, witnessing extended live musical performances.

During the annual **Waitangi Day Celebrations** (www.waitangi.org.nz, Feb. 6, free), the treaty buildings close as the grounds host live performances accompanied by market stalls selling arts, crafts, and food.

RECREATION

Taiamai Tours (09/405-9990, www.taiamaitours.co.nz, 9am Tues., Thurs., and Sat.-Sun. summer, adults $135, children $105) gives visitors the chance to paddle a 12m *waka* (war canoe) while learning traditional paddling techniques, maneuvers, chants, and history. The three-hour tours take in the Waitangi

River estuary and includes entry to the Waitangi Treaty Grounds.

Plunging in a perfect horseshoe shape in the Waitangi estuary, **Haruru Falls** were once surrounded by dozens of Maori villages. As the legend goes, a *taniwha* (water monster) still resides in the fall's plunge pool, but don't let that put you off taking a refreshing dip. The waterfall is well signed off Highway 11 (Putekona Rd.), 5km west of Paihia. It can also be accessed via the **Creek Mangrove Forest Boardwalk** (2 hours, easy) from the Waitangi Treaty House grounds.

GETTING THERE

The Treaty Grounds are 2km northwest of Paihia via Highway 11 and Te Karuwha Parade.

TOP EXPERIENCE

★ Dolphin Encounters

Bay of Islands is all about experiencing the seas, especially encountering wild dolphins. Numerous tour operators afford the chance to get up close and personal—and often even swim—with these benevolent marine mammals. While seeing dolphins is almost guaranteed (there's often a money-back or free return trip deal; check when booking), swimming with them is at your captain's discretion. If there are young dolphins in the marine pod, then human interaction is strictly forbidden. The dolphins tend to be very playful, though, and gladly show off their acrobatic skills.

DAY TOURS

Explore (Marsden Rd. and Williams Rd., 0800/365-744, www.exploregroup.co.nz) is the longest running of the big tour operators, with several cruises departing from Paihia (pickups from Russell are also available). The popular **Dolphin Discovery** (adults $115, children $65) is a four-hour cruise on a catamaran with large viewing windows and open decks; fins, snorkel masks, and wetsuits are included for the dolphin swim. You're also likely to encounter dolphins during **Discover the Bay** (adults $135, children $80), a four-hour cruise that takes in more of the islands and includes a pass through the Hole in the Rock, with a stopover at Otehei Bay on Urupukapuka.

Fullers (Maritime Bldg., Waterfront, 09/402-7421, www.dolphincruises.co.nz) is the other major tour operator in the area. They offer a handful of options, with free pickups from Russell. Their four-hour **Hole in the Rock Dolphin Cruise** (adults $105,

one of many Bay of Islands inquisitive resident dolphins

children $52.50, dolphin swim $30 extra, includes equipment) squeezes in encounters with a stopover on Urupukapuka Island and a pass through the Hole in the Rock, near Cape Brett.

Vigilant Yacht Charters (0800/334-662, www.vigilantyachtcharters.co.nz, $110) offers a more personal experience in smaller groups. Guest aboard skipper-chef Nik's gorgeous 13m classic cutter sailing yacht are invited to help hoist sails and other tasks. Features of the six-hour tour include island walking, kayaking, fishing, snorkeling, and of course, encountering wildlife.

A superb boutique option, ***Carino Sailing*** (09/402-8040, www.sailingdolphins.co.nz, $124) offers six-hour tours aboard a 15m catamaran. Guests can choose to help on deck or simply kayak, fish, snorkel, island hop, and swim with dolphins. A barbecue lunch is included, and there's an onboard bar.

OVERNIGHT TOURS

If one day on the bay isn't enough, consider a **Rock Adventure Cruise** (0800/762-527, www.rocktheboat.co.nz). These overnight tours are akin to a cozy floating hostel (actually a converted vehicle ferry), replete with its own log fire and a massive deck ideal for sunbathing and star-gazing. Tours depart from Paihia's wharf.

The **Bed and Breakfast Cruise** (adults $188, children $158) lasts 16 hours. Guests enjoy cruising the islands, a barbecue dinner, and a choice of activities, such as kayaking, fishing, and snorkeling. Breakfast is served before the cruise returns the following day. The **Classic Overnight Cruise** (adults $248, children $208) sails for 22 hours, with guided night kayaking (and bonus phosphorescence), snorkeling, diving for mussels, and the opportunity to hike remote islands. On both Rock Adventure Cruises, you'll see dolphins and plenty of sea birds. You can swap bunk beds for a private cabin ($20), rent towels and wetsuits ($5 each), and there's a fully licensed bar onboard. YHA discounts are available.

Bay of Islands Marine Mammals

Seeing bottlenose dolphins is practically a given year-round in Bay of Islands, closely followed by common dolphins. Orcas are more likely to visit April to October, while Bryde's whales enjoy the colder months of May to July—though they do occasionally swing by at other times. Other migrating species such as the humpback, long-finned pilot, and very rarely, blue whales may be spotted in March and April or August and September.

An upmarket overnight option, **Ecocruz** (0800/432-627, www.ecocruz.co.nz, 8am Tues. and Fri. Oct.-Apr., adults $725 s, $1,700 d, children $375) accepts a maximum of 10 guests for its three-day sail around some of the bay's underexplored nooks as well as classic sites like Cape Brett and the Hole in the Rock. The 22m ketch *Manawanui* sails all the way up to Cavalli Islands and Whangaroa Harbour. Accommodations include private doubles or four-berth cabins. All meals are included, as is the use of snorkel and fishing equipment and kayaks.

Sports and Recreation

KAYAKING

Coastal Kayakers (Te Karuwha Parade, 09/402-8105, www.coastalkayakers.co.nz) rents kayaks (1-6 hours, $15-60) and offers guided half- and full-day coastal tours (adults $89-139, children $69-139) of the Waitangi River and Haruru Falls. An unguided option is the **Haruru Falls One Way Paddle** ($45); walk to the waterfalls and then paddle back to Paihia via the Waitangi River (or vice versa). The free photo service is a nice touch.

SCUBA DIVING

Two of the nation's best wrecks await beneath the waves off Paihia: the *Rainbow Warrior* and the *HMNZS Canterbury,* a former

Tragedy on the *Rainbow Warrior*

On July 10, 1985, the Greenpeace ship the *Rainbow Warrior* was docked in Auckland in preparation for a protest voyage against French nuclear testing at French Polynesia's Moruroa Atoll. In an act of sabotage, under orders from their government (who initially denied it), French spies in diving gear bombed the boat, partially sinking it and killing one crew member. Two of the agents were caught and charged with manslaughter but, under a UN-negotiated settlement, freed after two years, while the rest of their team simply vanished. Two years after the disaster, the ship was scuttled near the Cavalli Islands and now serves as a dive site.

military vessel. **Paihia Dive** (Williams Rd., 09/402-7551, www.divenz.com) operates dive ($249-299) and snorkeling ($160) trips to the areas, which include volcanic reefs laced with caves and tunnels whose waters are thick with shoals of fish such as the blue maomao, rays, and moray eels. Trips depart from the Paihia Dive store at 7:30am daily and return at 3pm-4pm.

Northland Dive (3851 Russell Rd., 09/433-6633, www.northlanddive.com, $185) operates guided dives to the *HMNZS Canterbury* wreck, with plenty time for natural nooks like Cathedral Caves, Bird Rock, and Pigs Gully. All teem with fish, crustaceans, and coral. The company is located 34km southeast of Paihia and also provides accommodations.

FLIGHTSEEING

Salt Air (09/402-8338, www.saltair.co.nz, 20 minutes, $250) runs a handful of scenic helicopter flights over the Bay of Islands. The Hole Experience (35 minutes, $399) lands you on top of Motu Kokao (Piercy Island), home of the Hole in the Rock, for super seascape shots. The one-hour trip ($615) on the island is hosted by a Maori guide who is full of fascinating cultural facts. The Coastal Discovery (30 minutes, $335) extends The Hole Experience to venture east around Cape Brett.

PARASAILING

Glide at the end of a 366m towrope for stunning sea and island views with **Parasail Bay of Islands** (0800/334-566, www.bayofislandsparasail.com, adults $95-115, children $65). The adventures can be done solo, in tandem, or even dangling in a group of three people.

Shopping

At the **Paihia Farmers Market** (Village Green, www.bayofislandsfarmersmarket.co.nz, 2pm-5:30pm Thurs.), browse the stalls of local produce and arts and crafts while being serenaded by live musicians. It's a lovely way to pass the afternoon. The farmers market moves to Kerikeri (Hobson Ave.) on Sunday, 8:30am-noon.

The Cabbage Tree (Williams Rd., 09/402-7318, www.thecabbagetree.co.nz, 8am-6pm daily) stocks heaps of Kiwi-created gifts and souvenirs, such as bone and wood carvings, jade jewelry, and merino and possum wool clothing and accessories.

Festivals and Events

Paihia hosts the Bay of Islands **Sailing Week** (www.bayofislandssailingweek.org.nz, Jan.), the most significant regatta of its type in New Zealand—and one of the finest in the southern hemisphere. Among the best places to watch it is from the elevated grounds of the Waitangi golf course, or Tapeka Point in Russell.

During the joyful Bay of Islands **Bathtub Race** (www.bayofislandsbathtubbing.com, Apr.), a raft of boats are converted from household bathtubs and take to the waters to compete.

The Bay of Islands **Country Rock Festival** (www.country-rock.co.nz, mid-May) combines local acts with their Australian peers in venues around the bay, with additional street performances. The Bay of Islands **Jazz & Blues Festival** (www.jazz-blues.co.nz, Aug.)

also attracting acts from Australia, who play alongside their Kiwi counterparts in indoor and outdoor gigs.

Bay of Islands **Food & Wine Festival** (Village Green, Marsden Rd., www.paihianz.co.nz, Oct.) celebrates the best of New Zealand food, wine, and craft beers at a selection of stalls, accompanied by live music.

Food

Chilled-out **Alfresco's** (6 Marsden Rd., 09/402-6797, www.alfrescosrestaurantpaihia.com, 7:30am-close daily, $20-35) is the best way to start the day. A superb morning menu includes homemade granola or eggs and bacon, but go for the Fisherman's Breakfast: pan-fried dory, crushed potato, poached eggs, roasted tomato, and spinach. In the evening, order the aged scotch fillet. Exquisite offerings continue throughout the day from an open plan layout overlooking the ocean. A tap-beer and house-wine happy hour is offered (3pm-6pm daily).

★ **Charlotte's Kitchen** (The Wharf, 09/402-8296, www.charlotteskitchen.co.nz, 8am-close daily summer, 11:30am-close Mon.-Fri. winter, $25-40) is one of the bay's newest eateries in one its most pleasant settings—positioned on a pier jutting out over the lapping turquoise tide. A louvered ceiling plus floor-to-ceiling windows ensures views. Sunny days and night skies are uninterrupted as you tuck into a menu of seafood, grass-fed free-range meats, and wood-fired pizzas cooked from scratch. The setting befits its immaculate cocktail list.

All aboard **Darryl's Dinner Cruise** (0800/334-6637, www.dinnercruise.co.nz, adults $98, children $35, under age 5 free) for something a little different. This family-run business operates a boat-restaurant that cruises from Paihia Wharf up the Waitangi River to Haruru Falls; there guests can feast on meat and seafood as the sun goes down. Their lunchtime cruise (adults $68, children $25) serves Kiwi classics such as lamb and venison, while sailing to Russell. An abundance of birdlife and historical sites are guaranteed.

Accommodations

The sparkling and well-designed ★ **Haka Lodge** (76 Marsde Rd., 09/402-5637, www.hakalodge.com, 2-night minimum in peak season, dorm $31-33, $91 s or d) is a relaxed and airy affair with great touches like a sprawling reclining area that overlooks the bay through floor-to-ceiling windows with curtained-off bunks for privacy. The kitchen is very modern and the Wi-Fi is free. It's a short walk to the ferry to Russell and 10 minutes to downtown Paihia.

Saltwater Lodge (14 Kings Rd., 0800/002-266, www.saltwaterlodge.co.nz, dorm $27-42, $115 s or d) is a gleaming Paihia hostel, 50m from the beach and a five-minute stroll from the harbor. Comfortable beds are in pristine rooms; all have private baths, including the dorms. There's free Wi-Fi, a great kitchen, comfortable communal areas, and a games room with a foosball table and Ping-Pong. Triple and family en suite rooms ($160-175) are also available.

Great value lodgings at ★ **Bay Cabinz Motel** (32-34 School Rd., 09/402-8534, www.baycabinz.co.nz, $98-185) stand nestled within a bird-filled sub-tropical forest. The elevated cedar wood chalets are well-appointed and boast private patios with either sea or garden views. Amenities include cooking facilities, free Wi-Fi, and TVs and DVD players. It's only a 300m walk to the beach.

Cook's Lookout (9 Causeway Rd., 09/402-7409, www.cookslookout.co.nz, $205-325) is a delightful motel with jaw-dropping views over the Bay of Islands and Pacific Ocean. Ten of the 12 spacious en suite rooms have sea views (as does the solar-heated swimming pool), along with kitchenettes, free Wi-Fi, TVs, tea and coffee facilities, and private patios or balconies. Try to secure the corner studio room for the best view, and be sure to make use of the barbecue.

Swiss Chalet Lodge Motel (3 Bayview Rd., 09/402-7615, www.swisschalet.co.nz, $230-330) brings a touch of Alpine coziness to its timber-clad studios and family suites. Rooms feature angled roofs, balconies or patios with ocean views, en suite baths, and cooking facilities, and are equipped with free Wi-Fi and smart TVs. Luxurious two- and three-bedroom executive suites ($400-500) have two baths, double jetted tubs, and the best views in town. There's a communal hot tub, a barbecue area, and complimentary laundry. The wharf and downtown are just minutes away.

One of the Bay of Islands' best B&Bs is ★ **Decks of Paihia** (69 Upper School Rd., 09/402-6416, www.decksofpaihia.co.nz, $295). Set in a modern villa, the three en suite rooms have TVs, bathrobes, tea and coffee making facilities, toiletries, and free Wi-Fi. There's a swimming pool and a sunny deck area with ocean views. It's a 10-minute walk to the beach.

Surrounded by landscaped gardens next to the Waitangi River, **Bay of Islands Holiday Park** (678 Puketona Rd., 09/402-7646, www.bayofislandsholidaypark.co.nz) is an idyllic site. Accommodations include powered campsites ($34-38), basic cabins ($68) with access to communal kitchen and baths, and self-contained studio and motel units ($147-178) with TVs; some units have decks. Rent a kayak to paddle the river and enjoy the outdoor pool, barbecue area, and wood-fired pizza oven. It's a five-minute drive from Paihia.

Urupukapuka is the only island on which you can **camp** (DoC, 09/407-0300, www.doc.govt.nz, adults $13, children $6.50, under age 5 free).

Northland Dive (3851 Russell Rd., 09/433-6633, www.northlanddive.com, dorm $25, $60 s or d) operates an isolated lodge in a former milking shed. Separate men's and women's dorms are accompanied by double, twin, and family rooms ($60 for 2, $15 pp for more than 2), and camping ($15 pp) on the quaint grounds is also available. Rooms are modern, sparsely furnished, and well-kept; bring a sleeping bag for the dorms. Amenities include a large lounge and TV area with a log burner and a library. Home-cooked meals ($15 pp) are along the lines of steak or spaghetti Bolognaise with a basic breakfast ($6) of cereal, fruit, and toast. It's 34km west of Paihia.

Transportation and Services

Paihia is 17km (20 minutes) northeast of Kawakawa via Highway 11.

BUS

National bus operators **Intercity** (09/583-578, www.intercity.co.nz) and **Naked Bus** (09/979-1616, www.nakedbus.com) as well as North Island-wide operator **Mana Bus** (09/367-9140, www.manabus.com) all call at Paihia. **Paihia Transport** (09/402-7506, www.paihiatransport.co.nz) operates bus shuttle, tour, and charter services around the Bay of Islands.

FERRY

The Russell **passenger ferry** (09/403-7866, www.dolphincruises.co.nz, round-trip adults $12, children $6) connects Russell with Paihia's wharf. The first ferry departs Russell at 7am daily, then runs hourly 9am-9pm for the 15-minute trip to Paihia. Return ferries depart Paihia at 7:20am daily, then hourly 8:30am-9:30pm.

The **vehicle ferry** (6:50am-10pm daily, one-way $12.50 with driver, extra passengers adults $1, children $0.50) departs Opua 5.5km southeast of Paihia via Highway 11. Arriving at Okiato, it's a 10-minute drive south of Russell, along Russell Whakapara and Aucks Roads. The return ferry runs every 10 minutes (6:40am-9:50am daily). Buy tickets on board.

The **Bay of Islands Water Taxi** (0800/387-892, www.boiwatertaxi.co.nz) runs routes between Paihia and Russell to Cape Brett. **Explore** (0800/365-744, www.exploregroup.co.nz) operates daily ferries from Paihia to Urupukapuka Island.

BIKE

Paihia Mountain Bikes (156 Marsden Rd., 021/187-8192, www.paihiamountainbikes.co.nz) rents bikes for half, full, or multiple days. They also offer advice on local tracks and shuttle bus services. Book in advance.

SERVICES

Head to the Bay of Islands **i-SITE Visitor Information Centre** (The Wharf, Marsden Rd., 09/402-7345, www.northlandnz.com, 8am-5pm daily) for information about local activities and bus, train, and ferry services.

KERIKERI

In the northwest corner of the Bay of Islands, Kerikeri was one of the first stops for early European settlers. Today it's a favorite with local artists and craftspeople. Surrounded by orchards, it's an idyllic base to explore the region's historic sites.

Sights

Be sure to call in at the **Little Black Gallery** (394b Kerikeri Rd., 09/407-1311, www.artplace.co.nz, 10am-4pm Tues.-Sun. Oct.-Mar., 10am-4pm Tues.-Sat. Apr.-Oct.) and check out the eclectic bunch of unique Kiwi-created jewelry, ceramics, and paintings.

KERIKERI MISSION STATION

The **Kerikeri Mission Station** (246 Kerikeri Rd., 09/407-9236, www.stonestore.co.nz, 10am-5pm daily Nov.-Apr., 10am-4pm daily May-Oct., adults $10, children free) is of immense historical and cultural significance to the area. This picturesque riverside site was one of the first places where Maori and Europeans cohabited. It also houses two of the nation's oldest buildings.

The **Kemp House** was completed in 1822. It hosted missionary John Butler and his family, and was then home to blacksmith James Kemp, whose family cared for the property for the next century. It has been restored to its original humble Georgian-era glory. Tours are led by a guide who will enhance the experience by imparting tales of Maori warriors, European sailors, former convicts, and even the occasional ghost.

The **Stone Store** was built in 1832 and is the country's oldest stone structure. It originally served as a wheat warehouse, then later as a trading post, a general store, a school, a barracks, and a library. Today it's one of New Zealand's most unusual gift stores, offering authentic 19th-century goods like old-fashioned candy, copper and cast-iron pots, textiles, and tins of tea. Upstairs is a small museum with artifacts such as furniture, weapons, and a flour mill from the building's

Kerikeri Mission Station and Stone Store

previous life. This is a great spot to secure some quirky Kiwi souvenirs.

Admission includes a tour of Kemp House and access to the Stone Store Museum. The grounds host fragrant orchards, rose and vegetable gardens, and an old church and graveyard. Follow the riverside path (opposite the Stone Store) through a forest and up a gentle slope to **Kororipo Pa,** a former defensive Maori base that offers views of Kerikeri.

REWA'S VILLAGE

Terraces aside, there is often little left of New Zealand's historic *pa* sites, fortified settlements that were usually on a hill. **Rewa's Village** (1 Landing Rd., 09/407-6454, www.rewasvillage.co.nz, 10am-4pm daily, adults $10, children $5), across the footbridge from Kororipo Pa, provides welcome insights into how pre-European Maori lived. The full-scale fishing village is set within luscious bush with plenty of birdsong, a plant and herb garden for Maori medicinal uses, authentic *waka* (canoes), *pataka* (food stores), and a *marae* (meeting place).

TE WAIMATE MISSION

The nation's second oldest building is **Te Waimate Mission** (344 Te Ahu Ahu Rd., 09/405-9734, www.tewaimatemission.co.nz, 10am-5pm Fri.-Tues. Nov.-Apr., 10am-4pm Sat.-Mon. May-Oct., adults $10, children free). Built in 1832, the mission served to convert Maori to Christianity and introduce them to European farming methods. Today, the immaculately preserved kauri dwelling features original furniture and other artifacts accompanied by storyboards. The grounds are home to a church and a cemetery as well as a two-century-old oak tree, the oldest one in New Zealand. Charles Darwin spent Christmas 1835 here. The mission is a 20-minute drive southwest of Kerikeri.

Food

Stop by the sweetest smelling boutique store in Northland, **Makana Confections** (Kerikeri Rd., 09/407-6800, www.makana.co.nz, 9am-5pm daily), where you can watch chocolate being made by hand. Try the free samples, which are sure to lure you into the on-site café for a hot drink and sweet pastry.

Legendary Northland eatery **Café Jerusalem** (Cobblestone Mall, 85 Kerikeri Rd., 09/407-1001, www.cafejerusalem.co.nz, 11am-close daily, $17-19) serves great-value traditional Middle Eastern and Mediterranean meals. Opt to eat your falafel, kebabs, and *koftas* alfresco.

Located on the outskirts of town, there's a serene vibe to **Marsden Estate Winery** (56 Wiroa Rd., 09/407-9398, www.marsden.co.nz, 10am-5pm daily, $20-38). Sit beneath shady vines overlooking rows of grapes, meadows, waterways, and orchards as you dine on high-end fare like braised lamb shoulder and a superb seafood pasta, all served by attentive staff. A varied wine list includes both reds and whites.

The ★ **Pear Tree Restaurant and Bar** (215 Kerikeri Rd.,09/407-8479, www.thepeartree.co.nz, 10am-close daily summer, 10am-9pm Thurs.-Mon. winter, $18-38) rests in a stately villa surrounded by pristine lawns and towering trees on the banks of the languid Kerikeri River. Inside the airy white-walled interior, enjoy the log fire as you dine on stellar traditional dishes like lamb with truffle mash, or Malaysian-spiced fish and weekly curries.

Accommodations

The well-run **Hone Heke Lodge** (65 Hone Heke Rd., 09/407-8170, www.honeheke.co.nz, dorm $31, $54-64 s, $68-88 d) is a BBH hostel with a real community feel. Dorms sleep no more than six, with single and double rooms available with en suite baths. Wi-Fi is free; there's a pool table, a trampoline, plenty of outdoor space to kick back in (including a barbecue area), a TV room with free movies, and a fully equipped kitchen. The well-kept setup is popular with long-term seasonal fruit pickers.

At **Colonial House Motel** (178 Kerikeri Rd., 09/407-9016, www.colonialhousemotel.

co.nz, $149-199), you'll be struck first by the exotic colors of the tropical gardens, then the birdsong that fills them. The feel-good vibes continue inside the vibrantly furnished studio, one-bedroom, and two-bedroom suites equipped with free Wi-Fi and Sky TV; all have en suite baths with cooking facilities and private decks. A saltwater swimming pool, a spa, and a barbecue area are on-site.

Positioned on the fringe of the Historic Stone Store grounds and hemmed by whispering bush, the eco-friendly **Stone Store Lodge** (201 Kerikeri Rd., 09/407-6693, www.stonestorelodge.co.nz, $240) is one gorgeous getaway thanks in no small part to wonderful host Richard. Three suites are equipped with giant windows, free Wi-Fi, private decks, Sky TV, and luxurious baths with complimentary toiletries. Breakfast is included, and extras like massage, a wood-fire pizza, and an outdoor hot tub are available.

The riverbank ★ **Takou River Lodge** (660 Takou Bay Rd., 09/407-8065, www.takouriver.com, $280-350) is an idyllic slice of eco-luxury, with calming waters on one side and pastures, tropical gardens, and bird-filled forest on the other. Accommodations include cozy self-catering kauri cottages and lodges with outdoor claw-foot baths with river or bush views. All spaces are totally secluded. There's free Wi-Fi, but if you'd rather disconnect, opt for glamping—these luxury tents with timber floors, private kitchens, baths, and decks are ideal for staring at the stars. Guest are offered use of kayaks to paddle the river. The lodge is a 20-minute drive from Kerikeri.

Transportation and Services

Kerikeri is 23km (20 minutes) northwest of Paihia via Highways 11 and 10.

AIR

Bay of Islands Airport (KKE, 218 Wiroa Rd., 09/407-6133, www.bayofislandsairport.co.nz) is a 10-minute drive from Kerikeri and a 25-minute drive from Paihia. Daily flights to Auckland are operated by **Air New Zealand** (www.airnewzealand.co.nz). For airport shuttles and taxis, contact **Kerikeri Taxi Shuttle & Tours** (09/407-9515, www.kerikeritaxis.co.nz). They also operate guided trips around the Bay of Islands.

BUS

National bus operator **Intercity** (09/583-578, www.intercity.co.nz) stops at Kerikeri. The **Hokianga Link Bus** (09/405-8872, www.buslink.co.nz, Tues. and Thurs. Dec.-Mar., Thurs. Apr.-Nov.) connects Bay of Islands to Hokianga via Omapere, Opononi, Rawene, Kaikohe, Okaihau, and Kerikeri. Buses can also be booked in advance. **Fullers** (Maritime Bldg., Waterfront, 09/402-7421, www.dolphincruises.co.nz, 1pm daily, adults $60, children $30) runs a Discover Kerikeri guided bus tour than takes in historic sites such as Kemp House along with wine and chocolate tastings.

The Far North and Cape Reinga

Blissful isolation and some of New Zealand's best weather awaits in the Far North—or "top of the north." The largely uninhabited and unspoiled Karikari Peninsula is fringed by white beaches reached via a series of gravel roads and dusty tracks. Running parallel to its western flank, the more visited Aupouri Peninsula is home to drivable Ninety Mile Beach, backed by gigantic dunes steep enough to "surf." The peninsula protrudes more than 100km, terminating at Cape Reinga, a place of great spiritual significance to Maori.

The region's main hubs are **Whangaroa, Mangonui,** and **Kaitaia,** the gateway to Cape Reinga. Many find the coastal settlement of **Ahipara** (a few kilometers west) more appealing. The area's main attractions are easily reached by road and are well served by public transport.

MATAURI BAY

Matauri Bay arches around a golden bush-backed cove that faces the Cavalli Islands, the final resting place of the *Rainbow Warrior.* A walking path (20 minutes round-trip) off Matauri Bay Road leads up to a Rainbow Warrior memorial. The stone arch symbolizes a rainbow over the ship's propeller.

Matauri Bay is a 30-minute drive north of Kerikeri along Matauri Bay Road (off SH 10).

WHANGAROA HARBOUR

West of Matauri Bay, stunning **Whangaroa Harbour** is famed for marlin fishing and for its jagged coastline punctuated by enormous forest-clad 20-million-year-old volcanic rocky outcrops laced with walking trails.

St. Paul's Rock track affords some of the most accessible views as it climbs through manuka forest to a volcanic dome. The track is just 720m one-way but is steep enough to take 30 minutes round-trip—and to require fixed chains at the end to help haul yourself up. The track is in Whangaroa Township at the car park (Old Hospital Rd.).

Northland Sea Kayaking (Tauranga Bay Rd., 09/405-0381, www.northlandseakayaking.co.nz, $90-115) operates half-day and full-day guided tours around this wonderfully underexplored harbor. Tours are tailored to ability levels, with a good chance of dolphin encounters.

Accommodations

The superb ★ **Kahoe Farms Hostel** (1266 Hwy. 10, 09/405-1804, www.kahoefarms.co.nz, dorm $32, $81-105 s, $86-116 d) is in a lodge-like villa on a working farm 10 minutes west of Whangaroa. Polished hardwood floors and immaculate rooms elevate this BBH-affiliated lodging to B&B standards. The owners regularly cook pizza and pasta for guests, who can rent a kayak and explore the nearby mangroves. The Intercity bus can be booked to stop here on request.

DOUBTLESS BAY AND KARIKARI PENINSULA

The pretty fishing village of **Mangonui,** 30km northwest of Whangaroa Harbour, marks the beginning of Doubtless Bay. The sprawling arc reaches up to the eastern flank of Karikari Peninsula, punctuated by smaller bays and coves. White and golden beaches, often fringed by pohutukawa trees, drape the elbow-shaped 20km outcrop that can feel like earth's most remote paradise.

★ Coca Cola Lake

Don't leave without taking a dip in Rotopokaka Lake, nicknamed **Coca Cola Lake** (Ramp Rd.) thanks to its molasses-colored water stained by the surrounding peat-rich earth. The lake water is considered a tonic, believed by ancient Maori to hold healing properties. It's probably best to avoid drinking from Rotopokaka Lake, but its caramel hue makes for an enticing swim spot. If you stare long enough, you can almost picture its cola-colored water fizzing.

Rotopokaka Lake is 20km north of Mangonui along Highway 10. Look for the northern turnoff onto Inland Road, which forms the peninsula's spine, sporadically splaying into tracks that lead to deserted beaches and campsites. Turn north onto Inland Road and continue 3.5km to Ramp Road, the second turnoff on the right.

Food and Accommodations

Try the "world famous" fish-and-chips from the licensed ★ **Mangonui Fish Shop** (137 Waterfront Dr., Mangonui 09/406-0478, www.mangonuifishshop.com, 10am-8pm daily summer, $7-15), positioned on a wooden pier with a deck and seating overlooking the water. There's plenty of fresh seafood dishes and homemade burgers ($7-15) to choose from.

The ★ **Old Oak** (66 Waterfront Dr., 09/406-1250, www.theoldoak.co.nz, $175-325) is an exquisitely kept boutique motel. White-walled suites feature fashionable splashes of color and garden or harbor views (sometimes both). En suite rooms are equipped with Sky TV, free Wi-Fi, and hot-drink-making facilities. The rambling colonial villa is surrounded by a veranda and rose, vegetable, and herb gardens with a wraparound balcony above.

West of Mangonui, **Luxurious Doubtless Bay Villas** (20 Dudley Crescent, 09/406-1260, www.doubtlessbayvillas.co.nz, 2-night minimum, $220-595) overlooks the pink sands of Cable Bay. Hillside accommodations include one- to three-bedroom self-contained lodgings with ocean views. Guests enjoy use of free Wi-Fi, a tennis court, and Sky TV, and it's a short walk to the beach.

At the northern tip of the Karikari Peninsula, Maitai and Waikato Bays, tucked into the peninsula's jagged tip, are its crowning glory. Separated by a rocky headland, the pair of golden horseshoe coves are well sheltered and kissed by a cobalt tide. Spend the night at the **DoC campsite** (Maitai Bay Rd., 09/408-6014, www.doc.govt.nz, adults $13, children $6.50, under age 5 free), which has cold showers, flush toilets, and life-affirming coastal explorations.

KAITAIA

Kaitaia, 40km west of Mangonui, is New Zealand's northernmost town of note and the main launch point to windswept Ninety Mile Beach.

Far North Regional Museum

Te Ahu Centre is home to the impressive **Far North Regional Museum** (Mathews Ave. and South Rd., 09/408-9454, www.teahuheritage.co.nz, 8:30am-5pm Mon.-Fri., adults $7, children $3). Themed around the history of New Zealand's northernmost reaches, dapper displays include a fine greenstone collection, a 500-year-old skeleton of an extinct Polynesian dog, and early Maori carvings. The center also hosts the **i-SITE Visitor Centre** (09/408-9450, www.northlandnz.com, 8:30am-5pm daily), a cinema, and the **library** (09/408-9455, 8:30am-5pm Mon.-Fri.).

Food and Accommodations

Orana Motor Inn Restaurant and Bar (283 Commerce St., 09/408-1510, www.orana.co.nz) offers a hearty menu (7am-9:30pm daily, $25-38) with a European slant—think pork schnitzel, steak, and fish—along with curry and some splendid local seafood. Old-fashioned and basic rooms ($99-145) have en suite baths with free Wi-Fi, toiletries, tea and coffee, Sky TV, electric blankets, armchairs,

Coca Cola Lake

and desks. Guests can also make use of the swimming pool and the hot tub.

Transportation and Services

Kaitaia is 20km (20 minutes) southwest of the Karikari Peninsula along Highways 10 and 1.

AIR

Kaitaia Airport (KAT, Quarry Rd.) is served by **Barrier Air** (09/275-9120, www.barrierair.kiwi) with daily connections to Auckland.

BUS

National bus operator **Intercity** (09/583-578, www.intercity.co.nz) stops at Kaitaia. Far North public bus service **Busabout Kaitaia** (09/408-1092, www.busaboutnorth.co.nz, Mon.-Fri.) links Kaitaia to Mangonui, Ahipara, and Pukenui along the Aupouri Peninsula.

CAR RENTALS

For car rentals, contact **Far North Rentals** (0800/670-083, www.farnorthrentals.co.nz) or **Northland Rentals** (09/408-1905, www.northlandrentals.co.nz).

TOURS

Harrisons Cape Runner (114 North Rd., 09/408-1033, www.harrisonscapereinga-tours.co.nz, 9am-5pm daily, adults $50, children $25) operates tours to Cape Reinga along Ninety Mile Beach. Guests ride in a modified off-road bus that stops for kauri forests, the dunes, a drive across Te Paki Quicksand Stream, and a tour of Rawara Beach and Houhora Heads on the east coast. A picnic lunch and drinks are provided. Departure and pickup points include Harrisons' depot (with parking), the Te Ahu Centre, and Orana Motor Inn.

SERVICES

The Kaitaia **i-SITE Visitor Information Centre** (Matthews Ave. and South St., 09/408-9450, www.northlandnz.com, 8:30am-5pm daily) offers free Wi-Fi and tour, accommodations, and travel details for the Far North region. Along the Kauri Coast, there are no banks, few ATMs (some stores accept credit cards), and limited gas stations until you reach Dargaville in 174km.

AHIPARA

The scenic seaside settlement of Ahipara, 14km west of Kaitaia, makes for a more appealing Far North base. Positioned at the southern end of Ninety Mile Beach, the former gum digging village is famed for sweeping sand dunes that guard one of the world's best left-hand surf breaks; tubes can sometimes be ridden for nearly 500m. A shipwreck becomes partly visible at low tide, when mussels can be gathered from the rocks.

Recreation

Ahipara Adventure (15 Takahe St., 09/409-2055, www.ahiparaadventure.co.nz, 9am-9pm daily) rents beach equipment including surfboards, quad bikes, kayaks, stand-up paddleboards, BloKarts (a cross between a boat and buggy), and boards to surf the dunes at Ninety Mile Beach.

NZ Surf Bros (27 Kaka St., 021/252-7078, www.nzsurfbros.com, $599-799) operates five-day surf tours; meals and accommodations in a hip beachside lodge are included. Guests are supplied with a surfboard and a wetsuit and are ferried to the best waves in the region; lessons may be included, depending on the skill level. There is a pickup service from Auckland. The company also runs two-hour surf lessons (minimum 2 people, $60) and rents surfboards and wetsuits.

Food and Accommodations

Burgers at ★ **North Drift Café** (250 Ahipara Rd., 09/409-4093, 8am-2:30pm Mon.-Tues., 8am-3pm and 5pm-9pm Wed.-Sat., 8am-3pm Sun., $9-20) are named after local places like 90 Mile or Tui Street. Choose from exotic twists like Moroccan lamb, vegetarian options, fish-and-chips, or tacos. The classic breakfast dishes are the ideal way to prepare for a day at Ninety Mile Beach.

Beach Abode (11 Korora St., 09/409-2102,

www.beachabode.co.nz, $160-190) affords expansive ocean views from three immaculate self-contained apartments with decks, free Wi-Fi, hot drink facilities, and luxurious linens. The priciest apartment has its own garden. A private trail winds onto the sands.

A short walk from Ninety Mile Beach, **Ahipara Holiday Park** (168 Takahe Rd., 09/409-4864, www.ahiparaholidaypark.co.nz) covers a verdant 4ha. Campsites ($20-21) accompany a lodge-like YHA **hostel** (dorm $30, $75-95 s or d) with a sunny deck and barbecue area and a cozy TV room with an open fire. Some private rooms have en suite baths, while basic units ($70-75) share a kitchen and a bath; self-contained cabins and motel rooms ($105-135) are also available. Wi-Fi is free, and booking services include quad bike tours, surfboard rentals, horse trekking, and sandboard rentals to tackle those dunes.

Transportation and Services

Ahipara is 13km (10 minutes) southwest of Kaitaia via Ahipara, Pukepoto, Redan, and South Roads.

Ahipara is served by national bus operator **Intercity** (09/583-578, www.intercity.co.nz).

TOURS

Ultimate Sand Safaris (36 Wireless Rd., 09/408-1778, www.ultimatesandsafaris.co.nz, $150 pp, $400 for 4 people) rents 4WD beach buggies to drive along Ninety Mile Beach, or choose a 2.5-hour guided beach tour.

Tua Tua Tours (Main Rd., 0800/494-288, www.ahipara.co.nz, $100-175 for 1 person, $110-185 for 2) operates guided quad bike tours (1.5-3 hours) that explore local forests, beaches, and gum fields. There's also the option to toboggan some dunes.

Far North Outback Adventures (71 Foreshore Rd., 09/409-4586, www.farnorthtours.co.nz) offers full-day guided tours in luxurious 4WD vehicles. Itineraries include visits to Cape Reinga and Ninety Mile Beach, along with sand surfing, bird-watching, and visiting gum fields and ancient kauri groves. Morning tea and lunch with wine are included. Prices vary but run around $700 for 1-6 people. Pickups are around Ahipara and Kaitaia.

AWANUI AND VICINITY

The river port of Awanui ("Big River" in Maori), about 8km north of Kaitaia along Highway 1, marks the symbolic start of the peninsula. Highways 10 and 1 meet from the east and west, respectively, with Highway 1 branching north toward Cape Reinga.

Gumdiggers Park

Gumdiggers Park (171 Heath Rd., Waiharara, 09/406-7166, www.gumdiggerspark.co.nz, 9am-5pm daily, adults $12.50, children $6, under age 8 free), 15 minutes north of Awanui, is a compelling archaeological dig site of exposed ancient kauri forests. Marvel at 100,000-year-old kauri trunks, learn about the century-old gum industry, visit a gecko house, and stroll through a shady manuka grove.

★ NINETY MILE BEACH

At the very tip of the "top of the north," the land tapers into the 100km-long Aupouri Peninsula. The peninsula's west coast is dominated by Te Oneroa-a-Tohe ("The Long Beach of Tohe"), commonly called Ninety Mile Beach.

In the 1930s, Ninety Mile Beach served as a landing strip for early airmail services from Australia. It is now recognized as an official vehicle highway. The endless expanse of golden sand seems to unravel to infinity, guarded by a cliff of dunes that rises more than 140m to one side. It's great for **sandboarding** and tobogganing. The enormous dunes at the northern end of Ninety Mile Beach are the most popular sandboarding spot.

Rent sandboards from **Ahipara Adventure** (15 Takahe Rd., 09/409-2055, www.ahiparaadventure.co.nz) in Ahipara or **Ahikaa Adventures** (Te Paki Stream car park, 09/409-8228, www.ahikaa-adventures.co.nz, cash only, $15) at Te Paki Sand Dunes.

To drive the sands, book an official tour in hardy 4WD buses under the charge of professionals.

Accommodations

Wagener Holiday Park (214 Houhora Heads Rd., 09/409-8511, www.wagenerholidaypark.co.nz) overlooks the calm Houhora Harbour on the east side of Aupouri Peninsula. Tent and campervan sites ($34-38) are available, as are basic cabins ($65-68) with shared kitchen and bath facilities; some cabins have private toilets. An on-site tour desk can arrange trips to Cape Reinga and Ninety Mile Beach. There's a swimming pool, a barbecue area, and a pizza oven, as well as kayak and SUP rentals. It's a five-minute drive west of Pukenui and 10km from Ninety Mile Beach.

DoC-managed **Rarawa Beach Campsite** (off Hwy. 1, 09/408-6014, www.doc.govt.nz, adults $8, children $4, under age 5 free) is a short stroll from Rarawa Beach. The unpowered campsite accommodates 65 tents, with cold showers and flush toilets. Pay at the self-registration stand at the entrance. It's 15km north of Houhora, signposted down a gravel road off Highway 1.

Transportation and Tours

The main gateways to Ninety Mile Beach, via Highway 1, are Kaitaia (70km south) and Ahipara (80km south).

Ahipara Adventure (15 Takahe Rd., Ahipara, 09/409-2055, www.ahiparaadventure.co.nz) rents quad bikes for cruising along Ninety Mile Beach. **Cape Reinga Adventures** (09/409-8445, www.capereingaadventures.co.nz) offers tours of Cape Reinga and Ninety Mile Beach in 4WD minivans.

The **Full Day Cape Reinga Exclusive Helicopter Tour** (minimum 2 people, from $2,085 pp) arrives at Cape Reinga via helicopter and is followed by a three-hour bus tour of the cape, including Ninety Mile Beach.

★ CAPE REINGA

Cape Reinga is the most accessible northern headland. Overlooking the churning waters that mark the merging of the Pacific Ocean and the Tasman Sea, the cape is home to two iconic attractions: a historic lighthouse (not open to the public) and a lone pohutukawa tree that is said to be 800 years old and the mystical gateway that guides souls on their final journey into the underworld. Maori call

Ninety Mile Beach

the tip of this evocative peninsula Te Rerenga Wairua, "the leaping place of the spirits."

Walks

Highway 1 comes to an abrupt end at Cape Reinga car park, 112km north of Kaitaia. From the car park, the 300m **Lighthouse Walk** leads along the headlands to the base of the lighthouse with expansive sea views. A bright yellow signpost lists the distances to London and Los Angeles as well as the equator and south pole. (A similar signpost stands at Bluff on South Island.) East of the headlands is a lookout toward the pohutukawa tree.

The **Te Paki Coastal Track** (3-4 days one-way) runs 48km from Kapowairua, skirting the coastline past the Cape Reinga Lighthouse all the way to Te Paki Stream. The route can be broken into smaller sections. Popular options include the **Te Werahi Beach Track** (2km, 45 minutes) south from Cape Reinga car park along Te Werahi Beach. Extend the route by linking with the **Twilight-Te Werahi Loop Track** (16km, 5 hours) at the end of the beach. The challenging tramp crosses manuka scrub and climbs over dunes all the way to Te Paki Stream.

East of the lighthouse, the **Kapowairua/Spirits Bay to Pandora Track** (9km, 3 hours round-trip) leaves the Kapawairua campsite (Te Hapua Rd.) to walk the bay via the beach, or a slightly harder route behind the dunes. The track ends at Waiahora lagoon before scaling a rocky outcrop to the secluded Pandora Beach.

Camping

Cape Reinga has four DoC **campsites** (09/408-6014, www.doct.govt.nz) along the Te Paki Coastal Track. Bring insect repellent, as the mosquitoes are rampant here.

Kapowairua/Spirits Bay campsite (adults $8, children $4, under age 5 free) has 45 first-come, first-served sites with cold showers, running water, and flush toilets. It's on Spirits Bay Road, accessed via the Watiki Landing turnoff from Highway 1 onto Te Hapua Road.

Pandora campsite (free) has running water. It is accessible along the Te Paki Costal Track, or a two-hour walk from the car park on Highway 1.

Tapotupotu Campsite (adults $8, children $4, under age 5 free) overlooks a beach and a lagoon. The 45 first-come, first-served sites are unpowered, with cold showers and running water. It's 3km south of Cape Reinga, on Tapotupotu Road, off Highway 1.

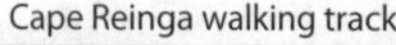

Cape Reinga walking track

Walking the Te Araroa Trail

Officially opened at the end of 2011, the **Te Araroa** (www.tearaoa.org.nz)—"the long pathway"—is a 3,000km walk that spans the length of the country, from Cape Reinga to Bluff. The route, usually tackled from north to south, links existing tramps and takes 100-160 days. In 2013, however, British ultramarathoner Jez Bragg completed the trail in 53 days, 9 hours, and 1 minute. Two years later, Auckland teacher Mina Holder polished off the Te Araroa in 77 days, 10 hours, and 44 minutes, believed to be the women's record, while raising thousands of dollars for her city's Starship Children's Hospital in the process.

Twilight campsite (free) is a basic campsite off the beaten path. Leave your vehicle at Cape Reinga car park and follow signs for the hour-long walk to Twilight Beach.

Transportation and Services

Cape Reinga is 112km (1 hour, 30 minutes) north of Kaitaia, via Highway 1.

TOURS

Salt Air (09/402-8338, www.saltair.co.nz) operates scenic helicopter and fixed-wing flights from Paihia's heliport on the wharf and the Kerikeri airport. The **Cape Reinga Half Day Tour** (minimum 2 people, $425 pp) is a 45-minute flight in a fixed-wing plane over Whangaroa Harbour, Doubtless Bay, and Ninety Mile Beach. The tour lands 20km from Cape Reinga, where guests board a 2.5-hour bus tour around the tip of Northland. You'll visit the cape and the beach where you can sand-surf the dunes. The climax of the tour is an hour-long flight back to the Bay of Islands, passing some of the more remote coastal landmasses.

The **Full Day Cape Reinga Exclusive Helicopter Tour** (minimum 2 people, from $2,085 pp) arrives at Cape Reinga via helicopter and is followed by a three-hour bus tour of the cape, including Ninety Mile Beach. Guests fly to Henderson Bay on the east coast of the peninsula for lunch and a coastal bike tour before returning to the Bay of Islands by helicopter.

Tour giants **Explore** (0800/365-744, www.exploregroup.co.nz, adults $150, children $110) and **Fullers** (09/402-7421, www.dolphincruises.co.nz, adults $149, children $74.50, under age 5 free) operate bus tours to Ninety Mile Beach and Cape Reinga from the Bay of Islands. However, these journeys start from the Bay of Islands and can take up to 11 hours.

The Kauri Coast

New Zealand's kauri tree has few peers, its colossal trunk layered in silvery bark and laced with green and leathery leaves. Before human arrival, more than 80 percent of New Zealand was blanketed in forest, with kauri among the most dominant species on North Island. A victim of its own success (its timber was used to craft canoes, build ships, fashion furniture, and shore up houses), logging and deforestation mean that figure now stands at 25 percent. Some of the finest remaining kauri forest is found along the 80km Kauri Coast that links Hokianga and Kaipara Harbours.

HOKIANGA HARBOUR

There's a real sense of majesty to Hokianga Harbour, a fiord-like formation south of Kaitaia that, according to Maori mythology, was the arrival point of their ancestors a thousand years ago. Known as Te Hokianga-a-Kupe ("the returning place of Kupe"), the jagged west coast harbor claws nearly halfway to the Bay of Islands, served by the sleepy port villages of Kohukohu, Rawene, Opononi, and Omapere.

The **Hokianga Vehicle Ferry** (09/405-2602, www.fndc.govt.nz, one-way vehicles $20-40, motorbikes $5, passenger $2 pp) departs from the Narrows Landing (7:15am-8pm Mon.-Fri., 7:45am-8pm Sat.-Sun.), 4km southwest of Kohukohu along Kohukohu Road, with a return ferry from Rawene (7am-7:30pm Mon.-Fri., 7:30am-7:30pm Sat.-Sun.). From the Narrows, the 15-minute crossing carries pedestrians and up to 24 vehicles and their passengers. The harbor can be crossed in 15 minutes aboard a vehicle ferry.

Kohukohu

The village of Kohukohu, 61km (1 hour) southeast of Kaitaia via Highway 1, is the gateway to Hokianga Harbour. This prime slice of picturesque real estate sits on the harbor's north shore, where the Mangamuka and Waihou Rivers emerge. Kohukohu has a smattering of historic Victorian timber villas.

FOOD AND ACCOMMODATIONS

The Tree House (168 West Coast Rd., 09/405-5855, www.treehouse.co.nz, dorm $32, $64-70 s, $82-88 d) is a timber lodge with cabins surrounded by native woodland. The wonderful all-natural environment is laced with walking paths. Basic units share bath and cooking facilities but boast private decks with peaceful views. Dorms in the main building sleep up to four people. Family rooms sleep three to six. A campsite and one powered van site ($20 pp) are available.

The **Night Sky Lodge** (6 Marriner St., 09/405-5841, www.nightskylodge.co.nz, $110-135) is a peaceful waterside retreat built from kauri. Most of the en suite rooms overlook the harbor. Relax on your private veranda and make the most of the free Wi-Fi, a communal kitchen, and a covered barbecue area.

Horeke

Horeke was the site of New Zealand's first commercial shipbuilding yard and is home to the country's oldest pub, Horeke Hotel. The hotel also marks the end of the Twin Coast Cycle Trail. Bike rentals are available from the hotel.

WAIRERE BOULDERS

The **Wairere Boulders** (70 McDonnell Rd., 09/401-9935, www.wairereboulders.co.nz, sunrise-sunset daily, adults $15, children $5, students and seniors $10), 4km south of Horeke via Taheke-Horeke Road, is a private park graced with amazing geological features. Set aside an hour to navigate this 2.8-million-year-old volcanic valley strewn with "floating" basalt boulders formed by the erosion of an ancient lava flow.

Several waterways bleed throughout the park, and kayak rentals (adults $15-30 per hour, children $10 per hour) are available. Self-contained RVs can park for one night for free, additional nights $10.

FOOD AND ACCOMMODATIONS

Built in 1826, the **Horeke Hotel** (2118 Horeke Rd., 09/401-9133, www.horekehotel.nz, 1pm-close Wed.-Fri., noon-close Sat.-Sun., $18-26) is New Zealand's oldest pub. A menu of classics features scotch steak or fresh-caught fish enjoyed in a dining room with an enormous brick fireplace, or on the deck overlooking the harbor. Live bands sometimes play.

The family-run **hotel** ($130-150) has three comfortable rooms with splendid harbor views. Amenities include TVs and communal pool tables. Bike rentals are available with a shuttle bus service along the Twin Coast Trail.

GETTING THERE

To reach Horeke sans ferry, take Highways 1 and 12 for an inland detour of 100km (1 hour, 15 minutes).

Rawene

CLENDON HOUSE

Rawene is home to **Clendon House** (14 Parnell St., 09/405-7874, www.clendonhouse.co.nz, 10am-4pm Thurs.-Mon. mid.-Dec.-mid.-Jan., 10am-4pm Sat.-Sun. Nov.-mid-Dec. and mid-Jan.-Apr., 10am-4pm Thurs.-Mon. July, 10am-4pm Sun. May-June and Aug.-Oct., adults $10, children $3.50, students $5), the former home of Captain James Reddy, a trader and ship owner with a remarkable life. Not only did Reddy witness the signing of the Waitangi Treaty, but he was chairman of New Zealand's first bank and the country's first U.S. consul. The dwelling marks his marriage to Jane, who was of local Maori descent. The modest abode has many original furnishings and possessions from the family who inhabited it for more than a century.

FOOD

Set in a gorgeous renovated boatshed on stilts over the sea, the ★ **Boatshed Café** (8 Clendon Esplanade, 09/405-7728, 8:30am-3:30pm daily) dishes up freshly made classic staples like pizzas and pancakes along with a super selection of tempting baked treats—best enjoyed with one of their excellent espresso coffees. Look for the specials on the blackboard ($9-17) where you can expect to see the likes of pasta and fish dishes. Be sure to browse the collection of locally made arts and crafts for a souvenir.

Opononi and Omapere

The tiny twin towns of Opononi and Omapere sit at the mouth of Hokianga Harbour on the north end of the Kauri Coast, fringed by golden sands, towering dunes, and coastal views. Look for a dolphin statue on the seafront at Opononi, a tribute to Opo, a bottlenose dolphin who frequented the harbor in the mid-1950s. Learn more about this legendary local courtesy of a short documentary film in the **i-SITE Visitor and Information Centre** (29 Hwy. 12, 09/405-8869, www.northlandnz.com, 8:30am-5pm daily).

GETTING THERE

Opononi and Omapere are 20km southwest of Rawene along Rawene Road and Highway 12. The two towns are a four-minute drive apart.

Transportation and Services

Public transport to and around Hokianga (and much of the Kauri Coast) is limited. The **Hokianga Link Bus** (09/405-8872, www.buslink.co.nz, Tues. and Thurs. Dec.-Mar., Thurs. Apr.-Nov., one-way $3-10, round-trip $6-25) connects Hokianga Harbour to the Bay of Islands via Omapere, Opononi, Rawene, Kaikohe, Okaihau, and Kerikeri.

Those without a vehicle should consider booking a tour instead.

TOURS

The **Hokianga Tour by Explore** (0800/365-744, www.exploregroup.co.nz, adults $154, children $77) is an eight-hour trip from Paihia that includes a harbor tour with swimming, a guided walk through Waipoua Forest, and lunch. There is an option to sand-surf the

Hokianga Harbour's giant dunes (adults $25, children $15, under age 5 $5), with a short boat transfer included.

From Paihia, the Giants and Glow Worms Tour (adults $129, children $64.50) from **Fullers** (09/402-7421, www.dolphincruises.co.nz) is an all-day excursion led by a Maori guide to Hokianga Harbour and the Waipoua Forest.

★ WAIPOUA FOREST

Waipoua Forest is the most well-preserved forest on the Kauri Coast. It's home not only to the world's finest kauri specimens—some trees are at least 2,000 years old—but also to towering stands of rimu and northern rata, explored via several easy tracks from well-signed car parks off the highway.

Tours

Footprints Waipoua (334 Hwy. 12, Omapere, 09/405-8207, www.footprintswaipoua.co.nz) tours are led by a Maori guide. These exquisite excursions merge science and myth as affable hosts recount the ecological and spiritual history of the forest. The four-hour **Twilight Encounter** (6pm daily Oct.-Mar., 5pm daily Apr.-Oct., adults $95, children $35) is the most moving; you'll meet mighty residents such as Te Matua Ngahere ("The Father of the Forest"), a 4,000-year-old kauri, and wildlife such as the kiwi, the weta, and the carnivorous kauri snail. The **Daylight Encounter** (1pm daily, adults $80, children $35) lasts 3.5 hours. Those short on time can opt for the **Meet Tane Day** (40 minutes, adults $25, children $25) or the **Meet Tane Night** (40 minutes, adults $70, children $35). Tours require a minimum of two guests; pickups are from Omapere and Opononi.

Walks

Walking through Waipoua Forest as the wind whispers, the limbs creak, and the birds tweet is an almost spiritual experience.

Tane Mahuta ("Lord of the Forest") is New Zealand's largest kauri with a girth of nearly 14m, and a height of more than 51m. The 10-minute walk starts from the Tane Mahuta road sign. The **Four Sisters Loop** (10 minutes round-trip) encircles a tightly packed grove of four kauri trees. It starts from the Kauri Walks car park. The **Te Matua Ngahere Walk** (30 minutes round-trip) loops to New Zealand's oldest kauri tree.

the oldest kauri tree, Tane Mahuta

Accommodations and Services

Te Roroa Waipoua Visitors Centre (1 Waipoura River Rd., 09/439-6443, www.teroroa.iwi.nz, 9am-3pm daily) is staffed by knowledgeable local guides. Stop here to book custom tours or plant a tree. An on-site **café** (9am-2pm daily) serves coffee and a no-nonsense menu of sandwiches, cakes, fries, and burgers. The complex also houses accommodations ranging from campsites (adults $15, children $7.50, under age 5 free) with access to hot showers and a basic camp kitchen to rudimentary kitchen cabins ($50-60) that sleep two to four. The self-contained holiday homes

($175-250) are cozier, with wood floors, private decks, and wood burners.

The visitors center is 9km south of the Kauri Walks car park off Highway 12. Highway 12 snakes 17km under the shade of these ancient giants, and even the drive demands hushed reverence.

Transportation

Waipoua Forest is about 16km (15 minutes) southeast of Omapere along Highway 12.

TROUNSON KAURI PARK

The 586ha **Trounson Kauri Park** (Trounson Park Rd.) is home to native critters such as the weta, the brown kiwi, kauri snails, and bats, and houses impressive kauri trees, kauri grass, and ferns. Explore it all via a loop track (1.6km, 40 minutes) from the car park.

Kauri Coast Top 10 Holiday Park (7 Opouteke Rd., 09/439-0621, www.kauricoasttop10.co.nz) operates a daily **night walk** (adults $30, children $20, nonguests adults $35, children $25) through Trounson Kauri Park. Tours last two hours; departure times vary but are usually 8:45pm daily in mid-summer and 6:30pm daily in mid-winter. Flashlights are provided.

Accommodations

Kauri Coast Top 10 Holiday Park (7 Opouteke Rd., 09/439-0621, www.kauricoasttop10.co.nz) has tent and RV sites ($44-54) and kitchen cabins ($114) with access to shared bath facilities, a Sky TV lounge, and communal kitchens. Fully self-contained units and motel rooms ($130-182) have Sky TV, private decks, and lounge areas. Guests enjoy free Wi-Fi, herb gardens, barbecue areas, and sports facilities. It's 5km from the Trounson Kauri Park, off Trounson Park Road.

The **Trounson Kauri Park Campground** (Trounson Park Rd., 09/439-3450, www.doc.govt.nz) is a DoC-maintained campsite with electric stoves, hot showers, and flush toilets. The 12 unpowered sites (adults $15, children $7.50, under age 5 free) and 8 powered sites (adults $18, children $9, under age 5 free) are first-come, first-served. Guests are charged a minimum fee of two adults per site.

Transportation

Trounson Kauri Park is 25km southeast of Waipoua Forest; 7km is along an unpaved road well-signposted off Highway 12.

KAI IWI LAKES

Fed by rainwater, **Taharoa, Waikere,** and **Kai Iwi Lakes,** known collectively as Kai Iwi Lakes, are bodies of indigo water nearly two million years old. They sit bordered by brilliant white beaches that are guarded from behind by pine trees. Rainbow trout, crabs, and freshwater mussels thrive in these waters that make an idyllic swimming and picnic spot.

Accommodations

Kai Iwi Lakes Camp (Domain Rd., Kaipara, 09/439-0986, www.kaiiwicamp.nz, $15 pp) operates Pine Beach and Promenade Point Campgrounds on opposite sides of Lake Taharoa. Both campgrounds have flush toilets and drinking water; only Pine Beach offers hot showers and Wi-Fi.

Transportation

The lakes are 25km (20 minutes) south of Trounson Kauri Park via Highway 12, Omamari, and Kai Iwi Lakes Roads.

DARGAVILLE

The port town of Dargaville developed in the late 19th century on the North Wairoa River as a hub of kauri logging, gum digging, and shipbuilding. Learn all about its illustrious history at the **Dargaville Museum** (Harding Park, 32 Mt. Wesley Coast Rd., 09/439-7555, www.dargavillemuseum.co.nz, 9am-5pm daily summer, 9am-4pm daily winter, adults $15, children $2, seniors $12) in Harding Park. Inside is a 16m hand-carved pre-European Maori war canoe, the masts of the *Rainbow Warrior,* and a replica gum diggers' camp replete with an operational gum-washing machine.

At the **Woodturners Kauri Gallery** (4 Murdoch St., 09/439-4975, www.

thewoodturnersstudio.co.nz, 9am-6pm daily), guests can witness master craftsman Rick Taylor manipulate kauri wood into bowls, pots, pens, and even hats. A one-on-one wood-turning workshop is offered for a minimum of one day ($425). Gallery hours vary; call or email Rick to confirm it's open before visiting.

Transportation

Dargaville is 35km (30 minutes) south of Kai Iwi Lakes via Highway 12.

RIPIRO BEACH

Uncoiling for more than 100km, **Ripiro Beach** may be New Zealand's longest drivable beach, but driving (and swimming) can be dangerous along this ferocious coastline due to shifting sands. It's well worth a stroll, and you might spot seals or the occasional bow or propeller from the scores of ships that have been lost here. Orcas and dolphins are known to patrol the waters.

Transportation

Baylys Coast Road offers the most convenient access point to Ripiro Beach, 13km directly west of Dargaville.

MATAKOHE

Tucked into the northeast corner of Kaipara Harbour, this small town is the birthplace of Joseph Coates, the first elected Kiwi prime minister. It's also known for its splendid museum.

Kauri Museum

Set aside half-a-day to explore the sprawling **Kauri Museum** (5 Church Rd., 09/431-7417, www.kaurimuseum.com, 9am-5pm daily, adults $25, children $8, under age 5 free), one of the nation's leading exhibitions. Lumber industry relics and machinery share space with a real steam sawmill, an enchanting collection of antique kauri furniture and carvings, and a world-renowned gum and amber display. In Volunteers Hall lies a jaw-dropping slab of felled kauri more than 22m long. The grounds host a kauri pioneer church and post office, and a 45,000-year-old kauri swamp log.

Transportation

Matakohe is 45km (30 minutes) southeast of Dargaville along Highway 12. From Matakohe, it's 136km (1 hour, 45 minutes) to Auckland via Highway 1.

Waikato, Bay of Plenty, and The Coromandel

Hamilton 134
Raglan and Vicinity 140
Waitomo 144
Matamata 149
The Coromandel Peninsula 151
Bay of Plenty 160

Look for ★ to find recommended sights, activities, dining, and lodging.

Highlights

★ **Hamilton Gardens:** New Zealand's finest city garden houses wonderful native flora and species from across the world (page 134).

★ **Surfing at Raglan:** Hang 10 at the edge of this laid-back black-beached town (page 140).

★ **Ta Puia Hot Springs:** Beneath the most secluded of black beaches bubbles a geothermal spa only accessible around low tide (page 143).

★ **Waitomo Caves:** Three hundred underground caves are illuminated by glowworms (page 144).

★ **The Pinnacles:** One of the best day walks on North Island rises high over Coromandel Peninsula to a collection of toothy limestone peaks (page 152).

★ **Cathedral Cove:** Marvel at this majestic coastal cave at the end of a pink-sand beach (page 157).

★ **Hot Water Beach:** Dig your very own thermal spa in the sand just meters from the Pacific Ocean (page 157).

★ **Donut Island:** Within an offshore collapsed volcanic crater blooms a secluded paradise (page 158).

★ **White Island:** Cruise or fly to New Zealand's only active marine volcano and walk among steaming vents and pools of bubbling mud (page 169).

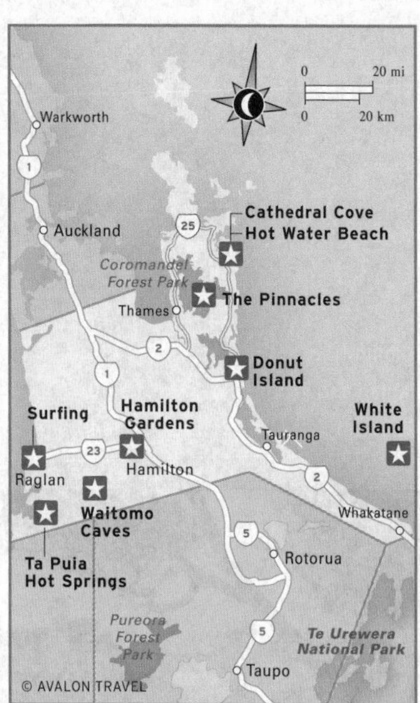

One of the most alluring aspects of Aotearoa are its wild landscapes. The region is home to verdant rainforests, tropical beaches, and enormous glowworm caves 30 million years in the making.

South of Auckland, the Waikato region is traversed by New Zealand's mightiest river, also named the Waikato. This was the site of some of the bloodiest battles of the New Zealand Wars, fought between Maori warriors and British troops in the late 19th century. Carpeted in rambling and ripe green pastures, Waikato is now the epitome of rustic paradise; there's good reason it was picked as the setting of the Shire in *The Lord of the Rings* and *The Hobbit* films.

Hamilton, the region's main hub, may not be the sexiest of New Zealand cities, but its internationally acclaimed gardens should not be missed. Directly west, the coastal town of Raglan attracts surfers from across the globe. To the south, the phenomenal glowworm caves of Waitomo sparkle like sun-kissed glitter. Here you can test your mettle rafting through underground caves or rappelling down lairs of near-black darkness.

On the northwest coast, the Coromandel Peninsula lures road-trippers with its tropical vibe. Blessed by golden beaches and dramatic rock faces, the coast is lined with former mining hubs and laid-back surf towns.

Curving southward, the east coast leads into the Bay of Plenty, home of Maori villages and a 1769 visit by Captain Cook. This sunny coastline is a favorite Kiwi getaway that harbors an active marine volcano and the historic coastal town of Whakatane.

PLANNING YOUR TIME

Start your exploration in the calming historic mining settlement of **Coromandel Town** on the west coast of the Coromandel Peninsula. Spend a day visiting the cavernous **Cathedral Cove** and **Hot Water Beach,** where you can dig your own hot spring.

On the way south to the **Bay of Plenty,** spend the night in the town of **Whangamata.** Once in the Bay of Plenty, make the vibrant coastal hub of **Mount Maunganui** a priority

Previous: the Coromandel Peninsula; sheep at a Waikato farm. **Above:** Bridal Veil Falls.

Waikato, Bay of Plenty, and The Coromandel

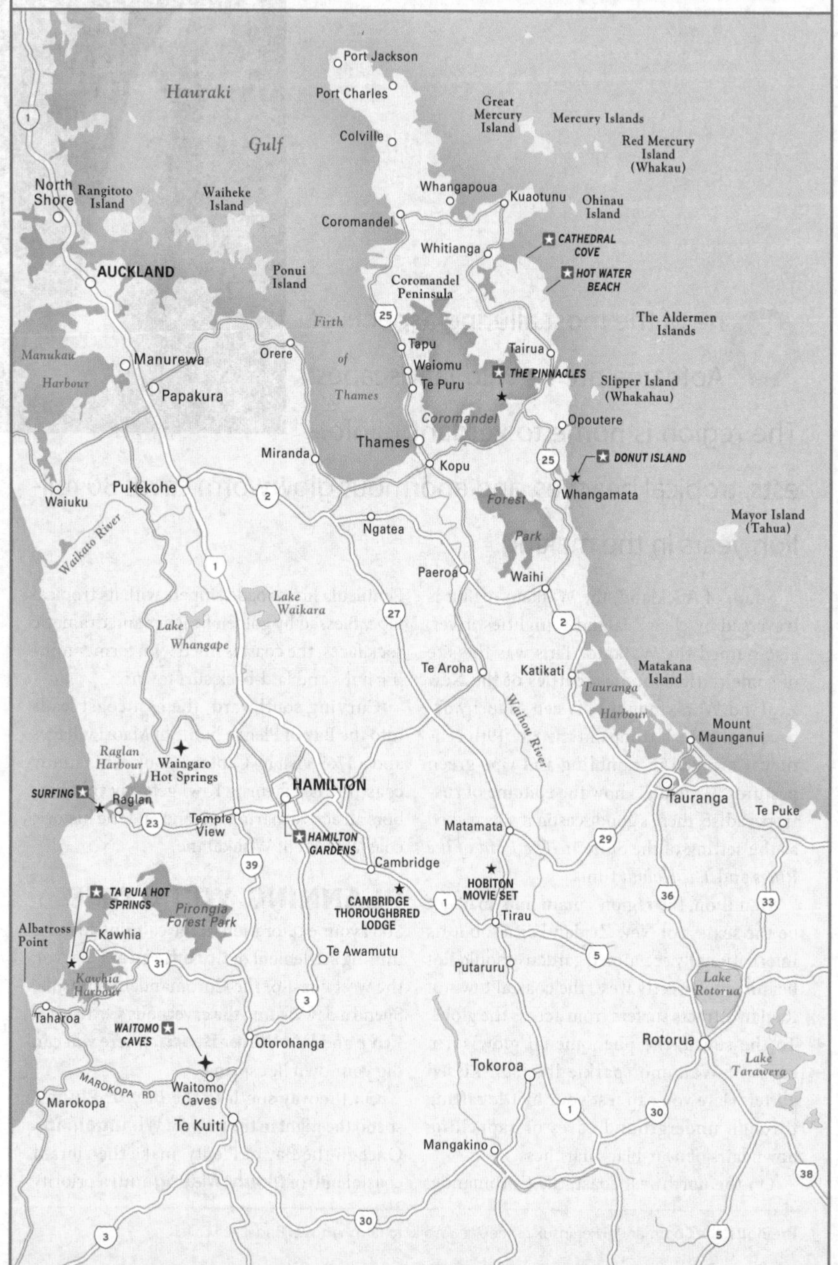
Port Jackson
Port Charles
Hauraki
Gulf
Colville
Great Mercury Island
Mercury Islands
Red Mercury Island (Whakau)
North Shore
Rangitoto Island
Waiheke Island
Whangapoua
Kuaotunu
Ohinau Island
Coromandel
Whitianga
CATHEDRAL COVE
AUCKLAND
Ponui Island
Coromandel Peninsula
HOT WATER BEACH
The Aldermen Islands
Firth of Thames
Tapu
Waiomu
Te Puru
Tairua
THE PINNACLES
Slipper Island (Whakahau)
Manukau Harbour
Manurewa
Orere
Papakura
Coromandel Forest Park
Opoutere
Thames
Miranda
Kopu
DONUT ISLAND
Pukekohe
Waiuku
Whangamata
Waikato River
Ngatea
Mayor Island (Tahua)
Paeroa
Waihi
Lake Waikara
Lake Whangape
Te Aroha
Katikati
Matakana Island
Tauranga Harbour
Waihou River
Mount Maunganui
Raglan Harbour
Waingaro Hot Springs
HAMILTON
Tauranga
SURFING
Raglan
Temple View
Te Puke
HAMILTON GARDENS
Matamata
Cambridge
HOBITON MOVIE SET
TA PUIA HOT SPRINGS
CAMBRIDGE THOROUGHBRED LODGE
Pirongia Forest Park
Tirau
Albatross Point
Kawhia
Kawhia Harbour
Te Awamutu
Putaruru
Lake Rotorua
Taharoa
WAITOMO CAVES
Otorohanga
Rotorua
Tokoroa
Lake Tarawera
MAROKOPA RD
Marokopa
Waitomo Caves
Te Kuiti
Mangakino
1
2
3
5
23
25
27
29
30
31
33
36
38
39

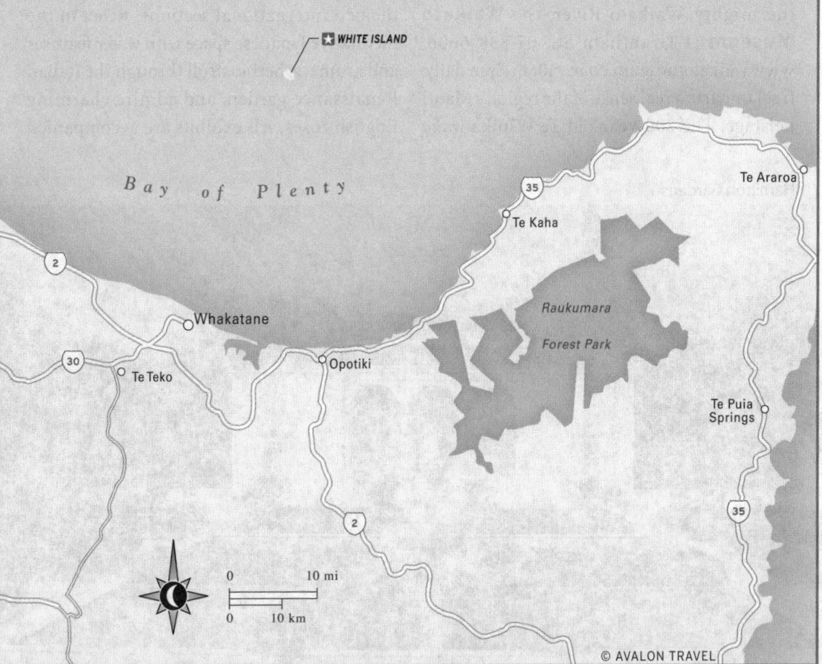
PACIFIC
OCEAN
WHITE ISLAND
Bay of Plenty
35
Te Araroa
Te Kaha
2
Whakatane
Raukumara
Forest Park
30
Te Teko
Opotiki
Te Puia
Springs
35
2
0
10 mi
0
10 km
© AVALON TRAVEL

and don't miss **Whakatane** for its rich Maori heritage. From here, you can take a flight or cruise to visit offshore volcano **White Island** (plan 2-3 days).

In **Waikato,** set aside a half day for the award-winning **Hamilton Gardens.** Add a day to explore **Waitomo's glowworm caves,** then kick back in the west coast surf town of **Raglan,** an idyllic seaside setting that you'll struggle to leave.

Hamilton

The magical Hamilton Gardens aside, there's little to lure the time-poor traveler to this city. However, it does serve as a decent base to explore Waikato attractions such as Hobbiton, Raglan, and the Waitomo Caves. Built along the banks of the Waikato River, 125km south of Auckland, Hamilton is the nation's fourth largest city. The backpacker-friendly hub hosts an easily walkable city center with free Wi-Fi plus a bounty of watering holes.

SIGHTS

Waikato Museum

Positioned high above the west bank of the mighty Waikato River, the **Waikato Museum** (1 Grantham St., 07/838-6606, www.waikatomuseum.co.nz, 10am-5pm daily, free) imparts a real sense of the region's Maori heritage. The 200-year-old Te Winika *waka taua* (war canoe), sits in galley 6, framed by an enormous window lined with Maori carvings. Exhibits highlight historical notes and imagery, while the contemporary facility holds fossils, art displays, and low-lit tributes to the fallen soldiers of World War I.

★ Hamilton Gardens

At **Hamilton Gardens** (Hungerford Crescent, Hwy. 1, off Cobham Dr., 07/838-6782, www.hamiltongardens.co.nz, 7:30am-8pm daily summer, 7:30am-5:30pm daily winter, free), internationally recognized and multi-award-winning exhibits are split into themed international sections. Relax in the meditative Japanese space with water features and aromatic herbs, stroll through the Italian Renaissance garden, and admire charming English roses. All exhibits are accompanied

Hamilton Gardens

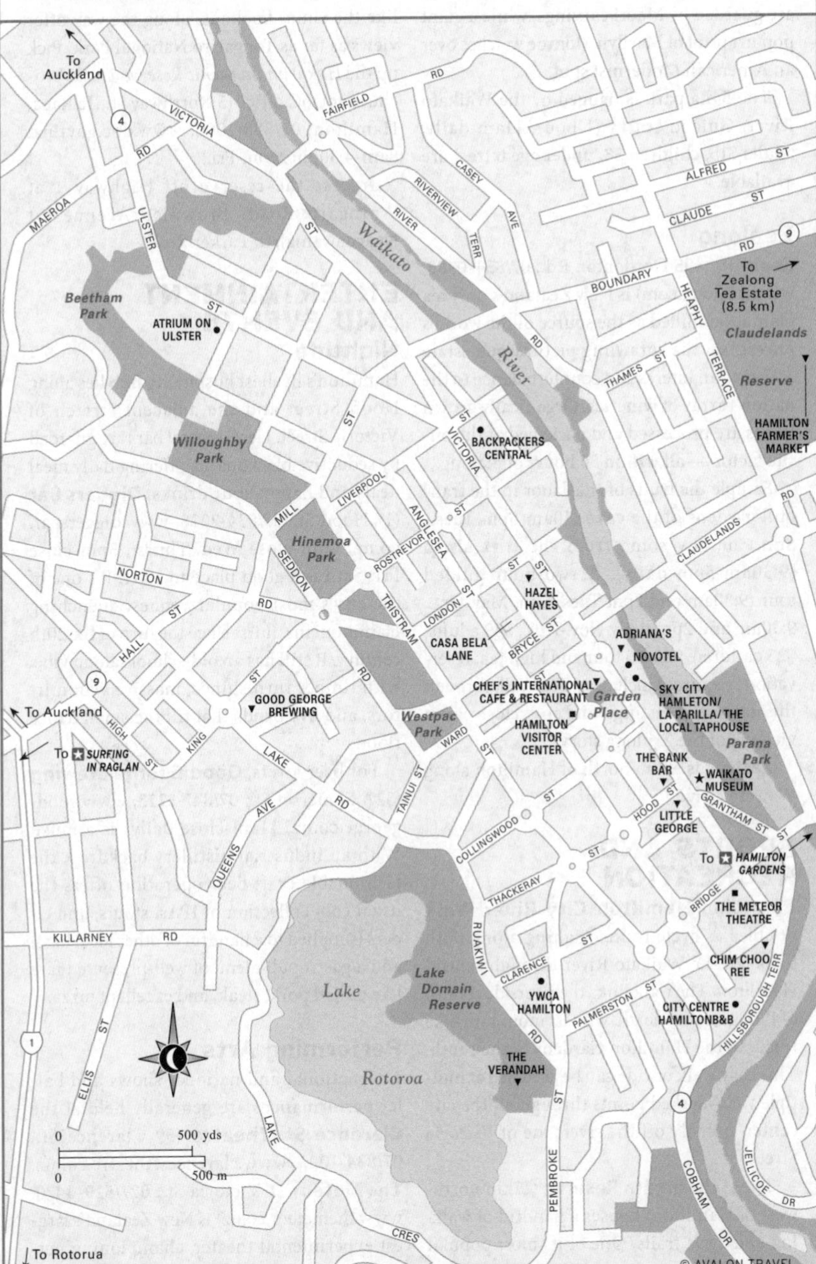
Hamilton
To Auckland
To Auckland
To Rotorua
To SURFING IN RAGLAN
To Zealong Tea Estate (8.5 km)
To HAMILTON GARDENS
Waikato River
Beetham Park
Willoughby Park
Hinemoa Park
Westpac Park
Claudelands Reserve
Parana Park
Garden Place
Lake Domain Reserve
Lake Rotoroa
ATRIUM ON ULSTER
BACKPACKERS CENTRAL
HAZEL HAYES
CASA BELA LANE
ADRIANA'S
NOVOTEL
SKY CITY HAMLETON/ LA PARILLA/ THE LOCAL TAPHOUSE
CHEF'S INTERNATIONAL CAFE & RESTAURANT
HAMILTON VISITOR CENTER
GOOD GEORGE BREWING
THE BANK BAR
WAIKATO MUSEUM
LITTLE GEORGE
HAMILTON FARMER'S MARKET
THE METEOR THEATRE
CHIM CHOO REE
CITY CENTRE HAMILTONB&B
YWCA HAMILTON
THE VERANDAH
VICTORIA RD
FAIRFIELD RD
CASEY AVE
RIVERVIEW TERR
RIVER RD
ALFRED ST
CLAUDE ST
BOUNDARY RD
HEAPHY TERRACE
THAMES ST
CLAUDELANDS RD
MAEROA RD
ULSTER ST
MILL ST
LIVERPOOL ST
VICTORIA ST
ANGLESEA ST
ROSTREVOR ST
SEDDON RD
TRISTRAM ST
LONDON ST
BRYCE ST
NORTON RD
HALL ST
HIGH ST
KING ST
LAKE RD
WARD ST
TAINUI ST
QUEENS AVE
COLLINGWOOD ST
HOOD ST
GRANTHAM ST
BRIDGE ST
THACKERAY ST
CLARENCE ST
RUAKIWI RD
PALMERSTON ST
HILLSBOROUGH TERR
PEMBROKE ST
COBHAM DR
JELLICOE DR
KILLARNEY RD
ELLIS ST
LAKE CRES
0 500 yds
0 500 m
© AVALON TRAVEL

by storyboards that explain the history and cultures that inspired them. Native offerings are guarded by Maori carvings, while a giant pop-art print of Marilyn Monroe watches over an American Modernist spot.

The 54ha park is fringed by the Waikato River. Guided **tours** (1 hour, 11am daily, adults $15, children $8, under age 6 free) are available.

Zealong

Zealong (495 Gordonton Rd., 07/854-0388, www.zealong.com) is New Zealand's only tea plantation. Billed as the source of the world's purest tea, the sprawling picturesque estate serves as an interesting counterbalance to the nation's array of wineries. Organically grown leaves are processed and packaged at the on-site factory—all within 36 hours of picking.

Sample the fruits of this labor in the tranquil gardens of the **café** (10am-5pm Tues.-Sun.) or buy some from the **gift shop** (9:30am-5pm daily). A two-hour guided tour (9:30am and 2pm Tues.-Sun. May-Oct., 9:30am and 2pm daily Nov.-Apr., $49 adults, $25 children, $60-85 tour and high tea, reservations required) includes a Tea Walk through the plantation, tastings, and an exclusive film viewing of the Zealong story.

Zealong is 10km north of Hamilton along Wairere Drive.

SPORTS AND RECREATION

The 10km **Hamilton City River Walk** doubles as cycle route, snaking along both banks of the Waikato River through central Hamilton. The walk links the riverside suburb of Pukete in the north, with its mountain bike track, to the Hamilton Gardens to the south. This easy walk or ride can be accessed at multiple well-marked points throughout the city center, notably off the river side of Victoria Street.

The **Hakarimata Reserve** (17km northwest of Hamilton) houses a handful of walking and cycle trails. One of its most popular walks is the well-formed 3km **Kauri Loop Track,** which passes a 1,000-year-old kauri tree along with other specimens and species like the rimu. Lookouts along the way offer views as far as Tongariro National Park. Pick up the *Hakarimata Scenic Reserve Tracks* brochure at DoC office (5 Northway St., Te Rapa, Hamilton, 07/858-1000, www.doc.govt.nz, 8am-4:30pm Mon.-Fri.).

Access the reserve off Highway 1 at Waingaro Road, Brownlee Avenue (at Ngaruawahia), or Parker Road.

ENTERTAINMENT AND EVENTS

Nightlife

Hamilton's liveliest hospitality hub lies along Hood Street and the adjacent stretch of Victoria Street. Here, several bars are guarded by seductive blackboards offering daily meal deals and happy-hour drinks. **Diggers Bar** (17 Hood St., 07/834-2228, www.diggersbar.co.nz, 4pm-close Wed.-Thurs., 3pm-close Fri.-Sat.) is a good place to start. It's one of the city's most popular venues, quenching Hamiltonians' thirst since the turn of the 20th century. It still has an old-school saloon vibe, with timber furnishings, massive wall mirrors, and live bands that fill the small dance floor.

For beer lovers, **Good George Brewing** (32A Somerset St., 07/847-3223, www.goodgeorge.co.nz, 11am-close daily) is a must. With an industrial distillery backdrop, the fashionable craft beer operation offers the usual cool collection of IPAs, stouts, and ciders (supplied to a handful of other local bars) and a gastropub menu of well-presented fare like pulled pork, steak, and excellent pizza.

Performing Arts

International and national shows and ballet performances are generally held at the **Clarence St. Theatre** (59 Clarence St., 07/834-1023, www.clarencesttheatre.co.nz). The **Meteor** (1 Victoria St., 027/529-4470, www.themeteor.co.nz) is New Zealand's largest experimental theater, championing performance arts such as poetry, dance, comedy,

Best Food

★ **Chim Choo Ree:** Imaginative fine dining in a trendy industrial setting in Hamilton (page 138).

★ **Coromandel Oyster Company:** A road- and harbor-side shack serving seafood straight from the sea near Coromandel Town (page 154).

★ **The Church:** A Mediterranean medley of tapas dished up in a former church not far from Hot Water Beach (page 158).

★ **Elizabeth Café and Larder:** Tauranga's regal café prepares fresh dishes with an international slant (page 162).

★ **Fish Face:** Delightful ocean dishes served in a marine-inspired environment in Mount Maunganui (page 166).

and improv, with a big slant on community projects. Buy tickets from the counter a few hours before the show starts.

Riverlea (83 Riverlea Rd., 0800/800-192, www.riverlea.org.nz) is an independent community-minded theater that hosts traditional performances. Recent shows include *The Witches* and *Rock of Ages*.

Cinema

To catch an art-house or foreign-language flick, head to **Victoria Cinema** (690-692 Victoria St., 07/838-3036, www.nzcinema.co.nz). **Metro by Hoyts** (12 Ward St., 07/850-3610, www.hoyts.co.nz) screens blockbusters, including 3-D films.

FOOD

While the interior of **The Verandah** (Hamilton Lake Domain, Rotoroa Dr., 07/838-0692, www.theverandah.co.nz, 8am-4pm daily, $14-25) is rather generic, seating on the outside deck offers views over the extensive palm-lined lawns to Hamilton Lake. Well-presented dishes such as French toast, pasta, and shepherd's pie make up the breakfast and all-day menus.

Hazel Hayes Cafe (587 Victoria St., 07/839-1953, www.hazelhayes.co.nz, 7am-4pm Mon.-Fri., 8am-2pm Sat., $10-20) serves the best breakfasts in town, with high-end organic offerings like hash browns with poached eggs and streaky bacon. All-day options include salmon salad or beef nachos and a cabinet lined with wraps. The café is named after the owners' grandmother, who is the inspiration behind the wholesome homemade menu.

You'll be well fed on a budget at **The Bank Bar & Brasserie** (Victoria St. and Hood St., 07/839-4740, www.thebank.co.nz, 11:30am-close Mon.-Fri., 11:30am-3am Sat., 10am-close Sun.) thanks to daily $12 lunchtime deals (nachos and burgers), $20 dinner deals (fish-and-chips), Thursday evening pizzas ($5), and weekday happy hours (4:30pm-6:30pm Mon.-Fri.). The stylish gastropub and former financial institution is furnished with oak paneling and mounted stag heads. There's an outdoor area out back.

Savor some spicy delights in the heart of Hamilton at welcoming **Chef's International Café** (27 Collingwood St., 07/839-6599, www.chefsinternationalrestaurant.com, 11:30am-11pm Mon.-Fri., noon-11pm Sat., $15-20), a well-priced, down-to-earth eatery whose rich decor and full tables add to a meals' warm glow. Indian dishes are accompanied by Malaysian and European fare; the lamb *jalfrezi* and the fish curry are especially good. It's BYO.

Best Accommodations

★ **Raglan Backpackers and Waterfront Lodge:** A welcoming, laid-back hostel befitting its surfing surroundings (page 143).

★ **Juno Hall:** Homey backpacker hostel set amid rolling farmland where you may get to bottle-feed some lambs (page 148).

★ **Colleith Lodge:** Luxurious eco-accommodations overlooking the Pacific Ocean in the tiny town of Tairua (page 158).

★ **Beach House Motel:** Minutes from Papamoa Beach, hot tubs and a pool add to the magic of this supercool motel (page 167).

★ **Driftsand Boutique Accommodations:** Sleep soundly to the sweet Pacific at these luxury lodgings overlooking secluded Ohope Beach (page 169).

Set in the historic Brewery Building with a chic industrial-minimalist backdrop of white tile walls, every creation on the ★ **Chim Choo Ree** (14 Anzac Parade, 07/839-4329, www.chimchooree.co.nz, 11:30am-2pm and 5pm-close Mon.-Fri., 5pm-close Sat., $36-38) menu is top-drawer, but the duck confit with licorice and salt-baked beets is especially delicious. Take fine-dining to the next level with a six-course tasting menu ($100) and optional wine pairing ($145).

ACCOMMODATIONS

Backpackers Central Hamilton (846 Victoria St., 07/839-1928, www.backpackercentral.co.nz, $30 dorm, $49-65 s, $82-87 d) is the city's best hostel, providing free unlimited Wi-Fi and a free breakfast of yogurt, fruit, cereal, and coffee. Communal areas are drab but spacious, with a full kitchen and a sunny deck area overlooking the street. Basic dorms are accompanied by well-equipped private single and double rooms (some with en suite baths) with mini fridges, TVs, and desks. Quads and family rooms ($89-125) cater to larger groups.

For privacy on a budget, head to **YWCA Hamilton** (Clarence St. and Pembroke St., 07/838-2219, www.ywca.org.nz, $30) near Hamilton Lake. Single and double rooms accommodate men and women; you'll never share a room with a stranger. Limited Wi-Fi is included, and there are stocked kitchens and cozy communal areas on each floor. Bedding, towels, and kitchen utensils are provided on arrival.

Proprietors Anne and Peter ensure the warmest of welcomes at the serene **City Centre Hamilton Bed & Breakfast** (3 Anglesea St., 07/838-1671, www.citycentrebnb.co.nz, $90-125), a pair of charming white wooden cottages with French doors that open onto a communal pool and garden area with a barbecue. The en suite lodgings are equipped with cooking facilities, free Wi-Fi, large LCD TVs, and some of the most comfortable beds in Waikato. It's minutes from the central business district and a stone's throw from the river.

On a road brimming with motels, the modern **Atrium on Ulster** (281/283 Ulster St., 07/839-0839, www.atriumonulster.co.nz, $125-175) stands out with first-class service. Swish en suite studio, one-, and two-bedroom units (some with spa tubs) sport leather armchairs or couches, HD TVs, walk-in showers, kitchenettes, and large windows filled with ample natural light. Guests can make use of a small but well-equipped gym and free unlimited Wi-Fi.

The only camping option close to the city center is the uninspiring **Hamilton City Holiday Park** (14 Ruakura Rd., 07/855-8255, www.hamiltoncityholidaypark.co.nz, $36-40) with well-kept powered and unpowered sites, plenty of shade, and a small kitchen and TV room. Cabins ($50-85) include kettles and seating; some have TVs and basic cooking facilities with access to shared kitchen and baths. Larger self-contained units ($88-125) have kitchenettes, private baths, and dining areas.

TRANSPORTATION AND SERVICES

Car

Hamilton is 125km (1 hour, 40 minutes) south of Auckland along Highway 1.

Air

Hamilton Airport (HLZ, Airport Rd., 07/848-9027, www.hamiltonairport.co.nz) is 20 minutes south of the city. Domestic carriers include **Air New Zealand** (www.airnewzealand.co.nz), with flights to Christchurch and Wellington, and **Sun Air** (www.sunair.co.nz), with flights to Whangarei, Great Barrier Island, and Gisborne.

Shuttles and Taxis

Super Shuttle (0800/748-885, www.supershuttle.co.nz) operates daily door-to-door services aboard a luxury minibus. For taxi service, call **Hamilton Taxis** (07/847-7477).

Car and Campervan Rental

Rental car options at the airport include **Avis** (www.avis.co.nz), **Hertz** (www.hertz.co.nz), and **Budget** (www.budget.co.nz). **Waikato Car Rentals** (www.waikatocarrentals.co.nz) are more centrally located. For well-priced campervans, consider **Nomad** (www.nomadnz.com).

Bus

The transport system in Hamilton is excellent. **Hamilton Transport Centre** (Bryce St. and Anglesea St.) is the main pickup and drop-off point for national bus services such as **Intercity** (www.intercity.co.nz) and **Naked Bus** (www.nakedbus.com). The CBD **shuttle bus** (www.busit.co.nz, every 10 minutes 7am-6pm Mon.-Fri., 9am-1pm Sat., free) operates in a one-way loop from the Transport Centre (via Caro St.), the i-SITE, Hood Street, and Liverpool Street.

Bike

Vello Espresso (11 Kent St., 07/839-0985, www.veloespresso.co.nz, 8:30am-5:30pm Mon.-Fri., 10:30am-2pm Sat.) offers a wide range of bikes for hire at competitive prices.

Services

The **Hamilton i-SITE Visitor Centre** (Caro St. and Alexandra St., 07/958-5960, www.visithamilton.co.nz, 9am-5pm Mon.-Fri., 9:30am-3:30pm Sat.-Sun.) is the first stop for information and services, or stop by one of the **DoC Offices** (73 Rostrevor St., Level 4; 9 Garden Place, 07/858-1000, www.doc.govt.nz, 8:30am-4:30pm Mon.-Fri.).

There is a **post office** (163 Commerce St., 07/847-9660, 8:30am-5:30pm Mon.-Fri., 9am-1pm Sat.) and medical services are available at **Waikato Hospital** (Pembroke St. and Selwyn St., 07/839-8899). For nonemergencies, try **Victoria Clinic** (750 Victoria St., 07/834-0333, 8:45am-4:30pm Mon.-Fri.).

CAMBRIDGE

Cambridge offers a quainter and quieter alternative to Hamilton. Known as "the town of trees and champions," Cambridge's tree-lined streets line the banks of the Waikato River. The town has a rich history of breeding superstar race horses.

Food and Accommodations

Homemade treats and an ever-smiling staff await at **Paddock** (46a Victoria St., 07/827-4232, www.paddockcambridge.co.nz, 8am-5pm Mon.-Thurs., 8am-8pm Fri.-Sat., 8am-4pm Sun.), a white-walled rustic café serving bagels, burgers, and a bounty of baked goods. The lemon-meringue cream doughnut is a must.

Quaint colonial architecture harbors a cornucopia of well-priced lodgings at **No. 1 Motels on Victoria** (89 Victoria St., 0800/166-842, www.no1motels.co.nz, $79-155). Guests can choose from en suite rooms or rooms with shared bath facilities. Amenities include air-conditioning, Sky TV, a beverage station, and Wi-Fi. While toast is complimentary, cooked breakfasts can be ordered. This is a basic but well-kept setup that is centrally located with ample free parking.

Transportation and Services

Cambridge is 23km (20 minutes) southeast of Hamilton along Highway 1 and the Thermal Explorer Highway.

Stop by the **i-SITE Visitor Centre** (Queen St. and Victoria St., 07/823-3456, www.cambridge.co.nz, 9am-5pm Mon.-Fri., 10am-4pm Sat.-Sun.) for local insights and to rent a bike ($10 per hour, $25 for 3 hours, $50 for 6 hours) to explore the town.

Raglan and Vicinity

There's a brief crest to Highway 23 before it winds down into Raglan, 48km west of Hamilton, that affords a magnificent glimpse of the coastal town and the momentous surf breaks beyond. The laid-back yet world-renowned surfing destination brims with boho boutiques, craft stores, and fashionable cafés along with a wealth of walks and water activities.

SIGHTS

Raglan Museum

Accessed via the i-SITE, the modest **Raglan Museum** (15 Wainui Rd., 07/825-0556, www.raglanmuseum.co.nz, 9:30am-6:30pm daily, adults $2, children $1) exhibits local history, from Maori inhabitance through to European settlement and contemporary surfers. Watch a short surfing documentary, see the region's first telephone exchange switchboard, and peruse an array of pharmacy items left by the town's first chemist. A sizable photography and postcard collection sits alongside numerous copies of the *Raglan Country Chronicle*, an early newspaper.

Raglan Old School Arts Centre

There's a thriving arts and crafts scene in Raglan; the picturesque coastal setting has long enticed creative types. Stop by the **Raglan Old School Arts Centre** (5 Stewart St., 07/825-0023, www.raglanartscentre.co.nz, office 10am-2pm Mon.-Fri.), whose eclectic collections include sculptures and paintings by local artists along with workshops and film screenings.

SPORTS AND RECREATION

★ Surfing

Despite Raglan's rep as a surfing mecca, there's ample opportunity for novices to have a crack at hanging 10. The coastline here is renowned for its year-round wave-generating consistency. The left-hand break at **Manu Bay** (8km west of Raglan) offers one of the world's longest water rides; it was filmed in the 1966 documentary movie *Endless Summer*. **Ngarunui (Ocean) Beach** is the region's largest beach and is the best for beginners. It's 5km west of Raglan and is patrolled by lifeguards in summer.

Whale Bay is a little farther west, accessed via a car park and a scramble over some rocks. It should only be tackled by experienced wave riders. The windswept **Ruapuke Beach** (30 minutes southwest of Raglan) is where punchy barrels roll even during relative calm elsewhere.

Beginners should make a beeline for the excellent **Raglan Surfing School** (5B Whaanga Rd., 07/825-7873, www.raglansurfingschool.co.nz). Daily lessons (3 hours, $89) include one hour honing your balance

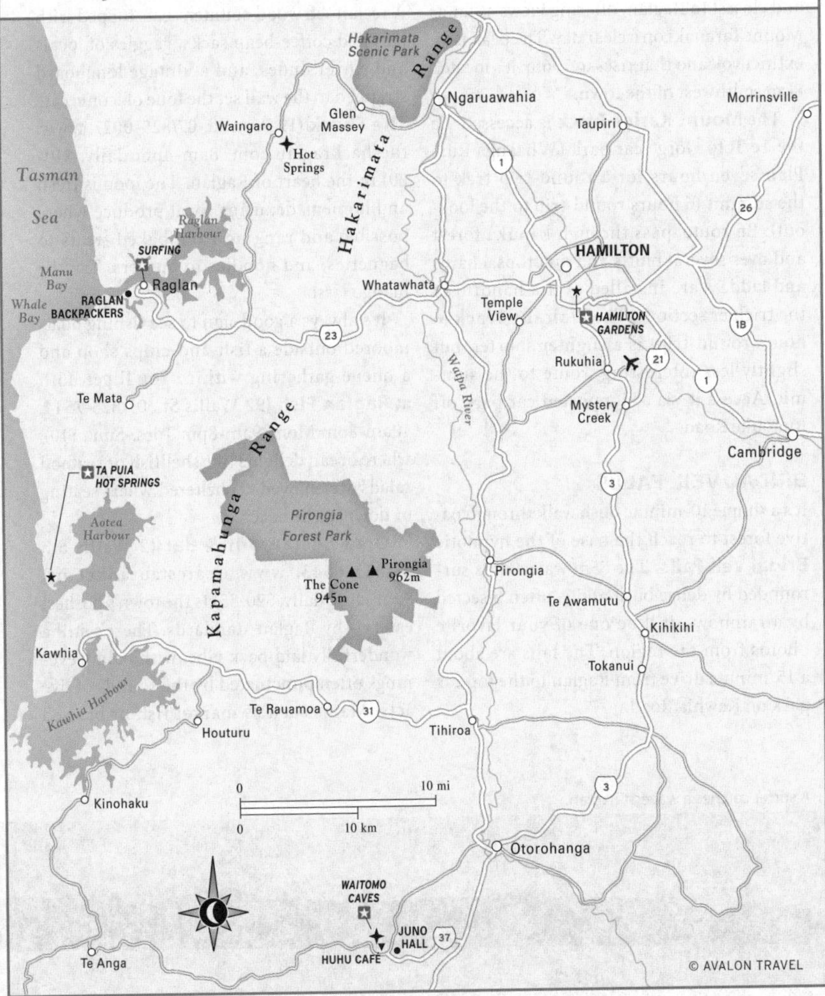

on land before heading to Ngarunui Beach. Private lessons ($149 one-on-one, $129-258 for a couple) are also available. Lessons must be booked in advance. Prices include free pick-ups as well as board and wet-suit rental. A rental service is also available. The school is 10 minutes outside Raglan.

In town, **Raglan Watersports** (5A Bankart St., 07/825-0507, www.raglanwatersports.co.nz, 8:30am-6:30pm daily) offers a bounty of equipment rentals, including surfboards, stand-up paddleboards, kayaks, and snorkels as well as guided tours.

Walks

MOUNT KARIOI

The surf town's rich forested and mountain surroundings are laced with a bounty of beautiful walking trails. The Mount Karioi Summit Tracks are among the most popular and closest to Raglan, offering views as far as Mount Taranaki on a clear day. The peak is an extinct volcano that rises to 756m; it's located 8km southwest of the town.

The **Mount Karioi Track** is accessed via the Te Toto Gorge car park (Whaanga Rd.). Plan seven hours for a round-trip trek to the summit (6 hours round-trip to the lookout). En route, pass through kanuka forest and over several bluffs and outcrops; chains and ladders are installed over a handful of the trickier sections. The **Wairake Track** (6 hours round-trip) is a slighter shorter, but slightly less interesting, route to the summit. Access it via a signposted car park off Ruapuke Road.

BRIDAL VEIL FALLS

It's a simple 10-minute bush walk through native forest to reach the base of the hypnotic **Bridal Veil Falls.** The 55m waterfall is surrounded by dense bush and is often bisected by a rainbow—it'll be one of your favorite photos from the region. The falls are about a 15-minute drive from Raglan to the top car park on Kawhia Road.

FOOD AND ACCOMMODATIONS

A reclaimed wood counter, seats topped with recycled coffee-bean sacks, gaggles of locals and surfer dudes, and a vintage longboard strapped to the wall set the tone of iconic café **The Shack** (19 Bow St., 07/825-0027, www.theshackraglan.com, 8am-4pm daily, $10-20) in the heart of Raglan. The food is fresh and homemade, using local produce where possible and ranging from baked treats to baguettes, and noodles to burgers. Try the mango lassi.

It's always a good sign to see fishing boats moored outside a fish-and-chips shop and a queue gathering within. You'll get both at **Raglan Fish** (92 Wallis St., 07/825-7544, 10am-8pm Mon., 9am-8pm Tues.-Sun., $10), where ocean delights like shellfish or seafood salads are enjoyed at sheltered wharf seating or down at the beach.

Orca Restaurant & Bar (2 Wallis St., 07/825-6543, www.orcarestaurant.co.nz, 9am-close daily, $20-35) is the town's poshest eatery—by Raglan standards. There's still a wonderfully laid-back vibe, with balmy evenings often punctuated by the sounds of live acts. Mains such as market fish or braised

A surfer catches a wave at Raglan.

pork belly are best washed down with local wine or craft beer.

Positioned on the edge of the estuary around an open grassy courtyard with hammocks, a pizza oven, and a hot tub, ★ **Raglan Backpackers and Waterfront Lodge** (6 Wi Neera St., 07/825-0515, www.raglanbackpackers.co.nz, dorm $29-33, $58 s, $68-78 d) takes some beating. Friendly staff offer tour advice and bookings as well as free use of kayak and fishing gear; mountain bikes rent for $2 per hour. The adjoining lodge has three bedrooms—one double and two small dorms. The comfortable, private facilities include private decks, gardens, and a barbecue. There is a designated area with limited space for camper vans ($19).

A mini community with a range of wacky and wonderful accommodations awaits at the bush-clad eco-retreat **Solscape** (611 Wainui Rd., 07/825-8268, www.solscape.co.nz) near Manu Bay. Accommodations comprise a collection of tipi tents ($30-110), mud earth domes ($100-120), and railway wagons converted into dorms and private rooms ($30-80). Communal facilities include baths, a fully stocked kitchen, and a lounge area with a log fire; eco-credentials such as solar showers, LED lighting, and composting toilets are part of the deal. Self-contained studios and holiday cottages ($140-200) have private facilities and outdoor areas. Camping ($20) is available, as are services such as a massage, yoga, and a surf school. Free shuttles are available into Raglan.

Near Ngarunui Beach, **Raglan Retreat** (349 Wainui Rd., 021/222-7922, www.raglanretreat.nz, $250-350) is a luxurious boutique complex cradled in a fern-rich forest fed by a mountain stream from the slopes of Karioi. En suite studios and chalets boast private balconies or courtyards, with log burners, spas, entertainment systems, complimentary high-end beauty products, and organic teas and coffees.

All are catered for at the lively **Raglan Kopua Holiday Park** (Marine Parade, 07/825-8283, www.raglanholidaypark.co.nz) on the harbor peninsula. Guests make use of the barbecue areas, a TV room, a fully equipped kitchen, and a game room with a pool table and arcade machines. Powered and unpowered sites ($22-24) share space with cabins and motel units ($45-160); most have private baths, lounges, and kitchen areas. The excellent booking desk can arrange activities such as surf lessons.

TRANSPORTATION AND SERVICES

Raglan is 46km (40 minutes) west of Hamilton along Highway 23. The **Bus It** (www.busit.co.nz, Mon.-Fri.) Raglan 23 service runs between Ragland and Hamilton.

For more information, visit Raglan's **i-SITE Visitor Information Center** (13 Wainui Rd., 07/825-0556, www.raglan.info). The town has a **library** (7 Bow St., 07/825-8929, 9am-8pm Mon.-Thurs., 9am-5pm Fri., 9:30am-12:30pm Sat.) and a **medical center** (216 Wainui Rd., 07/825-0956, 8:30am-5pm Mon.-Thurs.).

KAWHIA

This tiny far-flung harbor town rests in a region of Maori significance. It was the birthplace of revered warrior chief Te Ruaparaha and, according to legend, the final resting place of the ancestral canoe—or *waka*—Tainui.

★ Ta Puia Hot Springs

Dig yourself a hole in the black sand at **Ta Puia Hot Springs** and watch as the geothermal water bubbles to the surface, allowing you to recline in your very own hot water pool. Avoid venturing into the ocean, however, as the currents here can be dangerous.

To get here, head down to Ocean Beach at the end of Ta Puia Road, 4km west of Kawhia. From the car park, clamber over the dunes. Plan to arrive a couple of hours either side of low tide.

Kiritehere Beach

This region was formed from sedimentary rocks, and if you know where to look, the area is littered with marine fossils. Nowhere is this more evident than on **Kiritehere Beach** (Soundry Rd., 45km southwest of Kawhia). Scattered along the shoreline south of the stream is an abundance of polished sandstone rocks imprinted with fossilized shellfish.

Food and Accommodations

The **Oparau Roadhouse** (31 Kawhia Rd., 07/871-0683, www.oparauroadhouse.com, 6:30am-8:30pm daily) is a heartwarming community project that was built from scratch with an army of volunteers. It opened on Christmas Day 1990 and serves as a lonesome gas station, general store, and café (the homemade meat pies are spectacular), 15 minutes east of Kawhia. The spacious and soft grassy meadows are offered free of charge for camping and camper vans ($5 for power); they even throw in free Wi-Fi. It's a serene location, surrounded by rolling hills and a nearby river. There is a sink and a toilet, but no showers. They also rent shovels for the hot springs at Ocean Beach.

Transportation

Kawhia is 50km south of Raglan. The easiest way to get here is via Highways 23, 39, and 31, a journey that takes 1 hour, 40 minutes; the scenic—and most direct—coastal route via Kauroa-Kawhia Road takes 20 minutes less. However, stretches of this stunning route are little more than pothole-strewn gravel tracks; it's not recommended for nervous drivers or those in rental vehicles. There is no public transport.

Waitomo

Nestled in a region of Waikato called the King Country, Waitomo (90km southeast of Raglan) is the gateway town to the legendary limestone labyrinth of caves—many of which cradle vast colonies of glowworms. Above ground are several walks well worth investigating, and plenty of bars and eateries to kick back in come the end of adventuring. Self-catering travelers should stock up on supplies beforehand, as there is only one general store in town—with limited choices and a maximum markup.

SIGHTS

Waitomo Discovery Centre

Make the **Waitomo Discovery Centre** (21 Waitomo Village Rd., 07/878-7640, www.waitomocaves.com, 8:45am-5:30pm daily Mar.-Dec., 8:30am-7pm daily Jan.-Feb., $5) at the i-SITE your first stop. You'll get a feel for the region at this small museum that recounts the geological, natural, and human history of the caves with photography, fossils, rocks, and an informative documentary. You can even test your mettle through a mock cave crawl.

TOP EXPERIENCE

★ Waitomo Caves

Formation of the Waitomo Caves began 30 million years ago. The area under the ocean was uplifted through volcanic eruption and widened further, exposing the limestone to flowing water. Today the caves are home to underground rivers that can be gently sailed or rafted, cave walls that are climbed or rappelled, and caverns lit by sparkling glowworms.

Discover Waitomo (39 Waitomo Village Rd., 07/878-8228, www.waitomo.com) operates an efficient tour schedule led by professional guides. Tour options include the town's three main attractions: Waitomo Glowworm Cave, Aranui Cave, and Ruakuri Caves. Paved paths lead down hand-railed boardwalks ending in a short boat ride through the caves.

WAITOMO GLOWWORM CAVE

The **Waitomo Glowworm Cave** (tour every 30 minutes 9am-5pm daily Nov.-Mar., 9am-5:30pm daily Apr.-Oct., adults $51, children

$23.50) takes in two 30-million-year-old cave systems, first snaking through the 14m high Cathedral, an imposing cavern with fascinating acoustics. You'll then pass a beautifully lit 16m vertical limestone shaft known as the Tomo, formed by an ancient waterfall that links the top level of the cave to the underground Waitomo River. The journey concludes with a short boat ride beneath a mesmeric canopy of twinkling glowworms. Tours lasts 45 minutes.

ARANUI CAVE

The **Aranui Cave** (9am-4pm daily, adults $50, children $23) is positioned beneath the Ruakuri Scenic Reserve, 3.5km west of the visitors center. It is famed for its formidable grouping of stalactites—millions of them—that feather nearly the entire ceiling. There are no glowworms, but there is a colony of weta, New Zealand's iconic cave-dwelling insect that's been around since the dinosaurs. This tour option takes one hour and includes a 15-minute stroll through the surrounding bush.

RUAKURI CAVES

Carved beneath the reserve, **Ruakuri Cave** (2 hours, tours 9am, 10am, 11am, 12:30pm, 1:30pm, 2:30pm, and 3:30pm daily, adults $74, children $29) is said to have been accidently discovered five centuries ago by a young Maori hunter searching for birds. Ruakuri is the longest guided cave in New Zealand and among the most spectacular, featuring sprawling limestone features, fossilized seashells affixed to the walls, and masses of glowworms. The unnerving rumble of distant underground waterfalls is never far away, made more eerie in the knowledge that the site served as a sacred Maori burial ground.

MANGARONGAPU CAVE

One of the region's most authentic caves experiences, pretty **Mangarongapu Cave** houses no artificial lights or boardwalks. You'll likely get a little wet and muddy (protective clothing is provided) on this journey beneath a farm village. Tours are operated by family-owned **Glowing Adventures** (1199 Oparure Rd., 07/878-7234, www.glowing.co.nz, 8:30am and 11:30am daily summer, 2pm, 9am, and noon daily winter, $129) and groups are limited to no more than eight people. Visitors are led through native forest and untouched caves dappled with glowworms; there is some scrambling over boulders, so a reasonable level of fitness is required. Allow three hours

rappelling into Waitomo Caves

for the tour (two hours underground). Hot showers are provided when you're done.

Mangarongapu Cave is 12km west of Waitomo. Transportation is not provided.

FOOTWHISTLE CAVE

Caveworld (23 Waitomo Village Rd., 07/878-6577, www.caveworld.co.nz, hourly 9am-5pm daily, adults $59, children $35) operates 1.5-hour tours of **Footwhistle Cave**, 3.5km from Waitomo. Enter the cave via a short bush walk. Along with the limestone stalagmites and stalactites, you will encounter glowworms up close and witness the skeletal remains of the moa bird. The cave is lit rather romantically by carefully positioned candles (along with a few solar-powered ones). Another highlight is the brief illumination of the cavern with a magnesium torch.

SPELLBOUND

Spellbound (15 Waitomo Village Rd., 07/878-7622, www.glowworm.co.nz, 10am, 11am, 2pm, and 3pm daily, adults $75, children $26) runs three-hour tours of a couple of compelling private caverns with the region's highest concentration of glowworms (the BBC filmed a documentary series here). Tours include transport and take in two caves—one by inflatable raft, one by foot—with no more than 12 guests at a time.

The cave is located 12km south of Waitomo beneath a backcountry farm.

ADVENTURE CAVING

Several companies offer a variety of subterranean scares. A good place to start is **Waitomo Adventures** (654 Waitomo Caves Rd., 07/878-7788, www.waitomo.co.nz) with six options, three of which are guaranteed to get you soaked. All safety gear and protective clothing, including wetsuits, are provided.

The **Lost World Through the Window** (4 hours, 2pm daily, $200) is a fun-filled cave-top adventure that involves zip-lining at heights of up to 80m and scaling a few ladders. The **Lost World 4-Hour** (8am, 10am, 12:30pm, 1pm, 2:30pm, and 3pm daily, $380)

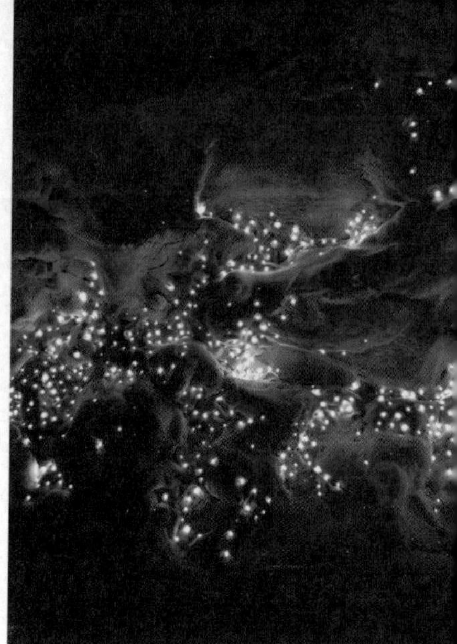

glowworms

begins with a 20-minute 100m rappel that's not for the faint of heart (you'll feel like Batman rappelling into a cave), but there's an instructor there the whole time. It's an incredible experience as you pass weird and wonderful rock formations adorned with plants and as the crashing of the Mangapu River echoes up from below. After that, there's ladder-climbing and glowworm-laded caverns to explore. The **Lost World Epic** (7 hours, 10:30am daily, $540) begins with that 100m rappel followed by walking, wading, and sometimes swimming through the waters of enormous caves. Tours include a packed lunch and barbecue dinner.

One of the most popular activities in the region is black-water rafting—experiencing rapids in the dark. The **TumuTumu Toobing** (4 hours, 9:30am, 10am, 1:30pm, 2pm, 2:30pm, and 3pm daily, $200) tour is among the best. Walk, wade, swim, and sit on a rubber ring as you're carried beneath a starlit ceiling of glowworms. A much-welcome hot shower follows.

The **Haggas Honking Holes** (4 hours,

Why Do Glowworms Glow?

There are many types of glowworms, none of which are worms; rather they are the larval stage of flying insects, and the ones in New Zealand represent the mosquito-like fungus gnat. They thrive in dark, damp environments, so aside from caves, they can often be found hanging from a forest canopy, which they affix themselves to by way of sticky silk attachments that are also used to trap food, like a spider's web. Their glow serves to lure small insects who then become snared in the silk. The light is the result of chemical reaction powered by their protein-rich diet.

9am, 10am, 1:30pm, 2pm, 2:30pm, and 3pm daily, $275) tour rappels down caves and rock climbs through waterfalls among an intricately carved limestone cave system lit by numerous glowworms.

St. Benedict's Caverns (9am, 9:30am, 10am, 1:30pm, 2pm, 2:30pm, and 3pm daily, $200) is a fascinating cave system with an array of contrasting formations explored via zip lines and rappels. It's dry and relatively easy going.

WALKS

The **Waitomo Walkway** is a relaxing 3km trek that begins opposite the Waitomo Discovery Centre. The walk follows the Waitomo River through bush, then across farmland and limestone landscapes to the Ruakuri Scenic Reserve. Here, the **Ruakuri Walk** (1km round-trip) makes its way through a bush-clad gorge, limestone arches, and along the Waitomo stream. Plan to make it there for nightfall and you'll see glowworms along the banks.

Otorohanga Kiwi House

Kiwi, kea, kaka (parakeets), and kakariki (parrots) are just some of the chirpy locals that reside at the conservational **Otorohanga Kiwi House** (20 Alex Telfer Dr., 07/873-7391, www.kiwihouse.org.nz, 9am-5pm daily, adults $24, children $8, under age 5 free). The site is surrounded by bush with wetland walks and waterways patrolled by long-fin eels that are fed each day at 2:30pm. Kiwi feedings are at 10:30am, 1:30pm, and 3:30pm daily; kea and kaka feedings are at 11am, and the parakeets are fed at noon. You'll also encounter tuatara, a reptile that's been around since the time of the dinosaurs.

Otorohanga Kiwi House is 16km (15 minutes) northeast of Waitomo along Highways 37 and 3.

Food and Accommodations

The on-site café at the **General Store** (15 Waitomo Village Rd., 07/878-8613, 9am-5pm daily) serves the usual array of muffins, baked cakes, wraps, rolls, and breakfasts, accompanied by the village's best coffee.

Tomo Bar (Hotel Access Rd., 07/878-8448, www.curlysbar.co.nz, 11am-close daily, $18-33) is the town's social focal point. It's heavy on sports, with pool tables, framed rugby jerseys, and events on the TV. The sizeable selection of local tap beers is accompanied by a typical gastropub menu of fish, poultry, and red meats.

The hillside **Roselands** (579 Fullerton Rd., 07/878-7611, www.roselandsnz.com, 9am-close daily, adults $36, children $18, under age 5 free) offers spectacular views of the surrounding bush canopy; guests can dine inside or outside at this fabled barbecue joint serving a buffet lunch and dinner. Hunks of meat are flame-grilled before your eyes and are accompanied by salads and dessert. Or opt for the all-you-can-eat beef casserole dinner buffet (6pm daily, $15) and come on Thursday for the big-screen movie night. Wine and beer is served, and there's free pickup and drop-off service from your accommodations. It's 3km from Waitomo.

Huhu (10 Waitomo Village Rd., 07/878-6674, www.huhucafe.co.nz, noon-close daily, $19-35, set menu $35-50) brings a touch of fine dining to the region. Enjoy roast duck leg or tea-smoked ora king salmon with New Zealand wines and a tempting collection of craft Kiwi beers. Enjoy it all on long leather sofas with views over the village.

★ **Juno Hall** (600 Waitomo Caves Rd., 07/878-7649, www.yha.co.nz, dorm $33, $80-90 s or d) is a YHA hostel positioned on ripe pastures that host orphaned farm animals; guests are often invited to bottle-feed lambs. The welcoming timber lodge sleeps up to 45 people in warm and comfortable rooms; en suite doubles are available. The open-plan communal area has a cozy potbelly fire, sink-in couches, and a well-stocked kitchen, and there's also an outdoor swimming pool. It's 1km outside Waitomo.

Great value accommodations are next to the Waitomo general store at **Waitomo Caves Guest Lodge** (7 Waitomo Village Rd., 07/878-7641, www.waitomocaves.co.nz, $110-150), a restful environment surrounded by a bounty of greenery. Each of the eight rooms come equipped with en suite baths, TVs, electric blankets, heaters, and tea- and coffee-making facilities. A generous continental breakfast accompanies the lovely rural views. Wi-Fi is free.

Te Tiro (970 Te Anga Rd., 07/878-6328, www.waitomocavesnz.com, $140) is a pair of welcoming pioneer-style timber cottages located on a 650ha sheep farm. The native bushland is laced with trails and a glow-worm grotto, with jaw-dropping rural views admired from a private deck. Breakfast is included, and there are barbecue facilities, best enjoyed at dusk while waiting for a blanket of stars to appear overhead. It's a 15-minute drive from Waitomo.

The well-run and well-equipped **Top 10 Holiday Park** (12 Waitomo Village Rd., 07/878-7639, www.waitomopark.co.nz) offers complimentary communal facilities like a hot tub, a swimming pool, trampolines, a stocked kitchen, a covered barbecue area, and a lounge with Sky TV and a library. Campers ($50-54) will be delighted at the abundance of shade and soft grass. More lodgings come in the form of cabins and motel units ($105-210) with TVs, kitchens, private patios, and baths. The tour booking desk is top-notch. The park is only 600m from the Waitomo Glowworm Caves.

Transportation and Services

Waitomo is 75km (1 hour) south of Hamilton, along Highway 39. **Intercity** (www.intercity.co.nz) runs daily bus service between Auckland's Intercity Sky City Bus terminal (102 Hobson St.) and Waitomo. The **Waitomo Wander** (www.travelheadfirst.com) operates shuttle buses between Auckland (pickup points vary) and Waitomo, as well as offering a range of guided tours. The drop-off and pickup point in Waitomo for both operators is the i-SITE.

Great Sights (www.greatsights.co.nz) is a major operator that runs guided tours between Auckland (102 Hobson St.) and the Waitomo Glowworm Caves. **Archers Tours** (www.archerstours.co.nz) operates guided trips between Hamilton and Waitomo, with options to take in Rotorua and Taupo.

The Waitomo **i-SITE Visitor Centre** (21 Waitomo Village Rd., 07/878-7640, www.waitomocaves.com, 8:45am-5:30pm daily) serves as a post office and museum.

Matamata

Less than an hour east of Hamilton, this farming town at the foot of the Kaimai Ranges has boomed thanks to the nearby Hobbiton movie set, which attracts visitors from across the globe.

SIGHTS

Hobbiton

The **Hobbiton Movie Set** (501 Buckland Rd., 07/888-1505, www.hobbitontours.com) is an authentic Middle-earth experience set on a lush sheep farm in the heart of Waikato, 15 minutes from Matamata. The setting served as the Shire for *The Hobbit* and *The Lord of the Rings* movies, and there's little need to suspend your disbelief that Frodo or Sam might appear around the corner at any turn.

TOURS

A two-hour **tour** (8:30am-3:30pm daily, adults $84, children $42, under age 9 free) takes in the rolling 5ha of greenery filled with Hobbit holes and ends at the Hobbit haunt the Green Dragon, where you can sample exclusive Hobbit ales and ciders. Tours run every 30 minutes, and guides brim with fun facts and film anecdotes. Additional tours are held 4pm and 4:30pm daily September-April and 5pm and 5:30pm daily December 27-February 28.

The **Evening Banquet Tour** (Wed. and Sat., adults $195, ages 9-16 $150, ages 5-8 $100, under age 5 free) is a dusk tour followed by a feast fit for a gluttonous huddle of Hobbits at the Green Dragon Inn. Diners sit at long medieval-style wooden tables heaving with whole roast chickens, baskets of steaming bread, vegetables, and oak barrels of booze. Following the banquet, guests stroll gently lit trails of the Shire, with handheld lanterns for added romance. Advance reservations are essential.

GETTING THERE

A free shuttle departs the **Matamata i-SITE** (every 45 minutes 9:30am-2:45pm daily; additional shuttles 3:30pm and 4:15pm daily Sept.-Apr., 5pm daily Dec. 27-Feb. 28). Allow three hours for the trip, including the tour.

From Rotorua, shuttles depart from 1235 Fenton Street (8am, 8:20am, 1pm, and 1:20pm

Hobbiton

daily, adults $119, children $77, under age 9 $35). Allow 4-5 hours for the tour and transport there and back.

Wairere Falls

Wairere Falls plunges 153m and is the highest waterfall on North Island. From the car park, a well-marked track (1.5 hours round-trip) winds through bush and across small bridged streams to a viewing platform at the base of the two-tiered falls. From there, another track leads to a high lookout that offers views across the Waikato Plains—but you'll need to add an extra two hours to the trip.

Wairere Falls is 15km northeast of Matamata. Follow Okauia Springs Road to Old Te Aroha Road and then Goodwin Road.

FOOD AND ACCOMMODATIONS

It's a little touristy—a giant Gollum peeks out over the awning and the pizzas are named after Middle-earth characters—but the atmosphere at the highly polished **Redoubt Bar & Eatery** (48 Broadway, 07/888-8585, www.matamata.redoubtbarandeatery.co.nz, 11am-1am daily, $24-37) is fun and welcoming without ever feeling forced. Servings are generous, and the burgers are especially good.

The sparkling **Matamata Backpackers** (61 Firth St., 07/880-9745, www.matamatabackpackers.co.nz, dorm $28, $70 s or d) has rooms with private reading lights, lockers, and power sockets, but no en suite rooms available. The private room can host three guests, and women-only rooms are available. The whole place feels fresh and modern, the kitchen is well-equipped and has a café vibe, and there's a fire in the lounge spot. Positioned just a couple of minutes' stroll from town, it also operates shuttles—and combo deals—to Hobbiton.

Three airy boutique rooms are up for grabs at **Arthouse Bed & Breakfast** (77 Duncan Rd., 07/880-9268, www.arthousebnb.co.nz, $160), a secluded villa adorned with art and positioned near Wairere Falls, with views of the Kaimai Ranges and their highest peak, Mount Te Aroha. The comfortable bedrooms have en suite baths with floor heating, Wi-Fi, TVs, robes, toiletries, hot drink facilities, and original paintings. The wonderful breakfast includes fruit juice, croissants, and eggs, served overlooking lush meadows.

Minutes from Hobbiton, **Brock's Place** (227B Buckland Rd., 0800/526-123, $8) offers sites for tents and motorhomes on soft green grass on private farmland, with toilet facilities and a coin-operated hot shower. It's very basic, but the views over the misty Waikato each morning are mesmeric.

TRANSPORTATION AND SERVICES

Matamata is 62km (50 minutes) east of Hamilton along Highways 1, 29, and 27. National bus operators **Intercity** (www.intercity.co.nz) and **Naked Bus** (www.nakedbus.com) service Matamata.

The **i-SITE Visitor Centre** (45 Broadway, 07/888-7260, www.matamatanz.co.nz, 9am-5pm Mon.-Fri., 9am-2:30pm Sat.-Sun.) is difficult to miss, as it looks like it has been lifted from Hobbiton.

The Coromandel Peninsula

Jutting from the northeast shoulder of the Waikato, the 400km Coromandel Peninsula tempts with its untouched, tropical vibe. The road-trip friendly coast is fringed by golden beaches. Dramatic faces of volcanic rock fold into a crooked range of rewarding hill walks with memorable ocean views. A handful of humble former gold-mining and lumber hubs, along with hip surf towns, are sprinkled along its outer route, offering a seductive air of indifferent isolation.

THAMES

Positioned around the point the Coromandel Ranges plunge into the Hauraki Plains, Thames was founded as a gold-mining town before becoming a logging town. It now serves as the gateway to the Coromandel Peninsula.

Sights

Marvel at the masses of majestic butterflies flitting about the **Butterfly Garden** (115 Victoria St., 07/868-8080, www.butterfly.co.nz, 9:30am-4:30pm daily Sept.-May, adults $12, children $6). The enclosed tropical paradise is brimming with aromatic flora like lilies, orchids, and torch ginger, all framed by a soothing collection of ponds and water features.

Recreation

BIKING

One of the easiest Great Rides, the **Hauraki Rail Trail** (www.haurakirailtrail.co.nz) follows the route of one of New Zealand's oldest railway corridors, passing through the iconic Karangahake Gorge. Along the way, the scenery includes old gold-mining towns and equipment, railway bridges, and native forest. The official route spans more than 80km—from Thames to Te Aroha—and is usually tackled over two days. Pick up the trail at the Thames Wharf (opposite Grey St.) off Highway 25.

Jollybikes (444 Pollen St., 021/0816-5000, www.jollybikes.co.nz) rents a range of bikes, including electric bicycles (the trail is e-bike friendly) and can advise shorter routes for those with less time. Guided cycle tours are also offered.

coast road near Thames on the Coromandel Peninsula

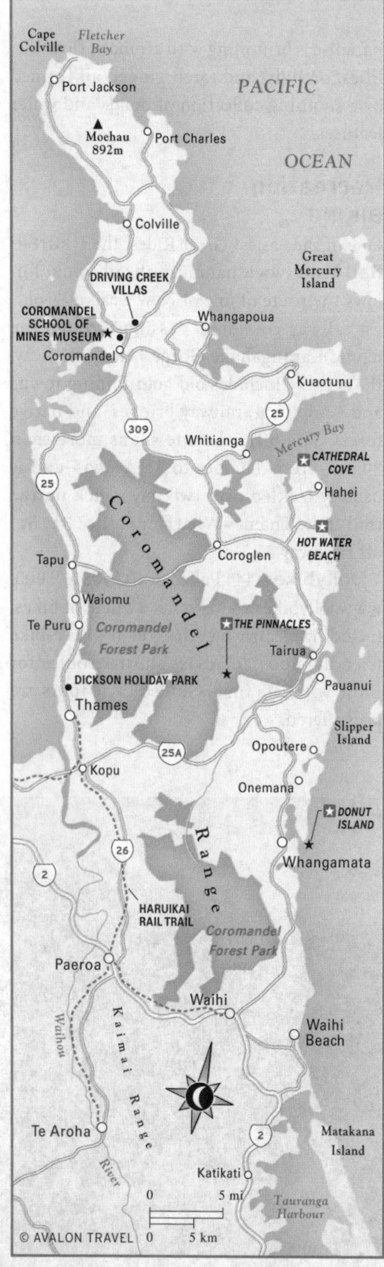

★ THE PINNACLES

The Pinnacles are a group of giant and jagged summits that reach 759m from the ranges around the glorious Kauaeranga Valley. Accessible via a lengthy day walk or overnight trek, the 12km hike is steep and slippery at times as it follows a well-marked route carved by early 20th-century kauri loggers. Historical remnants such as old tramlines, dams, and abandoned logs still reside along the edges of the forested trail. At the summit, 360-degree views span the peninsula across the Bay of Plenty, the Hauraki Gulf, and the Hauraki Plains. Plan to arrive for sunset or sunrise.

An 80-bed **DoC hut** (adults $15, children $7.50, under age 5 free) provides overnight accommodations about 30 minutes from the summit. It has lighting, cooking stoves, and a cold shower; bring a sleeping bag. Stays must be booked in advance through DoC (www.doc.govt.nz) or the **Kauaeranga Visitor Centre** (Kauaeranga Valley Rd., 07/867-9080), the end of which marks the beginning of the Pinnacles Walk.

Food and Accommodations

Plenty of polished timber and the constant hum of chatter emboldens the warm and traditional vibe at **Grahamstown Bar & Diner** (GBD, 700 Pollen St., 07/868-6008, www.thejunction.co.nz, 11am-close daily, $15-30). Feast on hearty dishes such as pizza, chunky fries, lamb shanks, and the fish of the day, then wash it all down with a beer on tap or local wine.

Located upstairs, the historic **Junction Hotel** has hosted guests since the late-19th-century gold rush—but accommodations have been thoroughly modernized since then. The heated dorm room ($30) sleeps five and has its own TV. This is accompanied by a selection of studio and one-bedroom twin and double units ($80-160) with private baths, TVs, and lounge or desk areas. The en suite single room ($65) overlooks the attractive St. James Church.

The well-maintained **Brookby Motel** (102 Redwood Lane, 07/868-6663, www.

brookbymotel.co.nz, $95-130) is in a super-chill setting surrounded by peaceful bushland with its own brook. Pristine studios and one-bedroom units come with en suite baths and private decks or balconies and free Wi-Fi, Sky TV, hot drink facilities, fridges, microwaves, and electric blankets. It's a brief stroll from the town center.

DoC operates a **visitors center** (www.doc.govt.nz, 07/867-9080) and basic **campsites** (adults $13, children $6.50, under age 5 free) along the Kauaeranga Valley, an ideal base from which to explore the Pinnacles and the region's other walks. The Kauaeranga Valley begins 10km northeast of Thames and is signposted from Kauaeranga Valley Road.

Transportation and Services

Thames is 115km (1.5 hours) southeast of Auckland along Highways 1, 2, and 25. **Intercity** (www.intercity.co.nz), **Naked Bus** (www.nakedbus.com), and **Go Kiwi** (www.go-kiwi.co.nz) operate bus services to Thames and the main towns of the peninsula.

Thames i-SITE Visitor Centre (200 Mary St., 07/868-7284, www.thecoromandel.com, 9am-4pm Mon.-Fri., 9:30am-2pm Sat., 9am-2pm Sun.) has information about the Coromandel Peninsula, along with DoC information for walks and huts.

COROMANDEL TOWN

Few Kiwi settlements capture or retain their gold mining past as quaintly as Coromandel Town. Its charming streets are lined with a bounty of colonial wooden buildings that now host a more artistic and bohemian crowd. The 54km drive from Thames hugs the Hauraki Gulf, passing mussel and oyster farms and pohutukawa trees—it is magical.

Sights

DRIVING CREEK RAILWAY & POTTERY

Driving Creek Railway & Pottery (380 Driving Creek Rd., 07/866-8703, www.drivingcreekrailway.co.nz, 9am-5:45pm daily summer, 10:15am-4:30pm daily winter, adults $35, children $13, under age 4 free) is a narrow-gauge train ride—the only one of its kind in New Zealand. It was built by local artisan Barry Brickell to access raw materials like clay from the looming hills. Today guests can enjoy the winding one-hour ride as it inclines through forests of kauri, rimu, and totara, passing pottery sculptures along the way. The ride ends at the cleverly named

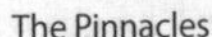
The Pinnacles

Eyefull Tower, a large wooden lookout with views over the peninsula. Pick up locally made pottery and craft souvenirs from the on-site store.

There are eight daily departures in summer and six in winter. Driving Creek Railway & Pottery is 3km north of Coromandel Town.

THE 309 ROAD

The legendary **309 Road** is a shortcut gravel-topped thoroughfare carved through dense bush across the peninsula's arching spine. Attractions along the scenic drive include a Kauri Grove, a collection of enormous kauri trees (accessed via a 15-minute walkway) and **The Waterworks** (471 309 Rd., 07/866-7191, www.thewaterworks.co.nz, 10am-6pm daily Nov.-Apr., 10am-4pm daily May-Oct., adults $25, children $20), a quirky collection of water-powered contraptions such as jets, cannons, and clocks constructed in part from recycled junk.

The 309 Road runs east for more than 20km, from Coromandel Town to Whitianga. If you happen to encounter an inquisitive group of semi-wild pigs en route, don't pull over unless you have some scraps to feed them. Otherwise, they will surround your car and stubbornly stay there—no matter how much you honk your horn or threaten to edge forward.

Food and Accommodations

It'd be a culinary crime to leave Coromandel Town without sampling the locally farmed shellfish. **Coromandel Mussel Kitchen** (309 Rd. and Hwy. 25, 07/866-7245, www.musselkitchen.co.nz, 9am-close daily mid-Sept.-mid-Apr., $19-32) grow their own salads and herbs and the hops for their in-house beer. Served in a bustling open-air setting, green-lipped mussels are the stars of a menu that also includes burgers and fish-and-chips. Patrons are sometimes entertained by live bands.

From a picturesque wooden shack, the ★ **Coromandel Oyster Company** (1611 Hwy. 25, 07/866-8028, daily 10am-5:30pm) dishes up the obvious straight from the sea, along with mussels, scallops, seafood chowder, and gourmet burgers enjoyed outside overlooking the coast.

A welcoming old-school hostel befitting the village vibe, the charming **Tui Lodge** (60B Whangapoua Rd., 07/866-8237, www.coromandeltuilodge.co.nz, dorm $29-32, $70 s or d) proffers plenty of cheer inside thanks to colorful decor and vibrant furnishings. Outside, the sprawling gardens include orchards from which you can pick fruit. Other freebies include bike rentals, tea and coffee, Wi-Fi, and laundry. Upgrade to an en suite double ($90), pitch a tent ($20 pp), or opt for the quirky on-site trailer ($80), replete with a queen-bed, a lean-to, a private toilet, and a shower.

Savor spectacular sea views from the serenity of **Harbour View Motel** (25 Harbour View Rd., 07/866-8690, www.harbourviewmotelltd.co.nz, $100-225). Reasonably priced en suite studios or one-bedrooms are dated but well-equipped with cooking facilities, dining spaces, and flat-screen TVs; some have private decks. Free perks include Wi-Fi and kayak and bike rentals. Communal amenities include a hot tub, a barbecue area, and laundry.

Long Bay Motor Camp & Cabins (3200 Long Bay Rd., 07/866-8720, www.longbaymotorcamp.co.nz) is a friendly, family-run setup overlooking a golden beach that spills into a sheltered turquoise cove. The site provides access to a couple of short scenic bush and coastal walks through a reserve that's open to the public. At the edge of the forest, cabins ($65-95) sleep up to six with kitchens, TVs, and barbecue areas. Tent and campervan sites ($10-25 pp) are also available. Beachfront units (Nov.-May, $110-130 per couple, plus $30 pp) accommodate up to four guests, with private decks, toilets, and kitchens. Bring your own sleeping bags and towels. The well-stocked kitchen and TV room have limited seating; an on-site store sells groceries and rents kayaks. It's a few minutes' drive west of town.

Transportation and Services

Coromandel Town is 54km (1 hour) north of Thames, along Highway 25. **Intercity** (www.intercity.co.nz) buses connect with Coromandel Town, as do **Go Kiwi Shuttles** (www.go-kiwi.co.nz).

From downtown Auckland, **360 Discovery Cruises** (www.360discovery.co.nz) sails to Hannafords Wharf, 10 minutes south of Coromandel Town, with a free shuttle to the center. Tours to other Coromandel hubs are available through **Coromandel Adventures** (www.coromandeladventures.co.nz), a shuttle bus company working in conjunction with 360 Discovery Cruises.

The **tourist information center** (85 Kapanga Rd., 07/866-8598, www.coromandeltown.co.nz, 10am-4pm daily) has free Wi-Fi, maps, and booking services.

PORT JACKSON

The northern tip of the peninsula is remote, rugged, and generally unpopulated. There are ample opportunities to explore the abundance of sandy and rocky nooks that punctuate the entire tip, including a handful of rudimentary camping sites.

Those planning on camping in the region should stock up on supplies and fill up with gas at **Colville,** the last settlement of note, 30 minutes north of Coromandel Town along the Colville Road. Beyond here, the roads are unpaved as they weave through ancient native forests and along windswept coasts. Contact DoC (www.doc.govt.nz) for road conditions, especially during or following heavy rain, as there may be fords.

Port Jackson is 30km northwest of Colville along Colville Road.

Recreation

The **Coromandel Coastal Walkway** (10km, 7 hours round-trip) is an easy hike that links Fletcher and Stoney Bays. It's one of the most rewarding seaside tramps you can do in New Zealand, with plenty of spots to stop and cool off in the Pacific en route. Vantage points allow for ocean and southward views all the way to The Pinnacles. The route also doubles as a grade 3 mountain bike track.

Campgrounds

Port Jackson has a spectacular DoC **campground** (Port Jackson Rd., 07/866-6932, www.doc.govt.nz, adults $13, children $6.50, under age 5 free) overlooking a sweeping 1km stretch of golden sands backed by green peaks with a sheltered beach ideal for swimming. A short coastal trail is signposted from the campsite. The campground has cold showers, barbecues, and a cooking hut. Sites must be booked in advance.

About 7km east of Port Jackson is the secluded Fletcher Bay, which houses another DoC **campground** (Oct.-Apr. 07/866-6685, May-Sept. 07/866-6932, www.doc.govt.nz, adults $13, children $6.50, under age 5 free) on coastal farmland. It has cold showers. Book in advance December-February.

Behind the campground is the DoC-maintained **Fletcher Bay Backpackers** ($26 pp), a ranch-style lodge set in idyllic grounds overlooking the bay. There are four bedrooms, each with two bunks. Facilities include bedding, hot showers, flush toilets, a lounge area, and a well-stocked kitchen.

Another DoC-maintained campsite awaits at **Stony Bay** (Oct.-Apr. 07/866-6822, May-Sept. 07/866-1106, www.doc.govt.nz, adults $13, children $6.50, under age 5 free).

WHANGAPOUA

Leave Port Jackson by following Port Jackson Road south toward Highway 25 and heading east. Look for the turnoff to Whangapoua Road at 12.5km, which leads to the isolated township of Whangapoua. At the northern end of the town's beach, follow the 1.5km route around the headlands through forest of pohutukawa and nikau palm to reach the white sands of **New Chums Beach.** Accessible only by boat or on foot, this remote sandy stretch is one of New Zealand's most beautiful.

Whangapoua is 73km (1 hour, 45 minutes) southeast of Port Jackson.

WHITIANGA

Whitianga—an abbreviation of Whitianga-o-Kupe (Kupe's crossing place)—is the largest hub of the Mercury Bay region at the peninsula's northeast. The harbor town and surrounding area hosts numerous natural wonders such as hot springs and unusual coastal formations. Many use Whitianga as a base from which to visit Cathedral Cove and Hot Water Beach.

The **Whitianga Scallop Festival** (www.scallopfestival.co.nz, Sept.) celebrates the region's seafood and marine heritage by way of street food stalls accompanied by live music and cooking demos and classes.

Sights

MERCURY BAY MUSEUM

Mercury Bay Museum (11A The Esplanade, 07/866-0730, www.mercurybaymuseum.co.nz, 10am-4pm daily summer, 11am-3pm daily winter, adults $7.50, children $2, under age 5 free) is in a stylish art deco building that first served as dairy factory. Inside are Maori artifacts along with exhibits dedicated to Captain Cook, the early kauri and gum loggers, and the original dairy factory.

LOST SPRING

The luxurious **Lost Spring** (121A Cook Dr., 07/866-0456, www.thelostspring.co.nz, 9:30am-5:30pm Sun.-Fri., 9:30am-7:30pm Sat., 90 minutes $40, all-day $70) is a collection of landscaped hot-spring lagoons, surrounded by tropical plants and sculptured rock, fed by a near 700m-deep geothermal well beneath Whitianga. If soaking in 32-40°C mineral water doesn't relax you, an on-site day spa offers a range of pampering treatments like massages and facials, along with a licensed eatery to bring you cocktails and platters poolside.

Food and Accommodations

The coolest café in Whitianga, **Café Nina** (20 Victoria St., 07/866-5440, 7:30am-3pm daily, 5:30pm-9pm Wed.-Sat., $10-20) is a tin-topped boho eatery hidden behind a mini native rainforest that gives way to glorious grounds round the back. Feast on all-day fried breakfasts, omelets, seafood chowders, or freshly baked muffins served with the best coffee in town. On the few sunless Coromandel days, the log fire will be roaring inside.

One of the region's premier eateries, **Salt Restaurant & Bar** (2 Blacksmith Lane, 07/866-5818, www.salt-whitianga.co.nz, 4pm-close Mon.-Thurs., noon-close Fri.-Sun., $27-40) serves fine-dining fare in a trendy and chill environment with a log fire and white-linen-topped tables. The deck overlooking the marina is the best spot to tuck into pan-seared oven-baked flounder drizzled in butter parsley sauce and a glass of pinot gris.

Friendly hostel **Turtle Cove** (14 Bryce St., 07/867-1517, www.turtlecove.co.nz, dorm $29-33, $77-90 s or d) has clean private rooms with en suite baths and comfortable beds. Enjoy complimentary unlimited Wi-Fi in the common areas, and a breakfast of coffee, tea, toast, and cereal served in a spacious well-equipped kitchen. The lounge and dining area opens onto gardens and a sunny deck. Make the most of the free boogie boards and spades to dig at Hot Water Beach.

A stone's throw from the sand and wharf, **Albert No. 6 Motel** (6 Albert St., 07/866-0036, www.albertnumbersix.co.nz, $140) is set around a villa with pristine en suite budget units equipped with free Wi-Fi and toiletries, tea- and coffee-making facilities, microwaves, toasters, TVs, and heaters. A simple continental breakfast is included.

Transportation and Services

Whitianga is reached via Highway 25 or the 309 Road. The town is 32-43km east of Coromandel Town and 35km southeast of Whangapoua.

Whiti City Cabs (07/866-4777) is a local taxi service, and **Coastal Campers** (www.coastalcampers.co.nz) offers good rates on camper van rentals.

Intercity (www.intercity.co.nz) buses serve Whitianga, as do **Go Kiwi Shuttles** (www.go-kiwi.co.nz), and **Naked Bus** (www.

nakedbus.com). **Cathedral Cove Shuttle** (www.cathedralcoveshuttles.co.nz) operates a bus service along much of the east coast, including to Hot Water Beach and Cathedral Cove.

For more information, visit the **Whitianga i-SITE Visitor Centre** (66 Albert St., 07/865-5555, www.whitiangainfo.co.nz, 9am-5pm Mon.-Fri., 9am-4pm Sat., 9am-2pm Sun.).

HAHEI AND VICINITY

Tiny coastal Hahei is just 6km southeast of Whitianga, but it takes more than half an hour on Highway 25 to navigate around Whitianga Harbor and Mercury Bay.

Sights

★ CATHEDRAL COVE

The iconic Hahei sands, revered for their pink tint (the result of crushed shells), lead north to the enormous rocky arch of **Cathedral Cove,** accessible via a 5km (1.5 hours round-trip) walk from the car park on Grange Road. The spectacular coastal track is hilly in places and takes in the lovely Gemstone and Stingray Bays.

Beyond the lapping emerald waves, the 9km **Whanganui A Hei Marine Reserve** harbors plants, sandy flats, and hard rock reefs home to an array of fish, including leatherjackets, rays, and red moki, as well as mollusks and crustaceans such as the rock lobster. Dolphins occasionally visit.

★ HOT WATER BEACH

A 10-minute drive south of Hahei, visitors can dig their very own hot pool just a seashell's throw from the ocean at **Hot Water Beach.** Plan to arrive two hours before or after low tide, when the exposed thermal waters rise through the sands. The subterranean spa doesn't stretch for the entire length of the beach, and it can get a little crowded in the section where the magic happens. Accommodations in the area provide guests with spades, or you can rent one locally. To get here, follow Link Road south to Hot Water Beach Road and turn left.

Recreation

Cathedral Dive and Snorkel (48 Hahei Beach Rd., 07/866-3955, www.hahei.co.nz, 9am, 1pm, and 3:30pm daily summer, 9am and 1pm daily fall-spring, $210) operates three-hour guided scuba diving tours to sites in and around the reserve. They also rent scuba and snorkeling equipment.

To experience the underwater world

Hot Water Beach

without getting wet, opt for the **Glass Bottom Boat Cathedral Cove Cruise** (16 Monk St., 07/687-1962, www.glassbottomboatwhitianga.co.nz, 8am, 10:30am, 1:30pm, and 4pm daily Dec.-Feb., 10:30am and 1:30pm daily Mar.-Nov., adults $95, children $50, under age 3 free), a two-hour cruise that takes in the cove and the reserve. Snorkels are provided for those who fancy a dip among schools of snapper. Tours depart from Whitianga Wharf.

Terrific half- and full-day outings with **Cathedral Cove Kayak Tours** (88 Hahei Beach Rd., 07/866-3877, www.seakayaktours.co.nz, daily, adults $105-170, children $65-120) navigate the marine reserve. The Classic Tour includes paddling through caves with a complimentary cappuccino on the beach. The Remote Coast Tour takes in the hard-to-reach volcanic cliffs, while the serene Sunrise and Sunset Tours include refreshments.

Food and Accommodations

Hot Waves Café (8 Pye Place, 07/866-3887, 8:30am-4pm Sun.-Thurs., 8:30am-8:30pm Fri.-Sat., $12-26) boasts a beachy laid-back interior that opens onto plush shady gardens with native plants and outdoor seating. It's just a brief stroll from Hot Water Beach. Freshly prepared offerings include salt-and-pepper squid and lamb shanks.

The Mediterranean-leaning menu at ★ **The Church** (87 Beach Rd., Hahei, 07/866-3797, www.thechurchbistro.co.nz, 3pm-close daily, $20-40) befits its paradisiacal surroundings. Enjoy tapas dishes such as smoked fish or pork belly, or large plates like lamb tagine couscous with mint yogurt, in an atmospheric converted 1916 timber Methodist Church.

The tropical haven of the 0.6ha surroundings blooms with colorful native bush and a collection of charming lumber **accommodations** (07/866-3533, www.thechurchhahei.co.nz, $140-230). Choose from self-contained en suite studios or cottages, with A-frame roofs, hardwood floors, and decks that overlook the gardens, with free Wi-Fi, beach towels, and spades for Hot Water Beach. Some rooms have a log burner.

TAIRUA

At the foot of volcanic peak Mount Paku, tiny Tairua was first established as a milling and farming town. Today, it serves as one of Coromandel's quieter surfing and tourist spots.

Across the estuary is **Pauanui,** a purpose-built holiday community with surfing and safe swimming beaches. The walk to Paku's summit is a relatively easy 45 minutes round-trip, reached via a signpost from the end of Tirinui Crescent.

For more information, visit the **tourist center** (223 Main Rd., 07/864-7575, www.tairua.co.nz). Tairua is 25km south of Hahei.

Accommodations

The luxurious ★ **Colleith Lodge** (8 Rewa Rewa Valley, 07/864-7970, www.colleithlodge.co.nz, $575) is one of the region's most impressive eco-boutique accommodations. Set among 0.6ha of native bushland, with a hot tub and an outdoor swimming pool, its three en suite bedrooms offer Pacific views. Each room has free Wi-Fi, a flat-screen TV, bathrobes, a private deck, and hot-drink-making facilities.

WHANGAMATA

The hip surf town of Whangamata is Coromandel's happy place. The shining settlement boasts an idyllic harbor and is surrounded by blue sea and green rainforest. Its white sands are easily accessed via several short passageways from a main drag alive with boutiques and eateries.

★ Donut Island

Extinct volcano **Whenuakura (Donut) Island** stands 1km offshore from Whangamata, its collapsed blowhole forming an enclosed fairy-tale-like tropical oasis that cradles a turquoise lagoon, native plants, and small beaches. Though you can make your way there on a kayak or paddleboard, the swell and tide waters in and around the island are unpredictable and dangerous—it's better to paddle with a guide.

Surfing and Stand-Up Paddleboarding

The beautiful white sands of **Whangamata Beach,** backed by gentle dunes and framed by forest-cloaked headlands, plunge to a break manageable by most. The bar near the estuary should only be attempted by seasoned surfers.

Surfs Up (101b Winifred Ave., 021/217-1201, www.surfsup.co.nz) offers two-hour introductory surf and SUP packages ($80) that include a one-hour lesson with a qualified instructor and an hour's solo board use. Equipment rentals, including kayaks, are also offered, as are guided kayak and SUP tours of the area.

Food and Accommodations

Head to cool **Argo Restaurant & Wine Bar** (328 Ocean Rd., 07/865-7157, www.argorestaurant.nz, 11am-close daily, $26-35) for an array of fresh fish, seared lamb loin, confit duck, or scotch fillet, washed down with craft beer or local wine. Whangamata's hippest eatery is just minutes from the beach—grab a table outside on a balmy Coromandel night.

Breakers (324 Hetherington Rd., 07/865-8464, www.breakersmotel.co.nz, $185-315) is an exceptional motel positioned next to the marina. Its wavelike two-story design overlooks a lengthy curved pool and tropical grounds. Comfortable and contemporary studio-, one-, and two-bedroom units boast Wi-Fi, Sky TV, cooking facilities, and a deck or balcony. Ground-floor units open straight onto the swimming pool, with private hot tubs.

Transportation and Services

Whangamata is a 30-minute drive south of Tairua along Highway 25. **Go Kiwi Shuttles** (www.go-kiwi.co.nz) provides bus service to Whangamata from Auckland.

For more information, visit the **Whangamata Information Centre** (616 Port Rd., 07/865-8340, www.whangamatanz.com, 9:30am-5pm Mon.-Fri., 9:30am-3:30pm Sat.-Sun.).

WAIHI AND WAIHI BEACH

At the end of the east coast, **Waihi Beach** marks the point where the Coromandel Peninsula merges into the Bay of Plenty; its 8km of sugary sands is a surfing haven. The southern end, known as Bowentown, harbors numerous hidden nooks and the remnants of an ancient *pa* where defensive trenches are still visible in the headland.

Ten minutes inland from Waihi Beach, along Highway 2, **Waihi** is a former gold-mining town that once boasted a population three times the size of Hamilton. There is still a working gold mine, known as Martha, easily visible on the edge of town on Martha Street. It looks like a giant meteor crater.

Waihi Gold Mine Tours (126 Seddon St., 07/863-9015, www.golddiscoverycentre.co.nz, 10:30am and 12:30pm Mon.-Sat., adults $34, children $17, under age 5 free) guides 1.5-hour tours to the Martha mine. Visitors learn of the gold's journey from extraction to crushing and final processing, along with the history of the site.

Accommodations

Bowentown Beach Holiday Park & Motels (510 Seaforth Rd., 07/8693-5381, www.bowentown.co.nz) sits surrounded by bush overlooking the Pacific, with a great range of accommodations and amenities. Communal facilities for campers ($50-84) include a spacious hot tub, TV lounge with Sky TV, full kitchen, and barbecue, along with bike, boogie board, and kayak rentals. Standard cabins ($85) sleep up to four in bunks and queens, with a TV and fridge, and use of the shared bath and kitchen facilities. For larger groups, the kitchen cabin ($95) sleeps up to six, with access to a shared bath; a self-contained unit ($125) with a kitchen, bath, and living area hosts up to four guests. Modern motel rooms ($145-300) come with a deck, separate dining and lounge areas, a kitchen, a private bath, and Sky TV.

Transportation and Services

Waihi is 40km south of Whangamata on Highway 25. To reach Waihi Beach from Waihi, turn left at Highway 2 and drive 2.6km to Waihi Beach Road. Turn left and continue 7.4km to Waihi Beach.

For more information, head to the **i-SITE Visitor Centre** (126 Seddon St., 9am-5pm daily).

PAEROA

Highway 2 snakes west from Waihi for 20km to Paeroa, en route to Karangahake Gorge and the Hauraki Rail Trail. The town of Paeroa is noted for its collection of antiques stores and is the birthplace of "world famous in New Zealand" soda, Lemon and Paeroa (L&P), a drink made using local mineral water and lemons. (It's now made by Coca Cola.) An iconic 6m **statue** of an L&P soft drink bottle pays tribute to the town's fizzy heritage; it stands at the intersection of Highways 2 and 26.

Karangahake Gorge

Highway 2 makes its way through the enormous and imposing **Karangahake Gorge** (www.doc.govt.nz/karangahake). The canyon was named after its eponymous blink-and-you'll-miss-it settlement that was once the most lucrative gold mining site in New Zealand (in 2017, prospectors discovered an 8,500-kg vein of high-quality gold). The gorge is home to a network of short walks and bike tracks that leave the car park at Karangahake, taking in old railway lines, tunnels, bridges, and mining relics.

The gorge is 7.2km south of Paeroa on Highway 2.

Food

The **L&P Café** (2 Seymour St., 07/862-6753, www.lpcafe.co.nz, 8am-5pm Mon.-Tues., 8am-10pm Wed.-Sun., $17-29) is a friendly establishment offering L&P bourbon barbecue ribs and L&P-flavored tempura-battered fish-and-chips. If you don't fancy a zingy twist, there's plenty of straight-up dishes like pastas, burgers, and egg breakfasts.

Bay of Plenty

The peninsula's east coast tumbles into the Bay of Plenty, christened in 1769 by Captain Cook after he viewed the abundance of food stores held at Maori villages along the coast. It was also one of the first regions where Maori settled. Blessed with sunshine, the 125km coastline is a wildly popular holiday destination with Kiwis—especially its two hubs of Tauranga and Mount Maunganui. Don't leave without exploring the active marine volcano of White Island and the historic coastal town of Whakatane.

TAURANGA

Buffered by one of New Zealand's largest natural harbors, Tauranga (the name means "place of anchorage" or "place of rest") is home to 125,000 people and its busiest port. It's the largest settlement in the Bay of Plenty and boasts a bounty of beautifully preserved historic architecture and seafaring adventures.

Sights

TAURANGA ART GALLERY

The **Tauranga Art Gallery** (Wharf St. and Willow St., 07/578-7933, www.artgallery.org.nz, 10am-4:30pm daily, free) epitomizes the city's ongoing cultural boom. The contemporary, airy open-plan space, set in a former bank, is spread over two floors that host permanent displays by Kiwi figures, most notably surrealist Edward Bullmore, along with vibrant rolling collections by international artists, with past exhibits including musings by Banksy.

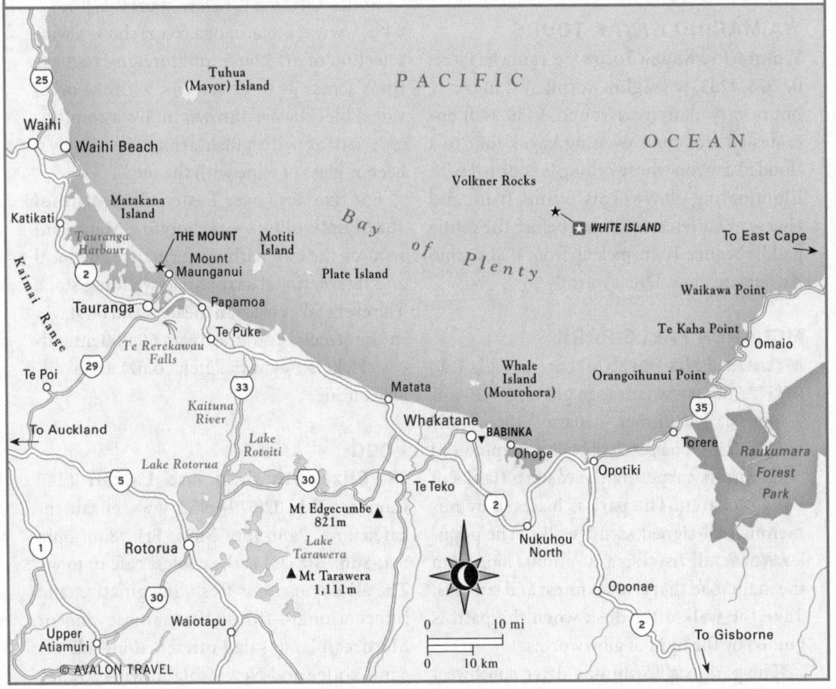

ELMS MISSION HOUSE AND GARDENS

The oldest Georgian home in Aotearoa, **Elms Mission House and Gardens** (15 Mission St., 07/577-9772, www.theelms.org.nz, 11am-3pm daily, tour $5, gardens free) were founded in the mid-1800s on land purchased for the Church Missionary Society to teach Maori about Christianity, trade skills, and to read and write. When the New Zealand Wars—a series of battles between Maori and the British—reached the region in the 1860s, British troops stationed themselves at the missionary station, and the archdeacon, Alfred Brown, and his wife, Charlotte, were eventually forced to tend to dead and injured friends from both sides. Information panels pertaining to the history are affixed around the house and garden—the grounds can be browsed at your leisure, while guided tours of the house operate on an as-needed basis.

Recreation

DOLPHIN TOURS

Bay of Plenty is one of the best places in New Zealand to spot orcas, especially between May and July, while dolphins reside here year-round. **Dolphin Seafaris** (Berth D1, Tauranga Bridge Marina, 07/577-0105, www.nzdolphin.com, 8am daily, adults $150, children $110) operates tours on a pair of nicely sized 15m luxury vessels with no crowds and a generous viewing deck. A swim platform is placed at the stern; conditions permitting, you can freely swim with wild dolphins (there's an affixed rail to hold on to). If you're lucky, you may even encounter whales. Tours last four to five hours and include fins and wetsuits along with snacks and hot drinks. Reservations are essential.

WAIMARINO KAYAK TOURS

Waimarino Kayak Tours (36 Taniwha Place, 07/576-4233, www.glowwormkayaking.com, hours vary, daily year-round, $130-140) operates a three-hour evening kayak tour to a flooded canyon whose ceiling is adorned with illuminating glowworms. Wine, fruit, and cheese are offered at sunset, before the gentle paddle begins. Tours pick up from Waimarino Adventure Park. Dress warmly.

MCLAREN FALLS PARK

McLaren Falls Park (McLarens Falls Rd., 07/577-700, www.tauranga.govt.nz, 7:30am-7:30pm daily summer, 7:30am-5:30pm daily winter) is a 190ha patch of bush with pine and rimu forests carpeting the eastern flanks of Lake McLaren. The park is bisected by numerous well-signed scenic walks. The popular **Waterfall Track** is a 20-minute loop from the main road that crosses forest and streams. Take the walk after dusk when the path is guided by the light of glowworms.

The park is a 15-minute drive southwest from Tauranga off Highway 29.

Entertainment and Events

The Strand is where all the magic happens, thanks to a gaggle of bars and eateries, all with vibrant outdoor areas overlooking the estuary. Craft beer lovers must head to atmospheric **Brew** (107 The Strand, 07/578-3543, www.brewpub.co.nz, 4pm-close Mon.-Wed., 11am-close Thurs.-Sun.), Tauranga's best bar. It has a rolling selection of Kiwi boutique ales and local wines, food (the Moroccan chicken is good), and live music on weekends.

Crown and Badger (91 The Strand, 07/571-3038, www.crownandbadger.co.nz, 10:30am-10pm Mon.-Thurs., 10:30am-1:30am Fri.-Sat., 10am-10pm Sun.) is a traditional English affair with lots of wood paneling. On weekend evenings, the place pulsates with live local and national bands. The menu is propped up by the usual pub fare (steak or fish-and-chips) and there are big-screen TVs to watch sports.

Rialto Cinema (21 Devonport Rd., 07/577-0455, www.rialtotauranga.co.nz) shows a wide selection of art-house and foreign-language films across its three screens, with the occasional blockbuster thrown in. It's a comfortable setting with plush armchairs. Enjoy a beer or glass of wine with the movie.

For five days over Easter, the **National Jazz Festival** (www.jazz.org.nz, Mar.-Apr.) seduces the city with performances by local and international saxophone-wielding stars. The event takes place in theaters and on stages in the streets, and it attracts 60,000 attendees. Tickets (www.ticketek.co.nz) are available online.

Food

★ **Elizabeth Café and Larder** (247 Cameron Rd., 07/579-0950, www.elizabethcafe.co.nz, 7am-3pm Mon.-Fri., 8am-3pm Sat.-Sun., $18-25) is the coolest café in town. The all-day menu is fresh, imaginative, and international—think Vietnamese pho or Moroccan lamb salad offered alongside organic coffee and New Zealand wines. Enjoy it under the watchful portraits of Queen Elizabeth II, painted à la pop art.

It's not the most sophisticated of settings, but for the best fish-and-chips in town, head on down to **Bobby's Fresh Fish Market** (1 Dive Crescent, 07/578-1789, 8am-7pm Mon.-Thurs., 8am-8pm Fri.-Sat., 8am-7:30pm Sun., $6-8) and unwrap your warm paper parcel on the jetty overlooking the sea.

Harbourside (150 The Strand, 07/571-0520, www.harboursidetauranga.co.nz, 11:30am-2:30pm and 5pm-close daily, $28-40) offers an elegant waterfront dining experience with a fine-dining seasonal menu along the lines of seared venison with charred figs and beet chutney, and a grill menu with pasture-fed Angus fillet and seared tuna. Book in advance to snag a table on the balcony.

A 10-minute drive west of downtown Tauranga, **Mills Reef Winery & Restaurant** (143 Moffat Rd., 07/576-8800, www.millsreef.

co.nz, 10am-close daily, $22-40) is one of the nation's most interesting eateries. Set in a majestic two-story art deco structure on 8ha of landscaped grounds, the restaurant offers seating inside or out, and you can enjoy European and Asian-inspired dishes like five-spice duck or beer-battered fish, paired with local produce and wine. Dinner reservations are essential.

Accommodations

Harbourside City Backpackers (105 The Strand, 07/579-4066, www.backpacktauranga.co.nz, dorm $30-36, $82-96 s or d) boasts one of the best budget locations in the city—in the heart of the hospitality hub and with great views of the water from a rooftop terrace. Accommodations include dorms, doubles, and twins, all available with en suite baths. Guest make use of free bikes, DVDs, and free Wi-Fi in most areas. Noise from the street can be an issue in some quarters.

There's a bohemian air to **Arthouse Backpackers** (102 Cameron Rd., 07/975-0963, www.art-house.nz, dorm $32-34, $88 s or d). Colorful lodgings with hand-painted furniture and an array of prints sleep up to 50 people in mixed and women-only dorms, alongside twin and double accommodations. Relax on mismatched bean bags in the TV room or cook in the fully stocked kitchen with timber work tops.

Choose from three rooms at the homey **Harbinger House** (209 Fraser St., 07/578-8801, www.harbinger.co.nz, $110-130), a boutique bed-and-breakfast where you'll arise each morning to the scent of freshly baked bread. Two rooms have balconies, but all overlook the well-tended gardens. Bath facilities are shared, and all rooms have carpets, kettles, and electric blankets for added coziness.

Peaceful lodgings are a brief stroll from downtown at **Tauranga on the Waterfront** (1 2nd Ave., 07/578-7079, www.thetauranga.co.nz, $170-350). The modern establishment has rooms ranging from studios to suites; most have private patios overlooking the adjacent inlet. All rooms have en suite baths and are equipped with seating areas, kitchenettes, fridges, walk-in power showers, Sky TV, and free Wi-Fi. Pricier options include a spa bath, and those on the shore boast a wonderful water view framed by cinematic windows.

Hotel on Devonport (72 Devonport Rd., 07/578-2668, www.hotelondevonport.net.nz, $250-350) is a slick setup where all rooms boast a city or sea view from a private balcony. A warm welcome includes a complimentary drink at the in-house bar. There's also free Wi-Fi and a newspaper on request, Sky TV, hot-drink-making facilities, and a minibar in every room.

Situated on the city outskirts, the cubic modernist architecture of **Trinity Wharf Tauranga Hotel** (51 Dive Crescent, 07/577-8700, www.trinitywharf.co.nz, $235-945) spreads across three piers with much of the structure positioned over water. There are 123 rooms split into 10 categories, some with floor-to-ceiling windows, balconies, and hot tubs. Amenities include free Wi-Fi, robes, private baths with heated tile floors, and Sky TV. The communal infinity pool almost spills into the sea, and there's a gym, a bar, and an eatery.

Tauranga Tourist Park (9 Mayfair St., 07/578-3323, www.taurangatouristpark.co.nz) has unpowered (adults $28, couples $38, children $8) and powered (adults $30, couples $38, children $8) sites around the water's edge, shaded by pohutukawa trees. Showers are hot and powerful, there's a library in the TV lounge, and the kitchen has all the gear. Cabins ($58) are a good value and come with fridges, kettles, and TVs; upgrade to a cabin with an en suite bath ($88), with a microwave, a toaster, and a seating area. It's 4km from the city.

Camping is permitted at **McLaren Falls Park** (McLarens Falls Rd., 07/577-700, www.tauranga.govt.nz, 7:30am-7:30pm daily summer, 7:30am-5:30pm daily winter, adults $10, children $5, under age 6 free).

Transportation

Tauranga is 105km (1.5 hours) east of Hamilton via Highways 1 and 29. From the north, it is reached in 90km (1.5 hours) from Whangamata along Highways 25 and 2.

Tauranga Airport (TRG, 73 Jean Batten Dr., 07/575-2456, www.airport.tauranga.govt.nz) has domestic routes on **Air New Zealand** (www.airnewzealand.co.nz) to Auckland, Wellington, and Christchurch. Call **Tauranga Mount Taxis** (0800/829-477) or **Tauranga Taxi Cabs** (0800/482-947) for transportation to the airport or around the city.

Car rental companies include **Thrifty** (www.thrifty.co.nz), **Avis** (www.avis.co.nz), and **NZ Rent a Car** (www.nzrentacar.co.nz). National bus carriers **Intercity** (www.intercity.co.nz) and **Naked Bus** (www.nakedbus.com) connect with Tauranga. For travel in Tauranga and along the Bay of Plenty, check routes via **Bay Bus** (www.baybus.co.nz).

Services

The **Tauranga i-SITE** (95 Willow St., 07/578-8103, www.bayofplenty.com, 8:30am-5pm Mon.-Fri., 9am-5pm Sat.-Sun.) serves as the visitors center for Mount Maunganui. There is a local **DoC office** (253 Chadwick Rd., 07/578-7677, www.doc.govt.nz, 8am-4:30pm Mon.-Fri.).

Tauranga has a **City Library** (91 Willow St., 07/577-7177, 9:30am-5:30pm Mon.-Tues. and Thurs.-Fri., 7pm-close Wed., 9:30am-4pm Sat., 11:30am-4pm Sun.) and **post office** (536 Cameron Rd., 07/571-1690, 8:30am-5pm Mon.-Fri., 9am-3pm Sat.). For medical services, visit the **City Hospital** (829 Cameron Rd., 07/579-8000) or the **health clinic** (19 2nd Ave., 07/577-0010).

MOUNT MAUNGANUI

Massively popular with surfers and Kiwi holidaymakers, the laid-back coastal settlement of Mount Maunganui is positioned on a narrow pointed peninsula framed by beaches. The dormant volcano Mount Maunganui is simply referred to as "The Mount."

Sights

Mauao (Mount Maunganui), or **The Mount**, is a sacred Maori summit that rises to 232m. It dominates a great swath of the coastline, offering breathtaking coastal views, especially at sunset. The path to the summit is a decent 45-minute hike along a well-trodden, sometimes paved trail shaded by forest much of the way. Another track circumnavigates its base and takes 45 minutes to complete.

Recreation

MOUNT HOT POOLS

One of only a handful of hot saltwater pools, the **Mount Hot Pools** (9 Adams Ave., 07/577-8551, www.mounthotpools.co.nz, adults $14, seniors and children $9, ages 2-4 $5.80, under age 2 free) are the ideal way to unwind following a surfing session or a hike up the Mount. The geothermal spring-heated waters are a muscle-relaxing 31-39°C and are split into pools of varying sizes, some with soothing jets. There are also private pools ($15.90) and massage treatments ($45-110).

SURFING AND KAYAKING

Mount Maunganui Surf Academy (021/150-2370, info@surflessons.co.nz, www.surflessons.co.nz) offers surf lessons ($50 for 1 hour, $80 for 2 hours, one-on-one $125 for 1.5 hours). Look for the yellow camper van at the corner of Marine Parade and Banks Avenue.

For kayak or SUP rentals, head to **Canoe & Kayak** (49 Totara St., 07/574-7415, www.canoeandkayak.co.nz).

Entertainment

One of the region's hippest bars, the Latin-inspired **Mount Social Club** (305 Maunganui Rd., www.mountsocialclub.co.nz, 8am-1am daily) has been a local stalwart since the 1970s, decorated in a colorfully painted array of reclaimed furnishings and recycled items, including a vintage Land Rover. Guests can savor an extensive list of craft beers, cocktails, and an exquisite tapas menu backed by mains like filet mignon and a rustic Greek salad.

Funky **Astrolabe** (82 Mount Maunganui Rd., 07/574-8155, www.astrolabe.co.nz, 10am-11:30pm daily) features mismatched thrift furniture, granny lampshades, and an

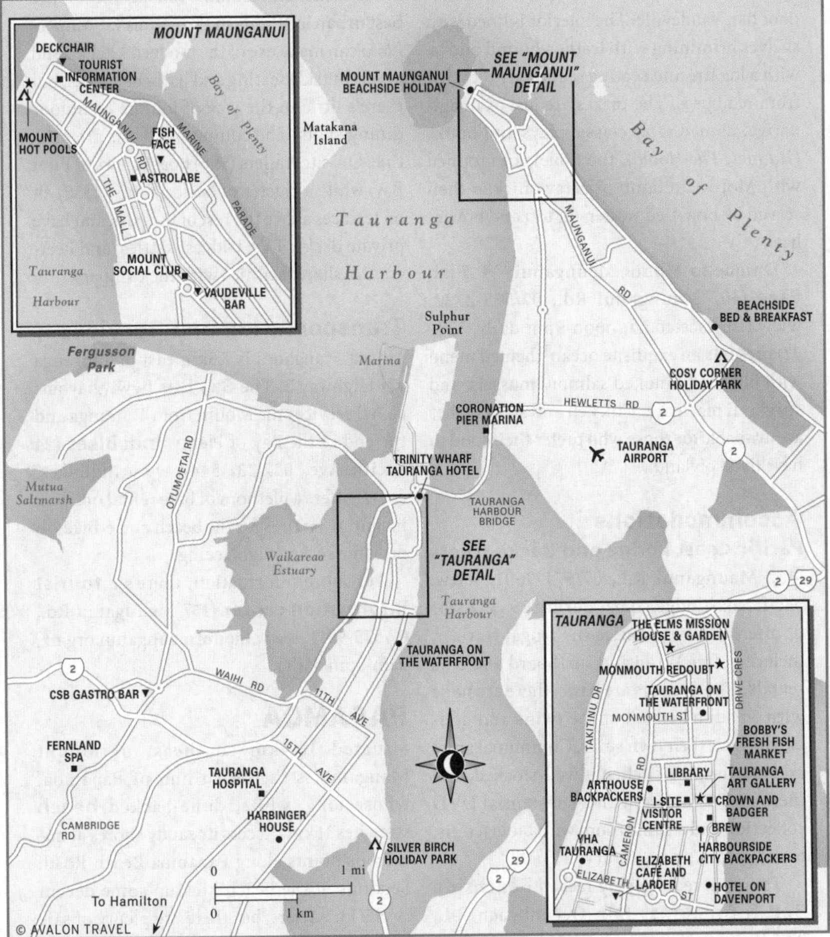

awesome timber bar shaped like a boat. A wide selection of Macs beers are on tap. This place holds regular happy hours and daily dinner deals with a menu of burgers, pizza, and fish.

It's all about cocktails and quirky entertainment like singing poets at **Vaudeville Bar** (314 Mount Maunganui Rd., 07/575-0087, www.vaudeville.co.nz, 4pm-close daily). The Victorian-themed, deliciously odd establishment is lined with high stools, tables, a leather-studded wall, and polished oak panels. Next door is the Pizza Library.

Food

Overlooking the ocean, **Deckchair** (2 Main Parade, 07/572-0942, www.deckchaircafe.co.nz, 6:30am-4pm daily, $10-20) is a relaxing café that prides itself on its freshly prepared wide-ranging fare that includes all-day breakfasts and gourmet burgers.

The Pizza Library (314 Maunganui Rd.,

07/574-2928, www.thepizzalibrary.co.nz, 5pm-9pm Mon.-Thurs., noon-3pm and 5pm-9pm Fri.-Sun., $25) is as quirky as its next-door bar, Vaudeville. The interior is lined with shelves brimming with leather-bound books, with a log fire and seating seemingly recycled from old buses. The pizzas are just as imaginative, named after classic plays and books (*Hamlet, The Hobbit,* the Bible), and topped with Moroccan lamb or satay chicken then served by bow-tied waiters in top and bowler hats.

Unique to Mount Maunganui, ★ **Fish Face** (107 Maunganui Rd., 07/575-2782, www.fish-face.co.nz, noon-9pm daily, $24-32) presents an exquisite ocean-themed menu with blue cod, smoked salmon, mussels, and spaghetti marinara. Chicken and steak dishes are available for those who prefer their food to have lived on land.

Accommodations

Pacific Coast Lodge and Backpackers (432 Maunganui Rd., 07/574-9601, www.pacificcoastlodge.co.nz, dorm $29, $82 s or d) offers plenty to entice the frugal traveler, including free Wi-Fi and surfboard and bike rentals. Clean rooms are basic; there are none with en suite baths, but the twins and doubles do have their own sinks. Communal areas are spacious, the kitchen is well-stocked, and there's a TV lounge with a substantial DVD collection and a game room with table tennis, board games, and a library.

There's a real holiday feel to **Beachside Bed & Breakfast** (21b Oceanbeach Rd., 07/574-0960, www.beachsidebnb.co.nz, $130 s, $125-150 d), thanks to the ocean views. Set in a modern home with agreeable hosts, the three guest rooms have private baths, heaters, and electric blankets; two rooms have TVs. The prize Rimu room has a couch, a DVD player, and movies, as does the comfortable communal guest lounge, where breakfast is served to sea views. It's seconds from the beach in a peaceful suburban location 3.5km from downtown.

Buttressed against the base of the Mount, **Mount Maunganui Beachside Holiday Park** (1 Adams Ave., 07/575-4471, www.mountbeachside.co.nz) boasts one of the best urban locations in the country. Campers ($65) can make use of the modern kitchen and ample outside seating and barbecue areas, but there's little in the way of lounge or indoor dining spots. The communal baths are pristine. On-site trailers ($90) boast views of Pilot Bay, while a cluster of basic cabins ($130) sit on terraces above the rest of the park and have private decks, TVs, fridges, kettles, and heaters. All share facilities with the campers.

Transportation and Services

Mount Manganui is 7.5km east of Tauranga via Highway 2. The **Bay Bus** (www.baybus.co.nz) services the Mount from Tauranga and the end of the Bay of Plenty. **Indi Bikes** (24 Pacific Ave., 027/231-5447, www.indibikes.co.nz) offers a plethora of bike rental options, including fat tires for the beach and e-bikes to do some serious sightseeing.

For more information, there's a **tourist information center** (137 Maunganui Rd., 07/575-9911, www.mountmaunganui.org.nz, 9am-5pm daily).

PAPAMOA

Situated 16.4km southeast of Mount Manganui is the beach hub of Papamoa, whose long, white, dune-backed **beach** stretches 15km. Access its sandy shores at numerous points along Papamoa Beach Road. Sections of the beach kick up some decent swells for surfers, but there are plenty of safe swimming spots also. In summer, look for the red flags on the beach in front of Papamoa Surf Lifesaving Club to ensure you'll be under close watch.

Sights

Blokart Recreation Park (176 Parton Rd., 07/572-4256, www.blokartcreationpark.co.nz, 10am-4:30pm Sat.-Sun., $30 for 30 minutes, $50 for 1 hour) blends go-karting and yachting. A sail is affixed above a three-wheeled buggy as the wind propels you around a track.

Or opt for the drift kart, an electric-powered three-wheeler.

The inland region south of Papamoa is the kiwifruit-growing capital of New Zealand, accounting for 80 percent of the country's harvest. (The fruit actually originates from China, but New Zealanders claimed it via clever marketing in the early 1900s). Family owned orchard **Kiwifruit Country** (316 Hwy. 33, www.kiwifruitcountry.com, 07/573-6340, adults $20, seniors and students $18, children $6, under age 5 free) celebrates the region's horticultural heritage with guided tours (hourly 9am-4pm daily Sept.-Apr.) of their 60ha grounds, followed by the opportunity to sample kiwifruit-crafted delights like wine, liqueur, and sweet treats.

Kiwifruit Country is 22km southeast of Papamoa, along Highways 2 and 33.

Accommodations

The ★ **Beach House Motel** (224 Papamoa Beach Rd., 0800/429-999, www.beachhouse-motel.co.nz, $155-220) epitomizes the chilled-out village vibe. A collection of 18 modern and welcoming units range from studios to one-bedrooms; some have hot tubs, but all have en suite baths with free Wi-Fi, cooking facilities, fridges, toiletries, and Sky TV. The communal facilities include a pool, a spa, a games room, and a barbecue area. Just minutes from the beach, this is one of the best motels on the coast.

Transportation

From Mount Manganui, take Highway 2 south for 13km to Te Puke Highway and turn right.

WHAKATANE

Whakatane is the last hub of significance on the coast. (Keep heading east and you'll soon be rewarded with numerous isolated bays and beaches and a handful of secluded townships.) Whakatane rests at the mouth of its eponymous river, a beautiful estuary that brims with boats. It is said to have been the site that the first Maori paddled to upon their arrival in the Bay of Plenty, and that heritage is still evident today. Whakatane is also the gateway to White Island. Less than one hour south is Te Urewera.

Sights

MATAATUA WHARENUI

Mataatua Wharenui (105 Muriwai Dr., 07/308-4271, www.mataatua.com, 11am-2pm daily, free, tours noon and 2pm daily, adults $49, children $15) provides one of the most

surfboards along Papamoa beach

authentic Maori experiences in New Zealand. Known as "the house that came home," the intricate *marae* (meeting place) was returned to Whakatane in 2011, having spent the previous 130 years exhibited at international museums and national sites. Constructed in 1875 as an expression of unity and goodwill to Queen Victoria, the stellar architecture incorporates ancestral carvings and legends of local history. Watch the documentary in the visitors center, then take a guided tour to learn more about the stories behind the carvings and to view sites of significance around the township.

TE KOPUTU A TE WHANGA A TOI

An intimate local library and exhibition center, **Te Koputu a te whanga a Toi** (Esplanade Mall, Kakahoroa Dr., 07/306-0509, www.whakatanemuseum.org.nz, 9am-5pm Mon.-Fri., 10am-2pm Sat.-Sun., free) houses a permanent museum collection with an emphasis on Maori heritage, along with stories of European settlement. It's accompanied by three galleries that display rolling collections of local and international art.

Recreation

This region was once the kingdom of legendary chieftain, Toi. **Nga Tupuwae o Toi** (the footprints of Toi) is a memorable walkway that laces an 18km loop track from Whakatane to Ohope Beach. En route, you'll pass ancient forests of pohutukawa and long abandoned *pa* (fortified Maori sites); you may even hear the call of a kiwi. The walk can be tackled in sections. The most popular branch heads along the shoreline to Ohope; from here, catch the Bayhopper Bus back to Whakatane. For more information and full details of the track, visit DoC (www.doc.govt.nz).

Food

L'Epicerie (73 The Strand, 07/308-5981, www.lepicerie.co.nz, 8am-3:30pm Mon.-Fri., 8am-3pm Sat., 9am-2pm Sun.) is an authentic French experience thanks to its freshly baked loafs, delicate pastries, and a selection of strong cheeses and cured meats served with fragrant coffee. The almond croissant is a must.

With down-to-earth fare served overlooking the sea, **Wallys on the Wharf** (2 The Strand, 07/307-1100, www.wallysonthewharf.co.nz, 11am-7pm daily, $8-10) prides itself on its crumbed fish-and-chips as well as an array of fresh-caught aquatic delights such as mussels, scallops, and whitebait fritters. There's limited bench seating outside and some seating within. This is a very casual affair among a run of harbor-side boatsheds.

High-backed leather seating, white walls and tablecloths, and polished wooden flooring enhance the sophisticated menu at **Roquette Restaurant & Bar** (23-29 Quay St., 07/307-0722, www.roquette-restaurant.co.nz, 10am-close Mon.-Sat., $29-37). The prawns, chicken, and chorizo risotto are good. Consider the super-value early-bird dinner (5pm-6pm Mon.-Sat., $23), which includes a glass of wine or beer.

In Ohope, stop by the excellent **Ohiwa Oyster Farm** (11 Wainui Rd., 07/312-4565, 9am-6:30pm daily, $5-10), a roadside shack that plucks oysters straight from the harbor and serves them alongside other delicacies like smoked fish. Hearty burgers and hot dogs are also on the menu, eaten at picnic tables near the waterfront.

Accommodations

Welcoming, modern accommodations are set around a sunny courtyard at **Windsor Lodge Backpackers** (10 Merritt St., 07/308-8040, www.windsorlodge-backpackers.co.nz, dorm $25, $49-84 s, $68-136 d). Dorms are clean, with individual bunk lights, while private rooms are available with en suite baths, TVs, fridges, and tea- and coffee-making facilities. The communal kitchen is well-stocked, and the TV lounge has a pool table. There's also bicycles to use for free.

Studios and apartments make up the slick **37 The Landing Motel** (37 Landing Rd.,

07/307-1297, www.landingmotel.co.nz, $149-250). Many rooms come with spas, but all include cooking facilities, king beds, modern baths, large Sky TVs, air-conditioning, heating, and free Wi-Fi. There's a communal barbecue and laundry.

At the terra-cotta **Tuscany Villas** (57 The Strand E., 07/308-2244, www.tuscanyvillas.co.nz, $139-400), a giant Pavarotti portrait hangs next to the outdoor pizza oven. Accommodations include comfortable beds in spa and studio suites and family-size rooms; all have en suite baths, and some have hot tubs. Wi-Fi is free and there's Sky TV and hot-drink facilities. The on-site private pizza and wine bar (Sun.-Wed. and Fri.) is open in summer.

You can hear the waves from secluded ★ **Driftsand Boutique Accommodations** (31 West End Rd., Ohope, 07/312-4616, www.driftsand.co.nz, $180-220), where five luxury rooms offer expansive views of the white sands of Ohope Beach. Fashionable units with modernist furniture are named after native birds like the tui and morepork. Rooms are modern and self-contained, with spacious walk-in showers or tubs, complimentary organic toiletries, and patio areas, backed by forests of pohutukawa.

The beachfront **Thornton Beach Holiday Park** (163 Thornton Beach Rd., 07/304-8296, www.thorntonbeach.co.nz) sprawls over glorious green grounds with views of Whale and White Islands. Campsites ($20 pp) are offered alongside basic cabins ($70) with TVs and private deck areas; bring your own bedding. Baths and kitchens are communal. Tourist flats ($95) and motel units ($120) are fully self-contained, with private decks with sea views. The park is a 15-minute drive northwest of Whakatane.

Transportation and Services

Whakatane is 77km southwest of Papamoa along Highway 2. **Whakatane Airport** (WHK, Aerodrome Rd., 07/308-8397, www.whakatane.info) has three flights daily to Auckland with **Air Chathams** (www.airchathams.co.nz). Same-day return flights to Gisborne and Hamilton are via **Sunair** (www.sunair.co.nz). For airport shuttles, call **JNP** (0800/872-555) or **Round Trip Passenger Services** (07/308-8028).

Both **Intercity** (www.intercity.co.nz) buses and **Naked Bus** (www.nakedbus.com) call at Whakatane, as does the coastal shuttle bus service **Bay Bus** (www.baybus.co.nz).

Make your way to the **Whakatane i-SITE Visitor Centre** (Quay St. and Kakahoroa Dr., 07/306-2030, www.whakatane.com, 9am-5pm Mon.-Fri., 10am-3pm Sat.-Sun.). For medical services, there's a **hospital** (Stewart St. and Garaway St., 07/306-0999).

★ WHITE ISLAND

Less than 50km from the coast, **White Island** (Whakaari) is New Zealand's only active marine volcano. Nestled in the Bay of Plenty, most of the volcano sits below sea level; access is via boat tour, helicopter, and scenic flights.

Boat Tour

White Island Tours (15 The Strand, 07/308-9588, www.whiteisland.co.nz, 8am daily, adults $219, children $130) operates boat trips to the island. The six-hour tour departs from Whakatane, arriving almost at the mouth of the horseshoe chasm to spend an hour exploring the inner crater.

Equipped with hard hats and gas masks, guests are guided past hissing steam vents, bubbling mud pools, volcanic streams, and an acid lake surrounded by a sulfur-tinged landscape of unusual yellow and orange hues. Other highlights include the remains of a stoic 1930s sulfur factory that has withstood several eruptions. The boat often encounters dolphins and whales. A light lunch and refreshments are included.

Flight Tours

Descending over the steaming crater mass by helicopter is akin to landing on another planet. **Frontier Helicopters** (216 Aerodrome Rd., 07/308-4188, www.whiteislandvolcano.co.nz, 8am, 10am, noon, 2pm, and 4pm daily, $695) operates two-hour tours. Enjoy a 20-minute scenic flight and then take a one-hour walk in and around the crater.

White Island Flights (216 Aerodrome Rd., 07/308-7760, www.whiteislandflights.co.nz, $249) offers one-hour fixed-wing scenic flights over the volcano. You'll also pass nearby Moutohora volcano, and the odds are that you'll see marinelife below, such as giant schools of fish.

Guests can combine a tour ($695) of White Island with a scenic flight over North Island's geothermal heartland—Lake Taupo and Mounts Tongariro and Ruapehu. All tours run daily by demand; call ahead or check online.

MOUTOHORA ISLAND

Moutohora (Whale) Island is a closely guarded wildlife sanctuary on an extinct volcano 9km north of Whakatane. Inhabitants include an array of rare and endangered native birds such as the saddleback, parakeet, and kiwi, along with the tuatara and a colony of fur seals.

DoC-approved tour operator **Moutohora Island Sanctuary with Peejay** (15 The Strand, 07/308-9588, www.moutohora.co.nz, 10am daily, adults $99, children $59) runs guided four-hour trips to the island for no more than 12 people at a time. Visitors are taken to the magical Sulphur Bay, where they can dig their own hot pools in the sand and cool off in the ocean.

White Island

Rotorua and the Volcanic Heartland

Rotorua 175
Taupo 191
Turangi 199
Tongariro National Park 202

Look for ★ to find recommended sights, activities, dining, and lodging.

Highlights

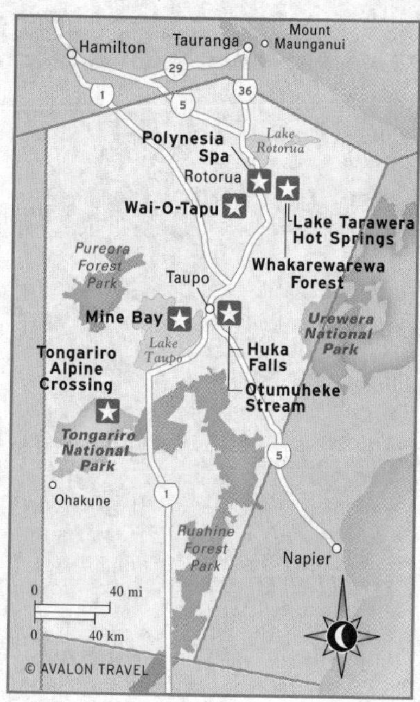

★ **Wai-O-Tapu:** Visit the region's most vibrant volcanic site (page 180).

★ **Lake Tarawera Hot Springs:** It's at least a four-hour hike (or a water-taxi ride) to this secluded hot water spring that flows into one of North Island's largest lakes (page 181).

★ **Whakarewarewa Forest:** A series of 12m-high suspension bridges are strung more than 500m between century-old redwood trees, along with world-class mountain bike trails down below (page 183).

★ **Polynesian Spa:** Soak in the warming waters of this historic spa, which has been soothing souls since the 19th century (page 184).

★ **Mine Bay:** A Maori face is carved into the rock rising 14m above Lake Taupo (page 191).

★ **Huka Falls:** This series of stupendously steep rapids and falls is New Zealand's most-visited natural attraction (page 192).

★ **Otumuheke Stream:** Under a bridge near the start of the Huka Falls walkway are the warming volcanic waters of this stream (page 193).

★ **Tongariro Alpine Crossing:** New Zealand's most spectacular day hike is 19.4km of ever-changing splendor (page 202).

The volcanic heartland of New Zealand is home to breathtaking landscapes of wildly contrasting textures, colors, noises, and smells.

The land is seemingly alive thanks to steaming vents, geysers, and pools of bubbling mud. Local Maori legend says that when their ancestors arrived in the magnificent Te Arawa *waka* (war canoe), their wise leader, Ngatoroirangi, headed to the summit of Mount Tongariro to claim the land—but nearly froze to death on its peak. He prayed to his family in his Pacific homeland of Hawaiki, who in turn sent fire demons to his aid. As they skimmed across the surfaces of the ocean and the land, they created a trail of volcanoes above and a geothermal path below, warming Ngatoroirangi and forever warming North Island's great heart.

Maori heritage is among the richest in New Zealand. Visitors are able to experience a real Maori village, watch cultural shows, and partake in a *hangi*—a traditional cooking method in which food is heated by hot stones underground. You can also soak in abundant hot springs around Rotorua.

The town of Taupo is home to the North Island's Lakes District. Formed in the caldera of an ancient volcano, Lake Taupo is New Zealand's largest, draining into the Waikato River via the legendary Huka Falls. At the lake's southern reaches is Tongariro National Park, New Zealand's oldest national park and home to iconic volcanic peaks, most notably Mount Ngauruhoe—otherwise known as Middle-earth's Mount Doom.

PLANNING YOUR TIME

The two must-do activities are: exploring the **volcanic parks** in and around **Rotorua** (you'll need a day at least) and hiking the **Tongariro Alpine Crossing** (another day-long endeavor). **Tongariro National Park** is an hour south of Taupo; base yourself here or stay at a gateway town like Ohakune.

Most of the region's attractions can be visited year-round, but the Tongariro Alpine Crossing requires mountaineering experience in winter; book a guide. For those without vehicles, the remaining sights are well served by shuttle buses.

Previous: Mine Bay rock carvings; Mount Ngauruhoe. **Above**: black swans on the banks of Lake Tarawera.

Rotorua and the Volcanic Heartland

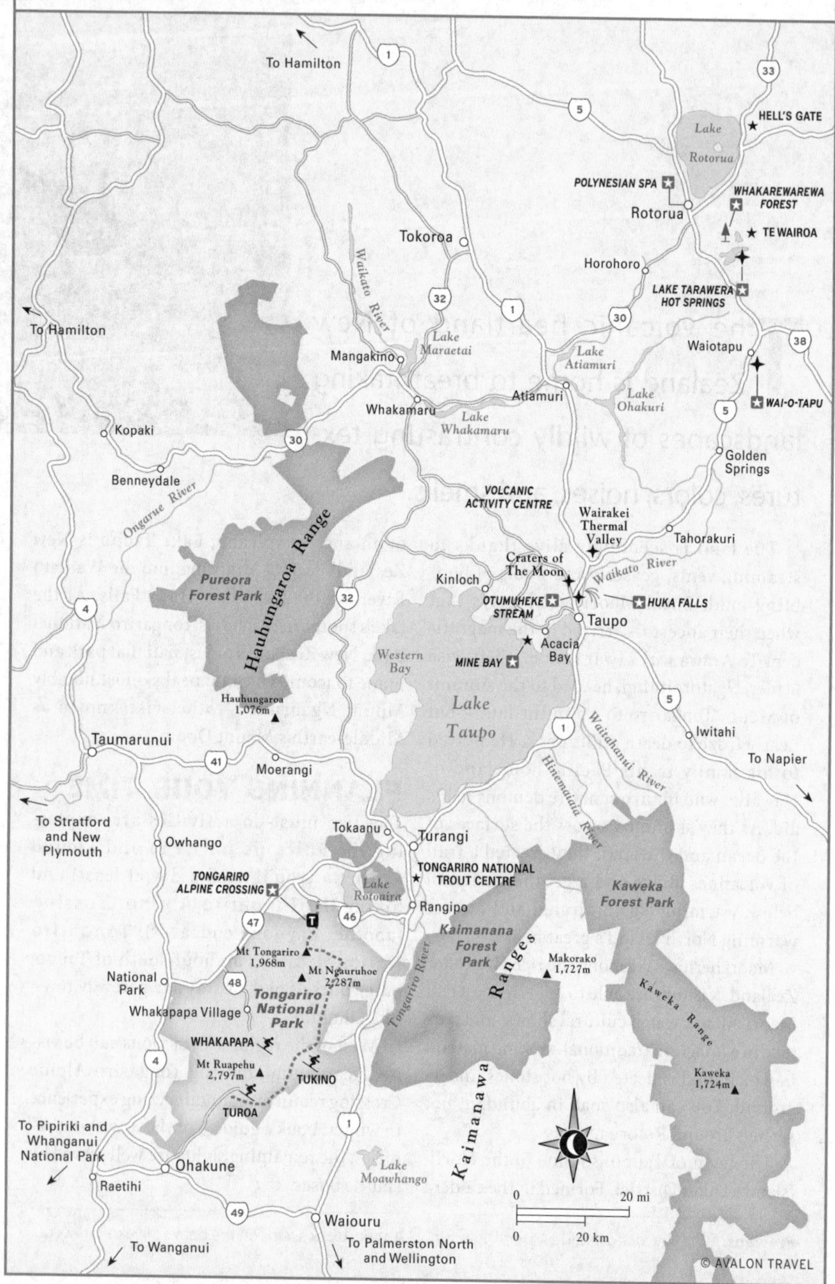
To Hamilton
Lake Rotorua
HELL'S GATE
POLYNESIAN SPA
Rotorua
WHAKAREWAREWA FOREST
TE WAIROA
Tokoroa
Waikato River
Horohoro
LAKE TARAWERA HOT SPRINGS
To Hamilton
Lake Maraetai
Lake Atiamuri
Waiotapu
Mangakino
Whakamaru
Atiamuri
Lake Ohakuri
WAI-O-TAPU
Lake Whakamaru
Kopaki
Benneydale
Golden Springs
Ongarue River
VOLCANIC ACTIVITY CENTRE
Wairakei Thermal Valley
Hauhungaroa Range
Tahorakuri
Craters of The Moon
Waikato River
Pureora Forest Park
Kinloch
OTUMUHEKE STREAM
HUKA FALLS
Taupo
Acacia Bay
Western Bay
MINE BAY
Hauhungaroa 1,076m
Lake Taupo
Iwitahi
Waitahanui River
Taumarunui
Moerangi
To Napier
Hinemaiaia River
To Stratford and New Plymouth
Owhango
Tokaanu
Turangi
TONGARIRO ALPINE CROSSING
TONGARIRO NATIONAL TROUT CENTRE
Lake Rotoaira
Rangipo
Kaweka Forest Park
Kaimanana Forest Park
Mt Tongariro 1,968m
Mt Ngauruhoe 2,287m
Makorako 1,727m
National Park
Tongariro National Park
Whakapapa Village
Tongariro River
Kaweka Range
WHAKAPAPA
Mt Ruapehu 2,797m
TUKINO
Kaimanawa Ranges
Kaweka 1,724m
TUROA
To Pipiriki and Whanganui National Park
Ohakune
Lake Moawhango
Raetihi
0 20 mi
0 20 km
Waiouru
To Wanganui
To Palmerston North and Wellington
© AVALON TRAVEL

Rotorua

It's not just the geothermal attractions that are Rotorua's biggest assets, but their concentration and accessibility—something that lured early Maori, whose thriving culture is now also a significant tourist draw. The city is not the nation's most attractive, but is easily navigable, and for those without transport, there are ample shuttle services to the surrounding mud cauldrons, spouting geysers, furious fumaroles, and iridescent mineral lakes. You can also make the most of world-class mountain biking trails, raft the world's highest commercially rafted waterfall, and get up close to local feathered natives like the kiwi or New Zealand falcon at a handful of conservation centers. When you're done exploring, take a load off soaking in the historic Polynesian Spa, natural hot springs overlooking Lake Rotorua.

SIGHTS

Rotorua Museum

The city's prettiest building opened in 1908 as an opulent bathhouse. Today the **Rotorua Museum** (Government Gardens, Oruawhata Dr., 07/350-1814, www.rotoruamuseum.co.nz, 9am-6pm daily Dec.-Feb., 9am-5pm daily Mar.-Nov., adults $20, children $8) houses some of New Zealand's finest Maori artifacts, most notably carvings pertaining to the local Te Arawa people, as well as a tribute to the legendary 28th Maori Battalion of World War II. Other highlights tell of the development of the geothermal spas and the eruption of Mount Tarawera by way of interactive and multimedia displays, as well as a pair of art galleries and a viewing platform on the roof that looks out over the surrounding Government Gardens and the lake. Free guided tours run hourly.

At the time of writing, the museum was closed due to earthquake damage. It is unlikely to reopen before 2021. Check the website for updates. In the interim, the museum operates **guided tours** (11am and 2pm Thurs.-Tues., 11am, noon, and 2pm Wed., weather permitting, free) of the Government Gardens, departing from the front of the museum.

Skyline Rotorua

Skyline Rotorua (178 Fairy Springs Rd., 07/347-0027, www.skyline.co.nz, 9am-close daily) covers a swath of Mount Ngongotaha, with guests ferried up to the 200m peak on a scenic gondola ride (adults $30, children $15) to enjoy stunning views, food, and adventures; 5km of gravity-powered-luge tracks (adults $44, children $29) of varying levels are complemented by the MTB Gravity Park, an exceptional downhill mountain biking area laced with more than 10km of trails for beginners through expert jumpers. The dual **Zoom Zipline** (adults $95, children $85) allows riders to race at 80km/h above the treetops for nearly 400m. The **Skyswing** (adults $40, children $30) sees daredevils suspended 50m above the Skyline before being released in a giant arch at 150km/h—the catch is that you have to pull the cord to release yourself for the ride.

The on-site Stratosphere Restaurant and Cocktail Bar sells refreshments and affords some of the best views in town. Skyline Rotorua is 4km northwest of downtown Rotorua.

Rainbow Springs Nature Park

Pouting trout are the undoubted stars of the show at **Rainbow Springs** (Fairy Springs Rd., 07/350-0440, www.rainbowsprings.co.nz, 8:30am-close daily, adults $40, children $20, seniors $36), a well-planned wildlife reserve. Four species of the fish—some rather monstrous—patrol winding streams, visible through an underwater viewing glass. A network of walkways leads visitors to native birds such as the kea and kiwi as well as a living dinosaur, the tuatara. For an extra $10, you can

Rotorua

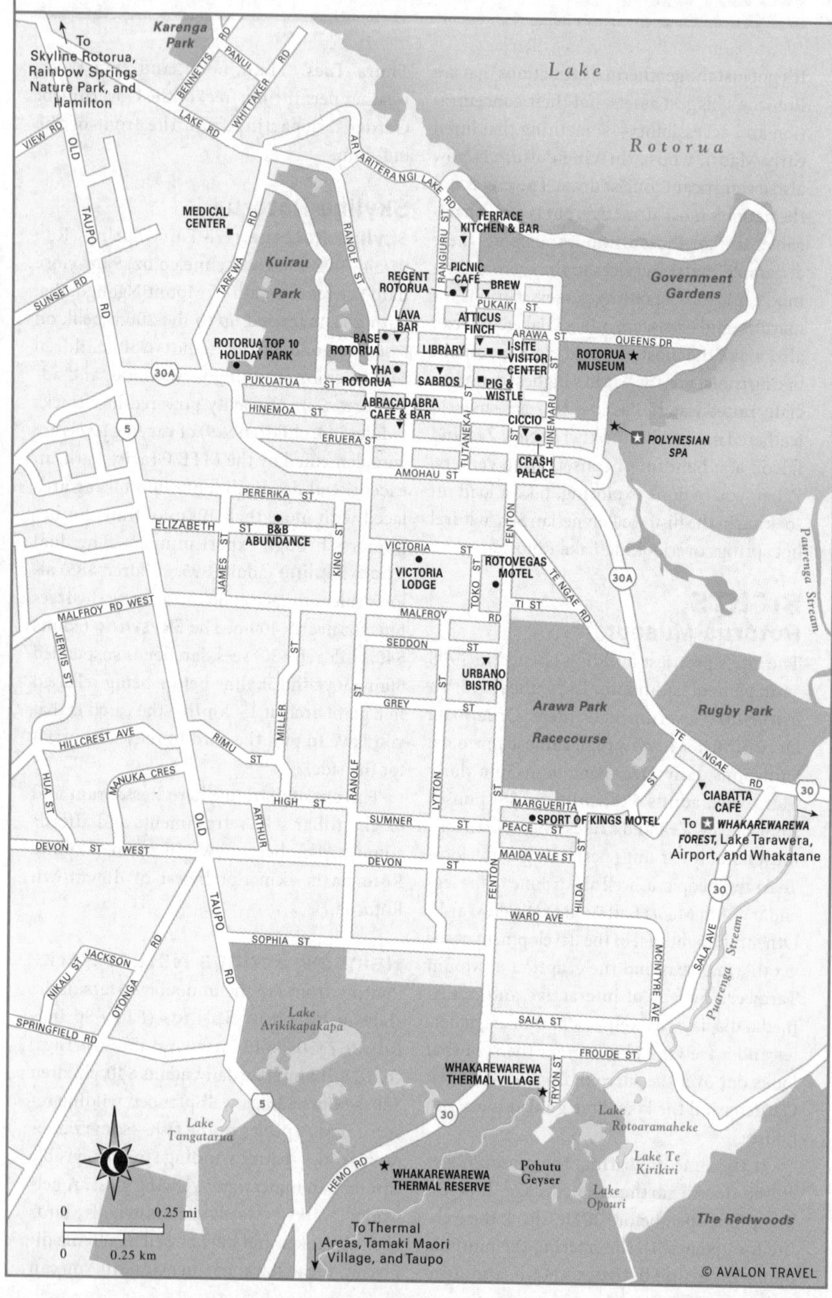
To Skyline Rotorua, Rainbow Springs Nature Park, and Hamilton
Karenga Park
Lake Rotorua
Government Gardens
MEDICAL CENTER
Kuirau Park
TERRACE KITCHEN & BAR
REGENT ROTORUA
PICNIC CAFÉ
BREW
LAVA BAR
ATTICUS FINCH
BASE ROTORUA
LIBRARY
I-SITE VISITOR CENTER
ROTORUA MUSEUM
ROTORUA TOP 10 HOLIDAY PARK
YHA ROTORUA
SABROS
PIG & WISTLE
ABRACADABRA CAFÉ & BAR
CICCIO
CRASH PALACE
POLYNESIAN SPA
B&B ABUNDANCE
VICTORIA LODGE
ROTOVEGAS MOTEL
URBANO BISTRO
Arawa Park Racecourse
Rugby Park
CIABATTA CAFÉ
SPORT OF KINGS MOTEL
To WHAKAREWAREWA FOREST, Lake Tarawera, Airport, and Whakatane
Lake Arikikapakapa
WHAKAREWAREWA THERMAL VILLAGE
Lake Tangatarua
WHAKAREWAREWA THERMAL RESERVE
Pohutu Geyser
Lake Rotoaramaheke
Lake Te Kirikiri
Lake Opouri
The Redwoods
To Thermal Areas, Tamaki Maori Village, and Taupo
Puarenga Stream
VIEW RD
LAKE RD
BENNETTS RD
PANUI RD
WHITTAKER RD
ARI ARITERANGI LAKE RD
OLD TAUPO RD
TAREWA RD
RANOLF ST
RANGIURU ST
SUNSET RD
PUKAIKI ST
ARAWA ST
QUEENS DR
PUKUATUA ST
HINEMOA ST
ERUERA ST
TUTANEKAI ST
HINEMARU ST
AMOHAU ST
PERERIKA ST
ELIZABETH ST
VICTORIA ST
FENTON ST
JAMES ST
KING ST
TOKO ST
TE NGAE RD
TI ST
MALFROY RD WEST
MALFROY RD
JERVIS ST
SEDDON ST
GREY ST
MILLER ST
LYTTON ST
HILLCREST AVE
RIMU ST
MANUKA CRES
HUA ST
HIGH ST
ARTHUR ST
SUMNER ST
MARGUERITA ST
PEACE ST
MAIDA VALE ST
DEVON ST WEST
DEVON ST
HILDA ST
WARD AVE
SOPHIA ST
JACKSON
NIKAU ST
OTONGA RD
SPRINGFIELD RD
MCINTYRE AVE
SALA AVE
SALA ST
FROUDE ST
TRYON ST
HEMO RD
30A
5
30
0
0.25 mi
0.25 km
© AVALON TRAVEL

go backstage to learn more about kiwi conservation and get up close to some eggs in the incubator—time it right and you may see some feeding. By day you can spot the flightless bird in its nocturnal house or hang around until sunset or come back after dark to see them wander outside to forage. The reserve is 3km north of downtown.

Paradise Valley Springs

Paradise Valley Springs (467 Paradise Valley Rd., 07/348-9667, www.paradisevalleysprings.co.nz, 8am-5pm daily, adults $30, children $15, under age 5 free) is an interactive wildlife park that began as a trout sanctuary in 1939. Rambling paths and treetops walkways lead visitors through native forest. You'll get up close to birds and farm animals, including unusual species such as emus and alpacas, some of which can be hand-fed. The highlight for many is the separate lion enclosure; arrive by 2:30pm to watch staff feed the lions large hunks of meat and to learn more about conservation efforts for the king of the jungle.

TOP EXPERIENCE

Wingspan National Bird of Prey Centre

It's tough to spot kiwis or raptors (up close, at least) in the wild. Fortunately, several conservation projects offer ample opportunities. The **Wingspan National Bird of Prey Centre** (1164 Paradise Valley Rd., 07/357-4469, www.wingspan.co.nz, 9am-3pm daily, adults $25, children $10, seniors $20) is an intimate museum, rescue center, and aviary dedicated to the New Zealand falcon. The museum houses harriers, barn owls, and morepork (the nation's only native owl), as well as taxidermy birds, falconry equipment, and the talons of the extinct Haast's eagle, a New Zealand native that was the largest bird of prey in the world, with a wingspan up to 3m and claws as large as a tiger's.

A highlight is the falconry demonstration (2pm daily), where you can watch trainers hone the falcons' hunting skills—and maybe even get to hold one of these majestic birds. The Centre is a 10-minute drive northwest of Rotorua.

Agrodome

Agrodome (141 Western Rd., 07/357-1050, www.agrodome.co.nz, 8:30am-5pm daily) is an authentic (if sometimes comical) rural New Zealand experience, a world away from city life. The farmland attraction is famed for its one-hour **Farm Show** (9:30am, 11am, and 2:30pm daily, adults $35, children $18) that includes sheep shearing and farm dog demonstrations as well as the opportunity to milk cows, feed lambs, or take part in a mock auction. During the one-hour **Farm Tour** (10:40am, 12:10pm, 1:30pm, and 3:40pm daily, adults $48, children $24, combo with Farm Show adults $66, children $34), guests hop aboard the trailer of a chugging tractor to explore the 140ha farm, fields, orchards, and its four-legged and feathered residents. Opt for the guided **Back Country Adventure** (10:45am, 12:15pm, and 3:45pm daily, adults $89, children $79, combo with Farm Show adults $110, children $89), an action-packed tear-up in a purpose-built six-seat buggy that's capable of really getting off the beaten track. Agrodome is a 10-minute drive from the city center.

Kuirau Park

Centrally located **Kuirau Park** (access from Ranolf St. or Lake Rd.) offers a free glimpse of geothermal fury. Walking paths meander past an array of belching fumaroles, bubbling mud pools, and a boiling lake (an early Maori woman was said to have been pulled to her death here by a mythical beast), and you can dip your feet into hot mineral springs. Heed warning signs and fences, as new geothermal activity can occur without warning.

Tamaki Maori Village

For an impressive, albeit staged, sense of ancient indigenous culture, visit the **Tamaki Maori Village** (Highlands Loop Rd., 07/349-2999, www.tamakimaorivillage.co.nz, 6:15pm

Best Food

★ **Terrace Kitchen & Bar:** Menu ingredients at this modern, airy space are picked from the restaurant's own garden (page 187).

★ **Urbano Bistro:** Rotorua's most fashionable establishment serves well-presented and imaginative European plates (page 187).

★ **Atticus Finch:** Flavorsome dishes with a Mediterranean twist are served at this literary-inspired eatery (page 187).

★ **Abracadabra Café & Bar:** Mexican meets Moroccan at this colorful bohemian villa (page 187).

★ **L'Arte Café:** Don't miss this visual and culinary feast in Taupo (page 197).

★ **Lotus Thai:** Book in advance to dine at Taupo's best exotic eatery (page 197).

★ **The Bistro:** Enjoy sophisticated and seasonal fine dining at Taupo's swishiest establishment (page 197).

★ **Ruapehu Room:** An elegant menu befits Whakapapa's poshest hotel (page 206).

and 7:30pm daily Nov.-Apr., 6:15pm daily May-Oct., adults $130, children $35-70, students and seniors $99, under age 5 free). Owned and operated by Maori, this replica village was built on sacred grounds. During the 3.5-hour evening experience, guests enjoy an immersive journey as they learn about Maori facial tattoos and traditional crafts, such as carving and weaving, and watch cultural performances with ceremonial dance. The surrounding native forest illuminated by the flickering light of decorative fires adds gravitas, and it is a wonderful environment to savor the traditional *hangi* (Maori dishes cooked while buried beneath hot stones). The site is 15km south of Rotorua. Complimentary transfers to and from your accommodations are included.

Whakarewarewa Thermal Reserve

The sprawling **Te Puia** (Hemo Rd., 07/348-9045, www.tepuia.com, 8am-6pm daily Oct.-Mar., 8am-5pm daily Apr.-Sept., adults $54, children $27) is where cultural and geothermal attractions merge. The magnificent natural features of the 60ha Whakarewarewa Thermal Reserve include bubbling mud pools and active geysers, such as Pohutu, the southern hemisphere's largest. Regular eruptions occur hourly, when visitors are treated to an explosive steam that blows 30m high. Don't miss the kiwi house, Maori architecture such as traditional and contemporary *waharoa* (carved entrances or gateways), and one of the nation's few *marae* (meeting place) where photography is allowed inside. You can also watch Maori craftspeople carve and weave. Cultural singing, dance, storytelling, and traditional food are available for an additional fee.

The standard day pass includes a 60- to 90-minute guided tour that runs hourly. **Upgraded tickets** (adults $69-163, children $44-82) include extras such as traditional food, cultural performances, and guided tours. **Evening tours** (6:15pm-9pm daily, adults $125, children $63) include a traditional *hangi* dinner, cultural performances, and a river cruise through the geothermal

Best Accommodations

★ **Crash Palace:** Adorned with hip artwork and graffiti, this is one of Rotorua's better budget lodgings (page 188).

★ **Victoria Lodge:** Warm and inviting rooms await at this colorful abode near the heart of Rotorua (page 188).

★ **Sport of Kings Motel:** This friendly motel has a range of room options and boasts a geothermally heated outdoor pool (page 188).

★ **Nicara Lakeside Lodge:** Indulge in tasteful extravagance at the edge of Lake Rotorua (page 189).

★ **Treetops Lodge:** This sanctuary estate features 1,000ha of native forest filled with trout streams, lakes, and walking trails (page 189).

★ **Haka Lodge:** Airy, spacious, and modern, this is Taupo's best backpacker hostel (page 197).

★ **Acacia Cliffs Lodge:** Luxurious modern rooms feature floor-to-ceiling windows overlooking Lake Taupo (page 198).

★ **Braxmere:** This peaceful scenic site hosts one of the region's best eateries (page 201).

★ **River Birches Lodge:** One of the North Island's standout boutique accommodations, set on the banks of Tongariro (page 201).

valley. Day and evening passes can be combined (adults $163, children $82).

The Reserve is a five-minute drive from downtown Rotorua.

WHAKAREWAREWA THERMAL VILLAGE

The **Whakarewarewa Thermal Village** (17 Tyron St., 07/349-3463, www.wakarewarewa.com, 8:30am-5pm daily, shows 11:15am and 2pm daily, tours 9am, 10am, noon, 1pm, 3pm, and 4pm daily, adults $40-70, children $18-40) has been home to a Maori community for more than 200 years. It is now the oldest family business in New Zealand. Today, residents go about their lives among plumes of steam and bubbling mud. Visitors can explore the brooding landscape and learn about traditional practices such as weaving, facial tattoos, and how this geothermal landscape helps cook food, heat homes, and even heal. Admission includes a guided tour and cultural performance; geothermally cooked meals and *hangi* are extra.

Waimangu Volcanic Valley

Waimangu Volcanic Valley (587 Waimangu Rd., 07/366-6137, www.waimangu.co.nz, 8:30am-5pm daily) is the world's youngest geothermal system. It was formed following the eruption of Mount Tarawera in 1886 (which, in geological terms, may as well have been this morning). The blast exploded Lake Rotomahana up to 20 times its original size and left a 6km scar across the land. Today, this rich native forest is filled with birds and punctuated by craters, marble terraces, steaming vents, and **Frying Pan Lake** (the world's grandest hot spring), all of it loosely laced by the winding Waimangu Stream.

A popular **self-guided walk** (1-4 hours, $38.50 adults, $12 children, under age 6 free) follows well-marked paths; pick up a map at the visitors center upon entry. A free shuttle bus patrols the valley to break up the strolls. A cruise of **Lake Rotomahana** (45 minutes, adults $45, children $12, under age 6 free) reaches otherwise inaccessible hot springs and the site of the Pink Terraces. Combine the cruise with a guided hike (3.5 hours, adults $83.50, children $24, under age 6 free). The Valley is 25km southwest of Rotorua.

TOP EXPERIENCE

★ Wai-O-Tapu

The region's most vibrant volcanic site is **Wai-O-Tapu Thermal Wonderland** (201 Waiotapu Loop Rd., 07/366-6010, www.waiotapu.co.nz, 8:30am-6pm daily Nov.-Mar., 8:30am-5pm daily Apr.-Oct., adults $32.50, children $11). An enormous pool of metallic mud—New Zealand's biggest—bubbles angrily alongside colorful lime-green lakes, hissing vents, terraces, geysers, and craters of ocher and azure, all surrounded by lush verdant forest, navigated via well-trodden tracks, and if you're lucky, covered by skies of cloudless royal blue. Be sure to have your camera ready for the display at Lady Knox Geyser at 10:15am when a 10- to 20-minute eruption is manipulated by way of the introduction of a harmless nonresidue soap powder into the vent by the staff (Lady Knox Geyser is a couple of kilometers' drive from the entrance, so arrive early). Wai-O-Tapu is a 20-minute drive south of Rotorua.

Hell's Gate

Considered Rotorua's most active volcanic field, the superbly named **Hell's Gate** (Hwy. 30, 07/345-3151, www.hellsgate.co.nz, 8:30am-10pm daily, adults $35, children $17.50) pales in scale and color when compared to its fellow geothermal parks. However, the snaking track sporadically winds through misty plumes for a real sense of immersion—you can often hear the water bubbling seemingly beneath your feet. Its waterfall, the largest in the southern hemisphere, is said to impart such physical and healing properties that Maori warriors bathed in it after battle. Today, you can dip your feet in volcanic mud or upgrade to the **Hells Gate Special Combo** (adults $90, children $45), which includes a 20-minute dip in a mud bath followed by an unlimited soak in a sulfur spa overlooking the geothermal park. Other combos include the New Zealand Special (adults $120, children $60), with private mud bath, and the Ultimate

Wai-O-Tapu Thermal Wonderland

Package (adults $240, children $185), with a one-hour massage.

Te Wairoa Buried Village

In 1848, a Christian missionary established a Maori and European community on the banks of Lake Tarawera called Te Wairoa. Less than four decades later it was no more. In 1886, nearby volcano Mount Tarawera blew its top, and the settlement suffered a four-hour onslaught as rock, mud, and ash rained down, burying the village and killing 150 people. Today, a pathway winds through the archeological site of **Te Wairoa Buried Village** (1180 Tarawera Rd., 07/362-8287, www.buriedvillage.co.nz, 9am-5pm daily summer, 9am-4:30pm daily winter, adults $35, children $10, students and seniors $32, under age 5 free), enabling a ghostly glimpse into the excavated homes and lives of its former residents. At the Museum of the Wairoa, peruse the village's relics and learn the science behind the eruption and the area's legendary pink-and-white terraces.

A steep path along Te Wairoa stream leads to **Wairere Falls,** which cascades 30m down Waitoharuru Cliffs. A flat track along Tarawera Road (a couple of kilometers past the village) offers views of Lake Tarawera, with Mount Tarawera looming ominously beyond. The buried village is a 15-minute drive from Rotorua.

★ Lake Tarawera Hot Springs

Twenty minutes southeast of Rotorua along Tarwera Road, the wonderfully secluded **Lake Tarwera** (Maori for "burned spear") is a sizeable deep-water lake. Tucked into its southwest corner, Te Rata Bay, is **Hot Water Beach.** A hot spring flows directly into the shallows here, where you can laze in the cool lake water as the warming tide passes through. Pick your spot for the best mix of temperatures, perhaps gathering some rocks to build your own private hot tub. Beware: the occasional extra hot blast may make you jump!

The bay can be accessed by a pre-booked water taxi. A better option is to take the **Tarawera Trail** (15km, 4-6 hours) in to the beach and take a scenic boat cruise out. The shady but tough track begins at Te Wairoa car park (Tarawera Rd.) and passes a number of waterways en route.

The water taxi is operated by **Totally Tarawera** (Mariners House, Tarawera Rd., 07/362-8080, www.totallytarawera.com, one-way adults $25, children $15, under age 5 free). To stay overnight, pitch a tent at the **Department of Conservation (DoC) campsite** (07/351-7324, www.doc.govt.nz, adults $13, children $6.50, under age 5 free). Book in advance either online or at the Rotorua i-SITE. The water taxi charges extra to ferry equipment: $5 for small items; $10 for a tent.

SPORTS AND RECREATION

Rotorua has a wealth of unique and fun options that explore the surrounding area. Save some time and cash with **Rotorua Combos** (1103 Hinemoa St., 0800/338-786, www.rotoruacombos.com). Their combo offerings mix and match two to three of Rotorua's most thrilling activities and fascinating sites, such as mountain biking, soaking in thermal pools, and rafting the Kaituna River.

Agroventures

Agroventures (1335 Paradise Valley Rd., 07/357-4747, www.agroventures.co.nz, 9am-5pm daily, rides $49-219) is a unique theme park with a mind-bending array of options. The most unusual offering is the Shweeb: Guests sit in a pedal-powered capsule as it dangles beneath a monorail, then race either the clock or another rider, reaching speeds of up to 45km/h. You can also work up a sweat (and your heart rate) on the 43m bungee jump. Don't miss the opportunity to fly or hover on the Xtreme Fall as your body is suspended in midair above a blast from turbo jets in an outdoor wind tunnel. Take a ride in the Agrojet, the fastest jet-boat sprint in the country—it zooms from 0 to 100km/h in 4.5 seconds. Agroventures is 8km north of Rotorua.

Canopy Tours

Experience New Zealand's ancient forest like a native bird with **Rotorua Canopy Tours** (173 Old Taupo Rd., 07/343-1001, www.canopytours.co.nz, 8am-8pm daily Oct.-Mar., 8am-6pm daily Apr.-Sept., adults $149, children $119). You'll dangle from zip lines and traverse suspension bridges up to 22m high, encountering an array of wildlife such as the tui and tomtit, enormous ferns, and trees up to 500 years old. The early morning tours, when the birds are at their most vocal, are the best. Groups are limited to 10 people and depart throughout the day. This three-hour tour is the only one of its kind in New Zealand.

Boating and Sailing

In operation since 1960, **Kawarau Jet** (Memorial Dr., 07/343-7900, www.nzjetboat.co.nz) is one of the country's most-respected adventure companies. Hold on tight for the half-hour Jet Tour (adults $85, children $54) that churns Lake Rotorua's waters at speeds up to 85km/h in a jet-boat. You'll take in landmarks like Kawaha Point and the small volcanic island of Mokoia, and a bird sanctuary replete with thermal springs. The tour includes occasional breaks, during which drivers can impart their knowledge.

The **KJet Parasail** (30 minutes, solo $115, tandem $85 pp) tethers you to the back of a speedboat for 120m-high views of the area; expect to spend around 12 minutes in the air. Or opt for the Skyjet Combo ($153), a one-hour package that combines parasailing with the jet-boat ride. The Mokoia Island Experience (adults $99, children $59) offers a 30-minute jet-boat tour of the lake and a guided 20-minute tour of the island. You'll learn about Maori history, bird-watch, and visit a hot pool.

Kick back on New Zealand's only sternwheel paddle-driven liner, the **Lakeland Queen** (lakefront, Memorial Dr., 07/348-0265, 9am-4pm daily). A range of daily one-hour cruises explore Lake Rotorua, while taking in the geothermal area of Sulphur Bay. The Coffee Cruise (8am and 1pm daily, $29) includes complimentary baked treats and unlimited tea or coffee, while the Breakfast, Lunch, and Dinner Cruises (8am, 1pm, and 6pm daily, $44-59) offer a buffet with free nonalcoholic beverages. The Twilight Wine Cruise (1pm and 6pm daily, $36) watches the sunset with appetizers and a complimentary drink from the bar.

White-Water Rafting

The world's highest commercially rafted waterfall is the 7m Tutea Falls. **Kaitiaki Adventures** (1135 Te Ngae Rd., 07/357-2236, www.kaitiaki.co.nz) navigates these rapids through spectacular canyons beneath overhanging native bush. The most popular tour is the Raft the Kaituna River (3 hours, 8:30am, 12:30pm, and 2:30pm daily, $109), which includes three falls, including Tutea, and 14 sets of rapids. This tour can even be tackled by first-timers. Complimentary pickups are offered from across Rotorua.

Kaitiaki also offers sledging (3 hours, $120), where you don a pair of flippers and tackle the white-water rapids while holding onto a body board. Rafting and hiking combos are also available.

Kayaking and Paddleboarding

Kaituna Kayaks (3G Trout Pool Rd., Okere Falls, 021/277-2855, www.kaitunakayaks.co.nz) operates several guided tours along local rivers whose white water ranges Class III-V. Most opt for the Kaituna River Trip ($150, tandem $280), a one-hour river paddle that barrels over the 7m-high Tutea Falls. A more serene option is the Lake Rotoiti Trip (1 hour, $90), which includes a swim in the hot pools. Pickups from Rotorua are available.

Choose from two stand-up paddleboard options with **Rotorua Paddle Tours** (761 Highway 33, Okere Falls, 0800/787-768, www.rotoruapaddletours.com, 9am, noon, and 3pm daily, $80); both last three hours and include pickup from central Rotorua. The Ohau Channel to Okere Falls Tour navigates a waterway that connects Rotorua and Rotoiti Lakes. Glide within the shadow of historic Maori buildings and native forest as you're serenaded by birds. The Lake Tikitapu (Blue Lake) Tour is a relaxed affair. After paddling to the center of the lake, the paddleboards are lashed together to form one big platform. Guests then swim and sunbathe at leisure.

Walks

There are several satisfying short treks in Rotorua to whet the hiker's appetite. Pick up the excellent *Walking and Hiking in Rotorua* leaflet from the i-SITE and DoC Visitor Centre (www.rotoruanz.com). The **Blue Lake Track** is an enjoyable 5.5km loop around Lake Tikitapu (Blue Lake), 9km southeast of Rotorua. The walk treks through native forest and past secluded beaches, affording views of the adjacent Green Lake (Rotokakahi), with plenty of spots to picnic and swim.

The wonderful **Hamurana Springs Walk** in the **Hamurana Springs Recreation Reserve** (773 Hamurana Rd., 0800/426-8726, www.hamurana.co.nz, 9am-6pm daily summer, 9am-5pm daily winter, adults $18, children $8, under age 10 free) winds through a redwood grove to a viewing platform that overlooks the North Island's largest spring. The unimaginably clear spring empties into Lake Rotorua. Allow 30 minutes for the round-trip walk, though you'll likely loiter by the water. The reserve is 15 minutes north of Rotorua, along Highways 5 and 6, or via Highway 30 to Hamurana Road.

★ WHAKAREWAREWA FOREST

A section of the whispering **Whakarewarewa Forest** (free), known as the Redwoods, is home to an impressive grove of magnificent California redwood trees that tower over the reserve's ferns, firs, and pine. Several well-signed walking tracks stretch into the 5,600ha forest and range from 30-minute to half-day treks. The **Redwoods Treewalk** (www.treewalk.co.nz, 9am-close daily, adults $25, children and seniors $15) is a must-do. Purchase tickets outside the visitors center, then follow a series of 12m-high suspension bridges that are strung more than 500m between century-old redwood trees. A nighttime Treewalk begins at dusk, when the bridges and surrounding bush are illuminated with brooding light—a scene lifted straight from the pages of a fairy tale.

Whakarewarewa Forest is also a mountain-biking mecca, laced with more than 145km of some of the finest two-wheel trails in the country.

The **Redwoods i-SITE Visitor Centre** (Long Mile Rd., 07/350-0110, www.redwoods.

rafting the Kaituna River

co.nz, 8:30am-6pm daily summer, 8:30am-5pm daily winter) is where you can get forest maps and information on the region. It also marks the entrance to the forest.

Mountain Biking

Rotorua is one of New Zealand's leading mountain biking centers and hosts several national and international competitions along its numerous trails. An abundance of mountain bike stores are scattered throughout the region; all can advise the best tracks, as can the good folks at the i-SITE Visitor Centres in downtown Rotorua. The website **Ride Rotorua** (www.riderotorua.com) is especially helpful.

For an unadulterated adrenaline rush, head to the downhill track at the Skyline Gravity Park at **Skyline Rotorua** (178 Fairy Springs Rd., 07/347-0027, www.skyline.co.nz, 9am-5pm daily, one lift $31). Fun awaits on the acclaimed trails of **Whakarewarewa Forest** (Long Mile Rd., 07/350-0110, www.redwoods.co.nz, 8:30am-6pm daily summer, 8:30am-5pm daily winter, free), where dozens of varied routes range from beginner to expert grades.

The **Te Aha Ari Cycle Trail** (www.nzcycletrail.com) is a fascinating "thermal" Great Ride that winds south from Rotorua for 48km, terminating at Waikite Valley. The full route usually takes two days to complete and encompasses four major geothermal attractions: Whakarewarewa, Waimangu Volcanic Valley, Wai-O-Tapu, and Waikite Valley Thermal Springs. You'll also cycle past the wetlands around Lake Okaro, Rainbow Mountain, and the Te Ranga Hot Pools.

BIKE RENTALS

Mountain Bike Rotorua (0800/682-768, www.mtbrotorua.co.nz, $35 for 2 hours, kids bikes from $20) rents bikes and operates the Skyline Gravity Park at **Skyline Rotorua** (178 Fairy Springs Rd., 07/347-0027, www.skyline.co.nz, 9am-5pm daily); the **Waipa MTB Carpark** (Waipa Mill Rd.), south of Whakarewarewa Forest; and the centrally located **Adventure Hub** (1128 Hinemoa St.). They also offer guided tours ($130-420) that include kayaking and hot pools.

Whakarewarewa Forest

Ogo

From the inventors of zorbing in Rotorua comes **Ogo** (525 Ngongotaha Rd., 07/343-7676, www.ogo.co.nz, 9am-5pm daily, $40-60 pp). What is Ogo, or zorbing? Imagine being thrown into a clear oversize inflated beach ball, doused with water, and then hurled down a zigzag trench along the slopes of Mount Ngongotaha as you're tossed around inside. Bring swimwear and a towel, and plan to finish with a dip in the nearby hot tub.

Thermal Pools

★ POLYNESIAN SPA

Nestled on the banks of Lake Rotorua, the warming waters of the historic **Polynesian Spa** (1000 Hinemoa St., 07/348-1328, www.polynesianspa.co.nz, 8am-11pm daily, $30-50) have been soothing souls since the 19th century. The collection of open-air hot mineral pools are fed by local springs and sit alongside the cold plunge and swimming pools. It's a heavenly spot to unwind, as you overlook Lake Rotorua hidden beneath a carpet of brooding mist. Private pool rentals ($20 for 30 minutes) are also available; a romantic couples option ($94) includes fresh-squeezed fruit juice. A gaggle of hot tubs surround the family pool ($10), while an on-site spa ($135-340) offers massage, health, and beauty treatments.

WAIKITE VALLEY THERMAL POOLS

New Zealand's largest single source of boiling water, **Waikite Valley Thermal Pools** (648 Waikite Valley Rd., 07/333-1861, www.hotpools.co.nz, 10am-9pm daily) boasts pure waters fed from Te Manaroa hot spring. A range of public tubs (adults $16.50, children $9, children under 5 $3) and private pools (40 minutes, minimum 2 people, $20 pp) are available. The pools are heated to 35-40°C and are surrounded by greenery; some overlook the Otamakokore River. The Spa Plus option (minimum 2 people) includes the use of other tubs, along with a complimentary towel and a bottle of spring drinking water.

Flightseeing

Volcanic Air (Memorial Dr., 07/348-9984, www.volcanicair.co.nz) operates several helicopter or floatplane tours departing from Lakefront Drive. The eight-minute Flight Experience (minimum 4 fares, $95 pp) affords spectacular views of Rotorua and the lake from the comfort of a helicopter. For a better sense and scale of the region's geothermal landscape, take the 15-minute **Crater Lakes Flight** (adults $195, children $146), which heads beyond the rim of Mount Tarawera for views of the surrounding lakes and volcanoes.

On the **Mount Tarawera Volcanic Landing** (40 minutes, adults $395, children $296), passengers are flown to the top of Mount Tarawera for views of its main crater and the lakes and domes beyond. The **Mount Tarawera Fly/Drive Combination** (3 hours, $565 pp) combines a flight landing on the mountain with a hike. On the combo tour, a 4WD vehicle leaves Lakefront Drive to drop you off close to the crater for a walk around its edge. If conditions allow, this is followed by a scenic helicopter ride back to base (Lakefront Dr.).

Volcanic Air also flies to New Zealand's only active offshore volcano, White Island. The **Volcanic Landing and Walking Tour** (adults $895, children $671) can be combined with the Mount Tarawera experience

Polynesian Spa

Vicinity of Rotorua

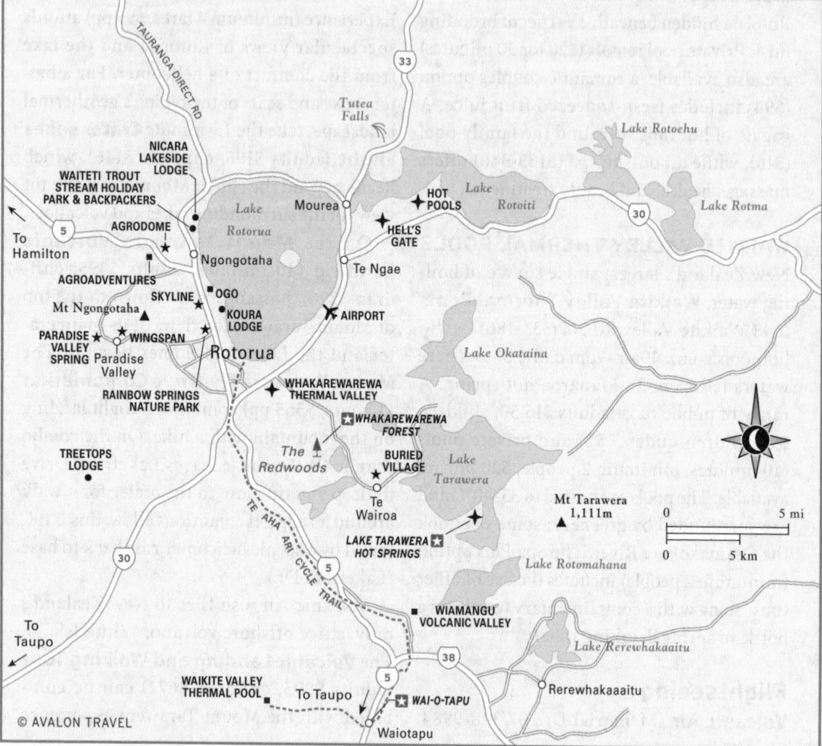

for a **Dual Volcano Landing** (adults $1,045, children $784), a 3.5-hour guided tour of both volcano craters with a scenic helicopter flight in between.

ENTERTAINMENT AND EVENTS

The lake end of Tutanekai Street, affectionately nicknamed "Eat Street," is home to a diverse range of restaurants with outdoor seating and some of the city's liveliest bars—but don't expect wild nights in town.

Nightlife

The city's best drinking den is the **Brew Craft Beers Pub** (1103 Tutanekai St., 07/346-0976, www.brewpub.co.nz, 11am-close daily). It's a hit with visitors and locals—especially beer aficionados, owing to the Croucher craft beers on tap that are backed by an array of ever-evolving local craft brews. The crowd usually spills into the outside area, soaking up and contributing to the Eat Street vibes.

Traditionalists should make for the **Pig and Whistle** (1182 Tutanekai St., 07/347-3025, www.pigandwhistle.co.nz, 11:30am-10:30pm Tues.-Wed., 11:30am-midnight Thurs., 11:30am-1:30am Fri.-Sat., 11:30am-10pm Sun.-Mon.), a historic pub with plenty of polished wood, beers on tap, and an open fireplace. Live sports are shown across seven big screens, and live bands play on weekends. The menu offers the usual hearty pub grub like burgers, steak pie, and fish-and-chips.

Local legend the **Lava Bar & Grill** (1286 Arawa St., 07/348-8636, 5:30pm-close daily) serves brightly colored cocktails under neon lights to obliging backpackers (it's right next to Base hostel). Live music, DJs, games, and drink and meal deals add to the deliciously unsophisticated and boisterous fun.

Events

Rotorua hosts **Crankworx** (www.crankworx.com, Mar.), the world's largest mountain bike festival. Over the course of nine days, the world's elite riders roll into town, tackling various bike tracks. The event is backed by freestyle competitions, live music, and Maori cultural performances.

FOOD

Cafés

Ciabatta Café (38 White St., 027/263-4050, 8am-1:30pm Mon.-Fri., 8am-3pm Sat.-Sun.) serves super coffee and a wonderful selection of pastries, but it is for their Long Dog—the "world's longest hotdog"—and artisanal breads that they are most famed; there's even a bread-making workshop. The local's local **Picnic Café** (1174 Whakaue St., 07/343-9239, 7:30am-4pm daily) dishes up some of the best breakfasts and lattes in town—try the French toast or the omelet—enjoyed in an inviting, all-white setting punctuated with fashionable crafts and artwork.

Contemporary and European

★ **Terrace Kitchen & Bar** (1029 Tutanekai St., 07/460-1229, www.terrace.kitchen, 7:30am-close daily, $28-34) is one of Rotorua's more recent culinary additions and it shows. There's a fresh feeling in the modern and airy white space that serves to enhance a menu filled with ingredients picked from the restaurant's own garden (the terrace heating is geothermally sourced). Pulled veal shank and chicken breast confit are among the menu highlights.

Be sure to book a window seat at **Stratosphere Restaurant & Bar** (178 Fairy Springs Rd., 07/347-0027, www.skyline.co.nz, 11:30am-close daily, gondola and lunch adults $64, children $35, gondola and dinner adults $85, children $45), perched atop Mount Ngongotaha overlooking Rotorua and accessed via the Skyline gondola. Choose from a superb buffet or cooked-to-order dishes including green-lipped mussels, steak, salmon, and pasta. Finish by toasting the twinkling city lights below with a cocktail.

Chilled-out **Ciccio** (1262 Fenton St., 07/348-1828, www.ciccio.co.nz, 11:30am-2:30pm and 5pm-9pm Tues.-Thurs. and Sun., 11:30am-2:30pm and 5pm-9:30pm Fri.-Sat., $17-28) is a family-run setup serving authentic Italian classics such as risotto and pasta, including spaghetti (the meatballs are good). Don't leave Rotorua without sampling their legendary "freak shakes," a thick and candy-topped shake—you won't need sugar, or sleep, for a week afterward.

The city's most fashionable establishment is ★ **Urbano Bistro** (289 Fenton St., 07/349-3770, www.urbanobistro.co.nz, 9am-11pm daily, $25-44). Within the brooding black decor, the friendly staff serves imaginative European offerings—heavy on the red meat—on square designer plates. The venison with truffle mashed potato and chocolate chili oil is out of this world. All of it is accompanied by an exquisite New Zealand wine list.

Sample fresh, flavorful dishes with a Mediterranean twist at ★ **Atticus Finch** (1106 Tutaneakai St., 07/460-0400, www.atticusfinch.co.nz, noon-3pm and 5pm-close daily summer, noon-3pm and 5pm-close Fri.-Sun. winter, $24-34). Located in the center of Eat Street, it's a wonderful place to share a meal with plenty of tapas on offer and a crackling atmosphere. The chili-caramel pork belly with pickled mango and coriander salad comes highly recommended. Pair it with a glass from the excellent wine list.

Latin American

Mexican merges with Moroccan at ★ **Abracadabra Café & Bar** (1263 Amohia St., 07/348-3883, www.abracadabracafe.com, 10:30am-11pm Tues.-Sat., 10:30am-3pm Sun., $26-36). Set in a colorful bohemian villa with cozy alcoves and a wraparound deck, this is the ideal setting to feast on sizzling fajitas, burritos, and seafood tagine. For something less substantial, the tapas ($13) are superb.

Cozy Sabroso (1184 Haupapa St., 07/349-0591, www.sabroso.co.nz, 5pm-9pm Wed.-Sun., $20-25) is adorned with decorative Spanish guitars and sombreros. Sumptuous Latin fare from Central and South America is served with the occasional Caribbean twist, resulting in hearty dishes such as Brazilian prawn stew along with light offerings like calamari or chicken tortillas.

ACCOMMODATIONS

Accommodations options are as varied as Rotorua's attractions, with plenty of lodgings dotting the lake and the city's entertainment district. If you find yourself in a bind, head for Fenton Street, which is lined with motels.

Under $100

Make the most of the free Wi-Fi, spa, and geothermal pool at **Base Rotorua** (1286 Arawa St., 07/348-8836, www.stayatbase.com, dorm $28-34, $85-95 s or d), a centrally located and sociable hostel with its own bar, Lava. It's a bit rough around the edges, and some of the larger dorms are cramped, but the staff are great and there's a useful tour service. Private en suite rooms are available, as is a women-only dorm.

One of Rotorua's better budget lodgings, ★ **Crash Palace** (1271 Hinemaru St., 07/348-8842, www.crashpalace.co.nz, dorm $24-30, $50 s, $70-78) is adorned with hip artwork and graffiti. Super single rooms include a desk, and there's a comfortable TV room to kick back in. Amenities include free unlimited Wi-Fi, a spacious and well-stocked kitchen, a pool table, DJ decks, a barbecue, a hot tub, and a small bar.

For a quieter stay, opt for the reliable **YHA Rotorua** (1278 Haupapa St., 07/349-4088, www.yha.co.nz, dorm $29-33, $75 s, $84-120 d), a purpose-built hostel that checks all the service boxes—but lacks in personality. The clean rooms have en suite options available; larger family rooms ($110-120) sleep four. There's an enormous stainless-steel kitchen, a pool table, a barbecue area, and a TV lounge with a sizeable movie library. Guests receive 2GB of free Wi-Fi per day.

Waikite Valley Thermal Pools (648 Waikite Valley Rd., 07/333-1861, www.hotpools.co.nz, 10am-9pm daily, adults $23, children $11) has a 26-site campground with showers, laundry, and kitchen facilities. Guests receive free access to the outdoor thermal pools.

$100-200

Colorful **Rotovegas Motel** (249 Fenton St., 07/348-5586, www.rotovegasmotel.co.nz, $138-304) comes with plenty of character thanks to retro-inspired furnishings and contemporary facilities. The self-contained units sport fully equipped kitchens or kitchenettes along with Sky TV and free Wi-Fi; some units boast private hot tubs. There's a heated outdoor pool, a sauna, and a barbecue area. It's a five-minute walk to downtown.

Well positioned near the heart of Rotorua, ★ **Victoria Lodge** (10 Victoria St., 07/348-4039, www.victorialodge.co.nz, $149-249) is a happy place. Warm and inviting rooms are splashed with vivid color that's mirrored in the vibrant compact grounds, peppered with tropical palms. Rooms range from studios to two-bedroom apartments; all have en suite baths. The larger units have full kitchens. Amenities include private hot pools, cooking facilities, Sky TV, and free Wi-Fi.

You're in for a restful stay at **B&B Abundance** (33 Elizabeth St., 027/044-004, www.bedandbreakfastrotorua.nz, $150-175), a traditional Kiwi villa set on an idyllic patch of shady lawn. Three homey rooms come with their own baths (one has a private entrance) and are adorned with warm, colorful furnishings, high-end linens, and inspirational quotes. There's free Wi-Fi and a continental breakfast included, though it's worth upgrading to the full English breakfast. It's a 10-minute walk from the center of Rotorua.

Laid-back and friendly, the ★ **Sport of Kings Motel** (6 Peace St., 07/248-2135, www.

sportofkingsmotel.co.nz, $169-255) boasts a palm-fringed geothermally heated outdoor pool and a comfortable barbecue area. Modern well-presented rooms have en suite baths with options ranging from studios to two-bedroom units. All have comfy beds and full kitchens; some rooms come with private spas. Amenities include free Wi-Fi, Sky TV, and DVD players with free movies to watch. Rotorua is a short drive away, as is the Whakarewarewa Forest; it's a 10-minute walk to the Te Puia Thermal Reserve.

$200-300

Fashionable **Regent Rotorua** (1191 Pukaiki St., 07/348-4079, www.regentrotorua.co.nz, $220-480) is well appointed and well positioned in the heart of town. Its 35 chic and original en suite rooms are festooned with designer wallpaper and wrought-iron framed mirrors, with toiletries, Sky TV, free Wi-Fi, and a docking station. Make use of the indoor mineral pool, the heated outdoor lap pool, and sample at least one cocktail from the onsite bar. In-house eatery the **Regent Room** (6:30am-close daily, $38-40) serves excellent seared salmon with clams and duck-leg confit.

Over $300

A short drive from downtown, **Koura Lodge** (209 Kawaha Point Rd., 07/348-5868, www.kouralodge.co.nz, $525-1,195) hosts a maximum of 20 guests across 10 sumptuous en suite rooms; balconies or verandas offer views across Lake Rotorua. All suites are equipped with free Wi-Fi, TVs, desks, Egyptian cotton bedding, and bathrobes; some have separate lounge areas, Sky TV, and billiard tables. Communal facilities include a sauna and an outdoor hot tub, along with complimentary kayaks and fishing equipment. Buffet and cooked breakfasts are included.

Indulge in tasteful extravagance at the water's edge at ★ **Nicara Lakeside Lodge** (30 Ranginui Rd., 07/357-2105, www.nicaralodge.co.nz, $550-580). This sustainable lodging houses three luxurious en suite rooms featuring original artwork and wonderful views over the water. Outside, the lawns and a sun terrace lead to a jetty protruding over the lake (away from the smell of sulfur). Amenities include bathrobes, fridges, hot drink facilities, docking stations for music devices, and free Wi-Fi. It's a 6km drive to Rainbow Springs and a 10-minute drive from Rotorua.

★ **Treetops Lodge** (351 Kearoa Rd., 07/333-2066, www.treetops.co.nz, $1,910-2,780) sits nestled among 200ha of centuries-old native forest with seven trout streams, four lakes, and more than 70km of walking trails. The sanctuary estate comprises ranch-like architecture and standalone rural villas with lofty ceilings, timber beams, open fires, antique furnishings, and stag heads mounted on the walls. Rooms are regal, replete with marble baths, Sky TV, free Wi-Fi, and bathrobes. For communal use are an antique billiards table, paneled library, and outdoor mineral hot tubs. The on-site spa offers a range of treatments and massages, including traditional Maori ones. An on-site restaurant dishes seasonal fare crafted with organic produce, much of which is grown in the estate gardens. They even make their own manuka honey! The lodge is a 20-minute drive southwest of Rotorua.

Campgrounds and Holiday Parks

Enjoy free kayak and dinghy rentals at **Waiteti Trout Stream Holiday Park & Backpackers** (14 Okona Crescent, 07/357-5255, www.waiteti.com), along with a swimming pool and a hot spa. Waterside gardens and woodland on 0.8ha are home to lovely tent and van sites (adults $21, children $12), but the self-contained units and motel rooms ($70-145) are very dated. Backpacker accommodations include a twin room ($35 s, $55 d) or a two-bunk lodge ($55 for 2 people, $15 per extra person) that sleeps four with access to communal facilities and a shared bath. Buy a fishing license and rent equipment from the office to try your luck in a stream fed directly from the mighty lake. Other amenities include a stocked kitchen, barbecues, games rooms, laundry, and a lounge area with Sky TV. The campground is a 10-minute drive outside Rotorua.

Rotorua Top 10 Holiday Park (1495 Pukuatua St., 0800/233-267, www.rotorua-top10.co.nz) is centrally located 1km from downtown Rotorua. Camp and van sites ($55-60) are available with power. Cozy motel units ($165-275) range from studios to two-bedrooms; all are self-contained and finished in pine. Modern facilities include free mineral pools, a swimming pool, gym access, bike rentals, stainless-steel kitchens, and Sky TV in a communal lounge with a fireplace.

TRANSPORTATION AND SERVICES

Rotorua is 228km (2 hours, 50 minutes) southeast of Auckland along Highways 1, 27, and 5, and 452km (5 hours, 35 minutes) northeast of Wellington via Highways 1 and 5.

Air

Rotorua Airport (ROT, Hwy. 30, 07/345-8800, www.rotorua-airport.co.nz) is 9km northeast of downtown Rotorua and is served by **Air New Zealand** (www.airnewzealand.co.nz) with connections to Auckland, Wellington, and Christchurch. **Super Shuttle** (07/345-7790, www.supershuttle.co.nz) and **Cityride** (www.baybus.co.nz) run shuttle buses into town.

Public Transportation

National bus carriers **Intercity** (07/348-0366, www.intercity.co.nz) and **Naked Bus** (09/979-1616, www.nakedbus.com) stop in Rotorua, as does North Island bus company **Mana Bus** (09/367-9140, www.manabus.com). For a cab, call **Rotorua Taxis** (07/348-1111, www.rotoruataxis.co.nz).

Car Rental

Car rentals at the airport include **Avis** (07/345-7133, www.avis.co.nz) and **Hertz** (07/348-4081, www.hertz.co.nz). **Rent A Dent Rotorua** (39 Fairy Springs Rd., 07/349-3993, www.radcarhire.co.nz) and **Rite Price Rentals** (105 Old Taupo Rd., 07/343-7919, www.ritepricerentals.co.nz) offer competitive rental prices.

Bike

Electric Bike Rotorua (1265 Fenton St., 07/460-0844, www.electricbikerotorua.co.nz, 9:30am-4pm Mon.-Fri., 10am-4pm Sat., $25 per hour) offer electric bike rentals; the longer you rent, the better the deal. Add a gourmet picnic lunch ($18-22) with rolls, fruit, and desserts, complete with a pannier and a blanket.

Tours and Shuttles

Elite Adventures (07/347-8282, www.eliteadventures.co.nz, adults $155-290, children $105-190) runs half- and full-day tours in luxury vans to natural and cultural sites around the region. **Flexi Tours NZ** (09/336-1663, www.flexitoursnz.com, $89-185 pp) offers similar routes for those on a budget. For shuttle buses to and from sights, contact **Uncle Tim's** (021/667-215, www.taylorstours.co.nz) or **Thermal Land Shuttle** (0800/894-287, www.thermalshuttle.co.nz).

For a quirky tour of the city, check out **Rotorua by Segway** (289 Fenton St., 021/444-505, www.rotoruabysegway.com, 10am and 1:30pm daily, $139) for a guided 2.5-hour tour of the city along designated cycle paths past the lakefront and Government Gardens.

Services

Rotorua **i-SITE Visitor Information Centre** (1167 Fenton St., 07/348-5179, www.rotoruanz.com, 7:30am-7pm daily summer, 7:30am-6pm daily winter) has local and national tour and accommodations information along with DoC info, as does the Redwoods **i-SITE Visitor Centre** (Long Mile Rd., 07/350-0110, www.redwoods.co.nz, 8:30am-6pm daily summer, 8:30am-5pm daily winter) outside Rotorua.

Rotorua has a central **library** (1127 Haupapa St., 07/348-4177, www.rotoralibrary.

govt.nz, 9am-5:30pm Mon.-Wed. and Fri., 9am-8pm Thurs., 10am-4pm Sat.-Sun.), a **post office** (1218 Tutanekai St., 0800/081-190, www.nzpost.co.nz, 9am-5pm Mon.-Fri., 9am-1pm Sat.), a **medical center** (19 Tarewa Rd., 07/349-1995, 9am-5pm Mon.-Fri.), and a **hospital** (Arawa St. and Pukeroa Hill, 07/348-1199).

Taupo

Lake Taupo sits in an ancient crater, filling an area the size of Singapore. The freshwater lake is the source of the Waikato River, the longest in New Zealand. The caldera that now cradles the lake was formed in AD 186 following an eruption so powerful the Romans and Chinese reported that the skies changed color. Today, the volcanic peaks of Tongariro National Park create a spectacular frame over the lake's southern end.

One of the region's most interesting attractions are the Maori rock carvings at Lake Taupo's Mine Bay. The 14m cliff-side icon was chiseled in honor of legendary navigator Ngatoro-i-rangi, said to be one of the first settlers of these sacred lands. The carvings can only be accessed via boat.

The resort town of Taupo lies at the lake's northeastern corner, 80km south of Rotorua. Local highlights include geothermal attractions, roaring waterfalls, adrenaline sports, and trout fishing in Lake Taupo—one of the world's top spots to do so.

SIGHTS

Lake Taupo Museum and Art Gallery

A highlight of the **Lake Taupo Museum and Art Gallery** (Story Place, 07/376-0414, www.taupodc.govt.nz, 10am-4:30pm daily, adults $5, under age 16 free, seniors and students $3) are the Maori art and artifacts, including a beautifully carved *marae* and a 19th-century waka, or war canoe. Popular exhibits include a moa skeleton and a quirky mid-20th-century trailer that hints at how Kiwis used to holiday way back when. Don't miss the vibrant watercolor paintings and the equally evocative award-winning gardens outside.

★ Mine Bay

Kill two birds with one stone (and maybe feed some ducks) while checking out the Maori rock carvings in **Mine Bay,** home to one of New Zealand's most fascinating artworks. Starting in 1976, it took *marae*-taught carver Matahi Whakataka-Brightwell and his team of artists four years to chisel the tattooed face in honor of his Maori ancestor, Ngatoroirangi, into a sheer alcove. The extraordinary artwork rises 14m above the water, the stained lower chin bearing witness to the ferocity of the lake. The carved face is surrounded by a handful of smaller rock carvings, including a mermaid.

GETTING THERE

Mine Bay is only accessible by boat. Purists will enjoy the calming experience offered by **Sail Barbary** (Berths 9 and 10, Redoubt St., 07/378-5879, www.sailbarbary.com, cruises 10:30am, 2pm, and 5pm daily summer, 10:30am and 2pm daily fall-spring, adults $44, children $25) whose 2.5-hour tours include a hot drink or, for the 5pm cruise, pizza and a beer or wine—with a licensed bar on board. You can also BYO. Recline on deck or get hands-on by hoisting some sails or steering the yacht—there's also an opportunity to take a dip in the lake.

Ernest Kemp Cruises (Berth 2, Redoubt St., 07/378-3444, www.ernestkemp.co.nz, cruises 10:30am, 12:30pm, 2pm, and 5pm daily summer, 10:30am and 2pm daily fall-spring, adults $44, children $15, seniors $40) operate two-hour trips to the carvings aboard a replica steamboat with complimentary cookies and hot drinks during the day, and wine, beer, and pizza for the 5pm tour. There's also a bar.

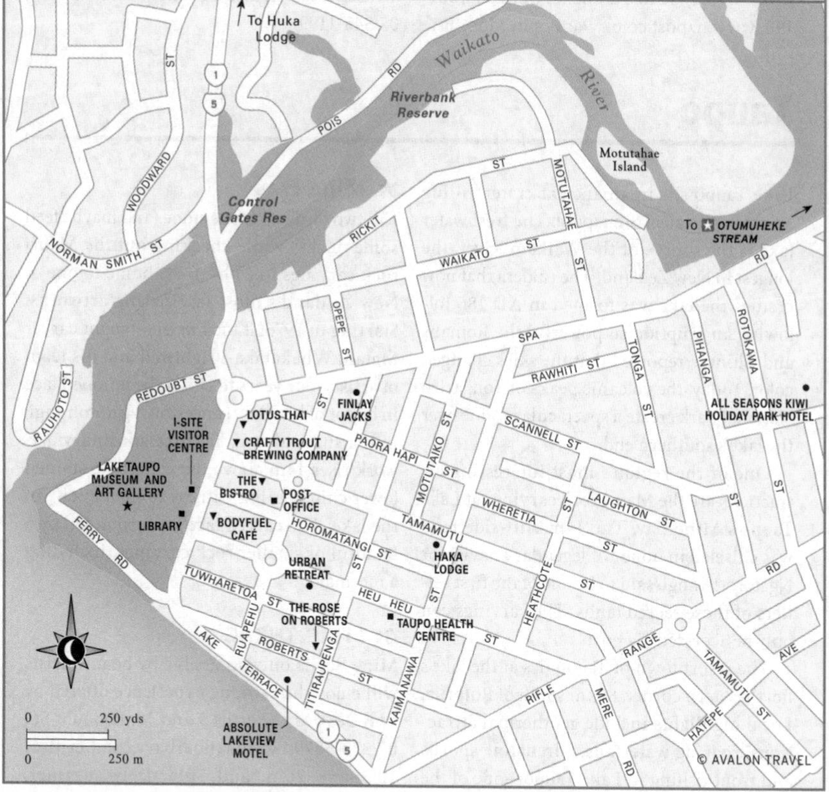

★ Huka Falls

A series of stupendously steep rapids that tumble toward a waterfall, **Huka Falls** (Huka Falls Rd.) is New Zealand's most-visited natural attraction. Metallic blue waters churn into a seething mass of froth as New Zealand's greatest river, the Waikato, is forced through a narrow chasm at a rate of 220,000 liters per second. The fury is such that you can feel the vibrations through your feet as you navigate the pathway to the lookout and cross over the viewing bridge. Huka Falls is 5km north of Taupo.

Get an eye-level display of the cascading waters with the **Huka Falls River Cruise** (Aratiatia Dam Car Park, Aratiatia Rd., 0800/278-336, www.hukafallscruise.co.nz, 10:30am, 12:30pm, 2:30pm, and 4:30pm daily summer, 10:30am, 12:30pm, and 2:30pm daily fall-spring, adults $39, children $15). The scenic 1.5-hour tour passes plenty of forest and steaming hot pools, with hot drinks included.

It's not just the thrill of the full-circle spins that'll have you howling with delight. With **Hukafalls Jet** (200 Karetoto Rd., 07/374-8572, www.hukafallsjet.com, adults $129, children $89), you will get close to the turbulent rapids of Huka Falls, alongside sights such as a prawn farm, a geothermal power station, and hot springs during the half-hour jet-boat tour (1pm and 2:30pm daily).

★ Otumuheke Stream

The warming volcanic waters of **Otumuheke Stream** (Spa Thermal Park, Spa Rd.) tumble into the frigid Waikato River, creating a handful of shallow hot pools that don't cost a dime to soak in. To find the stream, travel north along Spa Road and turn left on County Avenue. The stream is underneath the bridge near the beginning of the Huka Falls walkway. From here, you can follow the pathway alongside the Waikato River for 3km one-way.

Craters of the Moon

Operated by a charitable trust, **Craters of the Moon** (Karapiti Rd., 027/496-5131, www.cratersofthemoon.co.nz, 8:30am-6pm daily Oct.-Mar., 8:30am-5pm daily Apr.-Sept., adults $8, children $4, under age 5 free) is a lunar landscape peppered with vents and bubbling fumaroles. Though lacking the vibrant lakes around other geothermal parks, the relentless fog of volcanic steam that lingers over this rich land serves as a highly atmospheric substitute. Explore the landscape via a 45-minute track (mostly boardwalk) and a worthy 20-minute stepped path that leads to a raised lookout. It's 7km north of Taupo.

Wairakei Terraces

The **Wairakei Terraces** (Thermal Explorer Hwy., 07/378-0913, www.wairakeiterraces.co.nz, 8:30am-9pm daily Oct.-Mar., 8:30am-8:30pm daily Apr.-Sept., adults $15, children $7.50) navigate a collection of colorful and smoldering geothermal features—springs, vents, and mud pools—along with a small-scale reconstruction of the pink-and-white terraces destroyed by the 1886 eruption of Mount Tarawera. Steaming, mineral-rich, open-air hot-spring bathing pools (over age 14, $25) sit beneath bush and silica terraces. Massage treatments using local herbal oils are also available. The **Maori Cultural Experience** (3 hours, adults $110, children $55) includes traditional song and dance performances and a *hangi*. The terraces are a five-minute drive north of Taupo.

Orakei Korako

Orakei Korako (494 Orakei Korako Rd., 07/378-3131, www.orakeikorako.co.nz, 8am-4:30pm daily summer, 8am-4pm daily winter, adults $36, children $15, under age 6 free), also known as the Hidden Valley, is one of the most imposing thermal areas in the region. Visitors marvel at the massive and colorful silica terraces that appear to rust before their eyes. The

Huka Falls

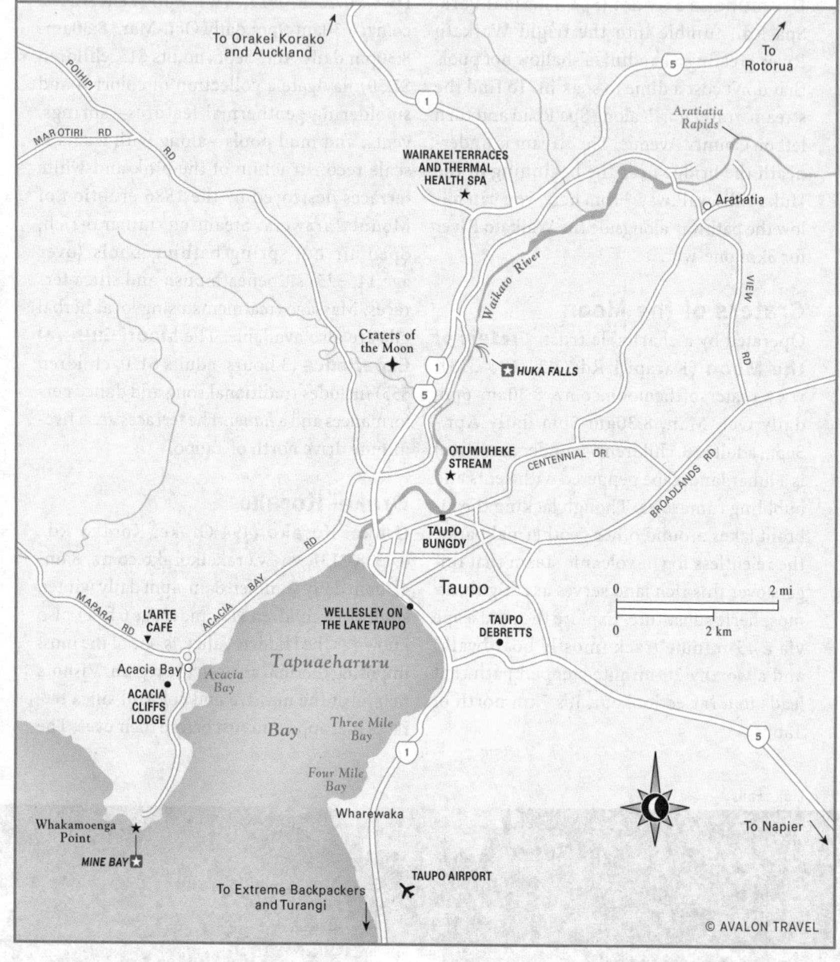

fizzing geysers and bubbling mud pools are reached via a ferry ride (included in the price). Hugging the banks of Lake Ohakuri and the Waikato River, the area's other jaw-dropping features include Ruatapu (Sacred Hole) Cave, the only hot-spring cave in the country, and one of only two in the world. It winds 35m down to the Waiwhakaata (Pool of Mirrors) hot pool.

Orakei Korako is a 25-minute drive north of Taupo. **Real Kiwi Tours** (027/935-9318, www.realkiwitours.nz) operates a shuttle bus from Taupo. From Rotorua, opt for **Tim's Tours** (021/667-215, www.taylorstours.co.nz) or **Grumpy's** (07/348-2229, www.grumpys.co.nz).

SPORTS AND RECREATION

Jet-Boating

Rapids Jet (Nga Awapurua Rd., 0800/727-437, www.rapidsjet.com, 10:30am, 12:30pm,

2:30pm, and 4:30pm daily, adults $115, children $65) is New Zealand's only white-water jet-boat operator. They offer a thrilling 35-minute experience in 500-hp V-8 vessels that spin you around, shooting you through the narrowest canyon on the Waikato River at up to 80km/h. The boats occasionally slow enough to take in the surrounding bush and hot springs. It's located 12km north of Taupo.

New Zealand River Jet (6 Tutukau Rd., 07/333-7111, www.riverjet.co.nz) offers three jet-boat tours along the Waikato River. The 36km **Scenic Blast** (50 minutes, 10am daily, adults $115, children $75) takes in forest and farmland—sometimes behind a blanket of volcanic steam—before passing through 50m-high Tutukau Gorge. You might sight trout in the crystal waters. Allow up to three hours for **The Squeeze** (11am and 2pm daily, adults $169, children $89), a scenic jet-boat tour through the gorge followed by a fun boulder scramble as you squeeze through crevasses to soak in a hot spring beneath waterfalls and surrounded by forest. The **Thermal Safari** (2.5-3 hours, 11am and 2pm daily, $179, children $99) speedily navigates Tutukau Gorge en route to Orakei Korako Thermal Reserve (entry included). Tours are based 35km from Rotorua.

Kayaking

Taupo Kayaking Adventures (876 Acacia Bay Rd., 07/376-8981, www.tka.co.nz, $90-235) runs several guided tours, ranging from a few hours to multiple days. Among the most popular option is the paddle out to Mine Bay to view the Maori rock carvings. The evening lake tour witnesses the sun set behind the mountains, with geothermal kayaking over steaming waters. The Squeeze Trip entails a float down the Waikato River followed by a soak in natural hot pools.

Fishing

Try your hand snagging some trout in this world-renowned fly-fishing region. **Central Plateau Fishing** (21 Glenn Mohr, 027/681-4134, www.cpf.net.nz) offers more options than you can shake a stick—or rod—at. The most popular are the half- and full-day tours ($350-700) in the spawning tributaries of Lake Taupo, where the odds are good to catch trout. Other options include day-long helicopter ($1,950-2,450) and multi-day rafting (from $1,150) tours to some of the region's most remote and scenic fishing spots.

Fish Taupo (Berth 1, Redoubt St., 0800/347-482, www.fishtaupo.co.nz, $110 per hour) is an excellent value, especially for small groups interested in heading onto Lake Taupo. All equipment is included in the rates.

If you'd rather head solo to the lake or river banks, make for **Taupo Rod and Tackle** (7 Tongariro St., 07/378-5337, www.tauporodandtackle.co.nz, 8am-5pm Mon.-Fri., 8am-4pm Sat.-Sun., adults $17, children $4.50) to rent equipment and buy a fishing license.

Biking

The **Great Lake Trail** (www.nzcycletrail.com) is a 71km Great Ride completed over two days. The path follows the northwestern shoreline starting from the Waihaha River carpark (Western Bay Rd.) connecting to Whakaipo Bay. A reasonable level of fitness is required to complete the Grade III route, which navigates native bush around the lake and includes spectacular vantage points over Tongariro. If you don't fancy completing the whole route, **Chris Jolly Outdoors** (Kinloch Marina, 07/378-0623, www.chrisjolly.co.nz) operates boat transfers to points along the track, with space on the boat for bikes.

A local Great Ride, the **Timber Trail** (www.thetimbertrail.com) is a Grade II-III track. The two-day jaunt stretches 85km between Pureora Forest Village and Ongarue, 130km west of Taupo. It rises to 980m along old tramlines, through native bush, and over eight thrilling suspension bridges. The track begins from the car park on the eastern side of the Waihaha River Bridge on Western Bay Road (Hwy. 32).

Bungee Jumping

New Zealand's tallest water-dunk bungee jump, **Taupo Bungy** (202 Spa Rd., 0800/888-408, www.taupobungy.co.nz, 9:30am-5pm daily summer, 9:30am-4pm daily winter, $169) towers 47m above an exceptionally scenic section of the Waikato River, its sapphire waters framed by silver cliffs fringed with forest. Keep your eyes peeled as you plunge from the platform toward the water's surface—you may spot trout. The company also operates the Cliffhanger ($145), an extreme swing with a nearly 180-degree arc that launches you out and over the water at speeds of up to 70km/h. Count down to your release or opt for the surprise drop. Both activities can be combined with a friend ($264).

Skydiving

Taupo is one of the world's best skydiving regions, as you're rewarded with coast-to-coast views that frame Lake Taupo and several other lakes, along with iconic volcanic peaks like "Mount Doom." Weather permitting, **Skydive Taupo** (Anzac Memorial Dr., 07/378-4662, $279-659) operate daily tandem jumps from 12,000 to 15,000 feet, taking off from Taupo airport, with photo and video packages offered. The free shuttle service collects from Taupo and Rotorua. Allow two to three hours for the entire experience.

Flightseeing

Passengers aboard Taupo's **Floatplane** (Ferry Rd., 07/378-7500, www.tauposfloatplane.co.nz, adults $109-830, children $55-415) may choose from numerous flightseeing options ranging from 10 minutes to two hours, covering the airspace above the lake and town of Taupo and its geothermal surrounds to the snowy peaks of Tongariro National Park, and as far as White Island, New Zealand's only offshore active volcano. All flights are bookended by the thrill of taking off from, and landing on, the lake. **Inflight Charters** (33 Anzac Memorial Dr., 07/377-8805, www.inflitetaupo.co.nz, $99-695) operate helicopter tours that stretch from 9 to 90 minutes, hovering over iconic sites like the Maori rock carvings, Mounts Tongariro and Tarawera, and the Kaimanawa Ranges.

FESTIVALS AND EVENTS

This supremely scenic location attracts a raft of world-class events that belies the town's relatively puny size. The ever-expanding **Taupo Summer Concert** (www.greenstoneentertainment.co.nz, Jan.), a one-day rock and pop extravaganza, takes place in the open-air Taupo Amphitheatre, with the lake, Waikato River, and mountains as a backdrop. Alanis Morissette is among its previous headline acts.

The wondrous **Wanderlust** (www.wanderlust.com, Mar.) brings its New Zealand leg to the shores of Lake Taupo for three days of yoga, meditation, music, and all things wellness. **Ironman** (www.ironman.com, Mar.) sees finely tuned triathletes battle it out around town, luring thousands of spectators.

The five-day **Taupo Winter Festival** (www.taupowinterfestival.co.nz, July) includes art exhibitions and music and comedy performances in venues across town.

Summer starts in style thanks to **Graffiato** (www.greatlaketaupo.com, Oct.), the nation's top street-art festival. International artists work their magic on more than 100 public sites over three days.

Around 7,000 bike riders—from kids through to professionals—take part in the street and off-road races of the **Lake Taupo Cycle Challenge** (www.cyclechallenge.com, Nov.), the largest event of its kind in New Zealand.

FOOD

The best eating and drinking joints are along the lakefront and the blocks directly behind. In the heart of town, **Bodyfuel Café** (67 Tongariro St., 07/378-9555, 7am-4pm Mon.-Fri., 7:30am-3:30pm Sat.-Sun., $7-21) is an unassuming, industrial-inspired space that prides itself on fresh organic fare and great coffee. Try the eggs florentine with smoked salmon—and it's never too early for carrot cake.

A little way out of town, bucolic ★ **L'Arte Café** (255 Mapara Rd., 07/378-2962, www.larte.co.nz, 8am-4pm Wed.-Sun., $12-18) is as much a visual feast as a culinary one, and an absolute Taupo must-do. Tuck into a bacon-and-avocado breakfast or an antipasto platter as you sip on wine surrounded by gardens adorned with colorful sculptures and Gaudí-esque mosaics.

The **Rose on Roberts** (92 Roberts St., 07/376-8030, www.roseonroberts.co.nz, 5pm-close daily, $27-32) is an inviting mock-Tudor gastropub. Contrasting modern dishes like braised lamb with *boulangère* potato or venison sausages with colcannon mash and seasonal greens arrive exquisitely presented. Pair your meal with one of the craft beers.

Crafty Trout Brewing Company (135 Tongariro St., 07/929-8570, www.craftytrout.co.nz, noon-close Wed.-Mon., $18-28) offers a respectable selection of in-house brewed beer and cider in a quirky fishing lodge-cum-alpine chalet setting. A nicely priced menu includes pasta, burgers, and ribs, but the wood-fired pizzas are the stars of this show. Enjoy the street view from the wonderful buzzy balcony.

If you're hankering for some spice, book a reservation at Taupo's best exotic eatery: ★ **Lotus Thai** (137 Tongariro St., 07/376-9497, www.lotusthai.co.nz, 6pm-9:30pm Mon., noon-2pm and 6pm-9pm Wed.-Fri., 6pm-9:30pm Sat.-Sun., $19-30). A smattering of Southeast Asian knickknacks and pictures lend a cozy feel, enhanced by warm and colorful curries and Thai broths. There are plenty of light dishes as well, like lotus noodles and an excellent duck salad.

Taupo's most upscale establishment, ★ **The Bistro** (17 Tamamutu St., 07/377-3111, www.thebistro.nz, 5pm-close daily, $26-39) is a relaxed affair with a terrific staff. Sophisticated and seasonal fine-dining selections include strip-loin of lamb wrapped in bacon and grilled-eye scotch fillet with spiced cauliflower chutney. The extensive wine list features some of the best tipples from New Zealand.

ACCOMMODATIONS

This ever-thriving town has an ever-expanding selection of lodgings. Be warned that they fill fast owing to the plethora of year-round activities in the region.

Under $100

YHA hostel **Finlay Jacks** (20 Taniwha St., 07/378-9292, www.finlayjacks.co.nz, dorm $25-30, $40 s, $80 d) is well-priced, with en suite dorms, women-only lodgings, and a family room ($94). Pop-art images and vinyl records line the walls, lending a boutique vibe. There's a comfortable TV lounge with bean bags, a cheerful courtyard area, a café-inspired communal kitchen, and free Wi-Fi.

Away from the town center, the pristine ★ **Haka Lodge** (56 Kaimanawa St., 07/377-0068, www.hakalodge.com, dorm $28-33, $69-79 s or d) is Taupo's best backpacker lodging. Airy, spacious, and modern, it boasts an extensive deck with lake and mountain views, a colorful and well-stocked kitchen, comfortable communal areas, free Wi-Fi, and a hot tub. Private rooms are hotel standard, while dorms have curtained bunks for privacy; some have en suite baths.

For a hostel in the heart of Taupo, head to lively **Urban Retreat** (65 Heu Heu St., 07/378-6124, www.tur.co.nz, dorm $24-30, $75-80 s or d), a sociable backpacker hostel with free limited Wi-Fi, a pool table, a TV room filled with couches, and a sunny and well-maintained garden and deck area with a bar with regular happy hours. Dorms come with lockable storage; some private rooms are available with en suite baths.

$100-200

Absolute Lakeview Motel (58 Lake Terrace, 07/378-4440, www.absolutelakeview.co.nz, $115-240) offers modern affordable lodgings, from en suite studios to two-bedroom suites. Several rooms come with private spas, balconies, and views of the lake. Amenities include

Sky TV, free Wi-Fi, tea- and coffee-making facilities, heating, and air-conditioning. Cooking equipment is available. The small indoor swimming pool is solar-heated, and there's communal exercise equipment, a spa, and a sauna.

Pine-paneled walls ensure a cozy environment at the **Wellesley on the Lake Taupo** (100 Lake Terrace, 07/376-0116, www.wellesleyhoteltaupo.co.nz, $122-225), an excellent value. En suite rooms include plush bedding and feature Sky TV, free Wi-Fi, hot-drink-making facilities, and toiletries; some rooms come with lake views. Guests are invited to use the hot tub and outdoor swimming pool. The beach is a one-minute stroll away.

$200-300

The classy **Phoenix Resort** (212 Lake Terrace, 07/378-7216, www.phoenixresort.co.nz, $200-350) offers some old-school charm, thanks to its ornate white architecture surrounded by rose gardens. All rooms feature a private mineral hot tub and bath, along with free Wi-Fi, cooking facilities, and Sky TV. Some units have balconies overlooking Lake Taupo.

Over $300

The architecturally fascinating ★ **Acacia Cliffs Lodge** (1/133 Mapara Rd., 07/378-1551, www.acaciacliffslodge.com, $650-750) sports floor-to-ceiling windows that reach the very corners of its angular roof overlooking Lake Taupo. Four luxurious and modern rooms boast private decks with views of the lake and Tongariro National Park. Amenities include Sky TV, free Wi-Fi, bathrobes, slippers, and toiletries. A gourmet breakfast is included, and guests receive a bottle of wine upon arrival. The bush-clad cliff-top lodge is a 10-minute drive from downtown.

Campgrounds and Holiday Parks

Much-loved **Taupo DeBretts** (Hwy. 5, 07/377-6502, www.taupodebretts.co.nz, 8:30am-9:30pm daily, adults $22, children and seniors $11, students $13, under age 3 $3, water slide $7) is a popular daytime destination thanks to its sprawling complex of geothermal mineral pools, spa, and water slides. The adjacent holiday park is family-oriented, with tent and RV sites ($27) and access to free Wi-Fi, barbecue areas, bike rentals, a full kitchen, and a TV room. There's an enormous range of cabins, motel rooms, chalets, and lodges ($90-270) with cooking facilities, private decks, and Sky TV; some units are fully self-contained and have lake views. Package deals include entry to the spa and pools. The campground is 4km southwest of Taupo.

Well-managed **All Seasons Kiwi Holiday Park** (16 Rangatira St., 07/378-4272, www.taupoallseasons.co.nz) is a restful site with powered and unpowered camp and van sites ($24-48) and fringe cabins and motel rooms ($72-165) that range from basic bed-only configurations to fully self-contained units with private decks overlooking the distant mountains. Amenities include a comfortable lounge area with Sky TV, a games room, plenty of outside seating, a barbecue area, a fully equipped kitchen, and a hot plunge pool. There is a fee for Wi-Fi. It's 1.5km from Lake Taupo; consider renting a bike for a leisurely ride.

TRANSPORTATION AND SERVICES

Taupo is 81km (1 hour) southwest of Rotorua along the Thermal Explorer Highway.

AIR

The **Taupo Airport** (TUO, 1105 Anzac Memorial Dr., 07/378-7771, www.taupoairport.co.nz) is 8km south of the city and is served by **Air New Zealand** (www.airnewzealand.co.nz) with connections to Auckland.

Public Transportation

National bus carriers **Intercity** (07/348-0366, www.intercity.co.nz) and **Naked Bus** (09/979-1616, www.nakedbus.com) stop in Taupo, as does North Island bus company **Mana Bus** (09/367-9140, www.manabus.com). For a cab, call **Blue Bubble Taxis**

(0800/228-294, www.taupo.bluebubbletaxi.co.nz) or **Great Lake Taxis** (07/377-8990, www.greatlaketaxis.co.nz).

Shuttles

Taupo Tours and Charters (308 Clearwater Lane, 027/767-8675, www.taupotoursandcharters.nz) operates a shuttle service between Taupo and the regional sights, as does **Adventure Shuttles** (1/504 Mapara Rd., 022/547-0399, www.adventureshuttles.co.nz). They also offer a bike rental service as well as biking and hiking tours.

Services

The **Taupo i-SITE Visitor Information Centre** (30 Tongariro St., 07/376-0027, www.greatlaketaupo.co.nz, 9am-5pm daily summer, 9am-4:30pm daily winter) has expert tour and accommodations advice. There's a central **post office** (46 Horomatangi St., 0800/081-190, www.nzpost.co.nz, 9am-5pm Mon.-Fri., 9am-noon Sat.), a **medical center** (37 Kaimanawa St., 07/378-4080, www.taupomedicalcentre.co.nz, 8am-5pm Mon.-Fri.), a **hospital** (38 Kotare St., 07/376-1000), and free Wi-Fi throughout town.

Turangi

If you want to get specific about the nation's trout fishing capital, then Turangi is it. The chilled-out town at the southern end of Lake Taupo serves as the northern gateway to Tongariro National Park and the launchpad to plenty of biking and rafting adventures on the nearby Tongariro River. If you're planning on staying overnight in the national park, this is the last stop to stock up on supplies.

SIGHTS

Tongariro National Trout Centre

Gawk at giant graceful trout via an underwater feeding chamber at the **Tongariro National Trout Centre** (Hwy. 1, 07/386-8085, www.troutcentre.com, 10am-4pm daily Dec.-Apr., 10am-3pm daily May-Nov., adults $15, children free), a hatchery that helps replenish local stocks. Check out other species, such as eels and mud fish, then amble along a selection of walking trails while being serenaded by birds. There's also a fishing pond for the kids. The Centre is 4km south of Turangi.

Tokaanu Thermal Pools

Tiny Tokaanu once served as the region's hub in pre-European times. Today the soothing mineral waters of **Tokaanu Thermal Pools** (Mangaroa St., 07/386-8575, 10am-9pm daily, adults $8, children $6, seniors $7, under age 5 free, private chlorine-free pools 10am-8pm daily, adults $12, children $8, seniors $10) offer an ideal post-hike soak. A 20-minute loop walk leads from Tokaanu Thermal Pools to some bubbling springs and mud pools among the native bush. See if you can spot rainbow trout in the adjacent cold stream. The pools are 6km west of Turangi.

RECREATION

Walks

The **Tongariro River Trail** is a 15km loop that follows the waterway through Waikari Reserve and past the Tongariro National Trout Centre. The easy track has numerous entries and exits that can be hiked or biked in sections. The most common entry point is from the Turangi i-SITE; use the underpass to avoid crossing Highway 1.

Lake Rotopounamu is a blissful 5km walk that circles the crater lake west of Mount Pihanga. You'll pass the occasional beach as you ramble through dense bird-filled forests, home to the North Island robin, kaka, and kereru. Begin the track opposite the parking area off Highway 47 (on the south side of Te Ponanga Saddle), 11km west of Turangi.

Mountain Biking

Tongariro River Rafting (95 Atirau Rd., 0800/101-024, www.trr.co.nz, 2 hours $30, half-day $40, full-day $50) operates an excellent mountain bike service for all riding levels. You'll enjoy exclusive access to a 3,800ha area (including a high-country sheep station) laced with well-marked tracks through ancient forests and alongside rivers and volcanoes. Transportation is provided to and from the trails. Guided tours include the **Tongariro River Track** ($50), a family-friendly 10km round-trip along the banks of the winding river, and the **Tree Trunk Gorge** ($85), a 10km round-trip that includes river crossings over old wooden bridges (or sometimes straight through the water). Rafting and biking combo deals are available.

Rafting

The region's rivers afford some of North Island's most joyous rafting adventures. **Rafting New Zealand** (41 Ngawaka Place, 0800/865-226, www.raftingnewzealand.com) operates half- and full-day tours for all levels. The most popular is the half-day **Tongariro White Rafting** (9am-2pm daily Nov.-mid-Apr., noon daily late Apr.-Nov., adults $179, children $149), a 14km Class-III voyage via 50-plus sets of rapids through a volcanic gorge. A hot shower, a hot dog, and hot chocolate are included. Free pickups are available. For greater thrills and spills, opt for the "extreme" **Wairoa River Rafting** (times vary Oct.-May, adults $179), a Class V tour that tackles notorious rapids with ominous names like Devil's Elbow and Mother's Nightmare.

Tongariro River Rafting (95 Atirau Rd., 0800/101-024, www.trr.co.nz) runs the gentle **Family Float** (adults $95, children $79, 10:30am and 3:30pm daily summer, 9am daily winter), a 1.5-hour raft along the lower Tongariro River punctuated with occasional benevolent rapids. The 2.5-hour Class-III **white-water tour** (9am and 2pm daily summer, 9am and 1pm daily Apr.1-20, noon daily winter, adults $139, children $125) takes on more than 60 thrilling rapids through a highly scenic bush-clad stretch of waterway.

Fishing

The professional anglers at **Ken Drummond Fishing Guide** (209 Hwy. 1, 07/386-0411, www.troutfish.co.nz, half-day $380, full-day $680) know the best spots to find brown and rainbow trout. Equipment is included, as is lunch if you opt for the full-day option. Prices are for one or two people, so bring a friend.

Lake Rotopounamu

If you'd rather go it alone and unguided, head down to **Sporting Life** (The Mall, 07/386-8996, www.sportinglife-turangi.co.nz, 8:30am-5:30pm Mon.-Sat., 9:15am-5pm Sun.) to rent equipment and buy a fishing license ($65 for 24 hours, $99 full season). Licenses are also available online from DoC (www.doc.govt.nz).

FOOD

Travel back in time at the **Cadillac Café** (35 Ohuanga Rd., 07/386-0552, 8:30am-3pm daily, $7-22), a local icon with a quirky take on a 1950s American diner. Sit amid vintage furniture and pop-culture prints as you tuck into pancakes, toasted sandwiches, burgers, smoothies, and shakes.

Turangi Tavern (17 Ohuanga Rd., 07/386-6071, 11am-close daily, $13-24) is a no-nonsense drinking den that hosts live music and sports on the TV. Traditional pub grub includes staples like burgers, steak, and bangers and mash alongside a lengthy pizza list. There's a respectable row of beers on tap.

The **Parklands Restaurant & Bar** (Parklands Motor Lodge, 25 Te Ahrahori St., 07/386-7515, www.parklandsmotorlodge.co.nz, 6pm-close Mon.-Sat., $25-34) is open to nonguests and serves super fish dishes, a T-bone steak, and mouth-watering apple-glazed lamb cutlets. The old-school dessert list includes classics like banana split, knickerbocker glory, and chocolate fudge cake.

The peaceful scenic Braxmere holiday complex hosts one of the region's best eateries, the **Lakeside House** (88 Waihi Rd., 07/386-6442, www.braxmere.co.nz, 10am-3pm and 6pm-close daily, $20-40). Tuck into a contemporary menu of pasta, venison, and snapper, all enjoyed while overlooking the lake.

ACCOMMODATIONS

These lodging rates listed reflect summer rates. Some of the region's lodgings may cost more during ski season; check prices when booking.

Rich timbers with reds and purple furnishings lend warmth to BBH-affiliated **Riverstone Backpackers** (222 Te Rangituatahanga Rd., 07/386-7004, www.riverstonebackpackers.com, dorm $35, $76-82 s or d), a homey hostel with free Wi-Fi, a cozy communal area, an herb garden, and a sunny deck with hammocks. En suite private rooms are available.

Near the town center, inviting **Parklands Motor Lodge** (25 Te Ahrahori St., 07/386-7515, www.parklandsmotorlodge.co.nz, $125-155) is surrounded by pristine gardens with views of Mount Pihanga. Guests choose between fully self-contained motel rooms or studio units with tea and coffee facilities. All have Sky TV and paid Wi-Fi, with use of the swimming pool, spa, sauna, and barbecue.

On the southern shores of Lake Taupo, ★ **Braxmere** (88 Waihi Rd., 07/386-6442, www.braxmere.co.nz, $189-300) is a boutique holiday complex that boasts modern waterside apartments with private patios, kitchens, and lounge areas.

★ **River Birches Lodge** (19 Koura St., 07/386-0445, www.riverbirches.co.nz, $650-950) is one of North Island's standout boutique accommodations. This woodland paradise is positioned on the banks of Tongariro River, where cedar-clad luxury suites (one has its own hot tub) sport comfy king beds. Views overlook the gardens. Amenities include bathrobes, free Wi-Fi, tea and coffee, and toiletries.

TRANSPORTATION AND SERVICES

Turnagi is 131km (1 hour, 40 minutes) southwest of Rotorua along Highway 1 and the Thermal Explorer Highway. National carrier **Intercity** (07/348-0366, www.intercity.co.nz) buses stop daily at the Turangi i-SITE. **Turangi Alpine Shuttles** (0508/427-677, $50 round-trip, $35 one-way) operates a bus service between the Turangi i-SITE and

Tongariro National Park, including the alpine crossing walk.

The **Turangi i-SITE Visitor and Information Centre** (1 Ngawaka Place, 07/386-8999, www.greatlaketaupo.co.nz, 9am-4:30pm daily) doubles as the DoC information bureau, offering regional and national travel advice and updates on local track and weather conditions.

Tongariro National Park

Tongariro National Park is the North Island's majestic, mountainous heart. It boasts dual UNESCO World Heritage Status, both for its cultural significance and its sheer beauty. Maori gifted the land to the British Crown in 1887; it officially became New Zealand's first national park in 1894. It is among New Zealand's most accessible natural attractions, luring one million visitors annually for hiking and skiing.

Tongariro covers the southern reaches of the Taupo Volcanic Zone, part of the Pacific Ring of Fire, a volcanic network that stretches from the tip of South America to the west coast of North America, across the Bering Strait, down to Japan, and to New Zealand. The first lava flows emerged 270,000 years ago; regular eruptions occurred over the following 200,000 years.

Three commanding peaks dominate the smoldering 80,000ha site: **Tongariro, Ruapehu,** and **Ngauruhoe.** To the north, the sprawling and somewhat disheveled Tongariro is the oldest volcano. It comprises a collection of smaller cones and craters, some of which erupted in 2012, the region's most recent volcanic activity of note.

Adjacent Mount Ngauruhoe is the beautifully formed, bruised cone that starred as Mount Doom in *The Lord of the Rings* films. At 2,500 years old, it is the region's newest volcano and the most active, erupting on average every nine years, although it has been silent since 1975.

Ruapehu is New Zealand's tallest volcano and the North Island's highest point, at 2,797m. From its mass protrudes a handful of smaller peaks. The mountain hosts the North Island's best skiing and its only glaciers. Its last eruption was in 2007, preceded by a couple of major blasts in 1995 and 1997. Prominent features include steaming fumaroles, mineral springs, lava deposits, volcanic desert, and glacial valleys.

Local *iwi*, Ngati Tuwharetoa, tell of North Island's godly mountains, once clustered together, battling for the love of Pihanga, a 1,350m peak to the north of the park, between lakes Rotoaira and Taupo. Tongariro, the "Warrior Mountain," emerged triumphant, forcing other peaks into retreat, including the mighty Mount Taranaki, who was banished to the west coast, carving out the Whanganui River in its wake. Maori consider the mountains guardians of the land.

RECREATION

★ Tongariro Alpine Crossing

New Zealand's most spectacular day hike is the **Tongariro Alpine Crossing** (www.doc.govt.nz), 19.4km of ever-changing gorgeousness. Though the trek can be completed in either direction, most begin at the Mangatepopo car park (Mangatepopo Rd., off Hwy. 47) and end at Ketetahi. Allow seven to eight hours for the challenging crossing, which begins at 1,120m. The crossing should be manageable by anyone with a reasonable level of fitness.

A relatively straightforward first hour follows the Mangatepopo Stream and past the fizzing Soda Springs. The track then rises steeply to the Mangatepopo Valley across the saddle between mounts Tongariro and Ngauruhoe—a.k.a. "Mount Doom." Hikers can no longer take the arduous side trip to scale Mount Ngauruhoe due to its sacred status. After passing through the rusted South Crater, the track rises again to Red Crater, the trail's highest point at 1,886m elevation. To go higher still, look for the signed side-trip to 1,967m Mount Tongariro summit, which adds 90 minutes to the trek.

The short, steep scree slope that follows sees many hikers slip onto their backsides as they head toward hypnotic Emerald Lakes that glimmer in the volcanic earth below. After reaching the northern slope of Tongariro, past Blue Lake, a well-formed trail marks the beginning of the zigzag descent as it snakes through tussock then under the shade of native bush.

GETTING THERE

During peak season (Oct.-Apr.), there is a four-hour parking limit at either end of the track to reduce congestion. Shuttle buses must be booked to and from the hike; ample services from nearby hubs are available. Outside the peak season, those with their own vehicle can park at Ketetahi car park (Hwy. 47) and arrange a shuttle bus with **Tongariro Expeditions** (07/377-0435, www.tongariro-expeditions.com) to the other end of the track at Mangatepopo.

Walks

World-class walks await at this UNESCO site. It's worth heading to the Turangi, Whakapapa Village, or Ohakne i-SITEs or DoC Visitor Centers for a Tongariro National Park brochure (or download it online at www.doc.gov.nz). The hiking season runs November-April. Those hiking outside the summer season should have alpine experience and carry equipment such as ice axes and crampons. Even during peak season, exposed sections of the park can suffer sudden deterioration in inclement weather, so always pack extra layers and a waterproof jacket.

The **Ridge Track** starts 150m above the DoC Whakapapa Visitor Center (Hwy., 48, Whakapapa Village), next to the public shelter. The 1.2km round-trip (2 hours) travels through beech forest to shrub lands and offers views of the iconic peaks of Mounts Ruapehu and Ngauruhoe. The **Taranaki Falls Trail** leads to a 20m waterfall that plunges over a 15,000-year-old lava flow into a boulder-strewn pool. The trailhead is 100m beneath the visitors center.

TONGARIRO NORTHERN CIRCUIT

If you're keen to do the Tongariro Alpine Crossing and then some, consider the

Tongariro Alpine Crossing

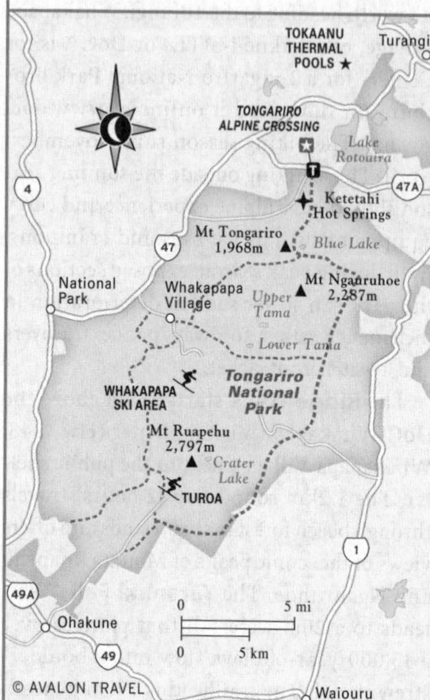

Tongariro Northern Circuit (3-4 days, 43km). The Great Walk circumnavigates Mount Ngauruhoe, starting and ending in Whakapapa Village. During peak season (Oct.-Apr.), huts (adults $32, under age 18 free) and campsites (adults $14, children free) must be booked in advance either from the Whakapapa Visitor Centre or any DoC office (www.doc.govt.nz).

CRATER LAKE

The **Crater Lake Track** is a six-hour round-trip hike that takes in views of Mount Ruapehu's crater lake, the national park's iconic ridges, and even Lake Taupo on a clear day. From the Whakapapa ski area chairlift, the trail rises 650m to the top of Mount Ruapehu. The route is not signed; at the ski lift, look right for the Knoll Ridge T-bar over to Restful Ridge. Follow the ridgeline to the crater area and return the same way. The track should only be attempted in summer; conditions can change quickly, so pack extra warm layers and waterproof clothing.

Adrift (53 Carroll St., National Park Village, 07/892-2751, www.adriftnz.co.nz, $255 pp) operates summer and winter guided tours of the Crater Lake Track. The eight-hour tours include transportation, lunch, and winter equipment.

ROUND THE MOUNTAIN

The magnificent **Round the Mountain Track** (4-6 days, 66km loop) begins 100m below Whakapapa Visitor Centre (Hwy. 48, Whakapapa Village) where it circumnavigates Mount Ruapehu. This dramatic and diverse trek takes in the park's iconic three peaks, plus beech forests, glacial gorges, waterfalls, suspension bridges, river crossings, and the Rangipo Desert. This multi-day hike can be walked in either direction. DoC-maintained huts and campsites (www.doc.govt.nz) are scattered along the route. During peak season (Oct.-Apr.), huts should be booked in advance. Visit the DoC visitors center (Hwy. 48, Whakapapa Village) for tickets, maps, trail updates, and weather conditions.

Skiing

The North Island's highest peak is home to its only ski hills of note. Whakapapa and Turoa both offer 700m vertical descents and ski runs for all levels. The season generally runs late June to mid-October, though it sometimes stretches into November. **Mount Ruapehu** (06/385-8456, www.mtruapehu.com, adults $79-119, children $47-69) sells day passes to both Whakapapa and Turoa and can hook you up with clothing, skis, snowboards, and toboggans. They are represented at **SLR @ Vertigo Adventure Centre** (27 Ayr St., Ohakune, 06/385-9018, www.slr.co.nz, 9am-5pm daily) and **Snow Depot** (29 Tongariro St., 07/892-4000, 9am-5pm daily). They can also arrange ski and snowboard lessons. There are no accommodations on the mountain.

Tongariro Flora and Fauna

Tongariro National Park's volcanic soils host a diverse eco-system, especially in the alpine zone. Podocarp forest carpets the lower levels of the park, along with the indestructible shrubbery that fringes parts of the Rangipo Desert to the east. Climb above 1,000m and life gets more interesting.

Mountain beech forest is abundant, along with the twisted trunked mountain cedar and cabbage trees. During summer, daisies, buttercups, foxgloves, and gentian bloom. Gold and red tussock competes with introduced heather, while red—and sporadically white and orange—mistletoe occasionally creeps up the beech trees. Leek-leaved orchids, green-hooded orchids, and sun orchids are also found at altitude.

The North Island brown kiwi scavenges the forest floors, and though you're unlikely to spot them in the daytime, you may catch glimpses of another endangered native bird, the *whio*, or blue duck, cruising a mountain stream. Other rare species include the kaka, falcon, and parakeet, while the tomtit, tui, rifleman, fantail, and wood pigeon are more common.

WHAKAPAPA

On the northwest slopes of Ruapehu sprawls New Zealand's largest ski area, **Whakapapa.** Runs stretch over 550ha, housing first-class beginner slopes, most notably in the Happy Valley section. An abundance of steep chutes, gullies, secret powder stashes, and backcountry trails cater to the more advanced skier. On clear days, carve up the pistes with a mind-blowing view of snowcapped Mount Doom in the distance. The on-site **Knoll Ridge** (07/892-4000, www.visitruapehu.com, 9:15am-4pm daily) is the highest mountainside café in New Zealand. Whakapapa is a 10-minute drive south of Whakapapa Village. The **Whakapapa chair lift** (Bruce Rd., 06/385-8456, www.mtruapehu.com, adults $35 children $20) runs year-round, but closes during adverse conditions.

TUROA

Carpeting Ruapehu's southwest slopes are the ski hills of **Turoa,** where you'll find the nation's longest vertical descent (720m). There's a massive variety of tempting terrain for the skilled skier, as well as natural half-pipes and chutes for skiers and snowboarders. The Alpine Meadow area caters to novices, with wide sweeping tracks that will keep all entertained. Turoa is most easily accessed 19km southwest from Okahune along Okahune Mountain Road.

Flightseeing

Mountain Air (Chateau Airstrip, Hwy. 47, 07/892-2812, www.mountainair.co.nz, from 8am daily, 2-person minimum, $120-295 pp) operates a handful of fixed-wing flights that cruise 10,000 feet over Tongariro's peaks, lakes, rivers, and craters. Flights range 15 minutes to one hour.

WHAKAPAPA VILLAGE

Whakapapa Village was purpose-built in the 1920s to serve skiers and outdoors enthusiasts—a role it still enjoys to this day. Positioned at the foot of Mount Ruapehu, the tiny alpine town is the only official settlement within the national park's borders.

Food and Accommodations

Fuel up for a day of hiking at **Fergusson's Café** (Hwy. 48, 07/892-3809, www.chateau.co.nz, 7am-6pm daily), across from the visitors center. The all-day menu includes egg breakfasts, meat pies, sandwiches, and proper coffee. Positioned at 2,020m atop Mount Ruapehu, **Knoll Ridge Café** (07/892-4000, www.visitruapehu.com, 9:15am-4pm daily) has mind-blowing views and a belly-filling menu packed with hearty offerings, such as toasties and curries and a splendid selection of sugary baked treats.

Whakapapa's local drinking den is the **Tussock Bar and Tavern** (12a Hwy. 48,

07/892-3809, www.chateau.co.nz, 7am-11pm daily, $23-27). This is where folks kick back and relax after a day hiking or skiing the slopes. There's sports on the big screen and a menu of burgers, pizza, steak, and bangers and mash to quickly replace those expended carbs.

Skotel (Ngauruhoe Place, 0800/756-835, www.skotel.co.nz) offers all the trappings you'd expect from an alpine resort complex—a ski-drying room, a hot tub, and a bar with a scenic terrace and an open fireplace. Accommodations for backpackers include cozy cabin-like dorms ($60) with three or four beds and sinks or en suite doubles ($100) with TVs and hot-drink facilities. Stand-alone self-contained cabins ($181) have decks overlooking the park, TVs, and a lounge area. The timber-clad en suite rooms ($138-230) come with tea- and coffee-making facilities, TVs, and private balconies with stunning mountain views.

The visually imposing **Chateau Tongariro Hotel** (Hwy. 48, 07/892-3809, www.chateau.co.nz, $195-296) has few peers. The 1920s alpine retreat looks like something out of *The Sound of Music*, with a backdrop of snowy peaks. Comfortable rooms have TVs, desks, and armchairs, but don't quite tally up to the magnificence of the exterior. All have en suite baths, though some have showers and no tub; not all have alpine views. Elegant and enormous, this palace has its own golf course, tennis courts, gym, bar, games room, sauna, pool, and cinema.

Dine on Whakapapa's poshest nosh at the hotel's ★ **Ruapehu Room** (6am-10am, noon-2pm, and 6pm-9:30pm daily fall-spring, 7am-10am, noon-2pm, and 6pm-9:30pm daily winter, $32-38) where chandeliers dangle from high ceilings supported by columns and bordered by giant windows. The elegant menu befits its surroundings and changes seasonally. Expect the likes of seared Atlantic salmon or beef tenderloin. Reservations are essential, and there is a dress code; men must wear shirts with a collar.

Delightful **Whakapapa Holiday Park** (Hwy. 48, 07/892-3897, www.whakapapa.net.nz) is perfectly positioned for both the Tongariro Alpine Crossing and the Whakapapa ski area. Guests choose from powered or unpowered tent or RV sites ($23) set in a beech forest or beside a stream. Amenities include free Wi-Fi (but the signal can be sketchy), a kitchen, a ski-drying room, barbecues, and a general store. Bring your own bedding for the basic dorm rooms ($28)

Chateau Tongariro Hotel

and lodges ($76). Lodges are equipped with a full kitchen but share bath facilities. There's a shuttle bus service to the alpine crossing and ski hills.

Transportation and Services

Whakapapa Village is 48km (35 minutes) southwest of Turangi along Highway 47; it's 50km northeast of Ohakune along Highway 4. **ROAM** (0800/762-612, www.roam.net.nz, adults $35, children $25, one-way) offers shuttle bus services from Whakapapa Village to the Tongariro Crossing.

The **Tongariro National Park Visitor Centre** (Hwy. 48, 07/892-3729, www.doc.govt.nz, 8am-5pm daily summer, 8:30am-4:40pm daily winter) doubles as a DoC information bureau and i-SITE tourist hub, with audio-visual and interactive guides to the region. Pick up trail maps, leaflets, tour information, and Hut tickets.

NATIONAL PARK VILLAGE

The nondescript National Park Village offers plenty of accommodations, most on Findlay and Carroll Streets, with some stunning volcanic views. There's little else to capture the imagination, unless being New Zealand's highest township (825m) counts.

Ski Biz Outdoor Shop (10 Carroll St., 07/892-2717, www.skibiz.co.nz, 7:30am-7pm Mon.-Thurs., 7am-midnight Fri., 7am-7pm Sat.-Sun.) rents summer and winter gear for tramping and camping, including skis, snowboards, and crampons.

Accommodations

The YHA- and BBH-affiliated **National Park Backpackers** (4 Findlay St., 07/892-2870, www.npbp.co.nz, dorm $28-30, $62-86 s or d) is the closest hostel to the Tongariro Alpine Crossing. Smiling staff and timber-panel decor create a certain warmth, and the basic rooms are meticulously kept. Double and twin beds are available in en suite rooms; tent sites cost $15 pp. Facilities include a well-stocked kitchen, a cozy communal area with a wood fire, and a shuttle bus to the alpine crossing. Don't leave without scaling their climbing wall.

All bases and budgets are catered to at **Plateau Lodge** (17 Carroll St., 07/892-2993, www.plateaulodge.co.nz, dorm $40, $78-165 s or d). Stellar accommodations include dorm rooms, hotel-style suites, and chalets with up to three bedrooms. Private lodgings are equipped with en suite baths and TVs; some have kitchens. Amenities include free Wi-Fi and a hot tub. RV sites ($40) are also available. A shuttle bus provides service to the crossing. Package deals with guided tours of the park are also offered.

Transportation and Services

National Park Village is 16km west of Whakapapa Village, at the intersection of Highways 4 and 47. Nationwide bus service **Intercity** (07/348-0366, www.intercity.co.nz) calls at National Park Village. The ***Northern Explorer*** (www.greatjourneysofnz.co.nz) train between Auckland and Wellington stops at the railway station (Station Rd.).

Adventure Outdoors (60 Carroll St., 07/892-2778, www.adventureoutdoors.co.nz) operates tours and services, such as guided walks through Tongariro National Park. Transportation and winter recreation equipment (ice axes and crampons) are included.

For bus service to and from the national park—and free secure storage of your vehicle while you're there—contact **Plateau Shuttle** (Carroll St., 07/892-2993, www.plateaulodge.co.nz). They also serve Whakapapa Village.

There's a visitor center and post office at **Macrocarpa Café** (3 Waimarino Tokaanu Rd., 07/892-2911, 6am-8pm daily).

OHAKUNE

Ohakune is the southern gateway town to Tongariro National Park. During winter, the thriving alpine town, brimming with chalets, serves as the most popular base for the Turoa ski hill, and once the snow has melted, it transforms into a chilled-out summer hub for trekkers and cyclists. Don't miss—well, you can't miss—the enormous fiberglass carrot on the side of Highway 49 on the way in or out, a nod to the local farming heritage.

Walks

The **Mangawhero Forest Walk** (Ohakune Mountain Rd.) is an easy one-hour trek that crosses the Mangawhero River before winding through a forest of rimu, matai, and kahikatea trees, some of which tower more than 30m. The trail starts at the bottom of Ohakune Mountain Road and crosses a volcanic crater past volcanic vents.

From Ohakune Railway Station (Thames St.) the wonderful **Old Coach Road** (15km one-way) follows an old rail route across cobbled roads, through an arching tunnel, and over enormous viaducts. It's an easy path, but a long one; you may want to cycle it.

Biking

Mountains to Sea (www.mountainstosea.co.nz) is a 200km three-day Great Ride that takes in the Tongariro and Whanganui National Parks. The trail descends 1,600m from Ohakune Railway Station (Thames St.) to finish at Whanganui and the Tasman Sea. Highlights include Tongariro's alpine views, the historic Old Coach Ride, and the majestic Whanganui River—crossed by jet-boat.

For bike, ski, and snowboard rentals, head to **TCB** (29 Ayr St., 06/385-8433, www.tcb.nz, 8am-6pm Sat.-Thurs., 8am-10pm Fri., $35 half-day, $50 full-day).

Food and Accommodations

Fuel up with excellent coffee and a legendary breakfast burrito at Ohakune's hippest café, **Eat Takeaway Diner** (49 Clyde St., 020/4126-5520, 8am-3pm daily, $7-15). The contagiously friendly staff take great pride in their menu of organic and free-range fare.

Replenish your calories spent white-water rafting at **The Blind Finch** (29 Goldfinch St., 06/385-8076, www.theblindfinch.co.nz, 9am-close daily, $17), a supercool no-nonsense industrial eatery that serves cocktails and craft beer, and cooks their handcrafted burgers over an roaring open cast-iron fire.

It doesn't get more alpine than at the **Powderkeg** (194 Mangawhero Terrace, 06/385-8888, www.powderhorn.co.nz, 3pm-close daily, $22-36), a timber-swathed bar and restaurant with an enormous brick fireplace and snowboards adorning the walls. Known as "The Keg," the eatery's menu includes scotch fillet, market fish, or crispy skinned duck breast. Upstairs is the resplendent **Powderhorn Chateau** ($260-800) where the timber-clad theme continues. Rooms are complemented by plush bedding and leather furniture and are equipped with free Wi-Fi, Sky TV, and hot-drink facilities. Some rooms have balconies. There's also an indoor heated swimming pool.

YHA backpacker hostel **Station Lodge** (60 Thames St., 06/385-58797, www.stationlodge.co.nz, dorm $28, $70 s or d) is a cozy budget option in a pristine villa surrounded by a sprawling garden. A women-only dorm is available, along with modern and fully self-contained one- and two-bedroom apartments ($130-220). There's a fire in the lounge area, barbecue facilities, a wood-fired pizza oven, and free Wi-Fi. It's a short stroll from the town center.

Choose from studio or one-bedroom units at **Peaks Motor Inn** (Mangawhero Terrace and Shannon St., 06/385-9144, www.thepeaks.co.nz, $139-298). Guests get free Wi-Fi and Sky TV in all of the fully self-contained rooms, which have private terraces; some also have a spa bath. Communal amenities include a fitness center, a barbecue, laundry, and bike rentals.

Transportation and Services

Ohakune is 135km (1 hour, 45 minutes) southwest of Taupo via Highways 47 and 1; it's 286km (3.5 hours) northeast of Wellington via Highway 1. Nationwide bus service **Intercity** (07/348-0366, www.intercity.co.nz) calls at

Ohakune daily. The **Northern Explorer** (www.greatjourneysofnz.co.nz) train between Auckland and Wellington stops at the railway station (Thames St.).

The Ohakune **i-SITE Visitor Information Centre** (54 Clyde St., 0800/647-483, www.visitohakune.co.nz, 8am-5:30pm daily) serves as a DoC hub, with information on weather, trails, bike tracks, tours, attractions, services, and accommodations. Contact **Dempsey Buses** (24 Seddon St., 06/385-4022, www.dempseybuses.co.nz) for a shuttle into Tongariro National Park, as well as regional biking and hiking trails.

East Cape and Hawke's Bay

East Cape.......................213
Gisborne.......................218
Te Urewera.......................223
Napier and Hawke's Bay.......226

New Zealand's easternmost region is a windswept wilderness steeped in Maori legend, hemmed by feral coastline on one side and Te Urewera on the other.

This evocative and unspoiled backcountry is filled with bountiful birdlife, towering ridgelines, and glistening waterways. To the south, the city of Gisborne ("Gizzy") marks the first land meeting between Maori and Europeans in 1769. It's also the first city in the world to see the sun rise and the chardonnay capital of New Zealand. The wine theme continues farther south as East Cape tumbles into Hawke's Bay. Its Mediterranean climate and nutritious soil are ideal for growing grapes. It was here. in 1851, that French missionaries planted New Zealand's first vines. Their spectacular winery, Mission Estate, still welcomes visitors today.

Hawke's Bay's arches into the Cape Kidnappers peninsula, home of the world's largest mainland gannet colony. The bay is fronted by two cities: Hastings and Napier, drenched in a collection of art deco architecture that has few rivals. The majesty of Tolkien's Middle-earth melds with the fashion of F. Scott Fitzgerald. Dust off your spats, sip on an old-fashioned, and dine like it's 1929.

PLANNING YOUR TIME

Napier offers a convenient base from which to explore this relatively compact region. You'll want your own transport—but don't pass up the chance to tour the city's **art deco** sights in a vintage car. Spend at least one night in Napier with a day spent touring the surrounding **vineyards.** Tour and shuttle operators offer experiences with a designated driver.

An abundance of historical and natural splendor lies north, in the city of **Gisborne.** You'll need at least a day each for the isolated **East Cape** and **Te Urewera**—and ideally your own transport.

Previous: a classic car in Napier; riding the Motu Cycle Trails. **Above:** sunset view from Te Mata Peak.

Look for ★ to find recommended sights, activities, dining, and lodging.

Highlights

★ **Rere Rockslide:** This smooth rock bed lies beneath the surface of a river and doubles as a natural water slide (page 218).

★ **Lake Waikaremoana Great Walk:** This peaceful multiday tramp follows along a mythic Maori lake in Te Urewera (page 224).

★ **Art Deco Architecture:** Napier is home to one of the largest concentrations of art deco architecture in the world (page 226).

★ **Wine Tasting:** Taste exceptional wines at the place where the nation's viniculture industry was born (page 229).

★ **Te Mata Peak:** This 399m-high lookout affords awe-inspiring views of Hawke's Bay (page 234).

★ **Bird-watching at Cape Kidnappers:** This stunning, windswept headland is home to the world's largest gathering of Australasian gannets (page 236).

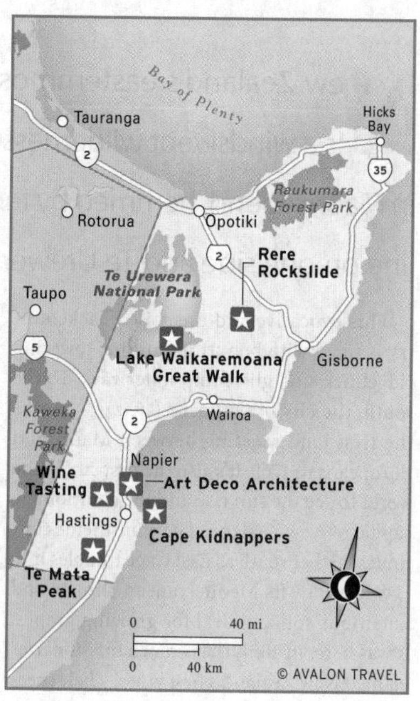

East Cape

East Cape is the northeast knuckle of North Island. Often referred to as Eastland or "out east," it separates the Bay of Plenty from Hawke's Bay. The region has an almost mythical isolation—you're as likely to see locals riding horseback as driving a car. The population here is predominantly Maori, which is fittingly poetic: It was this cape that welcomed some of the very first waves of their Polynesian ancestors nearly 1,000 years ago. Its ancient sands, whispering forests, and regal ranges have seen little change since.

OPOTIKI

Opotiki is the last town of significance as the Bay of Plenty merges into East Cape. It can serve as a launch point south to Te Urewera, though most choose to access that area from the eastern flanks of East Cape or from Hawke's Bay.

Sights

The volunteer-staffed **Opotiki Museum** (123 Church St., 07/315-5193, www.opotikimuseum.org.nz, 10am-4pm Mon.-Fri., 10am-2pm Sat., adults $10, children $5) is well presented, spread over three floors with pieces of machinery such as sewing machines, wagons, and tractors displayed along with a mock shop and school scenes from the pioneer days. The Maori collection includes tools, weapons, and musical instruments made from bone.

Recreation

The **Motu Trails** (www.motutrails.co.nz) are a collection of coastal biking tracks that form one of the Great Rides. They can be tackled either separately or linked together to form a giant loop. Some of the trails are intermediate and expert levels, and so are not suitable for all riders.

The easiest and most accessible track is the **Dunes Trail** (20km round-trip, 2-3 hours) along the waterfront. It begins at the Pakowhai ki Otutaopuku Bridge at Memorial Park Reserve (off Albert St.) and offers ample opportunity to kick back on the beach for lunch and to cool off in the surf. It's also an e-bike friendly track.

Just 1km from the start of the Dunes Trail, **Motu Cycle Trails** (135 St. John St., 07/315-5864, www.motucycletrails.com, 6am-6pm daily summer, 9am-3pm daily winter) rents bikes and has maps and route information. The company also provides secure parking and shuttle bus service to the local trails.

Food and Accommodations

The best dining is at vibrant **Two Fish Café** (102 Church St., 07/315-5448, 8am-3pm Mon.-Fri., 8am-2pm Sat., $7-22), where hearty breakfasts—bacon, eggs, and hash browns—accompany homemade offerings like burgers and seafood chowder. For a quick sweet treat, grab an espresso and a blueberry muffin.

Motu Cycle Trails (135 St. John St., 07/315-5864, www.motucycletrails.com) has a no-frills **bunkhouse** (dorm $30, $30 s, $60-70 d) that is immaculately kept, with a communal kitchen and barbecue area; a double with an en suite bath is also offered. Upgrade to the self-contained unit (maximum 4 guests, $35 pp) with its own TV and a private deck with barbecue.

Transportation and Services

Opotiki is 44km (40 minutes) east of Whakatane via Highway 2. National bus company **Intercity** (09/583-5780, www.intercity.co.nz) calls at Opotiki daily en route between Gisborne and Auckland. Local operator **Bay Bus** (www.baybus.co.nz, Mon. and Wed.) connects Opotiki and Whakatane.

The **i-SITE Visitor Information Centre** (70 Bridge St., 07/315-3031, www.opotikinz.com, 9am-4:30pm Mon.-Fri., 9am-1pm Sat.-Sun.) offers tourist and travel advice, and

East Cape and Hawke's Bay

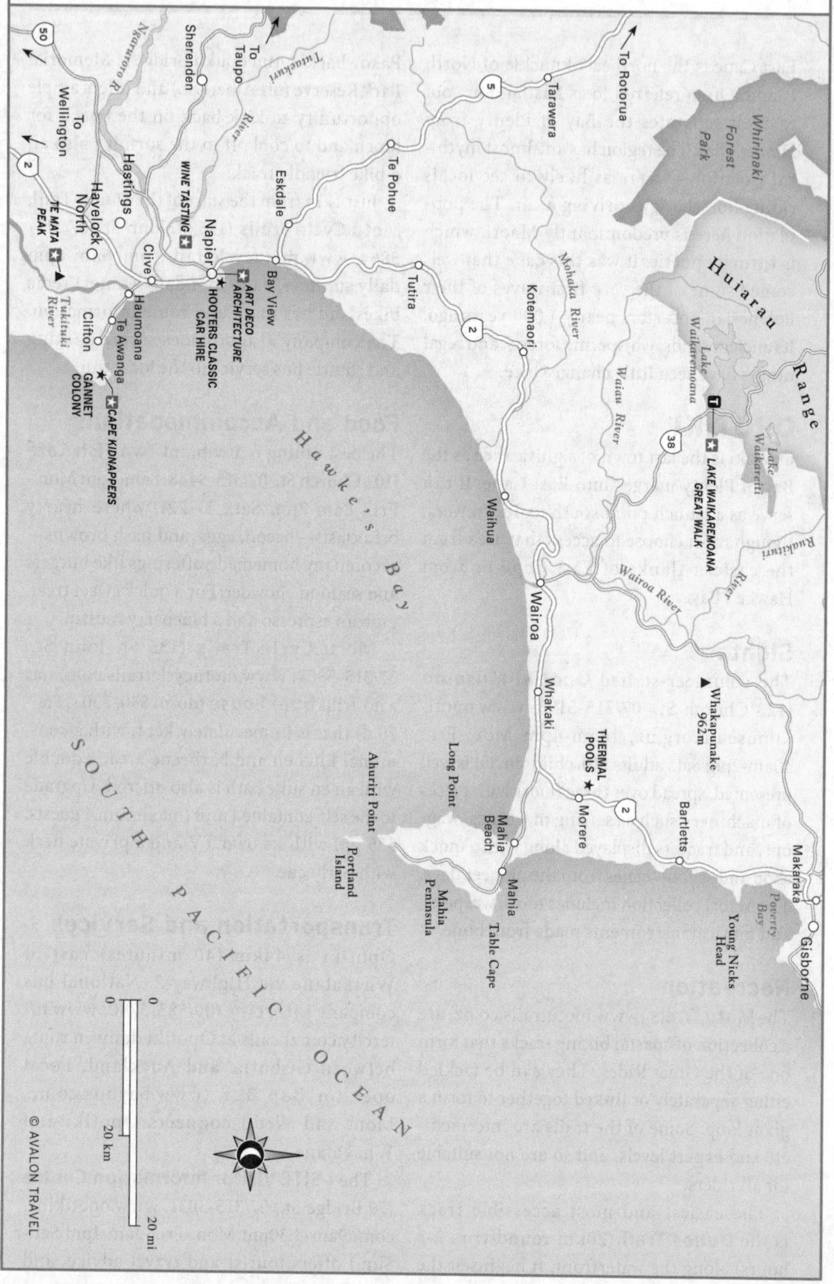

To Rotorua
Tarawera
5
Whirinaki Forest Park
Huiarau Range
Lake Waikaremoana
Lake Waikareiti
LAKE WAIKAREMOANA GREAT WALK
38
Ruakituri River
Wairoa River
Waiau River
Mohaka River
Te Pohue
Eskdale
Tutira
Kotemaori
Bay View
2
Waihua
Wairoa
Whakaki
Whakapunake 962m
THERMAL POOLS
Morere
Barletts
Makaraka
Poverty Bay
Gisborne
Young Nicks Head
Table Cape
Mahia
Mahia Peninsula
Mahia Beach
Long Point
Ahuriri Point
Portland Island
Hawke's Bay
SOUTH PACIFIC OCEAN
To Taupo
Tutaekuri River
Sherenden
Ngaruroro R.
50
To Wellington
2
WINE TASTING
Napier
ART DECO ARCHITECTURE
HOOTERS CLASSIC CAR HIRE
Hastings
Havelock North
TE MATA PEAK
Clive
Haumoana
Te Awanga
Clifton
Tukituki River
GANNET COLONY
CAPE KIDNAPPERS
0 20 mi
0 20 km

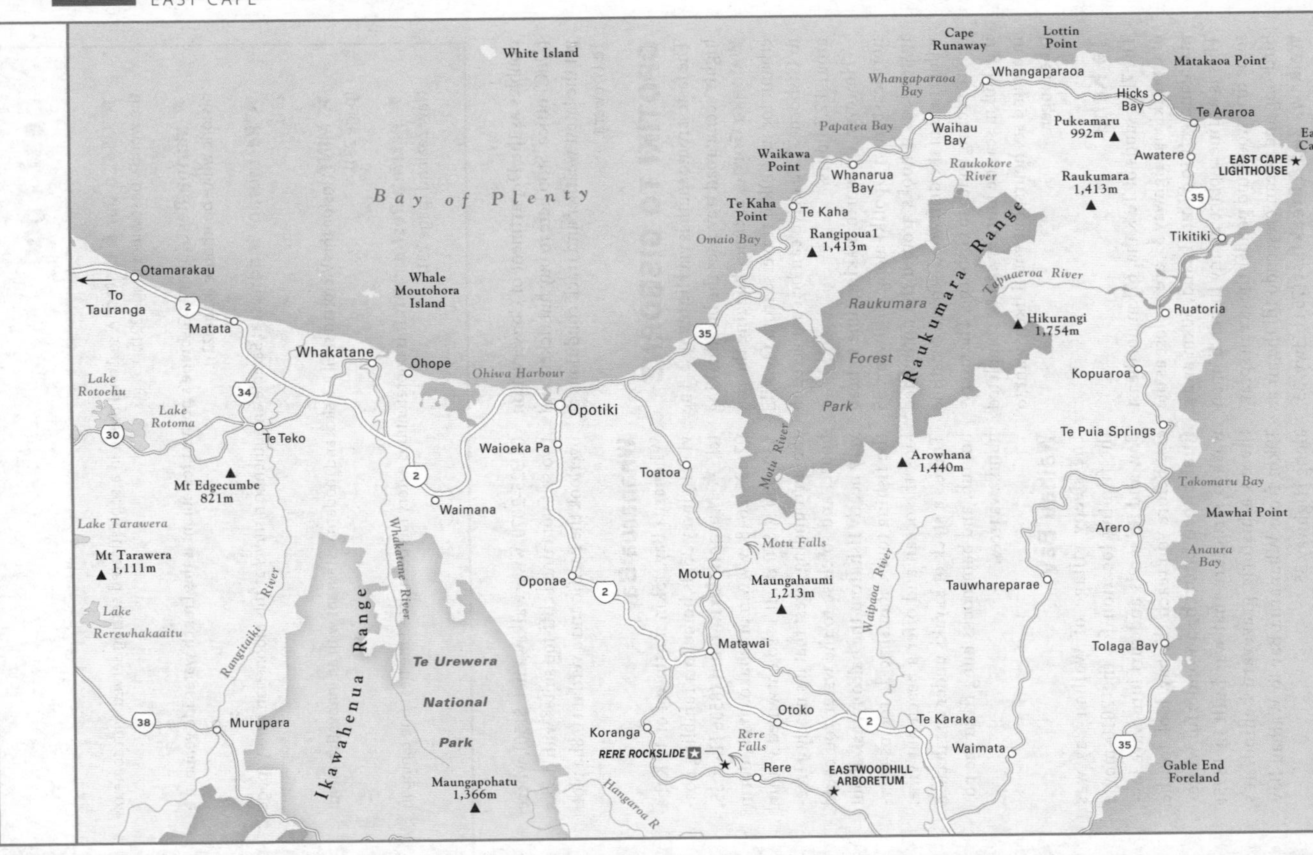
White Island
Bay of Plenty
Cape Runaway
Lottin Point
Matakaoa Point
Whangaparaoa
Whangaparaoa Bay
Hicks Bay
Te Araroa
East Cape
EAST CAPE LIGHTHOUSE
Papatea Bay
Waihau Bay
Pukeamaru 992m
Awatere
Waikawa Point
Whanarua Bay
Raukokore River
Raukumara 1,413m
Te Kaha Point
Te Kaha
Omaio Bay
Rangipoua1 1,413m
Raukumara Range
Tikitiki
Tapuaeroa River
Raukumara Forest Park
Hikurangi 1,754m
Ruatoria
Otamarakau
To Tauranga
Matata
Whale Moutohora Island
Whakatane
Ohope
Ohiwa Harbour
Opotiki
Kopuaroa
Lake Rotoehu
Lake Rotoma
Te Teko
Waioeka Pa
Te Puia Springs
Motu River
Arowhana 1,440m
Toatoa
Mt Edgecumbe 821m
Waimana
Tokomaru Bay
Mawhai Point
Lake Tarawera
Arero
Anaura Bay
Motu Falls
Mt Tarawera 1,111m
Whakatane River
Oponae
Motu
Maungahaumi 1,213m
Waipaoa River
Tauwhareparae
Rangitaiki River
Lake Rerewhakaaitu
Ikawahenua Range
Te Urewera National Park
Matawai
Tolaga Bay
Murupara
Otoko
Te Karaka
Koranga
Rere Falls
RERE ROCKSLIDE
Waimata
Rere
EASTWOODHILL ARBORETUM
Gable End Foreland
Maungapohatu 1,366m
Hangaroa R
2
30
34
35
38

Best Food

★ **USSCo Bar & Bistro:** A seasonal menu in a sophisticated setting served with some of the world's best wines (page 221).

★ **Marina Restaurant:** Gisborne's poshest restaurant is this French waterside venue in a historic white boathouse (page 221).

★ **Restaurant Indonesia:** Sample an authentic *rijsttafel* at this Indonesian eatery (page 231).

★ **MINT:** Inside this Victorian shell is a slick and modern restaurant with an innovative menu (page 231).

★ **Pacifica Restaurant:** This unpretentious eatery has been voted the best fine dining in New Zealand (page 231).

doubles as the Department of Conservation (DoC) office. Stop here to buy hut tickets and get the latest weather and track conditions at Te Urewera.

OPOTIKI TO GISBORNE

The fastest route south is via **Highway 2.** The highly scenic road traverses the breathtaking **Waioeka Gorge,** at times hugging the riverbank for its 140km traverse from Opotiki to Gisborne. The drive can be completed in around 2.5 hours.

However, it's worth making time to head northeast from Opotiki along **Highway 35** instead, as it hooks around the untouched wilderness of the driftwood-strewn coastline before veering south to Gisborne. The swerving 330km seaside journey can be completed in around six hours, but you'll likely want to take longer.

Te Kaha

The 7km sands of Te Kaha, 67km northeast of Opotiki via Highway 35, are as close as the mainland gets to White Island, 50km away. This is as fine a place as any to perch upon some driftwood and ponder the ocean spray. Birdsong and ocean crescendo fill the air at **Waikawa Bed & Breakfast** (7541 Hwy. 35, 07/325-2070, www.waikawa.net, $150), where two self-contained cliff-top suites with decks overlook the Pacific and a verdant 0.8ha plot.

Whanarua Bay

Whanarua Bay, 15km northwest of Te Kaha via Highway 35, is home to a rambling hostel, ★ **Maraehako Retreat** (8536 Hwy. 35, 07/325-2648, www.maraehako.co.nz, dorm $30, $50 s, $70 d). It is so entwined within the surrounding forest that it's nearly a treehouse, and so close to the water you could very nearly fish from the balcony; ask about the fishing tours. Ramshackle rooms overlook the ocean and offer a beach hut vibe. There's a stack of kayaks under the deck, a hot tub, and hammocks hung from the pohutukawa trees.

Waihau Bay

The sleepy village of Waihau Bay was the filming location for the 2010 movie *Boy,* and its sands and surf lure wave lovers. Before you reach the bay, look for the **Ruakokore Church,** a wonderful whitewashed structure that was built in 1895; there's a historic graveyard behind. It's 19km from Whanarua Bay to Waihau Bay along Highway 35.

Best Accommodations

★ **Maraehako Retreat:** This treehouse-entwined retreat is as close to the water as you can get (page 216).

★ **Stranded in Paradise Backpackers:** If you only have time to spend the night in one East Cape location, make it here (page 217).

★ **Whispering Sands Beachfront Motel:** A superb seaside value, fringing Waikanae Beach with views over Poverty Bay (page 221).

★ **Ridge House:** This exquisite B&B sits perched on 2.4ha of Gisborne farmland, with gardens, orchards, and ocean views (page 221).

★ **Mangapapa Hotel:** This colonial mansion oozes class, with regal suites, luxury amenities, and a fine-dining restaurant (page 236).

Te Araroa

You're halfway to Gisborne as you roll into Te Araroa, 56km east of Waihau Bay along Highway 35. The former whaling hub sprouts a gargantuan pohutukawa tree, said to be the largest in the land. South of the village's seafront, an unpaved road winds 22km past smaller pohutukawa trees and cliff faces to **East Cape Lighthouse.** The 360-degree view of Huatai Beach, across to Whangaokeno Island, and inland to the Ruakumara Ranges is worth the climb.

Tokomaru Bay

A little over an hour south of Te Araroa, 79km along Highway 35, idyllic Tokomaru Bay's commanding coastline promises to shoot straight to the top of your list of favorite Kiwi seaside spots. It's ideal for surfing and swimming, surrounded by a sprawling expanse of craggy green and gray hills and headlands. If you only have time to spend the night in one East Cape location, spend it here.

The fittingly named ★ **Stranded in Paradise Backpackers** (21 Potae St., 06/864-5870, www.stranded-in-paradise.net, dorm $32, $84 s or d) is a BBH hostel with free Wi-Fi, outdoor and indoor fires, barbecues, kayak rentals, and sea views from the veranda and rooms. Also available are basic single, double, and family cabins ($48-75) and nonpowered tent and van sites ($18 pp).

Tolaga Bay

Tolaga Bay is the first sign that you've made it back to civilization—by East Cape standards, anyway. The sleepy town's most prominent feature is its walkable 600m wharf, constructed in 1929 and said to be the longest of its kind in the southern hemisphere. The **Cooks Cove Walkway** starts at the car park on Wharf Road, 2km south of the township. It makes its way over farmland to a cliff-side track that snakes through forest to a cove where a plaque honors the visit by Captain James Cook in 1769. Allow 2.5 hours round-trip.

Tolaga Bay is 35km south of Tokomaru Bay along Highway 35. From here, it's a 45-minute drive south to Gisborne.

Gisborne

While Northland is known as the "Birthplace of the Nation," it's a title that could equally be applied to the city of Gisborne, or "Gizzy" to the locals. This site, overlooking Poverty Bay, is where Maori and Europeans first met on land when Captain Cook arrived in 1769.

SIGHTS

Tairawhiti Museum

Tairawhiti Museum (10 Stout St., 06/867-3832, www.tairawhitimuseum.org.nz, 10am-4pm Mon.-Sat., 1:30pm-4pm Sun., adults $5, under age 13 free) tells of the first Maori and Europeans to settle in New Zealand. There's a big maritime focus, including whaling equipment, carved whalebone, *waka* displays, the original wheelhouse and captain's quarters from the *Star of Canada* wreck that sank off the coast in 1912, and a wonderfully incongruous collection of vintage surfboards. It also houses the city's main art gallery. The museum is in Kelvin Park, adjacent to the river.

Cook Monument

Positioned on Kaiti Beach Road near the estuary, an **obelisk** marks the first landing site of Captain James Cook, believed to be the first European to step on New Zealand soil (it was also the landing point of the first Polynesian canoe, the Horouta *waka*). It's hardly the most attractive of tributes; head instead to the walking track that leads up nearby Kaiti Hill (also known as Titirangi Domain). Cook's Plaza overlooks the city and hosts a statue of the British explorer often mocked for bearing little resemblance to him.

East Coast Museum of Technology

At the **East Coast Museum of Technology** (67 Main Rd., 027/221-5703, www.ecmot.org.nz, 10am-4pm Sun.-Fri., 1pm-4pm Sat., adults $5, children $2), the technology on show is the kind that would help cultivate and process an apple as opposed to swiping at a screen. The volunteer-run establishment is full of character and showcases everything from vintage farm equipment, fire engines, and military vehicles to gas pumps and domestic appliances. The museum is a 5km drive northwest of downtown.

Eastwoodhill Arboretum

An upside-down record Down Under, **Eastwoodhill Arboretum** (2392 Wharekopae Rd., 06/863-9003, www.eastwoodhill.org.nz, 9am-5pm daily, adults $15, children $2, seniors $12, under age 5 free) is home to the largest collection of northern hemisphere trees (maples, oaks) in the southern hemisphere. The trees change dramatically in appearance between seasons—the autumnal hues are the most impressive. The resplendent 135ha plantation also hosts a native forest that is laced with 25km of walking trails and home to more than 40 species of exotic and endemic birds. The arboretum is 35km northeast of Gisborne via Wharekopae Road.

★ Rere Rockslide

The natural formation that is the **Rere Rockslide** is a super-smooth, 20m-wide rock face that slopes for 60m just beneath the surface of the Wharekopae River. Thrill-seekers can ride it either on an inflatable mattress, or, for more speed, a body board (bring your own). Afterward, saunter 2km downstream to where the beautifully symmetric **Rare Waterfall** plunges 5m. There's enough of a gap to walk behind the blanket of water. The rockslide is 10km past Eastwood Arboretum, off Wharekopae Road.

Wine, Beer, and Cider Tasting

Gisborne Wine Centre (Shed 3, 50 Esplanade, 06/867-4085, www.gisbornewinecentre.co.nz) is a welcome introduction to the

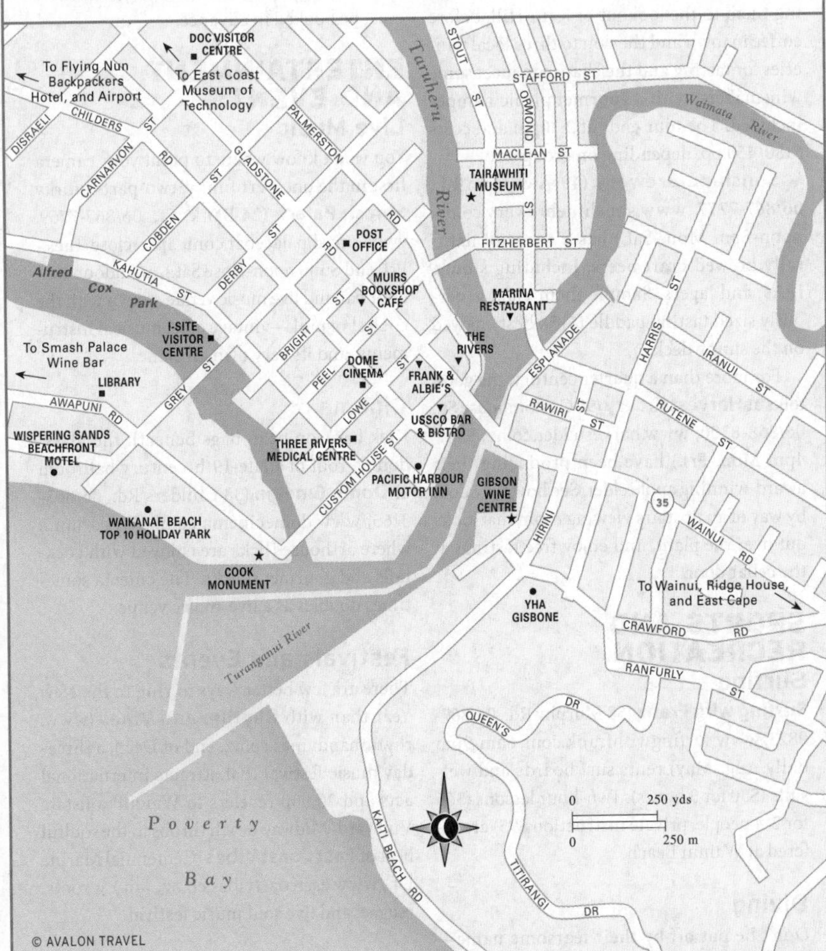

region's viniculture, collating the best local tipples and selling them for as little as $5 per glass, enjoyed overlooking the harbor.

It's all about the chardonnay at **Bushmore Estate** (166 Main Rd., 06/868-9317, www.bushmere.com, 11am-3pm Wed.-Sun. Sept.-May., by appointment Apr.-Aug.), and the gewürztraminer and pinot gris are excellent too. Enjoy live music on Sunday in summer, and feast on delectable offerings like fresh seafood or home-smoked lamb at the restaurant, **Vines** (11am-3pm Wed.-Sun., 6pm-9pm Thurs.-Sat., $26-30), with tables overlooking the grapes.

Famed for their organic approach to winemaking, if you happen upon the rustic cellar door of **Milton Vineyards & Winery** (119 Papatu Rd., 06/862-8680, www.milton.co.nz, 10am-4pm Mon.-Fri.) between November and March, order the artisanal platter of local cheese and cured meats.

Tairawhiti Tours (021/276-5484, www.

tairawhititours.co.nz) begin at 9:30am picking guests up from their accommodations, ferrying them to the lookout of Kaiti Hill, before coffee in town and then on to three local wineries for tasting and the chance to meet some winemakers, with a gourmet picnic hamper included. The tour ends at 2:30pm and costs $180-450 pp, depending on group size.

Sunshine Brewery (49 Awapuni Rd., 06/867-7777, www.sunshinebrewery.co.nz, noon-8pm Mon.-Sat.) has a range of naturally brewed craft beers, including stouts, IPAs, and lagers. Sample them via a generously sized tasting paddle ($15), best enjoyed on the sunny deck.

For more than a quarter century, the good folks at **Harvest Cidery** (91 Customhouse St., 06/868-8300, www.harvestcider.co.nz, 9am-4pm Mon.-Fri.) have been producing their award-winning apple cider. See how they do it by way of an upstairs viewing room that looks out over the plant, and enjoy free tastings at the cellar door.

SPORTS AND RECREATION

Surfing

Surfing with Frank (58 Murphy Rd., 06/867-0823, www.surfingwithfrank.com, 6am-9pm daily Aug.-May) rents surf boards and wetsuits ($30 for 3 hours). Two-hour lessons ($65 for 2-4 people, private instruction $95) are offered at Wainui Beach.

Diving

Don't be put off by their fearsome name—stingrays are so friendly that they can be hand-fed under guidance, even in the wild. Donning waist-high rubber waders at low tide, **Dive Tatapouri** (532 Whangara Rd., 06/868-5153, www.divetatapouri.com) take guests out onto the reef for the two-hour **Ecology Reef Tour** (adults $45, children $20) to hopefully encounter kingfish, crayfish, octopuses, and eels, as well as the rays. Your guide will also fill you in on interesting facts and information about ancient Maori fishing techniques. Those more confident should consider the super **Snorkeling with Stingrays Adventure** ($70); no experience is necessary, but tours must be booked in advance.

ENTERTAINMENT AND EVENTS

Live Music

You won't know where to point your camera first in the one-part funky, two-parts quirky **Smash Palace** (24 Banks St., 06/867-7769, www.smashpalacebar.com, 3pm-close Tues.-Fri. and Sun., noon-close Sat.), an indoor-outdoor bar and live music venue strewn with the coolest of junk—vintage cars, musical instruments, and its very own airplane.

Cinema

Kick back on bean bags beneath the glass-domed roof of a late-19th-century ballroom at **Dome Cinema** (38 Childers Rd., 06/863-3165, www.domecinema.co.nz, Wed.-Sun.), where arthouse flicks are enjoyed with cocktails and gourmet snacks. The cinema sometimes doubles as a live-music venue.

Festivals and Events

There are few better ways to ring in the New Year than with **Rhythm and Vines** (www.rhythmandvines.co.nz, end of Dec.), a three-day music festival that attracts international acts and 20,000 revelers to Waiohika Estate Vineyard. Midway Beach throbs to the soulful beat of **East Coast Vibes** (Centennial Marine Dr., www.eastcoastvibes.co.nz, Jan.), a roots, reggae, and live soul music festival.

FOOD

At **Frank & Albie's** (24 Gladstone Rd., 06/867-7847, www.frankandalbie.co.nz, 7:30am-2:30pm Mon.-Fri.), freshly prepared salads, sandwiches, and sticky treats are served in a busy, central setting. Enjoy some of the best coffee in town with home-baked bread amid the recycled furnishings and reclaimed wood decor.

★ **Muirs Bookshop Café** (62 Gladstone Rd., 06/867-9742, www.muirsbookshop.co.nz, 9am-3:30pm Mon.-Fri., 9am-3pm Sat.) is the place to lose yourself for hours as you sip an espresso and tuck into house-baked cake. Located above a bookstore, there's a plethora of reading material at hand. The enticing loft setting features dark wood and art with a lovely balcony that overlooks the street.

The Rivers (Gladstone Rd. and Reads Quay, 06/863-3733, www.therivers.co.nz, 11am-9pm daily, bar open late, $17-33) is a bustling Irish bar with a warm welcome. A dependable menu of well-priced pub staples includes chicken breast and surf and turf. The tasty Guinness pie is a Gisborne legend.

Bare brick walls and a black-tile bar set the mood for sophisticated seasonal dining at ★ **USSCo Bar & Bistro** (16 Childers Rd., 06/868-3246, www.ussco.co.nz, 4:30pm-close Mon.-Sat., $32-45), housed in the restored Union Steam Ship Company building. The beverage list does the menu justice, brimming with excellent Kiwi craft beers and the region's finest wines. Order the fresh fish with turmeric butter, clams, and truffle mash.

Gizzy's poshest eatery is a French waterside affair where guests can enjoy river views from the deck or a log fire from within the handsome high-ceilinged historic white boathouse. The ★ **Marina Restaurant** (1 Vogel St., 06/868-5919, www.marinarestaurant.co.nz, noon-2pm Thurs.-Sat., 6pm-close Tues.-Sat., $32-43) menu varies seasonally based on local produce. Expect dishes such as duck-leg confit or free-range 21-day-aged beef delivered to linen-topped tables by friendly staffers who know the best tipples to accompany them.

ACCOMMODATIONS

Accommodations in Gisborne are concentrated along Gladstone Road and along the waterfront near the estuary. Budget options are limited.

BBH-affiliated **Flying Nun Backpackers** (147 Roebuck Rd., 06/868-0461, dorm $25-27, $40 s, $60 d) is popular with the younger crowd and surfers and is well-priced for single travelers. The Gothic building is an old convent surrounded by huge grounds. Guests enjoy free Wi-Fi and a TV and games room. It's 15 minutes' stroll from downtown; free pickup is available.

YHA Gisborne (32 Harris St., 06/867-3269, www.yha.co.nz, $27-29, $52 s, $68 d) is close to Gizzy's center. Set in a cozy cabin-like building, some rooms sport sloping ceilings. An en suite double with twin bunks ($130) is available. There is limited free Wi-Fi, a spacious well-equipped kitchen, a deck, and a TV room. Other amenities include bike and surfboard rentals, an herb garden, and free movies.

Affordable **Pacific Harbour Motor Inn** (24 Reads Quay, 06/867-8847, www.pacificharbour.co.nz, $100-230) is a quality lodging that overlooks the Turanganui River and inner harbor marina. Well-presented accommodations range from studios to two-bedroom suites with free Wi-Fi, Sky TV, desks, fridges, and hot-drink-making facilities. Larger units have full kitchens, and some rooms have spa baths and balconies.

The terrific ★ **Whispering Sands Beachfront Motel** (22 Salisbury Rd., 06/867-1319, www.whisperingsands.co.nz, $135-195) is superb seaside value, fringing Waikanae Beach. Modern en suite units are equipped with kitchens, Sky TV, free Wi-Fi, and a private patio or balcony. First-floor rooms offer the best views over Poverty Bay. It's a 10-minute walk to downtown.

Gisborne's best B&B, ★ **Ridge House** (103B Wheatstone Rd., 06/868-5867, www.ridgehousenz.com, $250-800) is an exquisite modernist building perched on 2.4ha of farmland with olive groves, orchards, vegetable gardens, free-range chickens, and bee hives. One of the two private guest suites opens to the communal infinity saltwater pool; the other overlooks the sea. Both are equipped with free Wi-Fi, robes, and natural toiletries. Guests make use of the spa, library, and bespoke tour service.

Well-placed **Waikanae Beach Top 10 Holiday** Park (280 Grey St., 06/867-5634, www.gisborneholidaypark.co.nz) rests on the city's main beach minutes from downtown. Some of the tent and RV sites ($22) offer sea views. Standard cabin units ($85) come with hot-drink-making facilities. Rooms ($105) and fully self-contained units ($130-180) come with dining and lounge areas, TVs, kitchens, and private baths. Amenities include kayak, surfboard, and paddleboard rentals, barbecues, and a games room.

TRANSPORTATION AND SERVICES

Gisborne lies at the intersection of Highways 2 and 35 on Poverty Bay. It's 141km south of Opotiki via Highway 2, and 55km south of Tolaga Bay via Highway 25.

Air

Gisborne Airport (GIS, Aerodrome Rd., 06/867-1608, www.eastland.nz) is 3.7km west of downtown and is served daily by **Air New Zealand** (www.airnewzealand.co.nz) with flights to Auckland and Wellington.

Car rental companies at the airport include **Avis** (www.avis.co.nz), **Budget** (www.budget.co.nz), **Hertz** (www.hertz.co.nz), and **Thrifty** (www.thrifty.co.nz). For airport shuttle services, contact **Jayride** (www.jayride.com); for cabs, call **Gisborne Taxis** (06/867-2222, www.gisbornetaxis.co.nz). **RaD Care Hire** (1 Wainui Rd., 06/867-7532, www.rentadent.co.nz) offer an airport pickup and vehicle delivery service within Gisborne.

Public Transportation

Gisborne is served by national bus operator **Intercity** (09/583-578, www.intercity.co.nz), which stops outside the i-SITE Visitor Centre (209 Grey St.).

Tours

Gisborne Tours (021/204-1080, www.gisbornetours.nz) operates a shuttle bus around the region that includes Opotiki, Lake Waikaremoana, and Wairoa. Tours cover historical and cultural destinations with the option to create your own package.

Cycle Gisborne (124 Ormond Rd., 06/927-7021, www.cyclegisborne.com) rents bikes and offers guided tours of sights and vineyards.

Services

Head to the Gisborne **i-SITE Visitor Information Centre** (209 Grey St., 06/868-6139, www.tairawhitigisborne.co.nz, 8:30am-5pm Mon.-Fri., 10am-5pm Sat.-Sun.) for information regarding tours and accommodations as well as equipment rental and travel bookings.

Free Wi-Fi awaits at **HB Williams Memorial Library** (Peel St., 06/867-6709, www.gpl.govt.nz, 9:30am-5:30pm Mon.-Fri., 9:30am-1pm Sat.), and there's a central **post office** (127-137 Gladstone Rd., 0800/081-190, www.nzpost.co.nz, 9am-5pm Mon.-Fri., 9am-noon Sat.).

For medical services, head to **Three Rivers Medical** (75 Customhouse St., 06/867-7411, www.3rivers.co.nz, 8am-8pm Mon.-Fri., 9am-6pm Sat.-Sun.). For emergencies, try **Gisborne Hospital** (421 Ormond Rd., 06/869-0500).

Te Urewera

At 250,000ha, Te Urewera was once North Island's largest national park. Then, in 2014, it was granted human rights—meaning it was no longer owned by anyone (though it is under the guardianship of local *iwi*). This extraordinary slice of ancient land is blanketed by more than 650 species of native trees that shelter 35 protected native bird species, deer, and wild pigs. It affords a delicious glimpse into how New Zealand looked before humans arrived.

Te Urewera plays an important role in Maori legend. For centuries, it was home to the Tuhoe people (the "children of the mist"), said to be descendants of Tuhoepotiki (the mortal child of Hine-pukohu-rangi, the mist maiden) and her mountain husband, Te Maunga.

WAIROA

Tucked into the top corner of Hawke's Bay, unassuming Wairoa sits perched on the banks of its eponymous river. Wairoa is the gateway town to Te Urewera and is the last place to stock up on supplies before venturing into the wilderness.

Sights

The **Wairoa Museum** (142 Marine Parade, 06/838-3108, www.wairoadc.govt.nz, 10am-4pm Mon.-Fri., 10am-noon 1st Sat. of the month, donation) sits in a historic former bank. Wairoa has one of New Zealand's biggest Maori populations, something that is well represented in this museum rich in *toanga* carvings and a sprawling photography collection that dates to the late 19th century.

If visiting in early June, check out the four-day **Wairoa Maori Film Festival** (www.kiaora.tv, June), which celebrates indigenous movies with film screenings at **Kahungunu Marae** (Ihaka St. and Mataira St., 06/837-8501) and **Gaiety Cinema & Theatre** (Wairoa River Walkway, 06/281-5075, www.gaietytheatre.co.nz). The rest of the year, come for big movie releases and the occasional arthouse flick.

Food and Accommodations

Eastend Café (250 Marine Parade, 06/838-6070, 7am-4pm Tues.-Fri., 8am-3:30pm Sat., 9am-3:30pm Sun.) is the coolest hangout in town thanks to its thrift-store furniture and quirky driftwood sculptures and artwork. Located in the same building as the Gaiety Cinema, it serves traditional breakfast, pies, burgers, and espresso as well as craft beers and local wine.

Vista Motor Lodge (2 Bridge St., 06/838-8279, www.vistamotorlodge.co.nz, $120-240) has well-presented though dated units that range from studios to four-bedroom suites with Sky TV and private baths; some have full kitchens. There is limited free Wi-Fi throughout and a communal outdoor pool.

Vista Bar and Grill (2 Bridge St., 06/838-8279, www.vistamotorlodge.co.nz, 6pm-close Mon.-Fri., $22-30) is the restaurant of the Vista Motor Lodge. The traditional setting of polished wood furniture and chalkboard specials complements a menu of steak and fish-and-chips.

Modest accommodations are at **Wairoa Riverside Motor Camp** (19 Marine Parade, 06/838-6301, www.riversidemotorcamp.co.nz). A backpacker dorm ($30) sleeps 11 and has a private deck; cabins ($75) have basic kitchenettes, TVs, and small patios; and trailers ($40 s, $50 d) are equipped with a fridge and a TV. Tent and powered sites ($20 s, $34 d) are available. Visitors share baths and a fully stocked kitchen.

Transportation and Services

Wairoa is 98km (1 hour, 20 minutes) southwest of Gisborne and 116km (1 hour, 40 minutes) northeast of Napier along Highway 2. National bus operator **Intercity** (09/583-5780, www.intercity.co.nz) stops at the Wairoa i-SITE (Hwy. 2 and Queen St.) on its way from Gisborne to Wellington.

The **i-SITE Visitor Information Centre** (Hwy. 2 and Queen St., 06/838-7440, www.visitwairoa.co.nz, 8:30am-5pm Mon.-Fri., 10am-4pm Sat.-Sun.) has tourist and transport advice. It doubles as the DoC office, where you can buy hut tickets and get the latest conditions at Te Urewera. There is free Wi-Fi in the visitors center as well as at the **library** (212 Marine Parade, 06/838-8450, www.wairoalibrary.co.nz, 10am-5pm Mon.-Thurs., 9:30am-6pm Fri., 10am-noon Sat.).

LAKE WAIKAREMOANA

Te Urewera's most significant feature is Lake Waikaremoana ("the sea of rippling waters" in Maori), a jagged body of water surrounded by isolated beaches and towering native trees. The Tuhoe people refer to the lake as "Ko Waikaremoana te wai kaukau a nga tipuna," which translates as "the bathing water of our ancestors." It is said that the lake was formed when local chief Mahu sent his daughter Haumapuhia to collect water from a spring, but she refused. Overcome with anger, Mahu drowned his daughter and left her beneath the surface where she morphed into a *taniwha* (legendary monster). In a desperate attempt to reach the sea, Haumapuhia clawed at the land in all directions, creating the lake's chaotic shape. Ultimately, she failed, and remains in the waters in the form of a rock—her existence betrayed by the rippling waters that run through her being.

The scientific cause of the lake's formation isn't quite so compelling. The lake formed 2,200 years ago when a massive landslide collapsed from the Ngamoko range, blocking the Waikaretaheke River gorge, which eventually filled with water. The lake is nearly 600m above sea level and is up to 248m deep.

★ Lake Waikaremoana Great Walk

Along the **Lake Waikaremoana Great Walk** (46km one-way, 3-4 days, www.greatwalks.co.nz), you'll encounter native birds like the pukeko (listen for the call of the kiwi at Waiharuru hut), incredible views of the lake and forest canopy from Panekiri Bluff, and numerous opportunities to cool off in the lake.

Lake Waikaremoana Great Walk

The first 17km of the track from Onepoto Bay, rising from 600m to 1,180m at Panekiri Bluff, are the most challenging—tackle that section first. From there, it's a relatively flat hike along the water's edge and through valleys cloaked in native bush.

There are five **huts** ($32, under age 18 free) and five **campsites** ($14, under age 18 free) en route; book in advance through DoC (www.doc.govt.nz). The huts have mattresses, a wood burner, water supply, and toilets (no paper); bring a gas stove. Some campsites have cooking shelters and tables, and all have toilets and water; campers cannot use the hut facilities.

This walk does not circumnavigate the entire lake, just its south and western flanks. You'll need transport to get to the farthest point.

GETTING THERE

There are two trailheads, accessed via road or water taxi. Various boat landings offer an opportunity for prearranged pickups and drop-offs en route.

You get to the lake from the northwest via Murupara (along Waikaremoana Rd.), but there's a 90km section that takes two hours to drive. Head instead along Highway 38 (Lake Rd.) from the southeast. There is free secure parking at Waikaremoana Holiday Park if you'd rather not leave your vehicle in the car parks—it's an advisable option as car break-ins do happen.

Short Walks

The walk to **Lou's Lookout** (45 minutes round-trip) begins 6km southwest of the Te Urewera Visitor Center (along Hwy. 38). The trail winds though bluffs and around boulders before emerging to a panoramic view of Lake Waikaremoana.

The **Black Beech Walk** (30 minutes one-way) navigates an old highway past Panekire Bluff and black beech trees with some incredible views of the lake's Home Bay. The trail begins at the Lake Waikaremoana Holiday Park.

Two of the most worthwhile strolls begin around the junction of Highway 38 and Aniwaniwa Road, 2km northeast of the visitors center. The **Hinerau Walk** (30 minutes round-trip) leads to a trio of waterfalls known as the Aniwaniwa Falls. The **Aniwaniwa Falls Track** is another option; the lower riverside trail that winds to the base of the falls.

A short track leads the stunning **Papakorito Falls,** a 20m curtain of water that tumbles over a shimmering cliff face partly carpeted in moss and surrounded by rich green forest. The pullout is 2km along Aniwaniwa Road.

For a complete list of the area's extensive short hikes, grab a *Lake Waikaremoana Walks* leaflet from the local DoC office or the Lake Waikaremoana Holiday Park.

Accommodations

A handful of accommodations make for an excellent launch point for hikers. **Lake Whakamaino Lodge** (Hostel Lane, Tuai, 06/837-3876, www.lodge.co.nz, dorm $30, $50 s, $90 d) is near much smaller Lake Whakamaino, 10km southeast of Waikaremoana. Tranquil but basic lodges are housed in former dam worker lodgings. The hostel-like accommodations include shared kitchen and bath facilities; other offerings include private self-contained lodgings.

Lake Waikaremoana Holiday Park (6249 Lake Rd., 06/837-3826, www.waikaremoana.info) is on the shores of Lake Waikaremoana with nonpowered and powered campsites (adults $18-21, ages 5-17 $9-10.50, under age 5 free), as well as private units and chalets ($65-180) ranging from basic (shared kitchen and bath facilities) to fully self-contained. The restful location serves as a pickup and drop-off point for water taxis and has free secure parking, a general store, and a gas station. It's a couple of kilometers south of the visitor center.

Te Taita A Makoro (Hwy. 38, 06/837-3808, www.doc.govt.nz, free) is a rudimentary DoC-maintained campsite with 10 nonpowered sites. There are toilets and tap water, although the water should be treated. All sites are first-come, first-served. It's 4km north of Lake Waikaremoana.

DoC-run **Mokau Landing** (Hwy. 38, 06/837-3808, www.doc.govt.nz, adults $8, children $4, under age 5 free) campground is in a scenic spot between the forest and Lake Waikaremoana. Facilities include toilets and running water. It's located near the north shores of the lake, 10km west of the junction with Aniwaniwa Road; find it 1.5km from Mokau Falls, along Highway 38. There is parking at the waterfall.

Transportation and Services

Lake Waikaremoana is 58km (1 hour) northwest of Wairoa via Highway 38. It's 154km west of Gisborne via Highways 2 and 38, and

174km (2 hours, 45 minutes) north of Napier along Highways 2 and 38. From Rotorua, take Highways 5 and 38 southeast for 163km (3 hours).

Big Bush (06/837-3777, www.lakewaikaremoana.co.nz) operates bus shuttles between Wairoa and Lake Waikaremoana, as well as a water taxi on the lake.

From Rotorua, **Walking Legends** (07/312-5297, www.walkinglegends.com, adults $1,490, children $1,000) operates a four-day guided Lake Waikaremoana Great Walk. Meals, accommodations in DoC huts, and transportation are included. Support boats transport equipment, so you only have to carry a day pack.

The **Te Urewera Visitor Centre** (6249 Lake Rd., 06/837-3803, www.doc.govt.nz, 8am-4:15pm daily) is staffed by knowledgeable DoC rangers who can advise on the latest conditions. Find maps and book huts and campsites along the Great Walk at the Centre.

Napier and Hawke's Bay

With its rich, varied soils coupled with a lengthy dry summer cooled by a Pacific breeze, and a brief benign winter, it's little wonder Hawke's Bay is known as "the fruit bowl of New Zealand," its flat fertile plains laced with colorful orchards and eternal strings of grape vines.

Maori established settlements along the bay sometime before the turn of the 14th century, while Captain Cook likely became the first European to step on its shores in 1769, naming the coast Hawke's Bay after his childhood hero, Sir Edward Hawke, First Lord of the Admiralty. By the mid-18th century, the region had lured traders, a multitude of sheep farmers, and, most fatefully, Roman Catholic missionaries, who, in 1851, established the nation's first winery to supply the church. The first orchard of note was planted 40 years later. Now more than 70 wineries pepper the bay.

The apocalyptic Hawke's Bay earthquake of 1931 inadvertently created the region's other major tourist draw—an art deco architecture mecca in the bay's main hub, Napier.

NAPIER

Napier, the largest city in Hawke's Bay (population 62,000) is home to the largest concentration of art deco architecture in the world. What makes the city's spectacular collection even more compelling is the story of its defiance in the face of devastation.

Sights

On the north edge of downtown Napier, **Bluff Hill** stretches for 3km and is adorned with the city's poshest residences on a hard-to-navigate network of often dead-end streets.

Head to the eastern end of the hill at the end of Lighthouse Road, where a lookout affords a worthwhile port view right across to Cape Kidnappers. It's a 30-minute walk from the city center, but whether you're walking or driving, you'll need a map; the **i-SITE Visitor Centre** (100 Marine Parade, 06/834-1911, www.napiernz.com, 9am-5pm daily) will oblige.

★ ART DECO ARCHITECTURE

Wandering the streets of Napier is akin to stepping onto a Hollywood film set. The city's art deco architecture looks lifted straight from *The Great Gatsby.* There are 140 original art deco buildings in the city; most are along **Emerson, Tennyson, and Hastings Streets.**

The **Daily Telegraph Building** (49 Tennyson St., no public access) was built in 1932 and is revered for its ziggurat design emboldened by two-story columns adorned with fountain motifs. The pretty seaside suburb of Ahuriri (3km northwest of downtown) is home to the city's most alluring example of art deco: the **National Tobacco Company Building** (1 Ossian St.,

Napier

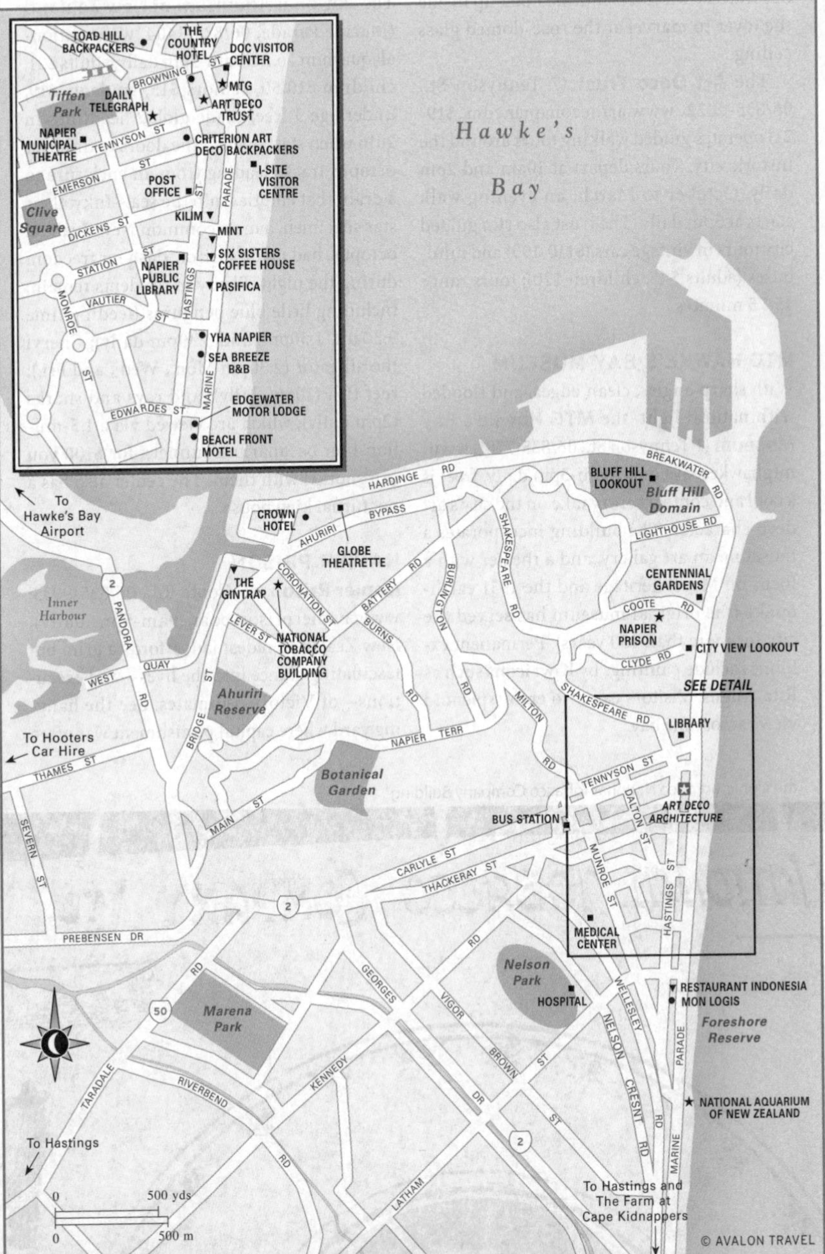
TOAD HILL BACKPACKERS
THE COUNTRY HOTEL
DOC VISITOR CENTER
BROWNING ST
MTG
Tiffen Park
DAILY TELEGRAPH
ART DECO TRUST
NAPIER MUNICIPAL THEATRE
TENNYSON ST
CRITERION ART DECO BACKPACKERS
I-SITE VISITOR CENTRE
EMERSON ST
POST OFFICE
PARADE
Clive Square
KILIM
DICKENS ST
MINT
SIX SISTERS COFFEE HOUSE
STATION ST
NAPIER PUBLIC LIBRARY
HASTINGS
PASIFICA
MONROE
VAUTIER ST
YHA NAPIER
SEA BREEZE B&B
MARINE
EDGEWATER MOTOR LODGE
EDWARDES ST
BEACH FRONT MOTEL
Hawke's Bay
To Hawke's Bay Airport
HARDINGE RD
BREAKWATER RD
BLUFF HILL LOOKOUT
Bluff Hill Domain
CROWN HOTEL
AHURIRI BYPASS
GLOBE THEATRETTE
SHAKESPEARE RD
LIGHTHOUSE RD
Inner Harbour
PANDORA
THE GINTRAP
CORONATION ST
BATTERY RD
BURLINGTON RD
CENTENNIAL GARDENS
COOTE RD
NAPIER PRISON
LEVER ST
BURNS
NATIONAL TOBACCO COMPANY BUILDING
CLYDE RD
CITY VIEW LOOKOUT
WEST QUAY
Ahuriri Reserve
BRIDGE ST
MILTON RD
SEE DETAIL
LIBRARY
NAPIER TERR
To Hooters Car Hire
THAMES ST
Botanical Garden
ART DECO ARCHITECTURE
DALTON ST
BUS STATION
MAIN ST
SEVERN ST
CARLYLE ST
THACKERAY ST
MUNROE ST
MEDICAL CENTER
PREBENSEN DR
Nelson Park
HOSPITAL
WELLESLEY RD
RESTAURANT INDONESIA
MON LOGIS
Foreshore Reserve
Marena Park
GEORGES
VIGOR BROWN ST
NELSON CRESNT
TARADALE RD
RIVERBEND RD
KENNEDY RD
NATIONAL AQUARIUM OF NEW ZEALAND
To Hastings
LATHAM ST
To Hastings and The Farm at Cape Kidnappers
0 500 yds
0 500 m
© AVALON TRAVEL

11am-4pm daily, donation). The terra-cotta structure is fronted by an intricate archway decorated with floral motifs. Look up inside the foyer to marvel at the rose-domed glass ceiling.

The **Art Deco Trust** (7 Tennyson St., 06/835-0022, www.artdeconapier.com, $19-21) operates guided walking tours around the historic city. Tours depart at 10am and 2pm daily. October to March, an evening walk starts at 5pm daily. The trust also run guided city tours in vintage cars ($110-195) and minibuses (adults $45, children $20); tours range 45-75 minutes.

MTG HAWKE'S BAY MUSEUM

With sharp angles, clean edges, and flooded with natural light, the **MTG Hawke's Bay Museum** (1 Tennyson St., 06/835-7781, www.mtghawkesbay.com, 10am-5pm daily, free) is a cool and contemporary take on the city's art deco character. The building incorporates a museum, an art gallery, and a theater with a focus on Maori heritage and the 1931 earthquake (the original museum has served the city for more than 150 years). Permanent exhibits include paintings by Kiwi icons such as Rita Angus. Visitors can also enjoy splendid views across the bay.

NATIONAL AQUARIUM OF NEW ZEALAND

The **National Aquarium of New Zealand** (Marine Parade, 06/834-1404, www.nationalaquarium.co.nz, 9am-5pm daily, adults $21, children $10.50, seniors $15, students $19, under age 3 free) made global headlines in 2016 when staff opened the doors to discover octopus tracks leading from an enclosure to a drain that empties into the sea—Inky, their star specimen, a male common New Zealand octopus, had made a heroic dash for freedom during the night. Plenty of residents remain, including little blue penguins (feeding time 9:30am, 1:30pm, and 3:30pm daily); Cheryl the alligator (2:30pm Mon., Wed., and Fri.); reef fish (10am daily); and rays and sharks (2pm daily), which are viewed via a 1.5-million-liter oceanarium tunnel—for $100 you can snorkel with them. The center also has a nocturnal kiwi house.

NAPIER PRISON

Napier Prison (55 Coote Rd., 06/835-9933, www.napierprison.com, 9am-5pm daily), New Zealand's oldest jail, affords a grim but fascinating glance into the lives—and executions—of Victorian inmates. See the hanging yard where capital punishment was often

the iconic, art deco National Tobacco Company Building

The Napier Earthquake and Art Deco Resurgence

On the morning of Tuesday, February 3, 1931, a magnitude 7.8 earthquake erupted with the power of 110 million tons of TNT. It lasted a terrifying 2.5 minutes. Much of Napier collapsed, killing 256 people. Perversely, as the city fell, an enormous mass of seabed along the fault line rose by as much as 2.7m to create 2,000ha of new real estate in the bay. In the city, brick buildings bore the brunt of the quake, while some of the reinforced concrete art deco constructions, which were fashionable at the time, stood stoic. It was decided the city's rebuild would adopt this art deco style.

Almost as striking as the film-set streets of central Napier is the pride that the residents take in their town, best exemplified during the **Art Deco Festival** (www.artdeconapier.com, Feb.). The colorful hub of Napier is swamped with classic cars and crowds of thousands dressed in Depression-era attire, attracting visitors from across the globe.

conducted at the hands of a fellow inmate, explore the psychiatric unit and the graveyard, and read the graffiti scrawled by gang members in several of the original cells during a self-guided daytime audio tour (adults $20, children $10). Some of the wings are said to be haunted.

If you'd like to truly test your mettle, take the **night tour** (usually last Fri. of the month, reserve ahead, over age 15, $25) of the prison asylum, patrolled by actors dressed in ghoulish costumes and straightjackets.

TOP EXPERIENCE

★ Wine Tasting

Hawke's Bay is New Zealand's oldest and second-largest grape-growing region. It's noted especially for its reds and supplies more than 80 percent of the nation's merlot, cabernet sauvignon, and syrah; the chardonnay is also excellent. Many of the cellar doors offer free tastings or charge a small fee ($5), and the winery restaurants are exceptional. Grab a wine trail map from the **i-SITE Visitor Centre** (100 Marine Parade, 06/834-1911, www.napiernz.com, 9am-5pm daily) for a full list of the vineyards, or visit www.hawkesbaywine.co.nz for the latest happenings.

A good place to start is where it all began. **Mission Estate Winery** (198 Church Rd., 06/845-9530, www.missionestate.co.nz, 9am-5pm Mon.-Sat., 10am-4:30pm Sun.) vines were planted in 1851 by French missionaries for the Roman Catholic Church, who still profit from the proceeds. The raised estate affords breathtaking views over Hawke's Bay. The on-site **restaurant** (11:30am-2:30pm and 6pm-close daily, $30-40) serves contemporary European fare with fresh, local produce.

Founded in 1937, **Brookfields Winery** (378 Brookfields Rd., 06/834-4615, www.brookfieldsvineyards.co.nz, 10am-4pm daily) was the nation's first boutique vineyard. The intimate handmade-brick winery sits along the Tutaekuri River, overlooking a rose garden. Its small, immaculate batches include an excellent chardonnay.

Crossroads (1747 Korokipo Rd., 06/879-9737, www.crossroadswines.co.nz, 11am-4:30pm daily) is an award-winning boutique winery famed for its flagship Talisman label, made from secret blends passed down from the winemaker to the heir. There's a good chance of bumping into chief winemaker Miles Dinneen—he's happy to chat, but don't expect him to impart any secrets.

Entertainment and Events

NIGHTLIFE

Low-lit and atmospheric, **Emporium** (Tennyson St. and Marine Parade, 06/835-0013, www.emporiumbar.co.nz, 7am-close daily) is a Napier time machine to the 1930s.

Perch atop a high stool at the classy marble bar and choose from a tasteful selection of classic and gin cocktails—the sazerac is dangerously good.

The **Gintrip** (64 West Quay, Ahuriri, 06/835-0199, www.gintrap.co.nz, 11am-close Mon.-Fri., 10am-close Sat.-Sun.) affords a laid-back drinking experience in a fashionable former boat shed overlooking the sea. The unpretentious menu has superb light bites and platters alongside traditional gastropub fare.

PERFORMING ARTS

The **Globe Theatrette** (15 Hardings Rd., Ahuriri, 06/833-6011, www.globenapier.co.nz, hours vary Tues.-Sun.) is an intimate and resplendent art-house cinema with 45 luxurious leather seats. Enjoy a film with beer, wine, and pizza. Hawke's Bay's main performance arts venue, **Napier Municipal Theatre** (119 Tennyson St., 06/835-1059, www.napiermunicipaltheatre.co.nz), hosts ballet, classical music, rock gigs, plays, and stand-up comics. Tickets are sold in-house or online.

FESTIVALS AND EVENTS

The weekend-long **Matariki Festival** (www.kahungunu.iwi.nz, June) is one of the nation's best Maori New Year celebrations. Head to Marine Parade to enjoy free live entertainment, cultural performances, fireworks, and the lighting of sky lanterns.

Food

The array of exquisite vineyard eateries is matched by a wide-ranging dining scene.

Hang with the locals at **Six Sisters Coffee House** (201 Marine Parade, 06/835-8364, 7:30am-4pm Mon.-Fri., 8am-4pm Sat.-Sun.). The row of six identical and colorful Victorian villas was built by an English architect in the late 1890s; they're much-loved, partly because they withstood the 1931 earthquake. The wonderful scent of baking greets coffee drinkers; good luck trying to leave without one of the scones.

Grab excellent fish-and-chips from **Westshore Fish Cafe** (112A Charles St., 06/834-0227, www.westshorefishcafe.co.nz, 11:30am-2pm Thurs.-Sun., 5pm-8pm Tues.-Sun., $10). Dine-in ($15-25) with BYO or enjoy your piping parcel down by the beach.

An open kitchen and attentive staff await at **Mister D** (47 Tennyson St., 06/835-5022, www.misterd.co.nz, 7:30am-4pm Sun.-Wed., 7:30am-close Thurs.-Sat., $25-38). The Italian-heavy menu includes risotto and a delectable bone-marrow ravioli alongside the finest

Be sure to sink a cocktail at the Emporium bar.

fillets of meat. The portions are generous, but leave room for the goat-cheese mousse with strawberry sorbet and brown-butter cake.

Don't leave Napier without sampling an authentic *rijsttafel* (a traditional Indonesian tapas-type meal) at ★ **Restaurant Indonesia** (409 Marine Parade, 06/835-8303, www.restaurantindonesia.co.nz, 5:30pm-9pm Tues.-Sun., $20-36). The selection of small dishes, kept warm over candles, includes curries and meats drizzled in sweet-and-sour sauces complemented by crunchy pickled vegetables. The cozy low-lit eatery is adorned with Indonesian paraphernalia like Balinese masks.

Spread over several levels, the intimate ★ **MINT** (189 Marine Parade, 06/835-4050, www.mintrestaurant.co.nz, 6pm-close Mon.-Sat., $30-32) sports a slick and modern setting that belies its Victorian shell—this is one of the historic Six Sisters villas. The innovative menu features seasonal pairings like duck-leg confit with blue cheese risotto, calamari, and pulled pork salad, and chocolate cake with dark chocolate mousse and salted ice cream for dessert.

You'd never guess that the odd blue bungalow that is ★ **Pacifica Restaurant** (209 Marine Parade, 06/833-6335, www.pacificarestaurant.co.nz, 6pm-close Tues.-Sat., $65-115) is one of the nation's best eateries. The fine-dining seafood-heavy fare is served in a Kiwi environment of simple furnishings and strategically placed driftwood. The five-course seasonal menu changes daily, but may include coconut-marinated lemonfish, venison carpaccio, steamed mussels, and scallop mousse.

Accommodations

There's a great range of lodgings around downtown Napier, especially along Marine Parade.

UNDER $100

YHA Napier Backpackers (277 Marine Parade, 06/835-7039, www.yha.co.nz, dorm $30, $45 s, $65-69 d) sprouts from a hotel that survived the 1931 earthquake. Today, this aging hostel offers well-priced rooms with sea views, shared baths, and a fully equipped kitchen. The TV room has a DVD player with plenty of free films, and there's a courtyard with a barbecue area. Before you leave, grab a stone from the beach and write a message on it to add to the collection in the lounge.

BBH hostel **Criterion Art Deco Backpackers** (48 Emerson St., 06/835-2059, www.criterionartdeco.co.nz, dorm $29, $53 s, $70-116 d) is in the heart of town in a fabulously ornate Spanish mission-style art deco building. Enjoy free breakfasts, herbs, spices, and hot drinks, along with a lounge room with pool table and TV room with Sky TV. Bath facilities are shared, but most rooms have a wash basin. The family room ($116) has an en suite bath and sleeps four.

There's a real sense of camaraderie at cozy **Toad Hall** (11 Shakespeare Rd., 06/835-5555, www.toadhall.co.nz, dorm $28, $65-90 s or d) thanks to welcoming communal areas like the rooftop terrace, which has a barbecue. Freebies include breakfast, baked treats, a pool, Ping-Pong, and Wi-Fi. A double room with an en suite bath is available. It's a 10-minute walk to downtown.

$100-200

In the seaside suburb of Ahuriri, **The Crown Hotel** (Bridge St. and Hardings Rd., Ahuriri, 06/833-8300, www.thecrownnapier.co.nz, $290-900) comprises 42 suites set in authentic 1932 art deco architecture with ocean views. Rooms ranging from studios to two-bedroom loft apartments; guest can enjoy floor heating, Sky TV, free Wi-Fi, and luxurious spacious baths. The on-site restaurant, **Milk and Honey** (7am-9pm daily, $24-32) tempts with dishes like aged scotch fillet or seared wild venison, all served overlooking the water.

Sea Breeze Bed & Breakfast (281 Marine Parade, 06/835-8067, www.seabreezebnb.co.nz, $135-145) is a charming Victorian villa overlooking the seafront. Three colorful and incongruous Asian-inspired suites include the Asian Imperial, Turkish, and Indian

Rooms. All are equipped with exotic knick-knacks and wall rugs, along with TVs, blow-dryers, and free Wi-Fi. Two rooms have en suite baths.

$200-300

Built in 1909, imposing **Country Hotel** (12 Browning St., 06/835-7800, www.country-hotel.co.nz, $285-1,120) was one of the few sizeable structures to survive the 1931 earthquake. Rooms with high ceilings have antique furniture and contemporary luxuries like Sky TV, Wi-Fi, and modern baths. Downstairs is an on-site bar and eatery.

OVER $300

Perfectly positioned overlooking Napier's shoreline, **The Dome** (101 Marine Parade, 06/835-0707, www.thedome.co.nz, $350-1,550), an iconic 1937 corner art deco building, offers a collection of fully self-contained modern suites equipped with designer furnishings, original artworks, free Wi-Fi, and balconies with sea views. Soundproofed rooms mean there's no need to worry about street noise (it's right in the heart of things), and there's a communal pool and hot tub.

CAMPING AND HOLIDAY PARK

Pitch a tent to the sound of the waves at **Napier Beach Kiwi Holiday Park & Motels** (10 Gill Rd., 06/836-7084, www.napierbeach.co.nz). Tent ($19-23 pp) and RV ($19-52 pp) sites are accompanied by basic cabins ($80-84) with TVs, kitchenettes, and shared baths; bring your own bedding. Also available are cabins ($110-119) with en suite baths, kitchenettes, TVs, and dining and picnic tables; fully self-contained units ($150-159); and motel units ($170-179) with private gardens. Guest facilities include a barbecue area, a children's playground, and laundry. The park is located 9km north of the city near the beach.

Transportation and Services

Napier is located on the south end of Hawke's Bay, 214km (3 hours) southwest of Gisborne along Highway 2. From Taupo, it's 141km (2 hours) southeast via Highway 5.

AIR

Hawke's Bay Airport (NPE, Main North Rd., 06/834-0742, www.hawkesbay-airport.co.nz) is 6km northwest of downtown via Highway 2. It is served by **Air New Zealand** (06/835-1130, www.airnewzealand.co.nz) with daily connections to Auckland, Wellington, and Christchurch. **Jetstar** (0800/800-995, www.jetstar.com) operates daily flights to Auckland. **Sounds Air** (0800/505-005, www.soundsair.com) flies to Blenheim three times a week.

There are two shuttle bus operators from the airport: **Super Shuttle** (0800/748-885, www.supershuttle.co.nz) and **Village Shuttle** (0800/777-796, www.villageshuttle.co.nz). Both offer services to Hastings and Havelock North as well as Napier.

Car rental companies at the airport include **Avis** (06/835-1828, www.avis.co.nz), **Budget** (06/835-6169, www.budget.co.nz), and **Thrifty** (06/835-8820, www.thrifty.co.nz).

PUBLIC TRANSPORTATION

Napier is served by national bus operators **Intercity** (09/583-578, www.intercity.co.nz) and **Naked Bus** (09/979-1616, www.nakedbus.com) as well as North Island-wide operator **Mana Bus** (09/367-9140, www.manabus.com). All services arrive and depart from the **Napier Bus Station** (12 Carlyle St.).

The local bus service is operated by **Go Bay** (www.hbrc.govt.nz) and covers the Hawke's Bay region, connecting Napier, Hastings, and Havelock North, and serving routes within those hubs.

For cabs, contact **Combined Taxis** (06/835-7777) or **Baywide Taxis** (06/843-4524).

TOURS

Husband-and-wife team John and Margaret run some of the region's finest guided tours via **Hawke's Bay Scenic Tours** (2 Neeve Place, 06/844-5693, www.hbscenictours.

co.nz). John's super anecdotes are accompanied by booklets with snaps of the city architecture and trips to some hidden spots—including one that affords a wonderful view of Napier.

Bay Tours & Charters (25 Coronation St., Ahuriri, 06/845-2736, www.baytours.co.nz) operate door-to-door minibus services around Hawke's Bay's attractions, including the wineries with informative—and often humorous—guides.

Centrally located **Napier City Bike Hire & Tours** (117 Marine Parade, 0800/245-344, www.bikehirenapier.co.nz) can point you in the right direction either by means of a guided tour or bike rental, and a bespoke itinerary with pickup and drop-off service. Choose from city, mountain, or tandem bikes.

Bike About Tours (47 Gloucester St., 06/845-4836, www.bikeabouttours.co.nz) have a great bicycle selection, including bikes with child seats, and a plethora of info and trail maps. Coach transfers via bus (with bikes) are available.

HOOTERS CAR HIRE

What better way to explore Napier's surrounding vineyards than in a roaring 1960s drop-top MG? Or how about crawling along the historic art deco streets in a classic 1920s Dodge? The automotive world is your oyster at **Hooters Car Hire** (68 Thames St., 06/835-1722, www.hooters-hire.co.nz, 9am-1pm Tues.-Sat.), the nation's finest collection of working vintage rides. The showroom is worth a browse even if you don't opt to rent; visit by donation ($1 or $2 gold coins).

The self-drive option (9am-5pm, $600, plus $1,000 refundable bond) may require a brief training session—some of the older cars have a double clutch or pedals in a different order. It's easy to pick up, and the roads aren't too busy. Chauffeur-driven **tours** (1-8 hours, $180-1,440 per car, 4 people maximum) take in the city's sights and wineries with drivers who are expert on all things Napier and art deco—and are dressed like it's 1930.

Services

The **Napier i-SITE** (100 Marine Parade, 06/834-1911, www.napiernz.com, 9am-5pm daily) has information on sights and vineyards, as well as an interesting art deco-themed gift shop. They can also advise on any DoC queries and hut bookings.

There is a central **library** (1 Tennyson St., 06/834-4180, www.napierlibrary.co.nz, 9:30am-5pm daily), a **post office** (1 Dickens St., 0800/081-190, www.nzpost.co.nz, 9am-5pm Mon.-Fri., 9:30am-12:30pm Sat.), and a **medical center** (76 Wellesley Rd., 06/834-1815, 24 hours daily). For emergencies, head to **Elmwood House Hospital** (44 Nelson Crescent, 06/834-4048).

HASTINGS AND VICINITY

Napier's smaller sibling, Hastings has its share of handsome art deco and Spanish mission architecture. It also serves as a gateway to top-drawer vineyards.

Wine Tasting

Ngatarawa Wines (305 Ngatarawa Rd., 06/879-7603, www.ngatarawa.co.nz, 10am-5pm daily summer, 11am-4pm daily winter) is a wonderful little winery where wine tasting takes place in a converted century-old horse-racing stable overlooking manicured lawns and a lengthy lily pond. Don't leave without sampling the merlot and dessert wines.

The exquisite angular architecture of the contemporary **Trinity Hill** (2396 Hwy. 50, 06/879-7778, www.trinityhill.com, tasting 11am-4pm Wed.-Sat.) offers a pleasing counterbalance to the array of historic estates. There are plenty of experimental wines to match the design, grown in the Grimblett Gravels.

Fashionable **Elephant Hill** (86 Clifton Rd., 06/872-6060, www.elephanthill.co.nz, 11am-5pm daily summer, 11am-4pm daily winter) is cradled in spectacular copper-clad architecture. Guests sip iconic red blends and chardonnay while overlooking orderly rows of vines framed by the Pacific Ocean and Cape Kidnappers beyond.

Food and Accommodations

There are few better ways to begin the day than at **Bay Espresso** (141 Karamu Rd., 06/876-5682, www.bayespresso.co.nz, 7am-4pm Mon.-Fri., 8am-4pm Sat.-Sun.), where ethically traded organic coffee is roasted in-house and served along with an extensive breakfast menu. The sprawling selection includes freshly made wraps, sandwiches, and baked goods; the carrot cake takes some beating.

The excellent restaurant at **Elephant Hill** (86 Clifton Rd., 06/872-6060, www.elephanthill.co.nz, noon-close daily summer, noon-close Sun.-Wed., 6pm-close Thurs.-Sat. winter, $36-42) offers a European-inspired menu whose highlights include seafood ravioli and confit pork belly.

The **Hawke's Bay Farmers Market** (027/697-3737, www.hawkesbayfarmersmarket.co.nz, 8:30am-12:30pm Sun.) is a must. The regional institution takes place at the **Hawke's Bay Showgrounds** (Kenilworth Rd.) and is one of the largest and oldest of its kind in the country. Grab a coffee and wander around the stalls of fresh produce as you shoot the breeze with friendly locals.

Stellar amenities—a private lake, a heated swimming pool, barbecue areas, and private jetted tubs—await at **Hastings Top 10 Holiday Park** (610 Windsor Ave., 06/878-6692, www.hastingstop10.co.nz). Accommodations options include tent and RV sites ($46-50); basic backpacker cabins ($80) with bunks, a fridge, and a kettle; cabins ($95) with fridges, seating areas, TVs, and shared bath and kitchen facilities; and fully self-contained motel units ($135) and apartments ($140-350) with up to three bedrooms, full kitchens, and large TVs, some with spas and private decks.

Transportation and Services

Hastings is 20km (20 minutes) south of Napier via Highways 50 or 2. Hastings is served by national bus operators **Intercity** (09/583-578, www.intercity.co.nz) and **Naked Bus** (09/979-1616, www.nakedbus.com) as well as North Island-wide operator **Mana Bus** (09/367-9140, www.manabus.com).

Car rental companies include **Hastings Auto Rentals** (808 Warren St. N., 06/878-7505, www.hastingsautorentals.co.nz) and **New Zealand Rent a Car** (405 St. Aubyn St. E., 06/835-0529).

Napier-based shuttle bus operators also cover the sights and vineyards of Hastings and Havelock North. **On Yer Bike** (2543 Hwy. 50, 06/650-4627, www.onyerbikehb.co.nz) rents bikes, including tandems, and offers guided two-wheel tours.

The **Hastings i-SITE** (101 Heretaunga St. E., 06/873-5526, www.visithastings.co.nz, 9am-5pm Mon.-Fri., 9am-3pm Sat., 10am-2pm Sun.) has information on sights and vineyards, as well as transport and accommodations.

HAVELOCK NORTH

Though Havelock North is a suburb of Hastings, it is its own satellite hub with a quaint, easily walkable center that brings to mind a charming English village. Havelock North is the launchpad to more wineries.

Sights

★ TE MATA PEAK

Te Mata Peak (www.tematapark.co.nz), 7.2km (15 minutes) southeast of Havelock North via Te Mata Peak Road, is part of a lengthy limestone ridgeline that rises 399m, offering 360-degree views of the luscious plains of Hawke's Bay, Cape Kidnappers, and as far as Mount Ruapehu in Tongariro National Park. Time your visit to coincide with the sunset and marvel as the ocher carpet creeps slowly over the surrounding land.

Te Mata Peak Road winds to the summit, where more than 30km of walking and biking tracks lace the 99ha grounds. The most popular trails begin from the Main Gates car park (Te Mata Peak Rd.). The **Piwakawaka Loop** (1.3km, 40 minutes) arches through groves of native trees as well as gum and redwoods frequented by fantail birds. The more challenging **Giant Circuit** (5.4km, 2 hours, 15 minutes) skirts the park's perimeter, then heads to the summit via the southern face.

Operated by local *iwi,* **Waimarama Maori** (021/057-0935, www.waimaramamaori.co.nz, 2 people minimum, $95 pp) runs two-hour walking tours at Te Mata. Guests can learn more about the land and the legends behind it. Transportation is from Havelock North, Hastings ($50), and Napier ($80).

ARATAKI HONEY VISITOR CENTRE

The **Arataki Honey Visitor Centre** (66 Arataki Rd., 06/877-7300, www.aratakihoneyhb.co.nz, 9am-5pm daily) makes for an interesting hour. The interactive museum is devoted to all things bees, with a fascinating peek into an enormous working hive (safely secured behind glass). There's free honey tasting, and a store sells honey-infused health, beauty, and edible goods.

BIRDWOODS

Birdwoods (298 Middle Rd., 06/877-1395, www.birdwoodsgallery.co.nz, 10am-5pm daily summer, 10am-4pm daily winter), 3km southwest of the village center, is a charming rustic complex. Gardens host a sculpture walk, and historic buildings house an art gallery with Kiwi works and African arts and crafts. There's also a café and an Old World candy store offering treats from glimmering glass jars.

Wine Tasting

Black Barn Vineyard (Black Barn Rd., 06/877-7985, www.blackbarn.com, 10am-5pm daily) is noted for its Bordeaux-influenced offerings, chardonnay, and sauvignon blanc. Sip a full-bodied red on the spacious elevated veranda on a sunny afternoon and you'll struggle to peel yourself away. During summer, an outdoor grassy amphitheater hosts films and concerts, and there's a weekly **farmers market** (9am-noon Sat.).

Positioned at the foot of Te Mata Peak, **Craggy Range** (253 Waimarama Rd., 06/873-7126, www.craggyrange.com) is visually spectacular. The wines are just as good on the palate as on the eyes thanks to a **cellar** (10am-6pm daily summer, 10am-5pm Wed.-Sun. winter) that offers tastings of their single-vineyard wines.

Food and Accommodations

All meals at **Black Barn Bistro** (Black Barn

Te Mata Peak

Rd., 06/877-7985, www.blackbarnbistro.com, 10am-5pm Sun.-Wed., 10am-9pm Thurs.-Sat. summer, 10am-5pm Sun. and Wed., 10am-9pm Thurs.-Sat. winter, $35) are prepared using Hawke's Bay produce. Light bites and cheese and olive platters accompany hearty mains like slow-cooked beef in red wine and duck confit. Luxury accommodations are also available.

Michelin-starred chef-run restaurant **Terroir** (noon-3pm and 6pm-close daily summer; noon-3pm and 6pm-close Wed.-Sun. winter, $35-40) serves line-caught fish, rib, lamb, and duck breast. The lunchtime boar belly platter is exceptional.

Few North Island establishments ooze as much class as secluded ★ **Mangapapa Hotel** (466 Napier Rd., 06/878-3234, www.mangapapa.co.nz, $550-1,200) a colonial mansion bordered by orchards and acres of landscaped grounds, with a pool, a sauna, a day spa, a tennis court, a gym, and bike hire. Twelve regal suites are uniquely furnished with antique armchairs and chandeliers that dangle from high ceilings; some rooms have balconies or private patios and spa tubs. All are equipped with tea and coffee facilities, luxurious baths with handmade toiletries, Sky TV with Netflix, free Wi-Fi, and robes and slippers. The fine-dining restaurant serves a revolving five-course seasonal degustation menu (6pm-8pm daily, $120) using local produce.

Transportation and Services

Havelock North is 5.5km southeast of downtown Hastings along Havelock Road. The **Havelock North i-SITE** (1 Te Aute Rd., 06/877-9600, www.hawkesbaynz.com, 10am-5pm Mon.-Fri., 10am-3pm Sat., 10am-2pm Sun.) has information on vineyards and local sights, including tide times at Cape Kidnappers, as well as transport and accommodations options throughout Hawke's Bay.

★ CAPE KIDNAPPERS

The southern reach of Hawke's Bay arches into a craggy claw-like peninsula known to Maori as Te Mata a Maui (The Fishhook of Maui). Maori cite it as the point by which Maui pulled North Island from the sea. It was renamed Cape Kidnappers by Captain Cook following a fatal misunderstanding with Maori traders in 1769, who wrongly believed the captain's Tahitian cabin boys were being held captive, so they smuggled one away in a canoe. Shots were fired, and some Maori were killed. In the ensuing confusion, the boy swam back to Cook's ship, *Endeavour.*

Today the stunning windswept headland is home to the world's largest and most accessible mainland gathering of **Australasian gannets.** The birds hatch here, fly to Australia after a few months, and return a few years later to spend the remainder of their 25- to 40-year lifespans exploring the Kiwi coast. Around 6,500 pairs of the graceful white, gold, and black birds are spread across several colonies. The two colonies open to the public are best viewed November-February; a third research colony is closed to the public. All colonies are closed to visitors during breeding season, July-October.

Walks

For those low on funds but high on energy, the DoC-maintained reserve can be accessed for free via the **Cape Kidnappers Walking Track** (19km round-trip, 5 hours), an easy though lengthy route that departs from Clifton, a small settlement at the foot of the

The Legend of Te Mata Peak

Te Mata Peak is said to have been formed when chief Te Mata O Rongokako was tasked with chewing his way through a mountain in order to win the hand of a Maori princess. Almost done, the chief choked to death on a boulder and fell to his death. His body formed the outline of Te Mata Peak. The legend goes that his distraught daughter then flung herself from the peak in a final act of grief.

peninsula. The track is well-marked but can only be tackled around low tide due to some beach walking. The best time to start is three hours after high tide; plan to return no more than 90 minutes after low tide.

Grab a *Cape Kidnappers Guide* from a local i-SITE, where staff can also advise on tide times or check the weather service online (www.metservice.com).

Tours

Gannet Beach Adventures (475 Clifton Rd., Clifton, 06/875-0898, www.gannets.com, hours vary daily Oct.-Apr., adults $44, children $24, students $34) tours operate via a novel method of transportation: Guests hitch a ride on a trailer towed by old-school red tractors. The trailers tour the Hawke's Bay coastline from Clifton to Cape Kidnappers, traveling through two gannet colonies before stopping for a break at the Cape. The viewing plateau at the end of the beach is a 20-minute walk. The four-hour tour is slow-paced, allowing you to take in the cliffs and the coast, and to dip your toes in the ocean. Pickups (adults $30, children $20) from the Napier or Hastings i-SITES are available and must be booked in advance. There is no public transport to or from Clifton.

For a more luxurious tour, without the steep trek from the beach to the headland, opt for **Gannet Safaris** (396 Clifton Rd., 06/875-0888, www.gannetsafaris.co.nz, adults $80, students and children $40). Their comfortable 4WD minibuses drive along the headland right alongside the gannet colonies. Pickups (adults $112, children $56) from Napier, Hastings, or the Havelock North i-SITES are available.

Transportation

Cape Kidnappers is 20 minutes east of Hastings and Havelock North via Clifton and Napier Roads, and 30 minutes southeast of Napier along Highway 2.

gannet colony on Cape Kidnappers

Taranaki and Whanganui

New Plymouth.................243
Egmont National Park..........251
New Plymouth to Whanganui..254
Whanganui....................256
Whanganui National Park......259
Palmerston North..............262

The most prominent features of this isolated region are the Whanganui River and Mount Taranaki, a beautiful and spectacularly symmetrical conical volcano permanently topped by ice.

A Maori allegory says that the volcano is a god that cleaved the path of the Whanganui River following a battle with mighty peaks to the east. The river is said to be the ancestor of these regional tribes.

The Whanganui River is the nation's longest stretch of navigable fresh water. It slices a path though Whanganui National Park, its age-old podocarp forest home to native birds like the kiwi, New Zealand wood pigeon, and the blue duck. Do not leave the region without exploring these sacred waters, whether aboard the historic paddle steamer *Waimarie* or kayaking deep into the national park.

The vibrant, verdant city of New Plymouth and the scenic city of Whanganui (the "Rhine of the Pacific") are the bases for this region. South of New Plymouth, the western flanks of Mount Taranaki spill onto the iconic Surf Highway, a coastal thoroughfare that links isolated sands pounded by year-round breaks. Where warriors once battled over this volcanic peninsula's fertile pastures, dairy cows now vie for the rich green grass.

PLANNING YOUR TIME

New Plymouth should be your base while exploring Taranaki. There's enough to keep you occupied here for a day or two, and it serves as a good launchpad to **Mount Taranaki.** Set aside a day to scale its peak or spend half a day exploring the lower trails and another half-day cruising the **Surf Highway** south of New Plymouth. If you don't have three days to conquer the **Whanganui Journey,** opt for a combined jet-boat and kayak tour. Most operators offer pickup and drop-off services in the region, and there are shuttle buses between many of the sights.

Previous: Taranaki dairy farm; the riverside city of Whanganui. **Above:** the Hawera Water Tower.

Taranaki and Whanganui

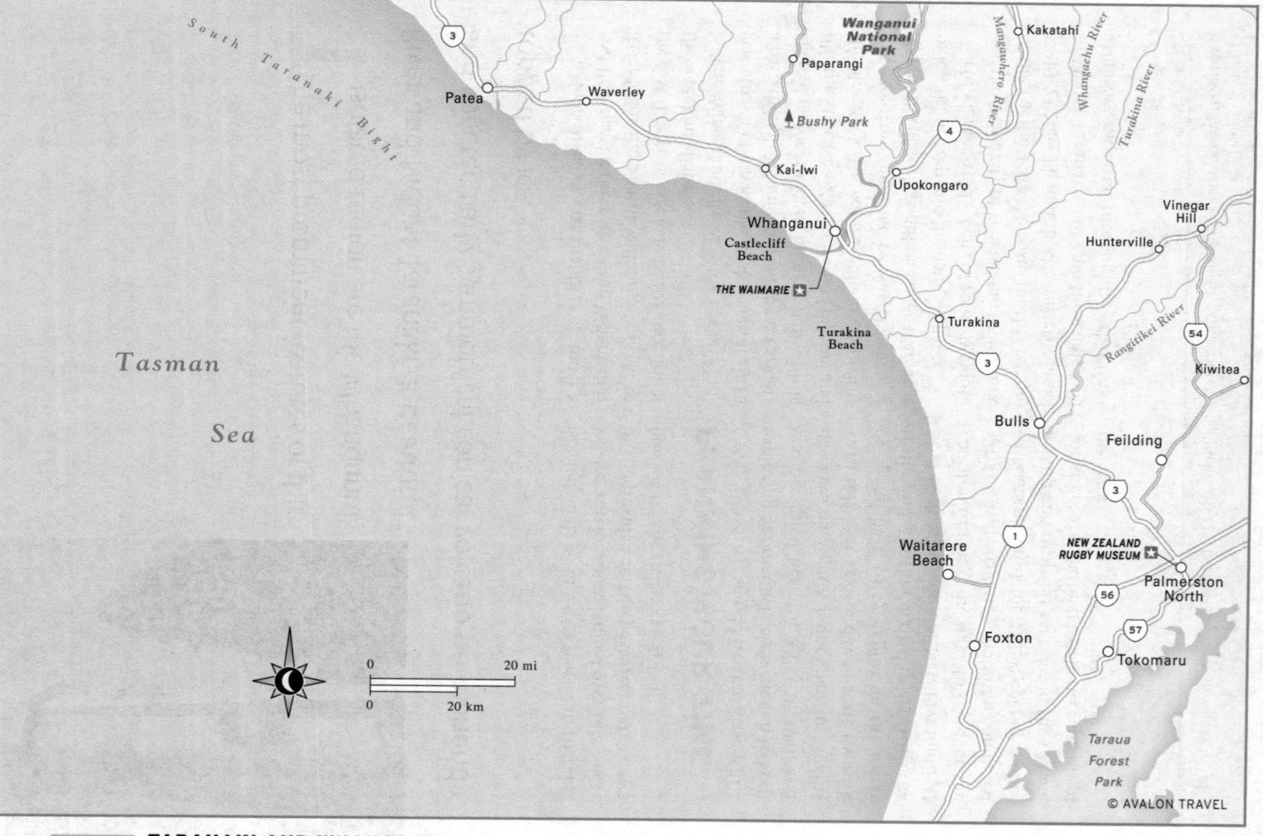

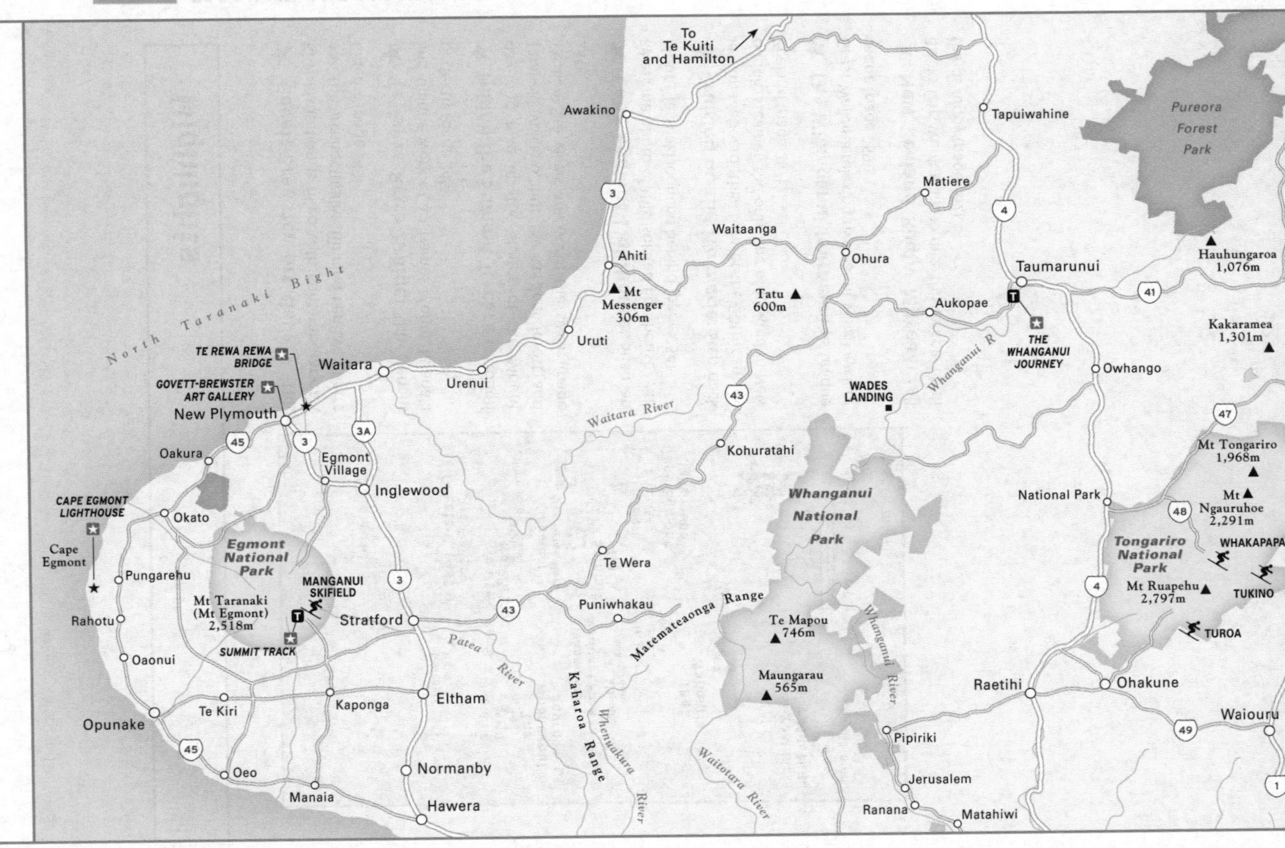
To Te Kuiti and Hamilton
Awakino
Tapuiwahine
Pureora Forest Park
Matiere
Waitaanga
Ahiti
Ohura
Hauhungaroa 1,076m
Taumarunui
Mt Messenger 306m
Tatu 600m
Aukopae
North Taranaki Bight
Uruti
THE WHANGANUI JOURNEY
Kakaramea 1,301m
TE REWA REWA BRIDGE
Waitara
Urenui
Owhango
GOVETT-BREWSTER ART GALLERY
WADES LANDING
Whanganui R
New Plymouth
Waitara River
Oakura
Egmont Village
Kohuratahi
Mt Tongariro 1,968m
Inglewood
CAPE EGMONT LIGHTHOUSE
Okato
Whanganui National Park
National Park
Mt Ngauruhoe 2,291m
Egmont National Park
Tongariro National Park
WHAKAPAPA
Cape Egmont
Te Wera
Pungarehu
MANGANUI SKIFIELD
Mt Taranaki (Mt Egmont) 2,518m
Puniwhakau
Range
Mt Ruapehu 2,797m
TUKINO
Rahotu
Stratford
Matemateaonga
Te Mapou 746m
SUMMIT TRACK
Patea River
TUROA
Oaonui
Kaharoa Range
Maungarau 565m
Whanganui River
Raetihi
Ohakune
Eltham
Te Kiri
Kaponga
Waiouru
Opunake
Whenuakura River
Pipiriki
Waitotara River
Normanby
Oeo
Jerusalem
Manaia
Hawera
Ranana
Matahiwi

Look for ★ to find recommended sights, activities, dining, and lodging.

Highlights

★ **Govett-Brewster Art Gallery:** This Kiwi institution is filled with contemporary art and the architecturally stunning Len Lye Centre Cinema (page 243).

★ **Te Rewa Rewa Bridge:** This elegant and unique work of art frames Mount Taranaki perfectly (page 245).

★ **Hiking the Summit Track:** It's a tough day-long hike up the slopes of the Mount Taranaki volcano, but the verdant forest and Tasman Sea views are worth the sweat (page 251).

★ **Cape Egmont Lighthouse:** Snag an awesome photo of this isolated lighthouse with Mount Taranaki looming behind (page 254).

★ **Cruising on the *Waimarie*:** Step back in time aboard this turn-of-the-20th-century paddle steamer, the only one of its kind in New Zealand (page 257).

★ **The Whanganui Journey:** This unique Great Walk is a relaxing river jaunt via a kayak or canoe (page 259).

★ **New Zealand Rugby Museum:** All Blacks fans won't want to miss this temple to all things rugby (page 262).

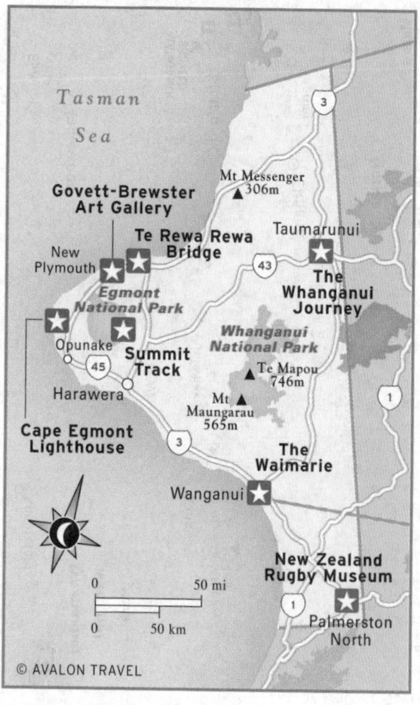

New Plymouth

New Plymouth is a relaxed yet sophisticated seaside city sitting in the shadow of a spectacular volcano. Punctuated by a collection of cultural enclaves and pummeled by year-round surf, New Plymouth has been named the nation's most livable city by esteemed Kiwi publication *North & South* magazine, and as the world's best small city by United Nations-endorsed Livable Communities. World-class galleries and exhibition spaces populate its countless parks, some of which are connected by walking trails, bike tracks, and a wonderful coastal route. New Zealand's only west coast deepwater port, New Plymouth is a place on the rise.

SIGHTS

Puke Ariki

Purpose-built **Puke Ariki** (1 Ariki St., 06/759-6060, www.pukeariki.com, 9am-6pm Mon.-Fri., 9am-9pm Wed., 9am-5pm Sat.-Sun., free) is a cultural and creative melting pot. This award-winning museum, gallery, and library are on an ancient *pa* site overlooking the shoreline. What shines brightest about Puke Ariki ("Hill of Chiefs") is its phenomenal collection of Maori artifacts, including bone and rock carvings, along with geological and wildlife exhibits. You'll learn about the region's vast subterranean oil and gas reserves and see a rather terrifying replica of a megalodon (an enormous, three-million-year-old species of shark) whose fossils have been found in South Taranaki.

★ Govett-Brewster Art Gallery

There's nothing else in the country quite like the **Govett-Brewster Art Gallery** (42 Queen St., 06/759-6060, www.govettbrewster.com, 10am-5pm daily, $15 adults, under age 16 free), an institution dedicated to Kiwi and international exhibitions of painting, sculpture, and kinetic art.

The on-site **Len Lye Centre Cinema** opened in 2015, its exterior resembling frozen waves of liquid metal. The Len Lye section houses a permanent collection of the experimental artist's work. The 9m-tall

the mirrored exterior of the Govett-Brewster Art Gallery

New Plymouth

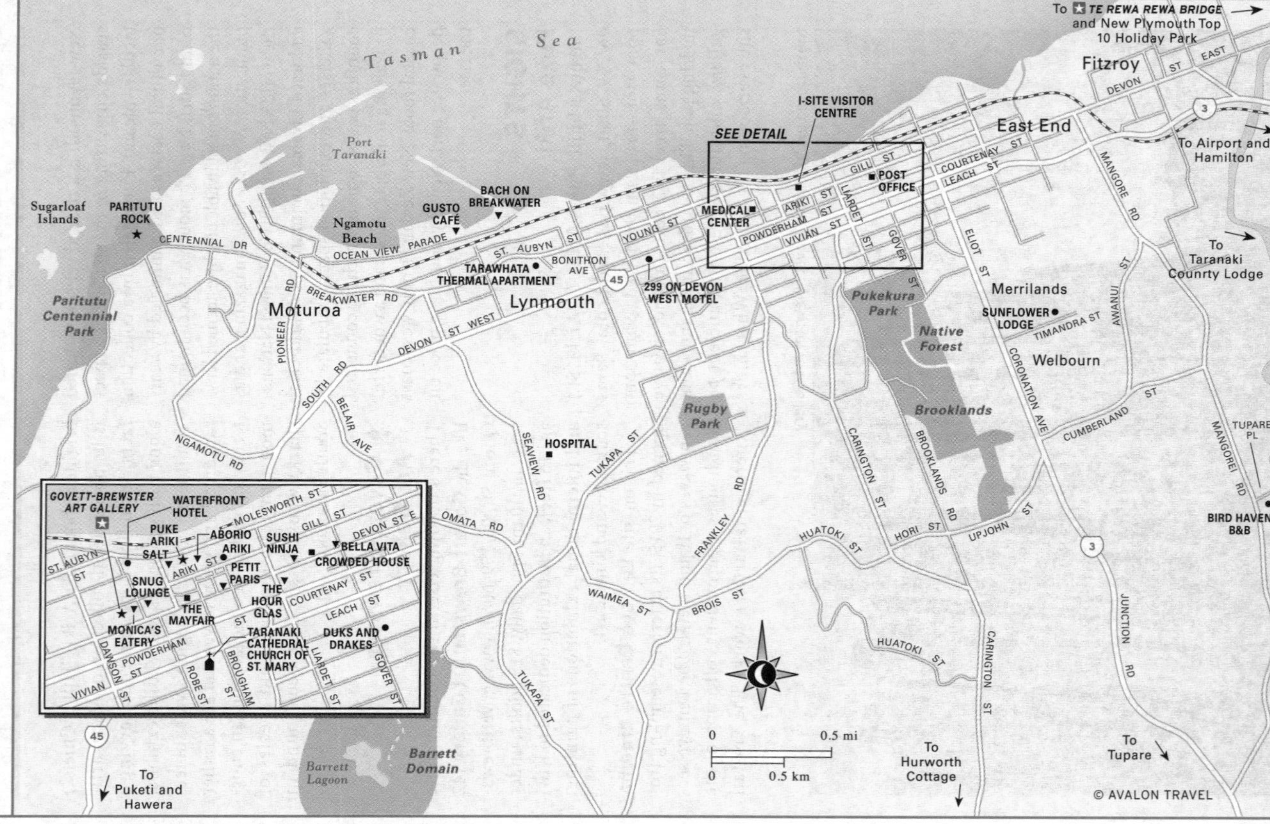

gallery and cinema showcases films along with arthouse productions from across the globe.

Guided **tours** (45 minutes, Thurs.-Sun., 2-person minimum, $25 pp) of the museum are available.

★ Te Rewa Rewa Bridge

The 83m **Te Rewa Rewa Bridge** is a working piece of modern art that supports foot and pedal traffic across the Waiwhakaiho River. An amalgam of blinding white shapes form a wave and a whale skeleton, meeting in an arch that perfectly frames Mount Taranaki in the distance. Find it on the New Plymouth Coastal Walkway (off Clemow Rd.).

Taranaki Cathedral Church of St. Mary

Built in 1846, **St. Mary's Church** (37 Vivian St., 06/758-3111, www.taranakicathedral.org.nz, 8am-6pm daily, free) is the oldest stone church in New Zealand, but its consecration in 2010 means that it is also the country's newest cathedral. Inside, beautiful arching timber beams reach from floor to ceiling, while pioneers, soldiers, and Maori warriors rest in the surrounding graveyard outside.

At the time of writing the cathedral was closed for earthquake strengthening renovations and due to re-open in 2020.

Hurworth Cottage

If walls could talk, **Hurworth Cottage** (906 Carrington Rd., 04/472-4341, www.historic.org.nz, by appointment, adults $5, children $2), 8km south of the New Plymouth city center, could tell some engrossing tales. Built in 1856 by pioneer farmer Harry Atkinson (who became prime minister four times), the house was one of only two to survive the New Zealand Wars. Today, it has been restored to its 19th-century glory, with family memorabilia and furniture. Most compelling is the old charcoal graffiti of Maori warriors on the wall.

Pukekura Park and Brooklands

The adjoining parks of **Pukekura Park and Brooklands** (10 Fillis St., 06/759-6060, www.pukekura.org.nz, 24 hours daily, free) were built on swampland in the late 19th century and are now among the city's best green sites. The park hosts two of the country's leading gatherings: **Womad** (http://tickets.womad.co.nz, Mar.) and the **Festival of Lights** (www.festivaloflights.nz, Dec.-Feb.).

Also on-site are a fernery, a small zoo of farm animals, reptiles, colorful birds, and a 23m-tall 2,000-year-old puriri tree. The historic Japanese-inspired Poets Bridge spans Main Lake for a wonderful photo with Mount Taranaki peeking over the tree line behind.

Pukeiti

A 30-minute drive from New Plymouth, the region's most impressive public garden, **Pukeiti** (2290 Carrington Rd., 0800/736-222, www.pukeiti.org.nz, 9am-5pm daily, free) is nestled on the lower slopes of Mount Taranaki. The 26ha rainforest clearing is home to more than 10,000 rhododendrons and azaleas, a colorful collection unrivaled elsewhere. Its extensive network of walking tracks weaves past forest, ferns, and mountain streams, where you're never far from a chorus of birds.

Tupare

The hillside grounds of **Tupare** (487 Mangorei Rd., 0800/736-222, www.tupare.info, 9am-8pm daily summer, 9am-5pm daily winter, free), which means "garland of flowers," were first cultivated in 1932 in the style of a traditional English garden. Today, the 1.6ha plot overlooking the Whaiwhakaiho River is carpeted with colorful blooms, redwoods, maples, and copper beeches.

Visitors can opt for a tour of the **Chapman-Taylor house** (11am Fri.-Mon. Oct.-Mar., free), built in the arts and crafts style. Free guided tours of the house and gardens are offered in summer high season, but

The Art of Len Lye

Innovative filmmaker and kinetic sculptor Len Lye was born in Christchurch in 1901 and spent some of his childhood living in a lighthouse in Marlborough—an experience that would shape much of his later work. After studying art in Wellington, he moved to Sydney, then Samoa, before settling in London in 1926, where he advanced his passion for the abstract and sculptures, developing a reputation in the media as a progressive thinker, the "futurist New Zealander" producing "mechanized art." Lye's animated filmmaking was equally challenging. Incorporating methods such as painting directly onto film saw him awarded the Medal of Honor at the Brussels International Cinema Festival in 1935. The following decade, the artist moved to New York, where he remained until his death in 1980, by which point he had forged a relationship with the Govett-Brewster Art Gallery in New Plymouth, who offered to realize large-scale versions of his work.

Built posthumously in 1996 from Lye's drawings, the *Wind Wand* sways on the seafront opposite Puke Ariki and is a much-loved New Plymouth landmark. The flexible 45m fiberglass and carbon fiber construction can give up to 20m in the wind, and takes on a whole new dimension come nightfall when the red orb at its tip, seemingly suspended in midair, gives off a warming glow.

must be booked in advance. Tupare is 6km southeast of downtown New Plymouth.

Sugar Loaf Islands and Paritutu Rock

Sugar Loaf Islands protrude west of the city, the craggy remnants of a substantial two-million-year-old volcano. The cluster of islands is 1km offshore and offers a predator-free bird paradise home to blue penguins. The surrounding marine reserve hosts migrating whales (Aug.-Sept.) and dolphins in summer.

Overlooking the islands from the mainland, **Paritutu Rock** rises steeply to 200m. A bike track leads to the top from the car park (Centennial Dr.).

While visitors are not allowed onto the islands, **Chaddy's Charters** (Ocean View Parade, 06/758-9133, www.chaddyscharters.co.nz, adults $40, children $15, under age 5 $5) operates one-hour cruises around them, as well as offering kayaks, stand-up paddleboards, and bike rentals.

RECREATION

For information on New Plymouth strolls, as well as walks in the wider region, pick up a copy of the free booklet *Taranaki: A Walkers Guide* from the **i-SITE Visitor Center** (Puke Ariki, 1 Ariki St., 06/759-6060, www.visitnewplymouth.co.nz, 9am-6pm Mon.-Tues. and Thurs.-Fri., 9am-9pm Wed., 9am-5pm Sat.-Sun.).

For bike rentals, head to the **Cycle Inn** (133 Devon St., 06/758-7418, www.cycleinn.co.nz, 8:30am-5pm Mon.-Fri., 9am-4pm Sat., 10am-2pm Sun.).

Walks

The **New Plymouth Coastal Walkway** runs along the shoreline for almost 13km and is shared by walkers, joggers, cyclists, skateboarders, and the occasional roller-skater. Inhale the salty air as you take in iconic sights like Len Lye's 45m *Wind Wand* (opposite Puke Ariki).

Pick up the track at Egmont Street and St. Aubyn Street and head east (turn right as you're looking at the sea) to **Te Rewa Bridge,** which spans the Waiwhakaiho River. The modern bridge amalgamates the shapes of a wave and a whale skeleton. It also provides a perfect frame for Mount Taranaki in the distance.

Puke Ariki (1 Ariki St., 06/759-6060, www.pukeariki.com, 1pm-3pm Sun. adults $25, under age 16 free) operates guided walks (2km, 2 hours) of city landmarks and historic buildings. The booklet containing historical photos and information is included and can also be purchased separately ($10). Book the walks through the i-SITE.

Surfing

Backed by the New Plymouth Coastal Walkway, mile-long **Fitzroy Beach** offers some of the greatest city surfing in the world. It's also popular with swimmers, and the beach is patrolled by lifeguards in summer. The **Beach Street Surf Shop** (39 Beach St., 06/758-0400, 10am-5pm Mon.-Fri., 10am-3pm Sat.-Sun.) rents surfboards and stand-up paddleboards. One-hour surf and stand-up paddleboard lessons ($100-120) are also available.

The beach is part of **Fitzroy Seaside Park** (end of Beach St.), 3km east of downtown.

Spa

Take a load off at **Taranaki Thermal Spa** (8 Bonithon Ave., 06/759-1666, www.pureone.co.nz, 10am-7:30pm Tues.-Sat. Dec.-Apr., 10am-9pm Tues.-Sun. May-Nov., adults $13-16, children $5-10), a historic bathhouse. The site was founded in 1914 after hot springs were discovered while drilling for oil. Today, guests can enjoy a public spa, five private pools, and an infrared sauna as well as massages and thermal wraps. Reservations are recommended. If you stay in the adjacent two-bedroom Tarawhata Thermal Apartment (021/062-2671, $220), spa entry is free.

ENTERTAINMENT AND EVENTS

Nightlife

It's called **Crowded House** (93-99 Devon St. E., 06/759-4921, www.crowdedhouse.co.nz, 10am-close daily) for good reason. This no-nonsense sports bar has big screens, pool tables, live music, and drink and meal deals galore. Classic, hearty pub grub includes ribs and wings.

Head to **Snug Lounge** (124 Devon St. E., 06/757-9130, www.snuglounge.co.nz, 4pm-close Mon.-Sat., noon-close Sun.) for sophisticated cocktails in a stylish Japanese-themed setting. Exquisite snacks include fresh modern dishes such as tempura prawns with wasabi mayo, steamed buns, wontons, and dumplings.

Discover dozens of craft beers at **The Hour Glass** (49 Liardet St., 06/758-2299, 4pm-close Tues.-Sat.), along with a healthy selection of wine and spirits. A good dose of tapas elevates the trendy lair-like setting. Live music plays on Friday nights.

In keeping with its previous incarnation as a theater, there's always something happening at **The Mayfair** (67-73 Devon St. W., 06/759-2088, www.themayfair.co.nz, 11am-close Wed.-Sun.), one of New Plymouth's buzziest bars. Come for live bands, DJs, comedians, and even classical acts as well as decent pub food, especially pizza.

Festivals and Events

A highlight of the Kiwi calendar, the World of Music, Arts and Dance festival, or **Womad** (Pukekura Park, www.womad.co.nz, Mar.), is a three-day music and cultural extravaganza that attracts local and international acts.

For two weeks, the **Taranaki International Arts Festival** (www.artsfest.co.nz, Aug.) offers a program packed with theater, comedy, art exhibitions, dance, and concerts all around the city. The event is held every other year in odd-numbered years.

The 10-day **Taranaki Fringe Garden Festival** (www.taranakigardens.co.nz, Oct.) takes place in the "Garden of New Zealand," promoting the region's finest public spaces at their most colorful.

The **Festival of Lights** (Pukekura Park, www.festivaloflights.nz, Dec.-Feb.) is a smorgasbord of live performances, plays, and music. The park's plants, trees, and ferns are all beautifully illuminated come nightfall.

FOOD

Cafés

Next door to Govett-Brewster, **Monica's Eatery** (King St. and Queen St., 06/759-2038, www.monicaseatery.co.nz, 6:30am-close daily, $15) is named after the founding patron of the gallery, Monica Brewster. Its

Best Food

★ **Bach on Breakwater:** Enjoy breakfast or lunch in a relaxed romantic seaside setting (page 248).

★ **Bella Vita:** Classic Italian food is served in a hip European-inspired environment (page 248).

★ **The Citadel:** Enjoy homemade burgers in this laid-back beach-house/restaurant (page 258).

★ **Bethany's:** Sample the seared ostrich at this contemporary airy eatery (page 263).

street-corner setting is hung with lights and wraparound windows welcome natural light, creating an airy, inspirational atmosphere. The menu is equally fresh, and fashionably presented; go for the cured salmon bruschetta and a smoothie for breakfast.

The region's coolest café, ★ **Bach on Breakwater** (Ocean View Parade, Port Taranaki, 06/769-6967, www.bachonbreakwater.co.nz, 9:30am-4pm Wed.-Fri., 9:30am-5pm Sat.-Sun., $12-22) has a relaxed, romantic vibe thanks to its seaside setting. The café is decked out with rich knotted wood—it's like chilling in a forest—with a menu heavy on vegan and gluten-free options. Order the superb pear, blue cheese, and walnut salad, or opt for more traditional breakfast and lunch options like pancakes and bacon or seafood chowder.

There's no better place to grab a morning coffee and croissant than at **Petit Paris** (34 Currie St., 06/759-0396, www.petitparis.co.nz, 7:30am-4pm daily), the region's best-smelling eatery. This bustling city joint has a counter heaving with sticky temptations like tarts, éclairs, and flans, as well as savory delights such as baguettes and salads. The onion soup is *très magnifique*.

Contemporary

Photo-worthy meals are offered in an artistic setting with sea views at **Salt** (1 Egmont St., 06/769-5304, www.waterfront.co.nz, 6:30am-close Mon.-Fri., 7am-close Sat.-Sun., $32-38), a fine-dining eatery beneath the Waterfront Hotel. The classic menu includes staples such as duck breast and the fish of the day. The staff are attentive and there's a happy hour (4:30pm-6pm daily).

Tucked into a trendy, industrial marina space, **Gusto Café and Restaurant** (Ocean View Parade, Port Taranaki, 06/759-8133, www.gustotaranaki.co.nz, 10am-close Mon.-Fri., 9am-close Sat., 9am-3pm Sun., $28-40) rises up from the seashore with a spacious balcony and floor-to-ceiling windows overlooking the water. An imaginative menu features plenty of seafood and classics with a twist like lamb rack with homemade venison sausage, garlic-buttered kale, and rosemary au jus.

Italian

Located in the Puke Ariki building, colorful **Arborio** (65 St. Aubyn St., 06/759-1241, www.arborio.co.nz, 9am-close daily, $21-38) offers modern dining with great service and sea views. Fresh, seasonal produce features prominently on a Mediterranean-inspired menu that includes pizza, pasta, and seafood. The ginger-glazed slow-cooked pork with caramelized rutabaga and pickled cucumber is a highlight. Secure a table on the terrace if you can.

Black tablecloths, atmospheric lighting, and bare brick walls set the tone at ★ **Bella Vita** (146 Devon St. E., 06/758-3393, www.bellavita.co.nz, lunch 11:30am-2:30pm Mon.-Sat., dinner 5pm-close daily, $24-38), the best

Best Accommodations

★ **Taranaki Country Lodge:** This blissful setting lets Taranaki's spectacular scenery soak into your soul (page 250).

★ **Opunake Motel & Backpackers Lodge:** This old-fashioned lodge boasts views of Mount Taranaki (page 254).

★ **Browns Boutique B&B:** Elegant airy rooms are within a short distance of downtown Whanganui (page 258).

★ **Fitzherbert Castle Motel:** This kitschy castle is fit for kings on a budget in Palmerston North (page 263).

Italian eatery in New Plymouth. Excellent pizza, pasta, and risotto plates are served alongside confit duck, pork belly, and an exquisite lamb rack. Portion sizes are generous but save room for the dessert—tiramisu.

Japanese

An authentic Japanese experience at **Sushi Ninja** (89 Devon St. E., 06/759-1392, www.sushininja.co.nz, 9am-5pm Mon., 9am-close Tues.-Sun., $12-37) arrives by way of rolled sushi, sashimi, teriyaki, and *donburi* dishes prepared by chefs behind an open bar. On top of that, the usual bamboo furnishing, paper lanterns, ornamental umbrellas, and a great sake selection makes for a warm and relaxed environment.

ACCOMMODATIONS

Under $100

Ducks and Drakes Boutique Motel and Backpackers (48 Lemon St., 06/758-0404, www.ducksanddrakes.co.nz, dorm $32-38, $68 s, $90-150 d) boasts a welcoming vibe thanks to its colorful decor, glass-clad sunroom, and lounge area with a log fire. Women-only dorms and en suite doubles are available. Facilities include free Wi-Fi and Sky TV. A long dining table encourages socialization, but there's plenty of quiet nooks to kick back in. The adjacent motel ($130-150) includes studio- and one-bedroom cottages with Sky TV and kitchenettes that open onto a shared garden.

Ariki Backpackers (9 Ariki St., 06/769-5020, www.arikibackpackers.com, dorm $27-30, $70 s, $70-90 d) has a wonderful sun deck with views of the *Wind Wand*. Beds are comfy, but the rooms could do with a sprucing up. A bar downstairs means you may wish to pack ear plugs. It's a social hostel, with plenty of amenities like free Wi-Fi, DVD and book libraries, a barbecue, a well-stocked kitchen, and Sky TV.

$100-200

Perched on the edge of town with magnificent views of Tupare Gardens, the Waiwhakaiho River, and Mount Taranaki, cozy **Bird Haven B&B** (10C Tupare Place, 06/758-1789, $120) is an affordable and rural escape. Amenities include a spa bath, free Wi-Fi, and a deck and patio space for enjoying a barbecue. The owners couldn't be more hospitable or the rooms more colorful, and plenty of native birds visit its rich expansive gardens, all within a five-minute drive of downtown.

With cast-iron rail balconies, colorful shrubbery, and clay walls overlooking a swimming pool, there's a Mediterranean feel to **299 On Devon West Motel** (299 Devon St. W., 06/757-9151, www.the299motel.co.nz, $150-210). Immaculate self-contained units range from studios to two-bedrooms, with Sky TV and a DVD player, free Wi-Fi, floor heating, and complimentary bicycle rental. Many of the city's main sights are just blocks away.

$200-300

Enjoy complimentary access to Taranaki Thermal Spa when you stay at **Tarawhata Thermal Apartment** (8 Bonithon Ave., 06/759-1666, www.pureone.co.nz, $220), a modern luxury lodging with two-bedroom units, Sky TV, free Wi-Fi, patio areas, and private hot-spring baths, with access to a full a kitchen.

The **Waterfront Hotel** (1 Egmont St., 06/769-5301, www.waterfront.co.nz, $240-550), is the city's only lodging on the seashore. Some of its modern, if generic, rooms come with spas and balconies and offer sea or city views. Amenities include free Wi-Fi and Sky TV. Guests can also make use of the 24-hour gym next door. Downstairs is the equally modern eatery, Salt.

A 15-minute drive from downtown, the innovative ★ **Taranaki Country Lodge** (169 Hursthouse Rd., 06/755-0274, www.taranakicountrylodge.co.nz, $200-300) features mountain and coastal views from architecturally designed chalet-like units with kitchen facilities, private patios, free Wi-Fi, and TVs. It's a blissful setting to sit and let Taranaki's spectacular scenery soak into your soul. Come nightfall, the sky bursts with stars.

Camping and Holiday Park

The well-placed **New Plymouth Top 10 Holiday Park** (29 Princes St., 06/758-256, www.nptop10.co.nz) is minutes from the sea and city center, with views of Mount Taranaki. Its many facilities include a heated swimming pool, a spa, a sauna, and a TV lounge where you can make friends over a giant game of chess. Tent and van sites ($52-56) have plenty of shade, and cabins ($95-115) come with a fridge and hot-drink-making facilities but share communal baths. Motel units ($120-330) range from studios to three bedrooms, with TVs and private kitchens and baths.

TRANSPORTATION AND SERVICES

New Plymouth is 160km northwest of Whanganui and 240km southwest of Hamilton along Highway 3. It's 277km west of Taupo along Highways 30 and 3.

Air

New Plymouth Airport (NPL, 192 Airport Dr., 06/759-6060, www.nplairport.co.nz) is 11km from downtown. **Air New Zealand** (www.airnewzealand.co.nz) operates daily flights from Auckland and Wellington, with weekday flights from Christchurch. **Jetstar** (www.jetstar.com) also serves New Plymouth. **Scott's Airport Shuttle** (0800/373-001, www.npairportshuttle.co.nz) operate a door-to-door minibus service. Airport-based car rental companies include **Budget** (www.budget.co.nz) and **Hertz** (www.hertz.co.nz).

Public Transportation

Citylink (0800/872-287, www.trc.govt.nz) runs buses around the city. **Southlink** (06/761-8363) operates a Friday bus service between New Plymouth's bus depot (Ariki St.) and Napier Street in Opunake. The minibus can be flagged down from anywhere along the road. **Connector** (0800/266-328) operates daily shuttles from New Plymouth to Opunake via Stratford and Hawera. For taxis, call **Energy City Cabs** (06/757-5580).

Services

The New Plymouth **i-SITE Visitor Centre** (Puke Ariki, 1 Ariki St., 06/759-6060, www.visitnewplymouth.co.nz, 9am-6pm Mon.-Tues. and Thurs.-Fri., 9am-9pm Wed., 9am-5pm Sat.-Sun.) has information on local accommodations and transport, conditions at Egmont National Park, and hut tickets.

The **library** (1 Ariki St., 06/759-6060, www.pukeariki.com, 9am-6pm Mon.-Tues. and Thurs.-Fri., 9am-9pm Wed., Sat.-Sun. 9am-5pm) is in the museum complex and has free Internet access. There's also a **post office** (21 Currie St., 0800/081-190, www.nzpost.co.nz, 9am-4:30pm Mon.-Fri.).

Medicross (8 Egmont St., 06/759-8915, daily 8am-8pm) is an urgent care and doctor's clinic, with a pharmacy, and no appointments needed. There's also a **hospital** (David St., 06/753-6139).

Egmont National Park

Egmont is New Zealand's second-oldest national park. It covers 35,000ha carpeted in native bush and alpine tussock, but it's really all about Mount Taranaki, a dormant volcano. This near-perfect cone dominates not only the park but the entire Taranaki peninsula along with a good chunk of the immediate North Island. (Such is its striking resemblance to Mount Fuji that it doubled as the Japanese peak in the Tom Cruise film *The Last Samurai.*)

The 2,518m Mount Taranaki formed more than 100,000 years ago. It is reported to have last erupted in 1775, but that may have actually been 25 years later. In 2017, the sacred peak was granted human rights.

Egmont National Park is a hiker's wonderland, with 300km of trails. Egmont Village provides entry from the north, while the main gateway town of Stratford connects to entry points from the east and south. All access is off the Inland Route, a section of Highway 3 that links New Plymouth to Whanganui via Hawera.

NORTH EGMONT

From Egmont Village, Egmont Road snakes 16km to the North Egmont Visitor Centre at the base of the volcano, where there are several well-signed walks.

Walks

The **Ambury Monument Walk** (10 minutes one-way) is a shady route past the Camphouse to a picnic spot and stone memorial of Arthur Ambury, who died trying to save William Edwin Gourlay on Taranaki in 1918. Return along the same path or hop onto the **Nature Walk** (25 minutes round-trip) through totara and kamahi forest to views across the Ngatoro Valley.

The **Ngatoro Loop** (1 hour) jumps onto the Summit Track for a time as it travels through a "goblin forest," so-named because of its otherworldly fern- and moss-covered tree trunks. There is a stream crossing that is generally dry or very low—though it may be impassable following a downpour.

★ SUMMIT TRACK

Egmont National Park attracts 300,000 visitors each year, and its star peak is New Zealand's most climbed mountain. The **Summit Track** can be hiked by most fit souls; mountaineering skills are not required, except in winter. Peak tramping season is January-mid-April, although you may still need an ice ax and crampons.

The track stretches 6.3km with an elevation gain of 1,600m and is one of New Zealand's most difficult day hikes. Two-thirds of the way, the private Taranaki Alpine Club hut, **Tahurangi Lodge,** offers a place to catch your breath, take in the views, and use the public restroom before continuing up the loose scoria face, along Lizard Ridge, to the edge of the icy crater and on to the summit rock. Maori consider the top of Taranaki *tapu* (sacred); don't step foot directly on to the summit stone.

As inviting as the slopes may appear from the base, Mount Taranaki is deceptively high, and conditions can change furiously. Check weather at the Department of Conservation (DoC) Visitor Center before you start, and allow at least five hours to summit and three hours to return. This hike is best done with a partner; advise someone of your plans and approximate time of return, or log your itinerary online (www.adventuresmark.org.nz).

Food and Accommodations

Mountain Café (Egmont Rd., 06/756-9093, 9am-3pm daily summer, 10am-3pm daily winter) is the region's highest café at 1,000m elevation. At the top are views of forest, farmland, and the alpine environment. The coffee is good, as is the soup, muffins, and burgers.

From the visitors center, it's a short stroll to the historic 34-bunk **Camphouse** (Egmont Rd., 06/756-0990, www.doc.govt.nz, adults $25, children $10, under age 5 free). It's pretty luxurious by DoC hut standards, with a hot shower, electric heating, and cooking facilities, includes utensils. Bring your own sleeping bag. It's positioned in front of the volcano and is one of the coolest slices of real estate on North Island.

Transportation and Services

Egmont National Park is a 10-minute drive from New Plymouth, southeast along Highway 3. **Top Guides** (0800/448-433 or 027/270-2932, www.topguides.co.nz, $35) runs the Taranaki Mountain Shuttle between New Plymouth and the North Egmont Visitor Centre. Custom guided walks and hikes ($99-349 pp) of the region are also available.

Intercity (09/583-5780, www.intercity.co.nz, $20-35 round-trip) operates daily shuttle bus services between New Plymouth (19 Ariki St.) and Egmont Village.

The **North Egmont Visitor Centre** (Egmont Rd., 06/756-0990, www.doc.govt.nz, 8:30am-4pm daily) offers maps, a full list of walks, and hiking and weather information along with hut tickets and a museum-like volcano exhibition that winds up to a sizable viewing window of the peak.

EAST EGMONT

Pembroke Road runs west from the town of Stratford into Egmont National Park. It continues another 3km to the 1,172m-high plateau. This is the park's highest road point, and an excellent spot to take photos.

Walks

The **Kamahi Loop Track** (20 minutes) is an easy stroll through the goblin forest of Taranaki's lower slopes. The more challenging **Curtis Falls Track** (2-3 hours round-trip) weaves through the steep Manganui Gorge, following the riverbed to the base

Summit Track

of Curtis Falls as it tumbles over ancient lava flows. Both tracks begin at Stratford Mountain House (Pembroke Rd.).

Stratford

Unassuming Stratford sits 20 minutes south of Egmont Village. Named after William Shakespeare's hometown, there are plenty of nods to the bard in the street names. New Zealand's largest **glockenspiel** is on Broadway, and the faux-Elizabethan clock tower plays Shakespeare quotes (10am, 1pm, 3pm, and 7pm daily) as figurines of Romeo and Juliet appear on the balcony.

FOOD AND ACCOMMODATIONS

Stratford Mountain House (Pembroke Rd., 06/765-6100, www.stratfordmountainhouse.co.nz, $160-200) is a lovely renovated lodge cradled by dense bush. The collection of chalets comes with TVs, hot-drink facilities, and private spa baths. The on-site **café** (breakfast 9am-noon daily, lunch until 2:30pm

The Legend of Mount Taranaki

Legend relates how Taranaki ("shining peak") was exiled to the west coast from the volcanic heartland following defeat to Mount Tongariro in a battle for the love of Mount Pihanga. As Taranaki retreated, he carved the Whanganui River in his wake before settling for eternity to watch over his lost love.

daily) serves traditional breakfasts, while the **restaurant** (6pm-9pm daily, $33-43) offers an exquisite evening menu of scotch fillet, seafood, and duck. Save space for the mud cake.

Transportation and Services

From Stratford, Pembroke Road runs west into Egmont National Park. National bus carrier **Intercity** (09/583-5780, www.intercity.co.nz) stops daily outside the i-SITE (Prospero Place) on the way to and from Wellington. **Eastern Taranaki Experience** (5 Verona Place, 027/471-7136 or 027/246-6383, www.eastern-taranaki.co.nz) operates shuttle services throughout region and offers guided tours.

Stop at the **i-SITE Visitor Centre** (Prospero Place, 06/765-6708, www.stratford.govt.nz, 8:30am-5pm Mon.-Fri., 10am-3pm Sat.-Sun.) for an update on weather and track conditions. Look for the sculptured bust of the famous playwright outside.

Forgotten World Highway

Running northeast for 155km, the **Forgotten World Highway** (Hwy. 43) connects Stratford to Taumarunui, 50km west of Lake Taupo. The isolated road was once a Maori trade route. It winds past the northern reaches of Whanganui National Park for 20km as it crosses four saddles and through valleys, native forests, and a historic tunnel. There are no gas stations en route, and the 12km stretch of road through Tangarakau Gorge is unpaved.

SOUTH EGMONT

Walks

The **Wilkies Pools Loop Track** (80 minutes round-trip) is a real treat. Walk through mystical goblin forests cloaked in moss and ferns to a collection of pools that have formed in ancient lava flows. Allow time for a blissful dip in the pools. The **Kapuni Loop Track** (1 hour) navigates more goblin forest alongside the Kapui Stream to the base of the 18m Dawson Falls as it plunges from petrified lava.

Food and Accommodations

The **Dawson Falls Mountain Lodge** (1890 Upper Manaia Rd., 06/765-5457, www.dawsonfalls.co.nz, $125 s, $19-230 d) has a cozy collection of rooms; some have garden views, and some overlook Mount Taranaki. Breakfast and Wi-Fi are included. The on-site **café** (10am-3pm daily) serves energy-boosting pre-hike offerings such as toasted sandwiches, wraps, and muffins.

Transportation

The **Dawson Falls Visitor Centre** (Manaia Rd., 027/443-0248, www.doc.govt.nz, 9am-4pm daily) is 25 minutes from Stratford. For those approaching the park from the south, turn off Highway 3 at the town of Eltham and head northwest toward the peak. The center marks the start of more walks.

Eastern Taranaki Experience (5 Verona Place, 027/471-7136 or 027/246-6383, www.eastern-taranaki.co.nz) provides shuttle services to the Dawson Falls area.

New Plymouth to Whanganui

South of New Plymouth, the Inland Route along Highway 3 heads directly toward Whanganui via Hawera, reaching the town in a little over two hours—but the Surf Highway (Hwy. 45) is far more fun.

The **Surf Highway,** officially Highway 45, winds 105km around the Taranaki peninsula from New Plymouth to Hawera, passing a handful of sleepy towns and villages en route. On one side of the highway, dusty roads snake to isolated coasts with clockwork crashing swells that have lured local and visiting surfers for decades; opposite rises that majestic volcano. Try to travel some of the route at dawn to marvel at the magical tricks the light plays as the sun peeks over the mount.

OAKURA

Chilled-out Oakura hosts one of the coast's most popular surf beaches, patrolled by lifeguards during the summer months, as well as a gaggle of arty cafés and boutiques popular with wave-loving folk.

Surfing

What surf master Gary Bruckner doesn't know about surfing isn't worth knowing, so where better to pick up a few tips than his **Tarawave Surf School** (021/119-621, www.taranakisurfschool.com)? Choose a 1.5-hour group lesson ($50-60) or opt for a private lesson ($75) and receive the benefit of more than 40 years of experience. Wetsuits and surfboards are included.

Accommodations

Just a short walk from the beach, **Oakura Beach Holiday Park** (2 Jans Terrace, 06/752-7861, www.oakurabeach.com) camp sites overlook the Tasman Sea. A wide range of units ($85-150) include basic cabins with bunks and shared baths to fully self-contained motel-style lodgings with kitchens, private decks, and TVs. You can also pitch a tent or park your RV ($44).

CAPE EGMONT

★ Cape Egmont Lighthouse

A 20-minute drive south of Oakura is the blink-and-you'll-miss-it township of Pungarehu. Look for the turn west onto Cape Road, which winds down toward the coast and past the **Cape Egmont Lighthouse** (you can't see the lighthouse from the highway). The lighthouse was built in London in the mid-19th century, then shipped in parts to Mana Island near Wellington. It moved to Taranaki in 1877. Today, it's a fantastic spot for photos, with Mount Taranaki looming in the distance.

OPUNAKE

Wonderful surf breaks await at Opunake, whose beach is also patrolled by lifeguards in summer. The town is home to an unusual **mural trail,** most of which is concentrated along the town's main street.

Opunake Mural Trail

A walk down the main drag reveals 23 pieces of street art, all depicting aspects of Kiwi life and culture. Look for ***The Wave Over Mount Taranaki Postage Stamp*** on the front of the old post office (93 Tasman St.) and the fish mural outside the swimming pool (Longfellow Rd.). A map and a complete list of artworks are available at the **i-SITE Visitor Center** (55 High St., Hawera, 06/278-8599, www.southtaranaki.com, 8:30am-5:15pm Mon.-Fri., 9:30am-4pm Sat.-Sun. summer, 10am-3pm daily winter).

Accommodations

Surrounded by expansive fields, the ★ **Opunake Motel & Backpackers Lodge** (36 Heaphy Rd., 06/761-8330, www.

Cape Egmont Lighthouse

opunakemotel.co.nz, dorm $30, $40 s, $75 d) boasts special views of Mount Taranaki. The endearingly old-fashioned lodge is festooned with floral furnishings in the bedrooms and thrift-store furniture in the kitchen and communal area. Motel units and cottages ($95-110 s, $110-130 d) come equipped with full kitchens and separate lounge areas. Free Wi-Fi is provided throughout, and some units overlook the volcano.

HAWERA

Tawhiti Museum

Often cited as New Zealand's finest private museum, the **Tawhiti Museum** (401 Ohangai Rd., 06/278-6837, www.tawhitimuseum.co.nz, 10am-4pm daily Dec. 26-Jan., 10am-4pm Fri.-Mon. Feb.-May, 10am-4pm Sun. June-Aug., adults $15, children $5, under age 5 free), a 10-minute drive east of town, has a multitude of awards to back it up. This innovative complex hosts life-size statues with lifelike features (friends and locals lent their features for the cast makers) that breathe life into historic scenes depicting Maori villagers, warriors, and whalers as well as European settlers tending to kitchens or carpentry, or poised on a candle- and lantern-lit waterway. Miniature dioramas of scenes from the New Zealand Wars are another impressive addition to this ever-burgeoning universe.

Hawera Water Tower

There's something rather noble about the historic **Hawera Water Tower** (High St., adults $2.50, children $1) as it protrudes skyward from a pretty garden behind the i-SITE Visitor Centre. The name of the town comes from the Maori *te hawera,* which means "the burned place." The town was named following a feud between two local tribes that culminated in one burning the other's village to the ground. After the arrival of the Europeans, several large-scale fires engulfed sections of the town, and thus the 54m water tower was built and opened in 1914. Today, visitors can climb its 215 steps for views of Hawera and the surrounding pastures.

Accommodations

A sharp-lined minimal exterior lends a modernist feel to **The Park Motel** (61 Waihi Rd., 06/278-7275, www.theparkmotel.co.nz, $140-170). The coolness continues inside, from the slick studios through the two-bedroom suites. All are equipped with free Wi-Fi, Sky TV, cooking facilities, desks, and electric blankets. Guests are free to use the nearby gym.

Transportation and Services

South Taranaki i-SITE Visitor Centre (55 High St., Hawera, 06/278-8599, www.southtaranaki.com, 8:30am-5:15pm Mon.-Fri., 9:30am-4pm Sat.-Sun. summer, 10am-3pm daily winter) has free Wi-Fi and info on tours, accommodations, and travel in Taranaki.

Whanganui

Photogenic Whanganui ("great bay") sits nestled on the banks of its eponymous river. The charming provincial hub was established in 1840 and is one of New Zealand's oldest cities. Known as the "Rhine of New Zealand," Whanganui is laced with a wonderfully colorful architecture that betrays its rich artisanal soul—it is home to hundreds of artists, sculptors, and glassblowers.

You may see the town name spelled "Wanganui." Though this is widely accepted, the Maori spelling with an "h" is the proper usage.

SIGHTS

Whanganui Regional Museum

The highly prized collection of ancestral *taonga* (treasures) at **Whanganui Regional Museum** (62 Ridgeway St., 06/349-1110, www.wrm.org.nz, 10am-4:30pm Mon.-Sat., free) has few peers in New Zealand. Opened in 1892, the museum's impressive collection of Maori artifacts includes carved war canoes *(waka)* as well as portraits of Maori leaders by Kiwi artist Gottfried Lindauer and weaponry like the beautiful brutal *mere*—a club made from greenstone.

Sarjeant Gallery Te Whare o Rehua

With more than 5,500 contemporary and historical artworks that date to the mid-19th-century, the **Sarjeant Gallery Te Whare o Rehua** (38 Taupo Quay, 06/349-0506, www.sarjeant.org.nz, 10:30am-4:30pm daily, free) is among New Zealand's most impressive and creative exhibitions of photography and art. Formerly housed in one of the city's most impressive buildings—a majestic dome-topped white Oamaru stone structure built in 1912—the gallery moved to Taupo Quay following earthquake damage.

Durie Hill Elevator and War Memorial Tower

Across the Whanganui City Bridge, a carved Maori *waharoa* (gateway) marks the entrance to a 213m-long pedestrian tunnel (enter at 42 Anzac Parade) under Durie Hill. Here you'll find the **Durie Hill Elevator** (one-way adults

the *Waimarie*

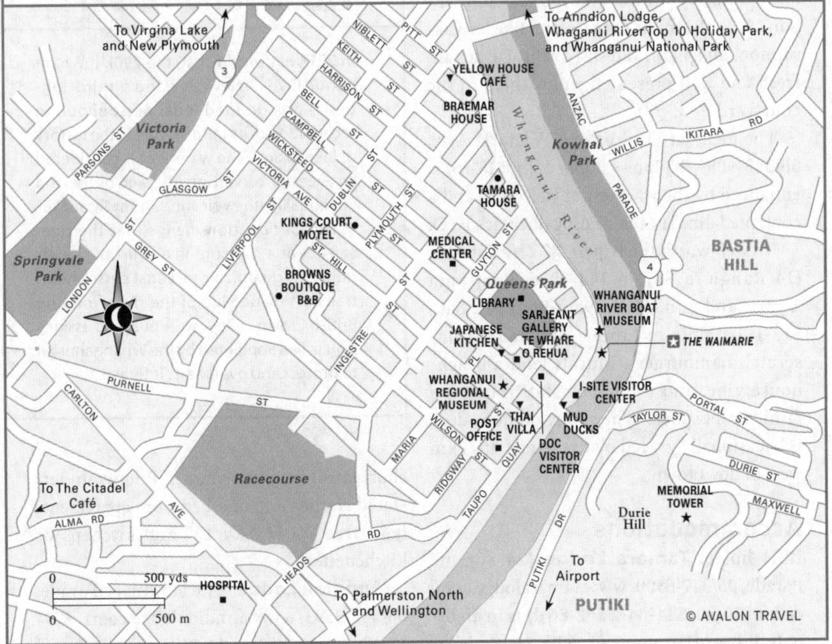

$2, children $1). Built in 1919, it rises 66m to the top of the hill. Emerge to splendid views over Whanganui and the river.

Enhance your exploration further by scaling the 176 spiral steps of the handsome **War Memorial Tower,** a Category 2 Historic Place that opened in 1925 in honor of the local soldiers killed in World War I. Either take the elevator back down or follow the 191-step walkway to more views to the river.

★ The *Waimarie*

Salvaged in 1993 from the depths of the Whanganui River, the ***Waimarie*** (1a Taupo Quay, 06/347-1863, www.waimarie.co.nz, cruise 11am daily, adults $45, children $15, under age 5 free) is New Zealand's only authentic coal-powered paddle steamer. The turn-of-the-century vessel was built in 1899 in London and shipped in parts to New Zealand, where it served to ferry tourists to Pipiriki. Follow in their footsteps on a two-hour **cruise** (5:30pm every 2nd Fri. Nov.-Apr., $30) across the legendary waterway, with live and recorded historical commentary. You can even take your turn shoveling coal in the boiler room.

Food

Shining from a sun-kissed villa, the **Yellow House Café** (17 Pitt St., 06/345-0083, www.yellowhousecafe.co.nz, 8am-4pm Mon.-Fri., 8:30am-4pm Sat.-Sun., $10-20) is equally enchanting inside thanks to local artwork. Indulge in treats like jam and cream scones or opt for the savory venison burger. There's a lovely and shady garden all around.

Mud Ducks (31 Taupo Quay, 06/348-7626, www.mudducks.co.nz, 8:30am-4pm daily, $12-20) serves breakfast, brunch, and lunch from a central riverside setting. Swing by in the morning for the French toast or a meatloaf burger later in the day. The smoothies are also excellent.

The menu at **Japanese Kitchen** (92 Victoria Ave., 06/345-1143, 11:30am-2:30pm and 5pm-8:30pm Tues.-Fri., 5pm-8:30pm Sat.-Sun., $13-20) tempts with classics like teriyaki salmon, *unagidon,* and sushi rolls. Dishes are fresh and well-presented; enjoy them in the courtyard.

The menu at **Thai Villa** (7 Victoria Ave., 06/348-9089, 4:30pm-9:30pm daily, $18-25) is enhanced by the warmest of welcomes and a contented din. Try the sizzling duck. It's BYO.

It's well worth the trip to ★ **The Citadel** (14 Rangiora St., 06/344-7076, 9am-8pm Thurs. and Sun.-Mon., 9am-9pm Fri.-Sat., $12-19) simply to sample the made-from-scratch hamburgers. Murals lend a beach-house vibe, and the happy staff imparts a family atmosphere. The sunny outdoor deck is occasionally graced by live bands. It's 7km west of downtown.

Long Live the Whanganui River

In 2017, in a world-first, the 290km Whanganui River—New Zealand's third longest—was granted legal personhood in recognition of its intrinsic role in the history of local Maori. The waterway is considered an ancestor, carved into the land by the god Pukeonaki—the volcano, Mount Taranaki.

This designation means that the river can act as a "person" in a court of law. Or rather, its guardian can. Legal personhood transfers ownership of the river from the British Crown to Te Awa Tupua, and assigns a guardian appointed by the Whanganui iwi to protect and oversee its interests.

Accommodations

BBH hostel **Tamara Lodge** (24 Somme Parade, 06/347-6300, www.tamaralodge.com, dorm $29-30, $44-64 s, $62-86 d) is in an ornate Edwardian mansion with river views. En suite rooms are available, and there's a TV room with plenty of DVDs, a fully stocked kitchen, and a barbecue. Wi-Fi and bike use is included. The pretty garden can be savored from the comfort of a hammock.

Braemar House (2 Plymouth St., 06/348-2301, www.braemarhouse.co.nz) merges a YHA backpacker hostel (dorm $30, $75-100) and B&B ($85 s, $100-140 d), with separate communal areas on the banks of the Whanganui River. Women-only lodgings are available, as are family rooms ($100-150). Hostel guests enjoy free Wi-Fi, bike rentals, a TV room, a herb garden, and a well-stocked kitchen. The historic guesthouse was built in 1895 and has a lovely lounge area with a piano, a library, and a TV. Some rooms are equipped with French windows overlooking gardens and the river.

Kick back on your personal deck at **Kings Court Motel** (60 Plymouth St., 06/345-8586, www.kingscourtmotel.co.nz, $140-180), a short stroll from downtown. Roomy understated studios and one-bedroom apartments have free Wi-Fi, Sky TV, and kitchens or kitchenettes.

Anndion Lodge (143-145 Anzac Parade, 06/343-3593, www.anndionlodge.co.nz, $79-175) is a premier motel with rooms equipped with colorful furnishings. Great value options include accommodations with shared baths and kitchen facilities as well as fully self-contained units. Everyone has access to a pool table, a sauna, a swimming pool, a barbecue area, and free Wi-Fi.

A pair of exquisitely curated airy pastel rooms lie within ★ **Browns Boutique B&B** (34 College St., 027/308-2495, www.brownsboutiquebnb.co.nz, $190), whose white walls bear local art. Guests enjoy free Wi-Fi, a gourmet breakfast, tea- and coffee-making facilities, toiletries, elegant gardens, and a private sunny courtyard. It's less than 1km from downtown.

Trappings at the waterside **Whanganui River Top 10 Holiday Park** (460 Somme Parade, 06/343-8402, www.wrivertop10.co.nz) include kayak rentals, paintball, a games room, barbecues, a spa, and a swimming pool. Basic cabins ($65-78) share communal baths and kitchens, though some have cooking facilities. Self-contained units and motel rooms ($115-155) come equipped with Sky TV. Camping sites ($36-44) are available with power. Free Wi-Fi is available for all guests.

Transportation and Services

Whanganui is one hour northwest of Palmerston North along Highway 3, two hours southeast of New Plymouth along Highway 3, and three hours southwest of Taupo along Highway 4.

AIR

Whanganui Airport (WAG, Airport Rd., 06/348-0536, www.whanganuiairport.co.nz) is 7km from downtown with daily flights to Auckland with **Air Chathams** (www.airchathams.co.nz).

Avis (06/348-7528, www.avis.co.nz), **Budget** (06/345-5122, www.budget.co.nz), and **Hertz** (06/348-7624, www.hertz.com) rent cars at the airport. For taxis, call **River City Cabs** (06/345-333); expect to pay $25 to downtown.

BUS

Nationwide bus carrier **Intercity** (06/583-5780, www.intercity.co.nz) calls at Whanganui. **Horizons** (06/952-2800, www.horizons.govt.nz) operates bus service between Whanganui and Palmerston North.

SERVICES

The Whanganui **i-SITE Visitor Information Centre** (31 Taupo Quay, 06/349-0508, www.whanganuinz.com, 9am-5pm daily) has local and national tourist information, booking services, and free Wi-Fi. The **DoC Visitor Centre** (35 Taupo Quay, 06/348-8475, www.doc.govt.nz, 8am-5pm Mon.-Fri.) provides information on Whanganui National Park conditions and sells hut tickets.

Whanganui District Library (Queens Park, Campbell St., 06/349-1000, www.whanganuilibrary.com, 9:30am-6pm Mon.-Fri., 10am-5pm Sat., 10am-3pm Sun.) has free Wi-Fi. There's a **post office** (100 Taupo Quay, 06/348-0351, www.nzpost.co.nz, 8:30am-5pm Mon.-Fri., 9am-4pm Sun.) and a **hospital** (100 Heads Rd., 06/348-1234). For nonemergencies, visit **Quay Medical Centre** (174 Wicksteed St., 06/345-2720, 8:30am-5pm Mon.-Fri., 9am-noon Sat.-Sun.).

Whanganui National Park

Whanganui National Park punches well above its weight. Its 742sq-km are home to the country's largest western brown kiwi population and the longest navigable river. North Island's second-mightiest tract of lowland forest is one of seven strongholds of the indigenous *whio,* or blue duck. The park's bounty of sandstone cliffs, gorges, towering ridges, beeches, and flowering rata trees can be explored on a bike and on hiking trails. A paddle along the Whanganui River is the most popular option.

Taumarunui is the northern gateway to the national park. **Pipiriki,** 113km north of Whanganui along Highway 4, provides access from the south.

★ THE WHANGANUI JOURNEY

The **Whanganui Journey** is classed as one of New Zealand's Great Walks, even though it takes place almost entirely on the Whanganui River. The route runs 145km from north to south, from Taumarunui to Pipiriki, and generally takes five days of three to nine hours each day. A popular option is to get on the water at Whakahoro, which reduces the journey to 87km, which can be easily tackled in three days. Note that it is not possible to stop or turn back from Whakahoro.

The geographical splendor is set to a soundtrack of birdsong and waterfalls. The meandering waters occasionally bubble into gentle rapids along the way, but these can be paddled by novice kayakers and canoers. Make sure to land at Mangapurua for the walk to the iconic **Bridge to Nowhere** (90 minutes round-trip), a lonely concrete structure built in the 1930s and abandoned before any connecting roads were laid to it.

Landing points en route lead to **DoC Huts** (0800/964-732, www.doc.govt.nz, adults $32, under age 18 free) and **campsites** (adults $20, under age 18 free). During the Great Walk season (Oct.-Apr.), these must be booked in advance. You'll need to carry your own food and camping gear (dry bags are provided by kayak rental companies).

Mangapurua Track

The **Mangapurua Track** is the trail to the Bridge to Nowhere and is part of the **Mountains to Sea Great Ride** (www.mountainstosea.co.nz). The 36km track can be biked or hiked. From its start off Ruatiti Road (30km northeast of Raetihi), it winds down through the forests of Mangapurua Valley to terminate at Mangapurua Landing via the bridge.

Whanganui River Canoes (10 Parapara Rd., Raetihi, 06/385-4176, www.whanganuirivercanoes, $115) runs a mountain bike shuttle service. Visitors are dropped at the beginning of the track and then picked up by jet-boat at the landing before heading to Pipiriki for a bus back to Raetihi. Bike rental is provided.

Whanganui River Road

Savor some of the river magic from the tarmac courtesy of the **Whanganui River Road,** which hugs the eastern banks from Whanganui to Pipiriki before turning east to Raetihi. It's a glorious 79km drive that takes two to four hours, depending on stops. Along the way, you'll pass historic and scenic sights such as the **Oyster Cliffs,** brimming with fossilized oysters; the three-sided spire of **St. Mary's Church of Upokongaro;** and the **Omorehu waterfall,** just before Pipiriki. Grab a detailed *Whanganui River Road Guide* from the **Taumarunui i-SITE Visitor Information Centre** (116 Hakiaha St., 07/895-7494, 8:30am-5pm daily).

Tours

Myriad adventures await at **Yeti Tours** (61 Clyde St., Ohakune, 06/385-8197, www.canoe.co.nz, adults $420-1,500, children $320-569), whose guided Whanganui River tours range 2-10 days. Meals and transportation to and from the launch site are included. Kayak and canoe rentals (from $175) are available; solo

kayaks and canoes on the shore of the Whanganui River

paddles are not allowed for safety reasons. Boats come with storage barrels or dry bags, buoyancy vests, paddles, bailers, and a river guidebook. Camping equipment (tents, sleeping bags, and cooking utensils) can also be rented ($50 for 2 people for 2 days).

Whanganui River Adventures (2522 Pipiriki Raetihi Rd., 06/385-3246, www.whanganuiriveradventures.com) runs half-day, one-day, and two-day canoe and jet-boat combos (adults $95-175, children $47.50-87.50), a 45-minute scenic jet-boat tour (adults $80, children $40), and a Bridge to Nowhere Tour (adults $135, children $67.50) that lasts four hours. The one-hour jet-boat ride is followed by a 40-minute walk to the bridge.

A quirky way to complete the journey is to hop aboard the **Mail Run,** a postal van whose driver doubles as a guide, imparting never-ending local knowledge as he delivers letters along the route.

FOOD AND ACCOMMODATIONS

Whanganui River

The only other riverside accommodations in the park are the **Bridge to Nowhere Lodge** (Ramanui Landing, 06/385-4622, www.bridgetonowhere.co.nz), 20km upstream from Pipiriki. The scenic complex offers comfortable accommodations that comprise dorms, double, and family rooms without meals ($55 pp, under age 5 $20). A meal package (adults $155, children $75, under age 5 $55) with breakfast and a buffet dinner is also available.

The **Bridge to Nowhere Retreat** (adults $285, children $145, under age 5 $75) includes meals as well as a jet-boat ride along the river and a trip to the Bridge to Nowhere. Space is limited, so reservations are essential. Those who book packages are given priority for private rooms.

There's also an adjacent campsite ($15 pp) with basic cabins ($30 pp) and bunks that sleep six to eight. The campsite has a shelter with cooking facilities, a barbecue area, and hot showers. Check out the walkway to the glowworm dell.

Taumarunui

There's a decent selection of Asian dishes at **Jasmine's Café & Thai Restaurant** (43 Hakiaha St., 07/895-5822, www.jasminestthai.co.nz, 8am-9pm daily, $16-25). Standout dishes include the beef panang curry and duck *pad khing*, but there are plenty of Western options like steak. It's open for traditional Kiwi breakfast as well.

Alexander Spa Motel (6 Marae St., 07/895-8501, www.alexanderspamotel.co.nz, $120-175) is a short walk from the town center. Self-contained units come equipped with hot-drink facilities, toasters, microwaves, fridges, TVs, and free Wi-Fi. Guests make the most of the communal spa.

Pipiriki

The **Flying Fox** (3081 Whanganui River Rd., 06/927-6809, www.theflyingfox.co.nz, $60-240), 32km south of Pipiriki along the Whanganui River Road, offers quirky lodgings so remote that they can be accessed only via the river (or by prebooking a rudimentary cable-car and zip line across the water). Accommodations include a private two-story cottage surrounded by orchards; a part hand-built wooden cart, part enormous tent; or glamping in a yurt. Campers may pitch a tent at the campsite ($15 pp), which is equipped with a fire pit, a hot shower, a kitchen shelter, and a barbecue. Amenities include a wood-fired bush bath, a solar shower, and Wi-Fi.

TRANSPORTATION AND SERVICES

The Whanganui River is accessible year-round. Book tickets online in advance through **DoC** (www.doc.govt.nz, Oct.-Apr.).

National **Intercity** (09/583-5780, www.intercity.co.nz) buses call at Raetihi daily, stopping outside the Caltex Petrol Station (Hwy. 4) heading north, and on the opposite side of the road heading south. Tour operators in Pipiriki run daily shuttles to and from Raetihi that stop at **Taumarunui i-SITE Visitor Information Centre** (116 Hakiaha St., 07/895-7494, 8:30am-5pm daily).

Palmerston North

Known as "Palmy," landlocked Palmerston North's population of 84,000 is bolstered by Massey University; a third of the city is 15 to 30 years old. Positioned 140km northeast of Wellington, most will pass through Palmy when driving to or from the capital.

SIGHTS

At the center of Main Street, **The Square** is the city's contemporary focal point. It boasts an enormous clock tower surrounded by geometrical lawns, a bridged pond, and some intriguing Maori figures.

Te Manawa

Make **Te Manawa** (326 Main St., 06/355-5000, www.temanawa.co.nz, 10am-5pm Fri.-Wed., 10am-7:30pm Thurs., free, charge for some exhibitions) your first stop. The 55,000-piece permanent collection of interactive exhibits focuses on natural history, science, art, and Maori artifacts.

★ New Zealand Rugby Museum

The **New Zealand Rugby Museum** (inside Te Manawa, 326 Main St., 06/358-6947, www.rugbymuseum.co.nz, 10am-5pm daily, adults $12.50, children $5) is home to some of the world's rarest sports memorabilia, most of which is connected to the national rugby team, the All Blacks. Exhibits include jerseys, leather balls, shoulder pads, photos, video footage, and the coin tossed (and the whistle blown) from the first World Cup.

FOOD

Don't leave Palmy without popping into energetic **Café Cuba** (236 Cuba Café, 06/356-5750, 7am-close daily, $15-32) to sample its legendary all-day breakfast. Later in the day, opt for a steak sandwich or Thai curry. There are plenty of vegan options, plus great cakes and coffee. Snag a table out front.

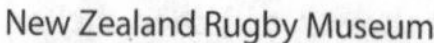
New Zealand Rugby Museum

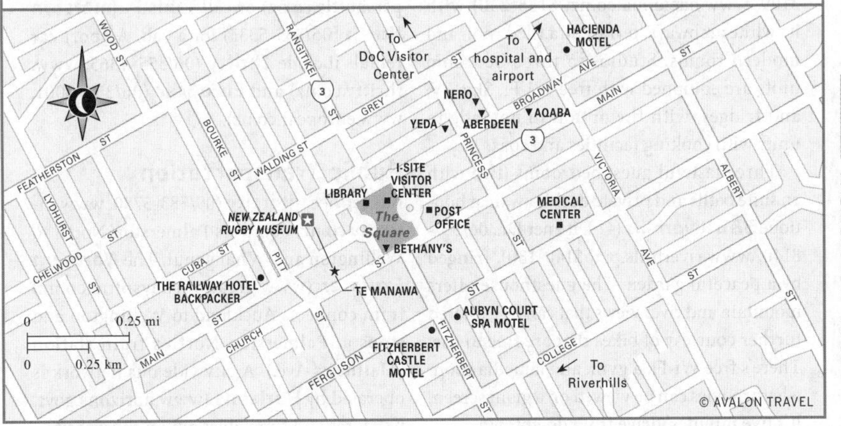

★ **Bethany's** (32a The Square, 06/351-6322, www.bethanys.co.nz, 9am-close Mon.-Sat., 9am-5pm Sun., $22-38) is a contemporary award-winning eatery. The innovative menu includes high-end standards like the catch of the day and beef fillet alongside the occasional surprise such as seared ostrich. Wraparound windows allow for an airy atmosphere and wonderful views of the square, or grab a seat outside for an even better look.

Aberdeen (161 Broadway Ave., 06/952-5570, www.aberdeenonbroadway.co.nz, 5:30pm-close Mon., 11:30am-close Tues.-Sun., $28-45) is the city's top eatery. Inside, guests are greeted with polished floors, a roaring fire, and a fine-dining menu specializing in steak. In addition to an excellent T-bone, offerings include duck confit salad, a pork cutlet, and a terrific Akaroa salmon with mint and coriander yogurt dressing.

Nero (36 Amesbury St., 06/354-0312, www.nerorestaurant.co.nz, 11am-2pm and 5pm-close Mon.-Fri., 5pm-close Sat., $28-44) sits in a Victorian villa surrounded by pristine gardens. Dine alfresco from a seasonal menu of delights like Angus beef fillet drizzled in black-garlic butter or duck-leg confit with red cabbage and pickled cherries.

Lovers of Asian cuisine will not be disappointed by ★ **Yeda** (78 Broadway Ave. 06/358-3978, www.yeda.co.nz, 11am-9pm daily, $15-20). The open-plan layout and long tables create a buzz that's backed by the sizzle of the open kitchen. Dishes include sushi, Hong Kong buns, Malay curries, and Chinese noodles.

ACCOMMODATIONS

The bohemian **Railway Hotel Backpackers** (275 Main St., 06/354-5037, www.railwayhotel.co.nz, dorm $33-35, $69-89 s, $89-120 d) is a mishmash of colorful decor, eclectic artwork, and knickknacks. Rooms have a fridge, a microwave, and a TV. There's a women-only dorm that has an en suite bath. The well-stocked kitchens include free snacks, breakfasts, and hot drinks. Wi-Fi is also free.

Sure, the ★ **Fitzherbert Castle Motel** (124 Fitzherbert Ave., 06/358-3888, www.castlemotel.co.nz, $125-148) looks kitsch, with its unconvincing mock turrets and steeple roof, but inside it's fit for a king—especially one on a budget. Nestled on a leafy street in the heart of Palmy, the spacious and spotless en suite rooms sport free Wi-Fi, Sky TV with a DVD player, tea- and coffee-making facilities, and basic cooking facilities. Some rooms have spa baths and kitchenettes.

There's an air of the Mediterranean to the **Hacienda Motel** (27 Victoria Ave., 06/357-3109, www.hacienda.co.nz, $125-230) with its white archways, terra-cotta tiled roof, and modern rooms. Studios to three-bedroom units are equipped with free Wi-Fi, Sky TV, and fridges, with the option to upgrade to units with cooking facilities and spas.

Three tasteful guest bedrooms (two with en suite baths and private decks) await at boutique **B&B Riverhills** (41 Dittmer Dr., 06/357-8140, www.riverhills.biz, $140-180), fringed by a peaceful garden. The guesthouse offers mountain and river views that can be explored further courtesy of bikes that are free to use. There's free Wi-Fi, a gym, and a media room where movies can be viewed on a giant screen. It's five minutes' drive from downtown.

There's a hot tub in every room at luxurious **Aubyn Court Spa Motel** (360 Ferguson St., 06/354-5757, www.aubyncourt.co.nz, $155-375). Guest have use of a communal sauna and fitness center along with Sky TV, unlimited Internet, kitchenettes, and DVD players.

TRANSPORTATION AND SERVICES

Palmerston North is 142km (1 hour, 40 minutes) northeast of Wellington along Highway 1. It's a little under an hour (73km) southeast of Whanganui along Highway 3. From Auckland, it's 514km south along Highway 1 (6 hours, 40 minutes).

Air

Palmerston North Airport (PMR, Airport Dr., 06/351-4415, www.pnairport.co.nz) is 3km northeast of downtown. Flights connect with Christchurch, Auckland, Wellington, and Nelson. For airport transportation, contact **Super Shuttle** (0800/748-885, www.supershuttle.co.nz) or call **Taxis Palmerston North** (06/355-5333) for a cab. Airport car rentals include **Thrifty** (06/355-4365, www.thrifty.co.nz) and **Europcar** (06/353-0001, www.europcar.co.nz).

Public Transportation

Bus service **Intercity** (09/583-5780, www.intercity.co.nz) connects Palmerston North to Wellington and Whanganui. The ***Northern Explorer*** (www.greatjourneysofnz.co.nz) train connects Auckland to Wellington and stops at Palmerston North's train station (Matthews Ave.). A citywide bus network is operated by **Horizons** (www.horizons.govt.nz); fares and timetables are on the website.

Services

Palmerston North I-Site Visitor Centre (The Square, 06/350-1922 www.manawatunz.co.nz, 9am-5:30pm Mon.-Thurs., 9am-7pm Fri. and Sun., 9am-3pm Sat.) has free daytime parking and Wi-Fi, in addition to local maps and information. You can also buy DoC hut tickets.

The Square is home to the **City Library** (06/351-4101, www.citylibrary.pncc.govt.nz, 9:30am-6pm Mon.-Fri., 9:30am-8pm Thurs., 10am-4pm Sat., 1pm-4pm Sun.), which has free Wi-Fi. There's also a **post office** (328 Church St., 0800/081-190, www.nzpost.co.nz, 9am-5pm Mon.-Fri., 9:30am-1pm Sat.). For medical services, try **Palmerston North Hospital** (50 Ruanhine St., 06/356-9169) or the **medical center** (445 Ferguson St., 06/354-7737, 8am-8pm daily).

Wellington and Wairarapa

Wellington 270
The Kapiti Coast 289
The Hutt Valley 293
Wairarapa 295

Look for ★ to find recommended sights, activities, dining, and lodging.

Highlights

★ **Museum of New Zealand Te Papa Tongarewa:** The capital's centerpiece museum explores Kiwi legends and histories in fascinating ways (page 270).

★ **Wellington Cable Car:** This historic funicular tram leads to a splendid view of the city, with a return route via the Botanic Gardens (page 275).

★ **Cuba Street District:** Don't leave Wellington without experiencing its scintillating nightlife (page 279).

★ **Craft Beer:** They take their craft brewing very seriously in the capital and it shows (page 280).

★ **Kapiti Island:** Tour an island paradise that's home to some of the world's rarest birds (page 291).

★ **Pencarrow Lighthouse:** The nation's first "manned" lighthouse was the first to be run by a woman (page 294).

★ **Wine Tasting:** Martinborough's boutique vineyards are a noteworthy stop on the region's wine trail (page 297).

★ **Patuna Chasm:** This stunning self-guided tour leads through a labyrinth of limestone gorges (page 298).

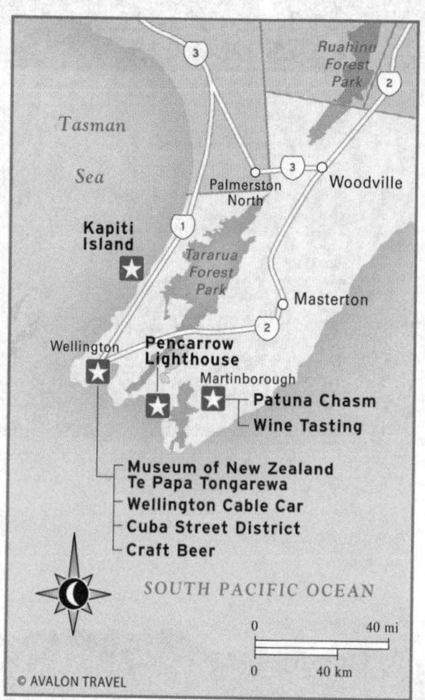

The world's southernmost capital is cultured and cosmopolitan, ridiculously laid-back, and achingly hip.

Wellington has also been scientifically proven to be the windiest city on earth, with record wind speeds at 247km/h (the daily average is 29km/h). Yet with more than 2,000 hours of sunshine a year, Wellington has few peers. Cradled within a craggy green amphitheater whose steep fertile slopes are sprinkled with pastel-roofed villas, the capital overlooks a seemingly ever-turquoise harbor alive with pleasure craft, ferries, and the occasional ocean liner. Beyond, the roaring 92km Cook Strait connects North Island to South Island via Wellington to Picton.

The Kapiti Coast stretches north of Wellington, a seaside extension of the capital favored by holidaymakers and commuters attracted by its relaxed vibe. Offshore is Kapiti Island, a lauded nature reserve and pest-free birdwatching paradise that hosts some of the world's rarest feathered critters—including the fabled kiwi.

Through the scenic Hutt Valley, luscious Wairarapa arches east of Wellington, the yin to the capital's yang. Its plains, fringed by rolling mountain ranges, are home to a collection of burgeoning boutique vineyards that have begun to steal some limelight from the country's more prominent grape-growing regions. At Wairarapa's foot is Cape Palliser, North Island's southernmost point, where a sizeable seal colony and an iconic red-and-white striped lighthouse stand guard.

PLANNING YOUR TIME

Spend at least **two days** in the capital to take in all the sights. Visit the **Te Papa** museum, enjoy the view from **Mount Victoria,** ride the **cable car,** and experience the café culture and vibrant nightlife of the **Cuba Street District.** Wine lovers should set aside another day to explore **Wairarapa,** either under their own steam or on a tour from Wellington. Those pressed for time should make for the **Kapiti Coast,** where Kapiti Island is one the region's must-dos.

Previous: the Wellington Blown Away sign; the view from Mount Victoria. **Above:** Old St. Paul's.

Wellington and Wairarapa

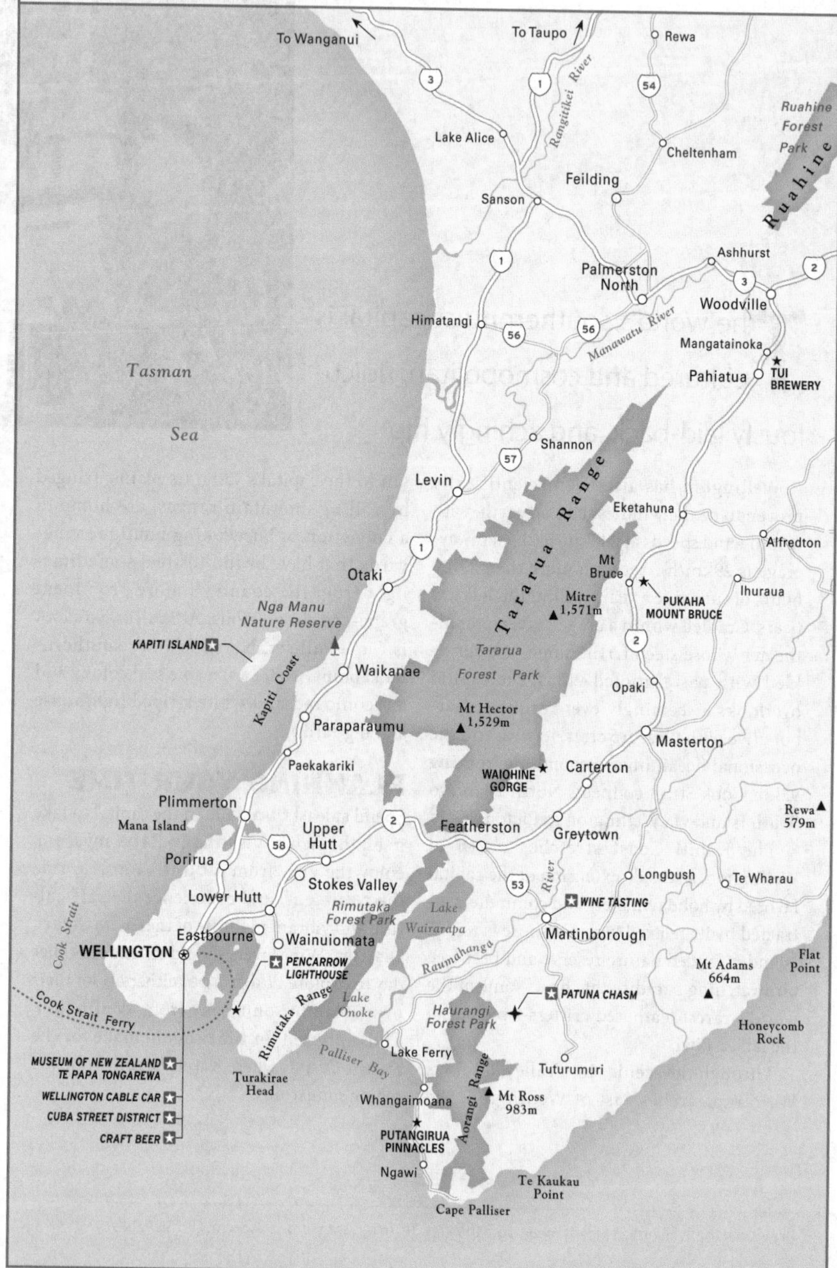

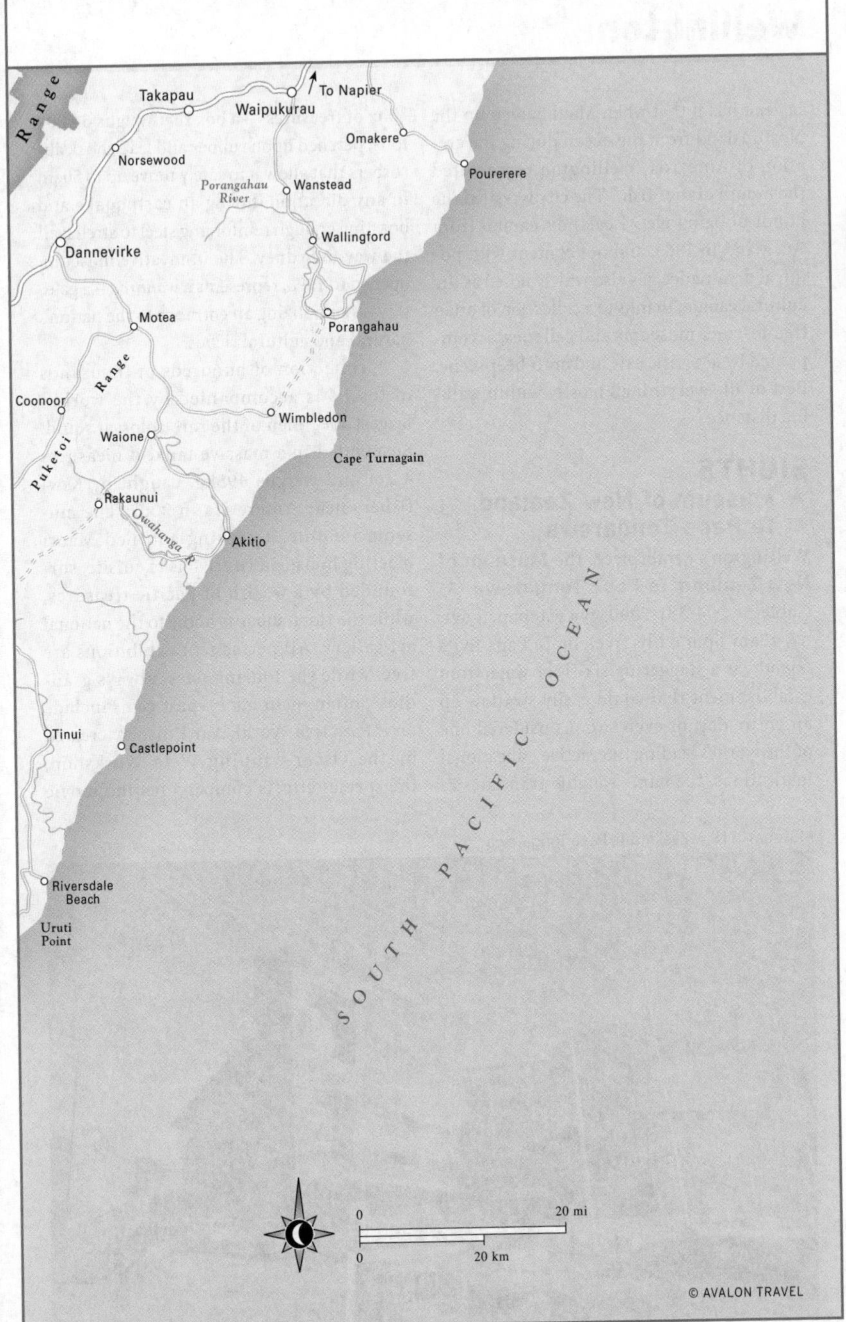
Range
Takapau
Waipukurau
To Napier
Omakere
Norsewood
Pourerere
Porangahau River
Wanstead
Wallingford
Dannevirke
Porangahau
Motea
Range
Coonoor
Wimbledon
Waione
Puketoi
Cape Turnagain
Rakaunui
Owahanga R.
Akitio
SOUTH PACIFIC OCEAN
Tinui
Castlepoint
Riversdale Beach
Uruti Point
0
20 mi
0
20 km
© AVALON TRAVEL

Wellington

Legend has it that when Maui hauled up the North Island from the ocean during the creation of Aotearoa, Wellington represented the mouth of the "fish." The city wrestled the honor of being New Zealand's capital from Auckland in 1865, and not content with political dominance, it's also widely noted as the cultural capital, thanks to a collection of often free-to-enter museums and galleries, accompanied by a terrific café and craft beer scene. Best of all, everything's mostly within walking distance.

SIGHTS

★ Museum of New Zealand Te Papa Tongarewa

Wellington's centerpiece, the **Museum of New Zealand Te Papa Tongarewa** (55 Cable St., 04/381-7000, www.tepapa.govt.nz, 10am-6pm daily, free), or Te Papa to its friends, is a staggering six-floor waterfront establishment that could easily swallow up an entire day, or even two. Considered one of the world's leading interactive educational institutions, the name roughly translates as "box of treasures"—a box that weighs 64,000 tons, perched upon rubber and lead shock absorbers that allow it to safely move up to 50cm in any direction during an earthquake and boasting enough reinforcing steel to stretch all the way to Sydney. The innovative museum, opened in 1998, represents a *waharoa*—a gateway—symbolizing an entrance to the nation's natural and cultural riches.

A collection of hundreds of thousands of fossils is accompanied by the world's largest specimen of the rare colossal squid. Suspended in a massive tank, it measures 4.2m and weighs 495kg, caught by Kiwi fishers near Antarctica in 2007. The museum's *marae,* a carving-adorned Maori meeting house on Level 4, is exquisite, surrounded by a wealth of Pacific treasures, while the floor above is home to the national art gallery. All permanent exhibitions are free, while the touring ones, always grandiose, often incur a fee—past gems include an interactive World War I display created by the Oscar-winning Weta Workshop, the special effects company behind movie

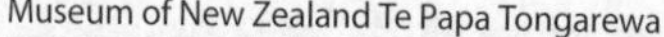
Museum of New Zealand Te Papa Tongarewa

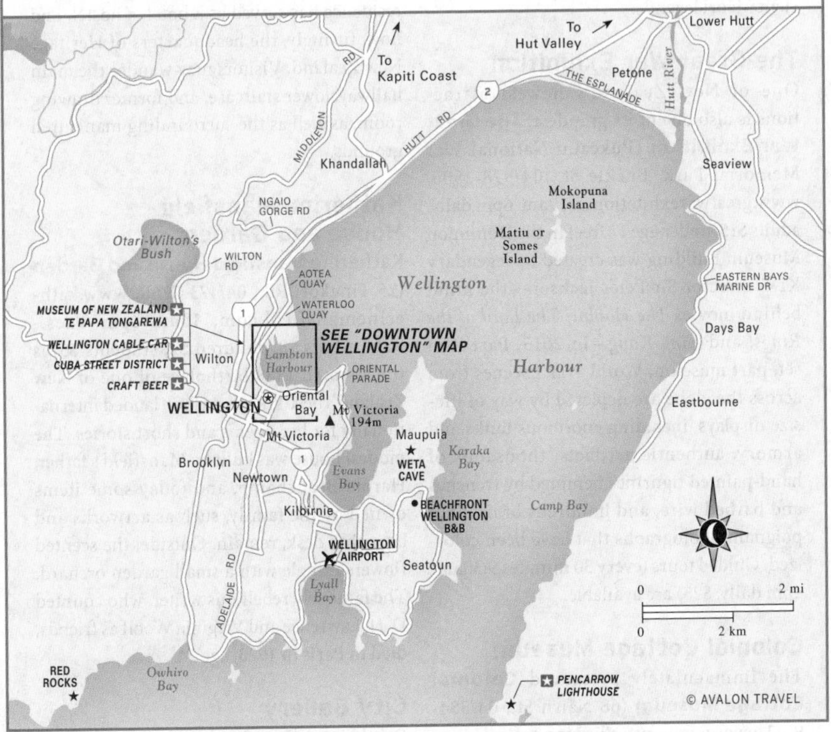

hits like *The Lord of the Rings*. Above the museum, a rooftop area affords wonderful views of Wellington Harbour.

Best to make your first stop the information desk on Level 2 to grab a map, and consider joining one of the worthwhile tours, before wandering around. The one-hour **Introducing Te Papa Tour** (approximately on the hour 10am-3pm daily Nov.-Mar., 10:15am, noon, and 2pm daily Apr.-Oct., adults $20, children $10) takes in the museum's most significant highlights, while the **Maori Highlights Tour** (2pm daily, adults $20, children $10), also one hour, concentrates on Maori cultural exhibits. The 45-minute **Twilight Express Tour** (5pm daily, adults $20, children $10) is an abridged highlights tour, ideal for those on a time budget.

Wellington Museum

Housed in the atmospheric Bond Store, a heritage building opened in 1892, **Wellington Museum** (3 Jervois Rd., Queens Wharf, 04/472-8904, www.museumswellington.org.nz, 10am-5pm daily, free) imparts a sense of history well before you're even through its doors. While its more famous big sister, Te Papa, looks at the big picture, Wellington Museum—named one of the top 50 museums in the world by Britain's *The Times* newspaper in 2013—takes a more intimate, local approach, examining the rich history of the capital's land and cultures and especially its relationship with the ocean. Standout displays include a replica of Wellington's 19th-century waterfront; the time-bending attic space with steampunk-inspired creations such as flying saucers; a poignant exhibit and film about the sinking of the ferry *Wahine* in 1968; and a state-of-the-art hologram show that tells ancient Maori legends.

The Great War Exhibition

One of New Zealand's newest attractions is also one of its grandest, **The Great War Exhibition** (Pukeahu National War Memorial Park, Buckle St., 04/978-2500, www.greatwarexhibition.nz, 9am-6pm daily, adults $15, under age 17 free) in the Dominion Museum Building was created by legendary Kiwi director Sir Peter Jackson—the mind behind movies *The Hobbit, The Lord of the Rings,* and *King Kong*—in 2015. Part film set, part museum, World War I scenes from across the globe are depicted by way of life-size displays, including enormous tanks and armory, authentic artifacts, thousands of hand-painted figurines hemmed by trenches and barbed wire, and hundreds of original poignant photographs that have been colorized. Guided tours (every 30 minutes 9:30am-4pm daily, $25) are available.

Colonial Cottage Museum

The immaculately preserved **Colonial Cottage Museum** (68 Nairn St., 04/384-9122, www.museumswellington.org.nz, noon-4pm Sat.-Sun., adults $8, children $4), also known as Nairn Street Cottage, is thought to be the capital's oldest surviving house, built in 1858 by William Wallis. Admission includes a guided tour (12pm, 1pm, and 3pm) where you learn of daily colonial life, such as making candles from animal fat. Out back, the colorful garden brims with flowers and vegetables originally grown by the Victorian family.

Antrim House

Antrim House (63 Boulcott St., 04/472-4341, www.antrimhouse.co.nz, 9am-5pm Mon.-Fri., free) is a historic home on what was once a mainly residential road—hard to imagine now in the shadow of the office blocks of the central business district (CBD). Built in 1905 by successful local businessman Robert Hannah in Italianate style, the house has kauri wood paneling and stairs along with stained-glass windows. Following his death in 1930, the residence has served as a hotel, a hostel, and now, fittingly, the headquarters of Heritage New Zealand. Visitors may wander the main hallway, lower staircase, and former drawing room, as well as the surrounding manicured grounds.

Katherine Mansfield House and Garden

Katherine Mansfield House and Garden (25 Tinakori Rd., 04/473-7268, www.katherinemansfield.com, 10am-4pm Tues.-Sun., adults $8, children $2, students $5) is the restored 1888 birthplace of one of New Zealand's best-known scribes, lauded internationally for her poems and short stories. The modest house was built by Mansfield's father, Harold Beauchamp, and today some items owned by the family, such as artworks and a writing desk, remain. Outside, the scented flowers mingle with a small garden orchard. The famously rebellious writer, who counted D. H. Lawrence and Virginia Woolf as friends, died in Paris in 1923, age 34.

City Gallery

Overlooking Civic Square, **City Gallery** (101 Wakefield St., 04/913-9032, www.citygallery.org.nz, 10am-5pm daily, free) is the city's premier contemporary exhibition space, set in a fittingly fashionable art deco-era building. The permanent collection of local works, including a plethora of Maori and Pacific Island paintings and sculptures, are joined by regular visiting international collections and film showings.

New Zealand Portrait Gallery

The strangely compelling, if modest, collection of artworks at **New Zealand Portrait Gallery** (Shed 11, Queen's Wharf, 04/472-2298, www.nzportraitgallery.org.nz, 10:30am-4:30pm daily, free) comprises resident paintings and sketches of iconic, celebrity, and everyday New Zealanders—as well as head of state Queen Elizabeth II—bolstered by

Downtown Wellington

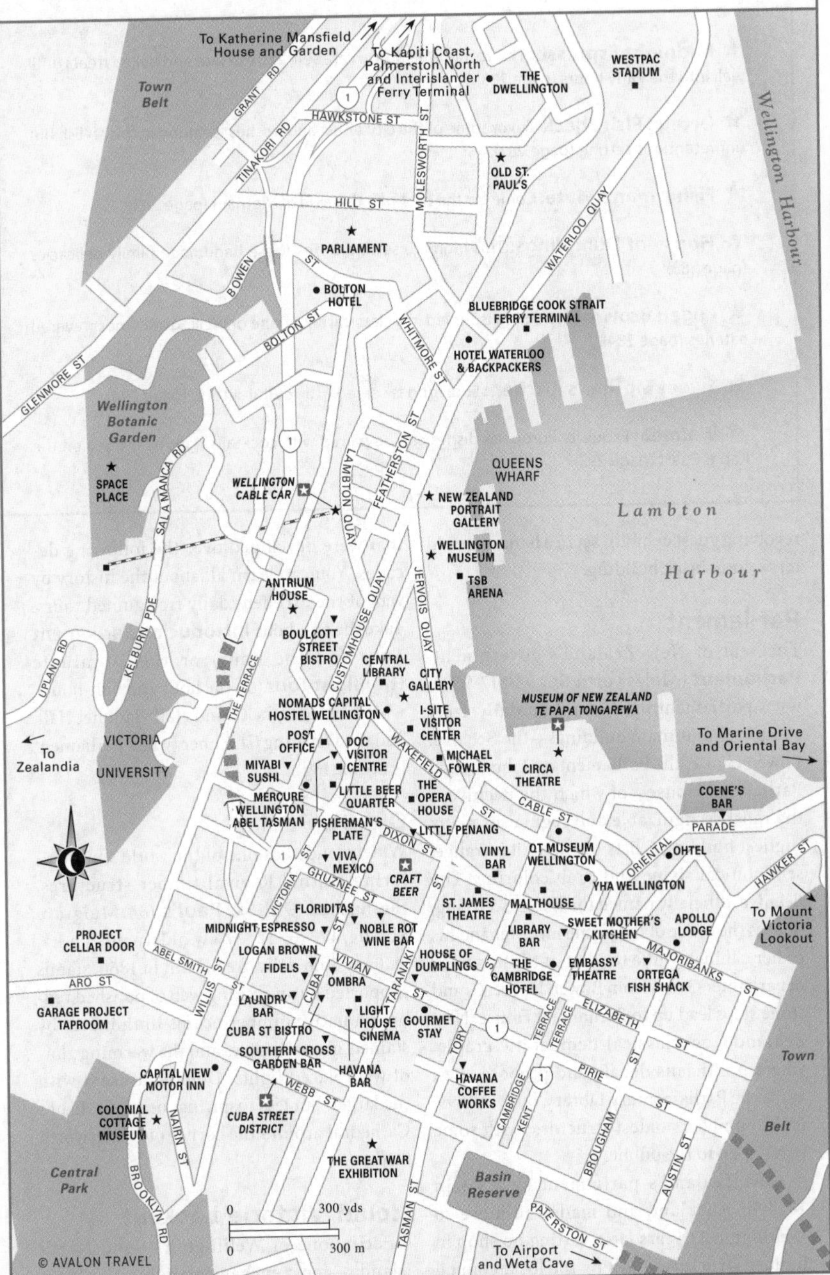
To Katherine Mansfield House and Garden
To Kapiti Coast, Palmerston North and Interislander Ferry Terminal
THE DWELLINGTON
WESTPAC STADIUM
Town Belt
Wellington Harbour
GRANT RD
HAWKSTONE ST
TINAKORI RD
MOLESWORTH ST
OLD ST. PAUL'S
HILL ST
PARLIAMENT
WATERLOO QUAY
BOWEN ST
BOLTON HOTEL
BOLTON ST
BLUEBRIDGE COOK STRAIT FERRY TERMINAL
WHITMORE ST
HOTEL WATERLOO & BACKPACKERS
GLENMORE ST
Wellington Botanic Garden
SALAMANCA RD
SPACE PLACE
FEATHERSTON ST
LAMBTON QUAY
WELLINGTON CABLE CAR
QUEENS WHARF
NEW ZEALAND PORTRAIT GALLERY
Lambton Harbour
WELLINGTON MUSEUM
TSB ARENA
ANTRIUM HOUSE
CUSTOMHOUSE QUAY
JERVOIS QUAY
BOULCOTT STREET BISTRO
KELBURN PDE
UPLAND RD
CENTRAL LIBRARY
CITY GALLERY
THE TERRACE
NOMADS CAPITAL HOSTEL WELLINGTON
MUSEUM OF NEW ZEALAND TE PAPA TONGAREWA
I-SITE VISITOR CENTER
To Marine Drive and Oriental Bay
VICTORIA UNIVERSITY
To Zealandia
POST OFFICE
DOC VISITOR CENTRE
WAKEFIELD
MICHAEL FOWLER
CIRCA THEATRE
MIYABI SUSHI
LITTLE BEER QUARTER
THE OPERA HOUSE
COENE'S BAR
MERCURE WELLINGTON ABEL TASMAN
CABLE ST
PARADE
FISHERMAN'S PLATE
DIXON ST
LITTLE PENANG
QT MUSEUM WELLINGTON
ORIENTAL
OHTEL
HAWKER ST
VIVA MEXICO
CRAFT BEER
VINYL BAR
YHA WELLINGTON
GHUZNEE ST
VICTORIA ST
FLORIDITAS
ST. JAMES THEATRE
MALTHOUSE
To Mount Victoria Lookout
MIDNIGHT ESPRESSO
NOBLE ROT WINE BAR
LIBRARY BAR
SWEET MOTHER'S KITCHEN
APOLLO LODGE
PROJECT CELLAR DOOR
ABEL SMITH ST
LOGAN BROWN
HOUSE OF DUMPLINGS
MAJORIBANKS ST
FIDELS
VIVIAN
OMBRA
THE CAMBRIDGE HOTEL
EMBASSY THEATRE
ORTEGA FISH SHACK
ARO ST
WILLIS
CUBA
TARANAKI
LAUNDRY BAR
LIGHT HOUSE CINEMA
GOURMET STAY
TERRACE
ELIZABETH ST
GARAGE PROJECT TAPROOM
CUBA ST BISTRO
TORY
SOUTHERN CROSS GARDEN BAR
PIRIE ST
CAPITAL VIEW MOTOR INN
HAVANA BAR
HAVANA COFFEE WORKS
Town Belt
WEBB ST
COLONIAL COTTAGE MUSEUM
CUBA STREET DISTRICT
CAMBRIDGE
KENT
BROUGHAM
AUSTIN ST
NAIRN ST
THE GREAT WAR EXHIBITION
Central Park
Basin Reserve
BROOKLYN RD
0 300 yds
0 300 m
TASMAN ST
PATERSTON ST
To Airport and Weta Cave
© AVALON TRAVEL

Best Food

★ **Midnight Espresso:** This iconic Wellington café serves fresh fare and baked treats until well into the early hours (page 283).

★ **Ortega Fish Shack:** Savor some of the city's best and freshest seafood in this stylish but unpretentious setting (page 283).

★ **Fisherman's Plate:** Come for the best *pho* this side of Vietnam (page 283).

★ **House of Dumplings:** This intimate setting befits these handmade family delicacies (page 283).

★ **Logan Brown:** Fine dining is served in a classical lair at one of Wellington's most revered eateries (page 284).

★ **Sweet Mother's Kitchen:** Soul food is served in a soulful setting (page 284).

★ **Waimea:** Exquisite European dishes can be paired with cocktails right by the sea on the Kapiti Coast (page 292).

revolving guest exhibits, set in a handsome old terra-cotta brick building.

Parliament

The seat of New Zealand's government, **Parliament** (Molesworth St., 04/817-9503, www.parliament.nz, 10am-4pm daily, free) comprises four main buildings—the Beehive, Bowen House, the Parliamentary Library, and Parliament House—of which the Beehive is the most recognizable and regular of many "ugliest buildings" lists owing to its strange, semiconical shape and drab coloring. The Beehive, officially named the Executive Wing, houses the office of the prime minister and his or her cabinet, while the rest of the members of parliament work from Bowen House. Grand stone steps lead up to Parliament House, New Zealand's neoclassical democratic cradle, where politicians debate and propose laws, while the Parliamentary Library, built in 1899, is the complex's oldest structure, with some parts open to the public.

New Zealand's parliament first sat in 1854 in Auckland and made the move to Wellington 11 years later, setting up shop in lumber structures built by the local council that were developed over the following decades. You can learn all about the history by way of the excellent daily free guided tours. Take the one-hour **Introducing Parliament Tour** (on the hour) or the 30-minute **Highlight Tour** (on the hour and half-hour), which includes the Grand Hall, Banquet Hall, and the Debating Chamber (when parliament is not sitting).

Old St. Paul's

Widely lauded as one of the world's most alluring Gothic Revival timber structures, the hushed **Old St. Paul's** (34 Mulgrave St., 04/473-6722, www.oldstpauls.co.nz, 9:30am-5pm daily, free), built in 1866, stands supported by an arching web of polished red-brown native lumber beams illuminated by stained-glass windows and the warming glow of well-placed lights. Don't confuse it with the larger, but less inspiring, newer St. Paul's Cathedral around the corner on Molesworth Street.

Mount Victoria Lookout

Offering one of Wellington's—and North Island's—most enchanting sights, the 196m

Best Accommodations

★ **YHA Wellington:** This clean, modern, and well-run gateway to the capital is perfectly positioned between the sights and the nightlife (page 284).

★ **The Dwellington:** This stylish, boutique-inspired hostel has an amazing kitchen and fantastic communal areas (page 285).

★ **Beachfront Wellington B&B:** Sea views and sweet treats are set in a serene, stylish, and secluded lodging away from the city (page 286).

★ **Ohtel:** This eco-warrior of a hotel boasts some of the most beautiful bedrooms in Wellington (page 286).

★ **QT Museum Wellington:** There's no escaping the artwork in this most creative of accommodations (page 286).

★ **Te Nikau Forest Retreat:** A magical Middle-earth-like escape is enclosed by a birdsong-filled forest on the Kapiti Coast (page 293).

★ **Atahuri Lodge:** Slotted in among some sand dunes, this luxurious retreat is as hard to find as it is to forget (page 293).

Mount Victoria rises from the eastern fringe of the city center, affording views of the bush-clad urban amphitheater around that ever-turquoise, ever-busy harbor and as far as the Hutt Valley. The 5km Mount Victoria Loop is a lovely stroll that requires average fitness. It begins at the top of Majoribanks Street and takes around 2.5 hours. You can also drive to the summit or catch the number 20 bus (www.metlink.org.nz, Mon.-Fri.).

★ Wellington Cable Car

Jaw-dropping views await at the climax of the historic **Wellington Cable Car** (280 Lambton Quay, 04/472-2199, www.wellingtoncablecar.co.nz, 7am-10pm Mon.-Fri., 8:30am-10pm Sat., 8:30am-9pm Sun., round-trip adults $7.50, children $3.50, one-way adults $4, children $2), New Zealand's only funicular railway and an absolute must-do while in the capital. Departing every 10 minutes, the tram makes its way from the CBD up a steep incline to the suburb of Kelburn, a journey that takes around five minutes for views across the harbor and to the Hutt Valley. From here, there is a free shuttle to Zealandia, and an easy route to the Carter Observatory and the Botanical Gardens (just follow the signs).

Next to the terminus, the **Cable Car Museum** (04/475-3578, www.museumswellington.org.nz, 9:30am-5pm daily, free) is located in the first winding house, in operation 1902-1978. Also on show are a pair of 100-year-old cars as well as oodles of information regarding the development of the capital's transport system and other cable cars around the world.

Space Place

Space Place (40 Salamanca Rd., 04/910-3140, www.museumswellington.org.nz, 4pm-11pm Tues. and Fri., 10am-11pm Sat., 10am-5:30pm Sun., adults $12.50, children $8, seniors and students $10) comprises intergalactic multimedia exhibits, including pieces of real moon rock and a replica spaceship module; the historic Thomas Cooke telescope, through which you can gaze into the ether; and an incredible full-dome planetarium screen that shows a range of educational and entertaining presentations regarding such things as space travel and the New Zealand skies.

Botanic Garden

Rather than make the return trip down to the CBD in the cable car, take a downhill stroll through the **Botanic Gardens** (Glenmore St., www.wellington.govt.nz, dawn-dusk daily, free) that stretch from the suburb of Kelburn all the way back down to the city. The 25ha site is home to native forest and colorful native and tropical plants, with an abundance of paths and places from which to look out over the city. Don't forget to pick up a free map while at the cable car station. Other entry and exit points to the gardens can be found on Glenmore Street, Salamanca Road, and Upland Road.

Otari-Wilton's Bush

Fifteen minutes from the city center, **Otari-Wilton Bush** (160 Wilton Rd., 04/499-1400, www.wellington.govt.nz, dawn-dusk daily, free) is the nation's only public botanic garden with only native plants. More than 10km of walking tracks meander through more than 100ha of native forest that cradles an 800-year-old rimu tree.

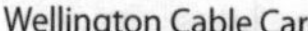

Zealandia

Long-term business plans pale into insignificance when compared with that of **Zealandia** (53 Waiapu Rd., Karori 04/920-9213, www.visitzealandia.com, 9am-5pm daily, adults $18.50, students and seniors $15, children $10, under age 5 free), a fenced city eco-sanctuary that aims to return its 225ha sprawl back to its prehuman state within the next 500 years. This most incongruous of projects cradles all manner of iconic Kiwi wildlife—some of which have been absent from the mainland for more than a century—including the kiwi, kaka, giant weta, and tuatara within its mass of rambling forest and weaving waterways. You'll hear birdlife everywhere, and numerous viewing hides and feeding stations along the tracks ensure you'll see plenty of the chirpers.

Plan to spend at least half a day here. Start with a free introductory guided tour (30-45 minutes, noon and 2pm Mon.-Fri., noon, 2pm, and 3pm Sat.-Sun.) to learn more of the sanctuary's sentient inhabitants. For a more in-depth experience, and to venture off the well-trod trails, consider the **Zealandia By Day Tour** (10am-2pm daily, adults $55, children $27.50), which departs from the visitors center. Tours last two hours; the tour time is given when you reserve.

Wellington Cable Car

Wellywood Blown Away

With New Zealand's much respected film industry based in the capital, it has bestowed upon itself the title Wellywood. As a nod to Hollywood, in 2011 plans were drawn up to erect a giant "Wellywood" sign on a hillside near the airport, but mass protests forced a rethink, with accusations that it made the nation look like "try-hards" and "Lord of the Cringe." A brewery even offered free beer to anyone who knocked it down, "no questions asked." After being put to a public vote, the following year, the current "Wellington—Blown Away" sign was constructed in its place, a nod instead to the city's legendary gales. Look for it on the Miramar Peninsula.

If you can, time your visit to coincide with the **Zealandia By Night Tour** (2.5 hours, daily, adults $85, children $20). The tour departs around dusk, when you'll be guided through the forest by flashlight to the sight of glowworms, weta, and possibly the little spotted kiwi and morepork, a native owl. There's nothing else in the country quite like Zealandia, named after the continental crust upon which New Zealand is perched.

Zealandia is just 10 minutes from downtown Wellington, in the hillside suburb of Karori.

Weta Cave

See how much of the Middle-earth magic was made for *The Lord of the Rings* and *Hobbit* movies, as well as models, costumes, and props for a slew of other productions, including the *Thunderbirds* film and *King Kong*, at the **Weta Cave** (1 Weka St., 04/909-4100, www.wetaworkshop.co.nz, 9am-5:30pm daily, adults $25, children $12, under age 6 free) in the suburb of Miramar, 20 minutes from downtown. Guided 45-minute tours leave every half hour, with visitors able to glimpse the Oscar-winning special effects team toiling in the Weta Workshop, get within touching distance of their wares, and enjoy a short documentary film.

Departing the **i-SITE** (Victoria St. and Wakefield St., 9am, 10:30am, noon, 1:30pm, and 3pm daily, adults $65, children $40, under age 6 free), the workshop offers a return bus tour to the cave, taking in some iconic Wellywood sights along the way, such as the Wellington Blown Away sign, filming locations, and Courtenay Place—the site of *The Hobbit* premieres.

SPORTS AND RECREATION

There's always something happening at Wellington's waterfront. **What NZ** (Frank Kits Lagoon, 04/499-9285, www.whatnz.co.nz, usually noon-6pm daily Dec.-Mar., noon-6pm Sat.-Sun. Apr.-Nov.) operates a range of waterfront activities, such as peddleboats, stand-up paddleboards, bikes, trikes, and roller-skates and blades. Several diving boards jut out over the water around the harbor—feel free to make use of them.

Beaches

Oriental Bay is the city's most popular beach, positioned 1.5km southeast of downtown—it's a cinch to find; just follow the pleasant waterfront walk, Oriental Parade, that leads from the end of Cable Street a couple of blocks east of Te Papa. The narrow golden arch (the sand was shipped in from Golden Bay in Nelson) spills into a safe swimming spot with the city looming in the background.

Positioned on the far side of the Miramar peninsula, just off Massey Road (10km east of the city center), **Scorching Bay** is a glorious sandy stretch that's highly sheltered and great for swimming. Surrounded by pohutukawa trees, it's a beautiful spot from which to watch the oceangoing traffic head in and out of Wellington Harbour.

Walks

Download the free **Welly Walks app** (www.wellington.govt.nz) for a comprehensive list of the capital's many tracks and trails. Walking

Matiu/Somes Island

You won't regret setting aside a day to visit **Matiu/Somes Island,** a Maori-owned, Department of Conservation (DoC)-maintained predator-free scientific and nature reserve in Wellington Harbour, whose native bush thrives with birdlife such as parakeets as well as the tuatara and the weta. There are also a couple of *pa* sites, all of which can be explored via a handful of short walks, including the 40-minute loop track—the island's longest—that weaves past the remains of World War II buildings and a lighthouse as well as incorporating a series of scenic lookouts. A rudimentary **campsite** (04/384-7770, www.doc.govt.nz, adults $13, children $6.50) has space for 12 tents, and there is a camp kitchen with a gas oven, but no fridge. Reservations are essential. The **East by West Ferry** (04/499-1282, www.eastbywest.co.nz, round-trip adults $23, children $12) serves the island daily from Queens Wharf and Days Bay.

maps are available from the **Wellington i-SITE Visitor Centre** (Civic Square. Victoria St. and Wakefield St., 04/802-4860, www.wellingtonnz.com, 8:30am-5pm daily).

CITY WALKS

Walk Wellington (04/802-4860, www.walkwellington.org.nz, adults $20, children $10) hosts guided 2.5-hour strolls around the city, catching highlights like Old St. Paul's and Parliament. Tours depart daily at 10am from the i-SITE Visitor Centre (Victoria St. and Wakefield St.); look for the guides wearing green vests. In summer, there are 90-minute evening walks (5:30pm Mon., Wed., and Fri. Dec.-Mar.).

Writers Walk weaves along the waterfront from Chaffers Marina, just east of Te Papa, around to Circa Theatre and across the City to Sea Bridge and Civic Square. The route is punctuated by 15 text sculptures adorned with quotes by revered Kiwi writers such as Katherine Mansfield and Maurice Gee. Consider linking up the walk with Oriental Parade at the southern end of Chaffers Marina.

Allow five hours to complete the **Northern Walkway,** a 16km trail that links the northern suburbs Johnsonville with Kelburn in the center, taking in a number of city parks—including the Botanic Gardens and Tinakori Hill, famous for its birdlife—and sweeping views of the capital. The walk begins at Truscott Avenue, 1.6km from Raroa Railway Station, and ends at Upland Road. There are numerous entry points, meaning it can be completed in stages.

The **Southern Walkway** is an 11km jaunt that will take at least four hours. It's a lower-level trail that hugs the harbor from Oriental Bay to Island Bay. This walk can also easily be tackled in stages.

RED ROCKS RESERVE

A pleasant day trip from Wellington, the historic **Red Rocks Reserve** is home to a fur seal colony and an incongruous collection of bruised rocks—200 million-year-old pillow lava formed by undersea volcanic eruptions. A couple of Maori legends pertain to the claret-colored coating: one is that explorer Kupe was injured while collecting shellfish, and his blood stained the rocks; the other is that Kupe's daughters cut themselves in grief over the absence of their father.

The coastal reserve runs between Owhiro Bay and Sinclair Head, 7km south of Wellington. From the Owhiro Bay car park, the flat seaside track is sometimes uneven; the rocks are around 30 minutes along the track. It's a 30-minute drive from Wellington to the reserve.

ENTERTAINMENT AND EVENTS

Nightlife

Most of the twilight magic occurs around the colorful Cuba Street District and more

Cuba Street District

raucous Courtenay Place—both within walking distance of each other.

★ CUBA STREET DISTRICT

Cuba Street is actually not Cuban at all—it was named after an early ship that arrived in Wellington in 1840. The street has always been a vibrant hub—its colorful street art, vintage clothing stores, and more recent Havana-inspired hangouts serve as a stark contrast to the grocers, locksmith, butcher, violin maker, and Victorian inn that first graced it.

Today the Cuba Street District is renowned for its übercool bohemian club and bar (and café and shopping) scene. It's all about Cuba at **Havana Bar** (32a-34 Wigan St., 04/384-7039, www.havanabar.co.nz, 11:30am-close daily), a cocktail and tapas joint spread across a couple of colorful cottages whose courtyards overlook the street, and who regularly host some of the city's best DJs. There's plenty of live music and plenty of soul at **Laundry** (240 Cuba St., 04/384-4280, www.laundry.net.nz, 4pm-close daily), a Latin living room-like setup with low-slung chairs, massive corner windows, and a wonderful menu, too—make sure you try a burger.

Everyone's catered for at **Southern Cross Garden Bar Restaurant** (39 Abel Smith St., 04/384-9085, www.thecross.co.nz, 8am-close Mon.-Fri., 9am-close Sat.-Sun.), a laid-back indoor-outdoor establishment. This place is an award-winner thanks to an enormous all-day menu of café and traditional pub meals and a sun-trap garden lit by lanterns come nightfall, often accompanied by live music and dance.

It's not all about the cocktails and craft beer in the capital. Wine lovers should make for **Noble Rot Wine Bar** (6 Swan Lane, 04/385-6671, www.noblerot.co.nz, 4pm-close daily), one of the capital's trendiest establishments. Choose from more than 500 mostly New Zealand wines paired with fine cheese, cured meat, and pâtés. The European-inspired dinner menu includes tagliatelle and beef bourguignon.

COURTENAY PLACE

You'll find happy hours and meal deals aplenty on this vibrant Wellington strip. Keep an eye out for the plethora of blackboards advertising drink specials outside the bars. The bar at foot-tapping **Vinyl** (66 Courtenay Place, 04/385-6713, www.ilovevinylbar.co.nz, 3pm-4am Sun.-Wed., noon-4am Thurs.-Sat.) is lined with thousands of record sleeves. They serve a decent collection of spirits that befit its hip vibe along with a rolling list of classic 1960s, 1970s, and 1980s tunes.

Discover dozens of beers from across the globe at the **Malthouse** (48 Courtenay Place, 04/802-5484, www.themalthouse.co.nz, 3pm-midnight Mon.-Tues., noon-3am Wed.-Sat., noon-1am Sun.). Its 29 taps and massive fridges heave with classic and craft brews, all enjoyed in a traditional pub setting.

One of the coolest bars in this coolest of capitals, the **Library** (53 Courtenay Place, 04/382-8593, www.thelibrary.co.nz, 5pm-2am Mon.-Thurs., 4pm-3am Fri.-Sat., 5pm-1am Sun.) imparts an air of sophisticated mystery from its tucked-away second-floor location. Inside, the polished bar and oak-panel walls are lined with rows of classic books. The Library is famed for its hard-to-find wines, exceptional cocktails (try the old-fashioned), and desserts.

TOP EXPERIENCE

★ CRAFT BEER

Wellington is the craft beer capital of New Zealand (just don't tell Nelson). For a complete list of establishments, check out www.craftbeercapital.com to see what beer-themed events are on while you're in town. A great introduction to the city's craft beer scene is **Hammonds' Capital Craft Beer Tour** (04/472-0869, www.wellingtonsightseeingtours.co.nz, $159), which stops at four microbreweries. Tours include talks about each brewery's history with tutored tastings and shared platters. The tour departs from the i-SITE at 1pm Friday and returns at 5pm. Reservations are essential.

Little Beer Quarter (6 Edward St., 04/803-3304, www.littlebeerquarter.co.nz, 3:30pm-close Mon., noon-close Tues.-Sat., 3pm-close Sun.), a few blocks west of Cuba Street, collates the cream of Kiwi craft beer. Its 14 revolving taps (plus a pair of hand pulls), more than 100 labels and international brews, and New Zealand wines are served in the cozy mismatched gastropub filled with stools, leather seats, and airy plants.

Garage Project Taproom (91 Aro St., 04/802-5324, www.garageproject.co.nz, 3pm-10pm Tues.-Thurs., noon-10pm Fri.-Sun.) boasts 18 taps and a couple of cask lines, along with a selection of cans and bottles served in a lair-like setting, hemmed in by artwork and mirrors. See where their tipples are brewed, and sample some free tastings at their **Garage Project Cellar Door** (68 Aro St., 04/384-3076, noon-7pm Sun.-Mon., noon-8pm Tues.-Wed., noon-8pm Thurs., 10am-9pm Fri.). The Garage Projects are in the inner-city suburb of Aro Valley.

Parrotdog (60-66 Kingsford Smith St., 04/384-8077, www.parrotdog.co.nz, 10am-7pm Mon.-Thurs., 10am-8pm Fri.-Sat., noon-6pm Sun.) offers seasonal in-house brews along with a standard range of pilsners and ales served with complimentary snacks. It's 6km southeast at Lyall Bay.

The **Occasional Brewer** (85 Adelaide Rd., 04/384-8268, www.theoccasionalbrewer.co.nz, 5pm-close Tues.-Thurs., noon-close Fri., 10am-close Sat.-Sun.), is the only one of its kind in the country. Guests are invited to brew their own beer from scratch under expert guidance. The process takes half a day, with another two to three weeks before the brew's ready for bottling. It's worth considering if you'll pass through Wellington on the way to or from South Island, but you can still stop by for tastings at the bar. The brewery is in the suburb of Mount Cook.

Performing Arts

Visit **WellingtonNZ** (www.wellingtonnz.com) or **Eventfinda** (www.eventfinda.co.nz) to see who's performing while you're in town. You'll also find listings in newspapers like the ***NZ Herald*** (www.nzherald.co.nz) and ***Dominion Post*** (www.stuff.co.nz). Tickets to most events are sold through Eventfinda or **Ticketek** (www.premierticketek.co.nz).

CLASSICAL ARTS

The **New Zealand Royal Ballet** (www.nzballet.org.nz) is based in Wellington, often performing out of the **St. James Theatre** (77-87 Courtenay Place, 04/801-4231, www.venueswellington.com), along with the **New Zealand Opera** (www.nzoperahouse.com). The **Opera House** (111-113 Manners St., 04/801-4231, www.venueswellington.com) also sometimes plays host to the ballet and opera as well as to plays and classical music performances. The **Michael Fowler Centre** (111 Wakefield St., 04/801-4231, www.venueswellington.com) is the home of the **New Zealand Symphony Orchestra** (www.nzso.co.nz) and hosts other performing arts, concerts, and comedy.

THEATER

Circa Theatre (1 Taranaki, 04/801-7992, www.circa.co.nz) is a leading creative light, attracting national and international shows of all stripes. **Bats Theatre** (1 Kent Terrace, 04/802-4175, www.bats.co.nz) is home to three intimate spaces for independent productions, with tickets rarely more than $16.

LIVE MUSIC

Large-scale rock and pop music concerts usually take place at the **TSB Arena** (Queens Wharf, Jervois Quay, 04/801-4231, www.venueswellington.com) or the **Westpac Stadium** (105 Waterloo Quay, 04/473-3881, www.westpacstadium.co.nz).

Cinema

Head to **Light House Cinema** (29 Wigan St., 04/385-3337, www.lighthousecinema.co.nz) for independent movies and well-considered blockbusters enjoyed with espresso coffee, craft beers, or local wines. Similarly, tantalizing refreshments are offered at the iconic **Embassy Theatre** (10 Kent St., 04/384-7657, www.eventcinemas.co.nz), where new art house and classic films are emboldened by some serious audio equipment. Built in 1924 and still with a wonderfully preserved auditorium, it's a Wellington institution and hosted the world premieres of some of *The Hobbit* and *The Lord of the Rings* movies.

The coolest picture palace in Wellington is **Roxy Cinema** (5 Park Rd., 04/388-5555), in the suburb of Miramar, whose 1928 art deco facade is complemented inside by a cocktail lounge and eatery, with sculptures by Weta Workshop and a pair of state-of-the-art screens.

Festivals and Events

JANUARY

Around 15,000 folks descend on the **Pasifika Festival** (www.wellington.govt.nz) at Waitangi Park (107 Cable St.) to watch live singing and dance, including the legendary haka, and enjoy authentic Pacific food.

The already sizeable Asian population is swelling in New Zealand, and the **Chinese New Year Festival** (www.chinenesenewyear.co.nz, Jan. or Feb.) is a big deal. Events at the **TSB Arena** (Queens Wharf., 04/801-4231, www.venueswellington.com) and Frank Kitts Park, at the waterfront, include fireworks, food, and dancing dragons.

FEBRUARY

The **Winery Tour** (www.winerytour.co.nz) sees musicians play various parks and vineyards across the country. Venues often change; check the website.

For three weeks from late February and into March, the **Fringe Festival** (www.fringe.co.nz) attracts local and international artists, comedians, dancers, musicians, poets, puppeteers, and more across the city's parks, clubs, cafés, and theaters.

MARCH

The **Wellington Wine & Food Festival** (www.wineandfoodfestival.co.nz) promotes the best of local fare, bringing together eateries, wineries, and microbreweries at Waitangi Park on the Waterfront.

During the first few of weeks of March, the **Pride Festival** (www.wellingtonpridefestival.org.nz, Mar.) marches into the Cuba District, celebrating all things LGBT across the area's bars and clubs, with street parades, too.

The **Newtown Festival Street Fair** (www.newtonfestival.org.nz), the country's largest free outdoor performance event, sees several blocks closed off to traffic around the suburb of Newton to host live music and dances on public stages.

CubaDupa (www.cubadupa.co.nz) is a cultural highlight, a yearly street festival that celebrates the capital's creative spirit throughout the Cuba District. Enjoy performance arts and eateries setting up shop outside their doors.

Top-drawer music festival **Homegrown** (www.homegrown.net.nz, Mar.) sees legendary local and up-and-coming acts take to a handful of stages at the Waterfront.

JUNE-AUGUST

One of the calendar's coolest happenings, befitting the city's Cuban vibe, the **Wellington Jazz Festival** (www.jazzfestival.co.nz) is a five-day event in June, with oodles of live music—including international artists—spread across hip venues and bars.

An August celebration of all things beer, for two days at the **Westpac Stadium** (105 Waterloo Quay, 04/384-3842, www.westpacstadium.co.nz), **Beervana** (www.beervana.co.nz) hosts an array of stalls offering hundreds of local and international beers, including hard-to-find and one-off brews.

SEPTEMBER-OCTOBER

Straddling September and October, the **World of Wearable Art** (www.worldofwearableart.com) invites creatives from across the world to design outfits that merge fashion and art, with some truly spectacularly weird and wonderful results showcased from catwalks and exhibit stands at the **TSB Arena** (Queens Wharf., 04/801-4231, www.venueswellington.com).

SHOPPING

Every Saturday near the waterfront, the vibrant **Wellington Underground Market** (Frank Kitts Park, Jervois Quay, www.undergroundmarket.nz, 10am-4pm Sat.) attracts local artists, craftspeople, designers, and bakers to sell their wares from stalls.

Books

A Wellington institution, **Unity Books** (57 Willis St., 04/499-4245, www.unitybooks.nz, 9am-6pm Mon.-Thurs., 9am-7pm Fri., 10am-5pm Sat., 11am-5pm Sun.) is a proudly independent bookstore that boasts possibly the country's best collection, including local and hard-to-find titles.

Clothing

There's an abundance of popular high-street fashion and sports brand stores along Lambton Quay. Even if it's just for a browse, take a meander through **Old Bank Arcade** (233-237 Lambton Quay, 04/922-0600, www.oldbank.co.nz). The sophisticated heritage building sports high ceilings, tiled mosaic floors, and fashionable boutiques framed by rich varnished woods—one such store is Kiwi men's streetwear label, **I Love Ugly** (04/472-0044, www.iloveugly.net, 9:30am-5:30pm Mon.-Thurs., 9:30am-6pm Fri., 10am-5pm Sat., 11am-4pm Sun.).

The Cuba Street District is a haven of all things vintage and boutique, with a cacophony of cool retro cats and artisans flogging their wares. **Madame Fancy Pants** (225 Cuba St., 04/385-0830, www.madamefancypants.com, 11am-5pm Mon., 10am-5pm Tues. and Sat., 10am-5:30pm Wed.-Thurs., 10am-6pm Fri., 10am-4pm Sun.) comprises a cozy boudoir-like layout displaying often limited edition, mostly women's goods, including clothing, stationery, and jewelry.

The owners at **Emporium Vintage Boutique** (103 Cuba St., 04/381-4544, www.emporiumnz.com, 10am-6pm Mon.-Fri., 10am-5pm Sat., 11am-4pm Sun.) handpick their high-quality retro clothing, often from the United States.

Gift and Home

For souvenirs, **Made It** (103 Victoria St., 04/472-7442, www.madeitwgtn.co.nz, 10am-5:30pm Mon.-Fri., 10am-5pm Sat., 11am-4pm Sun.) is a real find, curating a collection of clothing for guys and gals, along with candles, crafts, homewares, and stationery created by Kiwi artisans and small businesses.

One of the most interesting—and best-smelling—stores in the capital is **Wellington Apothecary** (110a Cuba Mall, 04/801-8777, www.wellingtonapothecary.co.nz, 10am-5pm Mon.-Thurs. and Sat., 10am-6:30pm Fri., 11am-4pm Sun.), where potions such as tonics, teas, and skin-care lotions are handmade from local natural ingredients and bottled before your eyes.

FOOD

Wellington's excellent culinary scene caters from the cheap and cheerful to fine dining and harbor views. The international food in the city is especially scrumptious. Foodies should consider **Zest Food Tours** (04/801-9198, www.zestfoodtours.co.nz, $185-485), a great introduction to the city's eateries, with half- and full-day jaunts around some of the coolest and most exclusive food joints to sample dishes and learn about the history of the establishments as well general Wellington insights. Tours depart from the i-SITE at Civic Square, and must be booked in advance.

Cafés

Not only is Wellington considered the craft beer capital of New Zealand, but also the café capital. A legendary haunt of the legendary Cuba District, atmospheric ★ **Midnight Espresso** (179 Cuba St., 04/384-7014, 7:30am-3am Mon.-Fri., 8am-3am Sat.-Sun.) entices with its superb coffee and great range of fresh quick eats, including super vegan options, all day and well into the early hours. It's a cozy but bustling establishment—give the nachos a try.

A Cuba District icon, steaming joe aside, the elegant, high-ceilinged **Floriditas** (161 Cuba St., 04/381-2212, www.floriditas.co.nz, 7am-9:30pm Mon.-Sat.) is famed for its European-inspired fare, including pasta and risotto, and exquisite desserts—notably the brown sugar pavlova served with tamarillo, pistachio, and cream, prepared in their own off-site bakery.

Havana Coffee Works (163 Tory St., 04/384-7041, www.havana.co.nz, Mon.-Fri. 7am-5pm) is one of Wellington's best-established java joints, roasting and grinding their own flavorsome exotic beans, served in a fashionable Latin setting with sticky baked treats, breakfasts, and awesome pies.

Seafood

It's almost worth swinging by ★ **Ortega Fish Shack** (16 Majoribanks St., 04/382-9559, www.ortega.co.nz, 5:30pm-11pm Tues.-Sat., $34-37) for a snap of the enormous swordfish on the wall, which, along with other marine-themed paraphernalia, sets the tone for this award-winning eatery. Go for the snapper or roasted sole with seaweed butter.

Enjoy some of the best cocktails and service in town at **Coene's Bar** (103 Oriental Parade, 04/385-7124, www.whg.co.nz, 11am-close Mon.-Fri., 9am-close Sat.-Sun., $24-33), a polished yacht club-like eatery with massive sea-facing windows and a seafood-heavy menu to match (there are red meats, too). The sesame-crusted tuna fillet is excellent. Snag a table on the balcony if you can.

Asian

An authentic no-nonsense Asian eatery with a sizzling open kitchen that prepares dishes with a mainly Vietnamese slant—the *pho* is outstanding—★ **Fisherman's Plate** (12 Bond St., 04/473-8375, 11am-9pm Mon.-Sat., $13-18) is a tucked-away Wellington gem. The portions are sizeable, the price not, and the hostess has the biggest smile in town. Consider one of the spicy wok stir-fries.

In keeping with its street-food vibe, vibrant **Little Penang** (40 Dixon St., 04/382-9818, 11am-3pm and 5pm-9pm Mon.-Thurs., 11am-3pm and 5pm-9:30pm Fri., 11am-9pm Sat., $13-17) isn't the kind of place you hang around (expect to queue at lunchtime). Service is fast and efficient, and there's no alcohol license, but the Malaysian fare is some of the best Asian cuisine in the capital thanks to dishes like *mee goreng*, clay-pot rice with chicken, and rolling daily specials (look for the blackboard).

BYO or order rice beer or sake at **Miyabi Sushi** (Shop 13, 142 Willis St., 04/801-9688, www.miyabisushi.co.nz, 11:30am-2:30pm and 5:30pm-9:30pm Mon.-Fri., noon-2:30pm and 5:30pm-9:30pm Sat., $15-28), where traditional Japanese dishes are beautifully presented and served in a friendly setting with East Asian art and paraphernalia such as decorative swords adorning the walls.

★ **House of Dumplings** (117 Taranaki St., 04/390-1039, www.houseofdumplings.co.nz, 11:30am-8:30pm Tues.-Sat.) offers steamed and pan-fried dumplings crafted using local ingredients and techniques passed through the generations. You can almost taste the tender love that goes into the preparation of the Cantonese chicken and coriander or Nepalese spiced lamb airy treats ($2-6 each), accompanied by a selection of spicy meat skewers ($4.50 each). The intimate setting is cramped but cozy and cloaked in stunning woods.

European

Wellington's best restaurant, ★ **Logan Brown** (192 Cuba St., 5:30pm-9pm Tues., noon-2pm and 5:30pm-9pm Wed.-Sat., 5:30pm-9pm Sun., $39-46) serves a *paua* (read abalone) ravioli that is the stuff of legend. Fine dining fare is spread across a handful of seasonal menus, including a chef's tasting set menu with wine pairings, and the Saturday degustation menus with delights like line-caught fish or wild venison. Stone columns, arches, and leather seating invoke a classical air.

With tasteful bare plaster walls, tiny tables, an open kitchen, and rows of vino behind the bar, **Ombra** (Vivian St. and Cuba St., 04/385-3229, www.ombra.co.nz, 10am-noon Mon.-Fri., 8am-10pm Sat.-Sun., $12-18) is the kind of intimate establishment you'd expect to stumble on in an Italian back alley. The super value Venetian-inspired menu offers an array of tasty classics and twists on traditional Italian tapas—*cicchetti*—alongside the likes of venison risotto and handmade sausages.

Boulcott Street Bistro (99 Boulcott St., 04/499-4199, www.boulcottstreetbistro.co.nz, lunch noon-2pm Sun.-Fri., dinner 5:30pm-close daily, $34-39) certainly wins the award for quaintest setting, in a wonderful historic white wooden villa that hints at its interior's coziness. Local seasonal produce is sourced to create modern European-leaning dishes—think citrus-braised beef cheeks or pan-roasted market fish—enhanced by a carefully curated selection of Kiwi wines. Start with the French onion soup and finish with a cocktail.

Proudly crafting French-inspired fare from locally sourced ingredients, **Cuba St. Bistro** (203-205 Cuba St., 04/890-3939, 11am-2pm and 5pm-9pm Mon.-Fri., 9am-2pm and 5pm-9:30pm Sat.-Sun., $25-34) is a warm welcoming eatery of rich woods, terra-cotta brick walls, and chatter. Fillet steak and free-range chicken is served alongside fresh market fish.

Latin American

A firm favorite with locals and visitors, iconic **Fidels** (234 Cuba St., 04/801-6868, www.fidelscafe.com, 7:30am-10pm Mon.-Fri., 8am-10pm Sat., 9am-10pm Sun., $15-20) serves classics with a Latin twist, including Cuban burritos and grilled haloumi with chili jam, as well as pizzas and burgers, accompanied by a well-selected New Zealand wine list and Wellington's best Bloody Mary. Its indoor and outdoor areas are adorned with colorful revolutionary imagery and the occasional cactus.

You'll find the usual visuals at **Viva Mexico** (210 Left Bank Arcade, off Cuba St., 04/382-9913, www.vivamexico.co.nz, noon-10pm Tues.-Sun., $23). Western-style "Wanted" art and dazzling religious imagery are accompanied by an authentic Mexican menu (no nachos) filled with fresh delights like chicken enchiladas and a folded tortilla with slow-cooked lamb.

A charmingly rambling eatery, ★ **Sweet Mother's Kitchen** (5 Courtenay Place, 04/385-4444, www.sweetmotherskitchen.co.nz, 8am-close daily, $15-27) epitomizes casual dining. A warm welcome foretells its well-priced soul food-inspired cooking philosophy, inspired by Mexico and New Orleans. Go for the Cajun blackened Tarakihi fish served with bourbon mash, but save room for the apple pie.

ACCOMMODATIONS

Fortunately, in Wellington you don't have to venture out to the suburbs for the better backpacker places. Further up the price bracket, the capital has some wonderfully creative boutique lodgings. Most are within walking distance of the best eateries and nightlife.

Under $100

One of the capital's slickest hostels, ★ **YHA**

Wellington (292 Wakefield St., 04/801-7230, www.yha.co.nz, dorm $33-38, $87 s, $99-133 d), is also among its best situated, positioned between Te Papa and Courtenay Place. Rooms are pristine, with dorms and privates available with en suite baths, paired with amenities like a lounge projection screen and free movie to borrow, a pool table, a superbly stocked kitchen, and an on-site café. Triple rooms ($97-133) are available.

Nomads Capital Hostel Wellington (118-120 Wakefield St., 04/978-7800, www.nomadsworld.com, dorm $32-43, $120-145 s or d) sits near Cuba Street and the waterfront, a sleek and clean backpacker lodging with a top-drawer tour desk. Plenty of freebies, like breakfast pancakes, tea and coffee, and a light evening meal, along with an adjacent bar with regular drink and meal deals, combine to attract a younger crowd. Rooms are fresh, and the kitchen is well-stocked.

Set in gorgeous historic art deco architecture, the relaxed **Hotel Waterloo & Backpackers** (1 Bunny St., 04/473-8482, www.hotelwaterloo.co.nz, dorm $26-33, $72-99 s, $89-129 d) offers a great range of well-priced rooms, some with en suite baths, including dorms, while all private rooms come with a desk and Sky TV. Communal facilities include a games room and an on-site café and bar. Positioned north of the harbor, the lodging is near Parliament, the train station, and ferry terminals, but it's a couple of kilometers from Cuba Street and Te Papa.

Positioned within walking distance of Oriental Bay and Te Papa, **The Cambridge Hotel** (28 Cambridge Terrace, 0800/375-021, www.cambridgehotel.co.nz, dorm $26-40, $69-99 s, $89-119 d) has been hosting travelers since 1883. The historic well-run corner building offers backpacker and reasonably priced hotel lodgings, with en suite baths available for all. Most rooms also sport Sky TV and tea- and coffee-making facilities. There is a bar and eatery on-site, and free barbecues from 6pm every Wednesday. Triple and quad rooms ($149-159) with en suite baths are available.

★ **The Dwellington** (8 Halswell St., 04/550-9373, www.thedwellington.co.nz, dorm $29-32, $85-93 s or d) is a real standout that raises the backpacker bar. Resembling a boutique hotel, timber bunks and double beds are complemented by mid-century furniture with artistic black-and-while photos by Kiwi artist Ans Westra. Free breakfast is served in New Zealand's coolest communal kitchen. Other amenities include a movie room, a game room, and a tennis court. Wi-Fi is free, and there's a triple room ($100). It's a little over 2km to Te Papa and Cuba Street.

$100-200

Look beyond the soulless Soviet-like exterior of **Capital View Motor Inn** (12 Thompson St., 04/385-0515, www.capitalview.co.nz, $130-260) and be rewarded with pleasant city views overlooking the harbor, a stone's throw from Cuba Street. Guests can make use of free parking and free Wi-Fi, with all 21 units boasting private baths, Sky TV, and cooking facilities.

Centrally positioned **Apollo Lodge Motel** (49 Majoribanks St., 04/385-1849, www.apolllolodge.co.nz, $150-200) is just a couple of minutes' stroll from entertainment district Courtenay Place and 10 minutes from Te Papa. The Edwardian villa houses clean, comfortable en suite rooms with heating, electric blankets, Sky TV, free Wi-Fi, a fridge, and at least basic cooking facilities like a microwave, a kettle, and a toaster—some rooms have a full kitchen. Choose from studio to three-bedroom units.

A lot of love—and fun—has gone into decorating and furnishing **Gourmet Stay** (25 Frederick St., 04/801-6800, www.gourmet-stay.co.nz, $160-439) a hip boutique hotel minutes from Courtenay Place. Rooms range from queen studios with shared baths through three-bedroom family lodgings, with a colorful Pacific vibe. Some rooms are equipped with a kitchen, all have free Wi-Fi, 14 TV channels, and tea- and coffee-making facilities. The top-floor room has an outdoor deck with a hot tub.

There's nothing else quite like the ★ **Beachfront Wellington B&B** (215 Marine Parade, 04/388-1646, www.beachfrontwellington.co.nz, $150-190), 15 minutes from the city in a secluded spot in the suburb of Seaton. Vibrant white and airy rooms all overlook the ocean, with TVs, free Wi-Fi, tea- and coffee-making facilities, bathrobes, and toiletries. Two of the three rooms share a bath, the other has an en suite bath, and breakfast consists of sweet treats like pastries and seasonal fruits.

$200-300

Bolton Hotel (Bolton St. and Mowbray St., 04/472-9966, www.boltonhotel.co.nz, $249-449) offers a plethora of stylish boutique rooms across budgets ranging from en suite studios to suites, some with stunning city views from floor-to-ceiling windows. Standard room amenities include free Wi-Fi, iPad minis, Sky TV, bathrobes, and hairdryers. Guests can also make use of the gym, hot tub, and lap pools. This is an elegant gem of a hotel.

Local author Jane Tolerton has converted her handsome Victorian home, a 10-minute walk from Te Papa, into the aptly named, and aptly restful, **Booklovers B&B** (123 Pirie St., 04/384-2714, www.booklovers.co.nz, $200-285). Three large en suite rooms are furnished with soft carpets, rich bedding, and floral drapes, the homey vibe emboldened by the scent of cooked breakfasts or baking each morning. Enjoy free Wi-Fi, and, of course, plenty of reading material—grab the room with the claw-foot bathtub if you can.

Vibrant, modern accommodations in the heart of downtown, **Mercure Wellington Abel Tasman** (169 Willis St., 04/385-1304, www.abeltasmanhotel.co.nz, $219-359) is within walking distance of the waterfront, Te Papa, and Courtenay Place. Airy rooms have en suite baths and are equipped with free Wi-Fi, a desk, Sky TV, hot-drink facilities, a fridge, and a microwave, and there's an on-site bar and restaurant.

★ **Ohtel** (66 Oriental Parade, Oriental Bay, Wellington, 04/803-0600, www.ohtel.com, $229) is a super-stylish Scandinavian-inspired boutique lodging in Oriental Bay. Decked out with antipodean furnishings and boasting serious eco-credentials like a solar-heated water system, rooms are equipped with free Wi-Fi, Sky TV, tea- and coffee-making facilities, and walk-in showers. Some sport a bath and views of Waitangi Park.

One of New Zealand's coolest lodgings and one that truly captures the capital's creative soul, ★ **QT Museum Wellington** (90 Cable St., 04/802-8900, www.qthotelsandresorts.com, $239-409), formerly Museum Art Hotel, is positioned on the waterfront near Te Papa, with sea views and adorned with fascinating artworks and sculptures. Designer rooms offer free Wi-Fi and Sky TV; there's a gym, a spa, a pool, a sauna, and an on-site French-inspired fine-dining restaurant and cocktail bar called **Hippopotamus** (04/802-8935, 6:30am-10pm Mon.-Fri., 7am-10pm Sat.-Sun., $38-48). Don't leave without trying the wild venison.

TRANSPORTATION AND SERVICES

Getting There

AIR

Wellington Airport (WLG, Stewart Duff Dr., 04/385-5100, www.wellingtonairport.co.nz) is 20 minutes southeast of the CBD. It hosts domestic flights from throughout the country, primarily with **Air New Zealand** (www.airnewzealand.co.nz). **Jetstar** (www.jetstar.com) and also connects the capital with Auckland and Christchurch. **Golden Bay Air** (www.goldenbayair.co.nz) connects with Golden Bay in Nelson. **Sounds Air** (www.soundsair.com) connects Wellington with Taupo, Westport, Picton, Blenheim, and Nelson. **Air Chathams** (www.airchathams.co.nz) flies to the Chatham Islands two or three times a week.

International flights go to Australia, some cities in Asia, and the Pacific Islands (at the time of writing, talks were underway to possibly extend the runway in order to attract longer-haul flights). The main carriers are **Air New Zealand, Jetstar, Qantas** (www.qantas.com), **Virgin Australia** (www.virgin-australia.com), **Singapore Airlines** (www.singaporeair.com), and **Fiji Airways** (www.fijiairways.com). Inside the terminal, the airport is famed for its collection of sizeable Middle-earth-themed sculptures.

Airport Flyer (every 10 minutes during peak hours Mon.-Fri., every 20 minutes at other times, adults $9, children $5.50) is an express shuttle bus that links the airport with the city and Hutt Valley. Expect to pay around $40 for a taxi—there will be plenty waiting outside.

CAR RENTALS

Wellington-based car hire outfits include **Apex Car Rentals** (186 Victoria St., 0800/300-110, www.apexrentals.co.nz), a Kiwi company with a good selection of vehicles at competitive prices. **Avis** (04/802-1088, www.avis.co.nz), **Thrifty** (03/359-2721, www.thrifty.co.nz), and **Budget** (04/388-0987, www.budget.co.nz) are all represented at the airport.

RAIL

Make a note of **Metlink** (0800/801-700, www.metlink.org.nz) for information regarding rail (as well as buses, cable car and ferries), including a handy journal planner on the website. Head to Bunny Street for the main access to **Wellington Railway Station.** Pay for tickets with cash on trains or at the ticket office (6:30am-8pm Mon.-Thurs., 6:30am-1:15am Fri., 7:45am-1:15am Sat., 6:30am-7:10am Sun.). All stations also have ticket machines that accept bank cards. The ***Northern Explorer*** (www.greatjourneysofnz.co.nz) is a scenic train route that connects Wellington and Auckland via the Kapiti Coast, Palmerston North, the Geothermal Heartland, and Hamilton. It runs southbound departing from Auckland (7:45am Mon., Thurs., and Sat.), and pulling into Wellington at 6:25am. Northbound it departs Wellington (7:55am Tues., Fri., and Sun.) and arrives in Auckland at 6:50pm. Daily services connect Wellington to the Kapiti Coast, terminating at Waikanae; the Hutt Valley, terminating at Upper Hutt Station; and Wairarapa, terminating at Masterton.

BUS

National bus carriers **Intercity** (04/385-0520, www.intercity.co.nz) and **Naked Bus** (09/979-1616, www.nakedbus.com) both operate daily routes to Wellington—the pickup and drop-off point is platform 9 of the railway station.

BOAT

Two ferry operators, the **Interislander** (1 Aotea Quay, 0800/801-700, www.greatjourneysofnz.co.nz) and **Blueridge Cook Strait Ferry** (50 Waterloo Quay, 0800/844-844, www.blueridge.co.nz) connect Wellington to Picton on South Island daily, and both take vehicles. The journey—which can be rather choppy—takes around 3.5 hours, but both boats show movies and have bars and eateries. Blueridge is generally slightly cheaper, while Interislander offers more luxury options like private lounges. Try not to book a nighttime journey, as you'll miss the incredible scenery as you sail into, or out of, the Marlborough Sounds on South Island.

Getting Around

BUS

There is an excellent bus network across Wellington, with routes, times, and journey planners available at **Metlink** (0800/801-700, www.metlink.org.nz). If you're in town for at least a few days, buy a Snapper card ($10) from i-SITE, which provides discounted bus service in the region. Kapiti Coast, Hutt Valley, and Wairarapa are well-served by buses and trains.

FERRY

East By West Ferries (04/449-1282, www.eastbywest.co.nz) operates a pair of vessels that travel between downtown Wellington, Matiu/Somes Island, and Days Bay.

BICYCLE

Switched On Bikes (Shed 1, Queens Wharf, 0800/386-877, www.switchedonbikes.co.nz, 9am-5pm daily) rents street, mountain, and electric bicycles. They also operate half- and full-day guided tours (from $95).

TOURS

Hop On Hop Off Guided Tours (0800/246-877, www.hoponhopoff.co.nz, 10am-2pm daily, adults $45, children $30) offers a super two-hour city tour that stops at 17 of the most iconic sights, including Te Papa, Parliament, Weta Cave, and the Cuba Quarter. Choose where to jump on and off, then get picked up by a later bus. The drivers are friendly and informative guides. Tours depart hourly from bus stop 101, next to the i-SITE on Wakefield Street.

A joyful way to experience the region's seaside sights is with the off-road **Seal Coast Safari** (64 Dixon St., 04/801-6040, www.sealcoast.com, 10am and 1:30pm daily, adults $125, children $62.50). Departing from the i-SITE (Wakefield St.), the three-hour 4WD tour travels among the turbines of the impressive wind farm on Brooklyn Hill with views of the blue-green Cook Straight across to South Island. The tour snakes through a private farm (home to goats, deer, and ostrich) and toward the coast to take in Red Rocks Reserve and the Leaning Lighthouse. Your trip ends with hot drinks and muffins in the company of idling fur seals.

Tolkien aficionados shouldn't miss **Rover Rings Tours** (04/471-0044, www.roverringstours.co.nz, adults $95-190, children $50-85). Their half- and full-day guided trips tour Middle-earth movie locations, Weta Cave, and Wellington spots such as Mount Victoria lookout. Trips must be booked in advance.

Services

The **Wellington i-SITE Visitor Centre** (Civic Square, Victoria St. and Wakefield St., 04/802-4860, www.wellingtonnz.com, 8:30am-5pm daily) is a font of knowledge about all things Wellington and the surrounding lands, with a free tour-booking service. The **DoC Kapiti Wellington Visitor Centre** (18-32 Manners St., 04/384-7770, www.doct.govt.nz) is the place to go for tramping information, hut passes, and permits for Kapiti Island.

Free Wi-Fi is provided throughout the CBD; look for the "cdbfree" network on your device. You can also try the **Wellington Central Library** (65 Victoria St., 04/801-4040, www.wcl.govt.nz, 9:30am-8:30pm Mon.-Fri., 9:30am-5pm Sat., 1pm-4pm Sun.). For mailings, there's a centrally located **post office** (2 Manners St., 0800/081-190, www.nzpost.co.nz, 9am-5:30pm Mon.-Fri., 9am-3pm Sat.).

Wellington Hospital (Riddiford St., Newtown, 04/385-5999) is on the edge of the CBD. Head to the corner of Victoria and Harris Streets for **Wellington Central Police Station** (04/381-2000). The **Wellington Accident and Urgent Medical Centre** (Adelaide Rd., 04/384-4944) offers after-hours medical care in the suburb of Newton.

The Kapiti Coast

This enchanting stretch of fertile shoreline north of Wellington is easily accessible thanks to its excellent road (Hwy. 1) and rail networks. Though the Kapiti Coast is fast expanding as more Wellington workers and creatives base themselves here, it'll be many lifetimes before it loses its laid-back rural allure, fringed by unspoiled surf and swimming beaches in the shadow of sloping green hills peppered with historic towns. Halfway along the 40km coastline, Kapiti Island—a bird sanctuary and the nation's oldest nature reserve—sits just offshore.

Getting There

Trains (www.metlink.org.nz) depart several times daily from Wellington to Paekakariki, Paraparaumu, and Waikanae with daily weekday service to Otaki (www.greatjourneysofnz.co.nz). The ***Northern Explorer*** (www.greatjourneysofnz.co.nz) train route arrives from Auckland (Mon., Thurs., and Sat., returns Tues., Fri., and Sun.).

PORIRUA

The small city of Porirua sits at the south end of the Kapiti Coast, a 20-minute drive north of Wellington along Highway 1. The seaside setting is a popular destination for water-sports enthusiasts. **Titahi Bay,** sandwiched between Porirua Harbour and the Cook Strait, is famed for its arching golden beach lined with colorful boatsheds. At low tide, a fossilized forest that is at least 100,000 years old is suddenly revealed.

The city's **Pataka Art + Museum** (Norrie St. and Parumoana St., 04/237-1511, www.pataka.org.nz, 10am-5pm Mon.-Sat., 11am-4:30pm Sun., free) exhibits some of the nation's most revered Maori and Pacific contemporary artists.

For more information, visit the **i-SITE Visitor Information Centre** (8 Cobham Court, 04/237-8088, www.poriruanz.com, 9am-5pm Mon.-Fri., 9am-4pm Sat., 10am-2pm Sun.). For emergencies, try the **Kenepuru Hospital** (Raiha St., 04/385-5999).

PAEKAKARIKI

North of Porirua 20km along Highway 1, Paekakariki is the Kapiti Coast's southern bookend, with a bulging population of artists.

Sights

The unassuming town was a significant rail hub in the late 1800s; in 1910, the local community had to step in to save the station and signal box from demolition. The fruits of their labor can be viewed at the charming **Paekakariki Railway Museum** (Hwy. 1, 04/904-9970, www.stationmuseum.co.nz, 11am-3pm Sat.-Sun., free). Housed in the town's working station, the museum details the region's former steam-powered glory, such as the transportation of troops during World War II along with Maori artifacts and carvings.

Marvel at the Kapiti Coast from the **Paekakariki Escarpment Trail** (enter via Ames St.), a 10km section of the 3,000km **Te Araroa Trail,** which runs south to Pukerua Bay. The well-marked track rises to 200m, weaving through the Akatarawa Ranges, along cliffs, and across a lofty swing bridge that proves especially interesting during Wellington's legendary winds. The track ends at the Pukerua Bay train station, with a 10-minute return to Paekakariki.

Queen Elizabeth Park (off Hwy. 1, Mackays Crossing Entrance) is home to two attractions and one holiday park. The **Wellington Tramway Museum** (04/292-8361, www.wellingtontrams.org.nz, 10am-4pm daily, adults $12, children $6) displays a fleet of working early- to mid-20th century tram cars, some of which can be ridden, along with photos, rail memorabilia, and short historical films. Next to the tramway, **Stables on the Park** (06/364-3336, www.stablesonthepark.co.nz, $70-140) offers the opportunity to take in this majestic stretch of coast on horseback. Inland treks tromp through bushland or across the sands. No experience is needed. Trips must be booked in advance.

Accommodations

Paekakariki Holiday Park (off Hwy. 1, 04/292-8292, www.paekakarikiholidaypark.co.nz) has ocean-side camping and van sites (adults $18, children $8) under the shade of pohutukawa trees. Cabins, lodges, and tourist flats ($70-110) are also available; many have en suite baths and include TVs, cooking facilities, and dining areas. The site provides easy access to an array of walking and biking trails.

PARAPARAUMU

Paraparaumu is the Kapiti Coast's most sizeable town. It also serves as the gateway to Kapiti Island. The town is 10km north of Paekakariki along Highway 1; Paraparaumu Beach is 4km northeast, at the end of Kapiti Road.

Sights

Paraparaumu's most imposing feature is the 14m-high statue of the **Virgin Mary,** which appears even taller from afar thanks to its position on a 75m knoll. The statue, built by Dutch artist Martin Roestenberg, was commissioned in 1958 to honor the 100th anniversary of the apparition at Lourdes.

Paraparaumu was the region's aviation center for a while in the mid-20th century, before Rongotai Airport was redeveloped and renamed as Wellington's present airport. Aviation enthusiasts should stop by the Paraparaumu airport, where the **Museum of Aviation** (227 Kapiti Rd., 04/905-2322, www.kapitiheritage.org.nz, 10am-4pm Sun., free) shows local and national flight history through imagery, text, memorabilia such as airplane parts and luggage, and small model airliners.

Southward Car Museum (Otaihanga Rd., 04/297-1221, www.southwardcarmuseum.co.nz, 9am-4:30pm daily, adults $18, children $5) is the coast's best museum—automobile aficionados especially may even consider it one of the country's most enjoyable, and its exquisite wide-ranging collection, stretching well beyond four-wheeled vehicles, is sure to hold the attention of everyone. Founded by Sir Len Southward, the first man to travel at 100mph on water, the 400-plus-piece exhibition includes an 1895 Benz Velo—the first car to arrive in New Zealand—as well as a $4 million Bugatti and a vintage British De Havilland Vampire fighter jet.

Recreation

Kapiti Four x 4 Adventure (334 Maungakotukutuku Rd., 04/299-0020, www.kapitifourx4.co.nz, $90-320) runs daily guided quad bike tours (1-6 hours), tearing up muddy trails, rivers, and rainforest with routes that traverse valley floors and up to ridgelines that afford views as far as Mount Taranaki.

The **Vintage Peddler** (81 Renown Rd., 027/440-2388, www.vintagepeddler.co.nz) provides a range of novel exploration options by way of a fleet of retro bikes. They also operate bespoke guided tour packages that take in sights such as the Tuatara Brewery. Stop by or call for a quote.

If e-bikes are more your thing, call in at **Dive Kapiti** (27 Milne Dr., 04/297-0075, www.divekapiti.co.nz, 9am-5pm Tues.-Fri., 9am-4pm Sat.-Sun.). They offer half- and full-day rentals along with kayak hire.

Food and Accommodations

Ambience Café (36 Marine Parade, 04/298-9898, 8am-4pm daily) covers all bases, its colorful all-day menu brimming with freshly made fare like fishcakes and sliders and heaps of vegetarian and vegan-friendly options, as well as probably the best coffee outside of Wellington. Some seriously indulgent ice coffees and hot chocolates are laden with the likes of ice cream and marshmallows—and enough calories for the entire week.

It's worth stopping by the tasting room at **Tuatara Brewery** (7 Sheffield St., 04/293-3351, www.tuatarabrewing.co.nz, 3pm-7pm Wed.-Thurs., 11am-8pm Fri.-Sat., 11am-7pm Sun.) to sample some beers and chat to the brewers while indulging in some light bar-type snacks such as platters ($16-27) or pizzas ($11-16).

The **Kapiti Lindale Motel** (3-7 Ventnor Dr., 04/298-7933, www.kapitimotel.com, $120-185) comprises a handsome gaggle of 10 peaceful and comfortable ground-floor self-contained units, surrounded by trees and manicured lawns, minutes from the railway station. Some units are equipped with spa baths, and all have kitchens or kitchenettes, free Wi-Fi, and Sky TV.

Transportation and Services

Kapiti Airport (PPQ, 60 Toru Rd., Paraparaumu, 04/298-1013, www.kapiticoastairport.co.nz) receives flights from **Air New Zealand** (www.airnewzealand.com) via Auckland and **Air 2 There** (www.air2there.com) and **Sounds Air** (www.soundsair.com) flights from Nelson and Blenheim. Car rentals are close to the airport; try **Rent Me Rentals** (www.rentmerentals.co.nz) or **Can Do Rentals** (www.candorentals.co.nz).

Intercity buses (www.intercity.co.nz) stops at the Paraparaumu Railway Station (Main Rd.). Local **Metlink** buses (www.metlink.org.nz) serve Kapiti from Wellington.

The Kapiti **i-SITE Visitor Information Centre** (175 Rimu Rd., 04/296-4700, www.kapiticoast.govt.nz, 8am-5pm Mon.-Fri.) offers information for the entire coast.

★ KAPITI ISLAND

A former whaling station, the DoC-maintained Kapiti Island is one of the nation's most important nature reserves, home to a stupendous variety of birds, including the kokako, the little spotted kiwi, the kaka, and the takahe. Few New Zealand destinations afford such a high chance of seeing the country's most fabled creatures in the wild.

The island's waters teem with an abundance of seals and dolphins, with the occasional visit from orcas. A handful of well-marked tracks navigate the island, offering hikes that range from a few minutes to four hours. Kapiti island is 5km off Paraparaumu Beach.

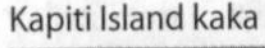
Kapiti Island kaka

Tours

Ferry passengers will arrive either at Rangatira or Waiorua/North End. A maximum of 160 visitor permits are issued daily and are included in the price of the ferry trip or guided tour.

The family that runs **Kapiti Island Nature Tours** (0800/527-484, www.kapitiislandnaturetours.co.nz, $80) have been guardians of a small private section of the island since the late 1800s. Their ferry service to the island leaves the Kapiti Boating Club (Paraparaumu Beach) at 9am daily and returns at 3pm. The **Kapiti Day Tour** ($180) includes a one-hour guided walk on the island, where visitors learn of its history and ecology. The six-hour tour includes a cooked lunch at the family lodge. The **Overnight Kiwi Spotting Tour** ($410-872) comprises one night and two days on the island with a guided Kiwi walk at night. Meals and guided tours are included. Guests stay in luxury tents or cabins nestled in the forest; there is also an en suite bungalow with sea views.

Kapiti Explorer (1 Manly St., 04/905-6610, www.kapitiexplorer.nz, Sept.-June 5, adults $75, children $40) operates ferry trips to Kapiti Island, departing from the Kapiti Boating Club (Paraparaumu Beach) at 8:45am daily for the 15-minute trip and returning at 3pm. The trip includes a 20-minute introductory talk about the island.

WAIKANAE

Waikanae is less than a 10-minute drive north of Paraparaumu along Highway 1. It is one of the Kapiti Coast's most scenic hubs.

Sights

Keeping the pre-digital era alive, the quaint and locally run **Kapiti Coast Museum** (9 Elizabeth St., 04/905-6313, www.kapiticoastmuseum.org.nz, 1pm-4pm Fri., 2pm-4pm Sat.-Sun., free) is housed in Waikanae's former post office. The museum boasts a kaleidoscopic collection of old-school clocks, radios, phonographs, and cameras displayed alongside Victorian clothing and domestic items such as Singer sewing machines and delicate china.

Recreation

Dozens of coastal and aquatic bird species—the heron, pukeko, little egret, and royal spoonbill—inhabit the Waikanae estuary year-round, making it one of the nation's best bird-watching destinations. Learn all about these creatures through **Waikanae Estuary Bird Tours** (20 Barrett Dr., 04/905-1001, www.kapitibirdtours.co.nz, 2 hours, $25). The two guided tours run daily and must be booked in advance.

The **Nga Manu Nature Reserve** (281 Ngarara Rd., 04/293-4131, www.ngamanu.co.nz, 10am-5pm daily, adults $18, children $8) houses domestic and native birds in walk-through aviaries. Dozens of feathered species visit the park's bush and wetlands, accompanied by lizards, frogs, eels, and tuatara. Among the 700 plant and tree species are 400-year-old kahikatea trees.

Food and Accommodations

Long Beach Café (40 Tutere St., 04/293-6760, 9am-11pm Mon.-Fri., 8:30am-11pm Sat.-Sun., $18-32) serves wholesome dishes featuring many homegrown ingredients. The pizzas never disappoint, and all baking is done on-site. Enjoy live music late Sunday afternoons.

★ **Waimea** (1 Waimea Rd., 04/293-4240, www.1waimea.co.nz, 11am-close Wed.-Thurs., 9am-close Fri.-Sun., $19-34) is an unforgettable experience. High-end plates are prepared by European chefs and feature duck-leg confit and *panko-* and parmesan-crumbed chicken. Finish with an espresso martini while taking in the sea view.

Dated but well-loved, **Ariki Lodge Motel** (4 Omahi St., 04/293-6592, www.arikilodgemotel.co.nz, $115-130) is fringed by colorful greenery and is a five-minute drive from Waikanae Beach. Lodging is in studio and one-bedroom units with free Wi-Fi and Sky TV. Cooking facilities include complimentary tea and coffee, while communal facilities offer a barbecue area and a swimming pool—better for cooling off than swimming laps.

Perched on the perimeter of a scenic reserve, ★ **Te Nikau Forest Retreat** (1B Tui Crescent, 04/299-2587, www.tenikauforestretreat.co.nz, $345, 2-night minimum), sits beneath a canopy of ferns, imparting a sense of Middle-earth majesty. Serenaded by birdsong throughout the day, the self-contained holiday home sports a covered outdoor spa that overlooks a mountain stream. Amenities include Sky TV, a DVD player, free Wi-Fi, and continental breakfast. The king double room has a private balcony with a spacious single bedroom.

★ **Atahuri Lodge** (Pingao Lane, 04/293-5555, www.atahuri.co.nz, $500-600) offers luxurious accommodations nestled among tussock-covered sand dunes. You can taste the salt of the sea in the air. Four sumptuous suites include private entrances, feather duvets, TVs and DVD players, Wi-Fi, bathrobes, and outdoor patios. Breakfast is included, as is a complimentary bottle of wine.

OTAKI

Northeast of Waikanae 15km along Highway 1, Otaki is the last town on the Kapiti Coast.

Sights

The **Otaki Museum** (49 Main St., 04/364-6886, www.otakimuseum.co.nz, 10am-2pm Thurs.-Sat., free) houses an extensive selection of historic photos alongside the town's earliest newspapers. New exhibits are introduced every three months.

Recreation

Otaki Beach offers some respectable year-round swells. **Otaki Surf School** (Pavilion Bldg., Marine Parade, 027/787-3464, www.epicsurfschools.co.nz) offers two-hour group lessons for beginners ($65). Or brush up on your skills with a private one-on-one lesson ($120). Surfboards and wetsuits are provided.

Accommodations

Savor some good old-fashioned hospitality at **Kemeni Cottage B&B** (11 Te Waka Rd., Te Horo, 021/577-091, www.kamenicottage.co.nz, $150). The self-contained setup includes twin or double beds, a kitchen, a lounge and dining area, a wood burner, a spa, and a swimming pool. Each morning a breakfast basket is delivered that includes fresh produce from the cottage orchards, eggs, and home-made jam. An extra fold-out bed can accommodate an additional guest ($35). The cottage is a five minute-drive south of Otaki.

The Hutt Valley

Adventure and beauty awaits under the shade of ancient forests in the Hutt Valley. The natural thoroughfare is traced by the Hutt River (Te Awakairangi) that runs northeast from Wellington, connecting the capital to Wairarapa. Beneath the valley, the geologic fault stretches to South Island and is responsible for the formation of the Southern Alps.

PETONE

Petone is New Zealand's oldest suburb. It sits at the north end of Wellington Harbour, 13km northeast of the capital via Highway 2.

Sights

The art deco **Petone Settlers Museum** (The Esplanade, 04/568-8373, www.petonesettlers.org.nz, 10am-4pm Wed.-Sun., free) celebrates the arrival of Maori and European immigration to the area. The museum's sizeable windows afford spectacular views over the waters by which so many arrived.

Recreation

The settlement serves as a jumping-off point for greater explorations of the Hutt Valley. Beginning at Hikoikoi Reserve on Marine

Parade, the **Hutt River Trail** is the only flat walk in the region. It stretches nearly 30km along the Hutt River to Upper Hutt, passing two *Lord of the Rings* film sites: one at Harcourt Park, the other between Moonshine and Totara Parks. The track is shared with part of the **Rimutaka Cycle Trail** (www.rimutakacycletrail.co.nz), a Great Ride that snakes 115km from Petone to Orongorongo to the south of the Rimutaka Ranges.

LOWER HUTT

North of Petone, 3km along Highway 2, Lower Hutt awaits.

Sights

Opened in 1971, the highly regarded **Dowse Art Museum** (45 Laings Rd., 04/570-5500, www.dowse.org.nz, 10am-4:30pm Mon.-Fri., 10am-5pm Sat.-Sun., free) showcases contemporary art. Its 2,000-piece collection is one of the nation's most significant, with revolving exhibits that often include sculpture.

Accommodations

Though it's 15km from downtown Wellington, the spacious **Wellington Top 10 Holiday Park** (95 Hutt Park Rd., 04/568-5913, www.wellingtontop10.co.nz, $50) is the closest campsite to the capital—and a world away from that city feel. Campers have use of a game room, a barbecue area, a Sky TV room, and a hot tub, with a full kitchen and a comfortable dining area. A range of modern units and motel rooms ($70-185), many of which are fully self-contained, include Sky TV and separate lounge and dining areas.

Services

The Lower Hutt **i-SITE** (25 Laings Rd., 04/560-4715, www.huttvalleynz.com, 9am-5pm Mon.-Fri.) is in the Pavilion. There's a drinking fountain outside to fill up your water bottle. For medical services, head to **Hutt Hospital** (High St., 04/566-6999).

Pencarrow Lighthouse

★ PENCARROW LIGHTHOUSE

Pencarrow Lighthouse, the nation's original permanent lighthouse, was built in 1859 and run by New Zealand's first—and last—female lighthouse keeper, Mary Jane Bennet. The light protrudes from Pencarrow Head and is accessed via a 16km coastal trail (4 hours on foot, 1.5 hours by bicycle). Begin the track at the end of Muritai Road, past the car park at Burdan's Gate.

The **Bike Shed** (04/562-7760 or 027/570-0108, www.bikeshedpencarrow.com, hours vary), 3km south of Eastbourne, rents mountain bikes and electric bikes for cruising the trail around Pencarrow Lighthouse.

Transportation

The lighthouse is 20km south of Lower Hutt. To reach it, follow Marine Drive south for 10km to the pleasant seaside setting of Days Bay. In another 1.5km south, you'll pass Eastbourne. In Muritai, the road becomes Muritai Drive until the Bike Shed at

Pencarrow. Pencarrow Head is reached in another 6.5km.

UPPER HUTT

Northeast along the Hutt Valley (19km from Lower Hutt along Hwy. 2), Upper Hutt is the gateway to a host of walking and biking tracks.

Recreation

Picturesque **Kaitoke Regional Park** (Waterworks Rd., www.gw.govt.nz, 6am-dusk daily) starred in all three *Lord of the Rings* movies as the home of the elves. Today, non-elves can explore the 2,500ha of forests filled with rata and rimu trees, some of which are thought to be more than 1,000 years old. The park also has plenty of swimming and picnic spots to enjoy. While wandering, keep your eyes peeled for kaka and parakeets.

Rimutaka Forest Park (Catchpool Stream Rd., off Coast Rd.) is a DoC-maintained wonderland that sprawls 22,000ha across the Rimutaka Range. Numerous well-marked walking tracks can be explored in half a day or less. A Great Ride, **Rimutaka Rail Trail** (www.rimutakacycletrail.co.nz), also weaves through the park.

Staglands Wildlife Reserve (2362 Akatarawa Rd., Upper Hutt, 04/526-7529, www.staglands.co.nz, 9:30am-5pm daily, adults $22, seniors and students $17, children $11, under age 4 free) offers the chance to get up-close with native critters like the kunekune pig, kea, kaka, and falcon. The reserve is set in a sprawling country estate replete with native bush and forest wetland walks.

Accommodations

Wallaceville Motor Lodge (2 Wallaceville Rd., 04/527-7785, www.wallacevillehouse.co.nz, $149-179) is a great value. The handsome country retreat was built in the early 1900s, and its white architecture contrasts beautifully with the luxurious gardens (host to many wedding parties). The hotel-style units have en suite baths and comprise studio rooms with kitchenettes, large spa rooms with a spa tub and full kitchen, and a family studio that has a kitchenette and can sleep four. All rooms are equipped with a private patio or balcony and include free Wi-Fi and Sky TV. Communal facilities include a laundry and a barbecue area with outdoor seating. Lake Wairarapa is a five-minute drive.

Transportation and Services

The large Upper Hutt **i-SITE Visitor Information Centre** (836 Fergusson Dr., 04/527-2168, www.visit.upperhuttcity.com, 9am-4pm Mon.-Fri., 9:30am-4pm Sat.-Sun.) can guide visitors around the valley.

Wairarapa

The Wairarapa region stretches from the southern end of Hawke's Bay down to the North Island's southernmost—and among its most isolated—coast at Cape Palliser. A visit here is an integral part of the Classic New Zealand Wine Trail, where 20-plus, mostly family owned, vineyards dot the town of Martinborough.

MASTERTON

Masterton is the largest town in the Wairarapa, most notable for its wool industry. Nearby are the Tui Brewery and the Pukaka Mount Bruce National Wildlife Centre.

Sights

In the heart of Masterton lies beautiful **Queen Elizabeth Park** (Dixon St., www.wairarapanz.com). Spread along the banks of the Waipoua River and populated with ducks and deer, it is famed as one of the most family friendly parks in the country. Activities in the park include mini golf and a miniature train ride (11am-4pm Sat.-Sun.).

Opposite the park is the **Wool Shed Museum** (12 Dixon St., 06/378-8008, www.thewoolshednz.com, 10am-4pm daily, adults $8, children $2, under age 5 free), the national museum of sheep and shearing. A bounty of historic shearing equipment, various wool samples, and shearing demonstrations await. Call ahead to book a demonstration. The fluffy garments in the on-site gift shop make for some splendid New Zealand souvenirs.

The **Aratoi-Wairarapa Museum of Art and History** (Bruce St. and Dixon St., 06/370-0001, www.aratoi.co.nz, 10am-4:30pm daily, gold-coin donation) is a small but sleek institution with an admirable contemporary collection of Kiwi and international art, with regular visiting exhibits.

The **Wings Over Wairarapa** (Hood Aerodrome, South Rd., www.wings.org.nz, Feb.) event witnesses dozens of aircraft taking to the skies in North Island's largest air show, held every two years.

Food and Accommodations

Café Strada (Regent Theatre Bldg., Queen St. and Jackson St., 06/378-8450, www.cafestrada.co.nz, 7:15am-close daily, $20-30) is one of the most popular eateries in town. The fully licensed café boasts sprawling menus featuring breakfast, burgers, curries, and fresh fish. The Movie Deal voucher ($30) includes a ticket to the adjacent cinema with your meal.

Guests can make use of free Wi-Fi, a swimming pool, and a barbecue area at the **Discovery Motor Lodge** (210 Chapel St., 06/378-9467, $125-195), well-presented lodgings near the center of town. Studio-, one-, and two-bedroom en suite units are equipped with Sky TV, cooking facilities, fridges, blow-dryers, and free toiletries. Opt for a room with a jetted tub.

Transportation and Services

Masterton is 100km northwest of Wellington and 66km north of Upper Hutt along Highway 2. The town is well served by **Metlink** (www.metlink.org.nz) trains and buses daily from Wellington. **Intercity** (www.intercity.co.nz) buses operate daily from Wellington and Palmerston North.

For information, visit **i-SITE Masterton** (Bruce St. and Dixon St., 06/370-0900, www.wairarapanz.com, 9:30am-4:30pm Mon.-Fri., 10am-4pm Sat.-Sun.).

North of Masterton

PUKAHA MOUNT BRUCE

The **Pukaka Mount Bruce National Wildlife Centre** (Hwy. 2, 06/375-8004, www.pukaha.org.nz, 9am-4:30pm daily, adults $20, children $6, under age 5 free), in partnership with DoC, is a leading wildlife breeding center, where long-fin eels and tuatara share space with some of the world's rarest birds, like the kokako, kaka, takahe, and the star attraction, the white kiwi. Throughout the day are talks by the rangers, and guests are invited to watch the feeding of some of the critters.

The **Guided Tour** (1 hour, 11am and 2pm daily, $45) may include an opportunity to help with animal feedings. The **Exclusive Behind the Scenes Tour** (11am daily, $125) gets more hands-on—you'll visit staff-only areas, watch a kiwi health check, or get into a stream with eels. Both tours must be booked in advance.

The center is surrounded by ancient podocarp forest alive with the chorus of wild birds. An easy 2-hour (4km round-trip) track leads to the summit of Mount Bruce (access to the track is via the center only). The Pukaha Mount Bruce National Wildlife Centre is located 30km north of Masterton on Highway 2.

TUI BREWERY

It doesn't get much more Kiwi than **Tui Brewery** (Hwy. 2, 06/376-0815, www.tuihq.co.nz, 11am-5pm Sun.-Thurs., 11am-6pm Fri.-Sat. Nov.-Apr., 11am-4pm Sun.-Thurs., 11am-5pm Fri.-Sat. May-Oct.) in the tiny town of Mangatainoka. The brewery has produced the nation's most iconic ale since 1889.

Guided **tours** (11:30am and 2:30pm daily, $20) last 40 minutes while taking in old and new equipment and landmarks. You'll learn the history of the brewery and finish with a beer tasting at the bar.

The Tui Brewery is 40km northwest of the Pukaka Mount Bruce National Wildlife Centre and 70km north of Masterton along Highway 2.

MARTINBOROUGH

What was once an unassuming colonial village has transformed into a noteworthy stop on the wine trail. Martinborough's boutique vineyards remain friendly and accessible. For more information about vineyards and tours, as well as maps, visit www.wairarapanz.com and www.martinboroughnz.com.

★ Wine Tasting

Most visitors are lured to the region for the grapes, so make **Martinborough Wine Merchants** (6 Kitchener St., 06/306-9040, www.martinboroughwinemerchants.com, 10am-5pm daily) your first stop. Not only do they stock a vast and varied selection of local beer, olives, and oils, the owners possess a wealth of vino knowledge and are more than happy to impart their wisdom.

Their guided **vineyard walks** (Oct.-Jan., minimum 6 people, $240) visit at least four establishments that are often not open to the public. Tours must be booked in advance and include tastings, food platters, and a lunchtime glass of wine.

Most of the region's 20-plus wineries are within easy walking or cycling distance of the village's beautiful central square. One of the closest and most alluring is **Palliser Estate** (96 Kitchener St., 06/306-9019, www.palliser.co.nz, 10:30am-4pm daily), a boutique setup boasting six vineyards across 85ha of the Martinborough Terraces. Tasting sessions ($5) at the cellar door include seating in a relaxing, shady courtyard with scrumptious platters of cured meats, cheeses, breads, and olives.

WINE TOURS

Martinborough Wine Tours (7 Campbell Dr., 06/306-8032, www.martinboroughwinetours.co.nz) operate customizable half-day ($85) and full-day ($180) vineyard tours in a luxury van; lunch and wine tastings are included. Advance booking is required.

If you'd rather burn some calories as you tour the vineyards, **Green Jersey** (16 Kitchener St., 06/306-6027, www.greenjersey.co.nz) provides a bike hire service as well as guided bike and van tours around the vineyards. Choose from mountain bikes, tandems, rickshaws, and e-bikes. Prior bookings are

Martinborough vineyard

required for tours. **Martinborough Wine Merchants** (6 Kitchener St., 06/306-9040, www.martinboroughwinemerchants.com) also offer a cycle hire service.

The **Martinborough Gourmet Wine Tour** (Hammonds, 04/472-0869, www.wellingtonsightseeingtours.co.nz, $209) takes guests on a scenic train ride from the Wellington Railway Station through the Wairarapa Valley to Martinborough. Visitors join an air-conditioned coach for travel to four boutique award-winning vineyards. Wine tastings, gourmet snacks, and an antipasto lunch are included. Bookings must be made in advance. The tour leaves Wellington in the morning (8:25am Mon.-Fri., 9:55am Sat.-Sun.) and returns between 5:20pm and 6:30pm daily.

EVENTS

Wine lovers descend on Martinborough for the **Toast Martinborough** (www.toastmartinborough.co.nz, Nov.), a wine festival with wine tastings, food, and live music at the town square and at nearby vineyards. Shuttle buses scurry among the locations.

Food and Accommodations

Lunch at **Poppies** (91 Puruatanga Rd., 06/306-8473, www.poppiesmartinborough.co.nz, 11am-4pm Fri.-Tues., $40) is the loveliest of gastronomical experiences—their seasonal sharing platters are the stuff of legend. Enjoy delicacies such as salmon, olives, cheeses, and pickles as you savor some of their boutique wines surrounded by cypress and bay trees. Make sure you save space for dessert—the chocolate chili and cinnamon tart is a must.

Positioned in the town's oldest and swankiest accommodations, the Martinborough Hotel, restaurant **Paddock to Plate** (The Square, 06/306-9350, www.martinboroughhotel.co.nz, 5:30pm-close daily, $26-40) serves famously fresh, locally sourced dishes to white-linen-topped tables, hemmed by a handful of French doors. Try the slow-roasted free-range pork with *kumara* ginger mash and wilted spinach.

The historic **Martinborough Hotel** ($250-310), built in 1882, is equally majestic, its grand staircase rising to 20 luxurious, rustic en suite rooms with high ceilings, high-end bedding, armchairs, gourmet teas and coffee, and Sky TV. Communal areas include a wonderful library brimming with old classics, soft seating, and a fireplace, along with a pretty courtyard with a rose garden and a handsome oak tree.

Transportation and Services

Martinborough is east of Upper Hutt and the Hutt Valley. From Upper Hutt, follow Highway 2 east for 27km. In Featherston, turn south on Highway 53 and continue on Route 53 for 18km.

Metrolink (www.metlink.org.nz) trains and buses run between Wellington and Martinborough, with limited service on Sunday.

Grab a wine map and a visitor guide from the **i-SITE Visitor Centre** (18 Kitchener St., 06/306-5010, www.wairarapanz.com, 10am-4pm Sun.-Mon., 9am-5pm Tues.-Sat.).

★ PATUNA CHASM

One of the best-kept secrets on North Island, **Patuna Chasm** is a 2km labyrinth of limestone caves and tunnels. Access is via **Patuna Farm** (236 Haurangi Rd., 06/306-9966, www.patunafarm.co.nz, adults $25, children $10, cash only) where you are ferried from the farmhouse to the beginning of the track as it meanders through native bush and limestone caverns cloaked in moss and soaked by the occasional waterfall. Look for ferns, fossils, and native birds—you may even encounter eels (the track and river often merge, so expect to wade through water up to 1m deep). There are two walks, at 10:30am and 11:30am daily; pickups are at 2pm and 3pm. Due to the river crossings, the track is open in summer only. Check online or call ahead for specific opening dates. Bookings are essential—as are a change of clothes and sense of adventure.

Patuna Farm is 20km south of Martinborough. Take Jellicoe Street south to White Rock Road and turn left. Continue 7.6km to Ruakokoputuna Road and turn right. Ruakokoputuna Road becomes Haurangi Road in 5.3km.

SOUTH TO CAPE PALLISER

South of Martinborough 60km, Cape Palliser represents the literal end of North Island. It is reached via Lake Ferry and Cape Palliser Roads south of Martinborough.

Hammonds **Off the Beaten Track Tour** (04/472-0869, www.wellingtonsightseeing-tours.co.nz, adults $235, children $118) of Palliser Bay is an all-day tour of the area's sights including the Cape Palliser Lighthouse and fur seal colony. The tour includes lunch at the Lake Ferry Hotel followed by wine tasting in Martinborough. Tours depart Wellington at 8:30am daily and return at 5:30pm. Book in advance at the **Wellington i-SITE** (Civic Square. Victoria St. and Wakefield St., Wellington, 04/802-4860, www.wellingtonnz.com, 8:30am-5pm daily).

Lake Ferry

The small town of Lake Ferry is a sleepy hub on the shores of Lake Onoke, whose waters are home to a variety of birdlife. To get there from Martinborough, follow Lake Ferry Road south for 35km.

ACCOMMODATIONS

Lake Ferry Hotel (2 Lake Ferry Rd., 06/307-7831, www.lakeferryhotel.co.nz, noon-3pm and 6pm-9pm daily, $35-75) has well-kept rooms with bunk beds and doubles, one of which is en suite; the remaining rooms share baths. The hotel has a lovely garden with water views, a restaurant (the fish-and-chips are the stuff of the legend), and a much welcome bar.

Lake Ferry Holiday Park (25-39 Lake Ferry Rd., 06/307-7857, www.lakeferryholidaypark.co.nz) offers unpowered ($15) and powered ($18-25) campsites, as well as basic cabins and studios ($60-90) with cooking facilities. Some cabins have private baths.

Putangirua Pinnacles

You may recognize the incredible **Putangirua Pinnacles,** whose otherworldly appearance was featured in *The Lord of the Rings*. These enormous gray pillars reach heights of 50m, their spiky peaks the result of 8 million years of erosion by rain, floods, and the Putangirua Stream. It's located 18km south of Lake Ferry on Cape Palliser Road.

The DoC-run **Putangirua Pinnacles Campsite** (04/384-7770, www.doc.govt.nz, adults $8, children $4, cash only) has 50 sites. It's located 13km along Cape Palliser Road, 20 minutes southeast of Lake Ferry. Pay at the self-registration kiosk on arrival.

Ngawi

The tiny fishing town of Ngawi is famed for its rows of **colorful bulldozers** lined up along its battered and black boulder-strewn beach. The bulldozers are used to winch boats up and down the steep coast. Ngawi is south along Cape Palliser Road, about 17km from the Putangirua Pinnacles.

Cape Palliser

Cape Palliser Road ends about 6.5km southeast of Ngawi. Here, the red-and-white **Cape Palliser Lighthouse** (closed to the public) adds a splash of color to this tormented shoreline. The lighthouse was first lit in 1897. Today, visitors must climb more than 250 steps for the lovely views from the 58m-high cliff—all of it worth the sweat.

Nearby is the largest **fur seal colony** on North Island. If you visit mid-November to mid-January, you might see some playful pups. Keep at least 20m away, as their parents are protective and can become aggressive.

South Island

Marlborough and Nelson

Picton 307
Marlborough Sounds 310
Marlborough Wine Region..... 315
Kaikoura....................... 319
Nelson and Vicinity 324
Abel Tasman National Park..... 331
Golden Bay 335
Nelson to the West Coast 340

The top of South Island is divided between the scenic regions of Marlborough to the east and Nelson Tasman to the west.

Most visitors arrive by ferry, crossing the Cook Strait from Wellington to the gateway port of Picton. The sea journey provides a first glimpse of the enchanting forested headlands of the iridescent Marlborough Sounds.

The sparkling, coastal community of Picton offers a tantalizing taste of the alluring lands beyond—wine-tasting in Marlborough, whale watching in Kaikoura, white-water rafting through the Buller Gorge—but this region is most known for Marlborough Sounds and the three national parks.

Snowy alpine peaks, clear lakes, and rainforest-clad coastlines of golden sand spill into the turquoise waters of isolated sounds. The easternmost, Queen Charlotte Sound, hosts the Queen Charlotte Track, widely considered the most spectacular of the country's Great Rides. It's unique in that it can be explored offshore by kayak. North along Tasman Bay, Abel Tasman National Park offers its own Coastal Track, a leisurely Great Walk that combines tramping and kayaking along the beachy coast.

One of New Zealand's longest and most isolated Great Walks lies west in Kahurangi National Park, where the 82km Heaphy Track follows an early Maori route across alpine saddles and through high-country and subtropical rainforest to terminate on the West Coast.

Midway between Picton and the West Coast, Nelson Lakes National Park is home to pristine Rotoiti and Rotoroa Lakes, the remnants of ancient glaciers. Here, the challenging Travers-Sabine Circuit crosses 80-90km of high-alpine peaks and lakes, climbing to its highest point of 1,780m.

Topping it all off is a microclimate that ensures 2,400 hours of sunshine per year. The region is an epicurean heaven, home to the "world's green-lipped mussel capital" in Havelock, craft microbreweries in bohemian Nelson, and world-renowned vineyards that produce some of New Zealand's best wines.

PLANNING YOUR TIME

Nelson, Blenheim, and **Picton** make for good bases in this region, but depending

Previous: Abel Tasman National Park; Lake Rotoiti. **Above:** bikes in Marlborough.

Marlborough and Nelson

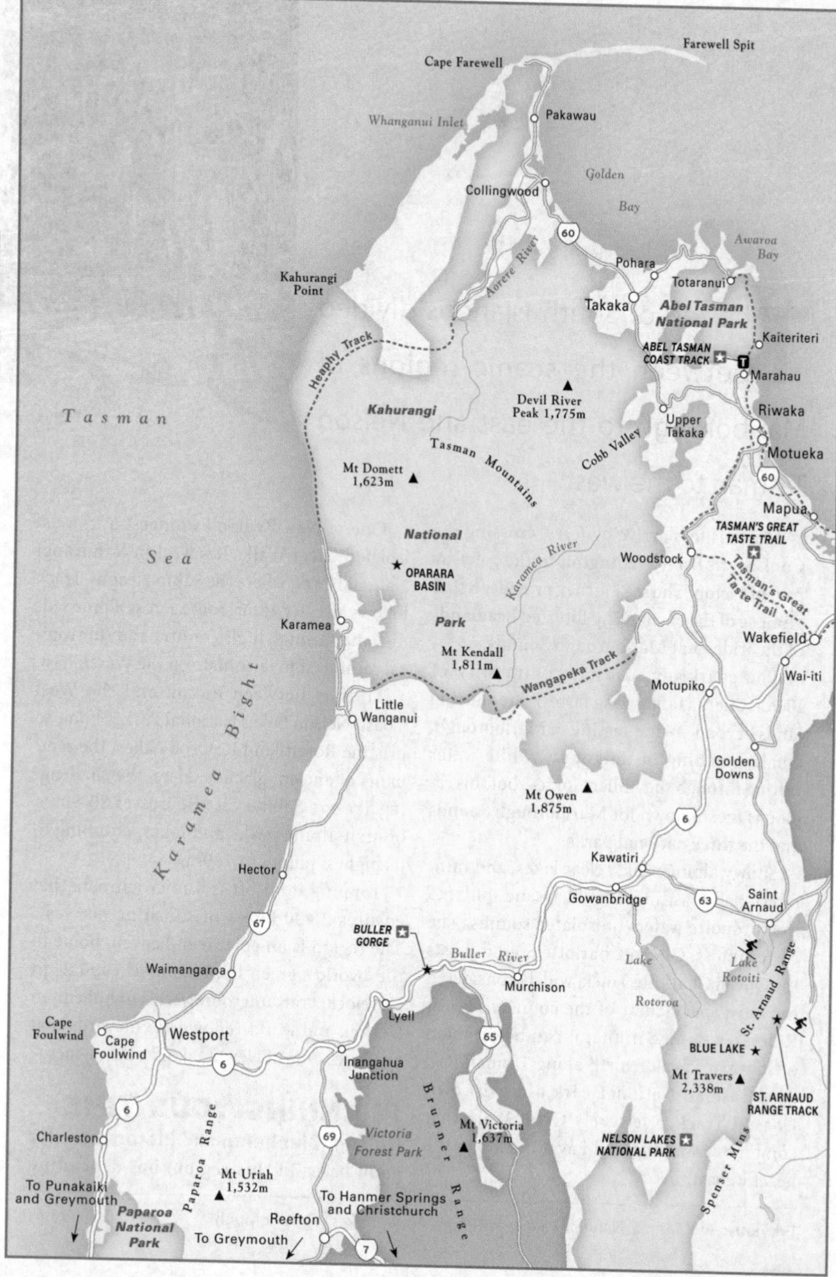

Farewell Spit
Cape Farewell
Pakawau
Whanganui Inlet
Golden
Bay
Collingwood
60
Aorere River
Awaroa
Bay
Pohara
Totaranui
Kahurangi
Point
Takaka
Abel Tasman
National Park
Kaiteriteri
Heaphy Track
ABEL TASMAN
COAST TRACK
Marahau
Devil River
Peak 1,775m
Riwaka
Tasman
Kahurangi
Upper
Takaka
Cobb Valley
Motueka
Tasman Mountains
Mt Domett
1,623m
60
Mapua
National
TASMAN'S GREAT
TASTE TRAIL
Sea
Karamea River
Woodstock
OPARARA
BASIN
Tasman's Great
Taste Trail
Karamea
Park
Wakefield
Mt Kendall
1,811m
Wangapeka Track
Wai-iti
Motupiko
Little
Wanganui
Karamea Bight
Golden
Downs
Mt Owen
1,875m
6
Kawatiri
Hector
Gowanbridge
63
Saint
Arnaud
67
BULLER
GORGE
Buller River
Lake
Lake
Rotoiti
Waimangaroa
Murchison
Rotoroa
St. Arnaud Range
Cape
Foulwind
Lyell
Cape
Foulwind
Westport
65
BLUE LAKE
6
Inangahua
Junction
Mt Travers
2,338m
ST. ARNAUD
RANGE TRACK
6
Paparoa Range
Brunner Range
Mt Victoria
1,637m
Charleston
69
Victoria
Forest Park
NELSON LAKES
NATIONAL PARK
Spenser Mtns
To Punakaiki
and Greymouth
Mt Uriah
1,532m
To Hanmer Springs
and Christchurch
Paparoa
National
Park
Reefton
To Greymouth
7

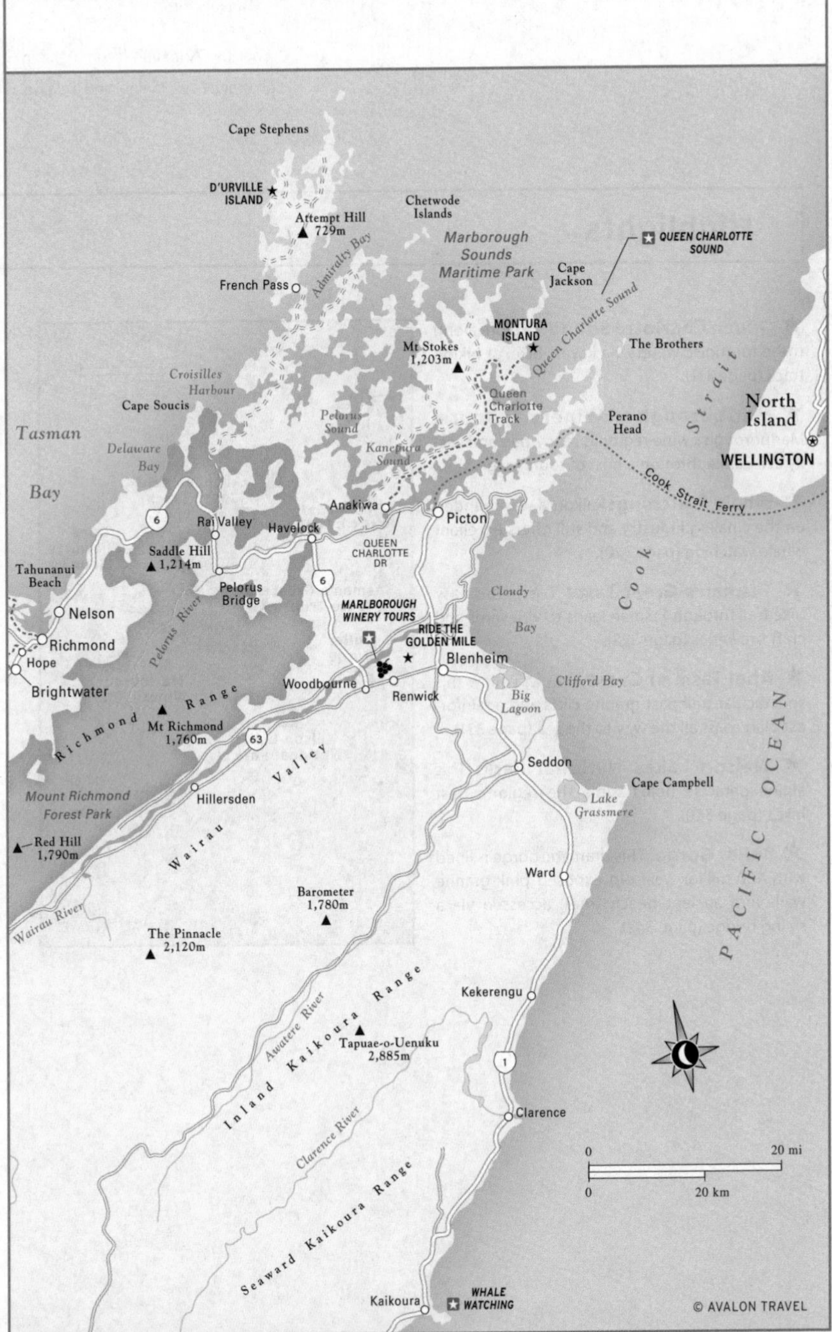

Cape Stephens
D'URVILLE ISLAND
Attempt Hill 729m
Chetwode Islands
Marborough Sounds Maritime Park
QUEEN CHARLOTTE SOUND
Admiralty Bay
French Pass
Cape Jackson
Queen Charlotte Sound
MONTURA ISLAND
Mt Stokes 1,203m
The Brothers
Croisilles Harbour
Queen Charlotte Track
Cape Soucis
Pelorus Sound
Perano Head
North Island
Tasman Bay
Delaware Bay
Kenepuru Sound
WELLINGTON
Cook Strait
Cook Strait Ferry
Anakiwa
Picton
Rai Valley
Havelock
QUEEN CHARLOTTE DR
Saddle Hill 1,214m
Tahunanui Beach
Pelorus Bridge
Cloudy Bay
Nelson
Pelorus River
MARLBOROUGH WINERY TOURS
RIDE THE GOLDEN MILE
Richmond
Hope
Blenheim
Brightwater
Woodbourne
Renwick
Clifford Bay
Big Lagoon
Richmond Range
Mt Richmond 1,760m
Seddon
Wairau Valley
Cape Campbell
Hillersden
Mount Richmond Forest Park
Lake Grassmere
PACIFIC OCEAN
Red Hill 1,790m
Ward
Wairau River
Barometer 1,780m
The Pinnacle 2,120m
Kekerengu
Awatere River
Inland Kaikoura Range
Tapuae-o-Uenuku 2,885m
Clarence
Clarence River
0
20 mi
20 km
Seaward Kaikoura Range
Kaikoura
WHALE WATCHING
© AVALON TRAVEL

Look for ★ to find recommended sights, activities, dining, and lodging.

Highlights

★ **Queen Charlotte Sound:** Explore along these turquoise waters via kayak, bike, or hiking track (page 311).

★ **Marlborough Winery Tours:** Marlborough's wine region is renowned and easily accessible through a host of tours (page 315).

★ **Whale Watching:** Kaikoura was founded on the whaling industry and still offers excellent whale watching (page 320).

★ **Tasman's Great Taste Trail:** This easy bike trail through Tasman leads to vineyards and craft breweries (page 328).

★ **Abel Tasman Coast Track:** Follow this spectacular trail past granite cliffs and a rainforest-clad coast all the way to the sea (page 331).

★ **Nelson Lakes National Park:** This alpine paradise holds some the region's best hikes (page 340).

★ **Buller Gorge:** This dramatic gorge is lined with 400 million-year-old exposed pink granite walls and ancient beech trees, accessed via a swing bridge (page 342).

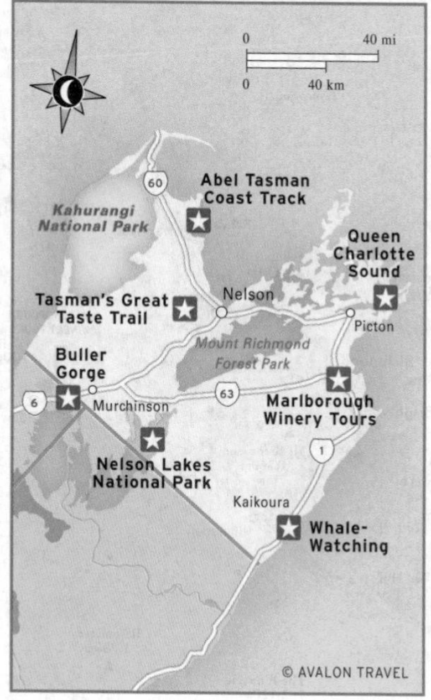

on how much time you have, you may have some difficult decisions. Nelson's microbreweries deserve a day of exploration, as do Marlborough's world-class vineyards; both can be done by bike. **Queen Charlotte Sound** and **Abel Tasman National Park** both boast superb scenic tracks that can be explored by kayak: the Queen Charlotte Track is also a Great Ride (by bike), while the Abel Taman Coastal Track is one of New Zealand's legendary Great Walks. Plan to spend at least one night along each. Lastly, set aside a day for whale watching in **Kaikoura.**

Fortunately, the region is well served by shuttle buses and water taxis.

Picton

South Island's first port of call, pretty Picton connects with Wellington via ferry across the Cook Strait, and sure makes an impression at the main terminus of the Marlborough Sounds. First settled by Maori in the mid-16th century, Europeans later developed the port as a whaling hub. It now serves as the main launchpad to Queen Charlotte Sound, dotted with pastel villas and white masts that contrast against the surrounding rainforest and emerald bay.

SIGHTS

Picton Heritage Museum

Springing from a former *pa* site, **Picton Heritage Museum** (9 London Quay, 03/573-8283, www.pictonmuseum-newzealand.com, 10am-4pm daily, adult $5, child $1, student $3) houses a 2,000-strong collection of Maori treasures, with maritime and whaling exhibits such as a harpoon gun, some fearsome-looking spears, toothy shark jaws, an abundance of photos, and carved whale bone.

Edwin Fox Ship and Visitor Centre

The **Edwin Fox Ship and Visitor Centre** (Dunbar Wharf, 1 Auckland St., 03/573-6868, www.edwinfoxsociety.com, 9am-5pm daily, adult $15, child $5) is a fascinating maritime monument and the final resting place of the gargantuan, gangrenous hull of the *Edwin Fox*—one of the world's oldest ships and the last surviving vessel that ferried convicts to Australia, immigrants to New Zealand, and troops to the Crimea War. The 1853 relic was built in Calcutta. Today, visitors can walk through the vessel, check out old paintings and photos, learn to tie knots, and try out replica bunks.

Eco World

Eco World (The Foreshore, 03/573-6030, www.ecoworldnz.co.nz, 9:30am-5pm daily, adult $24, child $12, student/senior $22) is your best chance for an easy sighting of the region's fish. The aquarium is home to the little blue penguin, giant weta, turtles, small sharks, and seahorses. Guided **tours** (11:30am, 12pm, 2:30pm and 3:30pm daily, $39, plus admission) allow guests to go behind the scenes and get up close to the critters. Don't miss the feeding times (11am or 2pm).

FOOD

Start the day with **Gusto** (33 High St., 03/573-7171, 7am-2:30pm daily, closed Sat. in winter, $10-23), an intimate and summery eatery famed for their hospitality and first-class egg breakfasts. Try the eggs benedict, or scrambled eggs with smoked salmon. Sweet treats include freshly baked pastries, pies, and a wonderful carrot cake.

Easy-going **La Café** (The Foreshore, 03/573-5588, www.lecafepicton.co.nz, 7:30am-10pm Mon.-Fri., 7:30am-close Sat., 8am-close Sun., $20-30) is a Picton institution. Enjoy outside dining, sea views, and a vibrant ambience aided by enthusiastic hosts and regular live music. The

Best Restaurants

★ **The Mussel Pot:** This place dishes up some of the best green-lipped mussels in New Zealand (page 314).

★ **The Burleigh:** These imaginative gourmet pies are among the best in South Island (page 317).

★ **Hislops Café:** A wholefoods menu includes an array of homemade breads and cakes using manuka honey and flour from the family farm (page 321).

★ **Kaikoura Seafood BBQ:** The best seafood dining awaits at this legendary roadside stall on the Kaikoura peninsula (page 321).

★ **Pier Hotel Restaurant & Bar:** Enjoy delicious crayfish with friendly locals (page 322).

★ **The Kitchen:** Healthy eating is easy thanks to whole foods and colorful seasonal produce (page 325).

★ **The Indian Café:** Nelson's best Indian eatery is also one of the city's best restaurants (page 325).

★ **Riverside Café:** A delectable seasonal menu awaits at this historic homestead along Tasman's Great Taste Trail (page 329).

consistently fresh menu changes regularly, but features steak, pasta, and seafood. Wash it down with some top-drawer local wine or craft beer.

Latin-inspired dishes meet Kiwi classics at **Café Cortado** (High St. and London Quay, 03/573-5630, www.cafecortado.co.nz, 8am-9pm Mon.-Tues., 8am-10pm Wed.-Sun., $27-48). Dine on fajitas, quesadillas, paella, and seafood chowder in the shade of palm and pohutukawa trees while overlooking the azure waters of Queen Charlotte Sound.

Gastro pub/sports bar **Mikey's Bar and Restaurant** (1 Wellington St., 03/573-7645, www.oxleys.co.nz, 9am-close daily, $16-30) serves great value fare—pizzas, burgers, and an interesting venison hotpot—prepared using local produce and plated with care. Regular meal and drink deals are offered throughout the week; swing by on a Sunday for roast dinner ($18) and Heinekens ($6). This one's a firm favorite with the locals.

ACCOMMODATIONS

Colorful, upbeat **Sequoia** (3a Nelson Sq., 0800/222-257, www.sequoialodge.co.nz, dorm $30-32, $76-94 s or d) is a gem of a hostel. There's an en-suite female dorm, family rooms ($98-120), plus free unlimited Wi-Fi, bike rentals, and a hot tub that's especially enjoyable under the stars. Guests enjoy herbs from the garden and some complimentary (and homemade) cake and ice cream in summer or soup in winter.

Positioned near the Picton cemetery (and entered via a casket-shaped door with a sign that states "rest in peace"), BBH-affiliated hostel **Tombstone Backpackers** (16 Gravesend Pl., 03/573-7116, www.tombstonebp.co.nz, dorm $31-39, $84-118) is anything but morbid. You'll be greeted by a super staff, sea views, and the sweet waft of freshly baked scones or muffins in the morning. Dorms and doubles are available en suite; private rooms are of high standard, both modern and spotless.

Best Accommodations

★ **Bay of Many Coves:** Five-star suites sit on a secluded hillside at the end of the Queen Charlotte Track (page 313).

★ **Havelock Motel and Motor Lodge:** Plentiful amenities and comfy lodgings are close to Marlborough Sounds (page 315).

★ **Albatross Backpacker Inn:** This former post office is Kaikoura's funkiest hostel (page 322).

★ **Tasman Bay Backpackers:** This relaxed and colorful hostel offers spotless rooms and perks like nightly hot chocolate pudding with ice cream (page 326).

★ **The Inn Between Lodge and Backpackers:** Boutique styling on a budget is housed in this beautiful villa in Nelson (page 326).

★ **Edens Edge Lodge:** Enjoy a community spirit at these sprawling grounds just minutes from the sea (page 329).

★ **Kimi Ora Eco Resort:** This eco-resort sits nestled within 12 hectares of native forest overlooking the national park (page 330).

Amenities include free Wi-Fi, a gym, and a spa tub, plus free transport to the ferry terminal.

Set in a historic villa, surrounded by—and in parts entwined in—rambling, charming gardens, **Jugglers Rest** (8 Canterbury St., 03/573-5570, www.jugglersrest.com, Sept.-May, dorm $35, $66 s, $80-90 d) is a quirky, colorful wonderland where you can take part in circus workshops, watch evening fire shows, and enjoy the free organic vegetable and herb garden, homemade bread and jam, Wi-Fi, fishing rods, and bike hire. This is one of the coolest hostels in New Zealand—but with only 15 beds (no bunks), it books up fast.

At the **Buccaneer Lodge** (314 Waikawa Rd., 03/573-5002, www.buccaneerlodge.co.nz, $80-110), the ground-floor budget room with en-suite is a great value, but the airy balcony suite comes with sea views, TV, hot-drink facilities, and a hairdryer. Amenities include a fully equipped kitchen, idyllic gardens, barbecue, free Wi-Fi, and free bike rental. The lodge is 4km from downtown Picton, across from Queen Charlotte Sound and Waikawa Marina.

Escape to Picton (33 Wellington Pl., 0800/693-722, www.escapetopicton.com, $350-495) offers boutique lodgings within shouting distance of the Picton marina. Three unique suites impart a classical feel, with elegant, handmade furniture, high ceilings, and polished floors. Enjoy free Wi-Fi, Sky TV, gourmet breakfast, and luxurious en-suite bathrooms. There's an on-site bar and a restaurant that serves an excellent duck breast along with other well-honed classics.

Parklands Marina Holiday Park (10 Beach Rd., Waikawa Bay, 03/573-6343, www.parktostay.co.nz) has pristine facilities including a sparkling kitchen, a swimming pool, and a TV and games room. Cabin units ($60-119) are equipped with a TV and private patio; some have cooking facilities and en-suites. Soft grass makes for comfortable camping ($17-38). The campground is less than 4km from the Picton ferry terminal and is a short walk from the marina.

TRANSPORTATION AND SERVICES

Picton lies west of Wellington across the Cook Strait on the South Island. Ferries from Wellington arrive in either the passenger terminal (1 Auckland St.) or the vehicle terminal (3 Auckland St.).

Air

Picton airport (Factory Rd.) is 9km (10 minute) southwest of Picton off State Highway 1. **Sounds Air** (www.soundsair.com) operates flights between the Wellington and Picton airports, with scenic 25-minute flights over Marlborough Sounds.

A1 Picton (0800/2174-2866, www.a1pictonshuttles.conz) runs shuttle buses from the airport, ferry terminal, and train and bus stations. It also ferries visitors to Havelock and Blenheim.

Coast to Coast Helicopters (296 Hwy. 1, 0800/282-4353, www.coasttocoasthelicopters.co.nz) operates flights over the Marlborough Sounds; options include the 20-minute Sounds Scenic ($340pp) and the Sounds Awesome ($495 per person), a 30-minute flight that includes cake and coffee.

Ferry

Two ferry operators, the **Interislander** (1 Aotea Quay, 0800/801-700, www.greatjourneysofnz.co.nz) and **Bluebridge Cook Strait Ferry** (50 Waterloo Quay, 0800/844-844, www.blueridge.co.nz) connect Wellington to Picton on South Island daily, and both take vehicles. The journey takes around 3.5 hours. Blueridge is slightly cheaper, while Interislander is more luxurious. Avoid booking a nighttime journey or you'll miss the incredible scenery into the Marlborough Sounds. The ferry terminal is less than one kilometer north of the town center, off State Highway 1.

Apex (03/573-7009, www.apexrentals.co.nz) and **Hertz** (03/520-3044, www.hertz.co.nz) rent cars at the ferry terminal.

Train and Bus

At time of publication, the *Coastal Pacific* route from Picton to Christchurch remained closed due to damage from the 2016 earthquake. Contact **Rail New Zealand** (www.railnewzealand.com) for updates.

National bus operators **Intercity** (04/385-0520, www.intercity.co.nz) and **Naked Bus** (09/979-1616, www.nakedbus.com) call at Picton. Regional bus operator **Atomic Shuttle** (03/349-0697, www.atomictravel.co.nz, $15-40) connects Picton to Blenheim, Nelson, Kaikoura, and Christchurch.

Services

The **Picton i-SITE** (The Foreshore, 03/520-3113, www.marlboroughnz.com/about/isite, 9am-4pm daily) offers information about exploring the Marlborough Sounds and can book tours and ferries. It also doubles as a **DoC office**. All buses stop outside.

Marlborough Sounds

So intricately carved is the northeast corner of South Island that it accounts for one fifth of New Zealand's entire coastline. Its four main bodies of water—the Queen Charlotte, Pelorus, Kenepuru, and Mahua Sounds (collectively called the Marlborough Sounds)—are separated from the forested headlands and punctuated by coves and caves. These ocean-drowned valleys are waters patrolled by dolphins, orca, and seals, and are home to king salmon, *paua* (abalone), oysters, clams, and enormous green-lipped mussels. The surrounding lands are laced with fig and cherry orchards, olive groves, fields of saffron and strawberries, and rows of vineyards, offering shelter for rare indigenous birds, including the kiwi.

Striking Picton serves as the gateway to

Queen Charlotte Sound. The sleepy town of **Havelock** steers visitors to the other sounds (Pelorus and the less-visited Kenepuru), with a smattering of idyllic accommodations accessible only by water.

★ QUEEN CHARLOTTE SOUND

Queen Charlotte Sound is the easternmost of Marlborough's turquoise sounds. Named Totaranui ("the place of the big totara") by Maori. Queen Charlotte's tempting waters, cacophony of coves, and adjacent hiking and biking tracks makes exploration a breeze, while its vastness ensures an air of tranquil isolation. Spend at least one night in a remote campsite or lodging, some of which are only reachable by boat.

Queen Charlotte Track

Considered by many to be the greatest of New Zealand's Great Rides, the **Queen Charlotte Track** (www.qctrack.co.nz, open year-round) is a 71km hiking and mountain biking trail that follows the headland separating the Queen Charlotte and Kenepuru Sounds. Sections of the track can be easily tackled by trampers and riders of all levels, with access points and accommodations en-route.

The track winds along Queen Charlotte Drive and Anakiwa Road, from Ship Cove in the north to the coastal settlement of Anakiwa, 20km west of Picton. The entire track can be completed in either direction; it takes 3-5 days to hike or 2-3 days to bike. The trail between Ship Cove and Kenepuru Saddle is closed to cyclists December-February. Crossing private land between Camp Bay and Anakiwa requires a **Queen Charlotte Track Land Cooperative Pass** ($10 one day, $18 five days, $25 one year), available from regional i-SITEs or Visitor Centers. Water taxis are available at numerous landing points along the route.

Motuara Island

Motuara Island is a DoC-managed nature sanctuary home to birds such as the saddleback, yellow-crowned parakeets, a handful of rowi kiwi, and the Maud Island frog. The island is explored via the **Motuara Island Lookout Track** (1 hr. round-trip) to the 128-meter summit for views of the sound. Several tours incorporate island stopovers, or you can rent a kayak and paddle there.

Motuara Island lies at the far end of Queen Charlotte Sound, across from Ship Cove. It bears historical significance as the

A ferry makes its way through the Marlborough Sounds.

site where Captain James Cook declared British sovereignty in 1770.

Tours and Cruises

An abundance of guided cruise operators offer transport to the sound. **Beachcomber** (The Waterfront, 03/573-6175, www.beachcombercruises.co.nz) operates several half- and full-day cruises and provides water taxi services to accommodations along the Queen Charlotte Track (or to those who walk or bike sections of it). The most popular trip is the four-hour Magic Mail Run (adult $99, child $55, child under 5 free). Guests board a New Zealand Post boat as it delivers mail and groceries to some of the sound's most isolated regions. It's a great chance to not only marvel at the beauty of the Marlborough Sounds, but to meet the locals and their pets; some pooches have been trained to venture to the wharf to collect their mail.

Cougar Line (The Foreshore, 03/573-7925, www.queencharlottetrack.co.nz, $65-105) is a major operator with a proliferation of tours. Their guided cruises of the Sound are combined with drop-offs and pick-ups for kayakers, hikers, and cyclists along various points of the Queen Charlotte Track. Tours range from one hour to a full-day. Trips to Motuara Island are also available; YHA and BBH discounts are offered.

E-Ko's (The Waterfront, 03/373-8040, www.e-ko.nz, adult $99-165, child $55-135) most popular tour is their Dolphin Encounter. Conditions permitting, guests can get in the water with these magical marine mammals but spotting the creatures at the very least is a near-certainty. This trip can also be combined with a visit to Motuara Island.

For a more personalized, and boutique, experience, **Uncharted Wilderness Tours** (03/579-9025, www.wildernesstours.co.nz, adult $180-1,400, child $120-990) has full day and multi-day packages available that include the chance to fish, snorkel, and hike some of the furthest reaches of the sound. Food and accommodations are included in the price.

Sea Kayaking Adventures (Anakiwa Rd. and Queen Charlotte Dr., 03/574-2765, www.nzseakayaking.com, $105-229) operates guided half- and two-day tours of the sound, along with kayak, hike, and mountain bike combination trips. If you'd rather go it alone, rent a kayak ($40/half-day, $60/full day). The more days you rent, the lower the price—the fifth day is free.

Marlborough Adventure Company (London Quay, 0800/283-283, www.marlboroughsounds.co.nz, $95 half-day, $130 full day) offers many custom guided services based on kayaking around the sounds. Hiking and biking the Queen Charlotte Track can also be incorporated, with overnight stays at lodges.

Scuba diving opportunities for all levels are aplenty in Queen Charlotte Sound, including a handful of shipwrecks ranging from 5-36 meters deep, and marine reserves home to abundant sea life such as cod, crayfish, and rays, some of which can be handfed. If you're keen to explore beneath these pristine waters, contact **Waikawa Dive Centre** (Rear Unit 2, Waikawa Marina, Marina Dr., 03/573-5939, www.waikawadivecentre.co.nz, $220-390), whose tours cater to all. All equipment is included, but minimum 2-4 divers are required.

Wilderness Guides (London Quay and Wellington St., Picton, 03/573-5432, www.wildernessguidesnz.com) rents bikes ($40 half-day, $60 full day, $125 three day). Their water taxi will drop you and your bike off at a landing point along the track and pick you up at a pre-arranged time and location. Multi-day options are available, as are kayak rentals and guided walks.

Accommodations

Nestled among native forest behind Lochmara Bay and overlooking Queen Charlotte Sound, **Lochmara Lodge** (03/573-4554, www.lochmara.co.nz, $115-324) offers a true taste of secluded paradise. Welcoming, light-filled suites and units overlook the bush and water, as does the onsite café. Guests make use of free Wi-Fi and kayak rentals. Highlights include a zipline, nature walks, an underwater observatory, with the opportunity to handfeed stingrays, and, elsewhere parakeets. Facilities are open to the public. The lodge is accessed only by boat or an hour's walk from the track.

Punga Cove (Akerbloms Rd., 03/579-8561, www.pungacove.co.nz, $63 s, $126-485 s or d) offers affordable accommodations in a million-dollar setting, ideal for the solo traveler. Budget single and double rooms open onto a shared deck, with shared lounge, kitchen, and bathroom facilities. More expensive units are fully self-contained with private decks or balconies. There's free Wi-Fi, hot tubs, and a swimming pool, as well as kayak and paddleboard rentals. It's a couple of hours drive from Picton.

The spectacular ★ **Bay of Many Coves** (03/579-9771, www.bayofmanycoves.co.nz, $900-2,250) sits on a secluded hillside surrounded by forest and overlooking azure seas at the end of the Queen Charlotte Track. Five-star suites sport balconies that hang over the bay. Guests enjoy free Wi-Fi, kitchenettes, living areas with sumptuous sofas and communal amenities like a heated outdoor pool, hot tub, and onsite day spa. Bed-and-breakfast and dinner options are available. It's a 30-minute cruise from Picton.

There are six **DoC campsites** (03/520-3002, www.doc.govt.nz, adult $6-13, child $3-6.50, children under 5 free) along the track: Schoolhouse Bay, Camp Bay, Bay of Many Coves, Black Rock, Cowshed Bay, and Davies Bay. The campgrounds have toilets and running water; some also have cooking shelters. Some sites are located next to the track, but none are more than a 10-minute (signposted) walk away. Most sites can be booked in advance at the Picton i-SITE (or leave payment in the self-registration box), but some sites only have space for a handful of tents and fill fast. Water taxis stop at Schoolhouse and Camp Bays.

Transportation

Queen Charlotte Drive is a 33.5km (50 minutes) coastal stretch that connects Picton and Havelock with wonderful views of the sounds.

Kenepuru Road shoots north from Queen Charlotte Drive for 75km, following the shore of Kenepuru Sound, parallel to the Queen Charlotte Track, with limited access points to the track en route. It's 21km (30 minutes) west of Picton,

Queen Charlotte Sound water taxi services include **Arrow Water Taxis** (1 London Quay, Picton, 03/573-8229, www.arrowwatertaxis.co.nz) and **Picton Water Taxis** (London Quay, Picton, 03/573-7853, www.pictonwatertaxis.co.nz).

HAVELOCK AND VICINITY

The harbor village of Havelock is the "green-lipped mussel capital of the world" and the gateway to Pelorus, Kenepuru, and Mahau Sounds.

Pelorus and Kenepuru Sounds

The **Pelorus Mail Boat** (Pier B, Havelock Marina, 03/574-1088, www.themailboat.co.nz, adult $128, child under 15 free) cruises different routes to deliver mail—and people—to the isolated communities along Pelorus Sound. Hop aboard for a narrated cruise with complimentary tea, coffee, and biscuits. The boat departs Havelock at 9:30am and returns 4pm-5pm (daily Nov.-Apr.; Mon., Wed. and Fri. May-Oct.).

Few locals know the hidden waterways of the Marlborough Sounds like Bruce Chamberlain and his team, who operate guided evening-, full-, and multi-day scenic cruises of Pelorus and Kenepuru Sounds. Chamberlain operates **Foxy Lady Cruises** (027/438-9866, www.foxyladycruises.co.nz), which tours the Sounds on the luxurious, 18-meter *Foxy Lady* (sleeps 12). Tours depart from Pier C at the Havelock Marina. Other options incorporate hiking and fishing trips and overnight stays in an isolated lodge.

Pelorus Bridge Scenic Reserve

Pelorus Bridge Scenic Reserve (www.doc.govt.nz) is a spectacular slice of natural wonder, where the Pelorus and Rai Rivers are lined by forests of beech, podocarp, and ferns alive with vocal native birds and a few rare bats. The sparkling green waters are often dotted with swimmers, while hikers explore a variety of trails.

The **Pelorus Bridge Café** (03/571-6019, 8:30am-4pm daily) serves sumptuous cakes and a decent espresso, as well as a selection of camping essentials. The DoC **campsite** (03/571-6019, www.doc.govt.nz, adult $18, child $9, children under 5 free) is one of the more glamorous offerings, with hot showers, electric cookers, and powered sites. Sites must be booked in advance and there's a three-night minimum (Dec. 26-Jan. 6).

Pelorus Bridge Scenic Reserve is 19km (15 minutes) west of Havelock on State Highway 6.

WALKS

The 800m **Totara Walk** (30 minutes round-trip) leaves the Kanuka picnic area to wind through woodlands to a massive, ancient totara tree. The 1.7km **Circle Loop Walk** (45 minutes round-trip) takes in the Pelorus River and forest before crossing a suspension bridge over the Rai River. The 1km **Tawa Walk** (30 minutes round-trip) loops through forest and past terraces formed by the Pelorus River, with access to a campground. One of the park's more challenging walks, the 1.5km **Elvy Waterfalls Track** (2 hours round-trip) borders the Pelorus River en route to a couple of waterfalls. There is a stream crossing that may be tricky following heavy rain.

Food

Start the day with breakfast and serene marine views at the **Slip Inn Café** (Havelock Marina, 03/574-2345, www.slipinn.co.nz, 8am-close daily, $21-35). Later in the day, choose from a range of fish dishes, including green-lipped mussels as well as pasta. If you can't get a seat outside, the impressive church-like interior still lets you look out over the water.

Book ahead to secure a table at local icon ★ **The Mussel Pot** (73 Main Rd., 03/574-2824, www.themusselpot.co.nz, 11am-2:45pm and 5:15pm-close daily Sept.-May, $20-31). They dish up some of the best green-lipped mussels in New Zealand, then use the shells as decorations. Mussels are served steamed, grilled, battered, or in a chowder. Other offerings include seafood, pastas, pizzas, and burgers.

view from Pelorus Bridge

The **Captain's Daughter** (72 Main Rd., 03/574-2440, www.captainsdaughter.co.nz, 8am-close daily, $24-40) serves the obligatory mussels along with high-end food like lamb rack and prawn risotto. The authentic old English pub has gorgeous stone walls, barrel tables, a roaring log fire, and the best selection of craft beers in town. Watch for the occasional live music nights.

Accommodations

Housed in a former school, **Rutherford Backpackers** (46 Main Rd., 03/574-2104, www.rutherfordbackpackers.com, dorm $25, $65 s or d) presents affordable accommodations and a large, open communal area with a wood burner, a fully equipped kitchen, and free Wi-Fi. It's popular with seasonal workers; for extra privacy, opt for the caravan option on the grounds.

Enjoy marina views, a heated swimming pool, and flawless gardens at ★ **Havelock Motel and Motor Lodge** (50-52 Main Rd., 03/574-2961, www.havelockmotel.co.nz, $114-184). Rooms come equipped with Wi-Fi, Sky TV, and kitchens; some have their own spa tub. Follow a session in the fitness center with a soak in the cedar hot tub.

Set on shady, five-acre grounds, the serene **Havelock Garden Motel** (71 Main St., 03/574-2387, www.gardenmotels.com, $135-150) has 12 immaculate units ranging from studios to two-bedrooms, all with a kitchen, private bathroom, Sky TV, and free Wi-Fi. It's a short stroll from Havelock.

Transportation and Services

Havelock is 33.5km (50 minutes) west of Picton via Queen Charlotte Drive, or 60km (40 minutes) via the less-scenic State Highways 1 and 6. Buses between Picton and Nelson stop at Havelock.

Pelorus Sound Water Taxi & Cruises (Pier C, Havelock Marina, 03/574-2151, www.pelorussoundwatertaxis.co.nz) operates pick-up and drop-off services throughout Pelorus and Kenepuru Sounds, with a range of scenic cruises.

Informed staff at the **i-SITE Visitor Centre** (61 Main Rd., 03/574-2161, www.marlboroughnz.com, 9:30am-4:30pm daily Sept.-May) can advise on local sights and accommodations and book tours of the sounds.

Marlborough Wine Region

Sauvignon blanc—the vino that put New Zealand on the palate of the international map—rules the roost in this region, but there are plenty of other worthy chardonnays and pinot noirs. More than two-thirds of New Zealand's wine is produced from the 20,000 hectares of vineyards that line the Wairua Valley, named *kei puta te wairua* ("the place with the hole in the cloud") by Maori.

The towns of **Blenheim** and **Renwick** serve as scenic bases from which to explore these revered vinicultural lands. Most visitors opt for winery tours and leave the driving to professionals.

TOP EXPERIENCE

★ Winery Tours

The i-SITE Visitor Information Centre and Vines Village have leaflets, brochures, and maps of vineyards, and can recommend excellent vineyard tour operators. Some useful websites include **Wine Marlborough** (www.winemarlborough.nz) and **New Zealand Wine** (www.nzwine.com). Most of the wineries offer snacks, while many also host exquisite eateries and free wine tastings. Any (usually small) charges are usually refunded if you make a food or drink purchase.

Highlight Wine Tours (03/577-9046, www.highlightwinetours.co.nz) offer door-to-door pickups from Blenheim, Picton, and Havelock, with half- and full-day tours in a choice of shuttle bus, or classic vehicles like a VW camper or drop-top Mustang.

Escape to Marlborough (33 Wellington St., Picton, 03/573-5573, www.escapetomarlborough.com, $195-245) offers custom vineyard tours in luxury shuttle buses. Combine your trip to include attractions like the Omaka Aviation Centre or a kayaking trip in the Marlborough Sounds.

Explore Marlborough (0800/397-627, www.exploremarlborough.co.nz) runs half- and full-day winery tours by bike or car; full-day tours include lunch at a vineyard. Tours pickup from Blenheim and Renwick.

The **Marlborough Wine & Food Festival** (www.wine-marlborough-festival.co.nz, Feb.) takes place at one of the region's oldest and most prestigious wineries, the **Brancott Estate** (180 Brancott Rd., Fairhall, 03/520-6975, www.brancottestate.com, 10am-4:30pm daily), home of New Zealand's first sauvignon blanc. Guests can sample a selection of local wines and dishes while serenaded by live music.

BLENHEIM

More than 20 vineyards lie within a 5km radius of Blenheim, Marlborough's main town and the heart of its wine region.

Sights

OMAKA AVIATION HERITAGE CENTRE

A vast chunk of the incredible world wars aircraft collection at the **Omaka Aviation Heritage Centre** (79 Aeordrome Rd., 03/579-1305, www.omaka.org.nz, 10am-5pm daily May-Nov., 9am-5pm daily Dec.-Apr.) is owned by *Lord of the Rings* director, Sir Peter Jackson. Scenes created in conjunction with the Weta Workshop (the company behind the magical Middle-earth special effects) lend this museum a cinematic feel.

Separate hangars display dioramas of World War One (adult $25, children $12, student and senior $23, children under 5 free) and World War Two (adult $20, children $10, student and senior $18, children under 5 free). Life-size mannequins operate airplanes, often suspended in action from lofty ceilings or in crash landings. The displays are enhanced by adjacent collections of memorabilia and documentary films. Combined ($39/16/35/free) tickets can be purchased for both exhibitions.

MARLBOROUGH MUSEUM

Familiarize yourself with the history of the region's viniculture courtesy of the **Marlborough Museum** (26 Arthur Baker Pl., 03/578-1712, www.marlboroughmuseum.org.nz, 10am-4pm daily, adult $10, child $5, child under 5 free). Behind cellar doors, winery equipment is displayed alongside a library of labels and bottles and a scent area where you can sniff the aromas of the various grapes. Look for the replica historic street scene and whaling and Maori exhibits with tools, jewels, and carved boats.

MOA BREWERY

For a change of scenery, head to nearby **Moa Brewery** (258 Jacksons Rd., 03/572-5149, www.moabeer.com, 10:30am-6pm daily) to choose from more than 20 craft beers to sample. There are some lovely shady gardens to

Wairau River Wines

kick back with a brew or two. The brewery was co-founded by Josh Scott, son of legendary local winemaker Allan Scott, whose winery is just across the road.

Recreation

More than 60km of walking and mountain bike trails await in the 11-sq-km **Wither Hills Farm Park** (www.marlboroughnz.com), five minutes' south of Blenheim. The tracks snake through working farmland and ridges with views over Cloudy Bay and the Cook Strait as far as Wellington, and inland down the Wairua Valley. Multiple entry points include Redwood Street and Taylor Pass Road. A map is available from the local i-SITEs.

Food

Meet friendly locals over sumptuous homemade pies at ★ **The Burleigh** (72 New Renwick Rd., 03/579-2531, 7:30am-3pm Mon.-Fri., 9am-1pm Sat., $6). The imaginative gourmet pies, such as steak and blue cheese, are among the best in South Island and the coffee is the best in town. The French baguettes are also *très* popular. The unassuming eatery fills fast.

Get your fill of Latin cuisine at **Gramado's** (74 Main St., 03/579-1192, www.gramadosrestaurant.com, 4pm-close Tues.-Sat., $28-40), a high-end South American eatery. Low lighting and candles set the stage for pan-fried fish or *feijoada*, a smoky Brazilian stew of black beans, bacon, chorizo, and pork ribs.

Accommodations

The Grapevine (29 Park Ter., 03/578-6062, www.thegrapevine.co.nz, dorm $26-27, $60-62 s, $$66-70 d) is a well-priced hostel with a fully stocked kitchen, bike and canoe rental, and free Wi-Fi. The hostel overlooks the Opawa River and is a 15-minute walk from downtown Blenheim. Savor a bottle of sauvignon blanc on the riverbank.

A stay at the pristine and modern **Knightsbridge Court Motor Lodge** (112 Middle Renwick Rd., 03/578-0818, www.theknightsbridge.co.nz, $145-220) won't dent the budget. Eighteen suites range from studios to two-bedrooms (some have spa bath suites) and come equipped with Sky TV, cooking facilities, a lounge area, private bathroom, and free Wi-Fi. Amenities include a spa pool, swimming pool, and a barbecue area.

Sprouting from five acres of vines, orchards, and farmland, **St. Leonards Vineyard Cottages** (18 St. Leonards Rd., 03/577-8328, www.stleonards.co.nz, $150-340) is a slab of bucolic Marlborough paradise with a slice of history to boot. The late-19th century farmstead is still patrolled by chickens (whose supply eggs for breakfast), sheep, and deer. Self-contained units are housed in converted, themed buildings such as a woolshed, stables and dairy and come with private garden areas and barbecues. Communal facilities include a heated outdoor swimming pool, tennis court, and free bike rentals.

Walnut Block Cottages (43 Blicks Ln., 03/577-9187, www.walnutblock.co.nz, $255) are nestled among rows of vines with mountain views and the area's oldest walnut tree. The modern, open layout features luxurious bathrooms, under-floor heating, Sky TV, free Wi-Fi, and bathrobes. Help yourself to fruit from the surrounding orchards or grab some cheese and a bottle of wine to watch the sun set behind the Wairua Valley. There's a minimum two-night stay in summer. It's 3km from the town center.

Transportation and Services

Blenheim is 28km south of Picton along State Highway 1.

The *Coastal Pacific* train between Picton and Kaikoura stops at Blenheim, but remained closed at the time of publication due to damage from the 2016 earthquake. Contact Rail New Zealand (www.railnewzealand.com) for updates.

AIR

Marlborough Airport (1 Tancred Cres., 03/573-5580, www.marlboroughairport.co.nz) is 11km (12 minutes) west of Blenheim via State Highway 6. **Air New Zealand** (www.

airnewzealand.co.nz) flies daily to Auckland and Wellington. **Sounds Air** (www.soundsair.com) offers less frequent flights to Nelson, Taupo, Napier, Christchurch, Westport, and Wellington. Car rentals at the airport include **Apex** (0800/500-660, www.apexrentals.co.nz) and **Budget** (03/572-8700, www.budget.co.nz).

PUBLIC TRANSPORTATION

National bus operator **Intercity** (04/385-0520, www.intercity.co.nz) stops at the Blenheim i-SITE (8 Sinclair St.). Regional bus operator **Atomic Shuttle** (03/349-0697, www.atomictravel.co.nz, $15-40) connects Blenheim, to Picton, Nelson, Kaikoura, and Christchurch.

For cabs and shuttles, contact **Marlborough Taxis** (03/577-5511) or **Blenheim Shuttles** (03/577-5277, www.blenheimshuttles.co.nz), who also offer rides to other local hubs such as Renwick.

SERVICES

For information about the Marlborough Wine Region and to book tours, visit the **Blenheim i-SITE** (8 Sinclair St., 03/577-8080, 9am-4pm Mon.-Fri., 9am-3pm Sat., 10am-3pm Sun.).

RENWICK AND VICINITY

The small town of Renwick serves as another launching point to Marlborough's vineyards. Northeast of Renwick, **The Vines Village** (193 Rapaura Rd., www.thevinesvillage.co.nz) is a welcome detour on your grape tour—or a fun destination in itself. The sunny, lakeside complex houses a gaggle of boutiques, bike hire, and a cellar door.

Brancott Estate

The legendary **Brancott Estate** (180 Brancott Rd., Fairhall, 03/520-6975, www.brancottestate.com) is the home of the original sauvignon blanc plantations that introduced New Zealand as a global wine player. The **cellar door** (10am-4:30pm daily) and **restaurant** (11am-3pm daily) are surrounded by floor-to-ceiling windows; an adjacent deck offers expansive views of the vineyards with mountains in the distance. Try a tutored sauvignon blanc tasting experience (11am and 2pm daily, min. 2 people, $18pp), which lasts 45 minutes. The 30-minute Premium Wine Tasting (enquire ahead, $6-15) includes exclusive vinos only available at the cellar door.

The **Vineyard Cycle Tour** (10:30am daily Sept.-Mar. by appointment, $35) is a 75-minute bike ride around the vineyard followed by a tasting session. The one-hour Living Land Falcon Encounter (11am Mon., Wed., and Fri. Dec.-Mar. by appointment, $40) lets guests get up close to an endangered New Zealand falcon, with a tasting session afterward.

Brancott Estate is 6km (7 minutes) south of Renwick via State Highway 6 and Godfrey, New Renwick, and Brancott Roads.

Ride the Golden Mile

For the independent traveler, the easiest way to explore Marlborough is to **Ride the Golden Mile** (www.ridethegoldenmile.com). The 6km bicycle route takes in nine wineries (don't aim for more than five in one day). Convenient starting points include the **Olde Mill House B&B** (9 Wilson St.) and the **Marlborough Vinters Hotel** (190 Rapaura Rd.).

Wineries to stop at include: **Nautilus Estate** (12 Rapaura Rd., 03/572-6008, www.nautilusestate.com, 10am-4:30pm daily Sep.-May), whose award-winning wines are served alongside artisan New Zealand cheeses; the super welcoming family-run operation **Wairau River Wines** (11 Rapaura Rd., 03/572-9800, www.wairauriverwines.com, 10am-5pm daily); and pioneering organic winery **Seresin Estate** (85 Bedford Rd., 03/572-9408, www.seresin.co.nz, 10am-4:30pm daily).

Bike Hire Marlborough (Vines Village, 0800/397-627, www.bikehiremarlborough.co.nz) provides bike rental services, maps, and information regarding local grape growers and where to stay.

Food

The Vines Village Café (The Vines Village, 193 Rapaura Rd., 03/572-7170, www.

vinesvillagecafe.co.nz, 8:30am-4:30pm) has an outdoor deck overlooking distant mountains. The Wine Maker's Breakfast ($22) of premium sausage and bacon, mushrooms, poached egg, hash browns, and sourdough toast is an ideal way to prepare for a day at the vineyards. There's also free all-day parking if you wish to tour the vineyards by bike.

The **Vinters Room** (190 Rapaura Rd., Renwick, 03-572-5094, www.mvh.co.nz, 11am-close daily, $33-36) uses only the finest local produce to craft exquisite dishes like scotch fillet, tempura cod, and pulled braised lamb shank—and the wine list is of course faultless.

Accommodations

Olde Mill House B&B (9 Wilson St., 03/572-8458, www.oldemillhouse.co.nz, $180-185) is surrounded by colorful gardens that can be enjoyed from numerous outdoor seating spots, including private patios. The restful, rural retreat has three en-suite bedrooms. Enjoy a glass of wine in the outdoor hot tub and make the most of the free Wi-Fi and bike hire. The sumptuous continental breakfast includes homemade muesli, jams and preserves, and fruit grown in the garden.

Marlborough Vinters Hotel (190 Rapaura Rd., 03/572-5094, www.mvh.co.nz, $170-310) five minutes north of Renwick, basks among sprawling vines. Its 16 modern, affordable suites boast scenic views, free Wi-Fi, Sky TV, boutique toiletries, private patios, under-floor heating and hot-drink facilities. Some suites come with an outdoor tub. Guests can make the most of the gym and outdoor spa, and bike hire is also available to tour nearby wineries.

Transportation and Services

Renwick is 15km (20 minutes) west of Blenheim via State Highway 6. From Picton, it's 38km southwest along State Highway 1.

Kaikoura

The seaside settlement of Kaikoura is a windswept coastal hub beneath the majestic Kaikoura Ranges. The waters here positively pulsate with marine life and the former whaling town today draws visitors for whale watching and swimming with dolphins. The Kaikoura Peninsula also hosts a massive fur seal colony.

The town's name comes from the ancient Maori title *Te Ahi Kaikoura a Tama ki Te Rangi*, "the fire that cooked the crayfish of Tama ki Te Rangi." *Kai* means "food" and *koura* is "crayfish," which are abundant. Don't leave without sampling this local delicacy.

SIGHTS

Fyffe House

Fyffe House (62 Avoca St., 03/319-5835, 10am-5pm daily, adult $10, child free, student $5) is Kaikoura's oldest surviving building—and what a survivor it is (it was closed for a year following the 2016 quake). The intimate pink cottage, perched at the tip of the peninsula, was built by the Fyffe family in 1844 as part of a whaling station. The fascinating foundations are partly whale bone and you can view these along with historical displays, texts, and audio recordings.

Kaikoura Museum

The **Kaikoura Museum** (96 West End, 03/319-7440, www.kaikoura-museum.co.nz, 10am-5pm daily, adult $12, $6 child) incorporates plenty of color and community input. The New Normal exhibit is dedicated to the 2016 earthquake with contributions from 30 local residents who convey the tragedy by way of photographs, damaged possessions, and a short documentary. The rest of the state-of-the-art museum leans heavily on Kaikoura's coastal exploits such as whaling—the building even resembles an enormous crayfish pot.

SPORTS AND RECREATION

★ Whale Watching

The town was founded on the whaling industry and now benefits from excellent whale watching. Expect at least 1-2 whale sightings, plus plenty of birdlife, seals, and dolphins with trips aboard Maori-owned and operated **Whale Watch Kaikoura** (The Whaleway Station, Whaleway Rd., 03/319-6767, www.whalewatch.co.nz, 7:15am-3:30pm daily, adult $150, child $60). Their daily 2.5-hour tours are aboard comfortable catamarans with indoor seating and raised outdoor viewing decks (and plenty of sea sickness medication).

Wings Over Whales Kaikoura (Kaikoura Airport, 617 State Hwy. 1, 03/319-6580, www.whales.co.nz, adult $180, child $75, under-3s free) operates half-hour ocean flights that enable you to marvel at the magnitude of these marine creatures from heights of 150 meters. Each passenger has their own window and the high-wing aircraft design means views are unobstructed.

Kayaking and SUP

Seal Kayak Kaikoura (2 Beach Rd., 0800/387-7325, www.sealkayakkaikoura.com, adult $85, child $65) operate two guided 2.5-3-hour tours on specially designed vessels that allow you to swap paddling for peddling at will. It'll give you plenty of opportunity to snap away at the abundant wildlife such as a fur seals (guaranteed) and albatrosses. Choose a daytime or sunset tour, and independent kayak hire is also offered.

Kayak or stand-up paddleboard with **Kaikoura Kayaks** (19 Killarney St., 03/319-7118, www.kaikourakayaks.nz, adult $99, child $70), whose half-day guided tours include seal-spotting and sunset options. There's always the chance of encountering some penguins, albatrosses, or dusky dolphins. Kayak and fishing rentals are also available.

Wildlife Tours

Dolphin Encounter Kaikoura (96 Esplanade, 03/319-6777, www.encounterkaikoura.co.nz) offers 3.5-hour daily swimming tours with dusky dolphin (swim: adult $175, child $160; view only $95/$50). The company also operates a 2.5-4-hour albatross encounter tour ($125-160/60-85); boats get up close to the birds and their young in the open ocean, as well as other seabirds, occasionally including the rare yellow-eyed penguin.

Seal Swim Kaikoura (58 West End,

whale-watching in Kaikoura

The Kaikoura Quake

In 2016, a 7.8 magnitude earthquake in Kaikoura killed two people and caused substantial structural and geological damage, isolating the town from the rest of the country for months. The rail line north and south of Kaikoura remains closed (estimated opening is 2019) and the number of damaged buildings forced a handful of businesses to close. Yet with a bit of planning and flexibility, you can still visit one of New Zealand's premier jewels.

03/319-6182, www.sealswimkaikoura.co.nz, adult $80-110, child $60-70) organizes guided ocean dips with playful and highly curious fur seals who never seem to tire of their snorkel-wearing human visitors.

Walks

The tramp up mile-high **Mt. Fyffe** (8 hours round-trip) reveals jaw-dropping views across the ocean. On a clear day, you'll see as far as North Island and Banks Peninsula near Christchurch. From the same carpark, the **Hinau Track** (45 minutes round-trip) provides a relaxing exploration of forest that is home to the hinau and kanuka.

Both tracks begin from the Mt. Fyffe carpark, 14km northwest of Kaikoura via State Highway 1 and Ludstone, Red Swamp, Postman's, and Chapman's Roads.

The DoC's *Kaikoura Peninsula Walkway* brochure is available at the i-SITE Visitor Centre.

KAIKOURA PENINSULA WALKWAY

The **Kaikoura Peninsula Walkway** (3 hours round-trip) is a magnificent coastal stroll that begins at the Esplanade in the town center. The track meanders south, wrapping around the head of the peninsula past the seal colony at Point Kean, then on to clifftop ocean views and wading birds. Thanks to numerous entry/exit points, shorter sections of the track can be walked instead.

Those who only wish to visit the **seal colony** can drive to the Point Kean carpark, which is right next to the lounging animals on Fyffe Quay. (Stay at least 10m away and avoid blocking their path to the sea.)

KAIKOURA COAST TRACK

Experience traditional multi-day Kiwi tramping without the hassle of a multi-day pack along the exceptional **Kaikoura Coast Track** (03/319-2715, www.kaikouratrack.co.nz, Oct.-Apr., $200). The self-guided, two-day, 26km trek slices through privately owned farmland with wild coastal views across crashing surf to the Kaikoura Ranges and misty valleys. Come nightfall, you'll be hosted in cozy family farm cottages where you can purchase supplies or book meals in advance (breakfasts $20, dinner $50). Transportation of your equipment is included. The track is closed May-September.

FOOD

Healthy haven ★ **Hislops Café** (33 Beach Rd., 03/319-6971, www.hislops-wholefoods.co.nz, Wed.-Sat. 8:30am-8pm, Sun. 8:30am-4pm) boasts a proudly wholefoods menu including an array of breads and cakes baked in-house using manuka honey and flour from the family farm. Other gastronomic treats include seafood, meats, and a slew of vegetarian options. Grab a seat on the outdoor deck.

Few have mastered fish-and-chips like the friendly folks at award-winning takeaway **Coopers Catch** (9 West End, 03/319-6362, www.chipshop.co.nz, 9:30am-10pm daily, $10). Order the classic and head down to the ocean to enjoy them.

The best seafood dining awaits at the legendary ★ **Kaikoura Seafood BBQ** (85 Fyffe Quay, 027/376-3619, 11am-7pm Sun.-Fri., 11am-3:30pm Sat., $5-9), a roadside stall on the Kaikoura peninsula a five-minute drive from the town center. Enjoy crayfish ($45, halves available), shellfish, and seafood fritters cooked to order and served with rice, salad, and bread. Grab a roadside table and savor the sea air.

Set beneath a historic lodge with peaceful, sea views, the ★ **Pier Hotel Restaurant & Bar** (1 Avoca St., 03/319-5037, www.thepier-hotel.co.nz, noon-close daily, $23-40) serves some of the best crayfish in town (half $45, whole $90). The sprawling seafood list also includes beef, lamb, and venison. Inside, you'll find polished wood, historic photos, an open fire, and friendly locals.

Green Dolphin (12 Avoca St., 03/319-6666, www.greendolphinkaikoura.com, 5pm-close daily summer, 5pm-9pm daily winter, $28-50) is a cozy seaside eatery with Pacific and mountain views. The seafood-heavy seasonal menu including *paua* (New Zealand abalone), along with red meats and a handful of exceptional pasta dishes (the pasta is crafted in-house). There's an impressive selection of boutique booze, too. It's a short drive from the town center.

ACCOMMODATIONS

Kaikoura's funkiest hostel, the ★ **Albatross Backpacker Inn** (1 Torquay Rd., 03/319-6090, www.albatross-kaikoura.co.nz, dorm $34-38, $84-89 s or d) is set in a former post office and takes great pride in its eco-credentials. Rooms burst with color and character; a female-only dorm is available as is a triple unit ($114). There's a barbecue area, and plenty of freebies such as bike rentals, hot drinks, and an herb and veggie garden. Try your hand at the multitude of instruments lying available and leave a message on the Wall of Art.

Rooms at bed-and-breakfast **Churchill Park Lodge** (34 Churchill St., 03/319-5526, www.churchillparklodge.co.nz, $110 s, $150 d) are bright and modern, with private bathrooms and balconies with ocean and mountain views. There's a lounge area, hot-drink facilities, free Wi-Fi, and TVs. The town center is a five-minute walk.

Bendamere House Bed & Breakfast (37 Adelphi Ter., 03/319-5830, www.bendamere.co.nz, $240-260) is spread over a couple of handsome white villas on a pristine half-acre plot lined with roses. Five stellar suites have private balconies or patios with sea and mountain views. There's free Wi-Fi, hot drink facilities, toiletries, and complimentary homemade shortbread, plus plenty of homemade treats for breakfast, including preserves and muffins.

Savor stunning mountain, ocean, and bush panoramas from **Nikau Lodge** (53 Deal St., 03/319-6973, www.nikaulodge.com, $220-280), a boutique B&B. This pretty 1925 villa is surrounded by pristine gardens. Rooms are equipped with free Wi-Fi, TVs, DVD players, hot-drink facilities and bathrobes. Guests are treated to home baked cookies and communal facilities include a hot tub and log burner in the lounge. Get an upper floor suite for the best views.

Kaikoura Top 10 Holiday Park (34 Beach Rd., 03/319-5362, www.kaikoura-top10.co.nz) comes with all the trappings of a modern holiday park: a heated pool and spa, barbecues, Wi-Fi, a game and TV room, and a full kitchen. Accommodations include camper and van sites ($46-50) that share amenities; fully self-contained cabins

Kaikoura Canyon

Less than a 10-minute cruise from the coastline, an underwater cliff plunges suddenly from the continental shelf into the Kaikoura Canyon. It is this underwater formation (up to 1.6km deep and 5km across) that is responsible for the region's vast and varied marine life. Two ocean currents collide in the canyon: a warm current from the tropical north, and a cool current from the Antarctic south. As they merge, settled nutrients surge upward, attracting a continual food chain that ensures sperm whales, dusky dolphins, and fur seals can feed year-round. Regular visitors include orca, humpback whales, and Hector's and bottlenose dolphins. Though elusive blue whales are known to pass though, they are rarely sighted.

Plant a Tree

Trees for Travellers (80 Scarborough St., 03/319-7148, www.treesfortravellers.co.nz) is a local project that offsets the carbon footprints of travelers by replenishing local forests. The organization plants native trees with basic packages beginning at $20. There are additional fees ($10-20) for larger species, certificates, or to plant the tree yourself.

and motel rooms ($95-200); and a historic beachside villa ($325) that sleeps six with a private garden and a log fire. It's close to the town center.

The area's only beachfront holiday park is **Peketa Beach Holiday Park** (665 Hwy. 1, 03/319-6299, www.kaikourapeketabeach.co.nz). The stunning 30-acre site is replete with mini-golf, beach volleyball, barbecues, Wi-Fi, and fishing equipment rentals—and ask about nearby surfing and kayak rentals. Tent and van sites (adult $36-44, child $5-10) are joined by basic cabins ($55s, $65 d) with fridges and private decks with access to shared kitchen and bathroom facilities. Don't miss the real-fruit ice cream from the on-site store. It's 7km south of Kaikoura.

TRANSPORTATION AND SERVICES

Car

Kaikoura is 156km (2 hours 10 minutes) south of Picton and 181km (2.5 hours) north of Christchurch, via State Highway 1.

State Highway 1 is open 7am-8:30pm daily; however, ongoing repairs from the 2016 earthquake may affect transportation. Contact the New Zealand Transport Agency (www.nzta.govt.nz) for updates and closures.

South from Kaikoura, Inland Route 70 remains open 24/7.

Bus and Train

National bus operator **Intercity** (04/385-0520, www.intercity.co.nz) services Kaikoura. Regional bus operator **Atomic Shuttle** (03/349-0697, www.atomictravel.co.nz, $15-40) runs north to Marlborough's main hubs. Heading south, **Kaikoura Express** (0800/500-929, www.kaikouraexpress.co.nz, adult $40, child $35) operates a daily bus service to Christchurch and offers combined transport and tour packages.

At time of publication, the *Coastal Pacific* train route from Picton to Christchurch via Kaikoura remained closed due to earthquake damage. Contact Rail New Zealand (www.railnewzealand.com) for updates.

Tours

You'll need a maximum of 10 friends for an excursion with **Maori Tours Kaikoura** (10 Churchill St., 03/319-5567, www.maoritours.co.nz, $975-1,300 per group), whose authentic cultural outings take in sacred sites. Local Maori, whose families have inhabited the region for centuries, teach guests traditional greetings, how to prepare a *hangi,* and how to weave flax. Book two weeks in advance; times are flexible, and tours range from half- to full-days.

Services

The **Kaikoura i-SITE Visitor Centre** (West End, 8:30am-6pm daily Jan-Apr., 9am-5pm Mon.-Fri., 9:30am-4pm Sat.-Sun. Apr.-Dec.) is the best source of information for the area.

Nelson and Vicinity

The Nelson Tasman region is an artsy, boho center bordered by three national parks, endless beaches, and plentiful microbreweries and vineyards.

(The Nelson Tasman region is often abbreviated to just Nelson which is also the name of its main city. The names are used interchangeably.)

SIGHTS

Christ Church Cathedral

Nelson's unusual **Christ Church Cathedral** (Trafalgar Sq., 03/548-1008, www.nelsoncathedral.nz, 9am-6pm daily, donation) sits on a hilltop formerly occupied by a wooden edifice erected on Church Hill in 1842. Foundations for the current concrete and Takaka marble structure were laid in 1925; its skeletal tower looks almost incomplete—a controversial design element. Inside are some splendid arches, an impressive organ, and colorful stained-glass windows.

Nelson Provincial Museum

Nelson Provincial Museum (Hardy and Trafalgar Sts., 03/548-9588, 10am-5pm Mon.-Fri., 10am-4:30pm Sat.-Sun., adult $5, child $3) is one of the nation's most modern museums. Inside are all manner of Maori artifacts, including carvings, Victorian antiques, and the Tyree Studio, an expansive photography compilation whose collection of 123,000 glass plate negatives has been recognized by UNESCO. Visiting exhibits may incur an addition fee.

World of Wearable Art and Classic Car Museum

Even those with only a passing interest in art or fashion will be awed by the mind-blowing costumes at the **World of Wearable Art and Classic Car Museum** (1 Cadillac Way, 03/547-4573, www.wowcars.co.nz, 10am-5pm daily, adult $24, child $10, student/senior $18, child under 5 free). The international collection was born from a quirky 1980s Nelson fashion show featuring creative outfits crafted from incongruous materials such as scrap metal or computer parts. (The show is now held annually in Wellington.)

Behind the museum, a hangar holds 120 beautiful and unusual automobiles, including American classics, European sports cars, and a 1908 Renault. Allow at least an hour to take it all in—though you'll probably stay for at least two. It's 10 minutes south of downtown.

Founders Heritage Park

Founders Heritage Park (87 Atawhai Dr., 03/548-2649, www.founderspark.co.nz, 10am-4:30pm daily, adult $7, children under 12 free) provides a glimpse into Nelson's colonial heritage. Pleasant gardens are surrounded by bush and are home to replica buildings such as a church and windmill. Take a scenic **train ride** (noon-4pm Sat.-Sun., adult $5, child $3) and check out an array of on-site artisan studios.

Botanical Hill

Protruding from Botanical Reserve, many believe **Botanical Hill** (Hardy St., www.nelson.govt.nz) to mark New Zealand's geographical center—there's even a plaque that states so. Alas, it's not quite the middle, but it does make for a satisfying walk with views of the sea and city. The reserve hosted New Zealand's first rugby match in 1870.

Suter Art Gallery

The **Suter Art Gallery** (Queens Gardens, 208 Bridge St., 03/548-4699, www.thesuter.org.nz, 9:30am-4:30pm daily, free) is a light-filled center that boasts three exhibition spaces and a contemplation garden. The building incorporates the brickwork and wood roof of the original gallery that opened in 1899. Suter's permanent works includes a significant collection of watercolors by the Victorian artist

Nelson

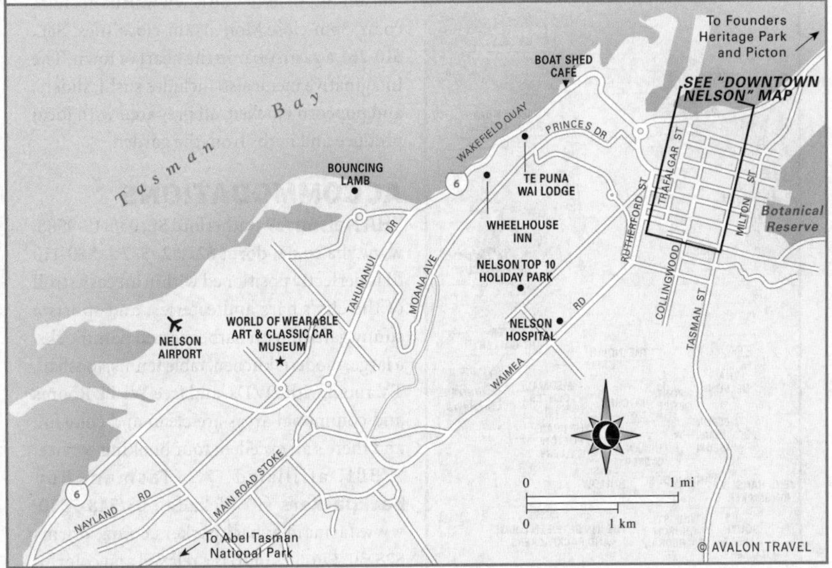

John Gully and paintings by British modernists William Gear and Bryan Winter. Outside, stroll the boardwalk sculpture trail to the eel pond.

SHOPPING

Nelson is a magnet for artists and craftspeople. The **Craig Potton Gallery** (255 Hardy St., 03/548-9554, www.craigpottongallery.co.nz, 10am-5pm Mon.-Fri., 10am-2pm Sat.) showcases works of the renowned Kiwi landscape photographer with prints, jewelry, and books available from the store.

Jens Hansen (Trafalgar Sq. and Selwyn Pl. 03/548-0640, www.jenshansen.com, 9am-5pm Mon.-Fri., 9am-2pm Sat., 10am-1pm Sun. summer) was the jeweler behind the world's most famous ring—the "One Ring" in the *Lord of the Rings*. Secure yourself an authentic replica or choose from other Kiwi-inspired creations.

For a complete list of the region's galleries and art trail maps, visit **Art Trails** (www.arttrails.nz).

FOOD

Set in a fashionable all-white industrial space, ★ **The Kitchen** (111 Bridge St., 021/195-8246, www.ktch.co.nz, Mon.-Fri. 7:30am-4pm, Sat. 8am-2pm) promotes delicious healthy eating. Dishes are crafted from wholefoods and feature colorful seasonal produce with plentiful vegan, gluten-free, and paleo options. Top it off with outstanding coffee and fresh juices.

Sip calming tea in **The Hollow** (144 Bridge St., 03/546-7935, www.thehollow.co.nz, Mon.-Sat. 10am-4pm, opens later during summer), a soothing tea house lined with shelves filled with exotic tea leaves and pots from around the globe, plus a collection of local art.

Nelson's best Indian eatery is also one of the city's best restaurants, period. Multi-award-winning ★ **The Indian Café** (94 Collingwood St., 03/548-4089, www.theindiancafe.com, noon-2pm Mon.-Fri., 5pm-close daily, $14-20) is set in a cozy historic villa with a constant hum. Well-priced meat and vegetable dishes are served in classic curry

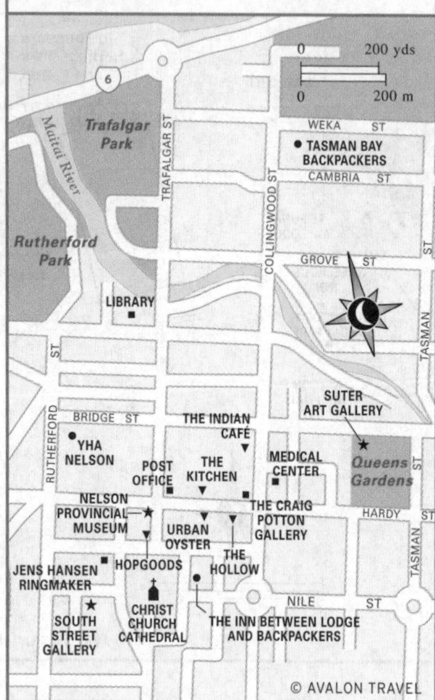

sauces like madras, korma, and vindaloo by a friendly staff. Book ahead.

The delightful **Boat Shed Café** (350 Wakefield Quay, 03/546-9783, www.boatshed-cafe.co.nz, 10am-close Mon.-Fri., 9:30am-close Sat.-Sun., $30-35) is the perfect spot to tuck into some freshly caught fish. If you're feeling adventurous, opt for the Trust the Chef Menu ($70-83) and they'll rustle up a selection of small courses. Time your dinner for sunset to enjoy the view over the water. It's a couple of kilometers west of downtown.

Hopgoods (284 Trafalgar St., 03/545-7191, www.hopgoods.co.nz, 5:30pm-close Mon.-Sat., $36-40) is a sophisticated bistro and wine bar set in a historic brick building. The changing menu includes slow-cooked lamb with black garlic and pea salsa, grouper with spiced cauliflower, and fresh produce delivered daily. Five-course tasting menus ($95) are available with wine pairing ($125). The narrow cluster of tables ensures a lively and ever-present din.

It's all about freshly shucked oysters and local craft beer at **Urban Eatery** (278 Hardy-Nelson St., 03/546-7861, www.urbaneatery.co.nz, 3pm-close Mon., 11am-close Tues.-Sat., $10-28), a gastro-bar in the heart of town. The imaginative menu also includes sushi, sliders, and popcorn chicken, all prepared with local produce and herbs from the garden.

ACCOMMODATIONS

YHA Nelson (59 Rutherford St., 03/545-9988, www.yha.co.nz, dorm $27-32, $77 s, $89-110 d) is perfectly positioned within an easy stroll of the city's bars and eateries, and sports a sunny garden with barbecue and hammocks, a large, modern kitchen, table tennis, foosball, TV room with DVDs, and free Wi-Fi. Rooms and communal areas are clean and colorful, and there's an excellent tour booking service.

BBH-affiliated ★ **Tasman Bay Backpackers** (10 Weka St., 03/548-7950, www.tasmanbaybackpackers.co.nz, dorms $28-30, $76-88 s or d) is a relaxed and colorful hostel with spotless rooms. Amenities include nightly hot chocolate pudding with ice cream, bike rentals, Wi-Fi, a well-equipped kitchen (free breakfast May-Oct.), and comfortable communal areas. Hammocks are slung outside and there's an open fire on chilly nights. It's a short stroll from downtown.

★ **The Inn Between Lodge and Backpackers** (335 Trafalgar Sq. East, 03/548-8335, www.innbetween.co.nz, $29-46, $90-130 s or d) offers boutique styling on a budget. Rooms sport designer wallpaper and feather duvets on comfy beds. En-suites and female dorms are available, and a family room sleeps four ($140). Communal areas have leather sofas, plus there's a 1950s jukebox, free Wi-Fi, an on-site café and bar, and a TV room. It's all housed in a beautiful villa close to Nelson's best restaurants.

Picturesque **Sussex House** (238 Bridge St., 03/548-9972, www.sussex.co.nz, $165-175 s, $185-200 d) is an elegant Victorian B&B with antique furniture and expansive lawns next to the Maitai River. Homey, en-suite rooms offer garden and river views and come with TVs and free Wi-Fi. The verandah is an excellent spot to kick back with a book.

The modern **Wheelhouse Inn** (41 Whitby Rd., 03/546-8391, www.wheelhouse.co.nz, $210-255) comprises five well-appointed and self-contained houses (and an apartment) with private balconies or patios, enormous windows, and sea views. Kitchens are fully stocked and the lounges are equipped with TVs, DVD players, and stereos. Free Wi-Fi is available throughout.

Te Puna Wai Lodge (24 Richardson St., 03/548-7621, www.tepunawai.co.nz, $265-395) affords ocean views from a Victorian villa home to three suites—one of which spans the entire third floor. Picture windows, polished wood floors, and marble-tiled en-suite bathrooms set an elegant scene. Each residence includes TVs, free Wi-Fi, and kitchenettes. Enjoy the on-site restaurant and barbecue and picnic area.

Nelson City Top 10 Holiday Park (230 Vanguard St., 0800/778-898, www.nelsoncity-top10.co.nz) serves campers and motorhomes ($45) thanks to amenities such as a TV room, barbecue area, and booking service. Standard cabins ($65) have private decks and share cooking and bathroom facilities with the campsites; kitchen cabins ($75) come with a TV. Cozy fully contained motel rooms ($109-170) come with lounge areas and Sky TV. It's a five-minute drive from downtown.

Transportation and Services

Nelson is 134km west of Picton via State Highway 6 or 107km west along Queen Charlotte Drive to State Highway 6.

Air

Nelson Airport (Trent Dr., 03/547-3199, www.nelsonairport.co.nz) is 8km (15 minutes) southwest of Nelson via Waimea Road or State Highway 6. **Air New Zealand** (www.airnewzealand.co.nz), **Jetstar** (www.jetstar.com), **Air2There** (www.air2there.com), **Sounds Air** (www.soundsair.com), **Golden Bay Air** (www.goldenbayair.co.nz), and **Origin Air** (www.originair.co.nz) connect Nelson with Auckland, Wellington, Christchurch, Blenheim, Palmerston North, and Paraparaumu.

Car rental companies at the airport include **Europcar** (03/265-5201, www.europcar.co.nz) and **NZ Rent A Car** (03/547-1270, www.nzrentalcar.co.nz). Airport shuttle buses are offered by **Supper Shuttle** (0800/748-8853, www.supershuttle.co.nz) and **Nelson Shuttles** (027/447-4818, www.nelsonshuttles.com).

Bus

Nelson is serviced by national bus operators **Intercity** (04/385-0520, www.intercity.co.nz) and **Naked Bus** (09/979-1616, www.nakedbus.com). Regional bus operator **Atomic Shuttle** (03/349-0697, www.atomictravel.co.nz, $15-40) connects Nelson to Picton, Blenheim, Kaikoura, and Christchurch. **NBus** (03/548-1539, www.nbus.co.nz) runs a daily bus service between Nelson and Richmond.

Car Rental and Taxis

Nelson Auto Rentals (31 Bolt Rd., 03/548-5125, www.nelsonautorentals.co.nz) offers a range of vehicles with unlimited kilometers, one-way trips, and airport pick-ups. They are located 1.5km northeast of the airport.

The city's main taxi company is **Nelson City Taxis** (03/548-8225).

Bikes

Trail Journeys Nelson (37-39 Halifax St., 03/548-0093, www.trailjourneysnelson.co.nz, 9am-4:30pm daily) rents bikes and operates a drop-off/pick-up service throughout the Nelson Tasman region. E-bikes are also available.

Services

The **Nelson i-SITE** (77 Trafalgar Sq., 03/548-2304, www.nelsonnz.com, 8:30am-5pm Mon.-Fri., 9am-4pm Sat.-Sun.) books tours and offers information on local attractions and accommodations. The location is shared with the local **DoC** office (03/546-9339, www.doc.govt.nz, 8:30am-5pm Mon.-Fri., 9am-4pm

Sat.-Sun.), which has information about Abel Tasman National Park.

Nelson has a **hospital** (Tipahi St., 03/546-1800) and **library** (27 Halifax St., 03/546-8100, www.nelsonpubliclibraries.co.nz, 9:30am-6pm Mon.-Fri., 10am-4pm Sat., 1pm-4pm Sun.). There's a central **post office** (209 Hardy St., 0800/081-190, www.nzpost.co.nz, 9am-5pm Mon.-Fri. 9am-1pm Sat.) and a **medical center** (2/105 Collingwood St., 03/548-8663, www.collingwoodhealth.co.nz, 9am-6pm Mon.-Fri.).

NELSON TO ABEL TASMAN

From Nelson, State Highway 60 shoots northwest to Abel Tasman National Park, along the coast of Tasman Bay. Along the way, the towns of Motueka, Kaiteriteri, and Marahau act as gateways to the national park, with services, food, and lodging options.

★ Tasman's Great Taste Trail

As Great Ride's go, **Tasman's Great Taste Trail** (www.nzcycletrail.com) is a breeze. What it lacks in physical demands, it compensates for with sensory stimulation. The bike trail passes a multitude of craft breweries, vineyards, boutiques, galleries, orchards, and eateries over its 175km-loop.

From Nelson, the trail heads north along the coast to Kaiteriteri then turns west inland. The slightly more challenging stretch offers a beautiful alpine backdrop en-route to the town of Woodstock before winding east toward Nelson via Wakefield.

NELSON TO MAPUA

While most won't have four days to complete the entire trail, the 33km stretch between Nelson to **Mapua Wharf** (www.mapuawharf.co.nz) is a scenic day-trip that should not be missed. The route follows the coastline overlooking Tasman Bay before reaching a boardwalk over the Waimea Estuary, patrolled by wading royal spoonbills and white herons. It soon enters the shady totara forests of **Rabbit Island** to emerge for the brief **Mapua Ferry** (03/548-0093, www.mapuaferry.co.nz, 10:10am-5:10pm daily summer, 10:10am-4:10pm winter, adult $8, student/senior $7, child $4 one-way; adult $12, student/senior $10, child $6 round-trip) crossing to the wharf.

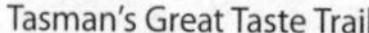
Tasman's Great Taste Trail

MAPUA

Mapua Wharf serves as a microcosm for all that makes the Nelson region so appealing. A tight collection of artisan galleries, bars, and cafes overlook the water, while outdoor seating and live music lends a festival air.

The Apple Shed (Shed 3, Mapua Wharf, 03/540-3381, 9am-10pm daily, $25-35) juts over the water with views of Waimea Inlet framed by the Richmond Ranges. Tuck into locally caught pan-fried fish or Canterbury Angus steak while sipping regional wine or a craft brew.

Mapua is 32km (30 minutes) northwest of Nelson via State Highway 60, Mapua Drive, and Higgs Road. Cyclists can book a shuttle bus back to Nelson.

BIKE RENTALS

Trail Journeys Nelson (8 Aranui Rd., Mapua Wharf, 03/548-0093, www.trailjourneysnelson.co.nz, 9am-4:30pm daily, from $40) rents bikes and operates a drop-off and pick-up shuttle service along the bike trail and throughout the Nelson Tasman region. The company can also help secure a place on the ferry and can arrange accommodations.

Motueka

Motueka serves as a gateway to Abel Tasman and Kahurangi National Parks. It is 46km north of Nelson along State Highway 60. From Motueka, it's 20.5km north to Marahau and Abel Tasman National Park.

SKY DIVING

Skydive Abel Tasman (16 College St., 0800/422-899, www.skydive.co.nz) bills itself as the nation's most scenic skydive. With contrasting views of snowy mountaintops, green rainforest, and crystal-blue oceans lapping at the Marlborough Sounds, it's a difficult claim to counter. Jumps range from 9,000-16,500 feet ($269-409) with USB video and photo packages available (from $219). Flights depart from Motueka Aerodrome.

FOOD

Set in a historic homestead along Tasman's Great Taste Trail, ★ **Riverside Café** (289 Main Rd., 03/526-7447, www.riverside-cafe.co.nz, 9:30am-4:30pm daily, 6pm-close Sat.-Sun., $25) dishes a delectable seasonal menu of wild meat and fresh seafood accompanied by organic produce grown in their idyllic gardens. You might even be serenaded by local musicians.

Motueka's only craft beer bar, the **Sprig and Fern Tavern** (Wallace St., 03/528-4684, www.sprigandferntaverns.co.nz, 2pm-close daily) offers a minimal, contemporary setting and a menu of pub classics like fish-and-chips and burgers accompanied by made-from-scratch pizzas—try the smoked salmon option. Sample a selection of local beer and cider or opt for a tasting paddle.

ACCOMMODATIONS

There's a community spirit at secluded ★ **Edens Edge Lodge** (137 Lodder Ln., 03/528-4242, www.edensedge.co.nz, dorm $32-33, $100 s, $105 d) set amid sprawling grounds with mountain views just minutes from the sea. Rooms are modern and immaculate; all privates are en-suite. There's a five-bed family room ($140), with access to communal facilities, and a triple en-suite ($134). Wi-Fi is free and there's a fully stocked kitchen and a sunny lounge area. Guests can help themselves to the herb garden and use the barbecue on the deck. Bike rentals are also offered.

Laughing Kiwi Backpackers (310 High St., 03/528-9229, www.laughingkiwi.co.nz, dorm $29-30, $68-76 s or d) has a laid-back beach vibe thanks to its native wood furnishings and palm-fringed grounds. There's free Wi-Fi, bike and kayak rentals, an ample deck, and barbecue areas. Camping equipment rentals are also available.

Motueka Top 10 Holiday Park (10 Fearson St., 03/528-7189, www.motuekatop10.co.nz) has campsites ($52) and cabins ($87-109) that share cooking and bathroom facilities (some cabins come with kitchens). Other communal amenities include a hot tub, heated swimming pool, and barbecue. Self-contained motel rooms and apartments ($140-345) range from studios to three-bedrooms; all are equipped with private decks and TVs. The larger units have separate lounge and kitchen areas. It's a short walk from the town center.

SERVICES

The **Moutueka i-SITE** (20 Wallace St., 03/528-65423, www.motuekaisite.co.nz) offers information and services for Abel Tasman and the coastal track.

Kaiteriteri

Kaiteriteri is a gateway to Abel Tasman National Park. It's 61km north of Nelson along State Highway 60; it's 16km north of Motueka and about 9km south of Abel Tasman National Park.

Split Apple Rock is a substantial boulder that is perfectly sliced in half. En-route to Abel Tasman National Park, look for the right turn from Kaiteriteri-Sandy Bay Road onto Tokongawa Drive and follow it to the carpark at the end. From there, it's a 10-minute walk to the beach that overlooks the rock. It's a little over 5km northeast of Kaiteriteri.

BIKING

More than 40km of thrilling trails lace 180 hectares of forest at the outstanding **Kaiteriteri Mountain Bike Park** (37 Martin Farm Rd., Kaiteriteri, 03/527-8010, www.bikekaiteriteri.co.nz, 24 hours daily, free). Trails range from beginner to expert and wind through forest and over ridgelines with mesmeric ocean views. Contact the Mouteka i-SITE Visitor Centre for a trail map.

FOOD AND ACCOMMODATIONS

Kai Restaurant and Bar (1 Kaiteriteri-Sandy Bay Rd., 03/527-8507, 8am-4:30pm Mon.-Wed., 8am-close Thurs.-Sun., $17-36) is a respectable gastropub with a spectacular beach view from its outside terrace. A sprawling menu includes seafood, pizza, and burgers.

★ **Kimi Ora Eco Resort** (99 Martin Farm Rd., 03/527-8027, www.kimiora.com, $199-279) sits nestled within 12 hectares of native forest overlooking the national park. Accommodations are in 23 alpine chalets with kitchenettes, balconies, TV, free Wi-Fi, sea views; some also have hot tubs. Guests enjoy the vegetarian eatery, indoor and outdoor pools, saunas, yoga classes, and a range of treatments like body wraps and massage at the wellness spa. Bike rentals are available for the Kaiteriteri Mountain Bike Park next door.

Two minutes from the beach, **Torlesse Motels** (8 Kotare Pl., Little Kaiteriteri, 03/527-8063, www.torlessemotels.co.nz, $180-340) offers a cluster of modern self-contained units—from studios to two bedrooms—with private patios or balconies, TVs, and free Wi-Fi; many rooms boast sea views. A hot tub soothes away the aches after hiking or kayaking. It's 2km south of Kaiteriteri.

Marahau

Marahau is the closest gateway to Abel Tasman National Park. It's 64km north of Nelson on State Highway 60.

FOOD AND ACCOMMODATIONS

One of the coast's coolest eateries, **Hooked on Marahau** (229 Marahau-Sandy Bay Rd., 03/527-8576, www.hookedonmarahau.com, 8am-9pm daily, $28-36) appears to be partly constructed from boat parts and reclaimed wood. The marine vibe complements the lovely sea views. The menu brims with squid, mussels, and fish, as well as pan-roasted lamb and a delicious Vietnamese chicken curry.

At Abel Tasman's southern entrance, **Old Macdonald's Farm Holiday Park** (Harvey Rd., 03/527-8288, www.oldmacs.co.nz) is a working farm set in 40 hectares of native and exotic bush. Tent and powered sites (adult $18, child $9, child under 5 free) share bathroom and fully equipped kitchen facilities as do those in dorm bunks ($30). There are also self-contained units ($70-150) with private kitchens; some have TVs, spa baths, and private decks. Secure parking is offered ($7/night). The grounds include 400-year-old rimu trees, a glowworm walk, and swimming spots on the banks of Marahau River.

The Barn (14 Harvey Rd., 03/527-8043, www.barn.co.nz, dorm $33, $89 s or d) offers an affordable base to explore Abel Tasman. Private cabins share bathroom and kitchen facilities and views look out over the foothills of the national park. You can also camp ($22-24). Amenities include a free herb garden, movie room, free Wi-Fi, pool table, barbecues, and outside fireplace.

The **Abel Tasman Lodge** (295 Sandy Bay-Marahau Rd., 03/527-8250, www.abeltasmanlodge.co.nz, $140) has immaculate, airy self-contained modern units with free Wi-Fi, luxurious bathrooms, and private decks that open onto bird-filled lawns. Guests enjoy the hot tub and sauna. It's 400 meters from the national park and a five-minute walk from the beach.

Abel Tasman National Park

Abel Tasman National Park opened in 1942, exactly 300 years after its Dutch namesake became the first European to sight New Zealand and encounter Maori. At 29,350 hectares, it is New Zealand's smallest national park, but its Great Walk is among the most popular—and accessible—with an abundance of beaches, consistent weather, and the chance to kayak along the scenic coast.

Beneath the sparkling sea, the Tonga Island Marine reserve harbors a multitude of marine life and a sizeable colony of seals.

★ ABEL TASMAN COAST TRACK

The sundrenched splendor of the **Abel Tasman Coast Track** (38-51km, 3-5 days) is a satisfying year-round tramp. The trail showcases the spectacular granite cliffs and rainforest-clad coastline as it winds its way through beech and manuka forests and across beaches and estuaries to the swirls of the crystal sea.

The whole track stretches from Marahau, in the southern section of the park, north to Wainui Bay, and is lined with DoC huts and

Abel Tasman Coast Track

campsites as it follows the coast of Tasman Bay. There are a handful of saddles and a fun 47-meter suspension to navigate. A popular option is to combine the hike with a kayaking tour.

The five-day trek can be tackled in sections:

- 12.4km: Marahau to Anchorage (4 hours)
- 8.4km: Anchorage to Bark Bay (3 hours)
- 13.5km: Bark Bay to Awaroa Inlet (4.5 hours)
- 16.9km Awaroa Inlet to Whariwharangi Bay (5.5 hours)
- 5.7-9km: Whariwharangi Bay to Wainui Bay carpark or Totaranui water taxi (2-3 hours)

When planning your trip, note that the Awaroa Inlet tidal crossing can only be navigated 1.5-2 hours on either side of low tide and may dictate the direction of your walk. Pick up a copy of DoC's *Abel Tasman Coast Track* at the Moutueka i-SITE (20 Wallace St.), which can advise on tide times, or check tide times at Metservice (www.metservice.com).

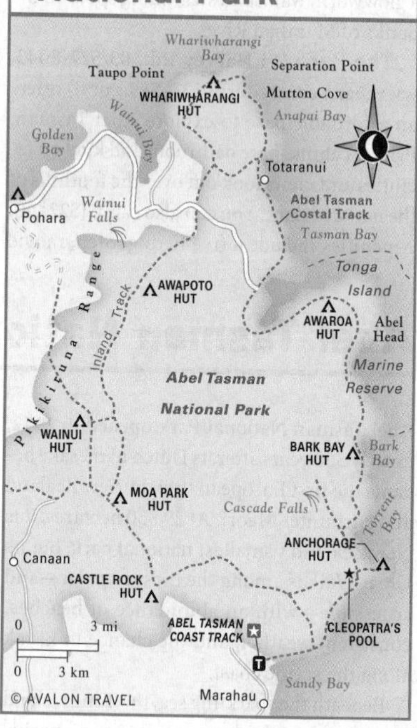

MARLBOROUGH AND NELSON
ABEL TASMAN NATIONAL PARK

Kayaking

Abel Tasman National Park offers a magical kayaking experience thanks to its luminous lagoons and marine reserve and the opportunity to explore the Coast Track at will. One of the coolest benefits of kayaking is that you can camp at isolated beaches otherwise inaccessible to the hikers on the Coast Track.

Guide operators rent kayaks and run water-shuttle pick-up services for a fee, or you can book your own.

KAYAK RENTALS AND TOURS

Some guide operators can also book overnight accommodations in the national park and rent camping equipment. Accommodations or camping are included when booking multi-day guided paddles.

Tasman Bay Sea Kayaking Adventures (TBK, 0800/827-525, www.tasmanbayseakayaking.co.nz) operates guided paddles along the coast, with the option to combine walking some stretches of the Abel Tasman Coast Track ($110-125). Ask about custom tours, kayak rentals (1 day, $75, 4 days $180, fifth day free), and camping at beaches ($15, youth under 18 free) or huts ($38/free) along the route. Bookings can be made at the local i-SITE or DoC office, or online (www.doc.govt.nz). All tours depart at 8:30am from Old Macdonald's Farm Holiday Park (Harvey Rd., Marahau).

Based out of Kaiteriteri, **Wilsons Abel Tasman National Park** (1 Sandy Kaiteriteri-Sandy Bay Rd., 03/528-2027, www.abeltasman.co.nz, adult $75-170, child $50-120) have been guiding visitors since 1841. Their kayaking excursions range from half- to full-days, with the option to combine a kayak trip with trekking, taking in sights such as Split Apple Rock and Pinnacle Island, famed for its seal colony. Wilsons also operates cruises and walking tours, as well as water taxis.

Awaroa Beach Goes Public

In 2015, a stunning seven-acre Abel Tasman block, including a stretch of sun-kissed sand called Awaroa Beach, became available for private sale causing brothers-in-law Adam Gard'ner and Duane Major to begin crowdfunding to buy the slice of paradise for the public. Around 40,000 Kiwis—and even some Aussies—chipped in, raising more than $2 million to buy the land, which was then gifted to the Department of Conservation for the people to enjoy.

Marahau Sea Kayaks (Franklin St., Marahau, 0800/529-257, www.msk.co.nz) runs 1-3-day guided paddles ($109-250) with walking combos available. Trips include DoC campsite passes, water taxi transfers, and some meals. The company also offers free parking, luggage storage, and equipment hire and shuttles to Nelson, Motueka, and Marahau.

Walks

Many short walks are simply sections of or side trips along the Abel Tasman Coast Track; all are easily accessed by kayak or water taxi. The walk to **Cleopatra's Pool** (1 hour one-way), is signposted off the main track, either from Torrent Bay or Anchorage. The idyllic swimming spot is surrounded by dense bush with a super-smooth, moss-lined all natural waterslide in the rocks.

The **Inland Track** (3-5 days) can be tackled separately or as part of a loop with the Abel Tasman Coast Track to Marahau. The 41km route snakes through beech forest and over ridges and saddles, with an optional side trip to Harwoods Hole. Road access is from the unsealed Canaan Road, off the Takaka Hill summit.

Accommodations

Abel Tasman National Park has four **DoC huts** (03/546-9339, www.doc.govt.nz, adult $32-38, child under 18 free) and 21 **DoC campsites** ($15/free). Campsites have water and toilets; some have cooking shelters. Huts do not have cooking facilities; bring a portable stove and utensils. All must be booked in advance, either through DoC or at a local i-SITE Visitor Centre.

The northerly **Totaranui campsite** is the only site with road access and vehicle parking; it can also be reached by boat. It's only available to those walking the Coast Track. There's a one-night maximum stay.

The national park offers a handful of private lodging options. **Aquapackers** (Anchorage Bay, 0800/430-744, www.aquapackers.co.nz, Oct.-Apr., dorm $85, $245 s or d) is New Zealand's only floating backpackers. Anchored off Anchorage Bay, stays include a barbecue dinner, continental breakfast, tea and coffee, and hot showers. To get there, guests must either hike 3.5 hours from Marahau and then wait to be collected in an inflatable boat, or book a kayak or water taxi for direct transport. Bookings are essential.

Awaroa Lodge (Awaroa Bay, 03/528-8758, www.awaroalodge.co.nz, $239-439) is set among dense, bird-filled bush a short walk from the beach. Rooms are equipped with free Wi-Fi, fridges, and hot-drink facilities; some rooms have private balconies or decks. An on-site café and restaurant serves local seafood and dishes that use ingredients from the lodge's organic garden. The luxurious accommodations are only accessible by foot, boat, or helicopter.

TRANSPORTATION AND SERVICES

Abel Tasman National Park juts between Golden and Tasman Bays, 66km northwest of Nelson. The southern entrance to the Coastal Track is from Marahau, 25 minutes north of

Motueka along State Highway 60; from the north, access is from Totaranui or Wainui Bay, via the town of Takaka 60km northwest of Marahau along State Highway 60.

Parking is available in DoC carparks at either end of track. Old MacDonald's Farm provides secure parking ($6 per day). Most tour operators offer secure parking for their guests.

Shuttle

Trek Express (67 Seaton Valley Rd., Upper Moutere, 03/540-2042, www.trekexpress.co.nz) operates 4x4 shuttle buses that cover the sprawling network of walking tracks throughout Nelson Lakes, Abel Tasman, and Kahurangi National Parks, along with the Marlborough Sounds and the far end of the Heaphy Track in Karamea.

Cruises and Water Taxis

Abel Tasman Sea Shuttle (2 Kaiteriteri-Sandy Bay Rd., Kaiteriteri, 03/527-8688, www.abeltasmanseashuttles.co.nz) is one of the region's main players. The most popular tour is the Discoverer Day (adult $76, child $38), an all-day trip that includes a scenic cruise followed by a 7-8km beach and forest walk. There are other half-or full-day tour options ($60-76/30-38) along with a water taxi service (adult $15-46, child half-price, child under 5 free one-way). Their **Three Day Park Passport** (adult $153, child $77) enables visitors to complete three days of walking with pick-up/drop off service at different points along the Abel Tasman Track, as well as from accommodations in Nelson, Motueka, Kaiteriteri, or Marahau.

Wilsons Abel Tasman National Park (1 Sandy Kaiteriteri-Sandy Bay Rd., Kaiteriteri, 03/528-2027, www.abeltasman.co.nz) runs half-and full-day sightseeing cruises with optional walking tours (adult $38-80, child half-price, child under 5 free; 1pm and 4:15pm cruise, children free) along with water taxis throughout the park (adult $15-47 one-way, child half-price, child under 5 free). The 3-Day Explorer Pass (adult $150, child $75) offers unlimited three-day boat travel over seven days.

Abel Tasman Eco Tours (0800/223-538, www.abeltasmanecotours.co.nz, adult $169-358, child $110-260, child under 7 free; 2 adult min. per tour) operates a personalized cruise service on a smaller boat, heading to destinations away from other tour groups. Tours last all day and depart from the boat ramp in Marahau (Sandy Bay-Marahau Rd.). Some trips are not recommended for children under age 7; check when booking. The team donates a portion of their profit (as well as their time) to local conservation projects.

Services

Motueka i-SITE Visitor Centre (20 Wallace St., 03/528-6543, www.motuekaisite.co.nz, 9am-4:30pm Mon.-Fri., 9am-4pm Sat.-Sun.) offers free tour bookings, accommodation, and travel advice, plus weather updates and tourist information regarding the Nelson region. Abel Tasman National Park DoC hut tickets and campsites can be booked here.

Golden Bay

Arching north of Abel Tasman National Park before tapering into the spindly Farewell Spit, the secluded Golden Bay (*Mohua* to Maori) is said to house the country's greatest concentration of artists and craftspeople. Unfurling beyond the imposing curl of road over Takaka Hill, this shimmering stretch of coastline shelters alternative communities and unspoiled backcountry. The region is backed by the majestic Kahurangi National Park.

TAKAKA HILL

Takaka Hill is 17km (25 minutes) west of Kaiteriteri via Riwaka-Kaiteriteri Road and State Highway 60.

Sights

From atop Takaka Hill, a 300-meter boardwalk navigates the **Ngarua Caves** (State Hwy. 60, 03/528-8093, www.ngaruacaves.co.nz, 10am-4pm daily summer, hours vary in winter, adult $20, child $8, under-5s free), leading through a sprawling trellis of stalactites and stalagmites. Tours also take in impressive moa skeletons.

The **Harwoods Hole** (45 minutes one-way) track winds for 2.9km through beech forest and limestone bluffs before terminating at the perimeter of Harwoods Hole, New Zealand's deepest vertical shaft. The sinkhole plunges 176 meters to an underground river—but you can't see directly down the shaft.

The trail begins from the carpark at the end of Canaan Road, an 11km unsealed route that branches off State Highway 60, 500m north of Ngarua Caves.

TAKAKA AND VICINITY

Takaka lies 40km northwest of Takaka Hill and Abel Tasman National Park along State Highway 60. This beachy, bohemian town serves as the gateway to the Golden Bay region and Kahurangi National Park.

Sights

GOLDEN BAY MUSEUM

Known as **Te Waka Huia O Mohua** (73 Commercial St., 03/525-6268, www.goldenbaymuseum.org.nz, 10am-4pm daily, closed Sun. in winter, by donation) is revered for its intricate diorama of Abel Tasman's disastrous arrival in Golden Bay in 1642 when he clashed with local Maori. At the time of writing, the museum was awaiting the installation of a full whale skeleton—the first provincial museum in New Zealand to harbor such an exhibit.

TE WAIKOROPUPU SPRINGS

Sparkling **Te Waikoropupu Springs** (www.doc.govt.nz) is one of the bay area's most alluring sights. The placid waters form the biggest freshwater springs in the country with some of the clearest waters in the world. A 1km partial boardwalk track (30 minutes round-trip) navigates the woodlands that surround the luminous blue ponds.

Access the springs from the carpark on Pupu Springs Road. It's located off Pupu Valley Road, off State Highway 60 and is 7km (10 minutes) west of Takaka.

Fishing

At **Anatoki Salmon** (230 McCallum Rd., 03/525-7251, www.anatokisalmon.co.nz, 9am-4:30pm daily, free), all fishing gear is provided for your lakeside angling adventure. After catching your salmon ($26 per kg), you can pay to have your fish smoked or sliced into sashimi ($5-10) (there's a café on-site). Or simply hand-feed the tame eels ($2) in the Anatoki River.

Antakoki Salmon is 7km (10 minutes) southwest of Takaka via State Highway 60 and Long Plain Road.

Food

Dangerous Kitchen (46 Commercial St., 03/525-8686, www.thedangerouskitchen.co.nz,

9am-close daily, $17-21) is a café by day and a restaurant by night. The menu of Italian and Mexican classics is made from scratch, including the pizza dough, burritos, and daily pastas featuring local produce. Local artwork adorns the walls and there's live music most nights.

The Mussel Inn (1259 State Hwy. 60, 03/525-9241, www.musselinn.co.nz, 11am-close daily, $24-30) is a local icon. The structure, built from reclaimed materials and local timber, resembles a Kiwi tramping hut-meets-woolshed. Adorned with decorative abalone shells, the inn serves hearty traditional pub dishes like steak and fish-and-chips with a range of craft beers on tap. It's 15 minutes northwest of Takaka.

Accommodations

A BBH backpacker, dated **Annie's Nirvana Lodge** (25 Motupipi St., Takaka, 03/525-8766, www.nirvanalodge.co.nz, dorm $29, $54 s, $68 d) offers the friendliest of welcomes at great prices. Basic rooms are colorful and cozy; there are a couple of kitchens, a comfortable chill-out area with plenty of board games, books and a TV and DVD player, bike rentals, barbecue, and free herbs in the gorgeous garden. Family rooms ($96-145) sleep 3-5.

Anatoki Lodge Motel (87 Commercial St., 03/525-8047, www.anatokimotels.co.nz, $140-160) has well-maintained units equipped with en-suite bathrooms, kitchenettes, free Wi-Fi and Sky TV. All rooms have small private patios with garden views. There's a swimming pool on-site.

Transportion and Services

Takaka is 39km (40 minutes) north of Takaka Hill via State Highway 60.

AIR

Adventure Flights Golden Bay (0800/150-338, www.adventureflightsgoldenbay.co.nz) operates scenic flights over Nelson, taking in attractions like Abel Tasman National Park and Farewell Spit. Those tackling the Heaphy Track can fly to Karamea or Brown Hut. Flights depart from Takaka Airfield (290 Takaka-Collingwod Hwy.).

Takaka Airport (State Hwy. 60, 03/525-8725) is serviced by **Golden Bay Air** (0800/588-885, www.goldenbayair.co.nz) with flights to Wellington, as well as scenic flights over Kahurangi and Abel Tasman National Parks and Farewell Spit. Flights to Karamea are also available.

Te Waikoropupu Springs

BUS

Golden Bay Coachlines (03/525-8352, www.gbcoachlines.co.nz) runs a daily bus service connecting Golden Bay with Nelson, Richmond, Motueka, Collingwood, Pahara, Abel Tasman National Park, and the Heaphy Track. Ask about custom charter and sightseeing options.

Maxicab Shuttles (0800/629-422, www.maxicabshuttles.com) offers bus shuttles and custom tours throughout the Nelson region, as well as car and van rentals.

SERVICES

The **Golden Bay Visitor Centre** (22 Willow St., 03/525-9136, 9am-3pm Mon.-Fri., Sat. 9am-2pm) offers advice about local tours, transportation and accommodations, and can book DoC huts and campsites.

POHARA

The coastal village of Pohara sits just 9km northeast of Takaka along Abel Tasman Drive with a sizeable sandy beach and views of Golden Bay.

Food and Accommodations

Infused with oodles of Mediterranean flair, the adobe **Sans Souci Inn** (11 Richmond Rd., 03/525-8663, www.sanssouciinn.co.nz, 7pm-close daily summer $35-59) varies its seasonal meal nightly, with an additional vegetarian option. Dishes like pork fillet with a tamarind and balsamic glaze are slow-cooked and use locally sourced ingredients from their own garden. It's all served in a romantic, rustic eatery with timber beams, French doors, and terra-cotta tile floors. Accommodations ($110 s, $130-140 d) carry on the Mediterranean theme with airy, spacious rooms. Amenities include free Wi-Fi, and hot-drink facilities, and serene gardens draped with hammocks.

★ **Ratanui Lodge** (818 Abel Tasman Dr., 03/525-7998, www.ratanuilodge.com, $395-425) offers spacious en-suite rooms that sport enormous beds with carved wood frames, luxurious bedding, and Sky TV. Amenities include free Wi-Fi, hot-drink facilities, and local toiletries. Make the most of the saltwater swimming pool, hot tub, and on-site eatery and cocktail lounge. It's a short stroll from Pohara Beach.

COLLINGWOOD

Collingwood is South Island's most northerly town of note and is the jumping off point for tours to Farewell Spit. It's 27km north of Takaka along State Highway 60, set near the Ruataniwha Inlet of Golden Bay.

Sights

Cozy **Collingwood Museum** (2 Tasman St., 03/524-8131, 9am-6pm daily, by donation) resides in an Edwardian council office building filled with historical photography. Peruse images of former industrial glories concerning coal, gold, and timber, backed by a sprinkling of farming equipment, Maori *toanga*, moa bones, equine equipment, and some cool vintage typewriters. The adjacent **Aorere Centre** recounts Golden Bay's history from Maori arrival through European settlement by way of storyboards with photos and accompanying texts.

Old-school farming machinery such as classic tractors, ploughs, and steam engines shore up the **Golden Bay Machinery & Early Settlers Museum** (869 Collingwood-Bainham Rd., 03/524-8131, 9:30am-5pm daily, by donation). Your visit may coincide with the occasional "Steam Up" day, when scones are cooked on an old-fashioned wood and coal range in the pioneer kitchen. It's 8km south of Collingwood.

Food and Accommodations

The **Courthouse Cafe** (11 Elizabeth St., 03/524-8194, www.thecourthousecafecollingwood.com, 8am-4pm daily, $15-20) offers a sophisticated menu that includes some impressively stacked burgers, soup with homemade toast, and takeout gourmet pizza (5pm-8pm Tues.-Sat.). The attractive former timber courthouse sits surrounded by peaceful lawns with outdoor seating and a white picket fence.

The wonderfully rustic ★ **Innlet Hostel and Cottages** (839 Collingwood-Puponga Main Rd., 03/5248040, www.theinnlet.co.nz, dorm $31, $75-180 s or d) accommodates a variety of budgets in homey lodgings. A collection of units and cottages pepper the forested grounds around a main hostel; some are fully self-contained. Communal amenities include free Wi-Fi, a barbecue area, and an enormous cargo net-hammock strung across a private mountain stream. A handful of walking trails dissect the expansive woodland and there's a beach 200 meters away. It's 10km north of Collingwood.

One of the region's finest motels is centrally located **Collingwood Park Motel** (1 Tasman St., 03/524-8499, www.collingwoodpark.co.nz, $120-190). A range of stylish self-contained units include free Wi-Fi and toiletries, cooking facilities, and garden and estuary views (the best are from the first floor). Those on a budget can opt for an Eco Pod; these cozy timber chalet-like domes sleep two with private decks and access to a shared kitchen and bathrooms. Powered motorhome sites ($45) have access to communal facilities and free Wi-Fi.

Golden Bay Kiwi Holiday Park (99 Tukurua Rd., 03/525-9742, www.goldenbayholidaypark.co.nz) is hemmed between beach and bush on a former farm overlooking a private beach. Choose from powered and non-powered camper and van sites ($45-49), modern cabins with fridges and basic cooking facilities ($78), and fully self-contained cabins and apartments ($175-315) with lounge areas, full kitchens, and private decks; many have sea views. Campers and those in basic cabins share bathroom and cooking facilities and a TV room. It's 8km south of Collingwood in the township of Tukurua.

FAREWELL SPIT

Farewell Spit gently curves 25km along South Island's northwest tip. It's the biggest spit in New Zealand and one of the longest sandbars in the world. With open ocean to the north and a sheltered bay to the south, the spit serves as a bird sanctuary for more than 90 species. In spring, thousands of migratory waders arrive from the northern hemisphere to join black swans and Caspian terns. The cliffs around Wharakiki Beach are punctuated by caves and arches that shelter colonies of seals. Dolphins and whales often pass by.

The spit is known as *Onetaua* ("heaped up sand") in Maori and has far-reaching dunes, salt marshes, mudflats, and a historic lighthouse. (Captain Cook bestowed its English name.)

Food and Accommodations

Farewell Spit Café (68 Freemans Access Rd., 03/524-8454, 9am-5pm daily summer, 10am-4pm Wed.-Mon. winter) offers mesmeric views over the spit. It's a scenic spot to savor cake and coffee before a day of exploration. The cafe also doubles as the **visitor and information center**.

The rudimentary **Wharakiki Beach Holiday Park** (Wharakiki Rd., 03/524-8507, www.wharakikibeachholidaypark.co.nz) is set in attractive grounds with standard and powered campsites (adult $20, child $12, child under 5 free) along with basic backpacker accommodations ($30) and four cabins ($100) with private decks. There's a communal kitchen, barbecue, lounge and dining areas, and hot showers ($2), as well as an on-site café. It's 8km northwest of the Farewell Spit Café.

Transportation and Services

Farewell Spit is 50km north of Collingwood via the Collingwood-Puponga Main Road.

Access is strictly limited. From the Triangle Flat carpark (end of Freeman Access Rd.) and Cape Farewell carpark (off Wharakiki Rd.), several well-signed walks offer views of Farewell Spit and the Tasman coast. To explore the spit proper, you'll need to book a tour.

TOURS

Farewell Spit Eco Tours (6 Tasman St., Collingwood, 0800/808-257, www.farewellspit.com, adult $130-165, child $58-120) operates

Heaphy Track

The **Heaphy Track** (www.heaphytrack.com) is the finest way to explore the magnificent diversity of Kahurangi National Park. The 78-82km Great Walk takes 4-6 days to complete and can be hiked in either direction.

The Heaphy Track follows a route used by early Maori to collect *pounamu* (greenstone). Most hikers begin from the public carpark at **Browns Hut** (34km southwest of Collingwood), in the northern end of the park, in order to tackle the steepest parts first. The challenging Great Walk climbs alpine saddles, wends through tussock-clad high-country, and passes river valleys and subtropical rainforest. The track finishes near **Karamea** on the West Coast. May-November, the track is also a Grade 4 mountain bike trail that takes 2-3 days.

DoC (03/546-9339, www.doc.govt.nz, adult $32-34, child under 18 free) manages all huts and campsites ($14/free) along the track. All huts and sites must be booked in advance through the DoC or a local i-SITE.

For guided day- and multi-day tours of Kahurangi National Park that include the Heaphy Track, contact **Bush and Beyond Guided Walks** (1544 Dovedale Rd., Wakefield, 03/528-9054, www.heaphytrackguidedwalks.co.nz) and **Kahurangi Guided Walks** (1204 Abel Tasman Dr., 03/391-4120, www.kahurangiwalks.co.nz), who also tour Abel Tasman National Park. Pick-ups throughout Nelson are available.

trips ranging from two hours to a full day. Off-road jaunts in their iconic red 4x4 minibuses mean that sands and towering dunes can be toured with ease. Take in sights such as the lighthouse, exposed fossils, and shipwrecks if the tide is right, as well as wildlife.

Cape Farewell Horse Treks (McGowan St., Collingwood, 03/524-8032, www.horsetreksnz.co.nz, $80-240) run guided tours north to Wharakiri Beach, famed for its massive dunes and rock arches, and along the Old Man Range with 360-degree views to Cape Farewell, Farewell Spit, and Kahurangi National Park. Rides last 1.5-5 hours and cater to all levels of experience.

KAHURANGI NATIONAL PARK

Kahurangi ("treasured possession" in Maori) is New Zealand's second-largest national park and is home to some of the nation's most ancient formations. Nearly a half-million hectares of wildly varied backcountry is undercut with gorges and cave systems and festooned with karst and forest home to indigenous fauna and flora, including the great spotted kiwi, giant land snail, and the giant weta. It houses 80 percent of the country's species of alpine plants.

Motueka and **Takaka** serve as gateway towns from the north; from the south, **Murchison** and **Karamea** act as gateways to the park.

Walks

The park's remote northwest corner is laced with several trails, most notably the Heaphy Track—one of New Zealand's longest and most isolated Great Walks. Those with less time can opt for the more-accessible **Flora Hut** and **Mt. Arthur Hut Tracks** (1-4 hours round-trip). Both are signposted from the Flora carpark. Shorter walks lead into the national park from the West Coast, including Opara Basin and a section of the Heaphy Track to Scotts Beach.

The Flora carpark is 31km (45 minutes) southwest of Motueka via College Street, Motueka Valley Highway, and Graham Valley Road. The final 6km of the road is unsealed; 4WD vehicles are recommended.

Grab a copy of DoC's *Kahurangi National Park* brochure from a local i-SITE or the DoC (www.doc.govt.nz).

Nelson to the West Coast

From Nelson, State Highway 6 undulates southwest all the way to the West Coast. Brace yourself for a breathtaking drive. Two natural attractions offer scenic excursions along the way.

★ NELSON LAKES NATIONAL PARK

Nelson Lakes National Park (www.doc.govt.nz) is a 102,000-hectare alpine paradise swathed in red and silver beech forests and dotted with pristine lakes said to have been gouged by the legendary chief Rakaihautu. Within the park are Rotoiti and Rotoroa Lakes, remnants of ancient glaciers that sculpted this backcountry, leaving a network of sheer-faced valleys with forested bottoms. Higher up, the dense bushline surrenders to alpine shrub, flax, and the snowy hebe. The park is home to robins, fantails, the forest parrot, kaka, the kea, the world's only alpine parrot, and the great spotted kiwi.

Tiny **St. Arnaud,** on the northern tip of Lake Rotoiti, serves as the gateway to the national park.

Walks

KERR BAY

The most accessible walks begin from Kerr Bay near the DoC Visitor Centre at Lake Rotoiti, a short stroll from the gateway town of St. Arnaud. The **Bellbird Walk** (15 minutes round-trip) loops through beech forest that's part of the Rotoiti Nature Recovery Project (a mainland bird sanctuary free of pests). Extend the walk by jumping on the adjoining **Honeydew Walk** (30 minutes).

The **St. Arnaud Range Track** (5 hours round-trip) snakes sharply from the eastern side of Kerr Bay through beech forest. The trail soon becomes gnarly underfoot thanks to slippery exposed roots. These eventually give way to tussock and herb fields as you approach the 1,650m ridgeline with 360-degree alpine views. It's a tough, steep, and rewarding climb.

LAKE ROTOROA

Lake Rotoroa is the largest lake in the national park. It's a 40-minute drive from St. Arnaud via State Highway 63 and Gowan Valley Road.

From the carpark at the end of Gowan Valley Road, the **Flowers Brothers Walk** (15 minutes round-trip) loops through native bush to the start of the Gowan River. The **Braeburn Walk** (2 hours round-trip) is an easy trek through beech forest filled with birdsong and beautiful stepped waterfalls. The track begins from Braeburn Road, 200m west of the Gowan Bridge.

TRAVERS-SABINE CIRCUIT

The 80-90km **Travers-Sabine Circuit** (www.doc.govt.nz) is a challenging, high-alpine

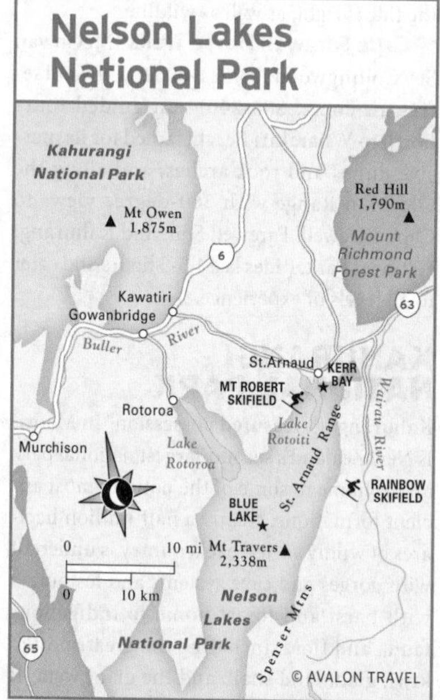

tramp for experienced hikers. The 4-7-day track begins and ends at Lake Rotoiti, taking in snow-kissed peaks, alpine lakes, and mountain streams as it winds through beech forest and tussock fields. The circuit peaks at its highest point of 1,780m over the Travers Saddle with jaw-dropping views of the national park.

It's worth the side trip to **Blue Lake** (1 day) to marvel at the world's clearest lake, where visibility stretches 80m, though it's only 7m deep. Its Maori name, *Rotomairewhenua*, means "the land of peaceful waters" and the sacred waters were once used to cleanse the dead.

The **DoC huts** (adult $15, child $7.50, child under 10 free) on the circuit must be booked in advance.

FOOD AND ACCOMMODATIONS

St. Arnaud services the park with a few places to eat and stay. The quaint **Clinker Café** (Beechnest Dr., 03/521-1040, www.clinkercafe.co.nz, 9am-4pm Thurs.-Mon.) is set in a modern chalet that is scented with the smell of freshly baked loaves. Hearty egg, bean, and bacon breakfasts are later replaced by a lunch menu of pizza, beef bourguignon, and meaty sandwiches.

The proudly family-run **Alpine Lodge** (75 Main Rd., 03/521-1869, www.alpinelodge.co.nz, July-May, dorm $35, $75-275 s or d) has rooms for all budgets. Backpackers have their own building with a shared bathroom and a spacious open communal kitchen and lounge area. Private en-suite rooms are housed in attractive motel lodges and have hot-drink facilities and mountain views; some rooms come with spas. The on-site bar and restaurant is open to the public and mountain bikes are available for rent.

Nelson Lakes Motel (Main Rd., 03/521-1887, www.nelsonlakes.co.nz) offers three levels of accommodations. The basic backpacker lodge (dorm $32, $75 s or d) has a cozy log fire in the communal lounge and a fully stocked communal kitchen. The fully self-contained motel rooms ($135-155) come with Sky TV, toiletries, and tea and coffee. The two-bedroom family cottages ($145-155) have TVs, separate dining areas, and full kitchens. Free Wi-Fi is available.

Tophouse (68 Tophouse Rd., 03/521-1269, www.tophouse.kiwi, $120 s, $135-150 d), 9km northeast of St. Arnaud, is a supremely romantic lodging, positioned in a historic white stone inn that looks shipped straight from rural Victorian England. Rooms are warm, and cozily old-fashioned with antique furniture and floral furnishings; none are en-suite. There is a shared TV lounge and Wi-Fi is free throughout. Fully self-contained stand-alone cottages come with TVs and mountain views. The on-site café serves Devonshire teas and coffee (noon-5pm Sat.-Sun.) and there's a tiny bar adjacent.

Positioned on the banks of Lake Rotoiti, scenic DoC campsite **Kerr Bay** (adult $18, child $9, child under 5 free summer, adult $8, child $4, children under 5 free winter) has tap water, toilets, cooking facilities, a barbecue, and picnic tables, and coin-operated showers ($1) and laundry ($2) in summer. Powered sites ($11-21) are available.

Transportation and Services

Nelson Lakes National Park is 90km (1.5 hours) south of Nelson. The gateway town of St. Arnaud is 88km (1 hour 15 minutes) southwest of Nelson via State Highways 6 and 63.

SHUTTLES AND TAXIS

Nelson Lakes Shuttles (67 Seaton Valley Rd., Upper Moutere, 03/540-2042, www.nelsonlakesshuttles.co.nz) operates a private bus service that connects St. Arnaud to trailheads throughout Marlborough and Nelson, as well as to Karamea at the end of the Heaphy Track and as far south as Christchurch.

For scenic cruises or water taxis to trailheads, contact **Rotoiti Water Taxis** (021/702-278, www.rotoitiwatertaxis.co.nz) or **Lake Rotoroa Water Taxi** (53 Porika Rd., 03/523-9199, www.lakerotoroawatertaxi.co.nz).

SERVICES

The **DoC Visitor Information Centre** (View Rd., St Arnaud., 03/521-1806, www.doc.govt.nz, 8am-5pm daily summer, 8am-4:30pm daily winter), near Lake Roitoti, has the latest weather and track conditions in Nelson Lakes National Park, and can help with transportation and accommodations. Hut and campsite tickets are sold here.

For gas or basic backcountry supplies, head to the **St. Arnaud Village Store** (74 Main Rd., 03/521-1854, 8am-6pm daily), which also operates a small café that serves coffee and fast food.

MURCHISON

The former gold mining township of Murchison is a relaxing stop before the adrenalin-fueled Buller Gorge. It's also a leaping off point into Kahurangi National Park.

Sights

MURCHISON MUSEUM

Sprouting from a wooden Edwardian post office, the **Murchison Museum** (60 Fairfax St., 03/523-9392, 10am-4pm Mon.-Sat., donation) honors the deadly Murchison earthquake of 1929 with photographs and written accounts. Exhibits include vintage machinery from the local mining and farming industries.

DUST AND RUST

Dust and Rust (35 Fairfax St., 03/523-9300, www.dustandrust.nz, 10:30am-4:30pm Wed.-Mon., free) is a vintage store set in historic stables. The dusty shelves brim with a compelling collection of artifacts such as gramophones, typewriters, saddlery, sporting goods, and toys. Abandoned rusted trucks and machinery loiter outside.

NATURAL FLAMES

Natural Flames (34 Waller St., 03/970-0026, www.naturalflames.co.nz, 9:15am or 2pm days vary, adult $95, child $65) is an ever-burning flame that flicks through a beech forest floor, fueled by an underground reservoir of natural gas. Accessible only by a guided 4WD tour, guests cross private farmland for an hour-long walk to the natural phenomenon, where the flames are used to cook pancakes and brew tea. The four-hour tours require a minimum of two guests.

Food and Accommodations

Rivers Café (51 Fairfax St., 03/523-9009, 8:30am-9pm summer, 8:30am-4pm winter, $17-32) is a down-to-earth eatery with a flower-filled interior, wicker chairs, and a spacious outdoor seating area. Locally sourced ingredients are used to craft generously portioned burgers, lamb shank, and tabouli salad with shredded chicken.

You're in for a restful stay at **Mataki Motel** (34 Hotham St., 03/523-9088, www.mataki-motel.co.nz, $125-230). Comfortable en-suite units are surrounded by gardens and bush-clad ranges and come with patios, Sky TV, and free Wi-Fi. Some rooms have full cooking facilities and spa baths. There's a barbecue area and an outdoor swimming pool.

Transportation and Services

Murchison is 59km (45 minutes) west of St. Arnaud via State Highways 63 and 6. From Nelson, it's 124km (1 hour 40 minutes) southwest via State Highway 6. On the West Coast, Westport is 98km (1 hour 25 minutes) west.

Murchison is serviced by national bus operator **Intercity** (04/385-0520, www.intercity.co.nz). Regional bus operator **Explore Murchison** (34 Waller St., 03/970-0026, www.naturalflames.co.nz) operates shuttles throughout the region, including the national parks, hiking trailheads, and Buller Gorge Swingbridge.

The **Murchison Information Centre** (47 Waller St., 03/523-9350, www.visitmurchison.nz, 10am-4pm daily) offers advice on local tours, travel, and accommodations. There's an array of tourist information and an amiable staff at the museum.

★ BULLER GORGE

The dramatic Buller Gorge, New Zealand's "white-water capital" and home to the swirling blue-green waters of the Buller River, was a significant trade and transport route for Maori and early Europeans—especially during the gold rush. Various excursions offer a chance to take in the splendor of the gorge's 400-million-year-old exposed pink granite walls and ancient beech trees. One of the best and most convenient ways to explore is via the swing bridge.

Swingbridge Adventure and Heritage Park

The 110m Buller Gorge **Swingbridge Adventure and Heritage Park** (Hwy, 6, Upper Buller Gorge, Murchison, www.bullergorge.co.nz, 03/523-9809, 8am-7pm daily Oct.-Apr., 9am-5:30pm daily May-Sept., adult $10, child $5) has the longest swingbridge in New Zealand. The swingbridge runs 17m above the water with a handful of short nature walks through bird-filled forests and river viewpoints.

Also in the park, the **Cometline** (adult $30, child $15) is a zip-line that propels guests back across the gorge—either seated, in tandem, or horizontally like Superman. Other activities include gold panning (adult $12.50, child $10) and the **Buller Canyon Jet** (03/523- 9883, www.bullercanyonjet.co.nz, adult $105, child $60, 10am-4pm daily in summer), a V8 jetboat ride that reaches speeds of 85km/hour complete with 360-degree turns and slaloming between rocky outcrops.

Rafting

If paddle power is more your thing, tackle the churning Buller River with a four-hour excursion via **Ultimate Descents White Water Rafting** (38 Waller St., Murchison, 03/523-9899, www.rivers.co.nz, departs 9:30am and 1:30pm daily Oct.-Apr., $160). For those with more time, money, and experience, heli-rafting tours transport guests (camping equipment provided) in a helicopter to a white-water rafting launch point. Bookings are essential.

Getting There

The Buller Gorge is 14km west of Murchison along State Highway 6, about an hour's drive east of Westport and 140km southwest of Nelson.

Buller Gorge

Christchurch and Canterbury

Christchurch 349
Akaroa and the Banks Peninsula 364
Arthur's Pass National Park 367
Lake Tekapo and the McKenzie District ... 372
Aoraki/Mount Cook National Park 376
Timaru 380

Christchurch is South Island's cultural capital and largest hub. From galleries to gastropubs and gardens, there is much to enjoy.

Christchurch will be forever linked to one of the country's darkest hours: the 2011 earthquake that razed its wonderful architecture and killed 185 people. Though parts of the city still await restoration, its people are filled with the spirit of productive defiance.

The gnarly and volcanic Banks Peninsula juts from the foot of Christchurch. This ocean reserve is home to 80 percent of the country's marine biodiversity, best explored by kayak. Here the idyllic French port of Akaroa retains an air of 19th-century English quaintness, replete with Gallic street signs and first-class eateries.

From Christchurch, the tan tussock grasslands and pastel meadows of the Canterbury Plains sprawl across the central eastern region of South Island. An anomaly in a nation fabled for its foreboding scenery, this vast flatland area is not without its wild side. Craggy mountain vistas with a light dusting of snow hem just about every horizon of the landscape. Come winter, a bounty of ski fields line an alpine spine of peaks and slopes.

Encircled by the Southern Alps, Aoraki/Mount Cook National Park offers a wealth of natural wonders, among them Tasman Glacier, the nation's largest and longest, and one of the world's great bike rides—the Alps2Ocean Cycle Trail.

PLANNING YOUR TIME

Set aside at least **two days** to explore Christchurch and the Banks Peninsula, home to a tiny French hamlet and lovely walks. Aoraki/Mount Cook National Park can be visited on a day trip owing to an excellent network of short hikes with plenty of opportunity to marvel at New Zealand's mightiest peak. Stop for half a day at Tekapo to see the impossibly blue lake from the top of Mount John.

Previous: Akaroa Lighthouse; Christchurch Botanic Gardens. **Above:** Lake McGreggor Campsite.

Christchurch and Canterbury

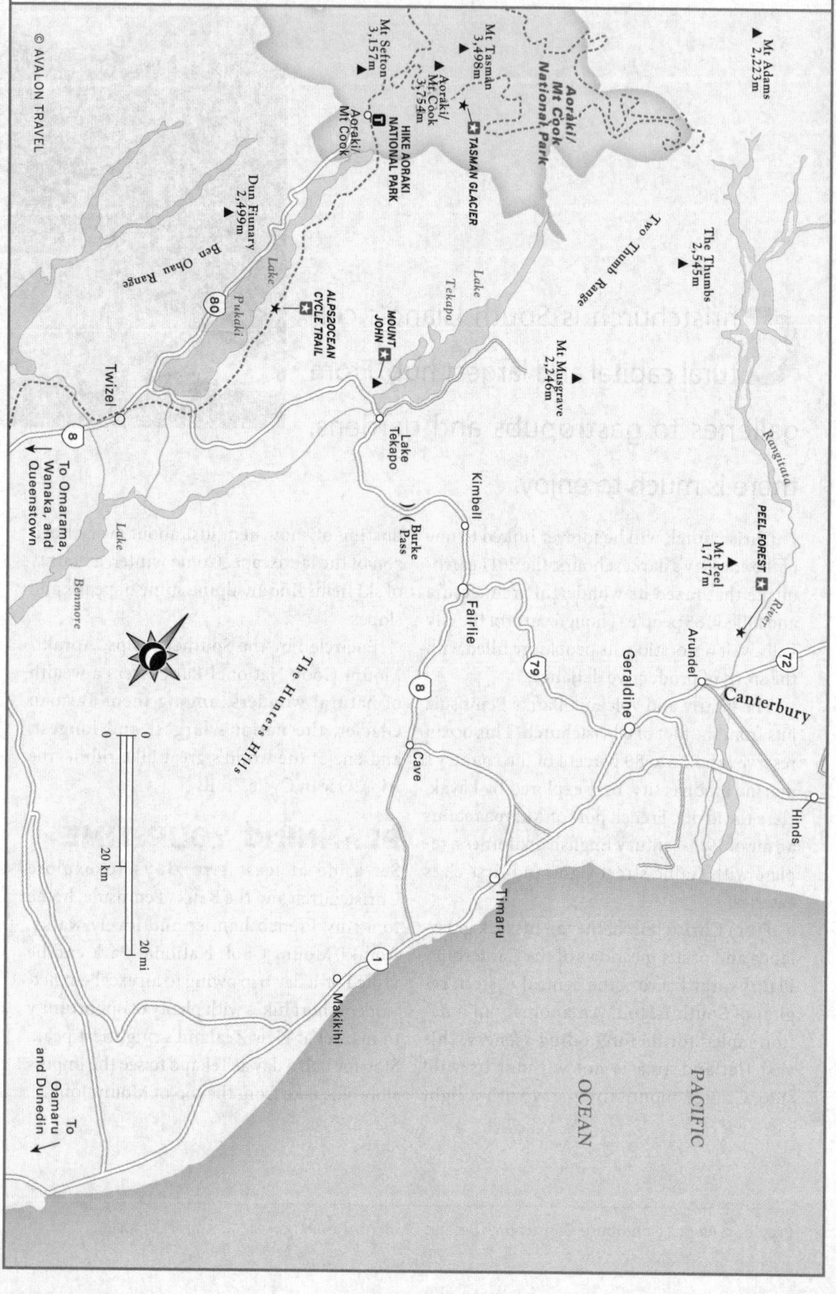

Mt Adams
2,223m
Aoraki/
Mt Cook
National Park
TASMAN GLACIER
Mt Tasman
3,498m
Aoraki/
Mt Cook
3,754m
Mt Sefton
3,157m
HIKE AORAKI
NATIONAL PARK
Aoraki/
Mt Cook
Two Thumb Range
The Thumbs
2,545m
Lake
Tekapo
MOUNT
JOHN
Mt Musgrave
2,246m
Dun Fiunary
2,499m
Ben Ohau Range
Lake
Pukaki
80
ALPS2OCEAN
CYCLE TRAIL
Lake
Tekapo
Twizel
8
To Omarama,
Wanaka, and
Queenstown
Lake
Benmore
Kimbell
Burke
Pass
Fairlie
79
8
Cave
The Hunters Hills
Rangitata
River
PEEL FOREST
Mt Peel
1,717m
Arundel
72
Canterbury
Geraldine
Hinds
Timaru
1
Makikihi
PACIFIC
OCEAN
To
Oamaru
and Dunedin
0 20 km
0 20 mi

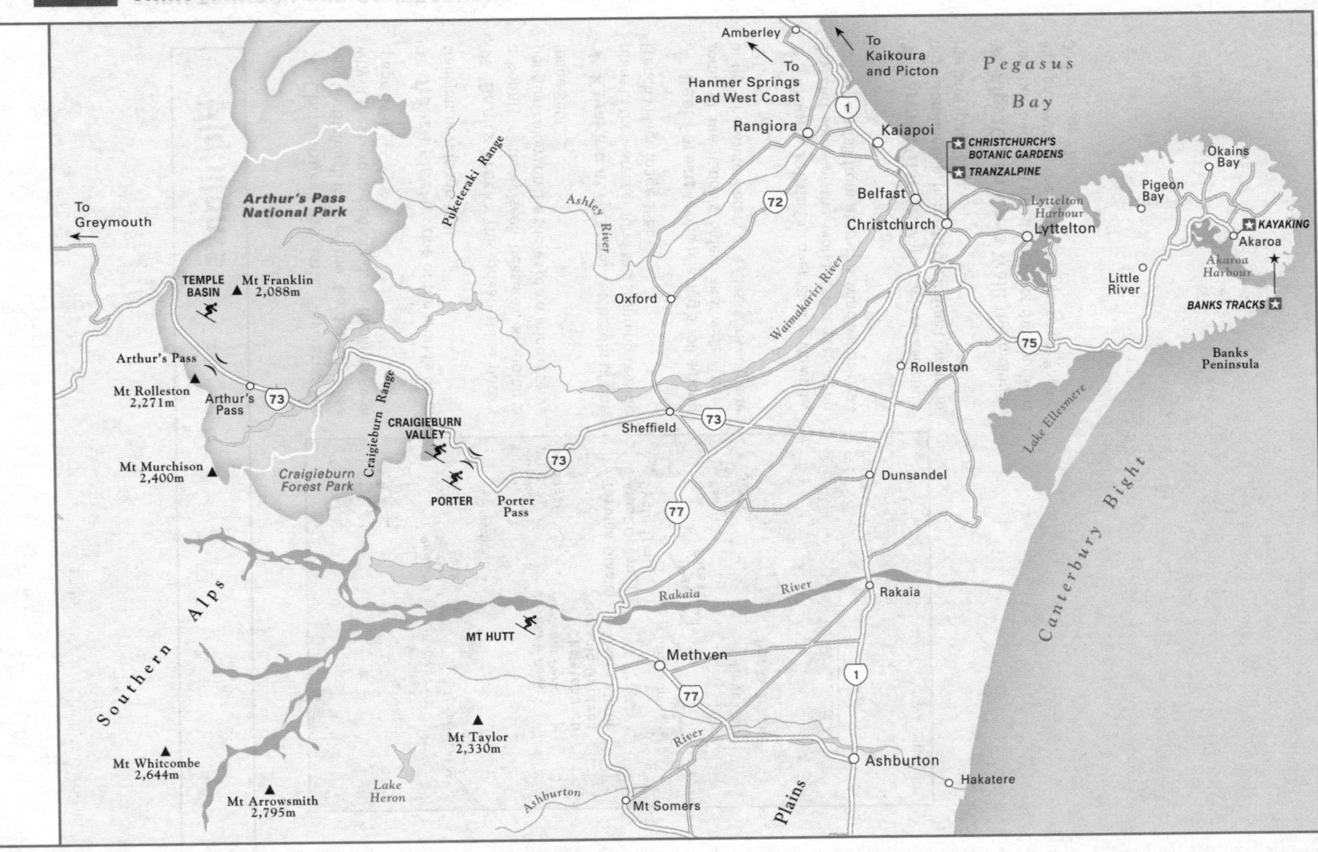
Amberley
To Hanmer Springs and West Coast
To Kaikoura and Picton
Pegasus Bay
Rangiora
Kaiapoi
CHRISTCHURCH'S BOTANIC GARDENS
TRANZALPINE
Okains Bay
Pigeon Bay
Belfast
Christchurch
Lyttelton Harbour
Lyttelton
KAYAKING
Akaroa
Akaroa Harbour
Little River
BANKS TRACKS
Banks Peninsula
Puketeraki Range
Ashley River
Arthur's Pass National Park
To Greymouth
TEMPLE BASIN
Mt Franklin 2,088m
Oxford
Waimakariri River
Arthur's Pass
Mt Rolleston 2,271m
Arthur's Pass
Craigieburn Range
CRAIGIEBURN VALLEY
Rolleston
Sheffield
Lake Ellesmere
Mt Murchison 2,400m
Craigieburn Forest Park
PORTER
Porter Pass
Dunsandel
Canterbury Bight
Southern Alps
Rakaia River
Rakaia
MT HUTT
Methven
Mt Taylor 2,330m
River
Ashburton
Hakatere
Mt Whitcombe 2,644m
Mt Arrowsmith 2,795m
Lake Heron
Ashburton
Mt Somers
Plains
1
72
73
75
77

Look for ★ to find recommended sights, activities, dining, and lodging.

Highlights

★ **Christchurch Botanic Gardens:** See why Christchurch is called the "Garden City." See why at these exquisite grounds on the River Avon (page 349).

★ ***TranzAlpine:*** It's one of the world's great train journeys (page 360).

★ **Banks Track:** This private hike passes a bounty of rarely seen treasures, including a penguin colony on the shores of a marine reserve (page 365).

★ **Kayaking at Akaroa:** Catch sight of dolphins in the waters around this stunning seaside French village (page 366).

★ **Peel Forest:** Take a relaxing stroll among some of the nation's oldest and widest trees or ride the white waters of a Class V river (page 371).

★ **Mount John:** Discover alpine views by day and some of the world's best stargazing come nightfall from atop this windswept peak (page 372).

★ **Tasman Glacier:** Marvel at New Zealand's highest mountain, home to the longest glacier in the land (page 377).

★ **Alps2Ocean Cycle Trail:** This multiday bike ride begins in the shadows of the Southern Alps and ends at the lapping waves of the Pacific Ocean (page 379).

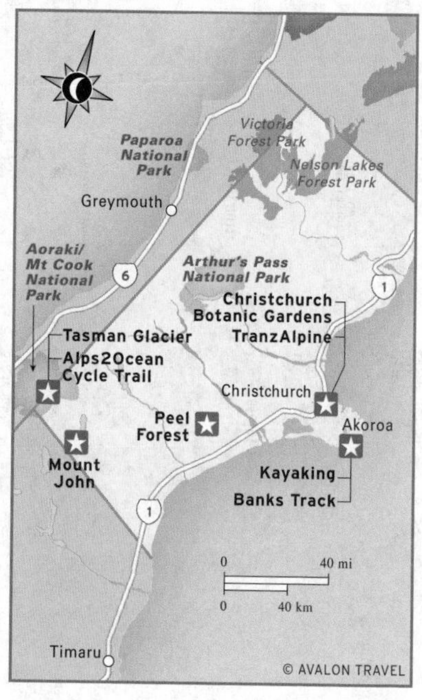

Christchurch

Devastating earthquakes in 2010 and 2011 destroyed much of Christchurch's city center, but its defiant population refuses to let it define their lives. Cathedral Square, one of the worst-hit spots, is adorned with moving messages from visitors from around the world whose words of hope outshine the tragedy. Though cranes may dominate the skyline, South Island's largest city remains a cultural hub awash with world-class museums, galleries, restaurants, and green spaces. It's the iconic "Garden City" of New Zealand.

SIGHTS

Canterbury Museum

The fabulously eclectic collection at the **Canterbury Museum** (Rolleston Ave., 03/356-5000, www.canterburymuseum.com, 9am-5:30pm daily Oct.-Mar., 9am-5pm daily Apr.-Sept., free) includes international artifacts like samurai swords and golden Buddhas alongside treasures such as wooden carvings, weaponry and tools, and Maori galleries with dioramas. Dinosaur fossils are complemented by well-planned displays of extinct and native birds. Christchurch's link to the South Pole (it's one of only a few gateway cities to Antarctica) is showcased by an exhibition that includes the vehicle driven by legendary mountaineer Sir Edmund Hillary. Guided **tours** (3:30pm-4:30pm Tues. and Thurs., free) depart from the information desk.

★ Christchurch Botanic Gardens

Behind the Canterbury Museum lies the **Christchurch Botanic Gardens** (Rolleston Ave., 03/941-8999, 7am-6:30pm daily, free) on the banks of the Avon River. Founded in 1863, the gardens host an array of vibrant seasonal blooms that include azalea and magnolia gardens hemmed in by giant oaks and silver birches. The highlight is the rose garden, alive with color from December onward. A handful of conservatories house exotic and tropical plants, including carnivorous specimens and more than 500 types of cacti.

Arts Centre

The **Arts Centre** (2 Worcester Blvd., 03/366-0989, www.artscentre.org.nz) sits opposite the Botanical Gardens and comprises a cluster of gothic revival buildings that formerly served the University of Canterbury. Today, the cultural hub hosts festivals, food stalls, boutiques, studios, and galleries.

Rutherford's Den (03/363-2836, 10am-5pm daily, adults $20, children $10, seniors $15, under age 5 free) honors the University's Nobel Prize-winning alumnus, Ernest Rutherford, the "father of nuclear physics." A reconstruction of the scientist's basement hideaway includes a lecture theater complete with original benches and state-of-the-art interactive exhibits. Footage of the man who first split the atom is beamed onto the walls and accompanied by recordings of his voice as you journey through the exhibits.

Christchurch Art Gallery

The **Christchurch Art Gallery** (Worcester Blvd. and Montreal St., 03/941-7300, www.christchurchartgallery.org.nz, 10am-5pm Thurs.-Tues., 10am-9pm Wed., free) is the South Island's leading art space. Inside the stunning undulating glass facade, a sweeping marble staircase links nine exhibition rooms home to visiting collections and permanent displays of classical and contemporary works. Peruse sketches, sculptures, and paintings from international and local minds such as pioneering Maori artist Dr. Buck Nin, the iconic Frances Hodgkins, and naturalist painter Julius Olsson, whose brooding oil on canvas, *Moonlight*, offers pause in the vast modern space.

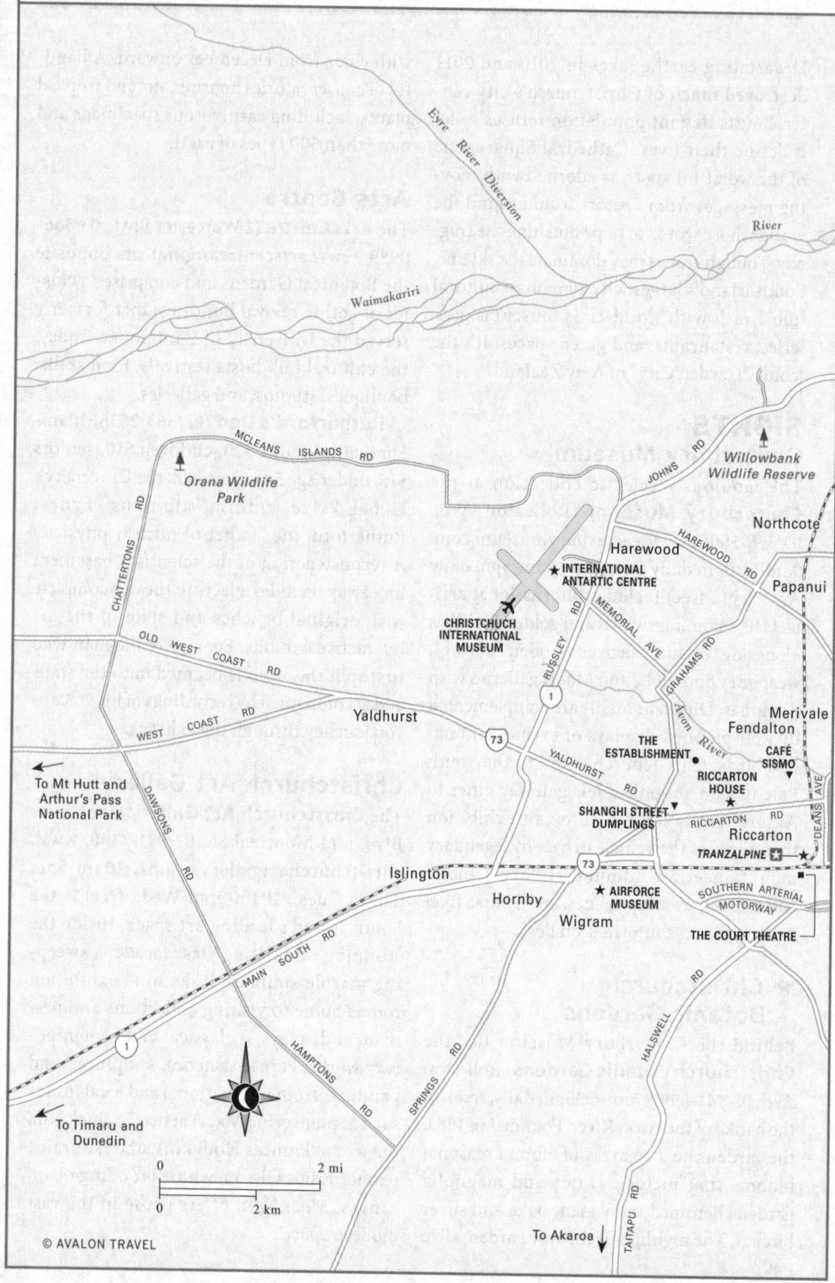
Christchurch
Eyre River Diversion
River
Waimakariri
MCLEANS ISLANDS RD
Orana Wildlife Park
CHATTERTONS RD
JOHNS RD
Willowbank Wildlife Reserve
Northcote
Harewood
HAREWOOD RD
INTERNATIONAL ANTARTIC CENTRE
Papanui
MEMORIAL AVE
CHRISTCHUCH INTERNATIONAL MUSEUM
RUSSLEY RD
GRAHAMS RD
OLD WEST COAST RD
WEST COAST RD
Yaldhurst
1
73
Merivale
Fendalton
Avon River
THE ESTABLISHMENT
CAFÉ SISMO
YALDHURST RD
RICCARTON HOUSE
To Mt Hutt and Arthur's Pass National Park
DAWSONS RD
SHANGHI STREET DUMPLINGS
RICCARTON RD
Riccarton
DEANS AVE
TRANZALPINE
Islington
73
Hornby
AIRFORCE MUSEUM
SOUTHERN ARTERIAL MOTORWAY
Wigram
THE COURT THEATRE
MAIN SOUTH RD
HALSWELL RD
1
HAMPTONS RD
SPRINGS RD
To Timaru and Dunedin
0
2 mi
0
2 km
To Akaroa
TAITAPU RD
© AVALON TRAVEL

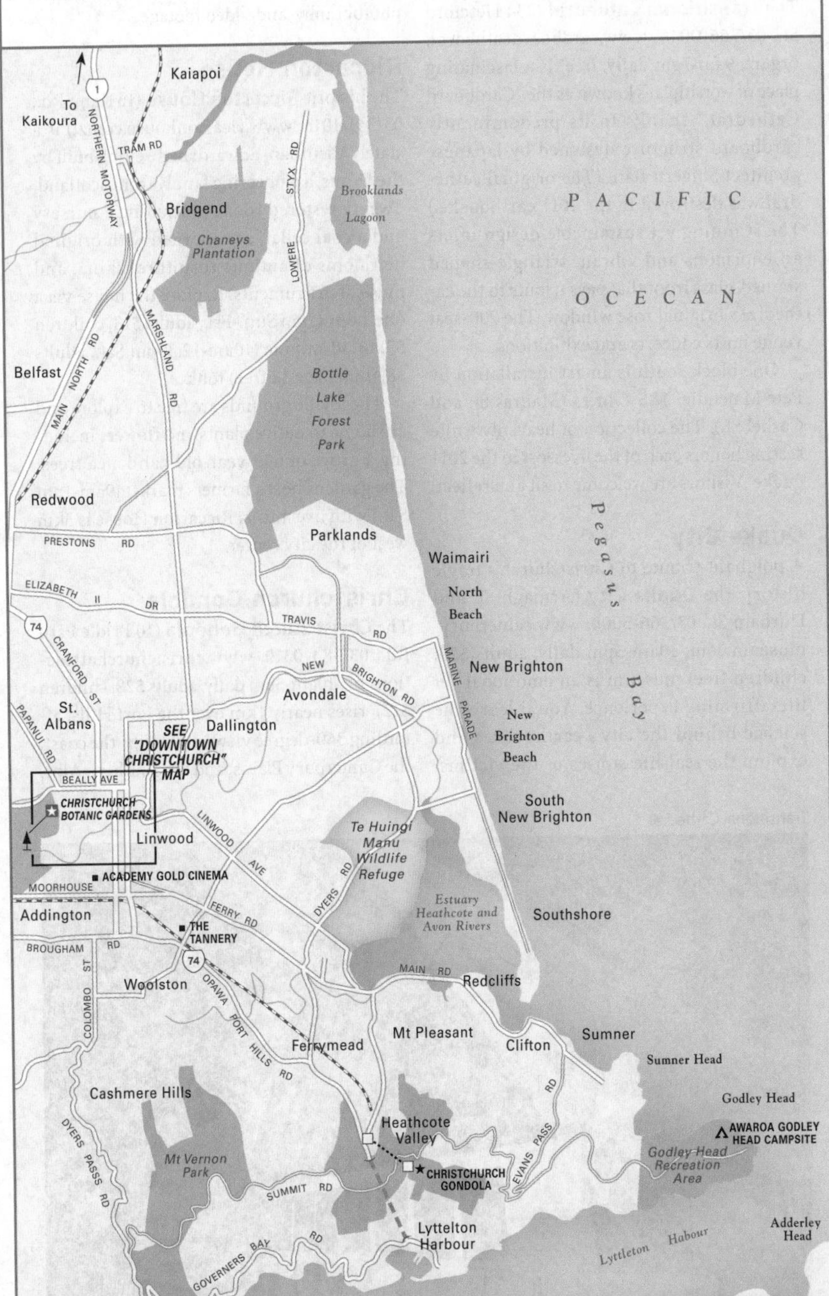
Kaiapoi
To Kaikoura
1
NORTHERN MOTORWAY
TRAM RD
STYX RD
Brooklands Lagoon
PACIFIC
OCEAN
Bridgend
Chaneys Plantation
LOWERE
MARSHLAND RD
MAIN NORTH RD
Belfast
Bottle Lake Forest Park
Redwood
PRESTONS RD
Parklands
Waimairi
North Beach
Pegasus Bay
ELIZABETH II DR
74
TRAVIS RD
CRANFORD ST
NEW BRIGHTON RD
MARINE PARADE
New Brighton
Avondale
PAPANUI RD
St. Albans
SEE "DOWNTOWN CHRISTCHURCH" MAP
Dallington
New Brighton Beach
BEALLY AVE
CHRISTCHURCH BOTANIC GARDENS
LINWOOD AVE
South New Brighton
Linwood
Te Huingi Manu Wildlife Refuge
DYERS RD
MOORHOUSE
ACADEMY GOLD CINEMA
Estuary Heathcote and Avon Rivers
Addington
FERRY RD
THE TANNERY
Southshore
BROUGHAM RD
74
MAIN RD
COLOMBO ST
Woolston
OPAWA
Redcliffs
PORT HILLS RD
Mt Pleasant
Sumner
Ferrymead
Clifton
Sumner Head
RD
Cashmere Hills
Godley Head
Heathcote Valley
AWAROA GODLEY HEAD CAMPSITE
EVANS PASS
DYERS PASS RD
Mt Vernon Park
CHRISTCHURCH GONDOLA
Godley Head Recreation Area
SUMMIT RD
Lyttelton Harbour
Adderley Head
Lyttleton Habour
GOVERNERS BAY RD

Transitional Cathedral

The **Transitional Cathedral** (234 Hereford St., 03/366-0046, www.cardboardcathedral.org.nz, 9am-7pm daily, free) is a fascinating place of worship. It's known as the "Cardboard Cathedral," thanks to its predominantly cardboard structure designed by Japanese architect Shigeru Ban. (The original cathedral was destroyed in the 2011 earthquake.) The stunning yet sustainable design offers an enormous and vibrant triangle-shaped stained-glass front that pays tribute to the cathedral's original rose window. The 700-seat venue hosts concerts and exhibitions.

One block south is an art installation by Pete Majendie, ***185 Chairs*** (Madras St. and Cashel St.). The collection of heavenly white seating honors each of the lives lost in the 2011 quake. Visitors are welcome to sit and reflect.

Quake City

A poignant tribute to Christchurch's tragic history, the **Quake City** (Armagh St. and Durham St., 03/366-5000, www.canterburymuseum.com, 10am-5pm daily, adults $20, children free) museum is an emotional yet life-affirming experience. You'll learn the science behind the city's earthquakes and explore the real-life stories of the victims, survivors, and rescuers by way of artifacts, photography, and video footage.

Riccarton House

The historic **Riccarton House** (16 Kahu Rd., 03/341-1018, www.ricartonhouse.co.nz,) is a stately Victorian-Edwardian dwelling built by the Deans, a pioneering family from Scotland. Twenty restored rooms, including a nursery and a coal cellar, are adorned with original heirlooms of antique furniture, china, and musical instruments. Explore the house via a one-hour (2pm Sun.-Fri., adults $18, children $5) or 30-minute (10am-12:30pm Sat., adults $8, under age 12 free) tour.

The idyllic grounds are free to explore and are home to native plants and flowers including a grove of 600-year-old kahikatea trees. The gardens host a farmers market (9am-1pm Sat.) with live music. Riccarton House is 3km west of the city center.

Christchurch Gondola

The **Christchurch Gondola** (10 Bridle Path Rd., 03/384-0310, www.christchurchattractions.nz, 10am-5pm daily, adults $28, children $12), rises nearly 1km over the Port Hills, affording 360-degree views of the city, the coast, the Canterbury Plains, and the Southern Alps.

Transitional Cathedral

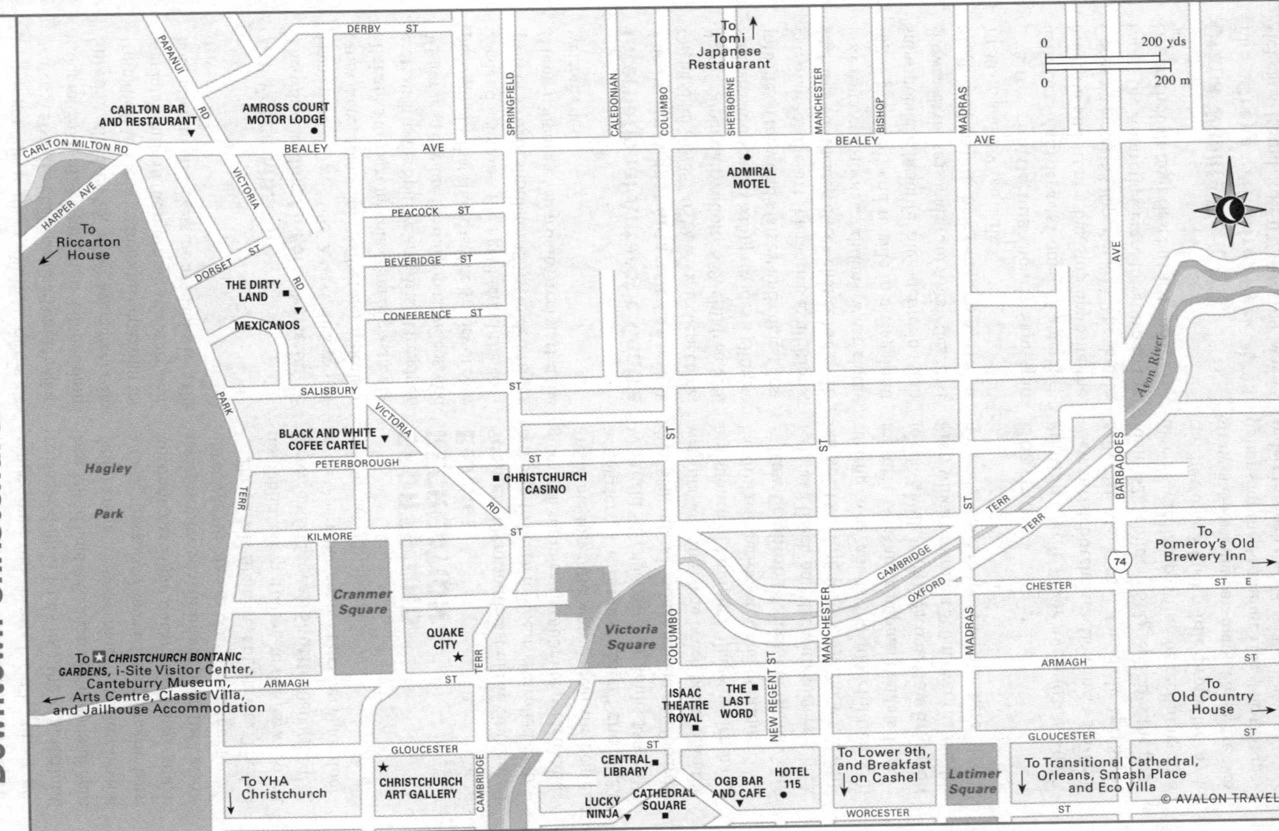
Downtown Christchurch
DERBY ST
PAPANUI RD
To Tomi Japanese Restaurant
0 200 yds
0 200 m
SPRINGFIELD
CALEDONIAN
COLUMBO
SHERBORNE
MANCHESTER
BISHOP
MADRAS
CARLTON BAR AND RESTAURANT
AMROSS COURT MOTOR LODGE
CARLTON MILTON RD
BEALEY AVE
ADMIRAL MOTEL
HARPER AVE
To Riccarton House
VICTORIA RD
PEACOCK ST
BEVERIDGE ST
CONFERENCE ST
DORSET ST
THE DIRTY LAND
MEXICANOS
SALISBURY ST
PARK TERR
VICTORIA RD
BLACK AND WHITE COFEE CARTEL
PETERBOROUGH ST
CHRISTCHURCH CASINO
Hagley Park
KILMORE ST
Avon River
BARBADOES
TERR
To Pomeroy's Old Brewery Inn
74
CAMBRIDGE
OXFORD
CHESTER ST E
Cranmer Square
QUAKE CITY
Victoria Square
COLUMBO
MANCHESTER
MADRAS
ARMAGH ST
To CHRISTCHURCH BONTANIC GARDENS, i-Site Visitor Center, Canteburry Museum, Arts Centre, Classic Villa, and Jailhouse Accommodation
ISAAC THEATRE ROYAL
THE LAST WORD
NEW REGENT ST
To Old Country House
GLOUCESTER ST
CENTRAL LIBRARY
HOTEL 115
To Lower 9th, and Breakfast on Cashel
Latimer Square
To Transitional Cathedral, Orleans, Smash Place and Eco Villa
To YHA Christchurch
CHRISTCHURCH ART GALLERY
CAMBRIDGE
CATHEDRAL SQUARE
OGB BAR AND CAFE
LUCKY NINJA
WORCESTER ST
© AVALON TRAVEL

Numerous walking tracks await at the summit of Mount Cavendish.

The gondola is 10km southeast of the city center. A **shuttle** (9:30am, 10:30am, 11:30am, 1:00pm, 2:00pm, 3:00pm, and 4:00pm daily, $10 adult, children $5, under age 5 free) runs from the Canterbury Museum, departing the gondola hourly in the morning and every half-hour after noon. Tickets are available from the driver.

Air Force Museum

The world-leading **Air Force Museum** (45 Harvard Ave., 03/343-9532, www.airforcemuseum.co.nz, 10am-5pm daily, free) appeals to all thanks to a strong collection of classic aircraft such as the Spitfire and Bristol freighter. Visitors can explore the dioramas, videos, and photography that showcase the history of New Zealand aviation—then get behind the controls of a flight simulator ($5). Guided **tours** (11am, 1:30pm and 3pm daily, free) start at the welcome desk.

International Antarctic Centre

The **International Antarctic Centre** (38 Orchard Rd., 03/357-0519, www.iceberg.co.nz, 9am-5:30pm daily, adults $59, children $29, students and seniors $45) provides a glimpse into life on the world's largest and coldest desert. State-of-the-art interactive exhibitions, such as a 4-D theater, offer a chance to experience Antarctic storm conditions (warm clothing is provided) and to ride in a Hagglund snowmobile. A beautiful high-definition film showcases the seasonal arc of Antarctica. Best of all, resident little blue penguins are fed at 10:30am and 3:30pm daily.

A free **shuttle bus** (hourly 9am-4pm daily Oct.-Mar.) departs from the Canterbury Museum and from a bus stop opposite the Cotswold Hotel (88 Papanui Rd.). The shuttle leaves the Antarctic Centre to return to the city on the half-hour (last bus at 4:30pm).

Orana Wildlife Park

The **Orana Wildlife Park** (793 McLeans Island Rd., 03/359-7109, www.oranawildlifepark.co.nz, 10am-5pm daily, adults $35.50) is New Zealand's only open-range zoo. Exotic beasts include rhinos, gorillas, and local icons like the kea, tuatara, and kiwi. Hand feed a giraffe (noon and 3pm daily) and see its enormous tongue, or book a first-come, first-served spot on the Lion Encounter (2:30pm daily, $45), where you're safely ensconced within a cage on the back of a truck as the big cats clamber on top.

The park is 20km west of the city. There is no public transportation to the park. To get there, contact **Steve's Shuttle** (0800/101-021, jaycee@paradise.net.nz, rates vary) for door-to-door service.

SPORTS AND RECREATION

Beaches

Sumner (10km southeast of the city center) is the go-to beach for locals. Patrolled by lifeguards in summer, the 400m of golden sands are home to gentle waves ideal for beginner surfers. The **Sumner Surf School** (32 Whitfield St., 0800/807-873, adults $80, children $30) offers lessons and rents surfboards, wetsuits, and fins. The beach backs onto the hip suburb of Sumner Village, which has a handful of eateries, bars, and boutiques.

New Brighton (8km east of the city center) has a beach popular with surfers. Check out **Soul Surfing** (020/453-7766, www.soulsurfing.co.nz, adults $60-100, children $30) for surf lessons and equipment rentals. Be sure to take a walk along the iconic **New Brighton Pier**, which protrudes 300m over the sea. It's not uncommon to spot dolphins here.

Boating

Punting on the River Avon (03/366-0337, www.christchurchattractions.nz, 9am-6pm daily Oct.-Mar., 10am-4pm daily Apr.-Sept., adults $28, children $12) replicates the popular Edwardian pastime of reclining on a flat-bottomed boat while propelled by a straw-hat-wearing oarsman. There are two options for the 30-minute ride. The first meanders through the classic English gardens of the **Mona Vale Estate** (40 Mona Vale Ave., 03/341-7450, www.monavale.nz, Sat.-Sun.). The second, and most popular, choice takes in the Christchurch Botanic Gardens and departs from the historic Antigua Boat Sheds (2 Cambridge Terrace, 03/366-5885, www.boatsheds.co.nz).

The charming **Antigua Boat Sheds** (2 Cambridge Terrace, 03/366-5885, www.boatsheds.co.nz, $12-35 per hour) have been servicing the city since 1882. You can rent kayaks, paddle boats, row boats, and Canadian canoes for exploring the River Avon, as well as bicycles ($10 per hour, $30 all day). The on-site Boat Shed Café serves light and tasty meals.

ENTERTAINMENT AND EVENTS

Nightlife

One of Christchurch's coolest bars, **Smash Palace** (172 High St., 03/366-5369, www.thesmashpalace.co.nz, 3pm-close Mon.-Thurs., noon-close Fri.-Sat., noon-8pm Sun.) serves booze and bar snacks from the side of an old bus overlooking a sun-trapped courtyard. At night, the space is illuminated by fairy lights.

Discover an array of house brews and New Zealand craft beers at **Pomeroy's Old Brewery Inn** (292 Kilmore St., 03/365-1523, www.pomspub.co.nz, 3pm-close Tues.-Thurs., noon-close Fri.-Sun.). Their award-winning stouts, pale ales, and pilsners are served in a traditional English pub setting with polished brass pumps, brick walls, and ingredients scrawled across a blackboard.

In the heart of Christchurch, historic New Regent Street is known as "New Zealand's most beautiful street," lauded for its concentration of eateries, bars, and boutiques positioned in pastel-colored Spanish Mission-style buildings. Here rests **The Last Word** (31 New Regent St., 022/094-7445, www.lastword.co.nz, 4pm-close Mon.-Wed., 4pm-close Thurs.-Fri., 2pm-2am Sat.), famed for its extensive whiskey and cocktail menu. The fashionable, intimate setting is decorated with dark-green walls, varnished wood, and potted plants, setting the stage for libations and snacks.

Victoria Street is a social focal point in the city center. **The Dirty Land** (131 Victoria St., 03/365-5340, www.thedirtyland.co.nz, 4pm-3am daily) is one of its hipper establishments. This late-night drinking den verges on the louche, with booth sofa seating, wrought-iron chandeliers, edgy artwork, and red-velvet curtains. Guests make use of the heated outdoor area as they sample delicious cocktails

Punting on the River Avon

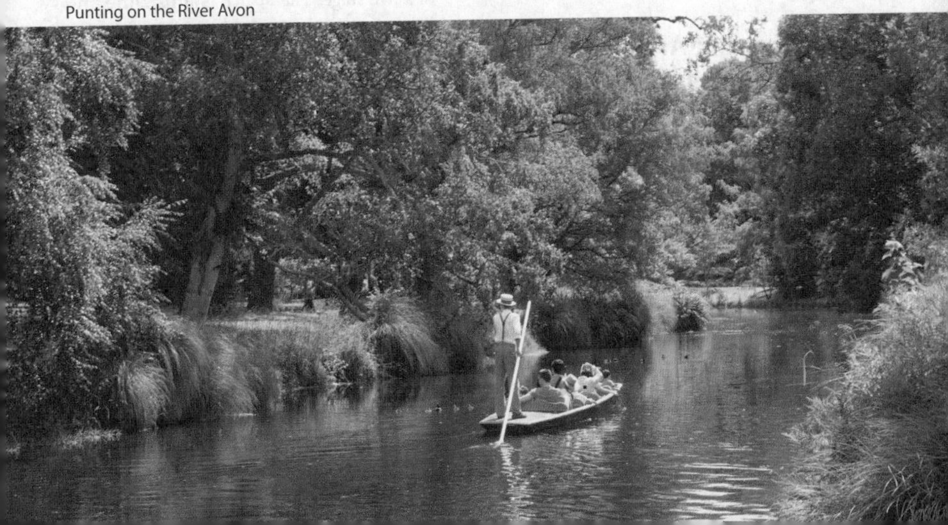

Best Food

★ **OGB Bar and Café:** Styled after a speakeasy, this classy eatery in Christchurch serves hearty high-end fare in a historic stone building (page 358).

★ **Roots Restaurant:** Enjoy seasonal fine-dining dishes on slabs of slate and wood in the port town of Lyttelton (page 362).

★ **The Little Bistro:** This intimate French restaurant delivers sophisticated Gallic delights in the seaside village of Akaroa (page 366).

★ **Kohan Restaurant:** Sample locally farmed freshwater salmon at this humble Japanese restaurant in Tekapo (page 373).

or a selection of local and imported beers. Bar snacks are prepared in the adjoining Mexican restaurant.

Slots, blackjack, and baccarat await at **Christchurch Casino** (30 Victoria St., 03/365-9999, www.christchurchcasino.nz, 11am-3am Mon.-Thurs., 11am-3am Fri.), where 36 table games and 500 machines are offered along with a handful of bars and eateries. Dress smartly.

The **Blue Smoke** (03/389-5544, www.bluesmoke.co.nz, hours vary) is a live-music venue and craft beer bar with a distinctly old-school dancehall vibe. Free folk gigs are held 3pm-close Sunday, with other concerts held regularly.

Performing Arts

The **Isaac Theatre Royal** (145 Gloucester St., 03/366-6326, www.isaactheatreroyal.co.nz) is an ornately furnished early-1900s auditorium. Diverse shows include plays, concerts, and comedy performances.

The city's leading performing arts venue is the **Court Theatre** (Bernard St., 03/963-0870, www.courttheatre.org.nz), in the suburb of Addington. It hosts an eclectic mix of shows—from fairy tales to horrors—as well as the weekly "Scared Scriptless" (10:15pm Fri.-Sat., $16-20), an improvised show that feeds off suggestions from the audience.

Academy Gold Cinema (The Colombo, 22/236 Colombo St., 03/377-9911, www.artfilms.co.nz) is a wonderful Old World picture house with art deco decor. Enjoy art-house movies across three screens from the comfort of luxurious armchairs.

Festivals and Events

The 10-day **World Buskers Festival** (Arts Centre, www.worldbuskersfestival.com, Jan.) showcases Kiwi and international artists such as street performers, comedians, dancers, and musicians. With a wonderful backdrop of the Port Hills, the **Nostalgia Festival** (Ferrymead Heritage Park, www.nostalgiafestival.co.nz, Mar.) features local food, drink, and music stalls while serving treats to the beat of a live stage. The **South Island Wine and Food Festival** (Hagley Park, www.winefestival.co.nz, Dec.) offers an array of stalls honoring great New Zealand recipes and tipples.

FOOD

Cafés

There's an industrial Victorian feel to **Black and White Coffee Cartel** (83 Victoria St., 027/511-7272, www.blackandwhitecoffee.co.nz, 7am-5pm Mon.-Fri., 8am-5pm Sat.-Sun.), where fashionable staff don old-school canvas aprons while tending to contraptions and beakers lifted from a science lab. Coffee is the main attraction (they roast their own beans), backed by an array of baked goods (scones or lemon cakes) and bagels as well as and salmon and spinach tarts.

Best Accommodations

★ **Jailhouse Accommodation:** Spend a night behind bars at this quirky hostel and former prison (page 358).

★ **Classic Villa:** Mediterranean hospitality awaits at this boutique B&B in the heart of Christchurch (page 359).

★ **Onuka Farm Hostel:** Peaceful budget lodgings are surrounded by native bush with incredible sea views from the Banks Peninsula (page 367).

★ **Wilderness Lodge:** Luxury eco-lodgings on this sprawling working sheep farm in Arthur's Pass National Park are replete with log fires, alpine views, and gourmet meals (page 370).

★ **YHA Mount Cook:** There aren't too many hostels that boast mountain views and a sauna; this one in Aoraki/Mount Cook National Park is a gem (page 379).

Sample homemade Danish pastries, French toast, and pancakes at **Café Sismo** (35 Riccarton Rd., 03/348-1984, 7am-3pm Mon.-Fri., 8am-3pm Sat.-Sun.), an intimate European-inspired café that serves lovingly crafted coffee in hand-painted crockery with plenty of smiles.

American

Carnivorous cravings are ably sated at **Carlton Bar and Restaurant** (1 Papanui Rd., 03/355-9543, www.carltonbar.co.nz, 11am-2am Sun.-Wed., 11am-2am Thurs.-Sat., $25-49), a saloon-like establishment with booth seating, mounted animal heads on the wall, and a meat-heavy menu of lamb racks, ribs, chicken, and a choice of six different steaks.

Christchurch's best Latin eatery is **Mexicanos** (131 Victoria St., 03/365-5330, www.mexicanos.co.nz, 11:30am-close Mon.-Fri., 10:30am-close Sat.-Sun., $8-28). It boasts a sprawling menu of tacos, tapas, and dishes such as braised beef rib *barbacoa*. The cavernous industrial setting is furnished with long timber tables, potted cacti, and vibrant Day of the Dead art.

Buzzing with character, **Orleans** (89 Lichfield St., 03/365-7312, www.orleans.co.nz, noon-close daily, $12-38) uses materials salvaged from a destroyed city villa. Its dark woods contrast against the stained-glass windows. Guests enjoy a menu of Southern favorites such as fried chicken, barbecue ribs, and duck wings. Sit at high tables on the balcony or in the cocktail bar, and enjoy the beat of live rhythm and blues.

Asian

Exquisitely presented dishes are served by attentive staff at **Tomi Japanese Restaurant** (76 Edgeware Mall, 03/377-8028, www.tomi.co.nz, 11:30am-2pm and 5pm-close Tues.-Sat., 5:30pm-close Sun., $20-40). Menu highlights include sizzling Japanese fish and lamb hot plates, flame-grilled scallops, and deluxe sashimi. Enjoy samples from the extensive sake list or BYO wine.

For an authentic taste of China, **Shanghai Street Dumplings** (Wairmairi Rd. and Riccarton Rd., 03/377-9223, www.shanghaistreetdumplings.co.nz, 11:30am-3:30pm and 5pm-10pm daily, $11-26) offers a well-priced menu featuring noodles, wonton soup, and pork buns. The superb dumplings contain free-range pork or chicken, prawns, or vegetables and are handmade using secret family recipes.

European

One of South Island's hippest eateries, ★ **OGB Bar and Café** (28 Cathedral Squ., 03/377-4336, www.ogb.co.nz, 6:30am-1am daily, $11-34) is styled after a speakeasy: it's set in a historic high-ceilinged stone building and adorned in dark polished wood. (Even the staff handsomely dress like it's the 1930s.) Order fresh fruit, cereal, or eggs and bacon for breakfast, or opt for a lunch of sticky ribs and burgers with hand-cut fries. The seasonal dinner menu includes market fish and aged rib-eye steak and is usually accompanied by live music.

The **Curator's House** (7 Rolleston Ave., 03/379-2252, www.curatorshouse.co.nz, 11am-11pm daily, $37-45) is set in a century-old building that springs from the corner of the Botanic Gardens overlooking the Avon River. Spanish-inspired fare includes tapas, Catalan slow-cooked chicken, and the house specialty, paella, prepared with herbs and vegetables grown in the on-site garden.

The **Tramway Restaurant** (Cathedral Junction, 03/366-7830, www.christchurchattractions.nz, $109 pp for 2) offers an elegant dining experience in a colonial tram. The four-course menu includes apple cider-marinated pork, slow-roasted lamb, and local salmon. The tram takes in the historic city sights like the museum, parks, and New Regent Street during its 2.5-hour tour.

Quick Eats

Traditional fast food cooked with lashings of Eastern panache await at **Lucky Ninja** (Cathedral Square, 021/832-1129, 10am-3pm Sat.-Thurs., 10am-7pm Fri., $10), a food truck serving spring rolls, fries, and gourmet burgers such as teriyaki beef or chicken.

You can build your own burger at **Lower 9th** (84 Lichfield Terrace, 03/365-7312, www.lower9th.co.nz, noon-close daily, $8-12), a fashionably grungy yet intimate diner with bare brick walls and an alcohol license.

ACCOMMODATIONS

Under $100

Old Country House (437 Gloucester St., 03/381-5504, www.oldcountryhousenz.com, dorm $36-38, $97-120 s, $92-122 d) is an über-chill and centrally heated hostel housed in a timber villa. Wood paneling lends a cozy air to the bedrooms; some have en suite baths. There's free unlimited Wi-Fi, a hot tub, and a sauna. It's a few kilometers east of the city center.

Centrally located **YHA Christchurch** (36 Hereford St., 03/379-9536, www.yha.co.nz, dorm $40-48, $80 s, $89-126 d) is a modern hostel set in a century-old villa. Private rooms have flat-screen TVs and baths; dorms are basic but well-kept and comfortable. Amenities include guest lounges with free movies, a fully equipped kitchen, laundry, and free Wi-Fi.

Find Kiwi quirkiness at its most hospitable at ★ **Jailhouse Accommodation** (338 Lincoln Rd., 03/982-7777, www.jail.co.nz, dorm $35-45, $90 s or d), a backpacker hostel housed within a former prison that was built in 1874. Immaculate, if cramped, rooms (well, they *are* former cells) are countered by the comfiest of beds, vibrant white walls, and hardwood floors. Spacious communal areas are well-lit and include a stocked kitchen, tea, barbecue, free unlimited Wi-Fi, Netflix, and a pool table.

Studio, one-, and two-bedroom units at **Admiral Motel** (168 Bealey Ave., 03/379-3554, www.admiralmotel.co.nz, $115-190 s or d) are equipped with private baths, fridges, satellite TV, free Wi-Fi, and cooking facilities and include complimentary tea, coffee, and hot chocolate. The value lodgings are individually heated and come with private patios or balconies. It's a short stroll to the city center, with a free shuttle to the railway station.

Charming **Eco Villa** (251 Hereford St., 03/595-1364, www.ecovilla.co.nz, $115-245 s or d) houses eight unique boutique rooms brimming with character; each is named after a tree (the oak, the cedar, the rimu, etc.). The environmentally friendly lodge is furnished with reclaimed materials such as the stunning centerpiece timber headboards in each room. Guests make use of free bikes, outdoor baths, a fully loaded kitchen, and an edible garden. Wi-Fi is free and unlimited. Bath facilities are shared for some rooms.

$100-200

Space-age **BreakFree on Cashel** (165 Cashel St., 03/360-1064, www.breakfreeoncashel.nz, $126-320 s or d) is one of the city's largest hotels, and one of its most interesting. Rooms come equipped with hot-drink facilities, fridges, private showers, and flat-screen TVs with Sky TV, and in-house movies. Vibrant colors and clever lighting compensate for the fact that some of the less expensive rooms have no windows. (Housed in a former high-rise office block, rooms with windows come with terrific views.)

Airy, well-appointed rooms await at well-priced **Amross Court Motor Lodge** (61 Bealey Ave., 03/377-1554, www.amross.co.nz, $160-255 s or d), located at the north border of the city center. Choose from modern studios (some with spa baths) or one- or two-bedroom units with private baths, cooking facilities, fridges, electric blankets, and TVs.

Beguiling **Hotel 115** (115 Worcester St., 03/928-2434, www.hotel115.co.nz, $140-310 s or d) rests in a heritage building that straddles a working tramline in the heart of Christchurch. Modern, richly colored en suite rooms feature large arched windows, a flat-screen TV, a minibar, an iPhone dock, tea- and coffee-making facilities, a blow-dryer, and all the Wi-Fi you can use.

Over $300

Pink exterior walls mean you can't miss ★ **Classic Villa** (17 Worcester Blvd., 03/377-7905, www.theclassicvilla.co.nz, $289-569 s or d), European-themed lodgings in a late Victorian townhouse opposite the Arts Centre. Inside, eight rooms with en suite baths boast high ceilings, polished hardwood floors, luxurious beds, Sky TV, and free Wi-Fi and toiletries. A luxurious lounge area replete with leather couches and a large fire invites relaxation. It's worth staying for breakfast alone—a Mediterranean medley of breads, cold meats, cheeses, fruit, and fish.

Located near Riccarton, **The Establishment** (50 Clyde Rd., 0800/378-225-474, www.theestablishment.net.nz, $525 s or d) is an exquisite B&B set in a modernist home on immaculate grounds. Three plushly carpeted suites sport Sky TV, linen and wool bedding, electric blankets, and capsule coffee makers. There's complimentary snacks and refreshments, plus free Wi-Fi.

Camping and Holiday Parks

Awaroa Godley Head Campsite (adults $13, children $6.50) is situated on a windswept cliff atop a former World War II battery site. Basic amenities include flush toilets and drinking water, but no electricity. The ocean views over Lyttelton Harbour, as well as walking and biking tracks and the nearby beach, make up for it. Bookings are through the **DoC Visitor Centre** (28 Worcester Blvd., 03/379-4082, www.doc.govt.nz). The campsite is off Summit Road, 20km southeast of Christchurch.

The **Top 10 Holiday Park** (39 Meadow St., 03/352-9176, www.top10.co.nz, $40) offers campers and motorhomes a centrally located base with shared bath facilities, a communal kitchen, an indoor pool, a hot tub, and free Wi-Fi.

TRANSPORTATION AND SERVICES

Getting There

AIR

Christchurch Airport (CHC, Durey Rd., 03/353-7777, www.christchurchairport.co.nz) is New Zealand's second-largest airport, 10km northwest of the city and offering international flights along with domestic routes to the North and South Island via **Air New Zealand** (www.airnewzealand.co.nz) and **Jetstar** (Wellington and Auckland only, www.jetstar.com).

Steve's Shuttle (0800/101-021, www.stevesshuttle.co.nz) operates a door-to-door service between the city and the airport (and the train station) with discounts for backpackers and groups. The **No. 29** and **Purple Line** buses (03/366-8855, www.metroinfo.co.nz) make multiple daily trips to and from the airport. Make eco-friendly **Green Cab** (0800/464-7336) taxis your first call, or try **Blue Star** (03/379-9799). Expect to pay $45-65 for a taxi at the airport.

TRAIN

From the **Christchurch Train Station** (Troup Dr., 0800/872-467, www.kiwirail.co.nz), the ***Coastal Pacific*** train (www.greatjourneysofnz.co.nz, late-Sept.-early May) snakes north along the east coast terminating at Picton, with stops at Kaikoura and Blenheim. At time of publication, the *Coastal Pacific* route remained closed due to earthquake damage. Contact **Rail New Zealand** (www.railnewzealand.com) for updates.

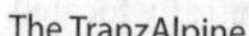

TOP EXPERIENCE

★ *TRANZALPINE*

Widely lauded as one of the world's premier train journeys, the ***TranzAlpine*** (www.greatjourneysofnz.co.nz, 8:15am daily, $139) travels 220km across South Island—from the Pacific east coast to the Tasman west. The trip starts in Christchurch, then creeps over the expansive Canterbury Plains with the snow-kissed Southern Alps looming in the background. Soon, you'll be snaking through those peaks as you pass through breathtaking gorges and valleys, Arthur's Pass National Park, and the 8.5km Otira Tunnel to end on the West Coast. Book tickets online well in advance and pay extra for refundable or transferable dates.

BUS

Intercity (www.intercity.co.nz) operate buses to Christchurch, with daily connections to the rest of the country. **Naked Bus** (www.nakedbus.com) and **Atomic** (www.atomictravel.co.nz) also offer daily bus service to South Island hubs.

Getting Around

CAR

The airport has car rental companies such as **Thrifty** (www.thrifty.co.nz) and **Avis** (www.avis.co.nz). **Quality Car Rentals** (2 Holt Place, 03/359-4612, www.qualityrental.co.nz) offers competitive prices for all budgets.

The TranzAlpine

BUS

The main **Bus Interchange** (Lichfield St. and Colombo St.) terminal is in the central business district. Here you will find maps and timetables for the city's extensive **Metro** (www.metroinfo.co.nz) bus network. Buy a **Metrocard** ($10) to receive 25 percent discount on fares, which are paid to the driver.

BIKE

Next Bike (03/390-1005, www.nextbike.co.nz, $4 per hour or $20 per day) operates a bike-sharing service with five pickup and drop-off stations around the city center. **Natural High** (690a Harewood Rd., 03/982-2966, www.naturalhigh.co.nz) rents bikes and guides single and multiday tours. If electric bikes are your thing, rent one at **City Electric Bike Hire** (64 Sandyford St., 027/715-9759, www.citybikehire.co.nz).

TOURS

The **Grand Tour** (7 Rolleston Ave., 03/365-8282, www.christchurchattractions.nz, 10am-3pm daily, adults $129, children $69) is a luxury shuttle bus that tours a selection of the city's sights and experiences: punting on the River Avon, the Botanic Gardens, the Christchurch Gondola, a trip to Sumner, and a ride on the historic tram. Prices includes all admissions costs.

Services

The **i-SITE Visitor Centre** (Arts Centre, 28 Worcester Blvd., 03/379-9629, www.christchurchnz.com, 8:30am-7pm daily) offers information on tours and travel around the South Island. It shares space with the **DoC Visitor Center** (03/379-4082, www.doc.govt.nz, 9am-4.45pm daily). There's a **post office** (67 Cashel St., 0800/501-501, 7am-5:30pm Mon.-Fri., 8:30am-noon Sat.) and the central **Christchurch Hospital** (2 Riccarton Ave., 03/364-0640).

LYTTELTON

Perched 12km southeast of Christchurch is the picturesque port town of Lyttelton, whose spectacular 11-million-year-old harbor lies carved at the foot of the Port Hills. A bounty of Victorian architecture houses cafés and eateries, and the town's population has an artistic bohemian streak. Important sites such as the Lyttelton Museum and Timeball Station were badly damaged during the 2011 quakes and are still under repair.

Harbor Cruises

Exploring Lyttelton Harbour is a must. **Blackcat Cruises** (03/304-7641, www.blackcat.co.nz) operates trips to uninhabited **Quail Island** (departs Lyttelton 10:20am and 12:20pm daily, returns 12:30pm and 3:30pm daily Dec.-Feb., departs 10:20am daily, returns 3:30pm daily Oct.-Apr., adults $30, children $15, under age 5 free). A scenic walk (2-3 hours) takes in volcanic cliffs, shipwrecks, and lovely swim spots. A walking map is included.

Another cruise heads to **Diamond Harbour** (departs Lyttelton 6:10am-10:30pm Mon.-Fri., 6:50am-10:50pm Sat.-Sun., returns 6:30am-10:40pm Mon.-Fri., 7:05am-11pm Sat.-Sun., adults $13, children $6.40) opposite the Banks Peninsula. Iridescent waters along with a beach, cliff-top walks, and cafés await. Both cruises are 10 minutes each way.

Food and Accommodations

Stalls assemble in Lyttelton for the **farmers market** (London St., 10am-1pm Sat.), which sells produce, arts, and crafts.

The charmingly ramshackle **Shroom Room** (48 London St., 03/328-9456, 8am-4pm daily, $9-20) sits beneath a clear arched roof propped up by corrugated-iron sheets. Inside, sit on mismatched furniture and tuck into the café's vegan and vegetarian menu, with delights like the Bless Up breakfast of smoked homemade beans, mushrooms, tomato, and salsa on toast. Don't leave without sampling the fruity "Dreamy Pash" smoothie.

You're in for a warm welcome at **Freemans Dining Room** (47 London St., 03/328-7517, www.freemansdiningroom.co.nz, 3pm-close Wed.-Fri., 9am-close Sat., noon-close Sun., $24-38), a trendy eatery whose hearty and wholesome European-inspired menu includes an array of pastas, pizzas, seafood, and red meat.

Meals at ★ **Roots Restaurant** (8 London St., 03/328-7658, www.rootsrestaurant.co.nz, noon-2pm Fri.-Sat., 6pm-11pm Tues.-Sat., $105-195) could be framed and hung in a gallery. Set 5-, 8-, and 12-course degustation menus are crafted from seasonal local ingredients in an open kitchen and served on hunks of stone or wood. The menu changes daily, but expect truffles, shellfish, venison, or lamb adorned with foams and flowers and paired with the best New Zealand wines.

Set in a grand villa with a garden and well-stocked kitchen, BBH hostel **Foley Towers** (208 Kilmore St., 03/366-9720, www.bbh.co.nz, dorm $27-32, $64-70 s or d) is a home away from home. Rooms are somewhat dated but clean; some rooms have en suite baths. The lounge and TV area is cozy and carpeted, and there is under-floor heating throughout.

The Rookery (9 Ross Terrace, 03/328-8038, www.therookery.co.nz, $130 s, $160-180 d) is housed in a hilltop cottage with jaw-dropping views across the harbor. The single room shares a luxury bath; the two double rooms have en suite baths. All come with bathrobes, underfloor heating, electric blankets, and hot-drink facilities. The colorful cottage is adorned with artwork and surrounded by vibrant gardens. Choose from a continental or hearty full English breakfast.

Transportation and Services

Lyttelton is about 13km southeast of Christchurch via Highway 74. Metro Bus 28 departs Christchurch (Colombo St., every 30 minutes to 1 hour) for Lyttelton. The trip takes 45 minutes with stops.

For more information, visit **Lyttelton Harbour Information & Resource Centre** (20 Oxford St., 03/328-9093, 10am-4pm Mon.-Sat., 11am-3pm Sun., www.lytteltonharbour.info).

HANMER SPRINGS

The alpine spa resort of Hanmer Springs, a two-hour detour north of Christchurch, is not to be missed. Thanks to its natural hot pools, pristine Hanmer Springs may be billed as "New Zealand's Alpine Spa Village," but there's plenty more to get the pulse going—bungy jumping, jetboating, and rafting.

Recreation

THERMAL POOLS

Hanmer Springs Thermal Pools (42 Amuri Ave., 03/315-0000, www.hanmersprings.co.nz, 10am-9pm daily, adult $24, child $12, senior $17) has been soothing weary souls since the mid-19th century. The sprawling outdoor complex holds an array of relaxing and natural open-air thermal streams and pools, ranging in temperatures from 33-42° (some have massage jets). Saunas and steam rooms ($32-42), private thermal pools ($32), a lap pool, and water slides ($10) are also available. For more pampering, book a hot stone therapy session, facial, or massage at the on-site spa.

WALKS AND BIKING

A bounty of well-marked biking and walking tracks of varying lengths and levels dissect the 13,000-hectare **Hanmer Forest**, 6km east of Hanmer Springs. The trails weave past waterways and waterfalls, over peaks and lowland tussocks, and through woodlands of beech, fir, and pine that are home to tui, fantails, bellbirds, and falcons.

The **Waterfall Track** (2.5 hours round-trip) is a popular option. From the carpark (Mullans Rd.), the track negotiates native forest, ferns, and orchids before arriving at the 41m-high Dog Stream waterfall. Take the Spur Track or Fir Trail to return.

The superb **Mt. Isobel Track** (6 hours round-trip) leaves the carpark (Clarence Valley Rd.) toward the summit via European and Japanese larch forest and subalpine scrub for a breathtaking view of Hanmer Basin and the looming plains and mountains beyond.

Ballooning Canterbury

Ballooning Canterbury (2126 Bealey Rd., Darfield, 0508/422-556, www.ballooningcanterbury.com, adult $395, child under 12 $320) operates serene, one-hour flights that showcase the stunning Canterbury landscape—from the Southern Alps through the tumbling plains to the Pacific coast and beyond. Departures are 55km west of Christchurch.

Hanmer Springs Adventure Centre (20 Conical Hill Rd., 03/315-7233, www.hanmeradventure.co.nz, 8:30am-5pm daily) rents mountain bikes.

JET-BOATING

Jet-boat through Waiau Gorge in its entirety at speeds of up to 80km/h with **Thrillseekers Adventures** (839 Hanmer Springs Rd., 0800/661-538, www.christchurchattractions.nz, adult $125, child $70), an exhilarating ride that features 360-degree spins, white-water rapids, and the navigation of narrow, sheer-faced passageways. The Waiau River's grade-II rapids can also be tackled in a raft ($169/99); gentler stretches are navigable in an inflatable canoe ($249/169). Return by jetboat, with a stop for a riverside picnic lunch.

Other activities include bungy jumping ($169) from the historic, 135-year-old, 35m-high Ferry Bridge.

WINTER SPORTS

Hanmer Springs Ski Area (www.skihanmer.co.nz, adult $30, child $15) caters mainly to intermediate skiers and snowboarders with a handful of runs for beginners and experts. The highest point is 1,769m with a 310m vertical drop. The season runs from early July to mid-September.

Hanmer Springs Adventure Centre (20 Conical Hill Rd., 03/315-7233, www.hanmeradventure.co.nz, 8:30am-5pm daily) rents clothing and equipment (including toboggans) and runs a **shuttle** (departs 9:15am, 11:15am; returns 4:15pm; adult $40, child $32 round-trip) to the ski fields.

The ski area is 17km north of Hanmer Springs village off Clarence Valley Road.

Food

Do not leave town without sampling the whiskey porridge at **Powerhouse Café** (8 Jacks Pass Rd., 03/315-5252, wwwpowerhousecafe.co.nz, 7:30am-3pm daily, $17-28), an attractive eatery set in a historic hydro-electric power station. The breakfast menu features French toast, grilled potato cakes, pancakes, and eggs Benedict. For lunch, order the seared salt-and-pepper calamari or the sourdough steak sandwich.

The attentive crew at **Malabar** (Alpine Pacific Centre, 5 Conical Hill Rd., 03/315-7745, www.malabar.co.nz, 5pm-10pm Tues.-Sun., noon-2:30pm Sat., $22-35) serve an Asian fusion menu backed by a rather tantalizing cocktail menu—just the thing to take the edge off some of the spicier delights. The honey-, garlic- and sesame-glazed duck breast is unforgettable.

★ **No. 31** (31 Amuri Ave., 03/315-7031, www.restaurant-no31.nz, 5pm-11pm daily, $29-39) is the town's best restaurant. Exquisitely presented à la carte offerings include rack of lamb, duo of wild hare, and a seared venison fillet. The quaint cottage setting is replete with a fireplace and French doors.

Accommodations

Intimate **Hanmer Backpackers** (41 Conical Hill Rd., 03/315-7196, www.hanmerbackpackers.co.nz, dorms $35, $80 s or d) exudes a Swiss-chalet vibe with an A-frame roof and mismatched furnishings. The largest room is a five-bed dorm; en-suite double and family rooms (both $95) are available. A sizeable library and board game collection is in the lounge area and the kitchen is well-stocked with complimentary spices, tea, and real coffee. Some Wi-Fi is free.

Kakapo Lodge Backpackers (14 Amuri Ave., 03/315-7472, www.kakapolodge.co.nz, dorms $33, $76 s or d) is close to the thermal springs, with splendid mountain views from the rooms and the courtyard. Snug beds come in single or double (no bunks) or upgrade to an en-suite ($95). Motel rooms ($115) with private kitchens and bathrooms are available.

The **Chalets Motel** (56 Jacks Rd., 03/315-7097, www.chaletsmotel.co.nz, $160-260 s or d) offers 10 one- and two-bedroom units with electric blankets, private bathrooms, and Sky TV. Private outdoor areas sit surrounded by coniferous trees and alpine views. One chalet has a spa bath. It's a short stroll from the thermal pools.

The **St James** (20 Chrisholm Cres., 03/315-5225, www.thestjames.co.nz, $245-655 s or d) is one of the region's most luxurious hotels. Studios and one- and two-bedroom suites are adorned with local art. Each self-contained unit has a private patio or balcony, free Wi-Fi, Sky TV, DVD players, bathrobes, and an underfloor-heated bathroom. Some rooms have gas fires.

Transportation and Services

Hanmer Springs is a 90-minute drive north of Christchurch via State Highways 1 and 7. **Hanmer Connection** (0800/242-663 adult $50 return, child $30) operates a daily bus service departing from the Christchurch Museum at 9am and leaving Hanmer Springs at 4:40pm. **Intercity** (03/365-1113, www.intercity.co.nz) operates a bus route between Nelson and Kaikoura.

Hanmer Springs i-SITE Visitor Centre (40 Amuri Ave., 03/315-0020, www.visithanmersprings.co.nz, 10am-5pm daily) doubles as the DoC office with booking services and information on walks and trail conditions.

Akaroa and the Banks Peninsula

Jutting east from Christchurch, the Banks Peninsula comprises two extinct volcanic cones. The dramatic, gnarly landscape contrasts vividly with the plains from which it protrudes. The area is home to a bounty of hiking trails that snake across rolling pastures and plunge straight toward sapphire seas. The waters around the peninsula teem with seabirds, seals, penguins, dolphins, and the occasional whale.

The town of Akaroa is the focal village of Banks Peninsula. First settled by Maori 800 years ago, its name translates as "long harbor." European and U.S. whalers arrived here in the late 18th and early 19th centuries, but it was the arrival of the French ship *Comte de Paris* in 1840 that had the greatest effect, bringing dozens of French settlers to the town. A Gallic community blossomed, and many of the road signs are still in French, a rather charming touch when coupled with the colorful Victorian stores and villas that line the streets.

Akaroa's harbor was formed by flooding the remains of an empty volcanic crater. The Akaroa Marine Reserve is thought to house up to 80 percent of New Zealand's underwater biodiversity, including rare specimens such as the Hector's dolphin and yellow-eyed penguin.

SIGHTS

Akaroa Lighthouse

First lit in 1880, **Akaroa Lighthouse** (Beach Rd. on Akaroa Head, 1:30pm-4:30pm Sun., adults $2.50, children $0.50) was bought for $1 by a preservation society and moved to its current site in 1980. On Sunday, guests can scale its two flights of stairs to check out the watch and lantern rooms and the outer balcony. This

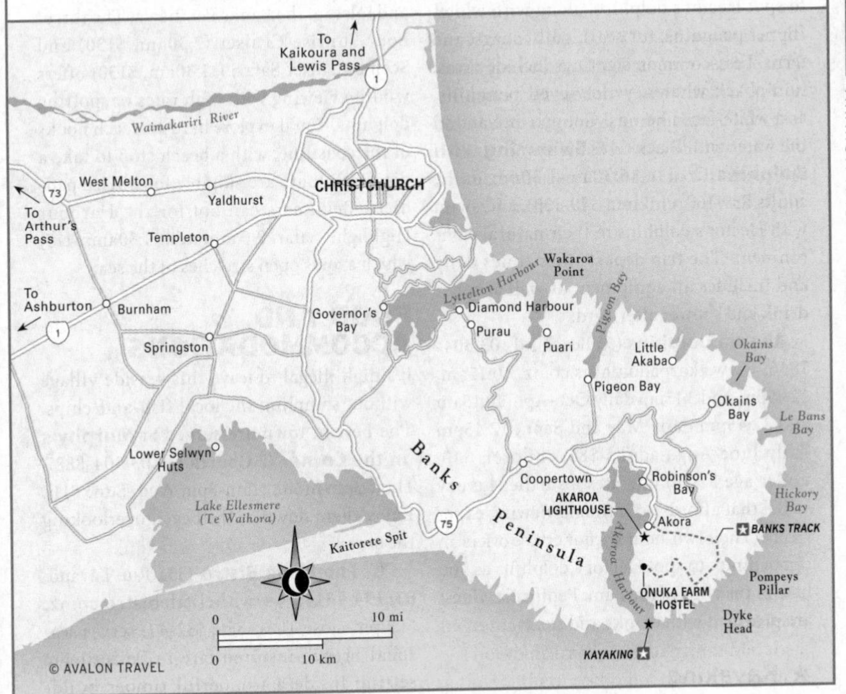

is the only lighthouse in New Zealand accessible to view in its original operational order. It's 1.5km southwest of the village.

Akaroa Museum

Founded in 1964 at the heritage Langlois-Eteveneaux cottage, **Akaroa Museum** (71 Rue Lavaud, 03/304-1013, www.akaroamuseum.org.nz, 10:30am-4pm daily, adults $4, children $1) has since expanded to include the historic Court and Custom Houses. The museum comprises three galleries, a research room, a theater, and a shop. The smashing setup recounts the geological and human histories of the Banks Peninsula through photos, costumes, tools, documents, artifacts, and a documentary video. There's also a display about local legend Frank Worsley, Shackleton's Antarctic navigator on the *Endurance*.

RECREATION

★ Banks Track

The **Banks Track** (29km, 2-3-days, www.bankstrack.co.nz) is a hike across the southeast corner of the peninsula. Along the way, take in volcanic coastlines, farmland, forests of red ferns, and waterfalls while visiting some of the area's hard-to-reach gems: Flea Bay, home to white-flipper and yellow-eyed penguin colonies, and a marine reserve frequented by Hector's dolphins and orcas. Accommodations along the route are in self-catering huts and cottages (Oct.-Apr., $150-260 pp).

Dolphin Cruises

Black Cat Cruises (main wharf, 03/304-7641, www.blackcat.co.nz, 11am, 1:30pm, and 3:40pm daily mid-Dec.-mid-Mar., adults $75, children $30, under age 5 free) runs an

18m catamaran in Akaroa Harbour. During the two-hour cruise, you're almost guaranteed to spot Hector's dolphins, along with white-flipper penguins, fur seals, gulls, shags, and terns. Less-common sightings include orcas, humpback whales, yellow-eyed penguins, and white-faced herons. Get up close and in the water with Black Cat's **Swimming With Dolphins Cruise** (6:30am-1:30pm daily, adults $89-160, children $49-130), and swim with Hector's dolphins in their natural environment. The trip departs four times daily and includes all equipment as well as a hot drink and shower afterward.

Akaroa Dolphins (65 Beach Rd., 03/304-7866, www.akaroadolphins.co.nz, 10:15am, 12:45pm, and 3:15pm daily Oct.-Apr., 10:15am and 12:45pm daily May and Sept., 12:45pm daily June-Aug., adults $85, children $40, under age 5 $20) operates a smaller luxury vessel that affords an intimate viewing experience. Their two-hour harbor cruise offers an opportunity to spot Hector's dolphins as you take in the cliffs of the Bank Peninsula. Guest are provided with drinks and treats.

★ Kayaking

Akaroa Guided Sea Kayak Safaris (Rue Lavaud, 021/156-4591, www.akaroakayaks.com, daily Nov.-Apr.) operate three fully guided sea kayaking tours around the bays and inlets of the Banks Peninsula. The three-hour Sunrise Cruiser (7:30am, $130) and Scenic Cruiser Safari (11:30am, $130) offers wildlife viewing with high rates of spotting dolphins. You'll explore hard-to-reach nooks of the coastline, with a beach stop to take a dip. Both tours are suitable for novice paddlers. Beginners can opt for the Harbour Highlights Safari (90 minutes, 11:30am, $115) which avoids open stretches of the sea.

FOOD AND ACCOMMODATIONS

It's nigh illegal to leave this seaside village without sampling the local fish-and-chips. The best in town are served at **Murphy's on the Corner** (7 Church St., 03/304-8887, 11am-3pm Mon., 11am-8pm Wed.-Sun., $11). Enjoy them down at the beach overlooking the ocean.

★ **The Little Bistro** (33a Rue Lavaud, 03/304-7314, www.thelittlebistro.co.nz, 5:30pm-close Tues.-Sat., $32-42) serves seasonal French-inspired fare in an intimate setting inside a wonderful timber building overlooking the ocean and surrounding hills. Dine on escargot with garlic and bacon

Akaroa village on the Banks Peninsula

vol-au-vent and lamb rack with goat cheese and potato terrine. It's all made using local produce and is accompanied by New Zealand wines.

Minutes from the beach, **Akaroa Village Inn** (81 Beach Rd., 03/304-1111, www.akaroavillage.co.nz, $200-325) offers an abundance of spacious modern lodgings. Choices within the luxury estate range from modern studio spa units to three-bed suites housed in apartment blocks and villas. All have en suite baths with underfloor heating, Wi-Fi, Sky TV, private patios or balconies, and access to a heated pool. Particularly charming is the converted shipping office with two bedrooms, a lounge with a gas fire, a living area, and a corner spa bath.

Set on 260ha of coastal farmland and native bush, ★ **Onuka Farm Hostel** (89 Hamiltons Rd., Onuka, 03/304-7066, www.onuku.co.nz, Oct.-Apr.) offers accommodations and activities for all, including the resident dogs and barnyard critters. The 19th-century farmhouse boasts dorms ($29 pp) and double or twin ($34 pp) and single ($64 pp) rooms, while the Tonga Hut ($80 s or d, $100 for 3) comes with sea views and a private kitchen and a bath in an adjacent hut.

The **campground** (Nov.-Mar.) fits 14 tents ($15 pp, $12.50 additional nights) and houses a seven-bed dorm (linens not provided, $19), plus "wooden tents" ($40 s or d) with see-through roofs that take in the night sky. The van park (Oct.-Apr., $15 pp, $12.50 additional nights) rests on a field with incredible sea views. Facilities across the entire complex include lounges with fireplaces, free Wi-Fi, barbecues, fully equipped kitchens, hot showers, and laundry. It's 7km from Akaroa.

TRANSPORTATION AND SERVICES

Akaroa is 82km from Christchurch via Highway 75. **Akaroa Shuttle** (0800/500-929, www.akaroashuttle.co.nz, round-trip adults $50, children $40) and **Akaroa French Connection** (0800/800-575, www.akaroabus.co.nz, round-trip adults $50, children $30) both operate daily bus service between Christchurch and Akaroa.

For more information, visit the **Akaroa i-SITE** (74a Rue Lavaud, 03/304-7784, www.akaroa.com, 9am-8pm daily summer, 9am-5pm daily winter).

Arthur's Pass National Park

Straddling the borders of Canterbury, the forested mountain ranges, braided rivers, and imposing gorges of Arthur's Pass National Park (www.arthurspass.com) have attracted adventurers since the late 1800s. The area was formally protected in 1929; it's the third national park in New Zealand and was the first on South Island.

Arthur's Pass National Park is separated by peaks that rise more than 2km. The west flank of the park is dominated by steep gorges, rainforests, and waterfalls; to the east, mountain beech carpets land that is intertwined with shingle-filled braided rivers. Above the bush line sprout snow tussock and alpine meadows. The trees are home to kea, fantail, and the great spotted kiwi, while the waters harbor black-fronted terns and wrybills.

The park's tiny alpine village sits surrounded by beech forest at an elevation of 740m. It's home to a handful of eateries and lodgings along with a permanent human population of just a few dozen. The resident kea population often entertains (and enrages) visitors by stealing food and the occasional car part or personal belonging.

Arthur's Pass Road

Arthur's Pass Road (Hwy. 73) is the highest crossing of the Southern Alps. From Christchurch, the scenic drive stretches 154km across the Canterbury Plains to climb

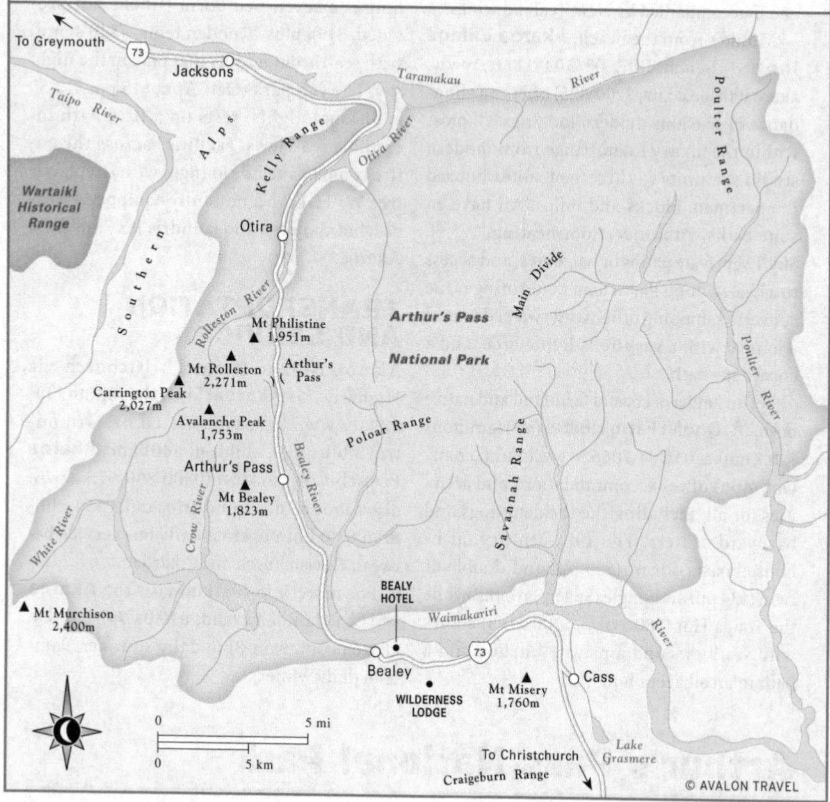

920m to the park village. Along the way, soak in the mountain views, river gorges, and the Otira Viaduct.

The mountain thoroughfare was first discovered by Maori; 1,000 pickax- and dynamite-wielding workers built a proper road across in 1856 to be used by horse-drawn coaches (an original stage coach is on display at the DoC Centre). In 1999, the impressive 440m-long, 35m-high Otira Viaduct opened to reduce the impact of major rock falls constantly damaging the road.

Walks

Day hikes and multiday treks are abundant throughout the park; most leave from the village or nearby. The **Arthur's Pass Historic Walk** (1.5 hours round-trip) takes an easy stroll around the village. You'll see various historic sites with photographs of how they once looked. Points of interest include Brake's store (the village's first shop where the YHA hostel now stands) and Arthur's Pass to the Otira rail tunnel.

The most popular walk is **Avalanche Peak** (6-8 hours round-trip), which climbs to 1,100m with mesmeric views of Mount Rolleston and Crow Glacier. **Devils Punchbowl Waterfall** (1 hour round-trip) is a much-loved track that leads through forest and over a river to the base of spectacular waterfalls.

Many of the overnight tramps require river-crossing and route-finding skills and are for experienced hikers only. Visit the **DoC office** (03/318-9211, www.doc.govt.nz, 8am-5pm daily summer, 8:30am-4:40pm daily winter) for a comprehensive list of tracks along with up-to-date weather conditions, as well as overnight hut tickets.

Ski Fields

Porters (Hwy. 73, 03/318-4731, www.skiporters.co.nz, late June-Oct., adults $99, youths and seniors $49, under age 11 free) is the closest ski field, with slopes for everyone across its 250ha fields. The highest point is 1,950m, with a maximum vertical drop of 610m. Facilities include a café and equipment rental. It's located just before the park boundary, 90km west of Christchurch. **Snowman Shuttles** (03/337-5750, www.snowmanshuttles.co.nz, adults $55, seniors and youths $50) operates once-daily buses to and from Christchurch.

Temple Basin (03/377-7788, www.templebasin.co.nz, adults $69, ages 13-17 $35, ages 10-12 $20, under age 10 free) offers an authentic all-natural alpine experience for adventurous skiers. The 320ha ski area is spread across four basins that max out at 1,753m with a vertical drop of 427m. There is no road access to the mountain. From the Temple Basin car park, 5km west of the village, it's a 45-minute trek up a steep track (there's a goods lift for gear) to the 1,400m base. Accommodations are in basic bunk lodges ($45) with no bedding; book in advance.

Food and Accommodations

In the village, **Wobbly Kea Café** (108 Main Rd., 03/318-9231, www.wobblykea.co.nz, 10am-8pm daily, $17-32) offers hearty meals ideal for stocking up on or replacing calories before or after hiking. Fill up on sizeable pizzas, fish-and-chips, or sausage with mashed potato and caramelized onion gravy. The cozy chalet-like environment includes an open fire.

Mountain House (84 West Coast Rd., 03/318-9258, www.yha.co.nz, dorm $33, $92 s or d) is an appealing YHA hostel at the forest's edge near the heart of the village. Alongside the main backpacker lodge (with dorms and double rooms) rests a pair of historic converted railway cottages ($142) with log fires that sleep four. Two self-contained motel units ($165) have private baths, TVs, and electric beds. Shared amenities include a well-equipped kitchen, a barbecue, a lounge, and laundry.

Bordered by dense beech forest, **Arthur's**

Arthur's Pass National Park

Pass Alpine Motel (52 Main Rd., 03/318-9233, www.apam.co.nz, $115-155) offers easy access to local walking tracks and is prone to visits from curious kea. (Come nightfall, you may also hear the call of a kiwi.) Dated but welcoming units are equipped with private kitchens and baths, electric blankets, Wi-Fi, satellite TV, and DVD players (a film library is available at the reception). All rooms are heated; some have gas fires.

The historic **Bealey** (Hwy. 73, 03/318-9277, www.thebealyhotel.co.nz, $80-185) has a bounty of lodging. Studio cabins come with en suite baths, a fridge, and hot-drink facilities, and include use of a fully stocked communal kitchen. Large cabins come with kitchenettes and private baths. The lodge offers backpacker-like accommodations with double beds and bunks, plus a shared kitchen, laundry, a lounge, and dining and bath facilities. The rustic on-site bar and restaurant ($22-32) serves hearty dishes like stuffed chicken breast and bacon-wrapped Angus filet mignon. The high-country complex is sheltered by forest and towering snowy peaks. It's 10km south of Arthur's Pass Village.

The ★ **Wilderness Lodge** (Hwy. 73, 03/318-9246, www.wildernesslodge.co.nz, $569-770 s, $938-1,240 d) is a special experience on a 1,600ha property home to 3,000 sheep, 120 Angus cattle, and several farmyard creatures. Accommodations are split between four sprawling luxury lodges with sundecks and spa baths that overlook peaks and bushland, and 20 mountain-view hotel rooms with alpine views, fresh fruit and flowers, and tea and coffee-making facilities. A gourmet dinner and full breakfast are included. There's free Wi-Fi, a library, and 25km of hiking trails. Activities include visiting the sheep farmer to hand-feed lambs, taking a guided nature walk, or stargazing come nightfall. The lodge is 16km southeast of Arthur's Pass Village.

Avalanche Creek Campsite (03/318-9211, www.doc.govt.nz, adults $8, children $4, under age 5 free) is conveniently positioned off Highway 73 opposite the village DoC office. Facilities are basic—tap water, toilets, and a cook shelter.

Transportation and Services

The village hub within Arthur's Pass National Park is 154km west of Christchurch via Highway 73. Once in the mountains, snow and black ice are common, and passes may close May-October. Carry snow chains, emergency clothing, and provisions when driving in winter.

Atomic Shuttles (03/349-0697, www.atomictravel.co.nz, $40) and **West Coast Shuttle** (03/768-0028, www.westcoastshuttle.co.nz, $42) operate daily shuttle bus services between Christchurch and Arthur's Pass. Plan three hours one-way for the trip. They also service walking trails en route.

Make the **DoC Visitor Centre** (03/318-9211, www.doc.govt.nz, 8am-5pm daily summer, 8:30am-4:40pm daily winter) your first stop for hiking, then peruse some local history at its tiny on-site museum. The **Challenge Arthur's Store** (03/318-9235, 8am-5pm daily) has the only ATM and gasoline pump in town.

INLAND SCENIC ROUTE 72

Heading south from Christchurch and Arthur's Pass, Highway 1 is the most direct route toward Aoraki/Mount Cook National Park. However, the 190km Inland Scenic Route 72 is a far more rewarding drive as it hugs the foot of the Southern Alps on one side and the Canterbury Plains on the other.

From Christchurch or Arthur's Pass, follow Highway 73 south, then east to its junction with Highway 77 near Darfield. From here, continue east on Highway 77, which becomes the Inland Scenic Route 72 near Mount Hutt.

Mount Hutt

A 1.5- to 2-hour drive west of Christchurch, turn north off the Inland Scenic Route 72 for the **Mount Hutt** (Mclennans Bush Rd., 03/308-5074, www.nzski.com, adults $99, children and seniors $50, under age 11 free) ski resort. The resort offers some of the best slopes in New Zealand for all skill levels; its lengthy season stretches from early June to early October. The 365ha fields reach 2,068m with a vertical drop of 648m and an epic long run of 2km. Equipment rentals are on-site, as are three eateries.

Most skiers and snowboarders stay in the pretty alpine town of Methven, 27km southeast. However, the **Mount Hutt Bunkhouse** (8 Lampard St., 03/302-8894, www.mthuttbunkhouse.co.nz, dorm $31, $80 s or d) is a great budget option that books fast. Cozy dorms come with timber bunks that sleep 6 to 8, with shared facilities such as a TV lounge with log burner, a covered barbecue courtyard, free tea and coffee in the communal kitchen, and a drying room for ski gear.

GETTING THERE

The **Mount Hutt Ski Bus** (160 Main St., 0800/684-888, www.methventravel.co.nz) runs three times daily between Mount Hutt and Methven and Christchurch. **Snowman Shuttle** (0800/766-962, www.snowmanshuttles.co.nz) operates a daily service to Mount Hutt from Christchurch and Methven and includes door-to-door service plus mountain packages with lift and equipment rentals.

★ Peel Forest

The **Peel Forest** (Peel Forest Rd.) branches off the Inland Scenic Route 60km southwest of Methven. Numerous well-marked trails lead through the 500ha ancient native bushland, which is home to 1,000-year-old totara trees up to 3m wide. Botanical highlights include white and black pine and around 70 species of fern. Bountiful birdlife includes the bellbird, tomtit, shining cuckoo, fantail, and falcons.

The **Peel Forest Store** (1202 Peel Forest Rd., 03/696-3567) doubles as an eatery and the DoC office. Buy a Peel Forest area brochure, which has information about all the walks. The DoC campsite is 3km away on the banks of the Rangitata River with basic **campsites** (adults $18, children $9, under age 5 free) and campsites with electricity (adults $21, children $10.50, under age 5 free) accompanied by rudimentary cabins ($50), with hot showers, tap water, and a shelter with cooking facilities. Several of the walking tracks depart from the campground.

Rangitata Gorge

Rangitata Rafts (0800/251-251, www.rafts.co.nz, noon daily, $215) operates a whitewater rafting trip through the steep-sided Rangitata Gorge. It's one of the few places in New Zealand with guaranteed Class V rapids (and easier routes; you won't be forced to tackle anything you're not comfortable with). Enjoy alpine and forest views during the two-hour tour through the canyon, which includes lunch and a celebratory barbecue. Rangitata Rafts is located 15km north of the Peel Forest along Rangitata Gorge Road.

South to Lake Tekapo

From the Peel Forest and Rangitata Gorge, follow the Inland Scenic Route 72 south for 26km to Highway 79 and turn east for Lake Tekapo and the McKenzie District. Alternately, continue south to Highway 1 on the coast and head to the town of Timaru.

Lake Tekapo and the McKenzie District

The McKenzie District covers the southwest corner of Canterbury and is famed for alluring attractions like Aoraki/Mount Cook National Park and sprawling, shimmering lakes hemmed in by snowy peaks and tussock plains.

LAKE TEKAPO

The tiny town of Lake Tekapo is known for its turquoise lake, whose hypnotic hue is caused by fine glacially ground rock flour suspended in the water—one of Canterbury's definitive natural features.

Sights

TEKAPO SPRINGS

Three blissful hot-spring pools at **Tekapo Springs** (6 Lakeside Dr., 03/680-6550, www.tekaposprings.co.nz, 10am-9pm daily, adults $25, children $14, seniors $20) offer massage jets and temperatures ranging 27-39°C. The pools are shaped like local lakes and are hemmed by rich native alpine shrubs, as well as snow in winter, with lake and mountain views. Other amenities include a kid's pool, a lap pool, and one of the world's largest inflatable waterslides. There's a steam room and sauna (adults $31, seniors $26), a bar and café, and a spa with facial treatments, massages, and hot stone therapy.

CHURCH OF THE GOOD SHEPHERD

Nestled on the southern shore of Lake Tekapo sits the picturesque **Church of the Good Shepherd** (Pioneer Dr., www.churchofthegoodshepherd.org.nz, 9am-5pm daily summer, 10am-4pm daily winter, free), built in 1935. The back window of the tiny stone church frames a cinematic view of Lake Tekapo bordered by the Southern Alps. Photography is forbidden inside, but there are plenty of spots outside to immortalize your visit.

★ MOUNT JOHN

The windswept apex of **Mount John** (Godley Peaks Rd., $5) affords a 360-degree view that has few peers, even on South Island. All around the 1,030m-high peak, the landscape merges from mountain ranges to the plains of the Mackenzie basin to Tekapo and Alexandria Lakes. Pay the nominal fee to drive to the top or hike the **Mount John Summit Track** (2 hours round-trip), a reasonably steep climb through larch trees and tussock that emerges onto a trail looping around the mountain.

Thanks to the region's stunning night sky, it has been named the **Aoraki Mackenzie International Dark Sky Reserve** (www.mackenzienz.com); it is the only one in the southern hemisphere. Due to the stability and transparency of its atmosphere, the mountaintop was chosen to host the renowned **University of Canterbury Mount John University Observatory** (03/680-6960, www.earthandsky.co.nz). The observatory operates guided tours (adults $75-125, children $50-75) that range from exploring research equipment to viewing the starlit skies through powerful telescopes. The on-site **Astro Café** (9am-6pm daily summer, 10am-5pm daily winter, $8-15) serves drinks and a light lunch to accompany the stunning views.

Mount John is 9km north of Tekapo off Highway 8.

Recreation

Mackenzie Alpine Horse Trekking (Godley Peaks Rd., 0800/628-629, www.maht.co.nz, late Sept.-May) runs guided horseback riding tours through this romantic wilderness. The Lake View (1 hour, adults $70, children $60) tour is a gentle trek through larch and pine forest with views of the plains, Mount John, and

Lake Tekapo, before returning though birdsong-filled forests. The Mountaintop Trek (2 hours, adults $110, children $100) begins with a circumnavigation of the base of Mount John before trotting to the north end of the peak to take in the Southern Alps and Mackenzie Basin. Combine this with a canter to Lake Alexandria through the basin for a full-day option (2 people minimum, includes lunch, $310 pp) that takes riders close to the Southern Alps and to a working sheep station.

Food

Good luck finding a café with a better view than that at **Astro Café** (Hwy. 8, 03/680-6960, www.earthandsky.co.nz, 9am-6pm daily summer, 10am-5pm daily winter), perched next to the observatory atop Mount John. If it's too windy to sit outside, take in the vista through the wraparound windows while enjoying a toasted sandwich or homemade soup. Get here early for coffee and breakfast to avoid the crowds.

Gourmet pork belly, salmon, or bacon pies are some of the gastro highlights at rustic **Run 76** (Hwy. 8, 03/680-6910, www.run76laketekapo.co.nz, 7:30am-4pm daily, $10-20), which doubles as a deli store and has outside seating overlooking the lake.

Fish-and-chips are one of the many lunchtime deals at **Reflections Café and Restaurant** (Hwy. 8, 03/680-6234, www.reflectionsrestaurant.co.nz, 7am-8:30pm daily, $19-31). The traditional menu includes roast pork loin on the bone and an incredible slow-cooked duck leg salad. Enjoy it with panoramic views of the lake. Local art for sale hangs on the walls.

The locally sourced salmon don is a must at the legendary ★ **Kohan Restaurant** (6 Rapuwai Ln., 03/680-6688, www.kohannz.com, 11am-2pm and 6pm-9pm Mon.-Sat., 11am-2pm Sun., $11-38), along with a super selection of tempura and sashimi dishes. Don't let the uninspiring decor deceive you—this is one of the best Japanese joints on South Island, and it comes with a lake view.

Accommodations

YHA Lake Tekapo (3 Simpson Lane, 03/680-6857, www.yha.co.nz, dorm $38-40, $105 s or d) is set on prime real estate overlooking Lake Tekapo. The view is shared by several of the cozy rooms, but is most enjoyed through the enormous window in the lounge area, complete with a piano, a TV, and a log fire. Laundry, a library, a barbecue, and bike rentals are other amenities at this efficient hostel.

view from Mount John

Lake Tekapo Motels & Holiday Park (Lakeside Dr., 03/680-6825, www.laketekapo-accommodation.co.nz) affords a range of sleeping options. The backpacker lodge (dorm $35-40, $90 s or d) provides modern heated rooms. Its picturesque and spacious grounds are surrounded by a mature pine forest. There's a large kitchen and a barbecue and lounge area with a wood burner.

Within the complex, upgrade to a double room ($110) with en suite baths or opt for stand-alone units ($150) with private baths, kitchens, and decks with lake views. The motel ($150-180) comprises studio-, one-, and two-bedroom units overlooking the lake, with en suite baths, Sky TV, kitchens, and free tea, coffee, and milk. A range of tent and van sites ($44-56 pp) include some on the water's edge. It's a short waterfront stroll to the village.

Charming **Creel House** (36 Murray Place, 03/680-6516, www.creelhouse.co.nz, $170-180 d, $130 s) replicates a Scandinavian chalet replete with A-frame ceilings and timber fittings overlooking pine trees and the lake. Rustic floral furnishings befit the three cozy bedrooms; all include private baths. One room has a balcony with lake views. The continental breakfast includes fresh seasonal fruit, croissants, jam, and coffee, served in a homey dining room and lounge area that gives way to a communal balcony.

Tiny **Lake McGreggor Campsite** ($5 pp) is a tranquil spot on the shores of a small, gorgeous lake surrounded by tussock and tan hills. It's frequented by plenty of friendly ducks and offers basic facilities like vault toilets and untreated running water. It's 10km northwest of Tekapo along dusty Lake Alexandria Road.

Transportation

Lake Tekapo is 228km southwest of Christchurch and 106km west of Timaru. From Christchurch, follow Highway 1 for 132km south to Geraldine and turn west onto Highway 8. From Timaru, it's a straight drive west on Highway 8.

TWIZEL

Twizel, on the shores of Lake Ruataniwha, was purpose-built in the late 1960s to service the development of the hydropower scheme in Waitaki Valley. Earmarked for bulldozing in the 1980s, the locals kicked up such a stink that it was saved. It now serves as a gateway to Aoraki/Mount Cook National Park.

The town is triangulated within three sizeable and scenic lakes: Benmore and Ohau to the east and west and 30km-long Lake Pukaki to the north. The svelte waterway resembles a catwalk welcoming superstar Aoraki/Mount Cook beyond. Twizel also provides the opportunity to pedal a section of the Alps2Ocean Cycle Trail.

Accommodations

Twizel Holiday Park (122 Mackenzie Dr., 03/435-0507, www.twizelholidaypark.co.nz) has powered sites ($40) and basic cabins ($52) with shared facilities that include baths, a fully stocked kitchen, a barbecue, and a TV lounge. En suite units ($99) come with TVs, couches, fridges, and hot-drink facilities. Self-contained cottages ($120-140) come with separate bedrooms that sleep up to four. The en suite two-bedroom tourist flat ($160) is a little more luxurious, with a full kitchen and a lounge area.

Transportation

Twizel is 58km southwest of Tekapo along Highway 8.

OMARAMA

The small town of Omarama sits at the intersection of two great Kiwi drives. First, the sweeping **Lindis Pass** navigates 115km of tussock-covered mountains south toward Wanaka. The second is through the **Waitaki Valley,** home to a sprawling hydroelectric power station replete with giant dams that you can drive over. The road rolls east for

120km across the Canterbury-Otago border. From here, head north for Timaru or south to Oamaru.

Recreation

Private timber spa baths overlook lakes, plains, and peaks at **Hot Tubs Omarama** (29 Omarama Ave., 03/438-9703, www.hottubsomarama.co.nz, adults $52, children $17, under age 5 $1). Guests soak in pure chemical-free mountain water that is heated in winter and cooled in summer. Massages and sauna packages are also available.

The **Clay Cliffs Scenic Reserve** ($5) harbors a rock formation seemingly sent from Mars. The reserve's towering cliffs were formed by two million years of uneven erosion of silt and gravel layers that were then lifted by the Ostler Fault. The Clay Cliffs are on private land; pay the vehicle fee at Hot Tubs Omarama. To reach the reserve, head north on Highway 8 for 3km and turn left at Qailburn Road. After 5km, turn onto unpaved Henburn Road.

Omarama is also a world-renowned gliding destination. **Glide Omarama** (Terminal Bldg., Airport Rd., 03/438-9555, www.glideomarama.com, $345-745) operates trial flights ranging from 30 minutes to 2.5 hours. You'll silently soar over the basin and mountaintops and deep into the Southern Alps.

Food and Accommodations

The **Wrinkly Rams** (24-30 Omarama Ave., 7am-4:30pm Mon.-Wed., 7am-8pm Thurs.-Sun., $10-20) is a quirky rustic eatery and art gallery serving central Otago wines, New Zealand craft beers, and fresh country fare like bacon and eggs and homemade soup. Don't miss the 30-minute shearing show (times vary daily, adults $25, children $12.50, under age 5 free) that culminates with a border collie herding sheep.

Accommodations at **Ahuriri Motels** (Hwy. 83, 03/438-9451, www.ahuririmotels.co.nz) include powered tent and RV sites ($36) with shared cooking and bath facilities; backpacker dorms ($35-45) with a fully equipped kitchen, a comfy TV lounge, and rooms that sleep up to four; and studio or three-bedroom units ($95-255) with private kitchens, baths, and TVs.

Transportation

Omarama is 30km south of Twizel along Highway 8.

Clay Cliffs Scenic Reserve

Aoraki/Mount Cook National Park

From Twizel, Highway 80 navigates the western banks of unimaginably blue Lake Pukaki, bordered by the Southern Alps. Here, Aoraki/Mount Cook, New Zealand's highest peak, rises to 3,724m.

Aoraki/Mount Cook National Park is part of the Te Waipounamu UNESCO World Heritage Area. It owes its dramatic landscape to glacial shifts: 40 percent of its lands are covered by more than 60 glaciers, including the 27km Tasman Glacier, New Zealand's longest—you can spot it from the highway on the way in.

Within the 70,000ha park rests five main valleys: Godley, Murchison, Tasman, Hooker, and Mueller, along with 140 peaks that are higher than 2,000m. The region is known for long warm summers and crisp snowy winters with blue skies. In Aoraki/Mount Cook Village, 4m of rain falls 160 days a year, with snowfall for a little more than 20 days. Temperatures range from 32°C to -13°C, but the average temperature is only 12°C (falling 1 degree every 200m in elevation).

The park is home to more than 300 species of alpine plants and more than 750 types of flowers—including alpine daisies and the world's largest buttercup, the Mount Cook lily. November-February, great swathes of the park's lower reaches are carpeted in color. Within the park is the kea (the only alpine parrot), the rock wren, and the kaki or black stilt—one of New Zealand's rarest birds (look for it around the braids of the Tasman River).

SIGHTS

Aoraki/Mount Cook Village

Aoraki/Mount Cook Village is a gleaming and compact complex with a population of 250. It sits encircled by the Southern Alps at the end of Highway 80 at an altitude of 750m. It's easily navigated thanks to one loop road. The village serves as a launchpad for most hikes and tours, and there is little in the way of shops, so stock up in Twizel beforehand. Most operations are overseen by the Hermitage Hotel or DoC.

The **Sir Edmund Hillary Alpine Centre** (Terrace Rd., 03/435-1809, www.hillarycentre.co.nz, 7:30am-8:30pm daily summer,

Tasman Glacier

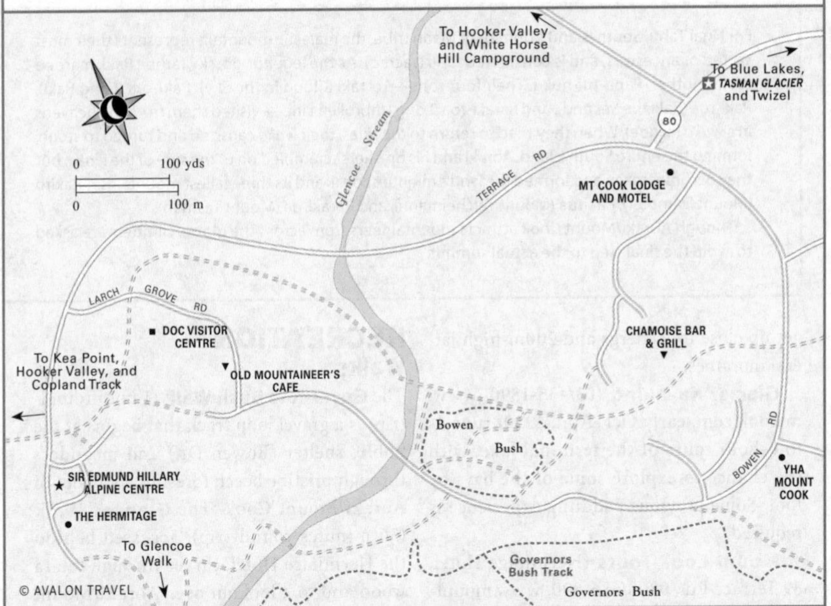

8am-7pm daily winter, adults $20, children $10) pays tribute to New Zealand's favorite son by way of mountaineering memorabilia and narration from the man himself. These legendary local landscapes are where he honed his climbing skills. The setup includes a planetarium and a 3-D cinema where documentaries include the epic tale of scaling Mount Everest.

★ Tasman Glacier

Tasman Glacier is the nation's largest and longest glacier. Probing from an altitude of 3,000m and stretching from 27km to 3km wide and 600m deep, the glacier covers an area of 101sq-km. It terminates at Tasman Lake, which is often dotted with icebergs—except in winter, when it freezes over.

WALKS

The easy **Blue Lakes and Tasman Glacier View Walk** (40 minutes round-trip) passes the small Blue Lakes (worth a swim if the weather's warm), southwest of Tasman Lake, for views of the lower reaches of the glacier.

The **Tasman Glacier Lake Walk** (1 hour round-trip) is an easy stroll that branches off from the Blue Lakes Track. The walk passes through the old terminal moraines that will give you an idea of the glacier's more glorious past—alas, the ice is receding at a steady rate. The tracks are accessed from the car park at the end of Tasman Valley Road (off Hwy. 80) before it enters the village. There are no shuttle services.

TOURS

Glacier Explorers (0800/686-800, www.glacierexplorers.com, 8am, 9:30am, 11am, 12:30pm, 2pm, 3:30pm, and 5pm daily mid-Sept.-late May, adults $155, children $77.50) operates cruises across the terminal lake of the Tasman Glacier. The 2.5-hour tour in customized powered MAC boats includes an easy alpine walk with one hour on the water. You'll

The Legend of Aoraki/Mount Cook

For Ngai Tahu, South Island's dominant Maori tribe, the majestic mountain represents their most sacred of ancestors, and is considered *tapu* (sacred). As the legends go, sky father, Raki, married earth mother, Papa-tui-nuku. Their four sons—Ao-raki (Cloud in the Sky), Raki-ora (Long Raki), Raki-rua (Raki the Second), and Raraki-roa (Long Unbroken Line)—visited them from the heavens in a *waka* (canoe). When they tried to return to the skies, their *waka* capsized and turned to stone, forming the entire South Island. Aoraki and his brothers scrambled on to the side of the *waka,* but they became frozen and formed the land's mightiest peak and its three tallest mountains—Rakiro (Mount Dampier), Rakirua (Mount Teichelmann), and Rarakiroa (Mount Tasman).

Though Aoraki/Mount Cook attracts mountaineers from across the globe, climbers are asked to avoid the final step to the actual summit.

get up close to icebergs and 200m-high lateral moraines.

Glacier Kayaking (03/435-1890, www.mtcook.com, early Oct.-Apr., $250) runs 4- to 6-hour tours of the terminal lake, with the chance to explore some of the bays by foot. Some previous paddling experience is required.

Mount Cook Tours (Hermitage Hotel, 89 Terrace Rd., 0800/686-800, www.mountcooktours.co.nz, 9am, 10:30am, 12:30pm, 2:30pm, and 4pm daily, adults $79, children $39.50) runs 1.5-hour tours aboard an Argo—an all-terrain eight-wheel vehicle that resembles an oversized quad bike. Local guides steer you through the Tasman Valley, up and over rocky slopes for splendid alpine and glacier views.

HELI-HIKING

The only way to get on to the glacier is by flight. **Helicopter Line** (Glentanner Park, Hwy. 80, 0800/650-651, www.helicopter.co.nz, 10am, noon, and 2pm daily Oct.-Apr., $555) operates a Tasman Glacier heli-hike from Mount Cook Airport. Guests are dropped onto the ice at 1,200m, then embark on a guided tour (2 hours) of ice caves, canyons, and crevasses. You'll fly by the incredible 1000m-high Hochstetter Icefall on the way back. Crampons and boots are provided.

RECREATION

Walks

The **Governors Bush Walk** (1 hour round-trip) is a gravel loop track that begins at the public shelter (Bowen Dr.) and meanders through pristine beech forest to a lookout of Aoraki/Mount Cook. The **Glencoe Walk** (30 minutes round-trip), accessed behind the Hermitage Hotel, carves through totara woodland to a lookout over Aoraki/Mount Cook as well as Hooker Glacier.

You can view Hooker Glacier, along with Mueller Glacier, via the **Hooker Valley Track** (4 hours round-trip). One of the region's most popular and rewarding strolls, the trail heads up the valley toward Aoraki/Mount Cook, crossing swing bridges and passing alpine flowers and tussock. The trailhead is opposite the DoC office.

Flightseeing

Heliworks (Mount Cook Airport, 03/435-1460, www.heliworks.co.nz) has a fleet of luxury helicopters that access exclusive landing sites around the park. Aerial tours include a snow landing. The Glacier Encounter (25 minutes, $280 pp) takes in the terminal face of Tasman Glacier before flying up the ice field. The Experience (35 minutes, $355), Paradise (45 minutes, $460), and Ultimate (55 minutes, $590) tours include more of the national park, plus a loop around Aoraki. The

Glacier Lake-Heli Combo package (3.5 hours, $490) offers a scenic flight with a landing on Tasman Glacier followed by a cruise along Tasman Lake.

★ Alps2Ocean Cycle Trail

The **Alps2Ocean Cycle Trail** (4-6 days, www.alps2ocean.com) is a life-affirming journey that begins in the shadow of Aoraki and heads east across the Mackenzie Basin to finish 300km later in the coastal town of Oamaru. The longest continuous ride in New Zealand, the trail stretches 306km and passes spectacular features such glaciers, lakes, hydroelectric dams, and ancient Maori rock art.

Numerous entry and exit points mean that the sections can be tackled separately. Accommodations are in towns and villages like Twizel and Omarama. The track is easy to intermediate (Grade 2-3) and follows mostly gravel or shingle trails, with some road riding. The trailhead begins at the White Horse Hill Campground (Hooker Valley Rd.).

FOOD AND ACCOMMODATIONS

Positioned above Mount Cook Lodge, the **Chamois Bar & Grill** (Bowen Dr., 03/435-1646, 4pm-late daily, $18-29) offers few surprises on its menu of steak, pizza, and fish-and-chips but is enhanced by alpine views, a pool table, and a big-screen TV.

Old Mountaineers Café, Bar and Restaurant (03/435-1890, www.mountcook.com, 10am-8pm daily, $25-35) feels like an authentic alpine affair, replete with old-school ice axes, gas burners, and an open log fire. The restaurant serves hearty breakfasts, lunches, and dinners using organic, local ingredients. The sourdough burger with a beer overlooking Mount Aoraki takes some beating.

★ **YHA Mount Cook** (4 Bowen Dr., 03/435-1820, www.yha.co.nz, dorm $40-44, $97-140 s or d) is a busy timber hostel with a friendly vibe and views of the Southern Alps from every room—and it fills fast. A fire adds to the coziness of the lounge area; there's a free DVD library, an on-site grocery store, bike hire, a barbecue, guitars, and a sauna—just the ticket after a day in the mountains.

Mount Cook Lodge and Motel (Bowen Dr., 03/435-1653, www.mtcooklodge.co.nz) is a modern complex with a variety of well-priced lodgings. Dorms ($40) have en suite baths, sleep four, and come with a fridge. En suite twins or doubles ($150) come with a TV and a private patio or balcony with spectacular views of the Southern Alps. Motel studio

YHA Mount Cook

deluxe units ($291) have private baths, well-stocked kitchenettes, TVs, patios, private parking spaces, and alpine views. Guest of the chalets ($260) are positioned under the mountains in lovely en suite A-frame structures with cooking facilities, plus full access to the Hermitage Hotel.

The sprawling luxury **The Hermitage Hotel** (Terrace Rd., 03/435-1809, www.hermitage.co.nz, $260-650) harbors a bounty of en suite accommodations, from alpine A-frame chalets to deluxe studios and suites with windows overlooking Mount Cook. Enjoy amenities like high-end toiletries, hot-drink facilities, Sky TV, and access to the hotel's collection of eateries and bars.

You'll likely be sharing space with wild rabbits at ★ **Glentanner Holiday Park** (Hwy. 80, 03/435-1855, www.glentanner.co.nz, $22-25 pp). Accommodations include 10-bed dorms ($40), basic units with beds and linens ($125), and self-contained motel-style units ($210) with private baths, kitchens, couches, and dining areas. Excellent facilities include a spacious sheltered barbecue area and a lounge with a log fire and Sky TV. The on-site information center books a range of national park tours. The park is 18km south of Mount Cook Village.

The DoC-maintained **White Horse Hill Campground** (Hooker Valley Rd., www.doc.govt.nz, adults $13, children $6.50, under age 5 free) has basic amenities like running water, flush toilets, and a cooking shelter. The campground in Hooker Valley offers easy access to walking trails, with priceless views of Aoraki and Mount Sefton. It's a couple of kilometers from Mount Cook Village.

TRANSPORTATION AND SERVICES

Aoraki/Mount Cook Village is 211km northwest of Timaru and 65km north of Twizel. From Highway 8 in Twizel, drive north for about 9km to the base of Lake Pukaki. Then follow Highway 80 north for 55km to the village.

Intercity (03/365-1113, www.intercity.co.nz) buses operate daily to Aoraki/Mount Cook Village. **Cook Connect** (0800/266-526, www.cookconnect.co.nz) buses link from Lake Tekapo daily.

The **DoC Visitor Centre** (end of Hwy. 80, 03/435-1186, www.doc.govt.nz, 8:30am-5pm daily Oct.-Apr., 8:30am-4:30pm daily May-Sept., free) is a spectacular affair with a cinematic view of Mount Aoraki. An array of artwork, interactive exhibits, and documentary films supplement the usual brochures and leaflets. Ask about weather and track conditions.

There is a public shelter (Bowen Dr., 8am-7pm daily Oct.-Apr., 8am-5pm daily May-Sept.) with coin-operated showers.

Timaru

Timaru is Canterbury's second-largest city. It was established as a whaling base in the early 1800s. Its sweeping Caroline Bay later attracted the attention of Victorian holidaymakers. Beautiful buildings built from bluestone (a local volcanic rock) remain from the Victorian and Edwardian eras. Today, it is home to a large harbor that offers protection from a treacherous tide that has wrecked numerous ships.

The golden arch of Caroline Bay is Timaru's focal point. Positioned off the northeast corner of the downtown area, its dunes are home to a small colony of blue penguins. Head east to Marine Parade at sunset to catch a glimpse of them as they exit the sea.

SIGHTS

Te Ana Maori Rock Art Centre

Te Ana Maori Rock Art Centre (2 George St., 03/684-9141, www.teana.co.nz, 10am-3pm daily, adults $22, children $11) houses

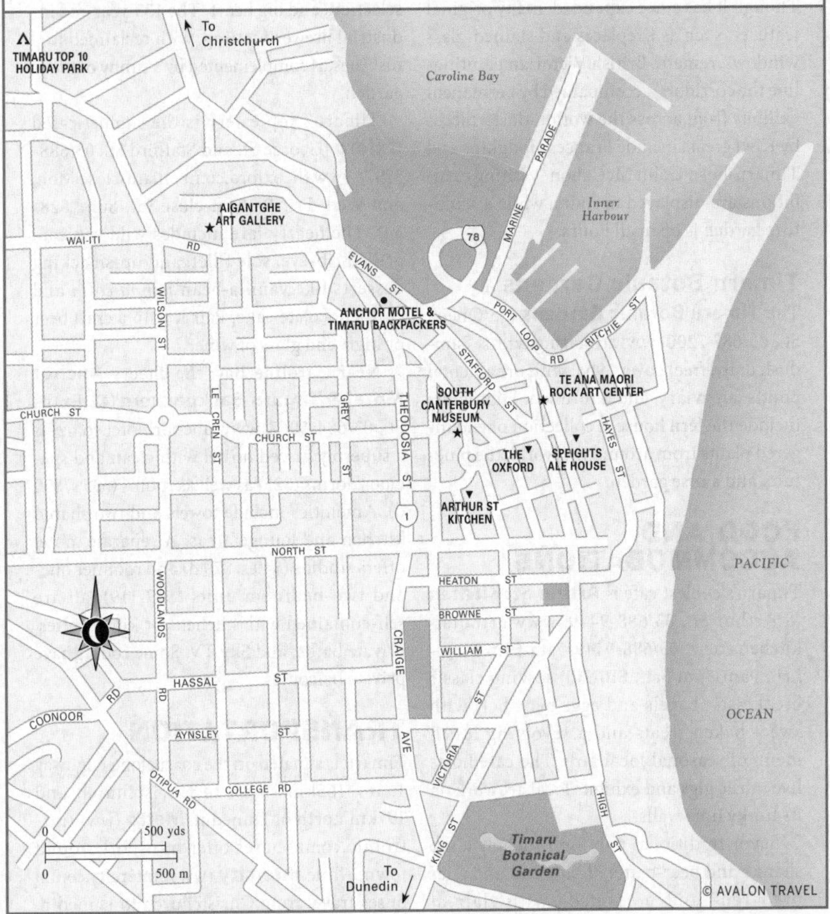

the nation's most important collection of ancient Maori rock art, created by Ngai Tahu Whanui—one of the oldest indigenous tribes. During your tour, guides regale with the history and the meaning of their work. There's also the opportunity to see original creations in situ on limestone cliff faces at the Opihi Rock Art Site (3 hours, 2pm daily Nov.-Apr., adults $130, children $52).

South Canterbury Museum

The engaging **South Canterbury Museum** (Perth St., 03/687-7212, www.museum.timaru.govt.nz, 10am-4:30pm Tues.-Fri., 1pm-4:30pm Sat.-Sun., free) offers a pleasant hour learning about the region's human and natural history. Notable exhibits include a replica of the 1903 aircraft built by local inventor Richard Pearse, along with fossils and Maori and whaling artifacts.

Aigantighe Art Gallery

The **Aigantighe Art Gallery** (49 Wai-iti Rd., 03/688-4424, www.timaru.govt.nz,

10am-4pm Tues.-Fri., noon-4pm Sat.-Sun., free) sprung from an Edwardian villa in 1956. Though it has since expanded, many original features, such as fireplaces and stained-glass windows, remain. British Victorian paintings line the corridors, accompanied by permanent exhibits from across the world. Masterpieces by Kiwi greats include Frances Hodgkins and Timaru-born Colin McCahon. Visiting exhibitions are displayed upstairs, while a sculpture garden is open all hours.

Timaru Botanic Gardens

The **Timaru Botanic Gardens** (35 Queen St., 03/687-7200, www.timaru.govt.nz, 8am-dusk daily, free) cover 19ha, with ornamental ponds, an aviary, and a rotunda. Highlights include the fern house, a collection of endangered plants from around the world, the pinetum, and a rose garden.

FOOD AND ACCOMMODATIONS

Timaru's coolest café is **Arthur St. Kitchen** (8 Arthur St., 03/688-9449, www.arthurstkitchen.co.nz, 03/688-9449, 7am-5pm Mon.-Fri., 9am-3pm Sat., $10-20), serving classic breakfasts (bagels and eggs benedict) with sweet baked treats and a revolving lunch menu of seasonal local fare. The café hosts live music gigs and exhibits local art work on its funky lime walls.

Savor traditional pub food such as lamb shanks and beer-battered blue cod and fries prepared—and presented—with flair at **Speights Ale House** (2 George St., 03/686-6030, www.thealehouse.co.nz, 11:30am-close daily, $20-35), one of the city's liveliest establishments owing to its big screens, big beer selection, and big heart. The 133-year-old industrial brewery setting, with reclaimed furnishings, is complemented by a sunny outdoor garden.

Timaru's top eatery is the sophisticated **Oxford** (George St. and Stafford St., 03/688-3297, www.theoxford.co.nz, 10am-close Mon. and Wed.-Fri., 9:30am-close Sat.-Sun., $28-34). The hearty fare includes wild venison, grilled rib-eye, sole fillet, and lip-smacking desserts like vanilla-bean *panna cotta* and chili-chocolate cake. Pair it with a craft beer or high-end glass of wine.

Near Caroline Bay, the cheery **Anchor Motel & Timaru Backpackers** (42 Evans St., 03/684-5067, www.anchormotel.co.nz) is a superbly priced hostel with clean and spacious dorms ($25) as well as rooms ($35 s, $50 d). Amenities include towels and two shared kitchen and lounge areas. A separate motel offers studios ($49 s, $79 d) and roomier one- and two-bedroom units ($99-119); all are self-contained with kitchens or kitchenettes, private baths, and Sky TV. Some rooms have private balconies.

TRANSPORTATION

Timaru is situated on the coast along Highway 1. It's 165km south of Christchurch and 197km north of Dunedin. **Metro** (www.metroinfo.co.nz) buses offer transport around town, while **Intercity** (www.intercity.co.nz) buses travel from Christchurch to Dunedin, stopping in Timaru (Travel Centre Railway Station, 1 Station St.).

West Coast

Westport and Vicinity............. 386
Paparoa National Park 392
Greymouth 395
Hokitika and Vicinity.................. 398
Westland Tai Poutini National Park..... 403
Haast and Vicinity 411

Look for ★ to find recommended sights, activities, dining, and lodging.

Highlights

★ **Oparara Basin:** An enormous network of caves in Kahurangi National Park harbors the largest stone arches in the southern hemisphere (page 391).

★ **Pancake Rocks:** This jaw-dropping collection of coastal cliffs is stacked to the sky like pancakes (page 392).

★ **White Heron Sanctuary:** New Zealand's only white heron nesting site is set in beautiful shallows in the shadow of the Southern Alps (page 401).

★ **Okarito Lagoon:** Kayak these expansive shallows to catch sight of some of New Zealand's rarest birds (page 402).

★ **Franz Josef and Fox Glaciers:** Two of the world's most accessible glaciers beckon travelers (pages 403 and 407).

★ **Copland Track:** A stunning overnight hike that leads to a natural hot spring where you can bathe with a view of the mountains (page 409).

★ **Haast Pass:** This breathtaking highway navigates mountain passes, gorges, rainforest, and blue glacial lakes in a UNESCO-designated region (page 411).

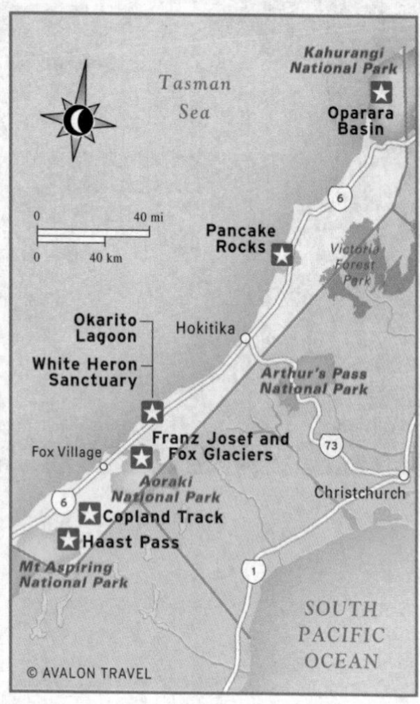

The sparsely populated West Coast deserves its reputation as the black sheep of the New Zealand family.

Cut off from the rest of the country by a towering alpine spine, it takes a certain determination to thrive in this moody region that simultaneously imparts a sense of freedom and claustrophobia.

The West Coast was an important source of *pounamu* (a sacred type of jade, or greenstone) for early Maori. When Europeans discovered coal and gold deposits here in the mid- to late 19th century, the economy exploded and was emboldened by a thriving timber industry. Greymouth, the coast's largest town, displays a sign that proudly tells how the West Coast provided the gold, coal, and wood that financed, powered, and built the nation. Fascinating mining relics accompany your journey, and some of the scenic walks and bike tracks follow routes first carved by pioneers.

Yet it's the natural wonders that are the stars of this show. The Franz Josef and Fox Glaciers, two of the most accessible glaciers in the world, snake from the peaks of the Southern Alps to the low-lying rainforest just 300m above sea level. Crammed into the region's northern recesses is a sprawling, magical network of underground caves. To the south, Haast, part of a greater World Heritage Site, has some of the world's best drives.

PLANNING YOUR TIME

It is essential to plan your drive through the West Coast. The winding mountain passes mean that relatively short distances take longer than expected. The nearly 800km journey from Nelson to Wanaka takes 14 hours without stops.

Most visitors will enter the West Coast at **Westport** and head south toward the glaciers, but the **Oparara Basin** (100km north of Westport) should not be missed. Set aside a day to explore the regions of Haast and Jackson Bay and prioritize the arts and crafts town of Hokitika. Allow at least half a day for the White Heron Sanctuary and Okarito Lagoon. If visiting in winter, spend a couple of days in glacier country.

West Coast weather is notorious. Though this coastal strip stretches for 400km, it is often no more than 30km wide. Battered by the raging waves and winds of the Tasman

Previous: the Haast Pass Highway; the Hokitika driftwood sign. **Above:** rock piles on the banks of Blue Pools.

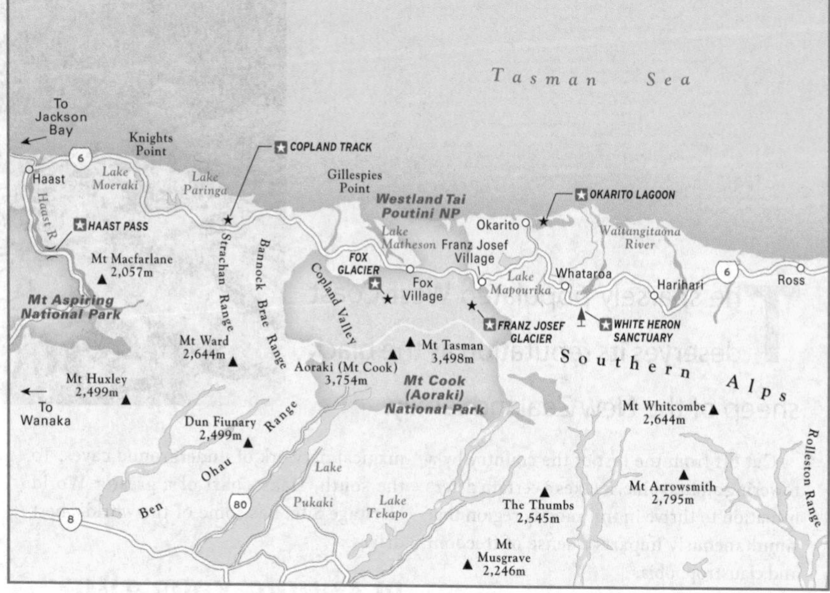

Sea and blocked by the impenetrable Southern Alps, it plays tricks on the climate. In spring, the rainfall here is comparable to that of the Amazon, much of it falling in violent bursts. Winter affords the clearest skies, when the region receives 1,845 hours of annual sunshine, rewarding with views of mountaintops and ocean vistas.

Westport and Vicinity

Visitors arriving from Nelson or Picton will enter the West Coast at Westport. The town hems the mouth of the Buller River, the region's largest waterway, and was of interest to early Maori who scoured the West Coast for *pounamu* (greenstone or jade). But it was the discovery of gold, and then coal, in the late 1800s that drew significant European investment.

The town itself harbors few points of interest for visitors, serving rather as a springboard to nearby activities such as rafting, jet-boating, caving, kayaking, hiking, and biking. A handful of mining attractions are worth a visit, while the seal colony and nearby Cape Foulwind are musts.

SIGHTS

Cape Foulwind and the Tauranga Bay Seal Colony

The **Cape Foulwind** headland was named by Captain Cook in 1770 following a particularly vile tempest. The rolling farmland and rocky shores jut into the Tasman Sea 10km southwest of Westport.

A thriving fur seal colony lies 3km south at **Tauranga Bay**. The seals (called *kekano* by Maori) were once hunted to the point

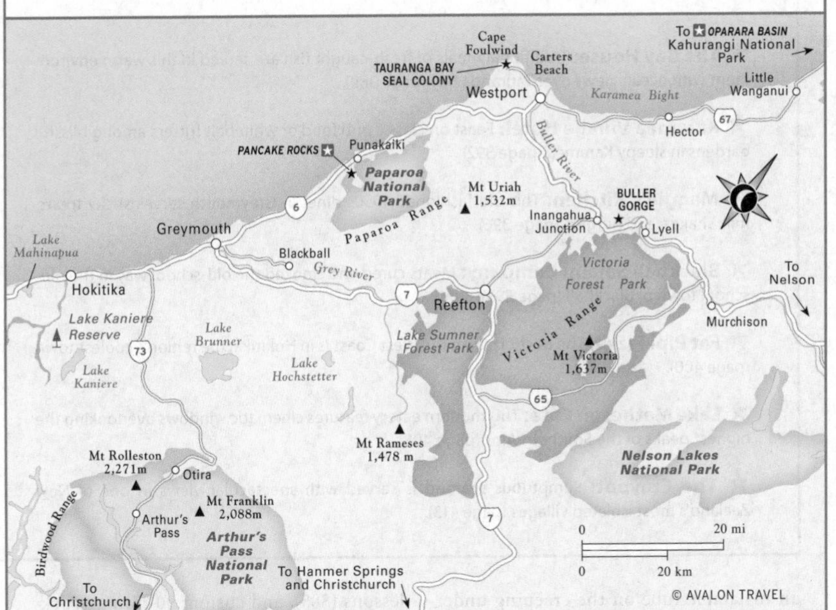

of extinction—by Maori for food and by Europeans for pelts. The seals are most numerous October-January, when they attend to newborn pups. From the raised viewing platform at the end of a windswept headland, you'll see them lounging on the rocks and taking the occasional dip. The seal colony is a 15-minute walk from the Tauranaga Bay car park (Tauranga Bay Rd.).

From the seal colony, the Cape Foulwind Walkway winds for another 3km along a clifftop trail, occasionally adorned with story boards that tell of the region's whaling and pioneer heritage, to a historic lighthouse. There is no public access inside the lighthouse. Allow an hour to walk each way.

Coaltown Museum

Coaltown Museum (123 Palmerston St., 03/789-6658, www.coaltown.co.nz, 9am-5pm daily Oct.-Apr., 9am-5pm Mon.-Fri., 10am-4pm Sat.-Sun. May-Sept., adults $15, seniors $13.50, children $7) is a well-informed and modern tribute to the region's mining heritage. Exhibits explain how coal is formed, extracted, and transported in the region, and details the history of the communities that benefited. Watch a documentary film, peruse extensive photos, and see a replica mine with actual equipment, including a Q wagon suspended at an impossibly steep incline.

SPORTS AND RECREATION

Underworld Adventures

Discover what's beneath this West Coast wonderland with **Underworld Adventures** (Charleston Adventure Centre and Cafe, Hwy. 6, Charleston, 03/788-8168, www.caverafting.com, 9am, 11:30am, and 2pm daily summer, 10am and 12:30pm daily winter). The award-winning eco-adventure firm offers a variety of activities: **Underworld Rafting** (4 hours, adults $185, children $150) is a fascinating stroll through the Nile River cave system followed by a solo ride on

Best Food

★ **The Bay House:** Traditional meals of fresh-caught fish are served in this warm environment with ocean views over Tauranga Bay (page 389).

★ **Karamea Village Hotel:** Feast on classic pub food or whitebait fritters among blissful gardens in sleepy Karamea (page 392).

★ **Maggie's Kitchen:** This old-fashioned 1950s diner in Greymouth serves sticky treats, milk shakes, and burgers (page 396).

★ **Blackball Salami Company:** Meats cured and smoked the old-school way in the old-school town of Blackball (page 397).

★ **Fat Pipi Pizza:** The best pizza on the West Coast is in Hokitika, the region's coolest town (page 400).

★ **Lake Matheson Café:** This modern eatery features cinematic windows overlooking the highest peaks of the Southern Alps (page 408).

★ **The Craypot:** Sumptuous seafood is served with spectacular views in one of New Zealand's most isolated villages (page 413).

an inflatable tube on the creeping underground waterways alight with glowworms. Depending on weather conditions (and your confidence), there's an option to tackle some rapids at the end.

The **Glowworm Cave Tour** (3.5 hours, adults $120, children $87.50) takes in the upper levels of the cave system, including glowworms. The **Adventure Caving Tour** (5 hours, adults only, $350) comprises a 30m rappel with boulder scrambling, waterfall scaling, and squeezing through some very tight gaps. It's a challenging, sometimes claustrophobic, endeavor that requires both physical and mental stamina.

Underworld Adventures is 20 minutes south of Westport in Charleston. Locations of each adventure vary based on the type of tour.

Surfing

West Coast Surf (299 Tauranga Bay Rd., 027/255-2651, www.wcsurf.co.nz) is an elite school offering 30-minute skill-sharpening sessions ($40), three-hour beginner's lessons ($85), and custom 90-minute packages ($120) in the waters of Tauranga Bay. Boards and wetsuit rentals ($10 for 2 hours, $80 all day) are also available. The school is located on Cape Foulwind, about 15km south of Westport along Highway 67.

Biking

A former gold mining route, the **Old Ghost Road** (www.oldghostroad.org.nz) stretches 85km from the Upper Buller Gorge north to the Mokihini River. The Great Ride (also open to hikers) weaves through rainforest, valleys, and four ghost towns with lodging huts (hut dorm $35, private $80 s or d) and tent sites ($20 s or d) scattered along the way. The demanding Grade 4 ride takes 2-4 days to bike and five days to hike.

Rent bikes from **Buller Adventure** (193 Palmerston St., Westport, 05/0848-6877, www.bulleradventures.com), which also offers transport to and from the trail. The bike track is best started from the south at Lyell (64km east of Westport).

Best Accommodations

★ **Gentle Annie:** Cabins and lodges at South Island's best campsite overlook a windswept driftwood-strewn beach in a secluded spot north of Westport (page 390).

★ **Rongo Backpackers and Gallery:** Everyone's happy place, this rainbow-covered hostel in Karamea has original artworks on the wall, a yoga studio, and vegetable garden (page 392).

★ **Punakaiki Beach Camp:** Bed down in this secluded rainforest clearing on the coast, with sea on one side and towering limestone cliffs on the other (page 394).

★ **Breakers Boutique Accommodation:** Luxury lodgings in Greymouth are adorned with native timber and art and furnished with local wool (page 397).

★ **Birdsong Backpackers:** The scent of baking bread fills the air at this coastal retreat in the laid-back town of Hokitika (page 401).

★ **Fox Glacier Lodge:** This idyllic alpine setting is replete with log fires, pine cabins, and mountain views (page 409).

★ **Collyer House:** French doors and antique furnishings are just some of the treats at this lodging in the World Heritage region of Haast (page 412).

FOOD

Freckles Café (216 Palmerston St., Westport, 03/789-8270, 7:30am-4pm Mon.-Fri., 9:30am-1:30pm Sat., $5-14) is a colorful little eatery popular among locals. It's famed for its high-quality coffee and homemade pastry and pies; the minced beef and cheese pie is especially scrumptious.

The **Denniston Dog** (18 Wakefield St., Westport, 03/789-5030, www.dennistondog.co.nz, 9am-late daily, $16-36) is a traditional pub with a generous selection of tap beers. Rib-eye steak, chicken Kiev, and green-lipped mussels along with daily baked treats are prepared and served with panache.

One the region's best bites, ★ **The Bay House** (Tauranga Bay Rd., Tauranga Bay, 03/789-4151, www.bayhouse.co.nz, 11:30am-4pm Wed.-Sun. June-Sept., 11:30am-4pm Wed.-Sun. and 5:30pm-close Wed.-Sat. Oct.-May, $30-36) is an idyllic eatery in a welcoming timber-clad environment overlooking the wild West Coast waves. The exceptional menu includes classic dishes like beer-battered fish-and-chips, rack of lamb, and fresh-caught seafood. In summer, book a table on the deck.

ACCOMMODATIONS

Bazil's Hostel and Surf School (54-56 Russell St., Westport, 03/789-6410, www.bazils.com, dorm $32, $72 s or d) offers warm colors and wood furnishings that lend a homey feel. Facilities include hammocks, a herb garden, free Wi-Fi, movie lounges, laundry, a hot tub, and barbecues. An extensive collection of outdoor equipment is available for rent, and the hostel is also an accredited surf school.

Set in a white Victorian villa, **Archer House** (75 Queen St., Westport, 03/789-8778, www.archerhouse.co.nz, $225 s or d) is the town's loveliest boutique B&B. Stained-glass windows, ornate lamps, and antique desks grace three spacious rooms, all equipped with modern baths, while communal areas comprise three lounges—one with a piano—and a watercolor-like garden. Continental breakfast is included.

Omau Settlers Lodge Motel (2 Omau Rd., Cape Foulwind, 03/789-5200, www.omausettlerslodge.co.nz, $159-169 s or d) rests far enough from the seal colony to evade the smell but is still close enough (4km) for a pleasant coastal stroll. Eight contemporary and roomy en suite studios boast mountain or sea views with private outdoor areas, a desk, a fridge, and tea- and coffee-making facilities. Admire the greenery from the outdoor hot tub.

The wooden **Beaconstone Eco Lodge** (115 Birds Ferry Rd., Westport-Charleston, 027/431-0491, www.beaconstoneecolodge.co.nz, Oct.-May, dorm $39, $88-96 s or d) sleeps up to 10 guests in doubles, twins, and two dorms with three futon beds. Surrounded by mountains and rainforest, the retreat sports solar power and composting toilets. Come nightfall, enjoy a stunning starlit view. The lodge is a 15-minute drive south of Westport.

Happiness abounds at ★ **Gentle Annie** (298 De Malmanches Rd., Mokihinui, 03/782-1826, www.gentleannie.co.nz, dorm $30, tent sites $12 pp), the coolest campsite in Kiwi land. This coastal haven spills onto a driftwood-strewn beach at the mouth of the Mokihini River. Behind the campsite are more accommodations among nikau palms. Lodges have decks, sea views, and sleep up to 27 guests. Cabins and cottages are equipped with baths and well-stocked kitchens and sleep up to 10 people ($75-180 s or d, $30 additional person). A quirky on-site café (summer only) is housed in a former cow shed. There's free Wi-Fi and hot showers for campers. It's a 30-minnute drive north of Westport.

TRANSPORTATION AND SERVICES

Westport is 285km (3 hours, 50 minutes) southwest of Picton along Highways 63 and 6. From Nelson, it's 222km (3 hours) southwest along Highway 6. From Christchurch, take Highways 7, 69, and 6 northwest for 332km (4 hours, 20 minutes).

Westport Airport (WSZ, Tiphead Rd., 03/280-8636, www.bullerdc.govt.nz) is 10 minutes northwest of the central business district. It is served daily by flights from Wellington via **Sounds Air** (03/520-3080, www.soundsair.com). **Avis** (www.avis.co.nz) and **Hertz** (03/789-7819, www.hertz.co.nz) provide car rentals at the airport. **Hertz** (197 Palmerston St., 03/789-7819, 8am-5pm Mon.-Fri.) also has an office downtown.

InterCity (03/365-1113, 123 Palmerstson St., www.intercity.co.nz) buses service destinations north to Nelson (departs 3:50pm daily) and south toward Greymouth and the glaciers (10:55am daily). **East West Coaches** (03/789-6251, 197 Palmerston St., www.eastwestcoaches.co.nz) offers shuttle buses that connect Westport to Christchurch via the Lewis Pass.

The Westport **i-SITE Visitor Information Centre** (123 Palmerstson St., 03/789-6658, 9am-5pm daily Dec.-Mar., 9am-4:30pm Mon.-Fri., 10am-4pm Sat.-Sun. Apr.-Nov.) provides maps and information about the region. Palmerston Street is also home to several banks and one of only three post offices on the West Coast.

NORTH TO KARAMEA

From Westport, Highway 67 runs north for 100km to Karamea. The beautiful coastal drive takes an hour straight through, but it's well worth the time to stop and explore one of the nation's most remote regions. Fill up the tank before you leave; there are no gas stations until Karamea.

Denniston

Weather-beaten Denniston rests above a former coal mine on a 600m plateau where the world's steepest tramway, the Denniston Incline, shifted coal and people. Old mining trails, scattered with rusted equipment, now serve as hiking and biking tracks.

The Denniston Experience (tours 3 times daily, Dickson St., Denniston, 03/789-9021, www.denniston.co.nz, adults $45-100, children $20-50) transports guests into the lives of 19th-century miners, journeying via a narrow-gauge train across viaducts and deep into the mines.

Oparara Arch

Denniston is a 30-minute drive east of Westport. To get here, take Highway 67 north and turn off at Waimangaroa. Enjoy the winding drive up Denniston Hill.

Charming Creek Walkway

The **Charming Creek Walkway** is a 19km (5-6 hours round-trip) hiking track that snakes along the Ngakawau Gorge past the Mangatini Falls. Along the way, you'll pass tunnels, a suspension bridge, abandoned mills, and old mine entrances strewn with industrial relics. The trail follows an old railway line partway and the Grade 3 track is shared with mountain bikers.

The walkway is 35km northeast of Westport. Take Highway 67 north for 32km to Ngakawau and then follow signs for the walkway.

Lake Hanlon

A tranquil respite, **Lake Hanlon** is one of New Zealand's youngest lakes, formed in the 1929 Murchison earthquake. The sheltered body of water is surrounded by dense rainforest that's mirrored in its glassy surface. An easy walk (1.5km round-trip, 30 minutes) leads to a lookout over the lake.

Lake Hanlon is an hour north of Westport along Highway 67. Keep your eyes peeled for the sign for Lake Hanlon on the side of the highway.

KARAMEA AND VICINITY

The sleepy northern settlement of **Karamea** is one of the best-kept secrets on the West Coast. The tiny town acts as a gateway to Kahurangi National Park (*kahurangi* means "treasured possession" in Maori), a subtropical hiking and biking paradise that brims with birdlife, including reef herons, kiwi, and kea; a substantial collection of fossils; and the largest stone arches in the southern hemisphere—35 million years in the making.

★ Oparara Basin

The **Oparara Basin** (www.doc.govt.nz) of Kahurangi National Park is a West Coast gem. A network of palm- and pebble-fringed tea-colored waterways flows through this limestone cave wonderland. Ferns, mosses, and algae unique to the area carpet great swathes of its delicate ecosystem. The basin is home to numerous well-signed walks that range from 10 minutes to a full day. The **Oparara Arch** (1km from the trailhead) is a magnificent limestone attraction, ably supported by the **Crazy Paving** and **Box Canyon Caves.**

The **Honeycomb Hill Caves** house skeletons of more than 50 species of extinct birds, including the moa and Haast's eagle. Access is via guided tour with Department of Conservation (DoC)-approved **Oparara Guided Tours** (Market Cross, Karamea, 03/782-6652, www.oparara.co.nz, $95-150).

The Oparara car park and trailhead is 22km north of Karamea off Karamea-Kohaihai Road (turn left at McCallums Road). The 30-minute drive is not suitable for RVs or buses.

Food and Accommodations

★ **Rongo Backpackers and Gallery** (130 Waverley St., Karamea, 03/782-6667, www.rongobackpackers.com) is Kiwi quirkiness at its best. Rainbow colors cloak the exterior while original artworks hang inside. A maximum of 22 guests are housed in themed "peace" dorms ($32-35) and rustic twin ($65 s, $40 pp) and double ($70 s, $90 d) rooms. Amenities include a yoga studio, a cinema room, and an organic vegetable garden. This backpacker hostel is also the home of the local community radio station—ask to host your own show.

The rainforest-themed **The Last Resort** (71 Waverley St., Karamea, 03/782-6617, www.lastresortkaramea.co.nz) is a popular hangout. Great-value accommodations include budget dorms ($37, $50 s, $74 d) and self-contained lodges ($107-130) equipped with a microwave, a TV, a fridge, and tea- and coffee-making facilities. The complex has an eatery (7:30am-8:30pm daily, $20-34) that stocks a selection of food with a snack menu and well-prepared staples like burgers and fish-and-chips. There's also a bar.

Whitebait fritters are a must at ★ **Karamea Village Hotel** (Waverley St. and Wharf Rd., 03/782-6800, www.karameahotel.co.nz, noon-9pm daily, $15-34), a charming establishment set in a beautiful green space. Traditional pub offerings include fish-and-chips and lamb dishes, with daily specials on chalkboards. Accommodations are in nine units with twins, doubles, and a family room. Three self-contained units ($125-150 s or d) include kitchens; the rest have en suite baths.

Transportation and Services

Karamea is 96km (1 hour, 20 minutes) north of Westport along Highway 67. The **Karamea Express** (03/782-6757, rates vary) operates a taxi-shuttle-bus service between Westport and Karamea. Buses depart Westport at 11:30am and Karamea at 7:40am Monday-Saturday.

The **Karamea Connections** (03/782-6667, www.karameaconnections.co.nz, $15) shuttle service transports travelers from Karamea to the Heaphy Track.

Community-owned and operated **Karamea Information & Resource Centre** (106 Bridge St., 03/782-6652, www.karameainfo.co.nz, 9am-5pm Mon.-Fri.) is the site of the area's only gas station (9am-5pm Mon.-Fri.) and has maps, information, and gas.

Paparoa National Park

Paparoa National Park (www.doc.govt.nz) comprises 30,000ha of fascinating rock formations and native bush that sprout from its limestone base. Molded in the soft rock, an intricate network of snaking caves, river canyons, and blowholes link to towering coastal cliffs. Inland rises the ancient granite of the Paparoa Range, carved by ice and carpeted in forests of beech and rimu trees alive with birds—including the great spotted kiwi.

The **Paparoa National Park Visitor Centre** (4294 Coast Rd., Punakaiki, 03/731-1895, 9am-6pm daily Nov.-Mar., 9am-4:30pm daily Apr.-Oct.) is opposite the entrance to Pancake Rocks. Stop here to learn how the bizarre rocks were formed and find Coast Road points of interests, plus local walks and activities.

★ PANCAKE ROCKS

The settlement of Punakaiki teems with tour buses thanks to the park's star attraction: **Pancake Rocks.** This bizarre coastal formation, 30 million years in the making, is punctuated by a handful of enormous blowholes. As the seabed was seismically raised and eroded by water and weather, the resulting mounds of limestone formations left unusual pancake-shaped piles of rocks.

The **Pancake Rocks and Blowholes Walk** (1.1km round-trip) is an easy saunter around a well-formed track. The plumes of sea spray forced through the blowholes are most impressive at high tide. The trailhead is opposite the Paparoa National Park Visitor Centre.

SPORTS AND RECREATION

Walks

The **Truman Track** (3.4km round-trip) is a rewarding trek past the powerfully hypnotic West Coast surf and a blowhole. Plan to arrive at low tide in order to explore the array of sea caves and rock pools. The trailhead is 3km north of the Paparoa National Park Visitor Centre.

The **Fox River Cave Walk** (3.7km one-way) is a moderate three-hour trek along the Fox River to a beautiful cave adorned with calcium formations. Bring a flashlight and allow at least 30 minutes to explore the cave, which reaches 200m into the hillside. The trailhead is signed 12km north of Punakaiki.

Horseback Riding

Punakaiki Horse Treks (4224 Hwy. 6, Main Rd., Punakaiki, 03/731-1839, www.pancakerocks.co.nz, $180, 2-person minimum) offers an engaging 2.5-hour journey across beaches and through bushland in the shadow of 100m limestone cliffs. Trips depart at 9:30am and 2pm (or 2:30pm) daily. No riding experience is necessary.

FOOD AND ACCOMMODATIONS

Brave the inevitable tour bus crowds at **Pancake Rocks Cafe** (4300 Hwy. 6, Punakaiki, 03/731-1122, www.pancakerockscafe.com, 8am-8:30pm daily Oct.-Apr., 8:30am-5pm daily May-Sept., $15-26) and reward your stomach with delectable stone-oven pizzas or fresh fish. Tasty pancake stacks are served with bacon, berries, or chocolate and are among the best-sellers.

Humming with chatter, **Punakaiki Tavern** (Hwy. 6 and Owen St., Punakaiki, 03/731-1188, www.punakaikitavern.co.nz, 8am-midnight Mon.-Sat., 8am-10pm Sun., $19-40) is open for breakfast, lunch, and dinner. Fare includes steaks, burgers, and bangers, with free Wi-Fi, a jukebox, outdoor seating, and a roaring fire in colder months. An on-site motel offers nine basic ground-floor studio units ($140 s or d) with en suite

Pancake Rocks

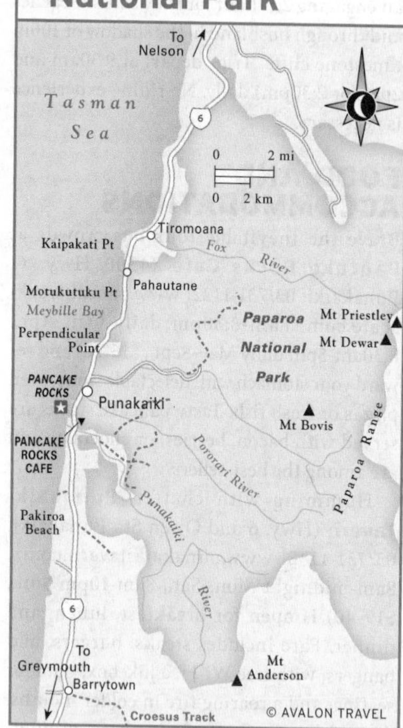

showers, fridges, and tea- and coffee-making facilities.

Set under imposing limestone cliffs, ★ **Punakaiki Beach Camp** (5 Owen St., Punakaiki, 03/731-1894, www.punakaiki-beachcamp.co.nz) has tent and campervan sites ($17-20 pp) and basic cabins ($68-78 s or d) with bunks or double beds that can sleep up to six. This secluded slice of West Coast paradise is minutes from Pancake Rocks and a stone's throw from the beach.

Budget accommodations with million-dollar views, **Punakaiki Beach Hostel** (4 Webb St., Punakaiki, 03/731-1852, www.punakaiki-beachhostel.co.nz, dorm $32, $83 s or d) has a gorgeous outdoor area that merges with the sand. Dorm beds come equipped with a reading light and a power outlet, but the star of the show is the House Truck ($130 s or d), a vintage lorry converted into a mini home for two, complete with a flat-screen TV, bath, and kitchen. Tent sites ($22 pp) are also available. Amenities include free Wi-Fi, tea, herbs, and spices.

You'll enjoy plenty of birdsong for your buck at **Te Nikau Retreat** (19 Hartmount Place, Punakaiki, 03/731-1111, www.tenikauretreat.co.nz, dorm $32, $62-160 s or d), a cluster of lodges tucked away in the bush. Dorm lodges and some of the less expensive private options (from rudimentary to fully self-contained units) share bath and kitchen facilities. Unlimited Wi-Fi is free to all guests. Some rooms have private decks overlooking the forest. YHA discounts are available.

Perched on a palm-carpeted hillside with ocean views, **Hydrangea Cottages** (4224 Hwy. 6, Punakaiki, 03/731-1839, www.pancake-rocks.co.nz, $230-325 s or d) comprise five unique lodgings built from native materials. Amenities include free Wi-Fi, a kitchen, and a TV and DVD player; barbecues can be rented. Some properties have sofa beds (up to 2 extra guests, $20 pp) or opt for the micro or rimu cottage with an outdoor bath on the veranda.

TRANSPORTATION AND SERVICES

Paparoa National Park is located along Highway 6 (the "Coast Road") between Westport and Greymouth. Services and park entrances are in the town of Punakaiki, 55km south of Westport and 45km north of Greymouth.

Intercity (www.intercity.co.nz) buses stop opposite the Pancakes Rock Cafe (300 Hwy. 6, Punakaiki): southbound at 12:35pm daily and northbound at 3pm daily.

Greymouth

Nearly half of the West Coast population lives in Greymouth, an industrial heartland that sits at the mouth of the Grey River. The waterway served the town well during the mining boom of the late-19th century, but it also caused a number of devastating floods that led to the erection of a flood wall that today doubles as a walking and bike path. Greymouth's proximity to rainforest and the Southern Alps means there's plenty of adventure activities to be found.

SIGHTS

History House Museum

Photographic exhibits recount mining, milling, and shipping triumphs and tragedies in the **History House Museum** (27 Gresson St., 03/768-4028, 10am-4pm Mon. and Thurs.-Fri., 10am-1pm Tues., 10am-8pm Wed., 10am-2pm Sat., adults $6, children $2). The handsome exterior is worth a photo in itself.

Shantytown

Shantytown (316 Rutherglen Rd., 03/762-6634, www.shantytown.co.nz, 8:30am-5pm daily, adults $33, children $16, seniors and students $26, under age 5 free) is a reconstructed 19th-century gold-rush-era settlement where visitors can pan for gold ($7), ride a steam train, and watch a sluice gun blast away at a cliff face. It's predominantly aimed at children and tour groups, but a handful of short walks take in the surrounding bush. Shantytown is 10km south of Greymouth along Highway 6.

RECREATION

For a picturesque view of the coast and town, make for **King Domain Walk** (enter at Mount St., 1.5 hours round-trip), a meandering uphill trek. Another fine short stroll is the relaxing waterside route along Greymouth's flood wall that runs west from Mawhera Quay along the estuary to **Blaketown Beach.** It's an hour's walk one-way with plenty of exit points en route.

Mawhera Quay also marks the start of the **West Coast Wilderness Trail** (www.westcoastwildernesstrail.co.nz), a four-day, 139km Great Ride that links Greymouth to Ross. The trail heads through rainforest and along glacial lakes and rivers, all in the shadow of the Southern Alps.

Get caked in mud (wear protective clothing) with **On Yer Bike!** (511 Hwy. 6, 03/762-7438, www.onyerbike.co.nz adults $50-180, children

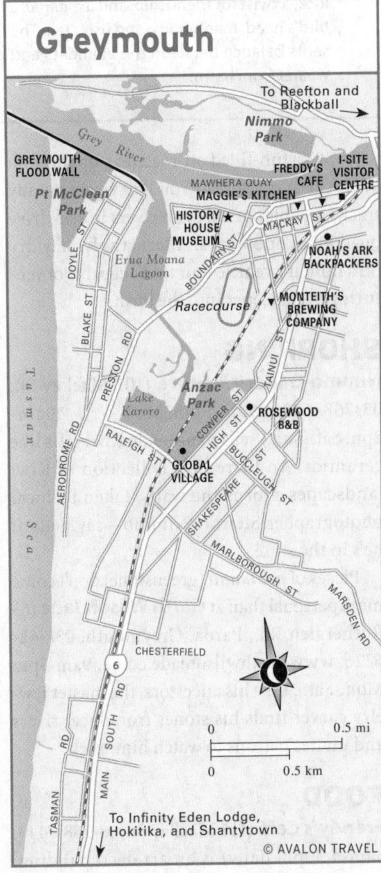

Greenstone: A Kiwi Gem

Jade, commonly referred to as greenstone in New Zealand, has bewitched people for thousands of years. Maori call the gem *pounamu*, historically using it for tools, weaponry, and decoration. The gemstone is respected for its beauty and durability. It is considered sacred *(tapu)*, and said to possess *mana*, or status. While gemstones are usually valued by carat weight, pieces of *pounamu* are examined individually to assess strength and color and to see how it could best be carved. Types of greenstone include: *kahurangi*, a translucent stone that is among the most treasured due to its scarcity; *kawakawa*, named after the leaf of a plant of the same name; and *totoweka*, a type of *kawakawa*, with red iron oxide flecks. Among the most commonly carved designs are the fish hook, which represents strength, peace, and luck; a twist for friendship; and a *manaia*, a figure with a bird's head, man's body, and fish's tail. The figure represents balance between the elements and protects the wearer from harm.

greenstone carving

$30-150), a fun-filled off-road tear-up through West Coast rainforest. You'll navigate muddy tracks and plunge through rivers in self-drive quad bikes or buggies. Alternatively, stay dry on a military vehicle tour that's capable of venturing even deeper into the bush.

SHOPPING

Nimmo Gallery + Store (102 Mackay St., 03/768-6499, 9am-5pm Mon.-Fri., 10am-2pm Sat.-Sun.) sells handmade Kiwi gifts like ceramics. An incredible collection of Kiwi landscapes adorns the walls, taken by local photographer Stewart Nimmo—say hello if he's in the store.

Pieces of *pounamu* (greenstone) don't come more personal than at **Garth Wilson Jade** (63 Rutherglen Rd., Paroa, Greymouth, 03/762-6226, www.garthwilsonjade.co.nz, 9am-5pm Mon.-Sat.). Like his ancestors, the master jewelry carver finds his stones from local rivers and invites patrons to watch him work.

FOOD

Freddy's Café (115 Mackay St., 03/768-7443, 8am-4:30pm daily) is an art deco building, with chandeliers and stylish 1930s artwork inside. Enjoy a wide range of decadent treats like cakes and ice-cream sundaes or more substantial fare like burgers and seafood chowder.

For 150 years, **Monteith's Brewing Company** (Turumaha St. and Herbert St., 03/768-4149 www.thebrewery.co.nz, 11am-9pm daily Nov.-Apr., 11am-8pm daily May-Oct., $13-23) has quenched the nation's thirst. You can see how the legendary beers are crafted with a 25-minute tour (11:30am, 3pm, 4:30pm, and 6pm daily, $25-35) or add your own tasting session ($13-23). Order sticky ribs from the excellent menu; they pair especially well with the booze.

Photographs and cute reviews from kids grace the walls of 1950s U.S.-style diner ★ **Maggie's Kitchen** (65 Mackay St., 03/768-5265, 5:30am-3pm Mon.-Fri., 7:30am-1pm Sat., $12-20). Taste traditional Kiwi fare such as meat pies or whitebait fritters but leave room for a caramel marshmallow slice.

You'd better be famished upon arrival at **Steamers Carvery and Bar** (58 Mackay St., 03/768-4193, 11am-8:30pm daily, $13-27). The no-nonsense eatery serves homey meals

Blackball Town

Tucked into the inland foot of the Paparoa Range, 20 minutes northeast of Greymouth, the town of **Blackball** is compellingly odd. Once a thriving mid-19th-century gold- and then coal-mining hub until the 1960s, now just 300 people call it home. Where people once dug for gold (some still do) to strike it rich to escape to another life, now a respectable collection of artists and hippies have escaped to a life in Blackball instead. **Kereru Crafts** (29 Hilton St., Blackball, 03/732-4048) showcases and sells a number of locally handcrafted goods like carvings, paintings, and jewelry.

Blackball has always had something of a rebellious stance—a number of early-20th-century strikes led to the formation of New Zealand's most significant trade union—streaks of such subversion still remain. It's most notable with the strategically placed "Formerly" sign nailed at a comical angle above the signage of the hotel, bar, and restaurant. **Formerly the Blackball Hilton** (26 Hart St., Blackball, 03/732-4705, noon-late daily summer, might close early in winter, $55 s, $110 d), which was forced to change its name following a legal dispute with a well-known international hotel chain. Once heaving with miners (the locals still know how to chuck back the beer), the historic building still serves old-fashioned pub fare ($28-34) before antiques-adorned walls and a roaring fire.

The ★ **Blackball Salami Company** (11 Hilton St., Blackball, 03/732-4111, www.blackballsalami.co.nz, 8am-4pm Mon.-Fri., 9am-2pm Sat.) is now the town's biggest exporter, and for good reason. Stop by to try their traditionally cured and naturally wood-smoked meats, including venison.

like roast meats and vegetables drizzled in gravy and in very generous portions. Don't leave without tasting the homemade apricot crumble.

ACCOMMODATIONS

A classy backpacker hostel minutes from the beach, **Global Village** (42-54 Cowper St., 03/768-7272, www.globalvillagebackpackers.co.nz, dorm $31, $78 s or d), has comfortable beds with private reading lamps and power outlets. The well-stocked kitchen offers free hot drinks, while the comfortable communal area houses opulent armchairs, a guitar, a piano, and a log fire. Free unlimited Wi-Fi, a gym, a hot tub, and a sauna round out the amenities.

Animal lovers are in for a treat at beast-themed **Noah's Ark** (16 Chapel St., 03/768-4868, www.noahs.co.nz, dorm $32, $82 s or d), where rooms are decorated in wall-mounted animal prints and striped sheets. Women-only dorms, family rooms ($109-136), and campsites ($21 pp) are housed in roomy sleeping quarters. Amenities include free Wi-Fi, bike rentals, and free tea, herbs, and spices. Enjoy the hot tub and hammocks outside. It's all a short stroll from downtown.

Paroa Hotel (508 Main South Rd., 03/762-6860, www.paroa.co.nz, $160-345) is one of the city's slickest lodgings. Modern suites (some have spa tubs) have balconies and sea views and come with cooking facilities, free Wi-Fi, and Sky TV. Guests make use of the garden, bar, restaurant, and communal barbecue area.

★ **Breakers Boutique Accommodation** (1367 Hwy. 6, Rapahoe, 03/762-7743, www.breakers.co.nz, $265-385 s or d) has four luxury rooms incorporating recycled native timber and furnished with local art. Rooms overlook well-kept gardens and the Tasman Sea. Enjoy complimentary hot drinks, home-baked treats, locally sourced breakfast, plus free Wi-Fi. Breakers is in Rapahoe, 14km north of Greymouth.

It seems little has changed at quaint **Rapahoe Bay Holiday Park** (10 Hawken St., Rapahoe, 03/762-7025, www.rapahoebeach.co.nz, tent sites $16, cabins $30 s, $45 d) since its 1970s inception. Basic cabins are equipped with a TV, a fridge, and a kettle.

The communal kitchen and lounge areas are well-stocked and full of mismatched furnishings, lending a beach-hut vibe. The holiday park is a 15-minute drive minutes north of Greymouth in Rapahoe.

TRANSPORTATION AND SERVICES

Greymouth is 101km south of Westport along Highway 6. Car rental companies in town include **Avis** (Mackay St., 03/768-0902, www.avis.co.nz), at the railway station, and **New Zealand Rent A Car** (170 Tainui St., 03/768-0720, www.nzrentacar.co.nz).

Intercity (www.intercity.co.nz) buses stop at the Greymouth Railway Station (164 MacKay St.) with service north to Westport and Nelson and south to Fox Glacier and Wanaka.

West Coast Shuttle Buses (03/768-0028, www.westcoastshuttle.co.nz) run to Springfield, Arthur's Pass, and Christchurch daily, departing from Greymouth (Regent Theatre, 6 MacKay St.) at 7:45am.

The *TranzAlpine* train journey connects Christchurch to Greymouth via the Arthur's Pass. Trains depart Christchurch daily at 8:15am and return at 6:30pm; a day trip is possible with a one-hour stop in Greymouth. Book departure and return dates separately though **KiwiRail** (04/495-0775, www.kiwirailscenic.co.nz, from $198) to allow time in the West Coast; one-way fares are available.

The expansive Greymouth **i-SITE Visitor Information Centre** (164 Mackay St., 03/768-7080, 9am-5pm daily Dec.-Apr., 9am-5pm Mon.-Fri., 10am-4pm Sat.-Sun. May-Nov.) is in the *TranzAlpine* Railway Station with baggage storage and a souvenir shop.

Hokitika and Vicinity

The arts and crafts mecca of Hokitika is the West Coast's coolest town with a delightful driftwood-strewn beach over which Mount Cook looms. A scattering of historical buildings prop up this sleepy town; its clock tower served as the setting for the Man Booker Prize-winning novel *The Luminaries* by Kiwi author Eleanor Catton.

Hokitika's population of 3,000 includes a sizable number of artists, and you can visit their studios to watch them at work. This is also the best place to purchase greenstone; the town's location is south of the Arahura River, which, according to Maori legend, is the birthplace of jade.

SIGHTS

Hokitika Museum

Exhibits in the **Hokitika Museum** (17 Hamilton St., 03/755-6898, www.hokitikamuseum.co.nz, 10am-2pm daily, adults $6, children $3) center around the area's gold-rush history, mining for greenstone, and whitebaiting. Much of the mining equipment sits alongside some impressive pieces of rare *pounamu*, with a plethora of black-and-white photos accompanied by informative historical texts. At the time of writing, hours were limited and not all exhibits were on display due to earthquake safety repairs.

Glowworm Dell

Find a slice of Middle-earth magic at the **Hokitika Glowworm Dell** (free) where a winding path leads to a grotto alive with hundreds of illuminating glowworms. Bring a flashlight or cell phone for light to navigate the trail, then switch it off when you enter the dell and watch the splendor begin.

The Glowworm Dell is 1.2km northeast of Hokitika along Highway 6. It is well signposted from the highway.

Hokitika Beach

Watch the sun set behind the iconic sculpture at **Hokitika Beach** (Beach St. and Weld

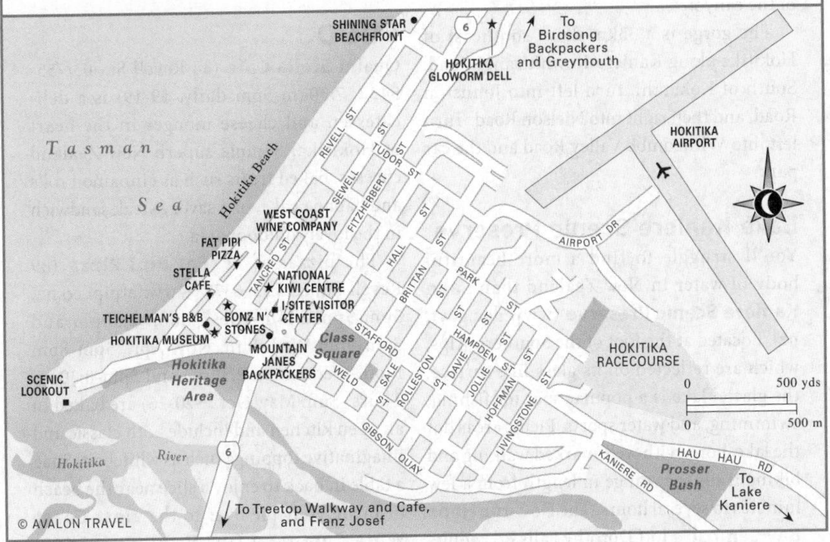

Lane) that spells out the town's name in driftwood. Then gather some driftwood of your own and light a bonfire on the sands. At the southern end of the beach (about a 10-minute walk south of town), **Sunset Point** is another romantic evening spot.

National Kiwi Centre

The **National Kiwi Centre** (64 Tancred St., 03/755-5251, www.thenationalkiwicentre.co.nz, 9am-5pm daily Nov.-Apr., 9:30am-4:30pm daily May-Oct., adults $22, children $13, seniors and students $19.50) is home to the *tuatara*, a reptile not much changed since the time of the dinosaurs; giant eels (feedings at 10am, noon, and 3pm daily); and a handful of foraging kiwi birds in viewing enclosures.

Bonz 'n Stonz

Craft the ultimate souvenir at **Bonz 'n Stonz** (16 Hamilton St., Hokitika, 03/755-6504, www.bonz-n-stonz.co.nz, 8am-5pm Mon.-Sat. Nov.-Mar., 9am-5pm Mon.-Sat. Apr.-Oct., $85-180) where you can design and carve your own piece of jewelry from jade, bone, or shell. Learn how to shape your stone with a bur, then sand, polish, and buff to a final finish using professional machinery under the watchful eye of an expert tutor.

West Coast Treetop Walkway and Café

Listen to the sounds of bristling foliage and birdsong at the **West Coast Treetop Walkway and Café** (1128 Woodstock-Rimu Rd., Hokitika, 03/755-5052, www.treetopsnz.com, 9am-5pm daily Oct.-Mar., 9am-4pm daily Apr.-Sept., adults $32, seniors and students $29, ages 5-15 $16). A 20m-high open tunnel network snakes among the peaks of rimu and kamahi trees as the Southern Alps stand watch from the horizon. Climb the 40m Hokitika Tower for a glimpse the Tasman Sea.

The West Coast Treetop Walkway is outside Ruatapu, 17.5km south of Hokitika along Highway 6.

RECREATION

Hokitika Gorge

The milky turquoise Hokitika River runs through granite **Hokitika Gorge** (www.doc.govt.nz). An easy walk (30 minutes round-trip) leads across a swing bridge and through rimu forests with ample viewpoints of the canyon.

The gorge is a 33km drive southeast of Hokitika along Kaniere-Kowhitirangi Road. South of Kokatahi, turn left into Johnston Road, and then right into Nielson Road. Turn left into Whitcombe Valley Road and the car park.

Lake Kaniere Scenic Preserve

You'll struggle to find a more beautiful body of water in New Zealand than **Lake Kaniere Scenic Preserve** (www.doc.govt.nz). Located at the foot of the Southern Alps, which are reflected on its glass-like surface, the glacial lake is a popular spot for fishing, swimming, and water sports. Picnic areas dot the lakeshore, with well-marked walking and biking trails that range in length from a few minutes to several hours. The DoC-run **Hans Bay Campsite** (off Dorothy Falls Rd., adults $8, children $4, cash only) and provides 40 scenic sites to pitch your tent.

The lake is 19km inland of Hokitika along Lake Kaniere Road.

SHOPPING

The **Hokitika Craft Gallery** (25 Tancred St., 03/755-8802, www.hokitikacraftgallery.co.nz, 9am-5:30pm daily) is owned and operated by a group of artists who work with flax, silk, wood, ceramics, canvas, and jade to create unique bags, scarves, and carvings.

Watch local artisans create traditional jade jewelry and *tiki* and *matau* sculptures at **Waewae Pounamu** (39 Weld St., 03/755-8304, www.waewaepounamu.co.nz, 8:30am-8pm Mon.-Fri., 9am-6pm Sat.-Sun. Nov.-Apr., 8:30am-5pm Mon.-Fri., 10am-4pm Sat.-Sun. May-Oct.).

Greenstone hogs so much of the limelight that few know of the revered local hand-blown glass. Family-run **Hokitika Glass Studio** (9 Weld St., 03/755-7775, www.hokitikaglass.co.nz, 8:30am-5pm daily) invites visitors to watch glass-blowing demonstrations (9am-4pm Mon.-Fri.) as intricate figurines such as penguins take shape.

FOOD

Quaint **Stella Cafe** (84 Revell St., 03/755-5432, 7:30am-5pm daily, $9-19) is a delicatessen and cheese monger in the heart of Hokitika. Sample superb New Zealand cheeses, baked treats such as cinnamon rolls and banana cake, or a savory steak sandwich in the lovely outdoor area.

The pizzas at ★ **Fat Pipi Pizza** (89 Revell St., 03/755-6373, www.fatpipi.co.nz, 5pm-9pm Mon.-Tues., noon-2:30pm and 5pm-9pm Wed.-Sun. Nov.-Apr., 5pm-8pm Mon.-Wed., noon-2:30pm and 5pm-8:30pm Thurs.-Sun. May-Oct., $20-26) are baked in an open kitchen and include both classic and imaginative toppings such as whitebait. Snag a table in back to enjoy a slice near the beach or bring your pie over to the **West Coast Wine Company** (108 Revell St., 03/755-5417, www.westcoastwine.co.nz, 4pm-close Mon.-Sat., noon-8pm Sun.) and pair it with a selection of high-end wines, cocktails, and craft beers.

ACCOMMODATIONS

Mountain Jade Backpackers (41 Weld St., 03/755-5185, www.mountainjadebackpackers.co.nz, dorm $26, $50 s, $65 d) offers great value lodging in Hokitika's city center. Accommodations include a range of dorms (6 beds women only, 8 beds mixed), double rooms, and self-contained family units. The kitchen, movie collection, and bookshelves are well-stocked, plus there's free unlimited Wi-Fi, laundry facilities, and a balcony with a lovely view of town.

Shining Star Beachfront (16 Richards Dr., Hokitika, 03/755-8921, www.shiningstar.co.nz) ranks as one of the most impressive and best value holiday parks on the West Coast. Self-contained motel rooms include spa baths, Sky TV, and private decks. En suite cabins ($119-202 s or d) come with fridges, tea- and coffee-making facilities, and farm views.

Wildfoods Festival

Since 1990, Hokitika has hosted the **Wildfoods Festival** (www.wildfoods.co.nz, Mar., adults $45, seniors $35, ages 5-17 $15), an internationally acclaimed culinary celebration that brings 15,000 people to town. This is an outdoor food festival with a difference—stalls promote weird, wonderful, and all-natural dishes such as chocolate worm truffles, crocodile bites, and crunchy crickets. There are also plenty of more conventional delights, including gourmet sausages, whitebait patties, and the traditional Maori *hangi*.

Tent and RV sites ($30 s, $40 d) share an immaculate kitchen, hot tub, barbecue area, and laundry. Wi-Fi is free, and there is an on-site petting farm.

Blissful ★ **Birdsong Backpackers** (124 Kumara Junction Hwy., 03/755-7179, www.birdsong.co.nz, dorm $34, $70 s, $89-140 d) is nestled at the edge of Hokitika. Rooms are decorated with murals and include beach or bush views. A 20-guest limit gives the hostel a private feel. Enjoy the superb kitchen and a picnic deck overlooking the ocean.

Book well in advance to secure one of six unique rooms at **Teichelmann's B&B** (20 Hamilton St., 03/755-8232, www.teichelmanns.nz, $190 s, $250-280 d), a historic white timber lodge opposite the Hokitika Museum. Spacious en suite quarters boast the comfiest king beds on the coast, complete with down covers and wool underlays, and complementary sherry and port in the lounge.

TRANSPORTATION AND SERVICES

Hokitika is 40km south of Greymouth along Highway 6. The **Hokitika Airport** (HKK, 1 Airport Dr., 03/755-6318, www.hokitikaairport.co.nz), 2km northeast of town, is the West Coast's main airport with flights from Christchurch via **Air New Zealand** (09/357-3000, www.airnewzealand.co.nz) twice daily.

Hokitika Taxis (03/755-5075, $12 airport to town) is the local taxi service. Car rental agencies **Budget** (03/768-4343), **Thrifty** (03/940-2501), and **Hertz** (03/768-0196) are located at the airport. **Intercity** (www.intercity.co.nz) buses depart the Hokitika i-SITE (36 Weld St.) at 2:57pm daily heading south, and 12:32pm daily north to Greymouth.

Visit the Hokitika **i-SITE Visitor Information Centre** (36 Weld St., 03/755-6166, 8:30am-6pm Mon.-Fri., 9am-5pm Sat.-Sun. Dec.-Feb., 8:30am-5pm Mon.-Fri., 10am-4pm Sat.-Sun. Mar.-Nov.) for more information about the town.

HOKITIKA TO FRANZ JOSEF

From Hokitika, Highway 6 continues 140km south to Franz Josef, initially hugging the coastline before sneaking through farmland, forest, and winding rugged mountain passes. There are a number of worthwhile stops along the way.

Ross

The claim to fame of the now tiny mining town of Ross's is as the source of the nation's largest gold nugget. Found in 1909 and weighing in at 3.1kg, it was named Honorable Roddy in honor of a local politician. To explore the area, follow the **Water Race Walkway** (4 Aylmer St., 03/755-4077), an easy 4km loop that takes in historic buildings, sea views, and the eerie town cemetery. Ross is a 20-minute drive south of Hokitika on Highway 6.

Whataroa

★ WHITE HERON SANCTUARY

New Zealand's only white heron nesting site sits among the low-lying rainforest at the foot of the Southern Alps. The only way to visit the site is thorough the **White Heron Sanctuary** (Hwy. 6, Whataroa, 03/753-4120, www.whiteherontours.co.nz, tours 9am, 11am, 1pm, and 3pm daily mid-Sept.-Mar., adults $135, children $65). The camouflaged viewing point in the Waitangiroto Nature Reserve is reached via a sleepy cruise along waterways hemmed by orchids, ferns, and pines. After a quick walk through Kahikatea rainforest, visitors can watch the long-necked birds tend to their young from a hidden observation point.

The rest of year, the company offers cruise and rain-forest tours for observing bird species such as bellbirds, fantails, tuis, and silvereyes. Tours are hosted by a DoC-approved guide and last 2.5 hours. Book ahead, especially during nesting season. Whataroa is 100km south of Hokitika along Highway 6.

Okarito

★ OKARITO LAGOON

Okarito Lagoon forms the biggest unmodified wetland in New Zealand, surrounded by rimu rainforest and home to bountiful bird species such as royal spoonbills and dotterels (if you're lucky, you may glimpse a white heron). The best way to explore these incredible shallows is via kayak. **Okarito Nature Tours** (1 The Strand, Okarito, 03/753-4014, www.okarito.co.nz) offer guided tours ($100-115) and rents single and double kayaks for paddling ($55-75 pp). If you have your own camping gear, opt for an overnight rental ($100) and you may get a chance to spot the elusive rowi kiwi.

Okarito Lagoon is 15km west of Whataroa. From Whataroa, follow Highway 6 for 13km to Forks-Okarito Road and turn right. Continue almost 10km to The Strand in Okarito.

White Heron Sanctuary

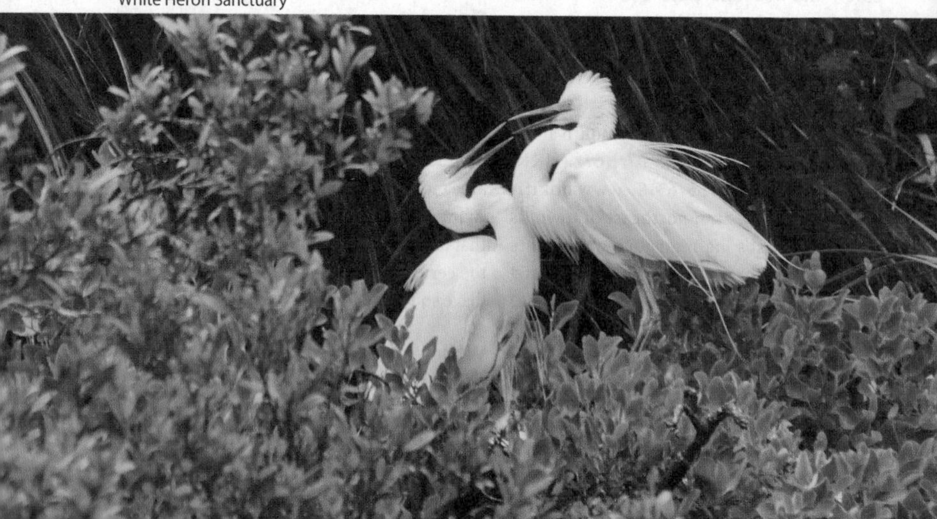

Westland Tai Poutini National Park

Most people visit the 127,541ha **Westland Tai Poutini National Park** (www.doc.govt.nz) to explore the glacier regions of Franz Josef and Fox; each region is served by an eponymous township. Of the 140 glaciers that seep from the Southern Alps, these are the only two that reach low-lying rainforest—making them among the most accessible glaciers in the world.

The park's dramatic scenery results from the alpine fault splitting the land—3,000m peaks rise cliff-like from low-lying plains. East of the fault, rainforests and alpine grasses sneak up the bases of the Main Divide (a range that includes 3,498m Mount Tasman, the nation's second-highest peak), before giving way to a permanent snow field across the Southern Alps. It is from these stoic ice sheets that Fox, Franz Josef, and dozens more glaciers creep, carving out high-altitude and mostly inaccessible gorges along the way. East of the range, beech and coniferous forests carpet the lowlands, dissected by rivers and dotted with glacial lakes.

The forest and wetlands attract birds like the tui, fantail, and the kea—the world's only alpine parrot. You may glimpse or hear a southern-crested grebe, white heron, and even the rowi kiwi (New Zealand's rarest), but don't bet on it.

Hundreds of plant species bloom throughout the park. Podocarp rainforests harbor rimu, totara, and miro trees, along with an array of New Zealand's iconic ferns. Closer to the coast, flax thrives. Changing seasons add vibrant colors as kamahi, fuchsia, and coprosmas bloom. The dense subtropical forest thins to subalpine scrub comprising herbs like edelweiss and hebe. Above the snow line, only lichens remain.

Planning Your Time

The weather in this region is notoriously fickle. While the West Coast generally receives around 3m of precipitation annually, up to 5m falls in "glacier country," rising to 10m (including snow) at altitudes of 1,500m. Conditions are usually clearer during the winter months, but even then, clear cold skies can fill with clouds without warning.

If you're planning any scenic flights or skydives (especially in summer), set aside a couple of days for weather delays. There's plenty of other sights and adventures to keep you occupied in the meantime.

SIGHTS

If bad weather delays your glacier plans, the **West Coast Wildlife Centre** (Cowan St. and Cron St., Franz Josef, 03/752-0600, www.wildkiwi.co.nz, 8:30am-close daily, adults $38, children $20) in the township of Franz Josef is just the tonic to escape the clouds. Established in partnership with DoC, the Centre allows visitors to get up close to the rowi—the rarest kiwi and one of the world's most endangered birds (less than 400 remain). Access into the impressive indoors is via a dimly lit native bush walk. The VIP Backstage Pass (reservation required, adults $58, children $35) provides a glimpse into the preservation work behind the scenes, such as tending incubating eggs in the lab.

★ FRANZ JOSEF GLACIER

The Franz Josef and Fox Glaciers bear many similarities, but when push comes to shove, Franz Josef is the bigger draw. It's quicker to reach via a helicopter tour, and its steeper gradient leads to more dramatic ice formations and crevasses, with easier access to the blue ice. Franz Josef township also offers more services, and many tour operators throw in a free pass to the hot pools after a glacier tour.

Glacier Walks

A variety of tracks follow bush-clad glacial

valleys whose walls are drenched by waterfalls. Hiking here affords a different view of the terminal face of Franz Josef Glacier, but none of the walks leads directly on to it. (To touch the ice, book a heli-tour that travels high up the glaciers.)

Sentinel Rock is reached via a 10-minute climb that affords a far-off but fantastic view of the glacier. The popular **Ka Roimata o Hine Hukatere Walk** (1.5 hours roundtrip) leads through rainforest before emerging in the glacier valley, whose steep sides are awash with waterfalls—it's especially spectacular following or during a heavy downpour. Entrance to both tracks is from the Glacier car park (end of Glacier Access Rd., 5km south of Franz Josef Village) off Highway 6.

The **Roberts Point Track** (5 hours, 11km) is for experienced hikers used to heights. The route traverses a high valley track over sometimes slippery rock, all of it stitched together by lengthy swing bridges. The reward is a bird's-eye view of the glacier. Access the track from the Alex Knob-Wombat car park (2km along Glacier Access Rd.) or via a 20-minute walk from Glacier car park (end of Glacier Access Rd., 5km south of Franz Josef Village).

For advanced trampers only, the **Alex Knob Track** (8 hours, 17km) rises through lowland forest to alpine landscapes with views of Franz Josef and the Tasman Sea. Access is from the Alex Knob-Wombat car park (2km along Glacier Access Rd.).

Embark on glacier trips in the mornings to minimize the risk of adverse weather that will obstruct views. Sturdy footwear is recommended; although most walks are along well-formed paths, there are loose rocks, and it's often wet and slippery. Check conditions at the DoC office as glacier valleys are prone to flash floods and avalanches.

Glacier Flightseeing Tours

The most rewarding (but expensive) way to see the glaciers is from the air. Flights are weather permitting; always book ahead and allow for more than one night's stay.

Franz Josef Glacier Guides (Glacier Base, 63 Cron St., 03/752-0763, www.franzjosefglacier.com) offers a variety of options. The **Ice Glacier Heli Hike** (4 hours, $449) departs regularly throughout the day. Visitors reach the glacier by helicopter where an ice-ax-wielding guide leads the crampon-clad line through tunnels of majestic white and blue ice. More confident adventurers can consider the guided **Heli Ice Climb** (5 hours, $525), a tough but thrilling jaunt that includes

Franz Josef Glacier

Glacial Ebb and Flow

Glaciers are formed through the constant accumulation of snow over thousands of years, either at altitude or near the poles. As a snow field, or neve, gets deeper, the weight of the snow compresses itself together to form ice—just like when you squeeze a snowball tightly in your hand. The power of the compression eventually forces out the air to give the ice its blue hue—occurring more deeply where the pressure is highest. As a glacier grows, it shifts, and when it is on a slope, like those of **Franz Josef** and **Fox,** it will slip under its own weight. Glaciers are in constant flux, cracking to form crevasses and ravines. New Zealand glaciers have retreated massively, thought to be caused by global warming. Analysis of aerial surveys published on the DoC website in 2014 showed that a third of the Southern Alps' permanent snow and ice had disappeared in less than 40 years.

helicopter transport and guided ice-climbing (no mountaineering experience necessary). Safety equipment is provided. Bring snacks, quick-drying layers, and sun protection.

Glacier Helicopters (Main Rd., Franz Josef, 03/752-0755, www.glacierhelicopters.co.nz, $240-450) offers four scenic flights ranging 20-40 minutes. Trips cross glaciers or Mount Cook, with snow landings for a high-altitude photo opportunity.

The Grand Traverse by **Air Safaris** (Main Rd., Franz Josef, 03/7520-716, www.airsafaris.co.nz, 50 minutes, $340) is a fixed-wing flightseeing tour with no snow landing. It captures the magnificence of Franz Josef and other glaciers, as well as an array of lakes, valleys, and Mount Cook.

Skydiving

Make New Zealand's highest jump (19,000 feet) with **Skydive Franz** (20 Main Rd., Franz Josef, 03/752-0714, www.skydivefranz.co.nz, $319-559). The 80-second free fall is followed by a five-minute ride with views that include the Tasman Sea and glacial and mountain landscape. There are also 13,000- and 15,000-foot options; photos and videos cost extra.

Glacier Hot Pools

The ideal way to end a day's exploring is with a soak in the idyllic **Glacier Hot Pools** (Glacier Base Building, Cron St., 03/752-0099, 11am-9pm daily, last entry 8pm, adults $27, children $23). Massage treatments and towel rentals are available.

Food

The small size of Franz Josef's township makes it easy to find an eatery, but its remoteness and popularity raises prices. Thus the $35 three-course menu at **Alice May Bar & Restaurant** (Cron St. and Cowan St., 03/752-0740, 4pm-9pm daily, $20-34) is a good value. Mains like whitebait and venison burgers are complemented by traditional desserts, notably pavlova, served in a homey country house replete with a wood fire.

Outdoor heaters and a crackling open fire mean that mountain views can be enjoyed from the deck any time at stylish **Landing Restaurant & Bar** (Main Rd., Franz Josef, 03/7520-229, www.thelandingbar.co.nz, 7:30am-1:30am daily, food until 10pm, $19-42). Thanks to the happy hours (4pm-6pm and 9pm-10pm daily), this is one of the town's livelier venues. The beautifully presented gastropub fare—lamb salad, pastas, and gourmet burgers—is served all day.

In the morning, grab a bacon bagel and coffee (or tea or a smoothie) from **Full of Beans** (Main Rd., Franz Josef, 03/752-0139, 7am-9pm daily, $10-27). Later in the day, the licensed café serves lunch and dinner (fish-and-chips, chicken and lime salad) with a great selection of take-out food.

Sate your spicy cravings at **King Tiger Eastern Eating House & Bar** (70 Cron St.,

03/752-0060, www.kingtiger.co.nz, 11am-10pm daily, $19-22), an Asian eatery with a menu that stretches from India to Thailand via China. Large portions of stir-fried meats and curries are easily shared, along with some well-chosen sides. Wash it down with a Far East cocktail like the Slumdog Millionaire mojito.

Accommodations

There's a chalet-like vibe at friendly **Franz Josef Montrose** (9 Cron St., 03/752-0188, www.franzjosefmontrose.nz, dorm $31-33, $79-109 s or d), a centrally located hostel. Dorms are basic but spotless; private rooms (some with en suite baths) come with towels, complimentary toiletries, and beds you won't want to leave. Relax with a free DVD rental and popcorn in the lounge room. There's also free breakfast, hot drinks, evening soup, and unlimited Wi-Fi.

Set in gorgeous bush surroundings, **Rainforest Retreat** (46 Cron St., 03/752-0220, www.rainforestholidaypark.co.nz) has a range of accommodations for all budgets. Dorm options ($27-35) include flashpacker four-bed en suite rooms with flat-screen Sky TV and hot-drink facilities. En suite units ($85-120) come equipped with a TV, iPod dock, and fridge. The Park Motel ($115-165) and cozy Tree Hut Log Cabins ($160-220) have en suite baths with kitchens and Sky Digital; the roomier Tree Lodge ($165-230) has a balcony and an extra single bed. Tent and RV sites ($16-24) offer use of a TV lounge, a kitchen, a laundry, a barbecue, a hot tub, and a sauna. There's an on-site bar and restaurant. The whole place is just a short walk from the main drag.

The closest motel to the glacier, luxurious **Alpine Glacier Motel** (17 Cron St., 03/752-0226, www.alpineglaciermotel.com, $130-199 s or d) comprises 24 stylish self-contained units; some have spa tubs, but all come with balconies or private decks and either a kitchenette or hot-drink facilities. Beds have electric blankets, and the Wi-Fi is free. Just two minutes to town, the rooms don't stay vacant long.

Tears of the Avalanche Girl

Franz Josef is an idyllic setting in a rainforest clearing just a few kilometers from the glacier. According to Maori legend, this place was born of lost love: Hine Hukatere shared her passion for the mountains with her soul mate, Tawe. When he fell to his death, the maiden's tears froze to form the glacier now known as Ka Roimata o Hine Hukatere—"The Tears of the Avalanche Girl."

10 Cottages (8 Graham Place, 03/752-0211, www.10cottages.co.nz, $205-225 s or d) feels a million miles from everywhere, yet is just minutes from the main street. The collection of detached unit studios, which sleep up to three, are located in a secluded cul-de-sac. Each unit boasts a kitchenette, an en suite toilet and shower room, and a deck with alpine views. The owners serve hot-baked treats come nightfall—a welcome touch.

Glenfarn Villas (Hwy. 6, 03/752-0054, www.glenfern.co.nz, $265-299) has self-contained alpine chalets with dining and lounge areas, free Wi-Fi, Sky TV, and a private deck with mountain views. It's 3km north of the Franz Josef township.

Akin to a country manor, **Holly Homestead B&B** (2900 Franz Josef Hwy., 03/752-0299, www.hollyhomestead.co.nz, $270-395 d) is a short drive from the village, surrounded by manicured lawns with mountains looming on the horizon. You'll be well looked after by owners Bernie and Gerard in their lovingly restored 1920s boutique B&B built from rimu timbers. Four cozy en suite rooms include coffee- and tea-making facilities, a blow-dryer, a TV, a stereo, plush linens, and bathrobes.

Surrounded by dense native forest, **Te Waonui Forest Retreat** (3 Wallace St., 03/357-1919, www.tewaonui.co.nz, $879) is an eco-friendly complex built with sustainable timbers. Luxurious spacious rooms are furnished with organic cotton bedding and fur cushions and offer alpine and bush views from a private deck or balcony. Amenities include movie-loaded LCD TVs, free Wi-Fi, a minibar, and hot-drink facilities. It's just a stone's throw from the hot-springs pools.

Transportation and Services

Franz Josef Village is 134km south of Hokitika along Highway 6.

BUS

Intercity (www.intercity.co.nz) buses stop at the Franz Josef bus stop (Main Rd.) at 9:15am daily northbound, and 5:05pm daily southbound toward Fox Glacier. This service turns around at Fox, but Intercity run another southbound service between the glaciers and Queenstown via **Newman's Coach Line** (book through Intercity). The service leaves Franz Josef bus stop at 8am daily.

SHUTTLES

Glacier Shuttles and **Charters Franz Josef** (0800/999-739) run a pickup service ($12.50 pp) between Franz Josef accommodations and the Glacier car park. Pickups are every two hours 8:45am-5:45pm daily, with return services from the car park 9am-7pm daily.

SERVICES

Glacier Base (Cron St.) is the meeting point for many tours and is the location of the hot pools and information centers, including **DoC Westland Tai Poutini National Park Visitor Centre** (69 Cron St., 03/752-0360, 8:30am-6pm daily Nov.-Mar., 8:30am-4:45pm daily Apr.-Oct.) and the Franz Josef **i-SITE Visitor Information Centre** (03/752-0796, 8:30am-6pm daily Dec.-Feb., 8:30am-5pm daily Mar.-Nov.).

★ FOX GLACIER

Fox Glacier's underdog status means fewer crowds and a more laid-back experience. The self-guided walk to Fox's terminal face is also shorter. Fox Glacier's hub of Fox Village is considerably smaller than that of Franz Josef (the glacier is actually bigger). The village is situated 6km from the ice formation.

Glacier Walks

For safety reasons, it is not possible to make your own way onto the glacier. To do so, book a heli-tour to explore farther up the ice. Visitors can opt instead for a free self-guided walk that follows Fox Glacier Valley to the glacier's terminal face. To reach Fox Glacier Valley, drive south along Highway 6 from Fox

Fox Glacier

township for 2km. Turn left before the Fox River bridge onto Fox Glacier Access Road.

The **Fox Glacier/Te Moeka O Tuawe Valley Walk** (1 hour round-trip, 2.6km) is an easy though uneven walk past "dead ice," the remnants of historic glacier retreat. After crossing a collection of streams, you'll get within 500m of the glacier terminal face. The walk leaves from the car park at the end of Fox Glacier Access Road.

The **Te Weheka Walkway/Cycleway** (2.5 hours round-trip, 8.4km) links Fox Village to the start of the Fox Glacier/Te Moeka O Tuawe Valley Walk. The trail winds partly through rainforest, and there's an interesting historic swing bridge crossing the Fox River. Some of the track is on the roadside and is not really worth walking on its own but can be an easy and enjoyable bike ride (1 hour). **Fox Glacier Top 10 Holiday Park** (Kerr Rd., Fox Glacier, 03/751-0821) rents bikes ($20 half-day, $40 full-day). Note that bikes are forbidden on the Fox Glacier Valley Walk.

Glacier Flightseeing Tours

The Flying Fox Tour (4 hours) with **Fox Glacier Guiding** (44 Main Rd., Fox Glacier, 03/751-0825, www.foxguides.co.nz, adults $425, children $399) includes a helicopter drop-off on the glacier followed by a guided hike through ice caves and arches. Guests then helicopter back out. Tours depart 8:50am and 11:50am daily year-round, with a 2:50pm daily departure in summer.

More challenging is the **Heli Ice Climbing Tour** (over age 13, 8am daily, $525) from the Fox Glacier Guiding for an eight- to nine-hour adventure of helicopter rides and ice wall climbs. There are routes for all skill levels; gear is provided.

Glacier Helicopters (Main Rd., Fox Glacier, 03/751-0803, www.glacierhelicopters.co.nz) offers a 20-minute scenic flight ($240) or a 30-minute flight ($310) over Fox and Franz Josef Glaciers. Both tours include a snow landing, where you can step onto the snowy alpine environment for a memorable photo.

Skydiving

Skydive Fox Glacier (1 Cook Flat Rd., Fox Glacier, 03/751-0080, www.skydivefox.co.nz, $249-399) was New Zealand's first glacier skydiving company. Choose to jump from 9,000-16,500 feet for a view of Fox Glacier and the Southern Alps, including Mount Cook. Photos and video cost extra.

Food

An eclectic menu at **Bigfoot Bar & Restaurant** (Fox Pod Hostel and Inn, 39 Sullivan Rd., Fox Glacier, 03/752-0022, 4pm-midnight daily, $18-26) covers curries, pizza, and traditional pub fare like burgers, steak, and ribs. A range of meal and drink deals, such as Friday beer jugs (4pm-close, $8), ensures there's always a lively atmosphere, while the sticky timber bar and tables lend a certain charm. Don't forget the obligatory snap with the yeti statue out front.

Enjoy alpine views framed by cinematic windows from the comfort of ★ **Lake Matheson Café** (1 Lake Matheson Rd., Fox Glacier, 03/751-0878, 8am-late daily Nov.-Mar., 8am-3pm daily Apr.-Oct., $29-36). It's ideal for grabbing a pre-trek breakfast or post-tramp lunch, but book ahead for dinner (5:30pm-close daily summer). Menu highlights include the parma ham bagel, salmon noodle broth, and merino lamb leg followed by a blueberry and chocolate mud pie as the sun descends behind the mountains.

Hobnail Café (44 Main Rd., Fox Glacier, 03/751-0005, 7:30am-4pm daily, $9-19) is located at Fox Glacier Guiding, making it convenient for a pre-tour munch. Hearty dishes are deserving of the rugged surroundings: well-presented breakfasts including bacon, egg, and vegetarian options backed by a generous selection of homemade food such as pies and wraps.

Accommodations

The **Rainforest Motel** (15 Cook Flat Rd., Fox Glacier, 03/751-0140, www.rainforestmotel.co.nz, $165-190 s or d) is a friendly and family-run lodge hemmed by verdant slopes just minutes from Fox Glacier township. Twelve individual and spacious en suite units come with kitchens, satellite TV, heaters, and electric blankets.

A block from the main street is well-run **Ivory Tower Backpacker Lodge** (33/35 Sullivans Rd., Fox Glacier, 03/751-0838, www.ivorytowers.co.nz, dorm $30-31, $65 s, $72-115 d). Three buildings offer dorms (mostly with four beds) along with doubles, twins, family rooms, and a lone single with its own TV. Each building is self-contained, with excellent kitchens, free tea, sugar and spices, free movies, and a book exchange.

★ **Fox Glacier Lodge** (41 Sullivan Rd., Fox Glacier, 03/751-0888, www.foxglacierlodge.com, $190-235 s or d) is a true alpine treat. Beautiful pine cabins include one-bedroom self-contained en suite units with kitchenettes, private decks, and flat-screen TVs. The B&B lodge has four en suite rooms with a sprawling breakfast served in the communal kitchen. The luxurious mezzanine units and king-spa chalets offer leather couches, spa baths, flat screen TVs, hot-drink facilities, gas log fires, and mountain views.

A hot tub with views of the Southern Alps is a good reason to stay at **Fox Glacier Top 10 Holiday Park** (Kerr Rd., Fox Glacier, 03/751-0821, www.top10.co.nz, tent and campervan sites $45-50 s or d, cabins $70-83 s or d, units $125-145 or d). Powered and unpowered sites are offered alongside cabins that can sleep up to six, as well as self-contained units with a kitchen, a separate lounge, and a private deck.

Transportation and Services

Fox Village is 157km south of Hokitika and 24km south of Franz Josef Village along Highway 6. Southbound **Intercity** (www.intercity.co.nz) buses leave opposite the Fox Glacier Guide (Main St.) at 8:45am daily; the northbound for Greymouth departs at 8:30am daily. A second northbound bus service terminates at Franz Josef, stopping in Fox at 3:24pm daily.

Fox Tours and Shuttles (0800/369-287, $12) provide return service from your accommodations to Fox Glacier car park or Lake Matheson. The Gillespie Beach service is priced upon request.

The **DoC Fox Glacier office** (Main Rd., 03/751-0807, 10am-2pm Mon.-Fri.) offers information but has limited hours.

LAKE MATHESON

Lake Matheson (www.doc.govt.nz) is one of New Zealand's most iconic and most photographed locations. Under the right conditions, it provides a picture-perfect reflection of mounts Cook and Tasman in its glassy surface. Get there early for the best shot, which needs to be taken from the far end of the lake, reached via an easy 4km track.

The trail access is conveniently located at the excellent **Lake Matheson Café** (1 Lake Matheson Rd., Fox Glacier, 03/751-0878, 8am-late daily Nov.-Mar., 8am-3pm daily Apr.-Oct.). Lake Matheson is 5km northwest of Fox Village along Cook Flat Road.

FOX VILLAGE TO HAAST

The winding 260km drive along Highway 6 from Fox Village to Wanaka via Haast can easily be completed in five hours. It's worth taking a full day or longer to visit some of the off-the-beaten-track stops. Haast is 121km (1.5 hours) southwest of Fox along Highway 6.

★ Copland Track

The **Copland Track** (Hwy. 6, 26km south of Fox Village) is a gorgeous and relatively straightforward 18km (7 hours one-way) tramp along the Copland Valley, with a second-day return the same way. The walk begins from the Copland Valley car park on the northern side of Karangarua River bridge. Guided by orange markers, the trail crosses creeks, scrambles over boulders, and passes through dense bush before emerging at the **Welcome Flat Hut** (DoC, 03/752-0360, www.doc.govt.nz, adults $15, children $7.50) where you can soak your weary body in natural hot pools surrounded by rainforest and the snowy Southern Alps.

The walk is accessible year-round, though

Catch of the Day: West Coast Whitebait

the Curly Tree Whitebait Company

One of New Zealand's most revered dishes, whitebait fritters (or patties) are created by adding whitebait to a seasoned beaten egg mixture and frying it in a pan or on a hot plate then garnishing as required (mint sauce is a favorite). Whitebait is often referred to as "White Gold" around here owing to its high price (which fluctuates depending on how much is caught in a season), and its tendency to arouse a gold fever-like competitiveness among fisherfolk. Whitebait are juveniles of five species of fish: giant *kokopu*, banded *kokopu*, shortjaw *kokopu*, *inanga*, and *koaro*, collectively known as galaxiids, all most numerous on the West Coast.

December-May is the best time. Parts of the route are prone to flooding and may become impassible following heavy rain. Check the weather forecast and conditions with DoC. The hut and **campsite** (adults $5, children $2.50, under age 11 free) must be booked in advance. The adjacent **Sierra Room** ($100), which sleeps one to four people and is equipped with a gas cooker, potbelly stove, and shower, must also be booked in advance.

Lake Moeraki

Lake Moeraki (off Hwy. 6, 30km south of Bruce Bay) affords a mountain reflection in its jewel-like surface. The adjoining **Monro Beach Walk** (40 minutes) is a shaded trail to a sandy shoreline with rocky outcrops favored by Fiordland crested penguins, the rarest of its kind. Arrive early in the morning or late afternoon during spring or late summer to increase your chances of seeing them. The walk begins from the car park at the northern end of the lake, just before the Moeraki River.

Knight's Point and Ship Creek

The lookout at **Knight's Point** (10km south of Lake Moeraki) gives way to splendid ocean views. Continue 10km farther to **Ship Creek,** the launching point for two fabulous 30-minute strolls: the **Kahikatea Forest Loop Walk,** a marshland boardwalk with plenty of birdlife; and the **Dune Walk,** which takes in a beach and a tiny dune-hemmed lake.

Curly Tree Whitebait Company

A well-deserved detour 10km north of Haast, **Curly Tree Whitebait Company** (www.curlytreewhitebait.com, 03/750-0097,

10am-5pm daily, $10) serves handmade whitebait patties sourced from local rivers and cooked on a hot plate while you wait. Follow the hand-painted signs from Highway 6 and look for the well-hidden ramshackle kitchen in a field.

Haast and Vicinity

So magnificent is the remote region around Haast, nestled on the western edge of Mount Aspiring National Park that it has been designated a UNESCO World Heritage Site. Haast comprises three tiny settlements: Haast Township, Haast Junction, and Haast Beach. All are within a few kilometers of each other along Highway 6.

HAAST

Waiatoto River Safari

Experience New Zealand's only mountain-to-sea jet-boat tour with the **Waiatoto River Safari** (1975 Haast-Jackson Bay Rd., Haast, 03/750-0780, www.riversafaris.co.nz, 10am, 1pm, and 4pm daily Nov.-Apr., 11am daily May-Oct., adults $199, children $139). For more than two hours you'll traverse turquoise glacial waters through alpine scenery draped in snow and beech trees as your host regales you with historical and geological information. You'll also visit a kiwi sanctuary to learn about breeding programs to save the endangered bird.

★ Haast Pass

The **Haast Pass** (142km) follow Highway 6 as it slices east through Mount Aspiring National Park (www.doc.govt.nz), linking the West Coast to Otago. Officially opened in 1965, the Haast Pass Highway is one of New Zealand's most thrilling mountain drives, winding past bluffs, gorges, and waterfalls. The journey is almost as dangerous as it is beautiful; your eyes can easily wonder from the road. Take the ample opportunities to safely pull over for photos and to let other drivers pass.

The Haast Pass Highway (Hwy. 6) is generally regarded as the route between Haast and Wanaka. The pass begins 10km southeast of Haast as the road enters Mount Aspiring National Park.

Haast Pass

WALKS

A number of easy and well-signposted short walks into Mount Aspiring National Park are accessible off the Haast Pass Highway; parking is usually plentiful.

Contrary to its name, **Roaring Billy Falls** (27km east of Haast along Hwy. 6) is one of the region's quieter waterfalls, unless it's been raining heavily. The falls are reached via a meandering stroll (23 minutes round-trip) through silver beech forest. **Thunder Creek Falls** (22.3km past Roaring Bill Falls) is the most spectacular, and busiest, stop. The 28m cascade is just a five-minute round-trip walk from the car park.

The **Gates of Haast** (1.2km east of Thunder Creek Falls) is a spectacular gorge with rapids that crash over boulders. Take pictures from the bridge viewpoint (but do not park on it). **Fantail Falls** (4.8km south of Gates of Haast) plunges into a clear cold pool ideal for swimming. It's an easy 10-minute round-trip walk from the roadside car park. The **Haast Pass Lookout Track** (12km south of Fantail Falls) is a 2km (1 hour) return track that leads to a viewpoint above the tree line for a stunning view of Mount Aspiring National Park.

The star of this show is undoubtedly **Blue Pools** (2km south of Haast Pass Lookout Track), where brown trout swim through glacial-fed crystal waters hemmed in by beech trees and pebble shores. As tempting as it is to jump from the swing bridge here, don't. People have been injured. Instead, walk down (1 hour round-trip) to take a dip in the pools from the safety of the banks.

Food

An excellent value, the **Prickly Gorse Cafe** (10 Marks Rd., 03/750-0055, 8am-2:30pm daily, $10-13) serves classics bites such as toasted sandwiches along with a selection of tempting treats like muffins and carrot cakes. The stars of the menu are the burgers and whitebait fritters (of course).

Antlers hung from the ceiling and stag heads mounted on the walls sets the tone of no-nonsense **Hard Antler Bar & Restaurant** (Marks Rd., 03/750-0034, 10am-11pm daily Nov.-Apr., 11am-7pm daily May-Oct., $26-32). The locals are sure to give you a fine welcome as you wash down fish-and-chips or beef nachos with a few pints of frothy beer.

Accommodations

Well priced and well kept, **Wilderness Accommodation** (Marks Rd., Haast, 03/750-0029, www.wildernessaccommodation.co.nz, dorm $28, $50-60 s, $65-70 d) offers a selection of spotless, colorful backpacker accommodations ranging from a single room to four-bed dorms. The plant-strewn indoor conservatory area is blissful. An adjacent motel offers twin and double rooms ($85-140 s or d); all have en suite baths with TVs and tea- and coffee-making facilities. Some rooms can accommodate an extra guest ($10).

Luxurious ★ **Collyer House** (Jacksons Bay Rd., Haast, 03/750-0022, www.collyerhouse.co.nz, $230-280 s or d) sports four en suite rooms with power showers, French doors, and antique furnishings. Nest-like beds boast a feather duvet and pillows, while a welcoming communal living area offers a fireplace crafted from local stones. The house is a 15-minute drive south from Haast en route to Jackson Bay.

Transportation and Services

Haast is 121km southwest of Fox Village along Highway 6. **Intercity** (www.intercity.co.nz) Queenstown-Franz Josef buses pass Haast, stopping opposite Wilderness Backpackers (Marks Rd.). The southbound bus stops at 11:20am daily, and the northbound bus stops at 12:50pm daily.

Stop by the **DoC Haast Visitor Centre** (Haast Junction, Hwy. 6 and Jackson Bay Rd., 03/750-0809, 9am-6pm daily Nov.-Mar., 9am-4:30pm daily Apr.-Oct.) to learn more about the area. The short documentary *Edge* *of Wilderness* ($3), about the local landscape and wildlife, is 20 minutes well spent.

JACKSON BAY

One of the remotest villages in New Zealand, sheltered Jackson Bay is awash with natural spectacles like dunes, lakes, and wetlands, while the town's natural deep harbor is noted for its fishing. Regular visitors to the region include rare and endangered species such as Hector's dolphins and Fiordland crested penguins, alongside native birds and fur seals.

There are a number of walks in the area: the **Wharkai-Te Koua Walk** (20 minutes) and the **Smoothwater Bay Track** (2 hours) will give you a good feel for the area.

Food

A visit to the ★ **The Craypot** (The Esplanade, 03/750-0035, www.thecraypotnz.com, noon-7pm daily Nov.-Apr., $16-29) is worth the trip to alone. Call ahead for the daily availability of the crayfish ($65-85), which sell out fast, and enjoy your seafood with a sea view.

Getting There

Jackson Bay is 50km southwest of Haast along scenic Haast-Jackson Bay Road.

Queenstown and Otago

Queenstown....................419
Wanaka.......................434
Mount Aspiring National Park.....440
Central Otago 443
Oamaru 446
Dunedin.......................449

Wildlife and world-class wineries. Watercolor scenery and gold-rush tales. Middle-earth and Maori myth. Otago serves as a microcosm for much of what makes New Zealand famous.

From the majesty of the Southern Alps, the Otago region tumbles east, spilling across the tussock-clad plains of Central Otago. This diverse landscape is stitched together by vineyards and legendary cycle trails that follow old gold mining tracks before plunging to the Pacific east coast. Here, two wonderfully preserved Victorian centers—Dunedin and Oamaru—straddle the Moeraki Boulders, an incongruous collection of spherical beached stones 60-million years in the making.

Tucked into the western reaches of Otago (informally labelled the Southern Lakes), Queenstown is the undisputed destination. The introduction of bungee jumping in 1988 spawned an adventure industry on such a scale that the resort town sells itself as the "adventure capital of the world," offering everything from paragliding to jet-boating to parachute jumps. Wanaka, 70km north, is another lakeside gem but on a far smaller scale than Queenstown and with a far more chilled-out vibe. There are spectacular ski hills and hundreds of miles of heavenly hikes—not to mention many of Middle-earth's most breathtaking shots.

From Queenstown, head to Dunedin, "the Edinburgh of the south," New Zealand's first city and home to its oldest university. An abundance of cool bars and eateries cater to the massive student population; the town is Gothic and atmospheric. From Dunedin, an eastern isthmus blooms into the jagged Otago Peninsula, home to the native yellow-eyed penguin, marine mammals, the world's only mainland nesting colony of royal albatross, and New Zealand's (kind of) only castle, Larnach.

PLANNING YOUR TIME

It's easy to get caught up in the thrill of **Queenstown,** blowing all your time—and money—in the process. Aim for two to four days to take in the town, some adventures,

Previous: the Otago Central Rail Trail; Queenstown from Bob's Peak. **Above:** the Queenstown gondola.

Queenstown and Otago

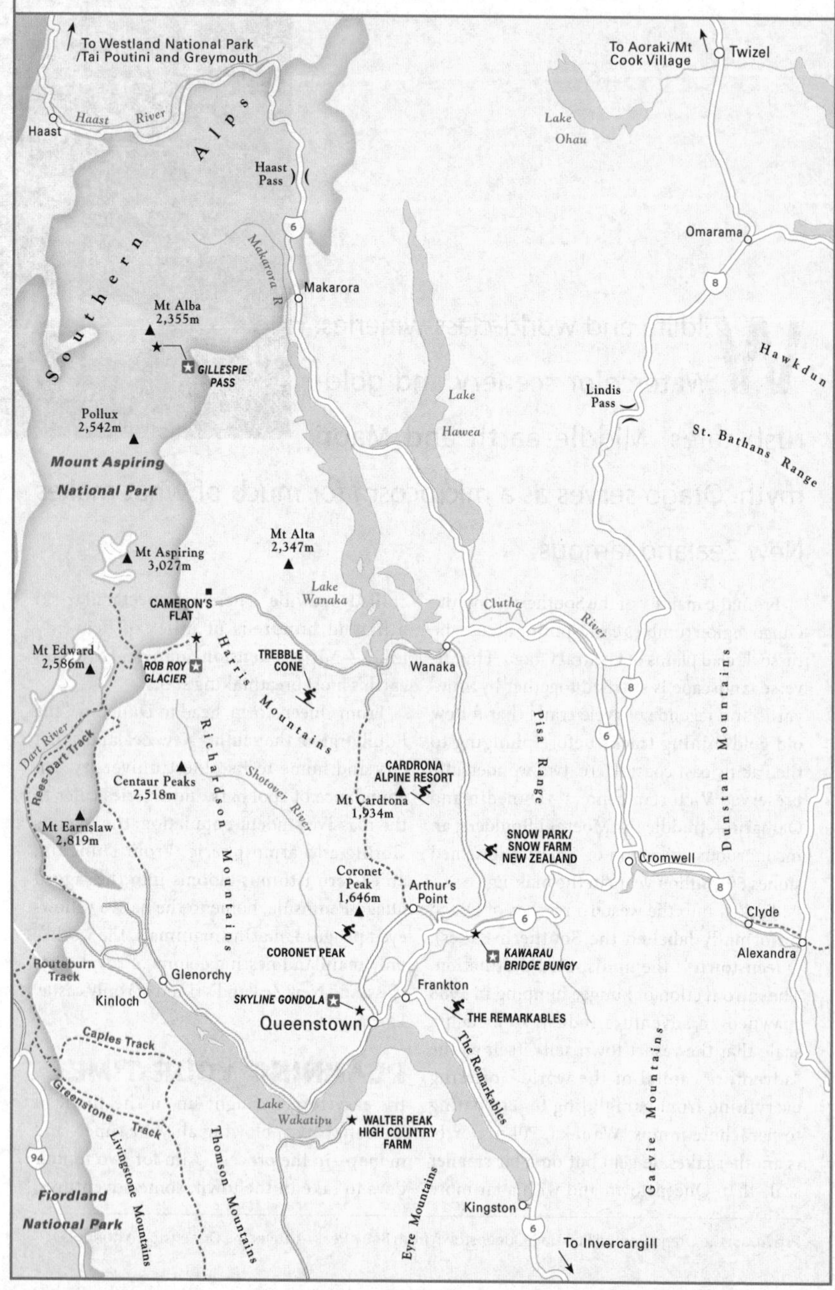
To Westland National Park /Tai Poutini and Greymouth
Haast
Haast River
Southern Alps
Haast Pass
6
Makarora R
Makarora
Mt Alba 2,355m
GILLESPIE PASS
Pollux 2,542m
Mount Aspiring National Park
Mt Aspiring 3,027m
Mt Alta 2,347m
Lake Wanaka
CAMERON'S FLAT
ROB ROY GLACIER
Mt Edward 2,586m
TREBBLE CONE
Harris Mountains
Wanaka
Dart River
Rees-Dart Track
Centaur Peaks 2,518m
Richardson Mountains
Shotover River
CARDRONA ALPINE RESORT
Mt Cardrona 1,934m
Mt Earnslaw 2,819m
Coronet Peak 1,646m
Arthur's Point
CORONET PEAK
KAWARAU BRIDGE BUNGY
Routeburn Track
Glenorchy
Kinloch
Frankton
SKYLINE GONDOLA
Queenstown
THE REMARKABLES
Caples Track
Greenstone Track
Lake Wakatipu
WALTER PEAK HIGH COUNTRY FARM
94
Livingstone Mountains
Thomson Mountains
Fiordland National Park
Eyre Mountains
The Remarkables
Kingston
To Invercargill
To Aoraki/Mt Cook Village
Twizel
Lake Ohau
Omarama
8
Hawkdun
Lindis Pass
St. Bathans Range
Lake Hawea
Clutha River
Pisa Range
Dunstan Mountains
SNOW PARK/ SNOW FARM NEW ZEALAND
Cromwell
Clyde
Alexandra
Garvie Mountains

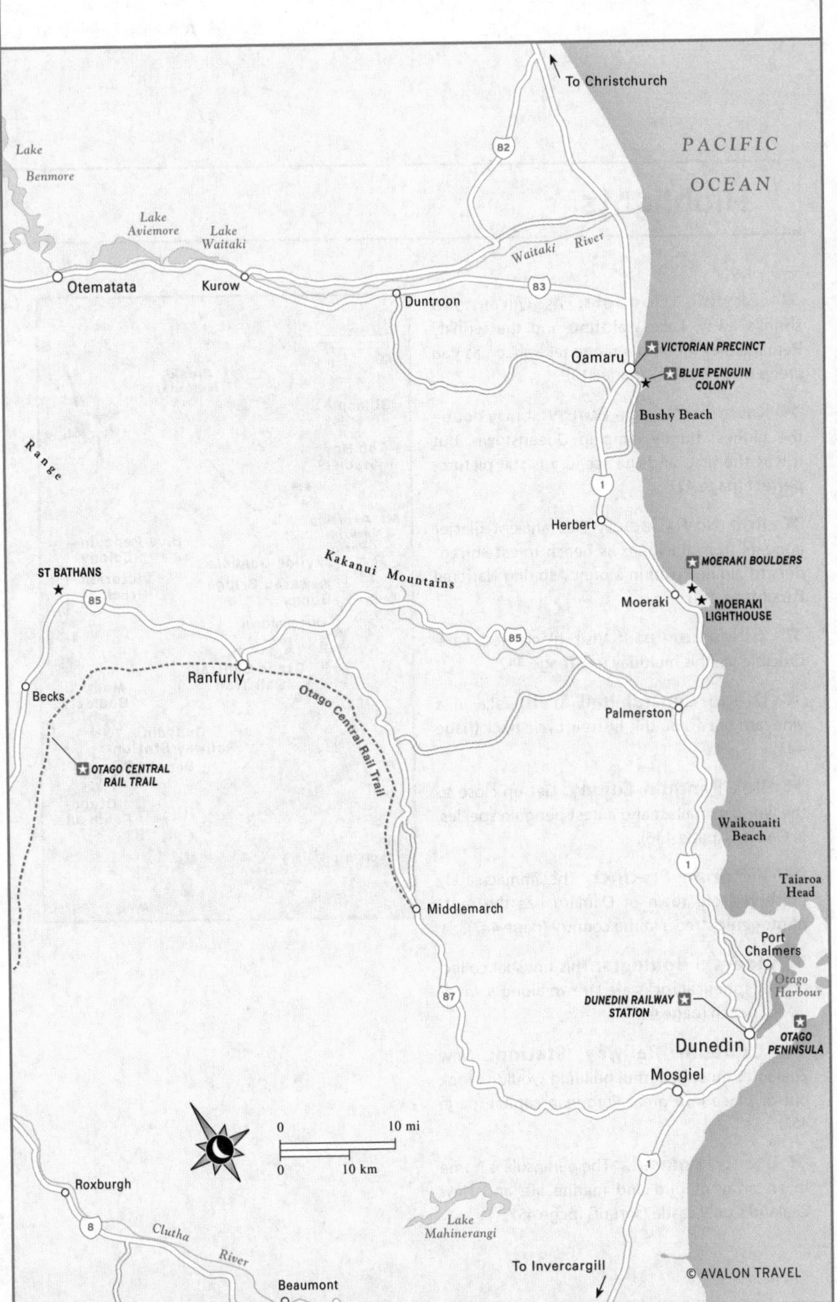
To Christchurch
PACIFIC OCEAN
Lake Benmore
Lake Aviemore
Lake Waitaki
Waitaki River
Otematata
Kurow
Duntroon
Oamaru
VICTORIAN PRECINCT
BLUE PENGUIN COLONY
Bushy Beach
Range
Herbert
Kakanui Mountains
ST BATHANS
MOERAKI BOULDERS
Moeraki
MOERAKI LIGHTHOUSE
Ranfurly
Becks
Otago Central Rail Trail
Palmerston
OTAGO CENTRAL RAIL TRAIL
Waikouaiti Beach
Taiaroa Head
Middlemarch
Port Chalmers
Otago Harbour
DUNEDIN RAILWAY STATION
Dunedin
OTAGO PENINSULA
Mosgiel
0
10 mi
0
10 km
Roxburgh
Lake Mahinerangi
Clutha River
To Invercargill
Beaumont
© AVALON TRAVEL
82
83
1
85
87
8

Look for ★ to find recommended sights, activities, dining, and lodging.

Highlights

★ **Skyline Gondola:** As Queenstown shrinks away, Lake Wakatipu and the wrinkly Remarkables mountain range take shape as you creep up Bob's Peak (page 419).

★ **Kawarau Bridge Bungy:** It may not be the highest bungy jump in Queenstown, but it was the first, and the scenery is still picture-perfect (page 421).

★ **Rob Roy Glacier:** This ancient glacier appears from nowhere as beech forest surrenders to alpine scrub in Mount Aspiring National Park (page 441).

★ **Gillespie Pass:** Visit glacier-fed Lake Crucible via this multiday trek (page 442).

★ **Otago Central Rail Trail:** Take in a vineyard or two on this historic cycle track (page 445).

★ **Blue Penguin Colony:** Get up close to the world's smallest and cutest penguin species, in Oamaru (page 446).

★ **Victorian Precinct:** The immaculately preserved old town of Oamaru has the most photogenic streets in the country (page 447).

★ **Moeraki Boulders:** This unusual collection of spherical rocks are strewn along a windswept beach (page 449).

★ **Dunedin Railway Station:** New Zealand's most beautiful building wouldn't look out of place in a great European capital (page 451)

★ **Otago Peninsula:** The peninsula is home to an array of bird and marine life and New Zealand's only castle (sort of) (page 457).

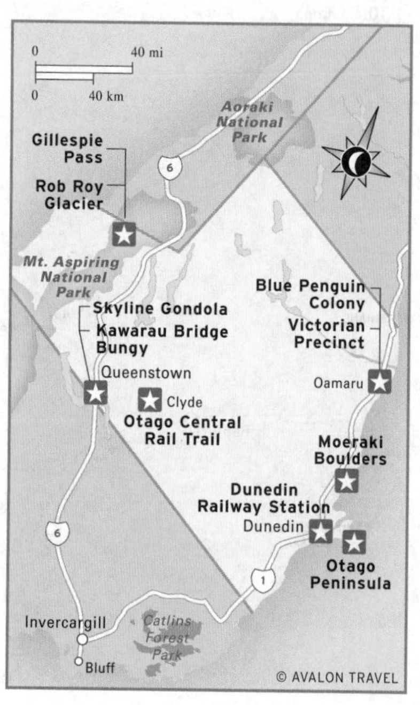

and explore some of the stunning countryside around—including the picturesque towns of **Glenorchy** and **Arrowtown. Wanaka** is worthy of at least a weekend—those seeking something a little more laid-back may wish to trade some extra time here from **Queenstown.** Spend at least a night in **Dunedin** and ditto the gorgeous **Oamaru.** Many only see **Central Otago** from the inside of a vehicle. If you have a day or two to spare, they'll be among the most relaxing of your trip.

Queenstown

The resort hub of Queenstown lies 280km northwest of Dunedin and 200km south of Haast. Take away its roguish reputation for scaring the hell out of all who visit, and Queenstown could simply be revered for its abounding beauty. Glistening on the shores of crooked cobalt Lake Wakatipu, the town is guarded by the towering wrinkled face of the Remarkables range, behind which spread some spectacular ski fields.

The town caters to everyone from backpackers to billionaires and boasts plenty of chills to counter its thrills. For every jet-boat and bungee jump, there's a relaxing river cruise, kayak tour, or a hike to a million-dollar view.

SIGHTS

★ Skyline Gondola

Set aside at least a couple of hours to take in the famed vistas from Bob's Peak, reached via the **Skyline Gondola** (Brecon St., 03/441-0101, www.skyline.co.nz, 9am-close daily, adults $35, children $22), a cable car that climbs 450m above Queenstown over pine forested slopes threaded by walking trails and mountain bike tracks. At the summit, outdoor decks afford unbroken views of Queenstown, Lake Wakatipu, and the Remarkables. Throngs of camera-happy tourists join the steady flow of mountain bikers attracted by more than 30km of trails. Up top, the **Luge** (with gondola adults $49-56, children $37-46), is a fun-filled gravity-powered toboggan-like ride along snaking concrete tracks. Come nightfall, guests can glimpse constellations like the Southern Cross courtesy of high-end telescopes with a **Stargazing Tour** (with gondola adults $93, children $49).

The **Market Kitchen Cafe** (9:30am-close daily) and the **Stratosphere Restaurant and Bar** (noon-close daily, with gondola adults $65-105, children $40-63) offer snacks and fine-dining, including homemade pastries, pizzas, and fresh seafood, along with beers, wines, and cocktails.

Kiwi Birdlife Park

A worthwhile sanctuary does its best to help preserve New Zealand's most beloved species. The **Kiwi Birdlife Park** (Upper Brecon St., 03/442-8059, www.kiwibird.co.nz, 9am-4:40pm daily, adults $48, children $23) affords a guaranteed glimpse of the elusive birds courtesy of nocturnal viewing houses. Enjoy one of four kiwi feedings (10am, noon, 1:30pm, and 4:30pm daily), and see other bird species such as the falcon and the kea, along with the tuatara. During Conservation Shows (11am and 3pm daily), the birds fly free.

TOP EXPERIENCE

SPORTS AND RECREATION

Bungee, Swings, and Zip Lines

AJ Hackett (Station Bldg., Shotover St. and Camp St., 03/450-1300, www.bungy.co.nz) operates three bungee sites. Sign up for a jump and you'll also get a free T-shirt (photos and videos cost extra). Pickup and drop-off service

Queenstown

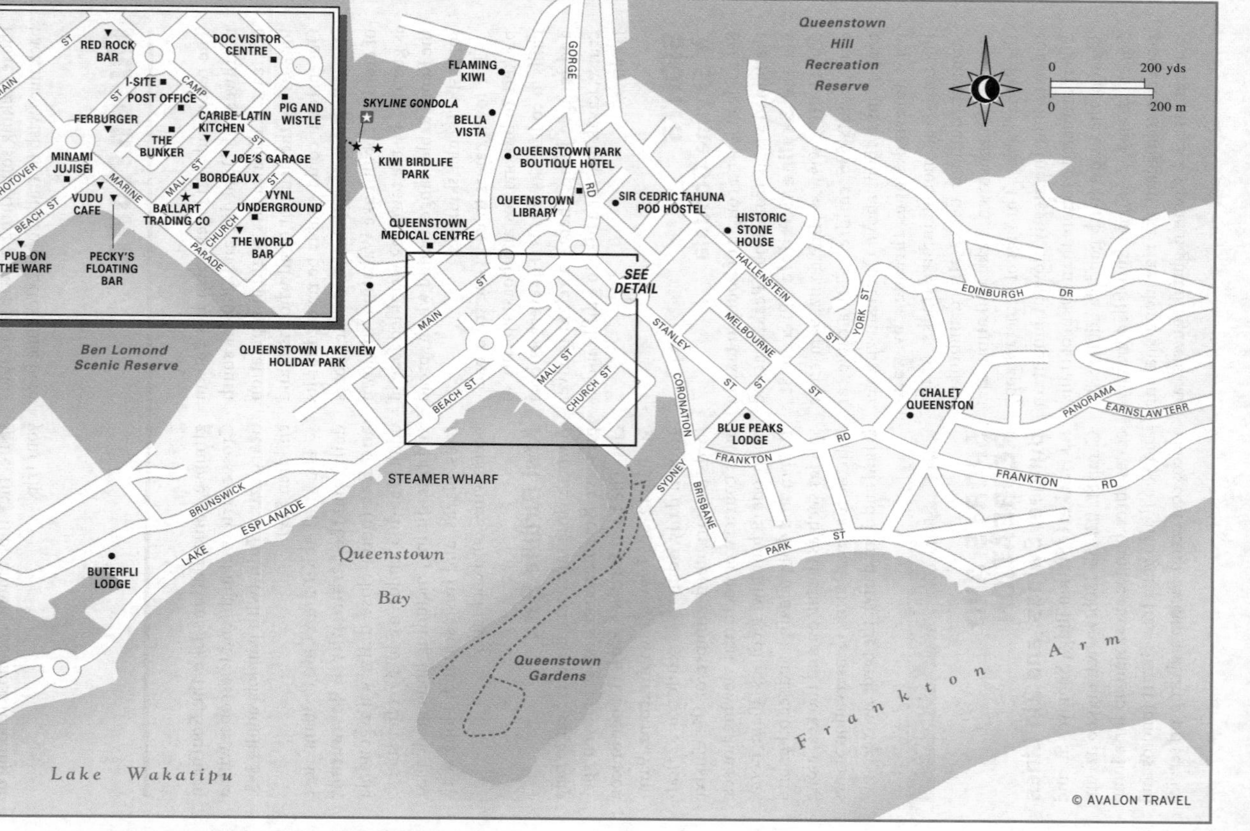

MAIN ST
RED ROCK BAR
DOC VISITOR CENTRE
I-SITE
CAMP ST
POST OFFICE
PIG AND WISTLE
FERBURGER
CARIBE LATIN KITCHEN
THE BUNKER
JOE'S GARAGE
SHOTOVER
MINAMI JUJISEI
MALL ST
BORDEAUX
MARINE
VUDU CAFE
BALLART TRADING CO
VYNL UNDERGROUND
BEACH ST
CHURCH ST
THE WORLD BAR
PARADE
PUB ON THE WARF
PECKY'S FLOATING BAR
SKYLINE GONDOLA
FLAMING KIWI
BELLA VISTA
KIWI BIRDLIFE PARK
QUEENSTOWN PARK BOUTIQUE HOTEL
GORGE RD
QUEENSTOWN LIBRARY
SIR CEDRIC TAHUNA POD HOSTEL
HISTORIC STONE HOUSE
QUEENSTOWN MEDICAL CENTRE
SEE DETAIL
Queenstown Hill Recreation Reserve
0 200 yds
0 200 m
Ben Lomond Scenic Reserve
QUEENSTOWN LAKEVIEW HOLIDAY PARK
HALLENSTEIN ST
MELBOURNE ST
STANLEY ST
YORK ST
EDINBURGH DR
CORONATION
CHALET QUEENSTON
PANORAMA
EARNSLAW TERR
BLUE PEAKS LODGE
FRANKTON RD
STEAMER WHARF
SYDNEY
BRISBANE
BRUNSWICK
LAKE ESPLANADE
PARK ST
Queenstown Bay
BUTERFLI LODGE
Queenstown Gardens
Frankton Arm
Lake Wakatipu
© AVALON TRAVEL

Kawarau Bridge

is available. There is also a booking center at the Kawarau Bridge site.

Get creative jumping **The Ledge** (adults $160, children $110). You are affixed to a full-body harness, which means your legs are free to take a running jump over the pine forests 400m up Bob's Peak. During winter it serves as New Zealand's only nighttime bungee. The nearby **Ledge Swing** (adults $160, children $110) dangles thrill seekers from its platform, with a lever allowing the rider to release themselves over the forest canopy when ready. The longer you wait, the harder it gets, and don't forget to holler like Tarzan.

Located 30km east of Queenstown, with a freefall of more than eight seconds, the 134m **Nevis Bungy** ($275) is the highest in Australasia, befitting its dramatic scenery of craggy cliff-like banks above the Nevis River. The cable car ride out to the launch pod promises to get your heart racing long before you jump. The 120m **Nevis Swing** (adults $195, children $145) is the highest in the world and boasts a 300m arc—opt to do it backward, upside down, or if you have a friend, tandem.

★ KAWARAU BRIDGE BUNGY

Leap 43m from the historic **Kawarau Bridge** (adults $195, children $145), 20 minutes east of Queenstown along Highway 6A and then Highway 6. Choose to touch turquoise waters beautifully contrasted by the gray and green bush-clad banks while camera-happy tourists snap away from the nearby viewing deck.

The adjacent **Zip Ride** (adults $50, children $40) propels guests up to 60km/h for 130m. Choose to go seated, fly like a superhero, or go upside down if you dare. The gravity-powered ride is less terrifying than the bungee, but heaps of fun.

Walks

The 3km **Tiki Trail** is a manageable local hike that zigzags its way up Bob's Peak, with views of town, the bungee, mountain bike tracks, pine forests, and the lake. Access is near the gondola entrance. **Queenstown Hill Walkway,** just a few minutes' drive from the city center, is a rewarding three-hour trek with 500m elevation gain to panoramic views of the Remarkables, Cecil Peak, Lake Wakatipu, and the Kawarau River. There's plenty of information en route regaling hikers with the history of the region. The loop begins at Belfast Street.

Starting on Skyline Access Road or at the Tiki Trail, the **Ben Lomond Track** weaves through bush then alpine grasses until it reaches the 1,748m summit of Ben Loman, one of the highest around. Savor views of Mount Earnslaw and Mount Aspiring. It's a six- to eight-hour trek. Pack extra layers as the weather up there can change quickly.

Biking

Queenstown Trail (www.queenstowntrail.co.nz) is the nation's most popular Great Ride, a network of 120km tracks around the Wakatipu basin, for beginners through intermediate. Highlights of the rides include river

Vicinity of Queenstown

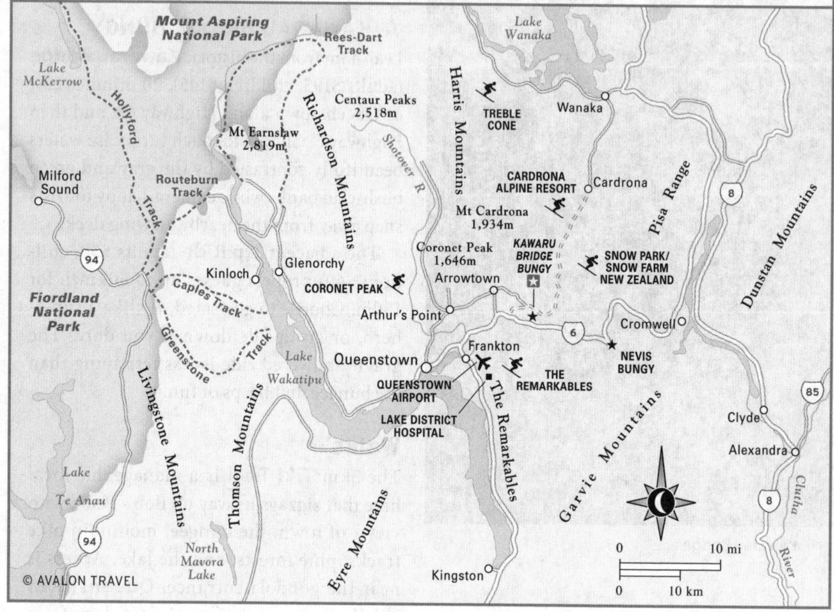

gorges, mining ruins, and suspension bridge crossings—with plenty of places to stop for food or wine at a vineyard.

Queenstown Bike Park (www.skyline.co.nz) comprises more than 30 tracks descending Bob's Peak, including black runs. Occasional breaks in the forest give way to incredible views—just try not to take your eyes off the track. Bikes can be transported up on the gondola.

Cycle Higher (9b Earl St., 03/442-9559, www.cycle.hire.com) is conveniently located by the lake near the start of the Queenstown Trail. Pedal and electric bikes are available, helmets are included, and you get a free coffee. **Charge About** (79 Peninsula Rd., 03/442-6376, www.chargeabout.co.nz) provides hybrid electric mountain bikes in packages with refreshments and taxis to trails. Find great deals on mountain and electric bikes at **Around the Basin** (0508/782-9253, www.aroundthebasin.co.nz), with tour info, maps, and free delivery to your lodging.

Horseback Riding

Moonlight Stables (69 Morven Ferry Rd., 03/442-1229, www.moonlightstables.co.nz, adults $120, children $95) conduct 1.5-hour horse treks for all abilities leading riders onto an 320ha working sheep farm and over lush pastures for incredible views of the alpine scenery. You'll also get up close and personal with rare white fallow deer.

Water Sports

Most aquatic adventures take place on the Kawarau River, which links to Lake Wakatipu, east of Queenstown, and the more challenging Shotover River, which joins the Kawarau River.

JET-BOATING

The jet-boat was invented in New Zealand, and **KJet** (Main Tower Pier, Marine Parade, 0800/529-272, www.kjet.co.nz, adults $129, children $69) was the world's first commercial company. Conveniently located at the central

Skipper's Canyon

Skippers Canyon is accessible only by 4WD vehicle via a sheer cliff-face gravel pass hand-carved by gold miners in the late 19th century. It is considered so risky that rental companies won't allow their vehicles there. Reaching this winding gorge is a real thrill, and perhaps the route's most notorious section is the rickety 90m-high, 96m-long suspension bridge that crosses the Shotover River. The canyon, 22km north of Queenstown, is where the river is narrowest, deepest, and fastest.

Nomad Safaris (37 Shotover St., 03/442-6699, www.nomadsafaris.co.nz, adults $185, children $90) offer a four-hour 4WD tour of the area taking in the rugged high-altitude landscape, visiting the ghost township of Skippers, and gold-panning in the river. The three-hour **Skippers Canyon Jet Tour** (03/442-9434, www.skipperscanyonjet.co.nz, adults $145, children $85), includes that hair-raising drive before a thrilling river-skimming journey at more than 80km/h, within touching distance of the canyon's face. See historic gold mining and movie sites. The 4.5-hour **Scenic Tour Combo** (adults $195, children $115) ventures deeper into the historic site, including a visit to Winky's mining museum.

pier, enjoy an hour-long tour across the lake, under the Kawarau Dam, and on to the Kawarau and Shotover Rivers. The 43km adventure is tackled at speeds of up to 85km/h, finishing with a complimentary viewing at the Queenstown's Underwater Observatory.

For a purely adrenaline-filled ride, head for the iconic red boats of **Shotover Jet** (Shotover Jet Beach, Gorge Rd., 03/442-8570, www.shotoverjet.com, adults $145, children $75) that travel often in turquoise water inches from a canyon rock face. Less than 10 minutes from Queenstown, rides depart every 15 minutes—just walk up and pay.

WHITE-WATER RAFTING AND CANOEING

Kawarau River's rapids are Class II-III rapids, while the Shotover, the most popular white-water rafting destination in New Zealand, is Class III-V. **Queenstown Rafting** (35 Shotover St., 03/442-9792, www.queenstownrafting.co.nz) offers rafting tours along the Kawarau and Shotover Rivers for $229, and a three-day tour of the Class III-IV Landsborough Valley ($1,799). The trip includes food, wine, and beer as well as a scenic helicopter flight in and out. More relaxing is the 7km guided canoe trip (adults $159, children $99) along the Kawarau River.

HYDRO ATTACK

A world first, the part-submarine, part-jet fighter **Hydro Attack** (Lapsley Butson Wharf, 0508/493-762, www.hydroattack.co.nz, summer 9am-6pm, winter 10am-4.30pm, $149) is a shark-shaped vessel that reaches 80km/h, skimming across and under Lake Wakatipu. The exhilarating ride can jump 5m in the air and dive 1.5m beneath the surface, and the glass roof affords stunning 360-degree views.

Skydiving

Fling yourself, in tandem, from 9,000, 12,000, or 15,000 feet, freefalling for up to 60 seconds at 200km/h with views of snow-topped mountains with **NZone Skydive** (35 Shotover St., 03/442-2256, www.nzoneskydive.co.nz, $299-439). Pay extra for a personal videographer to jump next to you.

Paragliding and Hang Gliding

Strapped in tandem, hanging from a wing-like parachute, paragliding affords a spectacular and serene experience—unless you allow for some aeronautical acrobatics from the instructor. Leap from the 500m summit of Bob's Peak with **GForce Paragliding** (03/441-8581, www.nzgforce.com, $199-219, including gondola), the only company with a permit to fly over the lake and town. Flights last 10 minutes.

Twenty minutes northeast of Queenstown, **Skytrek** (45 Camp St., 0800/759-873, www.skytrek.co.nz, $220-299) offers longer flights (up to 20 minutes), and strictly mountain and lake views, launching from Coronet Peak. Tandem paragliding or hang gliding options are available. Pay extra for an instructional flight, and you can take control of the hang-glider.

Flightseeing

Several Queenstown operators offer similar fixed-wing flights that venture northwest from Queenstown airport over the Southern Alps to Fiordland National Park.

Milford Flights (39 Lucas Place, 03/442-3065, www.milfordflights.co.nz, 10am and 2pm daily summer, 11am and 2pm daily winter, adults $385, children $224) takes in glacial lakes, rivers and valleys, and forests and fiords on a one-hour scenic trip.

With **Helicopter Line** (Lucas Place, 03/442-3034, www.helicopter.co.nz) choose from packages including 20-minute flights over Queenstown or the Remarkables (adults $240, children $168), a wine tour ($559) to Gibbston Valley that includes a scenic mountain flight, and a four-hour Milford Sound cruise package (adults $980, children $686).

Winter Sports

NZ Ski (9 Duke St., 03/442-4620, www.nzski.com) owns the ski hills of the Remarkables and Coronet Peak, along with Canterbury's Mount Hutt. Half-day to six-day passes (adults $89-570, children $42-288) cover Queenstown ski fields, while the season pass (adults $999, children $649) covers all three. Ski hills are generally open from mid-June until early October. Between the ski fields and the town, there are many equipment-rental stores. **Snow Rental** (39 Camp St., 03/442-4187, www.snowrental.co.nz) provides a great range of the latest gear for all budgets. **One Stop** (Duke St., 03/441-2085, www.onestopsnowshop.com) is another affordable option, with lift pass packages available.

THE REMARKABLES

Half an hour from Queenstown behind the Remarkables' lakefront facade, in a natural alpine north-facing amphitheater that's a stunning suntrap, spills a selection of slopes for everyone—wide runs, backcountry runs, narrow chutes, and rock drops. Lifts from the 1,622m base reach 1,943m, with a 357m vertical drop and access to plenty of off-piste spots. At the base building await three eateries and a bar with terrific views. Make your own way to the ski fields along Highway 6A. The final climb of the drive is along an unpaved road. The **Snowline Express** bus service runs from the Queenstown Snow Centre on Duke Street, making stops at designated points along the way.

CORONET PEAK

North of Queenstown 18km rises Coronet Peak. Though not as high as the Remarkables, it boasts a greater vertical drop (481m) and the only floodlit nighttime slopes in New Zealand. Famed for its expansive rolling pistes, Coronet Peak is ideal for novices and intermediate skiers and snowboarders, but it does have more advanced runs—hosting several international competitions. It's a 25-minute drive from downtown Queenstown, along George and Skippers Roads. Snowline Express also services the route.

Tours

NOMAD SAFARIS

Nomad Safaris (37 Shotover St., 03/442-6699, www.nomadsafaris.co.nz, adults $185, children $90) offer mud-filled motorized adventures in the mountains, through rivers and across ridges on tours to gold-mining sites and hard-to-reach movie locations around the Wakatipu basin. An instructor-led self-drive tour (adults $285, children $90) is available following a thrilling lesson around a purpose-built test track, while quad bikes (adults only,

$245) scramble up to the Queenstown Hill high country sheep station where more than 25km of trails show off the scenery, 1,000m high.

TSS *EARNSLAW* STEAMSHIP

The prestigious **TSS *Earnslaw* Steamship** (Real Journeys Visitor Centre, Steamer Wharf, 03/249-6000, www.realjourneys.co.nz, $59), a century-old vessel, is the most relaxing way to cross Lake Wakatipu. There's plenty of polished brass and wood adorning this luxurious coal-powered liner—known as the "Lady of the Lake" and the last of its kind in the southern hemisphere. For an additional $20, add the **Walter Peak High Country Farm Tour** to the cruise to witness the everyday workings of the farm, help feed the deer, and watch the dogs round up the sheep.

WINE AND CRAFT BEER TOURS

New Zealand Wine Tours Queenstown (0800/666-778, www.nzwinetours.co.nz, $199-385) prides itself on a small guest list, limited to seven people, and the diversity of outings, which include scenic stops in alpine country and historic sites such as the Kawarau suspension bridge, while visiting up to four Central Otago vineyards with tastings and a meal.

The five-hour Craft Beer Bike Tour (from $199) with **Fork & Pedal Tours** (51b McBride St., 027/344-1704, www.forkandpedal.co.nz), is a 5.5km easy evening ride that takes in the Kawarau and Arrow Rivers with three tasting stops at pubs in Queenstown and Arrowtown (you're driven between the two). Alternatively, the Bike the Wineries Tour (from $179) traverses part of the Gibbston River Trail taking in three wineries for tastings, with a picnic stop among some vines. Allow 4.5 hours. Tours begin daily at 11am.

ENTERTAINMENT

Queenstown pulsates come nightfall, boasting New Zealand's highest concentration of drinking dens—from backpacker bars to high-end bistros—all in a walkable area.

Bars and Pubs

A must, especially during winter months, is a cocktail in front of the roaring fire at **Bardeaux** (Eureka Arcade, The Mall, 03/442-8284, www.goodgroup.co.nz, 4pm-4am daily), a brooding bar furnished with brick, rich woods, and leather armchairs, boasting a super collection of spirits and South Island wines.

The achingly hip **Habana Rum Bar** (3 Searle Lane, 03/409-0290, 5pm-4am daily) infuses a little Cuba into Queenstown—a living-room feel with pictures frames of images of Castro and company. The low lighting come nighttime adds to the intimacy.

The Sundeck (2 The Mall, 03/441-8032, www.thesundeck.nz, 2pm-2am daily) is best enjoyed under the glorious sun due to its rooftop setting with a view of Lake Wakatipu and the Remarkables. Should things turn chilly, there's a cast-iron potbelly fire—and plenty of blankets—on hand. Behind it, the **Bunker** (14 Cow Lane, 03/441-8030, www.thebunker.co.nz, 5pm-4am daily) sits in an intriguing black cube building. Inside, discover a sophisticated cocktail bar with an extensive drinks list, jazz, leather furnishings, and an open fire. Reservations are recommended.

Choose from a generous range of tap beers at the **Pig and Whistle** (41 Ballart St., 03/442-9055, www.thepig.co.nz, 11am-close daily), an old-school English pub with a sun-trap outdoor deck and an abundance of big screens with rolling sports coverage and traditional pub meals.

Lakeside, the fashionable **Pub on Wharf** (88 Beach St., 03/441-2155, www.pubonwharf.co.nz, 10am-10pm daily) is a Queenstown institution thanks to its cheap meals (nothing over $20), nightly live gigs, and decent selection of tap Macs beers. The spacious outdoor area overlooks the lake.

A generally young, loud, and lively crowd squeezes into **Red Rock Bar & Cafe** (48 Camp St., 03/442-6850, 8am-11pm daily) thanks to $5 beers during happy hour (4pm-6pm daily). One of Queenstown's oldest

Best Food

★ **Ballarat Trading Co.:** Dark woods and leather booths set the tone at this fashionable Queenstown eatery (page 427).

★ **Caribe Latin Kitchen:** Treats are served with a smile at this colorful, feel-good establishment in the heart of Queenstown (page 428).

★ **The Remarkables Sweet Shop:** At this Old World candy store, jars of classic sugary treats line the shelves (page 433).

★ **Relishes:** Contemporary cuisine is served with craft beer and local wines, with views over Lake Wanaka (page 438).

★ **Cucina:** Dine on daring and delightful modern dishes in a dark, sophisticated setting in Oamaru (page 448).

★ **Dog with Two Tails:** Enjoy handmade classic dishes at this trendy music joint in Dunedin (page 455).

establishments, with a great central location, it hosts regular live bands and DJs. Meals are as little as $7.

There's nothing else quite like **Perky's Floating Bar** (Queenstown Bay, off Rees St., noon-midnight daily) in the whole of New Zealand—few bars afford such a view. Moored at the edge of Lake Wakatipu, the boat-cum-bar offers tap beers and wines and encourages guests to bring their own food. Drink, eat, and watch the sun slip behind the mountains.

Clubs

A live late-night venue known for attracting the best live rock in town, the cavernous **Vinyl Underground** (12 Church St., 8pm-4am daily) throbs with $5 drinks 10pm-midnight, and a pool table offers respite from the madness.

Clad in timber and serving frothy beer, there's an authentic air of a European alpine cabin to **Rhino Ski Shack** (Cow Lane/The Mall, 03/441-3290). It generally doesn't get going until later, when the DJs spin and the dance floor fills. The food is also good.

The World Bar (12 Church St., 03/450-0008, www.theworldbar.co.nz, 4pm-close daily) is a late-night burner, throwing open its doors at 4pm to serve pub meals, and with DJs from 10pm. Happy hour is 9pm-10pm daily, and the bar's teapot cocktails are nearly as legendary as the local adrenaline sports.

FOOD

Cafés

Vudu Café & Larder (16 Rees St., 03/441-8370, www.vudu.co.nz, 7:30am-close daily) is a delectable destination brimming with sticky baked treats like fruit tarts, muffins, and carrot cakes, along with a fresh contemporary breakfast and lunch menu that includes French toast, pulled pork, and plenty of vegan options.

Joe's Garage (Searle Lane, 03/442-5282, www.joes.co.nz, 7am-4pm daily, $10-20) is an automobile-themed diner whose long bar riffs on the iconic U.S. look—you can even purchase branded trucker hats and T-shirts. Breakfasts such as pikelets with lemon and vanilla sugar, or the Gorgeous George—bacon, eggs, and hash browns—are a must. The lunch menu includes burgers, salads, and schnitzels.

Asian

Cofounded by Michelin-star chef Josh Emmet, **Madam Woo** (5 The Mall, 03/442-9200, www.madamwoo.co.nz, 11am-close daily, $14-29) fuses Chinese with contemporary Malay street food. Shredded duck, cabbage salad, pulled pork, and pickled cucumber roti rolls are served on trendy wooden bowls and plates in a swish and airy setting.

Minami Jujisei (45 Beach St., 03/442-9854, www.minamijujisei.co.nz, 11:30am-close daily, $12-30) serves sushi and sashimi as well as tempura, teppanyaki, and *donburi* dishes. The locally sourced venison *tataki* is a treat.

Contemporary

There's a permanent queue outside iconic burger bar **Fergburger** (42 Shotover St., www.fergburger.com, 03/441-1232, 8am-5am daily, $12-19), a joint renowned for its inventive between-the-bun protein-packed creations, including beef, chicken, and venison patties. There's limited seating (take your boutique burger to the lakefront), and almost always a queue; call ahead to place your order. Check out **Fergbaker** (40 42 Shotover St.) next door for homemade meat pies, sweet pastries, cakes, and artisan breads.

The historic **Bathhouse** (Marine Parade, 03/442-5625, www.bathhouse.co.nz, 9am-10pm daily, $34-39) was built in 1911 as a royal commemoration. The colonial exterior of the former changing shed belies the eatery's modern fine-dining menu. Offerings include duck dumplings and prawn. It's the most romantic restaurant in Queenstown.

European

With dark woods, polished brass fittings, ornate ceilings, and leather booths, the ★ **Ballarat Trading Co.** (7-9 The Mall, 03/442-4222, www.ballarat.co.nz, 3pm-4am daily, $24-39) imparts an air of old-school sophistication. The gastropub's dishes, such as lamb rump and pan seared salmon, are beautifully presented, while the $15 lunch items, such as spaghetti carbonara, offer excellent value.

Winnie's (7-9 The Mall, 03/442-8635, www.winnies.co.nz, noon-close daily, $19-35) is set in a cozy alpine cabin replete with timber beams and a fireplace. Winnie's bakes unusual gourmet pizzas: bolognaise, tandoori

the ever-present queue outside the iconic Fergburger

Best Accommodations

★ **Butterfli Lodge:** This lovely laid-back lakeside hostel is on the edge of Queenstown (page 428).

★ **Queenstown Park Boutique Hotel:** A luxurious eco-friendly lodging purpose-built to embrace its environment (page 429).

★ **Aro Ha:** Slotted onto the slopes of Glenorchy's Southern Alps, this is one of the world's finest wellness retreats (page 432).

★ **Wanaka Backpaka:** Enjoy a well-priced, well-presented hostel with cinematic views (page 438).

★ **Highland House Boutique Hotel:** Affordable luxury awaits in a rich and welcoming 1911 Scottish home replete with creaking wood and lush carpets (page 456).

chicken, and the Peking pizza topped with chicken, shaved cucumber, spring onion, and an aromatic plum sauce.

Latin

Colorful ★ **Caribe Latin Kitchen** (36 Ballarat St., 03/442-6658, www.caribelatinkitchen.com, 10am-11pm daily, $10-15) serves a mouthwatering selection of Central and South American delights like arepas (try the beef), burritos, and quesadillas. The tunes, vibrant decor, and friendly staff are instant mood lifters, while the outside area is a fine spot to chill.

ACCOMMODATIONS

Queenstown's array of accommodations befits its array of activities. Rates reflect summer months (Dec.-Feb.), but may increase in winter (June-Oct.). Mid-priced lodgings book quickly.

Under $100

A sun-trap terrace, a log fire, and a mesmerizing lake view afford ★ **Butterfli Lodge** (62 Thompson St., 03/442-6367, www.butterfli.co.nz, dorm $34, $73 s, $77-82 d) a serene air at the fringe of town. Dorms come with single beds only (no bunks) in clean rooms with heat and free towels. There's a small kitchen and plentiful room in the communal areas. Guests enjoy free tea, coffee, and Wi-Fi. Campers can be accommodated, but space is limited. It's a 10-minute walk to town.

There's cozy lodging aplenty at **Sir Cedrics Tahuna Pod Hostel** (11 Henry St., 03/442-7052, www.tahunapodhostel.co.nz, dorm $50, double dorm $90, $94-179 d). Dorm beds (built as 6-12 individual pods) sport power and USB ports with shelves and reading lights; double pods are also available. The dorms are backed by private queen and penthouse dorm rooms. A colorful well-stocked kitchen is the place to enjoy free toast and cereal for breakfast and soup in the evening. Airy communal areas are adorned with local art and carvings, all topped by a lovely rooftop deck. There's free Wi-Fi.

Flaming Kiwi (39 Robins Rd., 03/442-5494, www.flamingkiwi.co.nz, dorm $38-36, $76 s, $84 d) is a terrific hostel just 500m from the gondola. Accommodations for up to 49 guests are spread across single and eight-bed dorms with clean modern baths. Amenities include free unlimited Wi-Fi, bike rentals, and international calls, plus three kitchens. Winter guests enjoy a wood burner and snow-gear drying room. Sleeping quarters come equipped with lockers and charging stations.

$100-200

A brief meander from downtown, **Blue Peaks Lodge** (11 Sydney St., 03/441-0437, www.bluepeaks.co.nz, $150-250 s or d) offers no-nonsense lodging that ranges from an en suite studio with a TV, a DVD player, a fridge, a microwave, and tea- and coffee-making facilities to studio-, one-, and two-bedroom motel units with kitchenettes and Sky TV. Clean and spacious rooms are equipped with complimentary refreshments and Wi-Fi. Ask for one with a mountain view.

Choose from a compact to a double spa studio at **Bella Vista** (36 Robins Rd., 03/442-4468, www.bellavistaqueenstown.com, $155-220 s or d), a superb value minutes from town. It's especially worth considering during the winter season as it's on the shuttle bus route to the ski fields and offers splendid views of the snowy mountains—a prime location to watch paragliders. All rooms have en suite baths and kitchenettes (in the large studio, a full kitchen), plasma TVs, in-house movies and DVD players, and limited free Wi-Fi.

$200-300

Aspen Hotel (139 Fernhill Rd., 03/441-0097, www.aspenhotelnz.com, $270-350 s or d) is a slick hillside operation with stunning views across Queenstown. There are three room types: Courtyard, Superior, and Lakeview. All come with smart modern decor, terrific power showers, iPod docks, blow-dryers, fridges, tea- and coffee-making facilities, flat-screen TVs with in-house movies, and Wi-Fi. An on-site eatery boasts floor-to-ceiling windows and a deck overlooking the enchanting alpine scenery. An open fire is in the bar.

Retaining every inch of its late-19th-century charm, the **Historic Stone House** (47 Hallenstein St., 03/442-9812, www.historicstonehouse.co.nz, $225-395 s or d) houses one-, two-, and three-bedroom apartments. Lodgings have classy decor, with flat-screen TVs and iPod docks, and plush beds adorned with feather duvets. Facilities include fully equipped kitchens, a hot tub, ski storage, and a colorful well-kept garden. Stone House is a few minutes from downtown.

Chalet Queenstown (1 Dublin St., 03/442-7117, www.chaletqueenstown.co.nz, $250 s, $270 d) boasts a beautiful traditional alpine construction replete with an A-frame roof and wraparound decking that looks over the lake and mountains. Inside this peaceful boutique lodging are seven pristine rooms with balconies or patios, feather duvets, flat-screen TVs, free Wi-Fi, and tea- and coffee-making facilities. The chalet is five minutes from town.

Over $300

Merging into the mountain environment, ★ **Queenstown Park Boutique Hotel** (21 Robins Rd., 03/441-8441, www.queenstownparkhotel.co.nz, $550-950 s or d) is a modernist and eco-friendly lodging five minutes from downtown. The cubic architecture incorporates massive glass panes for a wonderfully light-filled space. Choose from the Gondola Room or the Remarkables Room (both with kitchenettes), or the Tower Suite, a two-level penthouse with 270-degree views and a gas fireplace in the living room; some rooms come with patios or balconies. All rooms ooze luxury and are loaded with Wi-Fi, a minibar, and floor heating.

Camping and Holiday Parks

Even in summer, you may wake to a dusting of snow atop the peaks that tower over **12 Mile Delta Campsite** (DoC, Glenorchy Rd., first come, first served, adults $13, children $6.50), located on the shore of Lake Wakatipu. The astonishingly beautiful yet basic lakeside retreat has space for tents and RVs and comes with running water and a handful of toilets and picnic benches. It's a 10-minute drive from Queenstown.

Queenstown Lakeview Holiday Park (Upper Brecon St., 03/442-7252, www.holidaypark.net.nz) rests at the foot of Bob's Peak, just minutes from downtown. Tent and van owners ($55-63) can use the immaculate communal facilities, which include a modern well-stocked kitchen, a TV room, laundry, and showers. Units range from an en suite open-plan ($235) to one-bedroom studios ($245) with TVs and tea- and coffee-making facilities. Tourist flats accommodate larger groups ($255).

TRANSPORTATION AND SERVICES

Car

Queenstown is 206km (2 hours, 50 minutes) south of Haast along Highway 6. From Dunedin, it's 278km (3.5 hours) northwest along Highways 1, 6, and 8. The town is compact and walkable, but exploring the surrounding area requires a car.

Air

Queenstown Airport (ZQN, Sir Henry Wigley Dr., Frankton, 03/450-9031, www.queenstownairport.co.nz) hosts international and domestic flights with one of the most scenic landings in the world. Airlines include **Air New Zealand** (09/357-3000, www.airnewzealand.co.nz). Find deals on domestic flights at **Grab A Seat** (www.grabaseat.co.nz) and **Jetstar** (09/975-9426, www.jetstar.com). The airport is 8km from downtown Queenstown.

AIRPORT TRANSPORTATION

Car rentals at the airport include **Budget** (03/442-3450, www.budget.co.nz), **Thrifty** (03/442-3532, www.thrifty.co.nz), and **Hertz** (03/442-4106, www.hertz.co.nz). For camper vans, **Britz** (03/450-9510, www.britz.co.nz) and **Wicked Campers** (0800/246-870, www.wickedcampers.co.nz) are near the airport.

Connectabus (03/441-4471, www.connectabus.com, one-way adults $12, children $5.50) is Queenstown's public bus service. It runs every 15 minutes between the airport and downtown. **Super Shuttle** (09/522-5100, www.supershuttle.co.nz, $20) provides door-to-door shared rides. **Green Cabs** (0800/464-7336, www.greencabs.co.nz) run $25 from the airport to downtown.

Bus

Intercity (www.intercity.co.nz) buses link Queenstown to Franz Josef, Milford Sound, Christchurch via Mount Cook, and Dunedin. **Connectabus** (03/441-4471, www.connectabus.com, from $4.50) crosses Queenstown with daily service to Arrowtown, Wanaka, and Cromwell. **Info & Track** (03/442-9708, www.infotrack.co.nz, from $26) provides scheduled shuttles to Glenorchy and the Routeburn Tracks.

Services

The **Queenstown i-SITE Visitor Information Centre** (Camp St. and Shotover St., 03/442-4100, 8:30am-9pm daily) provides advice and booking services for local tours and activities. Head to the **Department of Conservation (DoC) Visitor Centre** (50 Stanley St., 03/442-7935, 8:30am-5pm daily) for advice on walking tracks and conditions. **BookMe** (www.bookme.co.nz) offers discounts on attractions and activities. It's a great site for the entire country, but is especially useful in Queenstown, where spending can easily spiral.

The small **Queenstown Library** (10 Gorge Rd., 03/441-0600, 9am-5:30pm Mon.-Wed. and Fri., 9am-7pm Thurs., 10am-5pm Sat.) offers Wi-Fi. There's also a **post office** (13 Camp St., 9am-5pm Mon.-Fri., 10am-2pm Sat.). The **Queenstown Medical Centre** (9 Isle St., 03/441-0500, 8:30am-5pm Mon.-Fri.) treats nonemergencies; the **Lakes District Hospital** (20 Douglas St., Frankton, 03/441-0015) emergency department is open 24-7.

GLENORCHY

The township of Glenorchy, 50km from Queenstown, is one of the gateways to Mount Aspiring National Park as well as to some of New Zealand's best hikes. Located on the northern tip of Lake Wakatipu, near the Dart and Rees Rivers, the setting appeared in numerous *Lord of the Rings, Hobbit,* and *Chronicles of Narnia* films.

Horse Treks

Explore the beautiful backcountry like an early pioneer with **High Country Horses** (243 Priory Rd., 03/442-9915, www.high-country-horses.co.nz). Half-day (adults $185, children $175) and full-day ($375) trips for riders of all levels take in movie sites while traversing glacial valleys, river crossings, gold mines, and beech forests. The overnight **Around the Mountain Tour** ($675) offers the world's only circumnavigation of a mountain on horseback and is the highest elevation ride in the region.

Jet-Boating and Kayaking

The **Dart River Company** (Mull St., 03/442-9992, www.dartriver.co.nz, adults $219, children $119) conducts jet-boat journeys from Lake Wakatipu deep into the Dart River Valley in Mount Aspiring National Park, skimming across turquoise waters past gray banks lined with ancient native forest as snowy peaks tower in the distance. A half-hour guided forest tour complements the 90-minute boat ride to learn about local nature and Maori legends. Combine the jet-boat experience with paddling part of the river in a **Funyak** (adults $349, children $239), an inflatable canoe capable of navigating smaller side streams, chasms, and rock pools. Pick-ups from Queenstown are available.

Walks

Scenic and historic trails cater to all hiking levels. **The Glenorchy Lagoon Walkway** (1-2 hours round-trip) begins north of town: start either on Oban Street or near the lakefront of Mull Street. A boardwalk crosses wetlands brimming with native birdlife like black swans and matuku.

The three-hour **Invincible Gold Mine Track,** built by miners in the 1880s, affords views of the Rees Valley and Mount Earnslaw and its surrounding ranges. Along the way rest a smattering of mining relics. To get here, follow gravel Rees Valley Road for 30 minutes from Glenorchy (check conditions online at www.doc.govt.nz, as there are fords).

EARNSLAW BURN

Reaching **Earnslaw Burn** glacier (4-6 hours one-way) is a challenging day-long tramp with a river crossing that should not be undertaken by novice hikers. From the trailhead, the track follows the true left bank of the Earnslaw Burn Valley, continuing through bush to a tussock basin where a viewpoint faces the massive ice-fall. (The glacier was used as a backdrop in

kayaks on Lake Wakatipu

The Hobbit: An Unexpected Journey.) To get to the trailhead, take Glenorchy-Paradise Road for 20 minutes and make a right turn at Lovers Leap Road.

Routeburn Track

The **Routeburn Track** (32km, 2-4 days one-way) is a Great Walk linking Mount Aspiring and Fiordland National Parks. The route can be completed in either direction, but most tackle it from Glenorchy.

From the Routeburn Shelter, the Routeburn Track works its way through some of New Zealand's finest alpine scenery—glacial valleys, bush, waterfalls, wetlands, and lakes—climbing to its highest point at 1,255m Harris Saddle a third of the way in. Along the way, look for birdlife such as the world's only alpine parrot, the kea, and the rifleman as well as rarer species like the yellowhead, blue duck, and rock wren. The world's largest fuchsia, the kotukutuku, grows up to 12m; look for it on the final section of the trip, which ends at The Divide, 85km from Te Anau.

DoC (www.doc.govt.nz) maintains four **huts** ($54) and a pair of **campsites** ($18) along the track. Book in advance during Great Walks season (Oct.-May). Off-season, parts of the route are impassable due to heavy snow and rainfall.

For those pushed for time, a popular day walk is to head from the Routeburn Shelter to Routeburn Falls Hut (3-4 hours one-way). The Routeburn Falls waterfall is a farther 3km. The Routeburn Shelter is a 25km drive from Glenorchy. Take Glenorchy-Routeburn Road and turn right onto Routeburn Road.

Food and Accommodations

Glenorchy Café (25 Mull St., 03/442-9780, 10:30am-4:30pm Sun.-Tues. and Thurs.-Fri., 10:30am-midnight Sat., $10-20) began life as a post office. Homemade pizza, pancakes, pasties, and pork belly have long since replaced the parcels and post, along with full breakfasts, soups, and sandwiches.

The country-style **Glenorchy Hotel** (42 Mull St., 03/442-9912, www.glenorchynz.com) offers incredible scenic views from rooms with shared baths ($99) as well as en suites ($120). The adjacent **Cosy Cottage** (03/442-9912, www.glenorchynz.com) contains dorm bunks ($35) and a twin single ($85) with shared bath facilities, a TV lounge, laundry, and a log fire. Free unlimited Wi-Fi is provided throughout both buildings.

Handsome **Glenorchy Lakehouse** (13 Mull St., 03/442-7084, www.glenorchylakehouse.co.nz, $295 s or d) is an idyllic luxury waterside B&B with dazzling views of snowy peaks that are best enjoyed from the outdoor hot tub. Rooms include a SuperKing (which can double as a twin) or SuperKing Ensuite, with floor heating, indulgent bathtubs, and flat-screen TVs with DVD players. The SuperKing Ensuite comes with its own private terrace with a mountain view.

★ **Aro Ha** (33 Station Valley Rd., 03/442-7011, www.aro-ha.com, $4,550-6,250 for 4-6 nights) is a self-sustaining luxury wellness retreat nestled on the alpine slopes of the shore of Lake Wakatipu. Rooms feature recycled timber and are adorned with organic cotton linens, woolen floor rugs, and natural latex mattresses. Vegan fine-dining fare is prepared using produce grown on-site. Daily yoga sessions and lengthy hikes are rounded off with a well-earned massage.

Transportation and Services

Glenorchy is 46km (50 minutes) northwest of Queenstown along the spectacular Glenorchy-Queenstown Road (pull over regularly to photograph the stunning scenery).

Stop by the **Glenorchy Information Centre** (42 Mull St., 03/442-9912, www.glenorchynz.com) for current walking track information and weather conditions.

ARROWTOWN

Arrowtown sits in the glacially carved Arrow Basin that was once frequented by early Maori for hunting and collecting *pounamu* (a sacred type of jade). Gold was discovered in the mid-19th century, and for a time the Arrow River contained among the world's highest

The First Chinese Kiwis

Appo Hocton arrived in New Zealand in 1842, the first Chinese person to do so—around 1,600 Kiwis are descended from him—and 20 years later, the first wave of mass Chinese immigration headed to the goldfields of Otago. They often worked abandoned mines whose spoils had been plundered by Europeans and lived in separate communities. Racism was rife, and few Chinese made enough money to bring their wives and families over—compounded by the introduction of a massive immigration tax in 1881 that meant most men died poor and alone. In 2002 the New Zealand government issued an official apology to China for the suffering such historical policies caused.

concentrations of the precious metal. Today, even the throngs of tourists can't detract from the beauty of its well-preserved streets that serve almost as a time machine to the gold-rush era.

Chinese Community

On the banks of Bush Creek sits the partially restored and partially recreated collection of buildings that were Arrowtown's 19th-century **Chinese Community** (Buckingham St., donation). Maintained by DoC, the settlement storyboards detail the site's history. One particularly fascinating tale tells of how local store owner Ah Lum became a local hero by saving a European man from drowning in the Shotover River, made all the more poignant considering how the Chinese were mistreated.

Lakes District Museum

Spread over two levels and across three historic buildings, the charming **Lakes District Museum** (39 Buckingham St., 03/442-1824, www.museumqueenstown.com, 8:30am-5pm daily, adults $10, children $3) recounts the region's history from early Maori through to European settlement, with a focus on gold mining. The museum contains an art gallery and a bookshop (well worth a browse for a souvenir) and offers panning for gold ($3, plus $10 deposit) in the Arrow River.

Food

★ **The Remarkables Sweet Shop** (27 Buckingham St., 03/442-1374, 8:30am-6pm daily) is an old-school candy store whose shelves heave with iconic and hard-to-find treats. Choose goodies from New Zealand fudge and nougat to British toffee.

Bare stone walls and kauri beams lend a rustic elegance to **Stables Restaurant** (28 Buckingham St., 03/442-1818, www.stables-restaurant.co.nz, 11am-11pm daily, $32-35). An inventive take on classic fares includes poached rabbit and fig pie. The star of the decadent dessert list is a sticky date pudding with salted caramel and vanilla-bean ice cream.

The Fork and Tap (51 Buckingham St., 03/442-1860, www.theforkandtap.co.nz, 11am-11pm daily, $19-29) borrows from the traditional British pub with beer-barrel tables, high stools, and a shady sprawling backyard often graced by live bands. The extensive selection of New Zealand craft beers and wines is accompanied by high-end pub grub like gourmet pizza and wild venison.

Accommodations

Arrowtown House Boutique Hotel (10 Caernarvon St., 03/441-6008, www.arrowtownhouse.com) raises the bed-and-breakfast bar with the awards to prove it. The immaculate timber architecture makes use of skylights. Large rooms come with a king bed, private laundry, a private terrace or balcony, a TV and DVD player, a kitchenette, tea- and coffee-making facilities with unlimited freshly ground beans, and homemade cookies (one of the owners is a chef). Wi-Fi is free and unlimited.

Viking Lodge Motel (21 Inverness Crescent, 03/442-1765, www.arrowtownvikinglodge.

co.nz, $150-160 s or d) is a good value. The collection of Swiss chalet-like units backs onto an outdoor swimming pool and is surrounded by majestic peaks. One- and two-bedroom lodgings are equipped with a full kitchen, Sky TV, and free Wi-Fi. The motel is less than 30 minutes from the region's main ski hills.

Framed by the Southern Alps, **Arrowtown Holiday Park** (12 Centennial Ave., 03/442-1876, www.arrowtownholidaypark.co.nz) provides powered and unpowered sites for tents and motorhomes ($40) with access to guest laundry and a barbecue area. En suite units ($130) are equipped with a kitchenette, heating, and a TV with in-house movies. It's 600m from the town center.

Transportation and Services

Arrowtown is a 20-minute drive from Queenstown along Highway 6A; from Highway 6, turn left at Arrow Junction. **Connectabus** (03/441-4471, www.connectabus.com, 7am-10pm daily) runs regular bus service between Queenstown and Arrowtown, with four buses daily to and from Wanaka.

The **Arrowtown Information Centre** is at the Lakes District Museum (49 Buckingham St., 03/442-1824, 8:30am-5pm daily).

Wanaka

A launchpad to Mount Aspiring National Park, laid-back Wanaka (www.lakewanaka.co.nz) is overshadowed by its more illustrious neighbor of Queenstown. The town was founded on the southeastern shore of Lake Wanaka during the gold rush, but it was the advent of mass tourism a century later that saw the settlement blossom. Few other towns in New Zealand are expanding so quickly, and few offer such natural splendor. The sight of snowcapped peaks rising above the nation's fourth-largest lake will be among your most enduring memories of Aotearoa.

SIGHTS

That Wanaka Tree

At Roy's Bay grows a lonesome willow that, thanks to the power of social media (#thatwanakatree), has become the **most-photographed tree** in New Zealand. The

That Wanaka Tree

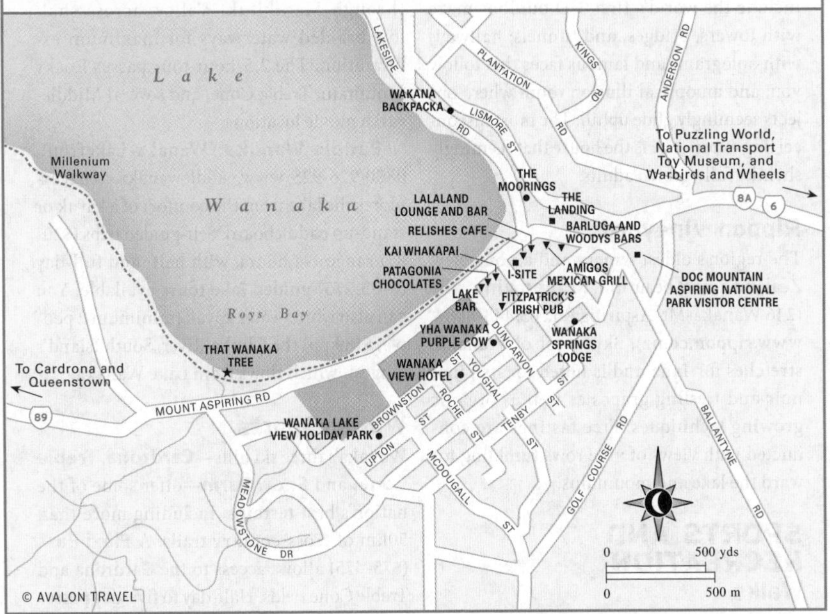

unlikely icon sprouted from a branch that was used as a makeshift fencepost. A century later, its drunken trunk leans lazily out of the water while skeletal limbs follow the peaks and ridgelines of the snowy Southern Alps beyond. Photographers from around the world come here to experiment with different angles and light. It's 2km west of Wanaka town center.

Warbirds and Wheels

Warbirds and Wheels (11 Lloyd Dunn Ave., 03/443-7010, www.warbirdsandwheels.com, 9am-5pm daily, adults $10, children $5) boasts an incredible collection of classic cars and airplanes. Aircraft on show include the RNZAF Skyhawk fighter jet and World War II Hurricane, along with antique automobiles like Lincolns, Rolls Royces, and the southern hemisphere's only Duesenberg. The "Fighter Ace Wall" is a tribute to the nations' aviators and displays pilot photos and bios.

National Transport Toy Museum

Marvel at one of the world's largest private museum collections at the **National Transport Toy Museum** (891 Wanaka-Luggate Hwy., 03/443-8765, www.nttmuseumwanaka.co.nz, 8:30am-5pm daily, adults $17, children $5). The sprawling exhibits are spread across four hangars and comprise more than 600 vehicles, 15 aircraft, 50,000 toys, and thousands of miscellaneous items—all collected by one man. Some of the pieces include 1930s cars, such as the Dodge Sedan; BSA motorbikes from the 1920s; an antique aircraft, the *Flying Flea;* and cabinets laden with rare toys like Star Wars figures and Barbie dolls in pristine condition.

Puzzling World

Puzzling World (188 Wanaka-Luggate Hwy., 03/443-7489, www.puzzlingworld.co.nz, 8:30am-6pm daily summer, 8:30am-5:30pm daily winter, adults $16, children $12) offers an amusing respite from reality thanks to its assortment of mind-bending activities that include the world's first 3-D outdoor maze with towers, bridges, and tunnels; hallways with holograms and famous faces that follow you; and an optical illusion room where objects seemingly glide uphill. The most disconcerting experience is the house that seemingly shrinks fully grown adults.

Rippon Vineyard

The region's oldest winery and among New Zealand's most beautiful, **Rippon Vineyard** (246 Wanaka-Mt. Aspiring Rd., 03/443-8084, www.rippon.co.nz), 3km west of Wanaka, stretches for 14ha and is noted for its pinot noir and riesling grapes as well as organic growing techniques. Free tastings are conducted with views of vine rows tumbling toward the lake and mountains.

SPORTS AND RECREATION

Walks

While most of the area's toughest hikes await at Mount Aspiring National Park, there are ample shorter and more accessible tracks in Wanaka. **Roy's Peak** (Nov. 11-Sept. 30) is the most famous of the local trails. The unique view from the 1,578m summit includes most of Lake Wanaka, along with peaks of Mount Aspiring National Park. The challenging 16km walk departs from **Roy's Peak Track** car park (6km west of Wanaka along Mt. Aspiring Rd.). Allow five to six hours for the return.

The rocky glacier-carved outcrop of **Mount Iron** rises almost 250m above the surrounding land. The easy 1.5-hour track to its peak weaves through kanuka scrubland and manuka forest alive with birdsong, ending with 360-degree alpine and lake views. The track starts from a car park 2km from Wanaka along Highway 84.

Water Sports

The Wanaka jet-boat tour with **Wanaka River Journeys** (99 Ardmore St., 03/443-4416, www.wanakariverjourneys.co.nz, adults $159, children $120) skims through Matukituki Valley, across shallow braided waterways for maximum exhilaration. The 2.5-hour tour passes Rocky Mountain, Treble Cone, and several Middle-earth movie locations.

Paddle Wanaka (Wanaka Lakefront, 0800/926-925, www.paddlewanaka.co.nz) explores the lake from the comfort of a kayak or stand-up paddleboard. Self-guided trips ($20-85) range 1-4 hours, with half- and full-day ($135-275) guided lake tours available. You can also white-water kayak (minimum 2 people, $189 pp) the Clutha River, South Island's longest, which flows from Lake Wanaka.

Winter Sports

Wanaka's three ski hills—**Cardrona, Treble Cone,** and **Snow Farm**—offer some of the nation's best terrains, including more than 50km of cross-country trails. A **Flexi Pass** ($75-475) allows access to the Cardrona and Treble Cone fields. Half-day to five-day passes are available online, on the mountain, or from the Wanaka i-SITE. The season runs mid-June to early-October.

Shuttle buses run between Cardrona, Treble Cone, and Wanaka, as well as Queenstown, stopping at various hotels en route. Prices and stops change seasonally.

Many rental stores, such as **SnoPro** (259 Lakeside Rd., 03/443-4456, www.snopro.co.nz) and **Base** (39 Helwick St., 0800/227-374, www.basenz.com), will deliver ski gear to your door. **Green Toad** (6 Pembroke Mall, 03/443-4315, www.greentoad.co.nz) rents toboggans and has competitive rates.

CARDRONA ALPINE RESORT

Cardona Alpine Resort (Cardrona Valley Rd., 03/443-8880, www.cardona.com, adults $75-101, children $45-51, season pass adults $799-999, children $299-349) is a family-friendly affair thanks to an abundance of gentle slopes that boast views from Lake Wanaka to Queenstown. The lifts peak at 1,860m from a 1,670m base, with a maximum 600m descent. Enjoy half-pipes, a gravity cross, and beginner freestyle features. The resort has several on-site bars and eateries, along with rentals, a ski and snowboard school, and 15 **apartments** ranging from plush studios to four-bedroom units ($300-399 s or d); all have en suite baths and are self-contained, with kitchens, lounge areas, and Sky TV. The resort is 25km south of Wanaka.

TREBLE CONE

The largest ski area on South Island, **Treble Cone** (Mt. Aspiring Rd., 03/443-1406, www.treblecone.com, adults $95-101, children $48-51, season pass adults $455-1,399, children $249) is spread across three basins. A handful of easy runs will keep novice skiers and snowboarders occupied, but more confident skiers come for some of the country's lengthiest trails, including a 700m vertical, along with open-powder fades, natural half-pipes, and fun drops. This is one of the best areas in the country for off-piste exploring. It's also among the highest (1,960m) fields and receives an abundance of high-quality powder snow. Facilities include three eateries, equipment rentals, and a snow sports school. There are no accommodations. Treble Cone is 22km west of Wanaka.

SNOW FARM

Snow Farm (Cardona Valley Rd., 03/443-7542, www.snowfarmnz.com, adults $35-90, children $15-45) is one of the leading cross-country ski destinations in the southern hemisphere. The resort offers 50km of ski trails, fat bikes, ski touring, dogsledding, and snow shoeing with tracks for all abilities. Nighttime skiing is available, and in summer, the farm opens for trekking, mountain biking, and nature watching.

Amenities include equipment rental, a ski school, and two accommodations: **Snow Farm Lodge** ($150-225) sleeps up to 50 guests; some rooms have en suite baths. Amenities include an on-site bar, an eatery, a gym and sauna, and stunning alpine views. A pair of basic **backcountry huts** (adults $30-35, children $15) with bunks and log fires are accessible via a 4km and an 8km ski.

Snow Farm is 33km from Wanaka. There is no shuttle, so visitors without transportation must book a taxi or private shuttle; try **Yello! Taxis** (03/443-5555) or **Alpine Connexions** (03/443-9120).

ENTERTAINMENT AND EVENTS

Nightlife

Barluga (33 Ardmore St., 03/443-5400, 5pm-2:30am Tues.-Sat.) is one of Wanaka's most sophisticated drinking dens. Sumptuous leather seats are positioned around an open fire pit that is best appreciated with one of their signature cocktails. Things get a little livelier as the night progresses, thanks to shared courtyard space with neighboring **Woodys** (03/443-5551, 4pm-2:30am daily), a casual sports bar with pool tables and giant TV screens. It's a popular local hangout and hosts live music.

Pulsating **Fitzpatrick's Irish Pub** (59 Helwick St., 03/443-4537, 4pm-1:30am Mon.-Sat., 4pm-midnight Sun.) has everything an Irish bar should: live bands, great atmosphere, and beers like Guinness and Kilkenny.

Wanaka's hippest hangout, **Lalaland Lounge Bar** (99 Ardmore St., 03/443-4911, 4pm-2:30am daily) broods with retro cool. Inside, comfortable vintage sofas sit beneath old-fashioned pull-cord lamps. Savor the lake view from the outdoor deck with a cocktail.

Festivals and Events

Rhythm and Alps (Cardrona Valley, www.rhythmandalps.co.nz, Dec. 31, $124-232) is South Island's largest New Year's Eve party. The multiday extravaganza attracts some of the nation's leading musicians as well as international acts. Overnight revelers can stay in a campsite in a field in Cardrona Valley, 15km south of Wanaka.

The Wanaka airport hosts the wonderful **Warbirds over Wanaka** (www.warbirdsoverwanaka.com, end of Mar.-early Apr., $60-180) air show. Classic Kiwi and military planes are joined by international aircraft like spitfires, P40 Kittyhawks, and P51-D Mustangs. Acrobatic air demonstrations delight the crowds.

FOOD

★ **Relishes** (99 Ardmore St., 03/443-9018, www.relishescafe.co.nz, 7am-close daily, $34-36) lures diners with its open fire, hanging Kiwi artwork, and mountain views across the lake. Sip a local craft beer while tucking into contemporary dishes like goat rack drizzled in sumac brown butter yogurt. Open for breakfast and lunch as well, this is one of the best dining experiences in Otago.

The Landing (80 Ardmore St., 03/443-5099, www.thelandinglakewanaka.co.nz, 5pm-close Tues.-Sun., $25-35) boasts a chic white wood-and-stone setting. Enjoy sophisticated seasonal dishes—like slow cooked venison shoulder with almond cream, pickled grapes, and pumpernickel—paired with great local wines along with craft beers and classic cocktails. Eat alfresco and watch the sun set over the lake.

Its name translates as "food made good" in Maori, and **Kai Whakapai** (Ardmore St. and Helwick St., 03/443-7795, 7am-11pm daily, $16-30) lives up to its name. A down-to-earth eatery by day and a bustling bar by night, Kai Whakapai serves superb breakfasts and pastries and beautifully presented pizzas and burgers. Grab a table outside when the sun is shining.

Tapas, Fiordland fair-game venison, and spare ribs are some of the hearty offerings at **Lake Bar** (155 Ardmore St., 03/443-2920, www.lakebar.co.nz, 11am-1am daily, $23-36), a friendly sports establishment with a pool table, big-screen TVs, and large windows framing the scenic lake and peak views.

Pasture-fed beef and free-range chicken sets family-owned **Amigos Mexican Grill** (71 Ardmore St., 03/443-7872, www.amigos-mexicangrill.co.nz, noon-close daily, $14-27) apart. Spicy delights include fajitas filled with sizzling chicken marinated in tequila and lime and char-grilled rib-eye steak in port wine jus. Wash it down with a couple of margaritas.

Forget the fresh forest air and alpine flowers—the sweetest scents in the Southern Lakes waft from **Patagonia Chocolates** (155 Ardmore St., 03/443-2380, www.patagonia-chocolates.co.nz, 9am-6pm daily), boutique chocolatiers who peddle espresso coffee, ice cream, truffles, and pastries. Enjoy it on a grassy spot outside in the sunshine.

ACCOMMODATIONS

Under $100

No other hostel sits as close to the water as ★ **Wanaka Backpaka** (117 Lakeside Rd., 03/443-7837, www.wanakabakpaka.co.nz, dorm $30-31, $64-92 s or d). Spacious dorms boast sturdy wooden beds with private reading lamps and some sinks. Well-kept private rooms range from the excellent-value twin-bunk room to the hotel-standard en suite doubles with a view. There's a high-quality kitchen along with complimentary tea and coffee, plus herbs from the garden. The lounge area affords a cinematic view of the lake. It's a five-minute stroll into town.

There are plenty of good vibes at the **YHA Wanaka Purple Cow** (94 Brownston St., 03/443-1880). Its open-plan, chalet-inspired design includes a log fire in the lounge and a free pool table. Timber-clad dorms sleep three to six in soft beds; all have en suite baths. Or choose from twins, doubles (plus one self-contained double), or a double en suite with a lake view.

$100-200

The Moorings (17 Lakeside Rd., 03/443-8479, www.themoorings.co.nz, $180-380 s or d) is a terrific modern two-story motel on the lakeside with marvelous views of the mountains. Fourteen studio units are equipped with king or queen beds, floor heating, an en suite bath, a kitchenette, a desk, a plush sofa, Sky TV, and a patio or balcony. Scenic views are restricted from some of the apartments. Communal facilities include a guest laundry and a ski-drying room.

Wanaka View Motel (122 Brownston St., 03/443-7480, www.wanakaviewmotel.co.nz)

options include modern studios ($130) with a fridge, a TV, and a private bath, or one- to three-bedroom self-contained chalets ($195-255) with kitchens and living rooms. (The studios and two-bedroom chalets lack lake views.) Guests enjoy free Wi-Fi, tea, freshly ground coffee, and bike rentals. It's located a stone's throw from the lake and the town.

Over $300

The stone **Lime Tree Lodge** (672 Ballantyne Rd., 03/443-7305, www.limetreelodge.co.nz, $395-595 s or d) is nestled in an avenue of lime trees among 4ha of prime pastureland with alpine views as far as the eye can see. Six en suite rooms sport French doors that open onto sprawling gardens, a swimming pool, croquet lawns, and a helipad. Rooms include beds adorned with designer linens, bathrobes, slippers, floor heating, baked treats, refreshments, and free use of bikes. Some rooms have private spas. The top suite is the Black Peak, which boasts black leather furnishings with black oak decor and a log burner.

You'd never guess that **Wanaka Springs Lodge** (21 Warren St., 03/443-8421, www.wanakaspringslodge.com, $295-330) is just minutes from the town center. Surrounded by enchanting gardens, the boutique lodging boasts an outdoor hot tub, a guest lounge with a log fire, and a deck with a mountain view. Eight en suite rooms are adorned with handmade furniture built from reclaimed local timber, as well as flat-screen TVs, local toiletries, New Zealand wool duvets, bathrobes, and slippers.

Camping and Holiday Parks

Luggate Cricket Club (Hwy. 6, Luggate, 03/443-7384) provides camping and RV sites for just $5. The unusual setup sees guests spread around the perimeter of the cricket field, with access to toilets and showers with limited hot water. Get there in the early afternoon to secure a spot. It is basic but has a fun festival atmosphere. It's a 15-minute drive from Wanaka.

The waterside **Wanaka Lake View Holiday** (212 Brownston St., 03/443-7883, www.wanakalakeview.co.nz) has powered and unpowered spots for tents and vans ($20 pp) with barbecues, a kitchen, and hot powerful showers. The spacious site is also home to basic units that are a good value for groups. Choose from a single cabin ($55) that sleeps up to four; a deluxe cabin ($75) that sleeps four, with a small fridge and a TV; a self-contained cabin ($100) that sleeps six, with a kitchen and a toilet; and an en suite tourist flat ($130) with a kitchen, a dining table, and a TV. The park is a few minutes' walk from the town center.

TRANSPORTATION AND SERVICES

Wanaka is 67km (1 hour) northeast of Queenstown along the Cardona Valley and Crown Range Roads.

Bus and Shuttle

The **InterCity** (www.intercity.co.nz) bus stops at 100 Ardmore St. on the Queenstown-Franz Josef route at 10:10am daily. On the way to Queenstown, it stops at 2:40pm daily. **Connectabus** (03/441-4471, www.connectabus.com) runs four daily services between Wanaka and Queenstown via the airport, Arrowtown, and Cromwell. **Alpine Connexions** (03/443-9120 www.alpineconnexions.co.nz) provide hiking shuttle transport into Mount Aspiring National Park and nearby tramping tracks.

Taxi and Bike

Explore Wanaka on two wheels with rented bikes from **Bike Lounge** (39 Helwick St., 03/443-7625, www.bikelounge.co.nz). **Wanaka Taxi** (0800/926-282, www.wanataxi.co.nz) can whisk you around town.

Services

For information about the town, visit the **Wanaka i-SITE Visitor Information Centre** (103 Ardmore St., 03/443-1233, 8:30am-7pm daily Jan.-Mar., 8:30am-5:30pm daily Apr.-Dec.). The **DoC Mount**

Aspiring National Park Visitor Centre (Ballantyne Rd., 03/443-7660, 8am-5pm daily Nov.-Apr., 8:30am-5pm Mon.-Fri., 9:30am-4pm Sat. May-Oct.) is the main information provider for conditions and activities within the park.

Wanaka Library is at 2 Bullock Creek Lane (03/443-0410, 9am-5:30pm Mon.-Wed. and Fri., 9am-7pm Thurs., 10am-5pm Sat.) and the **medical center** is at 23 Cardrona Valley Road (03/443-0710, 8am-6pm Mon.-Fri.).

Mount Aspiring National Park

Mount Aspiring National Park (www.doc.govt.nz) is the third-largest national park in New Zealand, carpeting 355,543ha of the Southern Alps from Haast Pass south to Fiordland. The land formed through glacial processes during the ice ages and incorporates river valleys, lakes, waterfalls, beech rainforests, and more than 100 glaciers. The World Heritage Site was also the filming location for Isengard in the *Lord of the Rings* movies. It harbors hundreds of moth and butterfly species and dozens of bird types, including parakeet, moreporks, blue ducks, and kea. The tallest peak is 3,033m Mount Aspiring, known as Titiea ("steep peak of glistening white") in Maori. The national park is a trekking mecca, with an abundance of half-day, full-day, and multiday trails. Mount Aspiring is considered one of the great Kiwi climbs. Although the park lies mainly in the West Coast region, most visitors access it via Otago.

MATUKITUKI VALLEY

Matukituki Valley lies northwest of Wanaka along the dusty unpaved Wanaka-Mount Aspiring Road, which winds 30km farther along the eponymous river and past grazing livestock. Cradled by a seemingly endless guard of craggy ridges and glistening mountaintops, the valley serves as a jumping-off point to a handful of trails into Mount Aspiring National Park.

Walks

The track from the Raspberry Creek car park to **Aspiring Hut** (5 hours round-trip) is an

Matukituki Valley

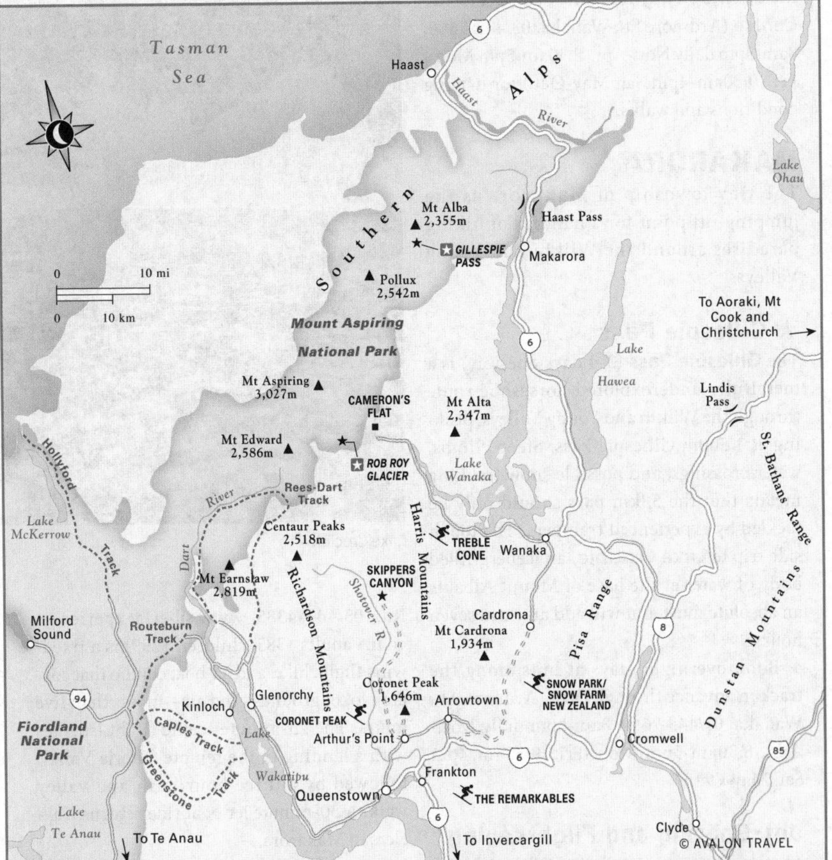

easy saunter through a grassy gorge, past the trout-filled turquoise waters of the Matukituki River as snowy peaks rise beyond the valley. The trailhead is at the terminus of Wanaka-Mount Aspiring Road.

★ ROB ROY GLACIER

The **Rob Roy Track** (3-4 hours round-trip) is one of New Zealand's best short hikes. From the Raspberry Creek car park, the 10km trail crosses a swing bridge over the Matukituki River and winds steeply through shady beech forest. Occasional breaks in the canopy reveal uncompromising cliff faces and plunging waterfalls. The trees suddenly fade to scrub in front of Rob Roy Glacier.

Eco Wanaka (03/443-2869, www.ecowanaka.co.nz) offers a guided tour of the glacier with pickup from Wanaka (adults $275, children $185) or Queenstown (adults $410, children 265). Lunch and refreshments are included.

Transportation

Matukituki Valley is 30km northwest of Wanaka along Wanaka-Mount Aspiring

Road. Deeper into the valley, the road makes several usually shallow fords. Check with the **Mount Aspiring National Park Visitor Centre** (Ardmore St., Wanaka, 03/443-7660, 8am-5pm daily Nov.-Apr., 8:30am-5pm Mon.-Fri., 9:30am-4pm Sat. May-Oct.) for driving conditions and walks.

MAKARORA

The tiny township of **Makarora** is the jumping-off point for a handful of hiking paradises around the Wilkin and Young Valleys.

★ Gillespie Pass

The **Gillespie Pass** (3-4 days one-way) is a mercifully underexplored horseshoe route through the Wilkin and Young Valleys, peaking at 1,500m Gillespie Pass. Steep climbs, water crossings, and possible snow trekking means that the 58km pass should only be tackled by experienced trampers. The tough side trip to **Lake Crucible,** an iceberg-filled body of water at the base of Mount Alba, is an absolute must, but will add an extra seven hours.

Book overnight stays at huts along the track in advance through **DoC** (Ardmore St., Wanaka, 03/443-7660, 8am-5pm daily Nov.-Apr., 8:30am-5pm Mon.-Fri., 9:30am-4pm Sat. May-Oct.).

Lake Crucible

Jet-Boating and Flightseeing

The scenic river safari with **Wilkin River Jets** (Makarora-Lake Hawea Rd., 03/443-8351, www.wilkinriverjets.co.nz, adults $130, children $75) is a thrilling way to take in the region's splendor. The 50-minute ride skims along the Wilkin and Makarora river valleys in Mount Aspiring National Park.

Trampers can make use of a drop-off service ($110) for the Gillespie Pass route to shave a day, and a river crossing, off their trek. Scenic helicopter flight, hiking, and jet-boat combination packages (adults $160-680, children $85-370) are also available.

The Siberia Experience (Makarora Tourist Centre, 5944 Haast Pass-Makarora Rd., 03/443-4385, www.siberiaexperience.co.nz, adults $385, children $299) is a fixed-wing flight, hike, and jet-boat combo that covers a lot of ground—and air—in less than five hours. The 25-minute scenic flight finishes with a landing in the remote Siberia Valley, followed by a three-hour bush and valley walk. A 30-minute jet-boat ride returns travelers to Makarora.

Transportation and Services

Makarora is 64km north of Wanaka along Highway 6. **Intercity** (www.intercity.co.nz) buses travel from Queenstown to Franz Josef, passing through Makarora. The southbound bus to Queenstown stops at 12:45pm daily, and the northbound bus to Franz Josef stops at 11:35am daily, next to the tourist center.

The small **Makarora Tourist Centre** (5944 Haast Pass-Makarora Rd., 03/443-8372, www.makarora.co.nz) visitor complex consists of a basic grocery store (8am-7pm daily), accommodations (dorm $30, $70-125 s or d), and an eatery (8am-8:30pm daily, bar until close daily, $18-29) serving traditional dishes like burgers and steak.

The Makarora DoC office has closed. The **Mount Aspiring National Park Visitor Centre** (Ardmore St., Wanaka, 03/443-7660, 8am-5pm daily Nov.-Apr., 8:30am-5pm Mon.-Fri., 9:30am-4pm Sat. May-Oct.) is the main information provider for conditions and activities within the park.

TO HAAST

From Makarora, the **Haast Pass Highway** (Hwy. 6) crosses Mount Aspiring National Park for 80km to the West Coast. It's a thrilling and winding mountain drive past bluffs, gorges, and waterfalls with access to numerous trails. Though the route travels between Haast and Wanaka, the pass begins 10km southeast of Haast at the West Coast entrance to Mount Aspiring National Park.

Central Otago

Central Otago is positioned between the Southern Lakes and the Pacific coast. The sparsely populated region was once a mining center, but grapes and orchards have long replaced gold. Its fabled land is stitched together by the world's southernmost vineyards and a smattering of modest historic settlements. A handful of world-class bike trails enable visitors to savor snowy peaks, sweeping rivers, and tussock plains as far as the eye can see.

CROMWELL

The former gold-mining town of **Cromwell** sits a mere 120km from the coast, but it is the farthest point from the ocean in New Zealand.

Sights

The **Cromwell Heritage Precinct** (Melmore Terrace, www.cromwellheritageprecinct.co.nz, daily, free) is a collection of historic buildings that were saved from flooding following the construction of Clyde Dam in 1990. Today, the 19th-century buildings house galleries and cafés.

The **Goldfields Mining Centre** (Hwy. 6, Kawarau Gorge, 0800/111-038, www.goldfieldsmining.co.nz) offers self-guided or one-hour guided tours (adults $25, children $10) around the town's historical mining sites. You'll see tunnels, a replica Chinese settlement, and tools such as a sluice gun and stamper battery used to crush gold-bearing rock.

Roaring Wine Tours (02/1056-1057, www.roaringtours.co.nz) embark upon your choice of excursions ($185-350) to boutique and exclusive Central Otago wineries for tastings. Pickup is from accommodations around Cromwell, Alexandra, Wanaka, and Queenstown.

Food and Accommodations

A modern eatery with panoramic mountain views, **Nichol's Garden Café** (11 Iles St., 03/445-0150, 8:30am-4:30pm daily, $12-20) serves freshly made fare including bacon and egg breakfasts, salads, and sandwiches alongside super coffee and a selection of local wines and beers.

The delicious plates coming out of **Armando's Kitchen** (71 Melmore Terrace, 03/445-0303, www.armandoskitchen.com, 9am-4:30pm Mon.-Wed. and Sun., 9am-8pm Thurs.-Sat., $20-25) include homemade Italian favorites such as lasagna and pizza alongside traditional Kiwi dishes like pork belly. Enjoy them all in a rustic environment surrounded by a veranda.

Cromwell Backpackers (33 The Mall, 03/445-1378, www.cromwell.org.nz, dorm $31-35, $80-90 s or d) is a clean hostel with five bedrooms. Options range from twin and double rooms to four-bed dorms with single beds (instead of bunks) and a women-only dorm. Guests have use of free towels, Wi-Fi, and tea and coffee in the well-equipped kitchen. It has a great location in the heart of town.

The contemporary **Colonial Manor Motel** (14 Barry Ave., 03/445-0184, www.colonialmanor.co.nz, $115-170 s or d) has 14 pristine rooms set amid meticulously manicured grounds. Rooms range from studios to family units, and most are equipped with kitchens; two of the studios have kitchenettes.

Transportation and Services

Cromwell is on the banks of Lake Dunstan, 60km east of Queenstown along Highway 6. **Connectabus** (03/441-4471, www.connectabus.com) stops via Cromwell on the Queenstown-Wanaka route four times daily. **InterCity** (www.intercity.co.nz) buses stop en route from Dunedin to Queenstown at 5:14pm daily and from Queenstown to Dunedin via Highway 8 at 8:40am daily. **Catch-A-Bus** (03/449-2150, www.otagorailtrail.co.nz, $15-60) is the only passenger service running through Ranfurly and the Otago Rail Trail. Buses operate daily between Cromwell and Dunedin via Highways 85 and 87.

The **Cromwell i-SITE Visitor Information Centre** (2 The Mall, 03/262-7999, 9am-7pm daily Nov.-Mar., 9am-5pm daily Apr.-Oct.) offers visitor services for the region.

CROMWELL TO COASTAL OTAGO

From Cromwell, Highways 8 and 85 head east toward coastal Otago, with sightseeing stops in the towns of Alexandra and Ranfurly.

Alexandra

The former mining town of **Alexandra** is famed for its fresh fruit orchards—notably cherries, peaches, and apricots—and its proximity to vineyards. A **Clutha River Heritage Cruise** (www.clutharivercruises.co.nz, adults $95, children $55) is a relaxing way to take in the region's mining history. The 2.5-hour tour travels through the Roxburgh Gorge to the Doctors Point and Butchers Point gold mines. Trips include refreshments and the chance to try your hand at gold panning.

FOOD AND ACCOMMODATIONS

Named after a wobbly wooden 19th-century river crossing, **Shaky Bridge Wine and Bistro** (65 Graveyard Gully, 03/448-8436, www.shakybridge.co.nz, noon-9pm Wed.-Sat., noon-5pm Sun., $20-30) sits in a picturesque old cottage. The exquisite menu includes duck-leg confit along with a selection of local wines. Grab a table outside in summer or in front of the log fire when the weather cools down.

Alexandra Motor Lodge (85 Centennial Ave., 03/448-7580, www.alexmotorlodge.co.nz, $120-150 s or d) offers well-appointed and well-priced studios as well as one- and two-bedrooms with kitchens, Sky TV, and free Wi-Fi.

TRANSPORTATION

Alexandra is a 20-minute drive southeast of Cromwell along Highway 8.

St. Bathans

Secluded **St. Bathans** was home to more than 2,000 people during its 1860s mining boom. Today, the population is less than 10. The tiny settlement serves as a living museum with a handful of historic buildings fringing its single street.

The Vulcan Hotel (St. Bathans Loop Rd., 03/447-3629, $60 pp) claims to be the most haunted hotel in New Zealand. The walls of its bar and billiard room are adorned with pioneer photos and mounted animal heads. The hotel sleeps up to eight guests across two comfortable double rooms and two twin rooms with shared bath facilities.

TRANSPORTATION

Situated 60km northeast of Alexandra off Highway 85, St. Bathans is just a 25km detour from the Otago Central Rail Trail.

Ranfurly

Ranfurly is notable for its art deco architecture that lines the main street and avenue. The best examples include the **Fenton Library building** (Pery St. and Northland

St.), now the home of the local radio station, and the **Centennial Milk Bar** (Charlemont St.). Though it's not on the scale of Napier, the town offers an easy hour-long stroll. Download the Ranfurly art deco brochure (www.maniototo.co.nz) for a map of the historic buildings.

Real Dog Adventure (5 Bypass Rd., 03/444-9952, www.realdog.co.nz) gets you up close to the largest kennel of Alaskan malamutes in the southern hemisphere. Take the 45-minute Kennel Tour ($30) and visit the dog kennels and workshop where the harnesses and sleds are crafted, then watch a short documentary before chatting with the team about their canines. Following the tour, experience the thrill of a dogsled ride ($85-120 pp) across the windswept Otago plains.

Old Post Office Backpackers (11 Pery St., 03/444-9588, www.oldpobackpackers.co.nz, Sept.-May, dorm $33, $50 s, $75 d) houses clean, vibrant rooms for up to 10 guests with shared bath facilities, a full kitchen, free tea and coffee, Wi-Fi, laundry, and a log fire.

TRANSPORTATION

Ranfurly is a one-hour drive east from Alexandra and a 40-minute drive from Dunedin via Highways 85 and 1 or 87. The **Ranfurly i-SITE Visitor Information Centre** (3 Charlemont St. E., 03/262-7999, 9am-5:30pm daily Jan.-Mar., 9am-5pm daily Apr.-Dec.) provides information about the area.

★ Otago Central Rail Trail

The **Otago Central Rail Trail** (www.otagocentralrailtrail.co.nz) is the original Great Ride. The 152km bike ride begins at the historic Old Clyde Station (Sunderland St.) and follows a defunct rail track that links the settlements of Clyde and Middlemarch via Alexandra and Ranfurly. The railway line was built between 1891 and 1907; riders can still traverse its tunnels and viaducts, tackling river gorges, high-country sheep stations, mining relics, country pubs, vineyards, and more than 20 historic townships.

It takes up to five days to complete the entire trail, or you can hop on and off at numerous points along the way for a shorter ride. Bike rentals, trip packages, and transportation are available from tour operators at towns en route. A good place to start is **She Bikes He Bikes** (Fraser St., 03/447-3271, www.shebikeshebikes.co.nz, 8:30am-5pm Mon.-Fri.,

the Otago Central Rail Trail

8:30am-12pm Sat.-Sun.), near the start of the trail in Clyde. They have bike rentals and offer a pickup and drop-off shuttle service along the track.

Catch-A-Bus (03/449-2150, www.otagorailtrail.co.nz, $15-60) runs a daily door-to-door service between Cromwell and Dunedin via Highways 85 and 87.

Oamaru

One of New Zealand's best-kept secrets, Oamaru is known for its populations of little blue- and yellow-eyed penguins, but its Victorian precinct is New Zealand's most photogenic urban spot and its steampunk capital.

SIGHTS

TOP EXPERIENCE

★ Blue Penguin Colony

Creatures don't come much cuter than the little blue penguin. For a guaranteed sighting that also aids their conservation, visit the **Oamaru Blue Penguin Colony** (2 Waterfront Rd., 03/433-1195, www.penguins.co.nz, adults $30, children $15) where you can browse the information center, watch informative videos, and see penguins nest in their boxes. It's when the sun sets that the magic happens. In summer, hundreds of the flightless birds emerge from the surf to waddle across a rocky beach to their nests, housed in an old quarry. A grandstand (adults $45, children $22.50) holds 350 guests with ringside seats within 3m of the birds' route.

Bushy Beach

A track at the end of **Bushy Beach Road** leads to an observation shelter for New Zealand's northernmost breeding colony of rare **yellow-eyed penguins,** a native species. The easy clifftop track (30 minutes round-trip) is surrounded by leafy green vegetation. Summer months are the best time to view them. Avoid accessing the beach 3pm-9am, when the penguins come to shore late afternoon to nest; the birds won't leave the water if they see someone on the sand.

Blue Penguin Colony

Oamaru's Victorian Precinct

★ Victorian Precinct

Oamaru's old-town **Victorian Precinct** (Tyne St. and Harbour St.) is a white-stone slice of perfectly preserved stoic Victorian history. (The white stone used to build the structures along these streets is a type of local limestone, quarried from around Oamaru and used throughout New Zealand.) Along these majestic blocks, imposing facades give way to an array of crafts stores, artisanal bakeries, bookshops, antiques shops, art galleries, and vintage clothing. Delve deeper and you'll discover Old World shopping arcades tucked into secret passageways hidden behind stable doors.

Steampunk HQ

The most notable building in the Victorian precinct, **Steampunk HQ** (Tyne St., 027/778-6547, www.steampunkoamaru.co.nz, 10am-5pm daily, adults $10, children $2) sits guarded by a menacing missile-clad steam train seemingly poised to launch into space. (Slip in some coins and flames and smoke will billow out.) Part weird art gallery, part museum, it houses an array of familiar yet otherworldly contraptions like tractors and steamboats with a decidedly dystopian slant.

ENTERTAINMENT AND EVENTS

Sample some rare South Island scotch at **The Whisky** (14 Harbour St., 03/434-8842, www.thenzwhisky.com, 10:30am-4:40pm daily). In 1997 the world's farthest southern whiskey distillery closed its doors, leaving hundreds of sprit-laden barrels adrift. In 2010, The Whisky purchased 443 of those barrels. Today you can sample them by the dram or buy a bottle from their boutique in the Victorian precinct. The wonderful setting resembles a traditional Highlands distillery, propped with timber beams and stag heads on the wall.

Scott Brewing Company (1 Wansbeck St., 03/434-2244, www.scottsbrewing.co.nz, 10am-close daily) pours premium craft beers that are brewed on-site and served in a fashionable industrial environment. Opt to sit in the shadows of the enormous stainless-steel brewing equipment, bask in the warming glow of a log fire, or soak in harbor views on the front deck.

For five days, Oamaru hosts the **Steampunk Festival** (www.steampunknz.co.nz, June). Celebrants dress in futuristic Victorian outfits to attend theater performances, fashion shows, teapot racing, and dances in the streets of the old town.

FOOD

Harbour St. Bakery (4 Harbour St., 03/434-0444, 10am-4pm Tues.-Sun.) serves the best meat pies in the southern hemisphere. The pies, sourdough loaves, pastries, and croissants are baked on-site in the heart of Oamaru's magical Victorian center.

Located in the historic precinct, **Tees St. Café** (3 Tees St., 03/434-5696, www.teesst.com, 7am-3pm Mon.-Fri., 7:30am-3pm Sat.-Sun.) has a seasonal menu that features carefully constructed dishes served in a vibrant setting. Choose from pancakes and fresh fruit, free-range eggs, or homemade lamb burger with beetroot relish, cheddar cheese, and fries.

The **Star and Garter** (9 Itchen St., 03/434-5246, 10am-close daily, $20-30) serves well-executed traditional fare such as bacon and eggs for breakfast, burgers for lunch, and lamb shank for dinner. Its seafood dishes (salmon or blue cod) are revered, and the seafood chowder is a local legend.

European-inspired ★ **Cucina** (1 Tees St., 03/434-5696, 5pm-10pm daily, $20-35) offerings include seafood and chorizo paella alongside such surprises as braised duck *ragù* with pappardelle, cherry tomatoes, red wine, truffle oil, and parmesan. The burnt plum crumble with coconut ice cream is a must. The black walls and polished wood setting add to the sophistication, as does the superb wine list.

Don't leave Oamaru without dipping into boutique ice cream at **Deja Moo** (4 Harbour St., 10am-4pm daily). Their freezer is filled with handcrafted flavors like salted caramel popcorn, hokey pokey, and vanilla.

ACCOMMODATIONS

★ **Oamaru Backpackers** (47 Tees St., 021/900-096, www.oamarubackpackers.co.nz, dorm $30) is the town's best hostel by a nautical mile. More akin to a B&B, the hostel dorm beds are arranged like a sailor's berth, complete with curtains, reclaimed marine-themed furnishings, and ocean views. Other sleeping options include a king-size single with storage and sink ($50), doubles and triples ($75-90), and the Quarry Room en suite ($120). Amenities include a spacious modern kitchen with continental breakfast included as well as dining and lounge areas. It is within walking distance to the town's attractions.

North Otago's only boutique luxury lodge, **Pen-y-bryn Lodge** (41 Towey St., 03/434-7939, www.penybryn.co.nz, $525-1,050 s or d) sits on a manicured hillside surrounded by gorgeous grounds peppered with colorful flowers and ornate water features. Lavish rooms feature hardwood floors and classic furniture with cotton linens with feather bedding, modern baths, iPod docks, and bathrobes. Communal facilities include a billiard room, a fitness center, a library, and a lounge with a log fire.

The historic **Mill House** (2358 Herbert-Hampden Rd., 03/439-5554, www.themillhouse.net.nz, $110-135 s or d) was built by a German settler in the late 19th-century using local stone. Lodge rooms in the original building include en suite modern double studios with heat, a gas fire, and complimentary tea, coffee, and TV in the welcoming guest lounge. In the newer motel section, four en suite units come equipped with a TV, a fridge, and a microwave. Outside the mill is a large shady garden with a barbecue. The house is 15 minutes south of Oamaru.

There aren't too many campgrounds that receive regular visits from a rare blue penguin, but **Oamaru Harbour Tourist Park** (8 Esplanade, 03/434-5260, www.oamaruharbour.co.nz, $23-30) offers a promising glimpse of one. Pitch a tent on thick soft grass, or secure a camper site; some sites afford harbor views. Amenities include a kitchen and a deck, plus the on-site café, Penguin's Nest (order the bacon roll). The park is within walking distance of all the sights.

TRANSPORTATION AND SERVICES

Oamaru is 113km (1.5 hours) north of Dunedin along Highway 1. It is 287km (3 hours, 40 minutes) east of Queenstown along Highways 6, 8, and 83.

InterCity (www.intercity.co.nz) buses depart for Dunedin at 12:05pm and 6:15pm daily, with the earlier service terminating in Te Anau. Two northbound buses depart for Christchurch at 9:30am and 3:05pm daily. **Whitestone Taxis** (03/434-1234, whitestonetaxis.co.nz) can take you to Bushy Beach ($15). For bike rentals, contact **Vertical Ventures** (021/894-427, www.verticalventures.co.nz, $45-110).

The **Oamara i-SITE Visitor Information Centre** (1 Thames St., 03/434-1656, 9am-6pm daily Jan.-Mar., 9am-5pm daily Apr.-Dec.) displays daily penguin arrival times.

OAMARU TO DUNEDIN

Fascinating wildlife and a beach strewn with fossils make this accessible stretch of coastline one of New Zealand's most compelling.

★ Moeraki Boulders

The alluring **Moeraki Boulders** are sizeable spherical stones scattered across Koehohe Beach. According to Maori myth, the stones are the remnants of eel pots that washed ashore from a shipwrecked canoe. In truth, these are concreted boulders 60 million years in the making, the result of the cementation of prehistoric marine mud that was buried in the cliffs, then eroded and exposed over time. Some of the cracked boulders reveal honeycomb centers. The area is best viewed 3.5 hours on either side of low tide. The Moeraki Boulders are a 30-minute drive south of Oamaru, along Highway 1.

Shag Point

The windswept headlands of **Shag Point** protrude from the Matakaea Scenic Reserve. A handful of coastal tracks overlook fur seals and sometimes yellow-eyed penguins frolicking among the kelp. The point is a 10-minute drive south of the Moeraki Boulders along Highway 1; turn at the sign onto Shag Point Road.

Dunedin

Brooding Dunedin, festooned with Gothic structures, is the main hub and New Zealand's oldest city. It was based on the Scottish capital, Edinburgh, and its Celtic heritage still abounds.

Named a UNESCO City of Literature, Dunedin is home to the prestigious University of Otago and a sizeable student population. The cultural hub strikes the perfect balance of measured wisdom and youthful exuberance with haunting Gothic architecture, fashionable eateries, museums, galleries, and street art.

A popular hunting and fishing location for Maori, Europeans later founded a whaling port here before the Scottish Free Church settled the city in the mid-19th century. The unimaginative name "New Edinburgh" was thankfully shelved in favor of its Gaelic translation, Dunedin, and locals are fiercely proud of their Celtic roots.

Dunedin is the gateway to the rugged Otago Peninsula, where colonies of yellow-eyed penguins, royal albatross, and New Zealand's only castle await.

SIGHTS

The Octagon is the city's central plaza and focal point. It's flanked by an array of Victorian stone buildings, along with a statue of the Scottish poet Robert Burns.

Otago Museum

The **Otago Museum** (419 Great King St., 03/474-7474, www.otagomuseum.nz, 10am-5pm daily, free) was founded in the mid-19th-century with a collection of rocks from a geological survey of Otago. Today, it holds a 1.5-million-piece collection from across the world, including rocks from the summit of Mount Everest collected by Sir Edmund Hillary and the camera Hillary used to photograph climbing partner Tenzing Norgay when they became the first people to scale the world's highest peak. Other permanent exhibits include the world's largest collection of moa bones, an eerie Victorian collection of stuffed exotic animals, Maori and Pacific artifacts like masks and carvings, dinosaur fossils, and a 17m fin whale skeleton. **Guided tours** (11am, 1pm, 2pm, and

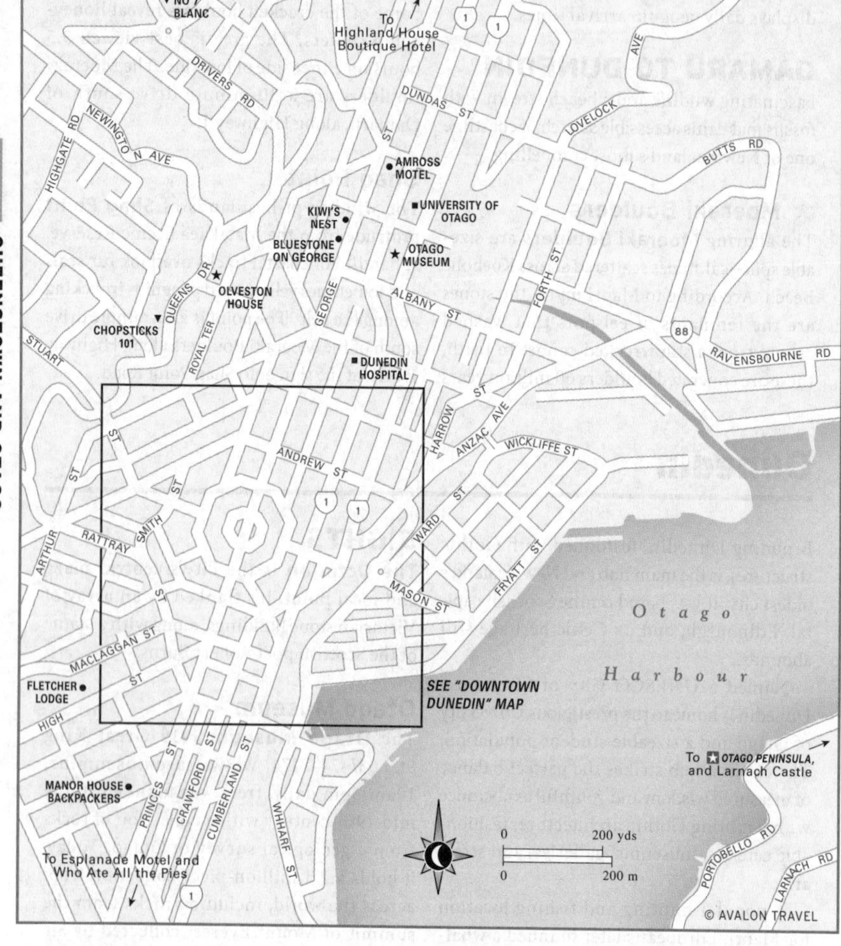

3pm daily, $15) can be booked online or at the information desk.

Toitu Otago Settlers Museum

The **Toitu Otago Settlers Museum** (31 Queens Gardens, 03/477-5052, www.toitu-osm.com, 10am-5pm daily, free) depicts Dunedin's gripping history from early Maori to European whalers to 21st-century arrivals. Cultural exhibits include classic vehicles, computers, and fashion items, while more absorbing displays offer a war memorial, the story of the Dunedin Study, and a room of 20th-century iconography. Interactive screens throughout reveal the stories of real-life Dunedin residents and their ancestors. Tours are available by appointment.

Dunedin Public Art Gallery

New Zealand's oldest public art collection resides at the **Dunedin Public Art Gallery** (30 The Octagon, 03/474-3240, www.dunedin.art.

museum, 10am-5pm daily, free). Works straddle the globe with art from Monet, Pissarro, and Turner. Pride of place is given to renowned local Frances Hodgkins, a neo-Romantic painter especially popular in Europe. Japanese prints and contemporary Australian pieces round out the works.

Olveston House

Built in 1904-1906, the historic **Olveston House** (42 Royal Terrace, 03/477-3320, www.olveston.co.nz, 9am-5pm daily, adults $20, children $11) affords a beguiling insight into Edwardian high society. Surrounded by fastidiously pruned hedgerows and manicured lawns, the 35-room mansion was gifted to the city in 1966 with all its original contents. One-hour **tours** (9:30am, 10:45am, noon, 1:30pm, 2:45pm, and 4pm daily) savor the splendor of its antique furnishings, priceless artworks, and 19th-century Japanese weaponry.

★ Dunedin Railway Station

The city's most recognizable structure, the **Dunedin Railway Station** (Castle St. and Anzac Ave.) was once the busiest terminal in the country. Opened in 1906, the Flemish Renaissance-inspired exterior was crafted from Oamaru white stone and contrasting black basalt. Inside, experience a hushed reverence for stained-glass windows and hundreds of thousands of Royal Doulton porcelain tiles that complete the mosaic floor.

Upstairs, the **New Zealand Sports Hall of Fame** (03/477-7775, www.nzhalloffame.co.nz, 10am-4pm daily, adults $6, children $2) celebrates the nation's greatest athletes from incongruous fields such as wood chopping and sheep shearing, as well as headline acts like rugby, cricket, and basketball.

Taieri Gorge Rail Journey

From the Dunedin Railway Station, the scenic **Taieri Gorge Rail Journey** (www.dunedinrailways.co.nz, adults $99, children $28) travels inland to Central Otago. Passengers traverse the alpine scenery and grassy plains in refurbished wooden 1920s carriages that travel through tunnels and giant viaducts built in the late 19th and early 20th centuries.

Service departs for the four-hour round-trip at 9:30am and 2:30pm Monday-Thursday and Saturday to Pukerangi, 9:30am and 2:30pm Friday and Sunday to Middlemarch October-April; and 12:30pm Monday-Saturday to Pukerangi, 9:30am Sunday to Middlemarch

Dunedin Railway Station

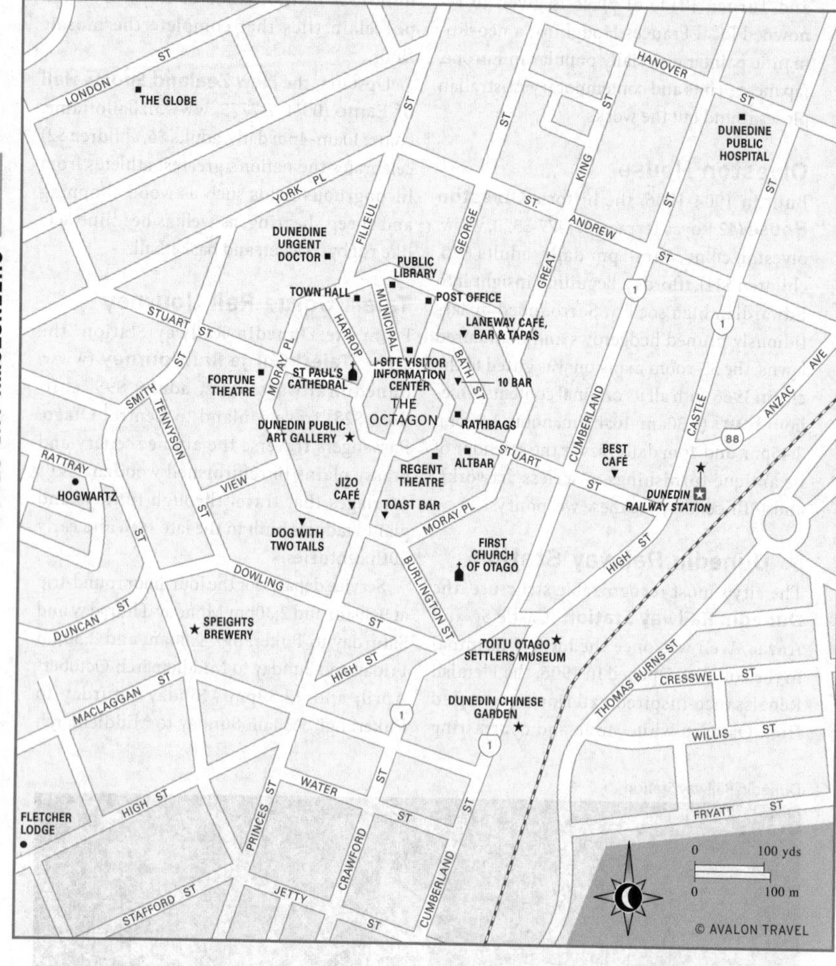

May-October. Middlemarch marks the start of the Otago Central Rail Trail.

Buses from Pukerangi and Middlemarch to Queenstown can be booked through **Dunedin Railways** (Dunedin Railway Station, Castle St. and Anzac Ave., 03/477-4449, www.dunedinrailways.co.nz, 8am-5pm Mon.-Fri., 9am-3pm Sat.-Sun.).

First Church of Otago

Opened in 1873, the **First Church of Otago** (415 Moray Place, 03/477-7118, www.firstchurchotago.org, daily) was built from brick and Oamaru limestone. Rows of turrets, pinnacles, and gables surround the roof, giving way to a 60m bell spire that can be seen all over Dunedin. Inside are timber beams, stained-glass windows, and a pulpit flanked by carved pillars depicting life and death. The church becomes mesmerizing come nightfall, when lights emphasize its Gothic design.

tea area of the Dunedin Chinese Garden

Dunedin Chinese Garden

Opened in 2008 by then-prime minister Helen Clark, the **Dunedin Chinese Garden** (Rattray St. and Cumberland St., 03/474-3594, www.dunedinchinesegarden.com, 10am-5pm daily, adults $9, children free) marks a fitting tribute Otago's Chinese, from early gold miners to the businesses of today. The garden is laid in the traditional *yuanlin* style, with pavilions and archways handcrafted by Chinese artisans and shipped from Shanghai.

Speights Brewery

Established in Dunedin in 1876, **Speights Brewery** (200 Rattray St., 03/477-7697, www.speights.co.nz, noon-8pm daily, adults $29, children $13, under age 5 free) is among the nation's oldest and most iconic brands. The 90-minute tour (noon, 2pm, 4pm, 5pm, 6pm, and 7pm daily summer, noon, 2pm, and 4pm daily winter, covered shoes essential) is an interactive guided journey where you'll learn about the history of brewing, marvel at the on-site machinery, and touch and taste the ingredients used to craft the booze. The tour ends with a tasting of six beers.

RECREATION

Centrally located **Cycle World** (67 Stuart St., 03/477-7473, www.cycleworld.co.nz, $50 per day) has a good range of road bikes and mountain bikes and can advise on interesting routes and trails.

Walks

City Walks (www.citywalks.co.nz, adults $30, children $5) organizes a pair of guided heritage walks around the city. The two-hour **Old Town Walk** (10:30am and 1:30pm Mon.-Sat.) takes in notable historic landmarks like The Octagon, the railway station, and the First Church. The **Heritage Highlights Walk** (4pm Mon.-Sat.) takes in a select sample of historical sights, followed by whisky and haggis. Book tours online.

Dunedin is famed for its commissioned graffiti. The **Street Art Trail** (www.dunedinstreetart.co.nz) directs visitors to the best samples of work in town. Grab a map of the 90-minute self-guided route from the i-SITE.

Baldwin Street is officially recognized by the Guinness Book of Records as the world's steepest residential street. It's only 350m long, but for every 2.86m it rises by 1m, which means that it takes 5-10 minutes to scale. Position your camera cleverly and have fun with the resulting weirdly angled images.

ENTERTAINMENT AND EVENTS

Nightlife

Dunedin's nightlife thrives thanks to a healthy arts scene and huge student population. **Albar** (135 Stuart St., 03/479-2468, 11am-2am Mon.-Sat., 11am-9:30pm Sun.) is one of the more interesting establishments. Whiskey bottles fight for shelf-space in this former butcher shop (you can still see butchery tiles on the wall). There are plenty of spirits on offer, as well as wine and some of the best tap beers in town.

One of Dunedin's most iconic drinking dens, **Inch Bar** (8 Bank St., 03/473-6496, 3pm-11:30pm daily) is a gloriously cozy, timber and wrought-iron-clad environment with an open log fire and regular live music. It's famed for its awesome selection of craft brews.

Bartenders at the award-winning **Toast Bar** (59 Princes St., 03/479-2177, 5pm-close Wed.-Fri., 5pm-close Sat.) mix top-notch classic cocktails like the espresso martini and are more than happy to take requests. An intimate Dunedin setting with low lighting the color of bourbon, it regularly hosts local DJs.

After-hours, head to the cavernous **10 Bar** (The Octagon, 03/477-6310, 10pm-4am Thurs.-Sat.), where live music, DJs, pool tables, and cheap drink deals attract a crowd.

Performing Arts

The **Fortune Theatre** (231 Stuart St., 03/477-8323, www.fortunetheatre.co.nz) productions include comedies, dramas, and kids shows in two auditoriums. **The Globe** (104 London St., 03/477-3274, www.globetheatre.org.nz) was formed in 1961 as an extension of someone's house. Today, amateur productions of Shakespeare, Greek tragedies, and Oscar Wilde play to an intimate audience of maximum 80.

The **Regent Theatre** (17 The Octagon, 03/477-8597, www.regenttheatre.co.nz) comprises three historic buildings, including an auditorium with 1,617 seats. Its eclectic show list includes operas, films, circuses, and live theater.

Festivals and Events

Arts Festival Dunedin (www.artsfestivaldunedin.co.nz, late Sept. even-numbered years) showcases theater, comedy, and dance for 10 days at various locations around the city.

The **Fringe Festival** (www.dunedinfringe.nz, Mar.) promotes 10 days of local and international talent in the performing and contemporary arts. The festival is produced by a nonprofit trust and brings in more than 10,000 visitors.

The Dunedin Study

The Dunedin Multidisciplinary Health and Development Study, commonly called the **Dunedin Study,** is a socio-scientific world first, with researchers studying the development into adulthood of more than 1,000 babies born in 1972-1973, retaining an astonishing 95 percent participation rate. More than 1,000 papers have been published concerning the mental and physical health of its subjects, a project that continues to benefit the global scientific community.

The city's moody architecture provides the perfect backdrop for the **Dunedin Midwinter Carnival** (www.midwintercarnival.co.nz, June) and its intriguing array of artistic lanterns and light sculptures.

FOOD

Cafés

A hidden gem in the back of The Octagon, **Laneway Café, Bar and Tapas** (7 Bath St., 020/422-8478, 6:30am-4pm Mon.-Tues., 6:30am-10pm Wed.-Thurs., 6:30am-11pm Fri.-Sat., $10-20) is set in a fashionable brick building with colorful artwork. Order inventive treats like eggs with chorizo, bacon, salsa, spinach, and jalapeños; ginger salmon; stuffed mussels; and buttermilk-popcorn chicken tapas. The interesting drinks list includes peppermint hot chocolate and spiced chai latte along with local and international wine, craft beer, and cider.

Best Café (30 Stuart St., 03/477-8059, 11:30am-2:30pm and 5pm-8pm Mon.-Thurs., 11:30am-2:30pm and 5pm-9pm Fri.-Sat., $16-26) is a pretentious-free peddler of seafood, including Bluff oysters, whitebait fritters, and the best fish-and-chips in town. Eat inside on the unabashedly retro vinyl-topped tables (BYOB) or get it to go.

Contemporary

Home of the one-meter pizza, **Ratbags and**

Innocent Bystander (11 The Octagon, 03/471-9222, www.ratbagsib.co.nz, 11am-10:30pm Sun.-Wed., 11am-3am Thurs.-Fri., 11am-4am Sat., $12-30) is a gastropub renowned for food and drink deals that ensure a lively atmosphere. Daring pizza toppings include chili prawn, mango, and coriander as well as the classics. Chicken wings and sticky ribs make up the rest of the menu.

No 7 Balmac (7 Balmacewen Rd., 03/464-0064, www.no7balmac.co.nz, 7am-close Mon.-Fri., 8:30am-close Sat., 8:30am-5pm Sun., $29-38) is a swanky suburban eatery perched atop Maori Hill. Contemporary cuisine includes offerings like Manuka-smoked salmon and wood-grilled lemon and thyme-infused chicken. Bread is baked in-house, and organic veggies are grown in their garden.

The ★ **Dog with Two Tails** (25 Moray Place, 03/477-4188, www.dogwithtwotails.co.nz, 8am-3pm Mon., 8am-close Tues.-Fri., 9am-close Sat., 10:30am-3pm Sun., $9-19) has a superhero-like double identity: humming café by day and thriving restaurant-cum-bar and live-music venue by night (most gigs are free). A piano, bookshelves, and maroon walls adorned with picture frames lend a homey living-room vibe. Choose from carefully created-from-scratch seafood chowder, burgers, and an organic lamb salad. They roast their own coffee, too.

Asian

A local favorite (especially with students), the fashionable **Jizo Café** (56 Princes St., 03/479-2692, www.jizo.co.nz, 11:30am-2:30pm and 5pm-9pm Mon.-Thurs., 11:30pm-2:30pm and 5pm-9:30pm Fri., 5pm-9:30pm Sat., $10-30) boasts traditional Japanese counter seating, along with regular tables and chairs spread over two levels. An exquisite menu brims with sushi rolls, sashimi, *donburi,* and noodles. BYO is possible.

Excellent value East Asian fare props up the sprawling menu at **Chopsticks 101** (380 George St., 03/477-1628, 11:30am-9pm Mon.-Thurs., 11:30am-10pm Fri., noon-10pm Sat.-Sun., $10-25). Opt for the large portions of stir-fries, dumplings, and noodle soups, which are big enough to share. The bustling eatery is a big favorite among locals.

ACCOMMODATIONS

Under $100

Dunedin's best hostel is the magical **Hogwartz** (277 Rattray St., 03/474-1787, www.hogwartz.co.nz, dorm $27-30, $61 s, $66-82 d). Built in the late 19th century as a former bishop's residence, the hostel's 17 immaculate rooms range from studios to five-bed dorms with single beds (no bunks); some rooms have splendid city views. The adjacent converted Coach House ($34-49 pp) and Stables ($56 pp) provide posher private en suite lodgings with separate kitchens. High ceilings and hardwood floors add to its hominess, as does a log fire in the lounge area, a cozy reading loft, and a communal piano. It's five minutes from The Octagon.

Manor House Backpackers (28 Manor Place, 03/477-0484, www.manorhousebackpackers.co.nz, dorm $23-30, $60-75 s or d) is set in a pair of early-20th-century colonial villas brimming with character. Spacious dorms sleep 4-12 in sturdy wooden bunks. Tea, coffee, and spices are in the kitchen, herbs are in the garden, and there's an extensive DVD collection, plus weekly movie nights with complementary popcorn. Wi-Fi and domestic calls are free.

The welcoming **Kiwis Nest** (597 George St., 03/471-9540, www.kiwisnest.co.nz) is a budget lodging in a century-old brick home with stained-glass windows. Accommodations include singles ($48) and doubles ($68) with shared baths; tidy en suite options ($68-88) with TVs, fridges, and tea- and coffee-making facilities; and a fully contained one-bedroom unit ($105) with its own kitchen. The six-bed dorm ($28) has its own sink and fridge. Communal facilities include a couple of sizeable kitchens, laundry, and free Wi-Fi.

$100-200

George Street is the place for motels in Dunedin. Reasonably priced **Amross Motel**

(660 George St., 03/471-8924, www.amrossmotel.co.nz, $165-230 s or d) is a stone's throw from Otago Museum. The modern establishment has studios as well as one- and two-bedroom en suite rooms with kitchenettes, large flat-screen TVs with Netflix and Sky TV, DVD players, and free unlimited Wi-Fi. Secure a spa suite for added luxury.

The lovely ★ **Highland House Boutique Hotel** (1003 George St., 03/477-2665, www.highlandhouse.co.nz, $160-215 s or d) springs from a 1911 Scottish heritage home in north Dunedin. Plush carpets welcome guests to 10 luxurious self-contained en suite studios with flat-screen TVs, kitchenettes, toiletries, and free Wi-Fi.

$200-300

Bluestone on George (571 George St., 03/477-9203, www.bluestonedunedin.co.nz, $230-270 s or d) is a modern establishment with self-contained soundproof studios sporting floor heating and high-end TVs; some rooms come with spas. Enjoy a gym, high-speed Internet, and wonderful views over the harbor and Otago Peninsula.

Over $300

With its oak paneling and secluded landscaped gardens, enchanting **Fletcher Lodge** (276 High St., 03/474-5551, www.fletcherlodge.co.nz, $355-650 s or d) appears lifted from a fairy tale. Five elegant en suite rooms have carved wooden beds, claw-foot tubs, antique furniture, and flat-screen TVs. Two luxurious self-contained apartments are also available. Continental breakfast is included.

Camping and Holiday Park

Leith Valley Holiday Park (103 Malvern St., 03/467-9936, www.leithvalleytouringpark.co.nz) is set on blissful grounds. Campers and RVers ($19) can use the sauna, barbecue area, and lounge with Sky TV, plus a kitchen and game room with Ping-Pong. A bunk room ($75 for 1-2 people, $20 per additional person) sleeps eight, with a fridge, a dining table, and a kitchen. A self-contained upstairs apartment ($125 for 1-2 people, $20 per additional person) comes with Sky TV and sleeps nine. An assortment of dorm-like cabins ($49 s, $59 d, $20 per additional person) sleep 3-5 with tables, chairs, a kettle, and a toaster. It's 1km from Dunedin.

TRANSPORTATION AND SERVICES

Car

Dunedin is 113km south of Oamaru via Highway 1. The drive takes about 1.5 hours.

Air

Dunedin Airport (DUD, Airport Rd., Momona, 03/486-2879, www.dunedinairport.co.nz) is 30km south of the city. **Jetstar** (09/975-9426, www.jetstar.com) operates one flight daily from Auckland, and **Air New Zealand** (09/357-3000, www.airnewzealand.co.nz) serves routes throughout New Zealand. There's no public bus service between the airport and the city. It's a 30-minute drive to the city center.

Super Shuttle (09/522-5100, www.supershuttle.co.nz, $25) is your best bet, with door-to-door shared rides. **Southern Taxis** (03/476-6300, www.southerntaxis.co.nz) and **Dunedin Taxis** (03/4777-777, www.dunedintaxis.co.nz) are located outside the airport terminal building; the ride to the city center runs around $90. **Budget** (03/486-2660), **Thrifty** (03/486-2537), and **Hertz** (03-477-7385) car rental agencies have offices at the airport.

Bus

InterCity (www.intercity.co.nz) buses provide service to Queenstown, Te Anau, Invercargill, and Christchurch. The main transport hub is at The Octagon, and timetables are on the **Otago Regional Council** website (www.orc.govt.nz).

For longer stays, consider picking up a GoCard ($5-10) to save 25 percent on bus fares. Two public bus companies (GoBus and Ritchies) have the same fare system and accept GoCard. Fares must be paid on the bus either with cash or GoCard.

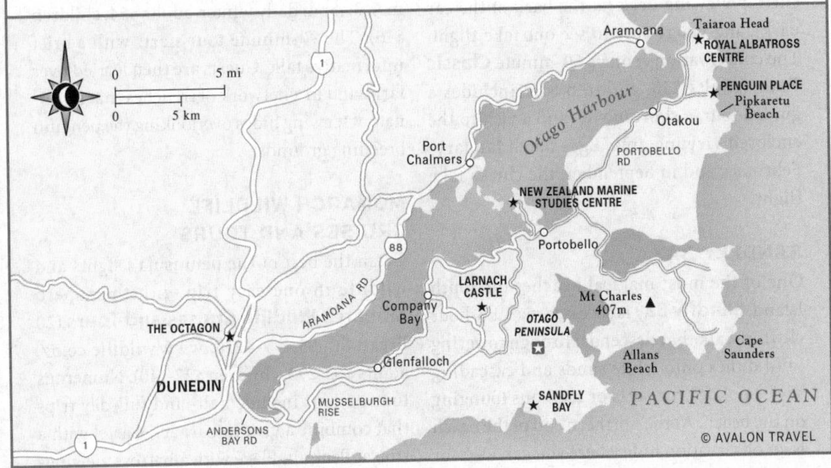

Services

The **Dunedin i-SITE Visitor Information Centre** shares space with the **DoC Dunedin Visitor Centre** (50 The Octagon, 03/474-3300, 8:30am-5:30pm Mon.-Fri., 8:45am-5:30pm Sat.-Sun.). Stop here for useful information especially about walks and wildlife on the Otago Peninsular. The **Dunedin City Library** (230 Moray Place, 03/474-3690, 9:30am-8pm Mon.-Fri., 11am-4pm Sat.-Sun.) offers free unlimited Wi-Fi, and there's a **post office** (310 Moray Place, 0800/081-190, 9am-5:30pm Mon.-Fri., 9am-1pm Sat.).

For emergencies, visit **Dunedin Public Hospital** (201 Great King St., 03/474-0999, 24 hours daily). For non-life-threatening health issues, visit **Dunedin Urgent Doctors** (95 Hanover St., 03/479-2900, 24 hours daily).

★ OTAGO PENINSULA

The Otago peninsula protrudes 20km northeast from Dunedin and possesses an astonishing concentration of wildlife, including the world's only mainland breeding colony of royal albatross and yellow-eyed penguins, a rare New Zealand native. Dolphins, whales, and orcas also visit its waters.

Sights

LARNACH CASTLE

Built in 1871 for banker and politician William Larnach, **Larnach Castle** (145 Camp Rd., 03/476-1616, www.larnachcastle.co.nz, 9am-7pm daily, adults $31, children $10, under age 5 free) is billed as New Zealand's only castle. It took three years to erect and another 12 years for master European artisans to perfect the interior.

After Larnach committed suicide in 1898, the 14ha estate was sold by his family. It later served as a lunatic asylum, a military barracks, and a nuns retreat. The castle was in a state of ruin when the Barker family bought it in 1967; the ballroom was being used to keep sheep. Now restored to its original glory, the historic building features stained-glass windows, unique marble and art, a dungeon, and a tower with coastal views. Top your visit off with high tea in the Ballroom Café.

ROYAL ALBATROSS CENTRE

Located at Taiaroa Head on the tip of the peninsula, the **Royal Albatross Centre** (1260 Harington Point Rd., 03/478-0499, www.albatross.org.nz, 10:15am-dusk daily) is the world's only mainland breeding colony of royal albatross, a majestic species whose wingspan stretches more than 3m. Head to the clifftop viewing deck (at the back of the car park), and you're sure to see one take flight. The conservation center's 60-minute **Classic Tour** (adults $50, children $15) includes a guided tour, a short movie, and a visit to the enclosed viewing area. Eggs hatch January-February, and in September, the chicks take flight.

SANDFLY BAY

One of the most magical beaches on South Island, **Sandfly Bay** is accessed via a 1.5-hour clifftop walk that descends through towering sand dunes onto white sands and cascading surf. Look for fur seals or sea lions lounging on the beach. At the northern end of the beach is an observation hide where you can look for yellow-eyed penguins coming to nest in the late afternoon.

Stay at least 10m from all wildlife, for their safety and yours. The track to the beach begins at the Sandfly Bay car park (end of Seal Point Rd.) off Highcliff Road.

PENGUIN PLACE

For a guaranteed sighting of the aloof yellow-eyed penguin, head to **Penguin Place** (45 Pakihau Rd., 03/478-0286, www.penguinplace.co.nz, tours 10:15am-6:15pm daily summer, 3:45pm daily winter, adults $54, children $16). The 90-minute tour starts with a brief informative talk. Guests are then ferried over farmland to a network of trenches that terminate at viewing hides overlooking the penguin breeding grounds.

MONARCH WILDLIFE CRUISES AND TOURS

Catch the best of the peninsula's sights and wildlife in one easy trip with the superb **Monarch Wildlife Cruises and Tours** (20 Fryatt St., 03/477-4276, www.wildlife.co.nz, adults $53-290, children $22-140). Numerous tour options include half- and full-day trips that combine a visit to Larnach Castel with a stop at Penguin Place with albatross viewings from a boat. You're likely to witness seals, sea lions, and other marine mammals such as dolphins—and occasionally whales.

Food and Accommodations

For a side-helping of information with a lashing of friendliness, stop at **Penguin Café** (1726 High Cliff Rd., 03/478-1055, www.penguincafe.net.nz, 8am-4pm daily, $9-15), where you can savor an array of homemade fare like

Sandfly Bay

toasted sandwiches, fish, and soup of the day, plus cake and ice cream. Outside are some lovely sea views.

Originally opened as a tea room in 1908, the historic **1908 Café** (7 Harrington Point Rd., www.1908cafe.co.nz, 5pm-8pm Mon.-Tues., noon-2pm and 5pm-8pm Wed.-Fri., 11:30am-8pm Sat.-Sun., $13-34) also offers wonderful harbor views from an elegant dining area with fireplaces and hardwood floors and furnishings. The extensive menu includes venison medallions, fresh local salmon, seafood chowder, and maple-syrup lamb shanks.

Family-run **McFarmers** (774 Portobello Rd., 03/478-0389) is a paradise with ocean views. Set on a small working sheep farm, the inn has two accommodations options. The Cottage ($120 s or d) comes with a queen bed and twin bedrooms, a fully loaded kitchen, a charming living area with timber beams, and a deck with panoramic views. The Backpacker Lodge ($33-55 pp) has a sunny deck overlooking the harbor, a log burner, a living area, and a well-stocked kitchen.

Local legend **Yellow House B&B** (822 Portobello Rd., 03/478-1001, www.yellowhouse.co.nz) is an eternal ray of sunshine thanks to its pastel shades and generously proportioned windows. A glass ceiling over the lounge area of the Starry Suite ($300) also doubles as a splendid stargazing spot. The suite is equipped with a two-person spa and sports splendid sea and garden views. The Bedroom ($250) has similar views from its private patio. High-end bedding in both rooms includes feather pillows and wool duvets. Breakfast is served with a view in the Tower, and a fairy tale-like garden is peppered with colorful flowers and reading nooks.

Transportation

To reach the Otago Peninsula from Dunedin, follow Wharf Street south until it becomes Portsmouth Drive. At Anderson Bay, turn north onto Portobello Road; the coastal route hugs the northern shoreline of Otago Peninsula. To return, take Highcliff Road to traverse the headland's spine. (Navigation can be confusing; pick up a map from the local i-SITE.)

Fiordland and Southland

Te Anau and Vicinity........... 465
Fiordland National Park........ 470
Southern Scenic Route......... 477
Invercargill 480
The Catlins Coast 486
Stewart Island 488

Nowhere better encapsulates New Zealand's isolation, mystery, and magnificence than the Southland's Fiordland National Park.

Slotted into the southwest corner of South Island, the vast Fiordland National Park is one of the wettest places on earth, famed for its jagged coastline punctuated by 14 fiords where rainforest-clad mile-high mountains burst straight from black seas. The centerpiece of the park is wondrous Milford Sound, which attracts half a million visitors per year.

Though the Southland area covers more than 3 million hectares, it is home to a mere 100,000 people. The South Island's southernmost reaches are stitched together by wondrous hiking trails, including four of New Zealand's nine Great Walks. Crystal rivers and bottomless glacial lakes set the scene for jet-boating, kayaking, and cruising. Marinelife and birdlife is abundant. The seas are patrolled by native dolphins, while the forests are graced by the flightless, prehistoric-looking takahe, thought to be extinct until 1948. Beneath rolling green farmland, a network of limestone caves begs exploration.

The Southern Scenic Route passes a 180-million-year-old petrified forest, where enormous trees bend in a perpetual lean thanks to relentless Southern Ocean blasts. Beaches sit beneath permanent mists of thick salty spray. Southland is one of the country's most peaceful regions. Driving its roads, you're more likely to get stuck behind a flock of sheep than in a traffic jam.

Invercargill is the region's largest city, home to 50,000 people, the World's Fastest Indian, and a breeding program of real-life dinosaurs. Across the Foveaux Strait, 30km south, rests sleepy Stewart Island, where 400 souls live alongside a giant open bird sanctuary—and one of your best chances of seeing a wild kiwi.

PLANNING YOUR TIME

Spend a night or two in the sleepy lakeside town of **Te Anau,** 2.5 hours south of Milford Sound, where hikers can explore local trails. Get to **Curio Bay** and explore the fossilized forest in the late afternoon as you wait for yellow-eyed penguins to waddle by. The next day,

Previous: Milford Sound; petrified forest at Curio Bay. **Above:** the Victorian Water Tower in Invercargill.

Fiordland and Southland

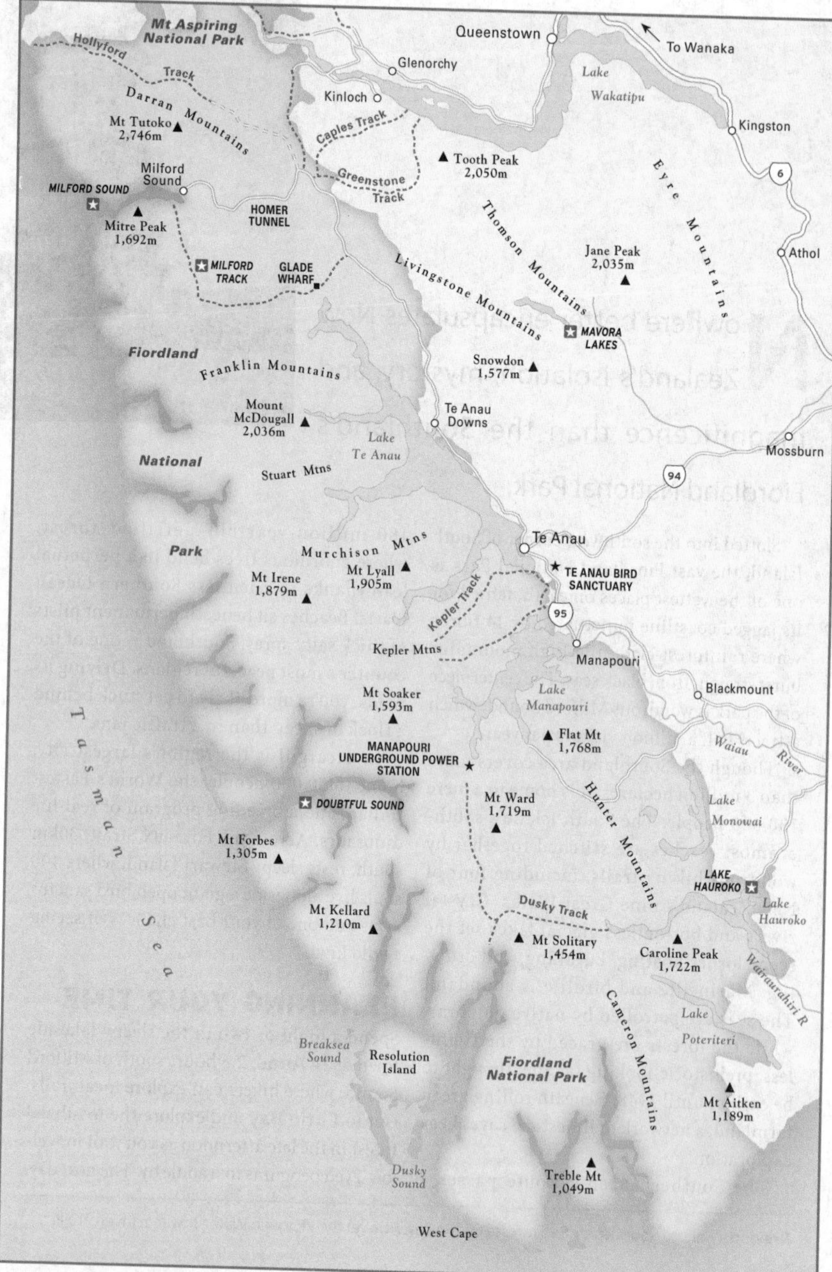
Mt Aspiring National Park
Hollyford Track
Darran Mountains
Mt Tutoko 2,746m
Milford Sound
MILFORD SOUND
Mitre Peak 1,692m
HOMER TUNNEL
MILFORD TRACK
GLADE WHARF
Queenstown
To Wanaka
Glenorchy
Kinloch
Lake Wakatipu
Caples Track
Greenstone Track
Tooth Peak 2,050m
Kingston
6
Eyre Mountains
Thomson Mountains
Athol
Jane Peak 2,035m
Livingstone Mountains
MAVORA LAKES
Snowdon 1,577m
Fiordland
Franklin Mountains
Mount McDougall 2,036m
Te Anau Downs
Lake Te Anau
Mossburn
94
National
Stuart Mtns
Park
Murchison Mtns
Te Anau
Mt Lyall 1,905m
TE ANAU BIRD SANCTUARY
Mt Irene 1,879m
Kepler Track
95
Manapouri
Kepler Mtns
Blackmount
Lake Manapouri
Mt Soaker 1,593m
Flat Mt 1,768m
Waiau River
MANAPOURI UNDERGROUND POWER STATION
Tasman Sea
Mt Ward 1,719m
Hunter Mountains
DOUBTFUL SOUND
Lake Monowai
Mt Forbes 1,305m
LAKE HAUROKO
Lake Hauroko
Dusky Track
Mt Kellard 1,210m
Mt Solitary 1,454m
Caroline Peak 1,722m
Wairaurahiri R
Cameron Mountains
Lake Poteriteri
Breaksea Sound
Resolution Island
Fiordland National Park
Mt Aitken 1,189m
Dusky Sound
Treble Mt 1,049m
West Cape

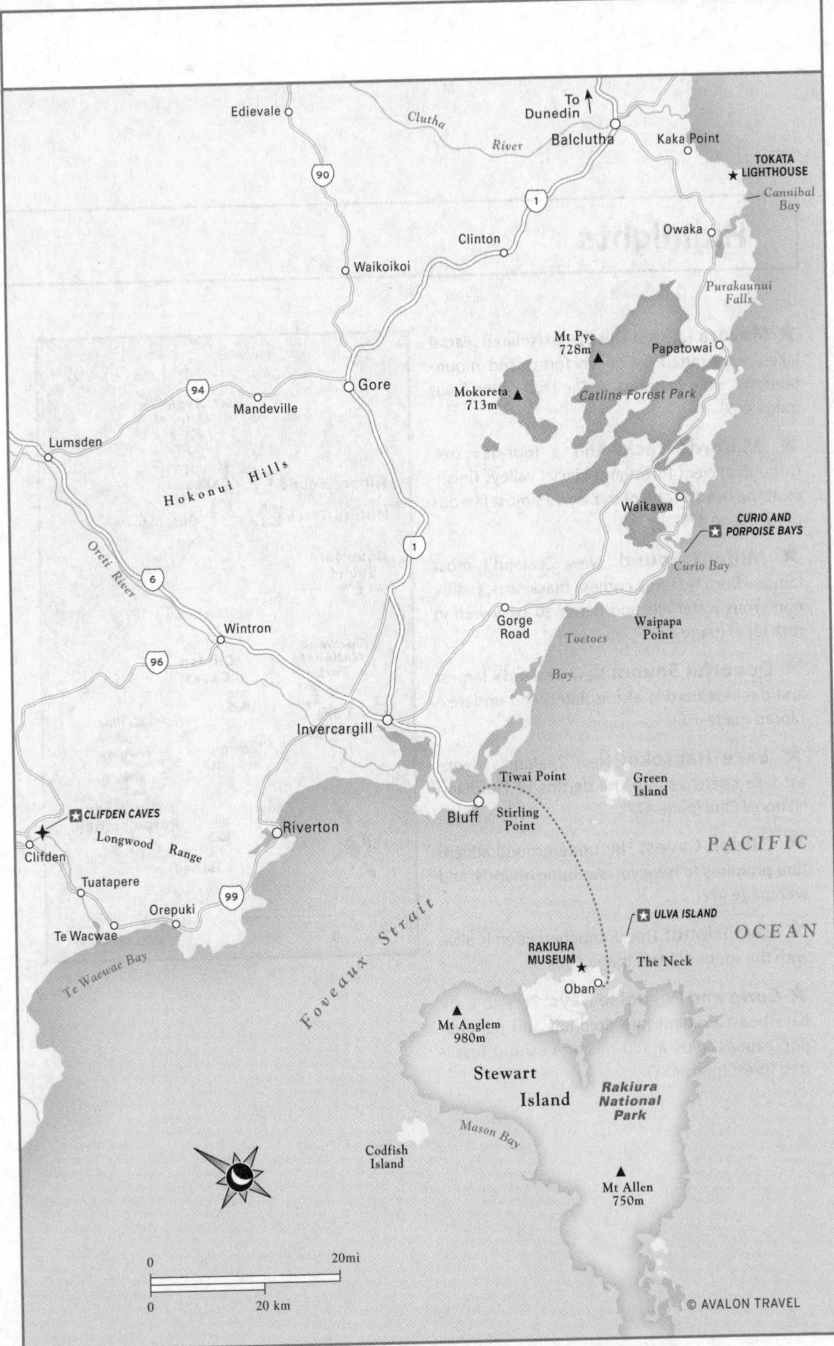
To Dunedin
Edievale
Clutha River
Balclutha
Kaka Point
TOKATA LIGHTHOUSE
Cannibal Bay
90
1
Owaka
Clinton
Waikoikoi
Purakaunui Falls
Mt Pye 728m
Papatowai
Gore
Mokoreta 713m
Catlins Forest Park
94
Mandeville
Lumsden
Hokonui Hills
Waikawa
CURIO AND PORPOISE BAYS
Curio Bay
Oreti River
6
Gorge Road
Waipapa Point
Toetoes Bay
Wintron
96
Invercargill
Tiwai Point
Green Island
Bluff
Stirling Point
CLIFDEN CAVES
Riverton
Longwood Range
Clifden
PACIFIC OCEAN
Tuatapere
99
Orepuki
ULVA ISLAND
Te Wacwae
Te Waewae Bay
Foveaux Strait
RAKIURA MUSEUM
The Neck
Oban
Mt Anglem 980m
Stewart Island
Rakiura National Park
Mason Bay
Codfish Island
Mt Allen 750m
0
20mi
20 km
© AVALON TRAVEL

Look for ★ to find recommended sights, activities, dining, and lodging.

Highlights

★ **Mavora Lakes:** This pair of isolated glacial lakes, surrounded by beech forest and mountaintops, were featured in *The Lord of the Rings* (page 469).

★ **Milford Track:** This a four-day trek through ancient forest and glacial valleys finishes at the head of one of the world's most famous fiords (page 470).

★ **Milford Sound:** New Zealand's most famous fiord features endless black seas, fed by numerous waterfalls and hemmed by towering rock faces (page 473).

★ **Doubtful Sound:** New Zealand's largest and deepest fiord is also isolated and underexplored (page 476).

★ **Lake Hauroko:** New Zealand's deepest lake stretches into the depths of Fiordland National Park (page 477).

★ **Clifden Caves:** This underground adventure promises to have you sweating, muddy, and wet (page 477).

★ **Ulva Island:** This untouched Eden is alive with the songs of birds (page 488).

★ **Curio and Porpoise Bays:** Back-to-back bays boast resident rare dolphins and penguin populations, plus a 180-million-year-old fossilized forest (page 487).

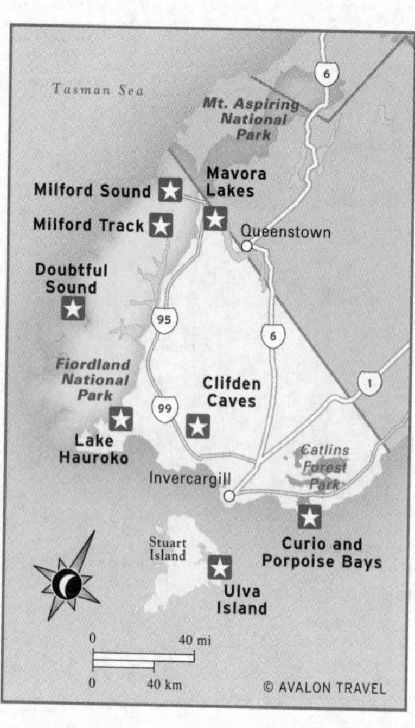

get up early to catch the resident Hector's dolphins frolicking and feeding in the surf just off shore of **Porpoise Bay**—or join them for a swim. Set aside at least two full days on sleepy **Stewart Island,** an untouched paradise. It will be time well spent.

Te Anau and Vicinity

One of New Zealand most far-flung towns, Te Anau is the gateway to Fiordland National Park and just a few hours' drive from Milford Sound. The town is set at the southern end of its eponymous lake, and the relaxed hub serves as a launchpad to a range of water activities and spectacular hikes, all under a watchful mountain backdrop.

SIGHTS

Te Anau Glowworm Caves

At 12,000 years old, the **Te Anau Glowworm Caves** (the Maori name Te Anau means "cave of rushing water") are mere geological infants. **Real Journeys** (Lakefront Dr., 03/249-6000, www.realjourneys.co.nz, tours daily, adults $88, children $22) operates guided two-hour tours into the caves—partly on foot, partly by boat. You'll travel through limestone tunnels and past underground waterfalls and whirlpools, finishing with the glowworms overhead. The tour is bookended by a scenic cruise on Lake Te Anau and an optional forest walk.

Te Anau Bird Sanctuary

See some of the region's elusive birdlife at the Department of Conservation (DoC)-run **Te Anau Bird Sanctuary** (181/209 Mapouri-Te Anau Hwy., 03/249-0200, www.doc.govt.nz, dusk-dawn daily, donation). The feathered residents are either recovering from injury or incapable of surviving in the wild. Celebrities include the kaka (a native parrot known to wolf-whistle at guests) and the prehistoric-looking takahe, a large flightless bird that was thought extinct until it was discovered in 1948 in the nearby mountains. The area is frequented by some of their free-flying friends like tui, fantails, and tomtits. Time your visit to coincide with regular feedings (9:30am daily Oct.-Mar., 10:30am daily Apr.-Sept.). The sanctuary is signposted from the Fiordland National Park Visitor Center on the shores of Lake Te Anau.

RECREATION

Boat Tours

Cruise Te Anau (Main Wharf, 03/249-8005, www.cruiseteanau.co.nz, 10am and 1pm daily Apr.-Nov., 10am, 1pm, and 5pm daily Dec.-Mar., adults $105, children $35, under age 5 free) is a terrific three-hour tour that includes a tranquil lake cruise in the shadow of Fiordland's peaks and a rainforest walk. Enjoy an onboard hot drink and homemade muffin on the journey back to base.

For something faster, **Luxmore Jet** (Lakefront Dr., 03/249-6951, www.luxmore-jet.com, 11am, 2pm, and 4pm daily Oct.-Apr., 11am and 2pm daily May-Sept., adults $120, children $60, under age 5 free) tours the Waiau River that links lakes Te Anau and Manapouri, taking in three *Lord of the Rings* locations. Look for rainbow and brown trout in the crystal waters during the hour-long trip.

Flightseeing

With **Wings & Water Te Anau** (Lakefront Dr., 03/249-7405, www.wingsandwater.co.nz, adults $225-605, children $130-360), passengers can choose from a variety of floatplane flights over fiords, glacial lakes, waterfalls, and historic sites such as Dusky Sound. Flight times range 20-75 minutes, and the floatplane lands at a variety of locations.

Southern Lakes Helicopters (Lakefront Dr., 03/249-7167, www.southernlakeshelicopters.co.nz, $240-1,995) offers a choice of routes, all with at least one landing. Take in

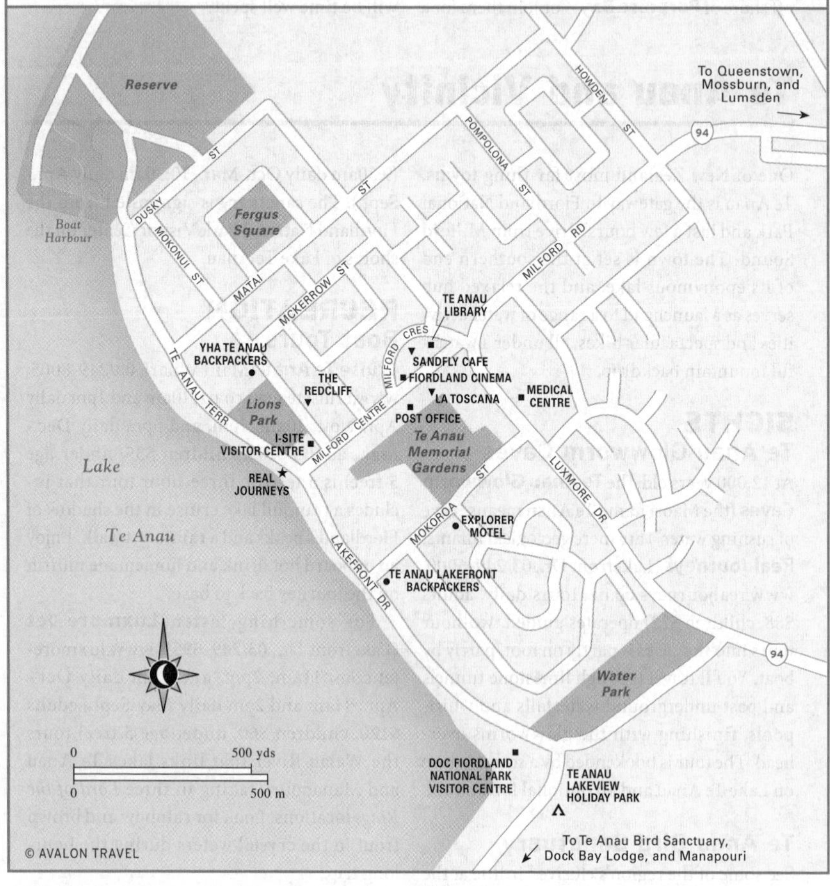

the region's alpine marvels and at *Lord of the Rings* locations. Flight times range from 30 minutes to three hours.

Kepler Track

On the eastern fringe of Fiordland National Park, the **Kepler Track** (45-70km, 4 days) sits sandwiched between Te Anau and Manapouri Lakes. The four-day trek crosses a swing bridge, small streams, beaches, and wetlands as it rises through beech and podocarp forest to ridgelines carpeted with alpine tussock. At the top, soak in the panoramic lake and mountain views. You'll encounter birdlife such as the kea, a cheeky alpine parrot.

Thanks to its loop design, the Kepler Track is one of the most accessible Great Walks. Enter or exit the track at three points: Kepler Track car park and control gates, Rainbow Reach swing bridge, or Lake Te Anau's Brod Bay. The car park is less than an hour's walk from the Fiordland National Park Visitor Centre (Lakefront Dr.).

Sections of the Kepler Track can also easily be tackled for those short on time. Follow the signposted **shoreline walk** (4km, 50 minutes one-way) from the visitor center in Te Anau to the Kepler Track car park and control gates for a relaxing stroll. From there, the rolling track heads north along the lake to **Brod Bay** (5km, 1.5 hours one-way), where you can cool off in the water.

Heading south from the car park, the track winds along the **Waiau River** (9.5km, 2.5 hours one-way), passing through red and mountain beech woodland before crossing the swing bridge to reach Rainbow Reach. Buses can also be booked to or from the swing bridge or car park.

CAMPING

DoC (www.doc.govt.nz) operates three **huts** ($54 pp, under age 17 free) and two **campsites** ($18 pp, under age 17 free) along the Kepler Track. Book in advance online or at the visitors centers.

GETTING THERE

Tracknet (03/249-7777, www.tracknet.net, $17) shuttle buses run between Te Anau accommodations and the car park or swing bridge. **Kepler Water Taxis** (03/249-8364, stevesaunders@xtra.co.nz, $25 one-way, $40 round-trip) covers Te Anau wharf to Brod Bay.

ENTERTAINMENT

The half-hour documentary *Ata Whenua—Shadowland* is an astonishing piece of cinema that will increase your anticipation for Fiordland National Park. Footage of snowy mountaintops, waterfalls, fiords, cliffs, and crashing waves are captured from the air and set to an evocative orchestral score. Watch it at the **Fiordland Cinema** (7 The Lane, 03/249-8844, www.fiordlandcinema.co.nz, 9am-7pm daily summer, 3pm-6pm daily winter, $10).

FOOD

Sandfly Café (9 The Lane, 03/249-9529, 7am-4:30pm daily) serves the town's best coffee (not that there's much competition) accompanied by comfort food and cool tunes. Choose from homemade muesli, bacon paninis, burgers, soups, and cakes, and head for a spot on the lawn out front.

Grab some hearty and warming fish-and-chips, onion rings, or homemade burgers from **Mainly Seafood** (106 Town Centre, 027/516-5555, 4pm-8:30pm Mon., 11:30am-8:30pm Tues.-Sat., 11:30am-9:30pm Sun., $8-18). Head down to the lake to enjoy the mountain views.

Discover down-to-earth Italian fare served in an unpretentious setting at **La Toscana** (108 Town Centre, 03/249-7756, www.

Kepler Track

Best Food

★ **The Redcliff:** Te Anau's most sophisticated eatery is one of Southland's best, serving local produce, homegrown vegetables, venison, and hare (page 468).

★ **Louie's Restaurant and Bar:** Enjoy European-inspired dishes and tempting sweets in a rustic setting in Invercargill (page 482).

★ **Thomas Green Public House and Dining Room:** This fashionable establishment in Gore puts a fine-dining twist on traditional fare (page 483).

★ **Kai Kart:** Stewart Island's iconic burger and seafood joint serves food with a seaside view (page 490).

latoscana.co.nz, 5:30pm-close daily, $14-30). Great value offerings take the form of classic pasta dishes alongside an extensive traditional pizza menu. Save space for one of the beautifully presented homemade desserts, such as tiramisu or dolce di vera.

One of Southland's finest restaurants, ★ **The Redcliff** (12 Mokonui St., 03/249-7431, www.theredcliff.co.nz, 5pm-9pm daily, $17-39) has a menu that mirrors its rustic environment. Local and seasonal products such as house-cured salmon, hare, or venison are paired with homegrown vegetables and local wines, and served in an old cottage, often to live acoustic music.

ACCOMMODATIONS

The town's only waterside hostel, **Te Anau Lakefront Backpackers** (48/50 Lakefront Dr., 03/249-7713, www.teanaubackpackers.co.nz, dorm $35, $88 s or d) is a well-appointed lodging in a former motel. Some dorms have private baths, but all rooms have lake or garden views. En suite doubles ($98) and camping ($20 pp) are available. Guests enjoy free unlimited Wi-Fi, a well-equipped kitchen, a barbecue area, and pristine grounds that attract birdlife.

Help yourself to free herbs and spices from the "edible garden" of **YHA Te Anau** (29 Mokonui St., 03/249-7847, www.yha.co.nz, dorm $37-43, $84 s, $100 d), an immaculate and efficient hostel whose angled roof, timber beams, and lounge create a chalet vibe. En suite private units and small dorms are available.

Sixteen bright modern en suite rooms comprise studio, one-bedroom, and two-bedroom apartments at the **Explorer Motel** (Mokoroa St. and Cleddau St., 03/249-7156, www.explorermotel.co.nz, $170-350 s or d). Each room comes equipped with a desk, a TV, a kitchenette, and electric blankets, and all have balconies or patios overlooking native gardens and the mountains beyond the lake. Guests make use of free Wi-Fi and a communal DVD library.

One of the region's finest lodgings, ★ **Dock Bay Lodge** (192 William Stephen Rd., 03/249-7709, www.dockbaylodge.co.nz, $650 s or d) overlooks Fiordland and Lake Te Anau. Luxury suites and spacious en suite rooms boast floor heating, bathrobes, TVs, and local toiletries. Communal areas feature antique furnishings, creaking leather couches, and log fires. Facilities include a gym, a spa and sauna, a barbecue area, and a library.

The **Te Anau Lakeview Holiday Park** (77 Manapouri-Te Anau Hwy., 03/249-7457, www.teanauholidaypark.co.nz) is well equipped with a professional tour-booking desk. The scenic 10ha expanse near the lakeshore houses campsites ($19-25 pp) and

Best Accommodations

★ **Dock Bay Lodge:** Relax in front of an open fire as you stare out over Fiordland National Park from this Te Anau lodge (page 468).

★ **Freestone Backpackers:** Get back to basics at this homebuilt hillside hostel in Manapouri with lake and mountain views (page 475).

★ **Beersheba Estate:** This boutique B&B near Invercargill boasts gardens, ponds, and woodlands filled with birds (page 482).

★ **Curio Bay Salthouse:** This modern motel with panoramic views of the Catlins Coast's Porpoise Bay is frequented by rare native dolphins (page 487).

★ **Stewart Island Lodge:** This hillside lodge with sea views is hemmed in by native bush home to curious kaka and parakeets (page 490).

backpacker rooms (dorm \$33-37, \$36-55 s, \$69-85 d) with shared facilities: barbecues, Sky TV, a sauna, and a hot tub. Also available are a range of cabins (\$85-135) and motel rooms (\$175-185); some have en suite baths and private kitchens. The deluxe motel offers self-contained studio (\$290) and family (\$396) rooms with lounge areas and TVs, plus private patios or balconies with jaw-dropping views of Fiordland National Park.

TRANSPORTATION AND SERVICES

Te Anau is 160km north of Invercargill via Highways 6, 96, and 94. It provides a decent base from which to explore Milford Sound, 120km north along Highway 94.

Te Anau's small airport is mainly for flightseeing operations. However, in summer **Air Milford** (03/442-2351, www.airmilford.co.nz) operates a weekly commercial flight between Queenstown and Te Anau.

Tracknet (03/249-7777, www.tracknet.net) and **Intercity** (09/583-5700, www.intercity.co.nz) run daily bus services to Te Anau from Queenstown and Invercargill; Intercity also offers service from Dunedin. Well-priced **Rent a Dent** (0800/736-823, www.rentadent.co.nz) is the town's only car rental. **Te Anau Transfers** (020/483-2628) offers a local taxi service.

If your hotel or hostel doesn't rent bikes, try **Wild Rides Fiordland** (03/280-0116), **Outside Sports** (03/441-0074, www.outsidesports.co.nz), or **Te Anau Bike Hire** (027/759-5985, www.teanaubikehire.nz).

The local **i-SITE** (19 Town Centre, 03/249-8900, www.fiordland.org.nz, 8:30pm-6pm daily) is best visited for local information. For updates on hikes, weather conditions, and to book huts for Great Walks, visit the **DoC Fiordland National Park Centre** (Lakefront Dr., 03/249-7924, www.doc.govt.nz, 8am-5pm daily Nov.-Apr., 8:30am-4:30pm daily May-Oct.).

In town, there's a **post office** (100 Town Centre, 03/249-7348, 8:30am-6pm Mon.-Fri., 9:30am-5pm Sat.), a **library** (24 Milford Crescent, 0800/732-732, 8:30am-5pm Mon.-Fri., 10am-3pm Sat.), and a **medical center** (25 Luxmore Dr., 03/249-7007, 8am-5:30pm Mon.-Fri., 9am-noon Sat.).

★ MAVORA LAKES

The 35,000ha **Mavora Lakes,** North Mavora and South Mavora, are surrounded by grasslands, forests, and mountains. The location is so spectacular that it was used in *The Lord of* *the Rings* films. The sprawling park is crisscrossed by hiking and biking trails as well as a 4WD track. The lakes teem with brown and rainbow trout, attracting anglers, while the surrounding forests are rich with deer, chamois, and wild pigs. A basic but beautiful lakeside **camping area** (adults $8, children $4) is maintained by DoC.

Mavora Lakes is 40km northeast of Te Anau. To get here, take Highway 94 east and turn left at either Centre Hill or Burwood Station. Follow the lake signs along 39km of unpaved roads. Allow 90 minutes for the drive from Te Anau. There is no public transport to the lakes.

Fiordland National Park

Fiordland National Park is one of four national parks (including Aoraki/Mount Cook, Mount Aspiring, and Westland) that make up Te Wahipounamu (Maori for "place of greenstone"), a UNESCO World Heritage Site. Spanning the southwest corner of South Island, Fiordland National Park's sheer-faced mountains rise straight from inky seas—a visage so dramatic that it should come with its own film score.

Fiordland's mountain ranges are tight, compact, and sheer-faced; they owe their devastatingly dramatic appearance to a composition of crystalline rocks (granite, gneiss, and diorite) that are more resistant to erosion—even when battered by up to 7m of relentless rainfall annually. It is after a downpour that Fiordland is at its most spectacular, when waterfalls gush from every nook, plunging straight into the sea.

Trees cling miraculously to steep cliffs, their roots stubbornly knotting to thin carpets of moss, lichen, and peaty humus. Throughout the park, dense and rolling rainforests are home to red and silver beech along with ferns and podocarps such as rimu and totara. At high altitude, the woodlands fade to alpine grass, herbs, and buttercups.

Fiordland is home to Milford, Doubtful, and Dusky Sounds; these coast-kissing valleys are actually fiords, carved by glaciers and flooded by the sea. Formed 20,000 years ago, the 14 fiords splinter the 215km of coastline that hems the 1.25-million-hectare national park.

TE ANAU TO MILFORD SOUND

Milford Road (Hwy. 94) weaves north from Te Anau for 120km, ending at Milford Sound—the only fiord accessible by road. Milford Sound is Fiordland National Park's most popular destination. The winding route to reach it is stupendously scenic; allow at least 2.5 hours for the journey. You may get stuck behind slow traffic (there are limited passing lanes) and there can be a 20-minute wait at Homer Tunnel. Fill up with gas before you leave—there are no gas stations north of Te Anau.

★ Milford Track

Te Anau Downs is where hikers must take a boat to Glade Wharf for the beginning of the famous Great Walk, the **Milford Track** (53.5km one-way, 4 days). From Lake Te Anau, follow the trail north through beech forest and an imposing valley, along the Clinton River to Lake Mintaro at the foot of Mackinnon Pass. The climb to the top of the 1,154m Mackinnon Pass is relatively arduous but is rewarded by spectacular views down sheer glacier-carved Clinton Canyon. In summer, look for flowering alpine plants such as the Mount Cook buttercup.

Descending the pass, take a side-trip to **Sutherland Falls** (1.5 hours round-trip), a 580m waterfall once thought to be the world's highest. (It can also be viewed between Quentin Shelter and Dumpling Hut.) The last section of the hike passes more waterways, finishing at Sandfly Point overlooking

Milford Sound. From here, it's a 15-minute boat trip to Milford Village.

ACCOMMODATIONS

Set on the lakeshore, **Fiordland National Park Lodge** (2681 Hwy. 94, Te Anau Downs, 03/249-7811, www.fiordlandnatparklodge.co.nz) offers backpacker accommodations with shared dorms ($28) and en suite doubles ($65-75) with heaters, fridges, and a communal kitchen and lounge area with a log fire. There are 20 motel rooms ($110-130) with electric blankets, private kitchens, and en suite baths. The lodge is 600m from the departure point to the Milford Track.

Camping is forbidden along the Milford Track, so the three overnight **huts** book fast. Make reservations months in advance through **DoC** (www.doc.govt.nz). During the Great Walk season (Oct. 24-Apr. 30), huts are $70 pp, free under age 17, and you must spend one night in each hut. Outside the Great Walk season, the price drops to $15 and bookings are not required (but tickets must still be purchased in advance). Transportation is limited, the huts are not heated, and track and weather conditions are often averse.

Ultimate Hikes (Station Bldg., Queenstown, 03/450-1940, www.ultimatehikes.co.nz, adults $2,295-3,300, children $1,720) operates a four-night guided walk along the Milford Track with transportation to and from your accommodations. Hikers are hosted in high-end cabins that come with drying rooms, private baths, hot showers, and a fully staffed kitchen. Daily meals (including a three-course dinner) are included. Local wines and beers are also available.

GETTING THERE

Te Anau Downs is 30km north of Te Anau along Highway 94.

Boats must be booked at the start and end of the Milford Track and should be reserved when booking hut passes. **Fiordland Water Taxi** (0800/347-4538, www.fiorldlandwatertaxi.co.nz) offers service from Te Anau Downs to Glade Wharf ($85 pp) and bus and boat service ($110) from Te Anau town, as does **Real Journeys** (0800/656-501, www.realjourneys.co.nz, $85 to Glade Wharf, $130 from Te Anau town). The boat from Sandfly Point to Milford Sound should be booked through **DoC** (www.doc.govt.nz).

Lower Hollyford Road

North of Te Anau Downs, Highway 94 makes its way into some of the widest parts of

Mackinnon Pass along the Milford Track

Davey Gunn

The region's rugged remoteness and heavy rain (and sandflies) mean that those who settle here must exude toughness and resourcefulness in equal measure. Local legend Davey Gunn epitomizes such hardiness. During the 1930s, the European pioneer was the first to bring tourists to Fiordland, notably the Hollyford Valley to the park's north. When visiting hikers complain of blisters or aching limbs, guides will regale them with the tale of Gunn tearing open his thigh on a branch while herding cattle. Gunn simply stitched himself up with a darning needle and continued on his way with his herd.

On Christmas Day, 1955, the bushman was crossing the Hollyford River on horseback when he fell into the ferocious current, to be swallowed into the valley he so adored. Gunn was never seen again.

Eglington Valley, a gaping glacial canyon with towering faces up to 2km apart. A few kilometers north are the **Mirror Lakes,** a collection of small tarns surrounded by wetland plants that perfectly reflect the looming Earl Mountains behind. The lakes are reached via an easy boardwalk stroll from a well-signed roadside car park.

Toward the head of the Eglington Valley, the road edges over **The Divide,** the lowest east-west crossing of the Southern Alps at 531m, and the start and endpoint of a handful of short and multiday hikes, including a Great Walk, the Routeburn Track. It's worth setting aside time for the **Key Summit Track** (3km) as it climbs through forest and past alpine lakes for wonderful views of the Eglington and Hollyford Valleys. The walks are accessed via a car park.

The Eglington Valley is 25km north of Te Anau Downs along Highway 94. The Divide is 85km north of Te Anau along the same road.

HOLLYFORD TRACK

Highway 94 splits past The Divide. The main route continues west to Milford Sound, while an offshoot heads north to the unpaved Lower Hollyford Road. The road leads into Hollyford Valley, an 80km canyon that stretches to the Tasman Sea. The well-regarded **Hollyford Track** (56km, 4-5 days) begins at the road's end.

The track follows the Hollyford River as it meanders north from the Darren Mountains to Martin's Bay. The trail exposes fine Fiordland features such as glacial formations, waterways, rainforests, and a rugged coast. Near the shoreline, it's not uncommon to encounter seals or penguins. The low-altitude route can be walked year-round with shelter in DoC **huts** (www.doc.govt.nz); buy tickets in advance.

Trips and Tramps (03/249-7081, www.tripsandtramps.com, $235-290) offers flights in a small fixed-wing aircraft from Martins Bay to Milford Sound. Visitors are then bused back to the car park at the end of the Hollyford Track. Those without transport can be picked up from Te Anau, bused to Milford Sound, and then flown to Martins Bay to hike the trail in the opposite direction. A bus picks up from the car park to head back to Te Anau. **Tracknet** (03/249-7777, www.tracknet.net) runs buses from the car park to Te Anau, Milford Sound, and Queenstown.

Guided Walks NZ (03/442-3000, www.hollyfordtrack.com) operate a two-night, three-day package that includes a 15km jetboat trip along the Hollyford River and Lake McKerrow, followed by a helicopter flight into Milford Sound. Guests stay in lodges complete with dining and lounge areas with log fires and hot water. All meals are included.

Lower Hollyford Road to Milford Sound

The final stretch of Highway 94 to Milford Sound threads between sheer-faced granite monoliths cloaked in beech forest and weeping waterfalls. The **Homer Tunnel** is a rudimentary passageway chiseled 1.2km through some serious rock at an altitude of nearly 1km. Prepare to wait at the traffic light for up to 20 minutes. Stop by the **Chasm,** 10km from the tunnel—you won't miss the tour-bus-bulging car park. Footbridges cross over the torrential Cleddau River that has eroded fascinating voids and sculptures into its rocky banks and base. Milford Sound is 10km farther north along Highway 94.

TOP EXPERIENCE

★ MILFORD SOUND

New Zealand's magnificent **Milford Sound** is the nation's famous and most accessible fiord. Located at the end of one of the world's southernmost highways, its hypnotic black waters are something of an abyss. The Milford Sound Marine Reserve stretches for 16km. Its 690ha cloak submerged mountain bases with unique coral, sponges, reef fish, rays, octopuses, eels, rock lobsters, starfish, sharks, and sometimes dolphins. The fiord's most famous feature is **Mitre Peak,** a pyramidal monolith that protrudes more than a mile into the sky. The saltwater is fed by a constant supply of fresh water from numerous waterfalls that tumble from its cliffs. This disorienting land of endlessly flat black seas is hemmed by towering rock faces where all sense of scale is lost.

View the marine reserve by way of the **Milford Sound Underwater Observatory** (Harrisons Cove, 03/441-1137, www.discoverycentre.co.nz, adults $36, children $18), whose viewing areas are accompanied by a wealth of informative displays.

Cruises and Tours

Cruises are the most popular and efficient way to appreciate the majesty of Milford Sound, but slicing across these ancient black waters by kayak is hard to beat—especially if it leads to a close-up encounter with curious seals, dolphins, or a Fiordland crested penguin.

The country's oldest kayak operator is the region's best. **Rosco's** (72 Town Centre, Te Anau, 03/249-8500, www.roscomilfordkayaks.com, $155-209) operates a range of half-day adventures around Milford Sound that are suitable for all skills. Small groups are led by expert (and humorous) guides. Some packages combine kayaking with short hikes through the rainforest and water taxis that take your kayak deeper along the fiord.

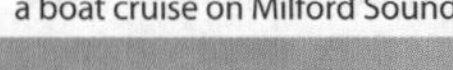

a boat cruise on Milford Sound

Go Orange (21 Town Centre, Te Anau, 03/249-8585, www.goorangecruise.co.nz) offers well-priced trek and kayak combos (4-5 hours, $118-180) and a kayak and cruise package (6 hours, $205) that sails guests out to the Tasman Sea. Two-hour cruises (adults $45-80, children $15) include commentary from the captain and head toward the open ocean; a hot snack-size meal is included. Pickups from Te Anau and Queenstown are available.

Family-run **Cruise Milford** (1 Milford Sound, Milford Sound Hwy., 0800/645-367, www.cruisemilfordnz.com, adults $90, children $18) is a boutique boat operator. Their vessels are among the smallest and least crowded on the fiord, making for a more comfortable sailing experience that is less invasive to the wildlife. Pickup from Te Anau (adults $169, children $80) and Queenstown (adults $175, children $120) are available.

Real Journeys (03/249-6000, www.realjourneys.co.nz, mid-Sept.-mid-May) operates an Overnight Cruise ($308) aboard a spacious replica scow with viewing decks, private en suite cabins, a lounge, and a bar. Kayaks are available for guest use, and meals are prepared by an on-board chef. The Wanderer Overnight Cruise ($385) includes a full-length fiord tour as well as a guided walk along part of the Milford Track. Two-hour scenic and nature cruises ($74-88) operate year-round. Coach transport to and from Te Anau or Queenstown is available.

Experience the underwater world with **Descend Suba Diving** (027/337-2363, www.descend.co.nz, $345), whose six-hour scenic cruise and diving tours include equipment, snacks, and refreshments.

The Tu-Te-Raki-Whanoa Legend

According to Maori mythology, while the demi-god Tu-te-raki-Whanoa was working his way from the bottom of Aotearoa, he carved Fiordland's deep wells and towering cliff faces from rock. By the time he reached the northern end, he had so perfected his craft that he created his masterpiece, Piopiotahi (Milford Sound). The goddess of the underworld, Hine-nui-te-po, was so overwhelmed by its beauty that she feared all who visited would never want to leave and so released swarms of *namu* (sandflies) to keep visitors at bay.

Getting There

Several bus companies serve Milford Sound from Queenstown and Te Anau daily, including **Tracknet** (03/249-7777, www.tracknet.net) and **Intercity** (09/583-5700, www.intercity.co.nz). Bear in mind it's a five-hour trip from Queenstown one-way.

Kiwi Discovery (03/442-7340, www.kiwidiscovery.com, adults $555, children $340) offers a coach, cruise, and flight package that includes a luxurious bus journey to, then boat ride on, Milford Sound, followed by a 40-minute scenic flight over Fiordland back to Queenstown. Flights are at the mercy of temperamental weather conditions.

MANAPOURI

The tiny settlement of Manapouri sits on the shores of its eponymous lake and the River Waiau. Even amid the region's breathtaking bodies of water, the splendor of **Lake Manapouri** stands out. Peppered with more than 30 islands, the lake is bordered by native bush and guarded by the magnificent Cathedral Mountains. Known as Roto-au (Rainy Lake) and Moturau (Lake of Many Islands) to early Maori, it is the gateway to wondrous Doubtful Sound.

Walks

A Great Walk, the Kepler Track, passes Lake Manapouri, but there are several gorgeous short strolls nearby. Most walks require water transport to reach the entry point, either across the river or farther down the lake. Download the DoC *Fiordland Day Walks* booklet online (www.doc.govt.nz) for comprehensive listings.

Flightseeing in Fiordland

Fly Fiordland (52 Town Centre, Te Anau, 03/249-4352, www.flyfiordland.com) operates flights from Te Anau and Milford Sound airstrips over some of the most inaccessible and untouched wilderness of New Zealand's most fabled national park. The Milford Sound overfly ($295) covers a 280km, 1-hour loop from Te Anau to Milford Sound, returning over several western fiords. Three Doubtful Sound flights ($195-345) last 25-75 minutes and may include Doubtful Sound, Lake Manapouri, and the Kepler Mountains, as well as the remote Dusky Sound, weather permitting. The 25-minute flight to Mount Tutoko from Milford Sound ($195) takes in the mile-high Kaipo rock wall and the huge glacial ice field of the Tutoko Plateau. The 25-minute valley flight to Lake Quill ($195) sees the 580m Sutherland Falls. A 35-minute flight combines the best trips for $245.

Frasers Beach Track is a short lakeside stroll best enjoyed as the sun sets behind Fiordland. It begins and ends at either Pearl Harbour, Manapouri, or at the Frasers Beach road entrance north of Manapouri township. You'll work up a sweat on the superb **Monument Track** (1km, 2 hours round-trip) thanks to a 290m climb through the forest to the summit of The Monument. The view of the lake and Kepler peaks is worth it. This track starts and ends at the lake's Hope Arm.

The **Pearl Harbour-Circle Track** (6.9km, half-day round-trip) begins from the jetty across the river and follows the waterside before heading through beech forest humming with birdlife to a viewpoint over the lake.

To hike the **Pearl Harbour to Hope Arm Track** (7.8km, 4-6 hours), follow the track along the lake edge for 15 minutes, ignoring the Circle Track. Instead, you'll head through the forest to the Hope Arm Hut, where a secluded bay awaits.

Food and Accommodations

Expect sizable servings of typical Kiwi fare at **Lakeview Café & Bar** (68 Cathedral Dr., 03/249-6652, www.manapouri.com, 11am-9:30pm daily, $20-34), including pancakes, chicken wings, and beer-battered blue cod with fries. The pub boasts stunning lake views, especially from its outdoor seating on the lawn.

The adjoining **Lakeview Motor Inn** (68 Cathedral Dr., 03/249-6652, www.manapouri.com) caters to all budgets with all rooms overlooking the lake. The en suite studios ($98) sleep up to three and come with a small fridge, TV, and tea- and coffee-making facilities. Hotel-standard queen and king rooms ($140-150) share the same amenities along with patio seating. The second-floor deluxe rooms ($150) sport comfortable armchairs and private balconies.

★ **Freestone Backpackers** (270 Hillside Rd., 03/249-6893, www.freestone.co.nz) offers a collection of well-priced cozy timber lodges (dorm $20, $60 s or d) overlooking the lake and mountains. Shared facilities include baths with hot showers, laundry, and a barbecue area. There's no TV room; instead, socialize on the veranda or explore the bird-filled 4ha hillside plot. The self-contained en suite lodge ($86) has a queen and bunk beds and a lounge with power outlets. The modern holiday house ($30 pp) serves as a more traditional hostel, with airy rooms (single to 3 beds), a well-stocked kitchen, a TV room with a woodburner, and a book exchange.

Getting There

Manapouri is 20 minutes south of Te Anau via Highway 95. **Tracknet** (03/249-7777, www.tracknet.net) and **Intercity** (09/583-5700, www.intercity.co.nz) buses stop in Manapouri on their way to and from Te Anau and Queenstown.

Adventure Manapouri (03/249-8070, www.adventuremanapouri.co.nz, 11am,

3pm, 6:30pm daily summer, $20 pp) runs a water taxi service from Pearl Harbour near the river mouth. Outside summer, call 022/192-5577 to book. They also rent rowboats ($40 for 1-2 people for 1 day, $60 overnight).

★ DOUBTFUL SOUND

At 421m, **Doubtful Sound** is New Zealand's deepest fiord, covering the greatest surface area across its three tentacles—First Arm, Crooked Arm, and Hall Arm—to Deep Cove, the fiord's terminus. Only slightly less striking than Milford Sound, but substantially less visited, Doubtful Sound must be accessed via a cruise along Lake Manapouri and then a bus across the Wilmot Pass via a spectacular alpine drive. The fiord is fed by numerous gigantic waterfalls and is frequented by seals and bottlenose dolphins, with Fiordland crested penguins known to visit.

Cruises

For those on a budget, **Go Orange** (03/249-8585, www.goorangecruise.co.nz) offers a great value. Guided day-long and five-day kayaking ($255-780) tours include camping overnight in the lakeside bush; all equipment is provided. Cruises (adults $230, children $115) across the fiord include free transfers from Te Anau and Manapouri (extra charge for Queenstown).

You're in for a personal experience with the local crew at **Deep Cove Charters** (03/249-6828, www.doubtfulsoundcruise.nz, Nov.-Mar., $550 s, $1,300-1,400 d, ages 10-14 $350), whose six private cabins accommodate a maximum of 12 guests. Their overnight cruise allows guests to relax, fish, and kayak the fiord, with a crayfish lunch, evening meal of local venison and vegetables, and a continental breakfast. Some nonalcoholic drinks are supplied; BYO is welcome.

The region's largest tour group, **Real Journeys** (03/249-6000, www.realjourneys.co.nz, Sept.-May, $445) operates an overnight cruise aboard a replica traditional scow. The old-school design is complete with dining room and a bar; a three-course buffet dinner and breakfast are included. Guests sleep in en suite cabins or quad bunks and have use of kayaks, or can explore the fiord in a boat with a guide. The all-day catamaran cruise ($260) begins at Lake Manapouri. Pickups from Te Anau and Queenstown are available.

Doubtful Sound

Southern Scenic Route

The fastest route from Te Anau to Invercargill is via Highway 94 and Wreys Bush-Mossburn Road. The 160km journey takes two hours. Jump instead onto the glorious **Southern Scenic Route** (www.southernscenicroute.co.nz) that skirts the eastern boundary of Fiordland to follow New Zealand's southernmost shoreline—it's twice the distance and immeasurably more spectacular.

The well-signed Southern Scenic Route stretches 610km, linking Queenstown and Dunedin by way of some of New Zealand's most underexplored and underpopulated country.

CLIFDEN

The **Clifden Suspension Bridge** is one of the nation's longest. An engineering marvel spanning the Waiau River, it was completed at the turn of the 20th century, and its 112m can be crossed by foot. The bridge is 90km south of Te Anau. Take Highway 94 south for 15km, then turn right onto Hillside-Manapouri Road. In 1km, turn left on Weir Road, continuing south on Blackmount-Redcliff Road for about 30km to Clifden.

★ Clifden Caves

Beneath lush pastures are the unlikely **Clifden Caves** (free). An impressive network of stalactites, stalagmites, and glowworms adorn these 20-million-year-old limestone caverns. Allow up to two hours to explore the caves and crawl through narrow spaces, getting muddy, cold, and wet. Bring flashlights (one handheld, one head), spare batteries, and a companion; there are no guides. The route is marked with orange arrows. Wear sturdy footwear and warm layers, and check the weather conditions—the caves can flash-flood during or following heavy rainfall.

The caves are 1km northeast of the tiny township of Clifden. Take State Highway 99, then State Highway 96. Look for the northern turnoff along Clifden-Gorge Road.

★ LAKE HAUROKO

South of Clifden, Lillburn Valley Road leaves Highway 99 and runs 35km (20km

Clifden Suspension Bridge

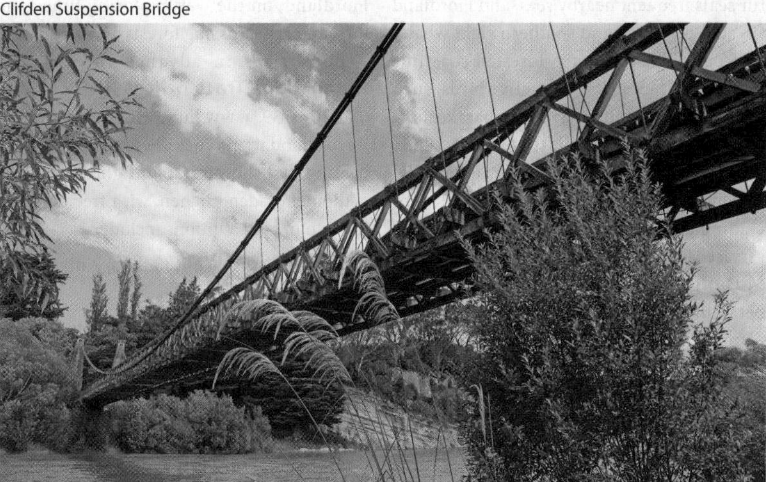

of it is unpaved) west to the hypnotic **Lake Hauroko,** an isolated, glacial body of water. New Zealand's deepest lake at 462m, Lake Hauroko is surrounded by unspoiled bush and mountains. Look for signs to the **Big Totara Walk,** a 600m trail among South Island's greatest totara trees, some of which are more than 1,000 years old. The **Lake Hauroko Track** (1.1km) is an easy loop from the car park. The trail follows the shoreline through forests of matai, rimu, and beech trees.

The six-hour **Wairaurahiri Jet Tour** (1260 Clifden-Orawia Rd., 03/225-5677, www.wjet.co.nz, adults $249, children $149) is a terrific 92km journey that delves deep into Fiordland. The jet-boat crosses the lake and is then followed by a 180m drop in elevation through 27km of the Wairaurahiri River, navigating Class III rapids. The trip includes a forest walk and barbecue lunch.

TUATAPERE AND VICINITY

The farming township of **Tuatapere,** 14km south of Clifden along Highway 99, sits wedged against the southwestern border of Fiordland and is the midway point of the scenic route. It serves as an idyllic base for trails and jet-boat tours as well as wildlife: The rare Hector's dolphins, blue penguins, and fur seals frequent nearby seas, and Fiordland Crested penguins and southern right whales also pass. The podocarp-forested coastline thrives with 25 species of native birds, such as tuis, fantails, moreporks, and parakeets.

The **Tuatapere Visitor Centre** (31 Orawia Rd., 03/226-6739, 7:30am-6pm daily) provides regional information about hikes, including transport advice and a hut-booking service. The on-site **Tuatapere Bushman's Museum** (donation) recounts the town's timber milling history by way of photographs and equipment displays.

Walks

Two walks depart from the Rarakau car park (1304B Papatotara Coast Rd.). A **bus** (03/226-6739, wwwhumpridgetrack.co.nz, $45 round-trip) transports hikers between Tuatapere and the Rarakau car park. The car park is on private land, and a $5 donation is appreciated.

SOUTH COAST TRACK

Carving along Aotearoa's southernmost shoreline, the **South Coast Track** (4 days) is a somewhat advanced tramp. Hikers begin from Rarakau car park and continue to Big River, staying in DoC-maintained huts along the way. At the end, hikers return the same way.

A popular option is to hike two days to the Wairaurahiri River and stay overnight at **Port Craig School Hut** (adults $15, children $7.50, under age 10 free) before hitching a boat ride and then a bus from Lake Hauroko. It's an easy walk that follows an old logging tramline and crosses a handful of rickety viaducts.

Wairaurahiri Wilderness Jet (0800/270-556, www.river-jet.co.nz, $180-230) operate half- and full-day jet-boat trips across Lake Hauroko and a selection of river rapids. A short forest walk is included in the full-day option. Departures are from the Rarakau car park.

HUMP RIDGE TRACK

The **Hump Ridge Track** (62km, 3 days) is a dramatic loop past wonderful vistas of the Southern Ocean, Stewart Island, and Fiordland, on the way exploring limestone tors, and crisscrossing forests and viaducts.

Book trips in advance through the **Hump Ridge Track office** (31 Orawia Rd., 03/226-6739, www.humpridgetrack.co.nz). Accommodations include plush bunks, gas heating, hot showers, solar lighting, and an equipment-laden kitchen, with free porridge in the morning. Options include:

- The **Freedom Walk** (3 days, 2 nights, departs Sat.-Thurs., $175).
- The **Prime Walk** (3 days, 3 nights, departs Thurs., $450), which includes pre-walk accommodations for one night in Tuatapere, dehydrated meals, and helicoptering your backpack to the first lodge.
- The **Guided Walk** (3 days, 3 nights,

Aurora Australis

While most are familiar with the northern lights or aurora borealis, you may be surprised to hear there's an identical phenomenon in the southern hemisphere known as aurora australis, the southern lights. The stunning spectacle is the result of high-energy solar particles colliding with the gases of earth's atmosphere, forcing atoms to emit vibrant multihued polar lighting displays. The south coast of New Zealand is one of the best places to witness the event, best viewed around midnight during moonless nights of the winter months—though they can occur any time of year.

departs Fri., bunk $1,645, $1,845 pp s or d) includes accommodations for one night in Tuatapere, a helicopter flightseeing trip over the bay, and cooked meals, breakfasts, packed lunches, and three-course dinners. Your backpack is helicoptered to the first lodge.

- The **Walk-Jet-Boat Combo** (from $189) links you with the Wairaurahiri River for a jet-boat ride to Lake Hauroko, followed by a bus back to Tuatapere.

Helicopters ($100-750) can be booked separately to transport either you or your bag to the huts.

Food and Accommodations

A big warm welcome awaits at **Yesteryears Café** (3A Orawia Rd., 03/226-6681, 8am-5pm daily). Masses of old china high-tea sets from generations of local families line the walls, and there's a coal range tucked in the corner. Homemade treats vary but include meat pies, pikelets, milk shakes, strudels, and scones.

Grab some fish-and-chips from **Hungry Hippo** (59 Main Rd., 03/226-6417, 10am-7:30pm Wed.-Thurs., 10am-8pm Fri.-Sat., $14-36) and then drive 10 minutes south to enjoy them with a sea breeze, salt air, and a sunset.

Shooters Backpackers and Holiday Park (4 Mcfeely St., 03/226-6250, www.tuatapereaccommodation.co.nz) sleeps up to 60 people in dorm ($30), single ($40), and twin and double ($65) rooms. Family rooms ($115-130) are also available. The homey timber-framed rooms are basic but immaculate, backed by a comfortable communal area with games, TV, DVDs, and a sunny deck. A spa and sauna ($25 per hour) are also available.

Private rooms at **Last Light Lodge** (2 Clifden Hwy., 03/226-6667, www.lastlightlodge.com) include cozy single ($55) and twin or double ($70) rooms with kitchenettes, heaters, and shared baths. Tent and RV sites ($14-16 pp) are spread across the 1.8ha grounds, with communal facilities: a fully equipped kitchen, a barbecue area, laundry, and a TV lounge. Free Wi-Fi is available in the on-site café, bar, and **restaurant** (8am-9pm daily, $10-25). The varied menu offers classic Kiwi fare such as seafood chowder along with breakfast, pasta dishes, and carrot cake.

RIVERTON

It's 50km of mainly coastal driving from Tuatapere to Riverton. Be sure to pull over at **Gemstone Beach**, an ever-changing wind- and wave-beaten stretch of sand that offers plenty of fascinating rocks and the occasional semiprecious stone such as jasper or quartz. The surf here is ferocious, and the sight of the Fiordland mountains through the salty mist kicked up by the swirling seas is breathtaking.

The sleepy seaside town of Riverton is one of New Zealand's oldest settlements. The former whaling and sealing base is now mainly inhabited by anglers and creatives.

The **Te Hikoi: Southern Journey** (172 Palmerston St., 03/234-8260, www.tehikoi.co.nz, 10am-5pm daily summer, 10am-4pm daily winter, adults $6, children free) museum is a wonderful surprise. Following a short documentary film, this modern exhibit recounts the region's heritage by way of art and photography galleries, plus a collection of imaginative dioramas showing hunters and whalers at work.

From Riverton, it's 40km along Highway 99 to Invercargill.

Invercargill

Southland's largest settlement is Invercargill. The town is perversely flat for a nation proud of its curves, and the unimaginative grid design is somewhat uninspiring. But the town hosts several worthwhile attractions—a drivable beach, one of the country's best city parks, a collection of classic vehicles, and a museum home to living dinosaurs.

SIGHTS

Queens Park

The 81ha **Queens Park** (between Queens Dr. and Kelvin St.) is one of New Zealand's finest city green spaces. Among its many treasures are a collection of animal enclosures home to rabbits, guinea pigs, ostriches, and alpacas. Discover unique New Zealand birds in the aviary, and marvel at pristine grounds fringed by tropical and native trees, vibrant rose and azalea gardens, and a botanical house and fountains.

Bill Richardson Transport World

The enormous **Bill Richardson Transport World** (491 Tay St., 03/217-0199, www.transportworld.co.nz, 10am-5pm daily, adults $25, children $15) carpets an entire city block. Its hangars hold more than 250 classic vehicles, amounting to the largest museum collection of its kind. It bulges with Kombis and Ford Model T's hemmed in by automotive paraphernalia such as vintage gas pumps. A wearable-arts gallery caters to those less car-inclined.

The adjacent **Motorcycle Mecca** (adults $20, children $10, both attractions adults $40, children $20) exhibits more than 300 two-wheel rides and related artwork from more than 60 manufacturers around the world. The collection ranges from the turn-of-the-20th century onward.

E Hayes and Sons

In 1967, Invercargill mechanic Burt Munro set the under-1,000cc world record at the Bonneville Salt Flats in Utah riding a 1920 Indian Scout motorcycle that he had spent two decades modifying. His story was immortalized in the movie *The World's Fastest Indian.*

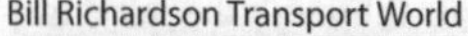

Bill Richardson Transport World

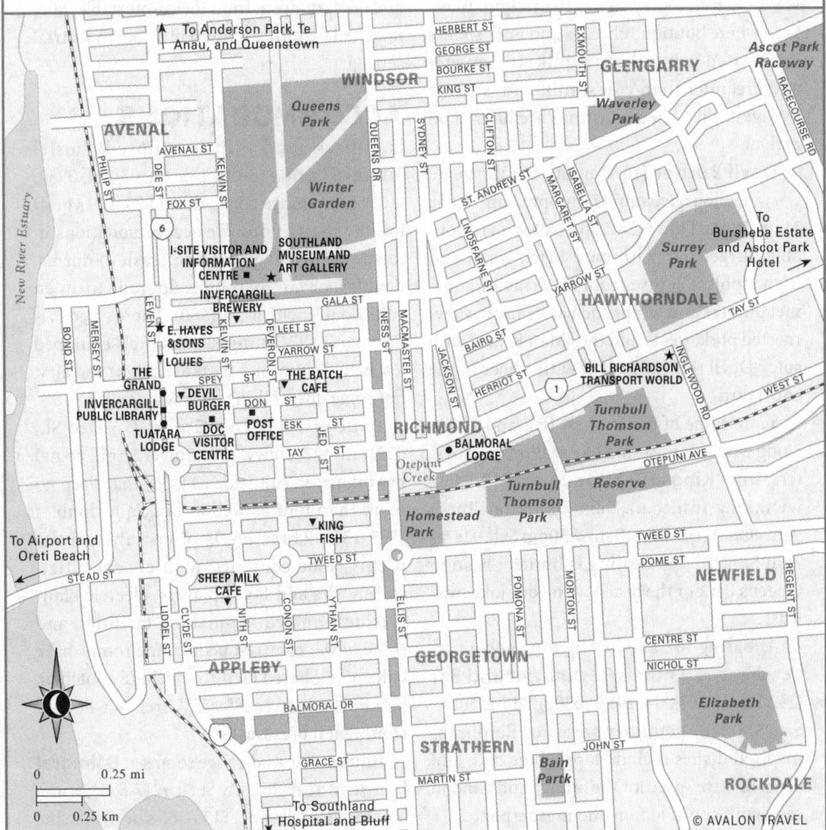

His bike is on display in the hardware store **E Hayes and Sons** (168 Dee St., 03/218-2059, www.ehayes.co.nz, 7:30am-5:30pm Mon.-Fri., 9am-4pm Sat., 10am-4pm Sun., free). Other classic cars and motorcycles include a 1910 Buick, a 1956 Morris J Commercial Van, and a 1923 Harley Davidson.

RECREATION

You'll need half a day and your own transport to tackle the **Heritage Trail,** which links the city's 18 most iconic spots, although the city center section is walkable. Highlights include the redbrick Victorian Water Tower, the 1906 baroque Civic Theatre, and the windswept sands of Oreti Beach, where you can gaze across the waves to Stewart Island. You can also drive along the beach! Grab a free trail map and brochure from the start at the Southland Museum.

FOOD

Don't leave without having breakfast at **The Batch Café** (173 Spey St., 03/214-6357, 7am-4:40pm Mon.-Fri., 8am-4pm Sat.-Sun., $10-20)—especially the bacon on French toast with maple syrup. Tempting treats like macarons and doughnuts are freshly baked on-site, backed by savory delights like brioche along with pork, fennel, and apple-sausage rolls.

For something different, herd yourself into **Sheep Milk Café** (111 Nith St., 03/211-5150, www.blueriverdairy.co.nz, 10am-2pm Tues.-Sat.) where boutique cheeses and milk shakes are crafted using sheep's milk. It's sweeter and creamier than cow's milk and is easier to digest. Free cheese tastings are offered on arrival.

Devil Burger (16 Don St., 03/218-9666, www.devilburger.com, 11am-9pm Sun.-Wed., 11am-10pm Thurs.-Sat., $10-20) is a fashionable burger bar with bare brick walls and high stools. Choose from an array of gourmet burgers and wraps such as venison, slow-roasted pork, steak, and the "Man Killer" with spicy Devil relish. Enjoy it with a beer in the courtyard.

Score some of the freshest fish-and-chips, along with local seafood like scallops and oysters, from **Kings** (59 Ythan St., 03/218-8450, www.kingsfish.co.nz, 9am-7pm Mon.-Tues., 9am-8pm Wed.-Fri., 10am-7:30pm Sat., 11am-7pm Sun., $7-24). Seating is limited; head to Queens Park or the beach with your takeaway feast.

A roaring fire and low lighting add a rustic vibe at ★ **Louie's Restaurant and Bar** (142 Dee St., 03/214-2913, 5:30pm-1am Tues.-Sat., $13-32). Exquisitely presented European-inspired dishes include tapas, blue cod, and venison. Save space for the orange and almond cake with confit lemon and mascarpone.

The elegant **Hideaway 201** (201 Lochiel Branxholme Rd., 03/221-7364, www.thehideaway201.co.nz, 11am-midnight Thurs.-Sun., $25-38), is a popular wedding venue with soft and shady lawns peppered with ponds, pebbled paths, and waterfalls. The menu comprises traditional and contemporary fare like duck salad, *dukkah*-spiced roasted salmon, and fish and bacon roulade. It's 15 minutes north of Invercargill.

From humble beginnings in the 1990s, Steve Nally has transformed his brewery hobby into a lauded craft operation. **Invercargill Brewery** (72 Leet St., 03/214-5070, www.invercargillbrewery.co.nz, 10am-6pm Mon.-Sat.) holds brewery tours (1pm Mon.-Fri., $25) with tastings of pale ale, pilsner, wheat beer, and stout beers. Or drop by and take your pick from the comfortable, mismatched furniture housed in a cool industrial setting.

ACCOMMODATIONS

Laid-back (and a little unloved) hostel **Tuatara Lodge** (30-32 Dee St., 03/214-0954, www.tutaralodge.co.nz, dorm $25, $69 s or d) has the most affordable accommodations in town. Up to 110 guests can crash in dorms, doubles, or family rooms; upgrade to an en suite double with a TV ($80). There's free Wi-Fi, a pair of TV lounges, and a well-equipped kitchen. Communal areas are bright and airy, but some dorms don't have windows.

Built in 1913, **The Grand** (76 Dee St., 022/123-4276, www.grandinvercargill.co.nz) has luxury en suite dorms ($35) that sleep no more than four as well as boutique doubles ($95-135). Three levels of en suite private rooms come equipped with couches, flat-screen TVs and DVD players, electric blankets, tea- and coffee-making facilities, and some of the comfiest beds; some rooms have balconies. Shared facilities include a kitchen, laundry, a lounge, Sky TV, free Wi-Fi, and continental breakfast.

Immaculate mid-range rooms at **Balmoral Lodge Motel** (265 Tay St., 03/217-5755, www.balmoralmotel.co.nz, $135-165 s or d) take the form of studios, one- and two-bedrooms, and luxury suites, with tea- and coffee-making facilities, fridges, blow-dryers, and flat-screen TVs in the lounge and bedrooms. Luxury suites are available with four-poster beds and corner spa baths. Balmoral is modern and a super value.

The blissful ★ **Beersheba Estate** (58 Milton Park Rd., 03/216-3677, www.beersheba.co.nz, $210-275 s or d) cradled within 1.6ha of glorious grounds with ponds and woodlands that sway to the calls of native birds. Contemporary en suite boutique B&B rooms come equipped with central heating, hot drink facilities, a fridge, and a private deck or patio. A self-contained cottage has

Side Trip to Gore

Gore is 50 minutes northeast of Invercargill along Highway 1. The town is guarded by gnarly hills and a river alive with brown trout. The improbable cultural hub has a proud rebellious streak—it was a center for illegal whiskey in the 19th and 20th centuries.

SIGHTS

Set in the town's heritage center, the **Hokonui Moonshine Museum** (16 Hokonui Dr., 03/203-9288, www.goredc.govt.nz, 8:30am-4:30pm Mon.-Fri., 9:30am-3:30pm Sat., 1pm-3:30pm Sun., adults $5, under age 18 free) celebrates Gore's illicit whiskey brewing by way of audio-visuals, artifacts, and life-size displays. You can even sample some "moonshine."

The **Eastern Southland Art Gallery** (Hokonui Dr. and Norfolk St., 03/208-9907, www.esgallery.co.nz, 10am-4:30pm Mon.-Fri., 1pm-4pm Sat.-Sun., free) boasts a graphics and paintings collection that includes pieces by Kiwi artists John Money and Ralph Hotere.

Experience flight's golden age at the **Croydon Aviation Heritage Centre** (1558 Waimea Hwy., 03/208-6046, www.experiencemandeville.co.nz, 9:30am-4:30pm Mon.-Fri., 11am-3pm Sat.-Sun., adults $10, under age 12 free). The spectacular collection of 1920s and 1930s aircraft harbors the southern hemisphere's greatest gathering of De Havilland airplanes. Visitors can take to the air in a Tiger Moth, Fox Moth, or Dominie/Rapide (03/208-9755, $75-300), where they'll be equipped with a vintage leather pilot's jacket and flying goggles for the 15-30-minute flight.

RECREATION

Gore's self-proclaimed reputation as the "Brown Trout Capital of the World" attracts keen anglers. Take a guided fishing trip to the pristine waters of the Mataura River with **Fly Fish Mataura** (86a Wentworth St., 03/208-6476, www.flyfishmataura.co.nz, $430-750). Trips last four to eight hours; transportation, equipment, food, and refreshments are provided.

FOOD

Café Ambience (51 Main St., 03/208-5888, 7:30am-4:30pm Mon.-Fri., 8:30am-1:30pm Sat.) serves fresh fare like banana bread, cinnamon rolls, quiches, salads, and smoothies, beautifully presented with edible flowers. It's a firm favorite with the locals.

Nachos, steak sandwiches, and fish-and-chips prop up the no-nonsense pub menu at **Howl at The Moon** (2 Main St., 03/208-3982, noon-2pm, 5:30pm-9pm daily, $22-38), served in a contemporary bar setting with a sunny courtyard.

The menu at ★ **Thomas Green Public House and Dining Room** (30 Medway St., 03/208-9295, www.thethomasgreen.co.nz, 10am-close daily, $32-39) doesn't pack too many surprises, but the execution is fantastic, with beef Wellington, grilled salmon, lamb striploin, and an exceptional surf and turf. High ceilings, large windows, and soft seating top the elegant surroundings, complemented by attentive service.

ACCOMMODATIONS

Modern lodgings are set in 1.2ha of grounds that overlook Gore at the hilltop **Reservation B&B** (16 Spittles Way, www.accommodationgore.nz, 03/208-1200, $140-225 s or d). The four fashionable rooms come with radiators, TVs, electric blankets, and free Wi-Fi. Guests enjoy complimentary tea and coffee in the lounge, along with continental breakfast.

Dolomore Park Camp (70 Dolamore Park Rd., 03/209-0330, adults $10, children $2, under age 5 free) is home to a podocarp forest that supports native birds as well as the Waimumu Stream, home to eels, freshwater lobsters, and trout. It offers 22 powered and unlimited unpowered sites for tents and RVs. Campers make use of picnic areas, bath facilities, and barbecues.

full kitchen facilities, a private veranda, a log fire, laundry, and a hot tub. It's 10 minutes from the city center.

The **Top 10 Holiday Park** (77 McIvor Rd., 03/215-9032, www.top10.co.nz) occupies quaint tree-hemmed grounds with campers ($40) invited to make use of a communal kitchen, a TV and lounge room, a barbecue area, and a pizza oven. Modern well-appointed studios, units, motel rooms, and cabins ($85-140) sleep two to six and have private baths, verandas, and TVs. It's a five-minute drive from the city center.

TRANSPORTATION AND SERVICES

Invercargill is 160km southwest of Te Anau via Highways 94, 96, and 6, and 190km south of Queenstown via Highway 6.

Air

Invercargill Airport (IVC, 106 Airport Ave., 03/218-6920) receives **Air New Zealand** (www.airnewzealand.co.nz) flights from Christchurch and Wellington; all flights to Stewart Island depart from here. **Invercargill Airport Shuttle** (03/214-3434, www.executivecarservice.co.nz) offers airport transport.

Bus

Nationwide **Intercity** (09/583-5700, www.intercity.co.nz) buses connect Invercargill to Te Anau, Christchurch, Dunedin, and Gore. **Tracknet** (03/249-7777, www.tracknet.net) operates buses between Invercargill, Queenstown, and Te Anau. **Catch-A-Bus-South** (03/479-9960) provides the region's only chartered door-to-door service between Invercargill or Bluff to Dunedin. A city bus route map and timetable (www.icc.govt.nz) is available online.

Car Rentals

Car rentals such as **Hertz** (03/218-2837, www.hertz.co.nz) and **Rent a Dent** (0800/736-823, www.rentadent.co.nz) are located at the airport. In town, try **Riverside Rentals** (03/214-1030). Head to **Wensley Cycles** (53 Tay St., 03/218-6206, www.wensleyscycles.co.nz) for bike rentals. Cab companies include **Blue Star Taxis** (03/217-7777) and **Invercargill Taxis** (03/216-5995).

Services

The **i-SITE** (108 Gala St., 03/211-0895, www.southlandnz.com, 8:30am-5pm Mon.-Fri., 8:30am-4pm Sat.-Sun.) is in the Southland Museum. The **DoC Visitor Centre** (33 Don St., 7th Fl., 03/211-2400, www.doc.govt.nz, 8:30am-4:30pm Mon.-Fri.) has information on Fiordland, Stewart Island, and the Catlins Coast. There is a **post office** (51 Don St., 0800/081-190, 9am-5:30pm Mon.-Fri., 9am-1pm Sat.), a **library** (50 Dee St., 03/211-1444, 9am-7pm Mon.-Fri., 10am-4pm Sat.-Sun.), and a **hospital** (Kew Rd., 03/218-1949).

BLUFF

There's an industrial feel to Bluff, one of New Zealand's oldest towns, and still a thriving fishing hub famed mostly for its oysters. This small port marks the termination of Highway 1, 30km south of Invercargill and the departure point for the ferry to Stewart Island.

Sights

BLUFF MARITIME MUSEUM

Delve into the region's whaling history and oyster industry at the **Bluff Maritime Museum** (241 Foreshore Rd., 03/212-7534, 10am-4:30pm Mon.-Fri., 12:30pm-4:30pm Sat.-Sun., adults $3, children $1), with stories of shipwrecks thrown in for good measure. The modest but intimate setting houses marine artifacts like old boat parts, a steam engine, and photographs, but the star of the show is the boardable oyster dredging ship *Monica* displayed outside.

STIRLING POINT

Stirling Point boasts New Zealand's most famous signpost. At the end of Highway 1, its multiple yellow arms display the directions and distances to major world capitals. The Foveaux Strait (the sea that separates South and Stewart Islands) lies behind.

Bluff Oysters

Many a seafood aficionado will tell you that Bluff oysters (sometimes called mud, dredge, or deep-water oysters) are the best in the world. The slow-growing oyster thrives in the clean frigid waters around New Zealand, but is most common around the Foveaux Strait. It is harvested here March-August, then devoured nationwide with aplomb.

In May, Bluff celebrates their famous shellfish with the **Bluff Oyster Festival** (0800/224-224, www.bluffoysterfest.co.nz, May, adults $30, children $10) with food stalls in the streets, which are later joined by parades and live bands.

A handful of well-signed walking tracks start from Sterling Point. The **Foveaux Walkway** (1 hour one-way) is an easy coastal trail that snakes its way to the 265m summit of Bluff Hill (Motupohue). To drive there instead, head for Flagstaff Road (signposted from Hwy. 1).

Food and Accommodations

It's all about the seafood in Bluff, but dining options are limited. **Galley Takeaways** (42 Gore St., 03/212-7391, 11:30am-7:30pm Sun.-Tues., 11:30am-8pm Wed.-Thurs., 11:30am-7:30pm Fri.-Sat., $5-10) serves fine fish, including blue cod, hoki, oyster, squid, and scallops; there are plenty of burgers if fish isn't your thing.

Set in an old post office, quirky **Bluff Lodge** (120 Gore St., 03/212-7106, www.blufflodge.co.nz, dorm $20, $45 s or d, linen rental $5) was built in 1899—and has not been updated much since. It's so old-school that there's a coal range in the kitchen. Accommodations include basic dorm, twin, and double rooms, with shared baths; upgrade to the King Room with your own private bath ($65). Enjoy complimentary tea and coffee, a communal TV room, and laundry.

Isolated **Land's End** (10 Ward Parade, 03/212-7575, www.landsendhotel.co.nz, $265 s or d) hotel rises over a rocky outcrop with views of Stirling Point. Four modern king rooms overlook the ocean; the twin room comes with a garden view. All rooms have TVs, tea- and coffee-making facilities, private baths, blow-dryers, and robes. Free Wi-Fi and breakfast are included, enjoyed in the on-site café.

Transportation

Bluff is 28km south of Invercargill via Highway 1. **Tracknet** (03/249-7777, www.tracknet.net) operates daily bus service between Invercargill and Bluff.

The Catlins Coast

The eastern stretch of the Southern Scenic Route links Dunedin and Invercargill along the Catlins Coast. The region is battered by Antarctic winds, bustles with wildlife, and boasts a fossilized forest that is 180 million years old.

There are no banks or ATMs on the Catlins Coast and little in the way of stores, so stop at the town of Balclutha for cash and supplies. The **i-SITE Visitor Centre** (4 Clyde St., 03/418-0388, www.cluthanz.com, 8:30am-5pm Mon.-Fri., 9:30am-3pm Sat.-Sun. summer, 8:30am-2pm Mon.-Fri., 9:30am-2pm Sat.-Sun. winter) serves the Catlins Coast region.

Balclutha is 80km south of Dunedin along Highway 1.

KAKA POINT

Kaka Point, 20km south of Balclutha, marks the official start of the Catlins Coast and is the gateway to a handful of attractions such as Nugget Point. The small holiday village overlooks golden beaches popular with surfers.

Nugget Point

Historic **Tokata Lighthouse** protrudes from the head of **Nugget Point,** 9km south of Kaka Point and overlooking a collection of offshore "nuggets," eroded rocky islets sticking up from the sea. An easy coastal track runs from Kaimataitai car park. From Roaring Bay car park (800m before Kaimataitai car park) another track (20 minutes round-trip) leads to a hide from which to view yellow-eyed penguins as they come ashore in the late afternoon. You'll encounter plenty of fur seals and sea lions lounging along this coastline—gannets, sooty shearwaters, and shags are frequent visitors. Time your trip to arrive at Nugget Point by sunset for the best photographs, after viewing the penguins.

Accommodations

Kaka Point Campground (34 Tarata St., 03/412-8801, www.kakapointcamping.co.nz) offers campsites ($29-32) and basic cabins ($56), all with free Wi-Fi. Shared facilities include a barbecue area, hot showers, a well-stocked kitchen, and laundry. The spectacular surroundings on the edge of a bird-filled nature reserve are worth every penny. It's a short stroll from the beach.

OWAKA

Owaka is the largest settlement of the Catlins. At the **Owaka Museum** (10 Campbell St., 03/415-8323, www.owakamuseum.org.nz, 9:30am-4:30pm Mon.-Fri., 10am-4pm Sat.-Sun., adults $5, children free), Maori history, pioneer tales, and shipwrecks are told by way of models, tools, artifacts, photos, and video. There's a small on-site information center staffed by friendly and informative volunteers.

Owaka is a 20-minute drive from Kaka Point along Highway 92.

Catlins River-Wisp Loop Track

The **Catlins River-Wisp Loop Track** (24km, 1-2 days) is the area's best-regarded trek. It incorporates silver beech forest filled with birdlife and wire-rope suspension bridges strung over waterways as they tumble into falls and rapids.

The route comprises two 12km loops; each can be completed separately, and there are multiple entry and exit points to break the trail into shorter hikes. The track is maintained by DoC (www.doc.govt.nz), but there are no huts; bring a tent to overnight.

To reach the main access point, turn off Highway 92 at Owaka onto Catlins Valley Road. Turn right onto Morris Saddle Road, then make a left at the cattle-stop onto Chloris Pass Road.

a yellow-eyed penguin at Curio Bay

PAPATOWAI

The township of Papatowai is a popular spot with the surfing community thanks to the area's incredible swells. Less than 20 minutes north of the town are some spectacular falls.

Purakaunui Falls

Mystical, three-tiered **Purakaunui Falls** (20 minutes) is a much-photographed waterfall set against black rock and surrounded by greenery—it looks lifted straight from a fairy tale. The easy track weaves under the shade of beech and podocarp forest. To reach the falls, drive 6km south of Owaka and turn left onto Purakaunui Falls Road to a car park.

Lost Gypsy Gallery

You've never seen anything like the roadside **Lost Gypsy Gallery** (Papatowai Hwy., www.thelostgypsy.com, 10am-5pm Thurs.-Tues. summer, free). The project, by local artist-inventor Blair Somerville, comprises a converted bus bulging with interactive animatronics and wind-up gadgets constructed from everyday items like toys, watches, and sea shells. Wander through a garden ($5) inhabited by bigger and bolder creations—the enjoyment comes with the surprise. A small on-site café sells snacks and espresso.

Cathedral Caves

The daunting **Cathedral Caves** (May-Oct., adults $5, children $1) penetrate the northern cliffs of Waipati Beach for 200m, reaching 30m high. You may see sea lions and penguins nearby. From the car park, a 1km track winds down though coastal forest; access is 7:30am-8:30pm, for two hours before and one hour after low tide. For tide charts, visit www.metservice.com.

It's 15km southwest from Papatowai along Chaslands Highway (Papatowai Niagara Rd.).

★ CURIO AND PORPOISE BAYS

Curio Bay is home to a 180-million-year-old petrified forest, formed while New Zealand was still part of supercontinent Gondwana. The fossilized remains of tree stumps and fallen trunks are visible at low tide on a rocky plain that's frequented by yellow-eyed penguins.

Sweeping, sheltered **Porpoise Bay** is a few minutes' walk northeast. It hosts a pod of 20 rare Hector's dolphins, who often spend early morning surfing the waves meters from the shore—but don't expect to see them in winter.

Curio Bay is 43km west of Papatowai along Chaslands Highway.

Accommodations

★ **Curio Bay Salthouse** (517 Waikawa Curio Bay Rd., 03/246-8598, www.curiobaysalthouse.co.nz, $140-180 s or d) is a contemporary motel with three spacious en suite units that open onto Porpoise Bay. Central heating and double-glazed windows fend off the coastal winds. Facilities include Sky TV, fully equipped kitchens, irons, and blow-dryers.

Nestled on the windswept headland that

separates the bays, **Curio Bay Holiday Park** (601 Waikawa-Curio Bay Rd., 03/246-8897, www.curiobayholidaypark.com, $20-30) offers extremely basic facilities—kitchen, toilets, and coin-operated showers—along with a rudimentary grocery shop. Well-positioned dense hedgerows admirably protect tent sites from the gales.

SLOPE POINT

New Zealand's southernmost mainland spot is **Slope Point,** which protrudes from a headland 15km west of Curio Bay. Reach it via a 20-minute meander across lush green pastures grazed by sheep. A couple of yellow arrows list the distance to the South Pole and the equator.

Stewart Island

Stewart Island is New Zealand's third-largest island. It sits 30km from the mainland across the Foveaux Strait and is of great significance to Maori. When demigod Maui fished up North Island, his canoe—South Island—was anchored in place by Stewart Island. Stewart Island is known as Rakiura, which translates as "the land of glowing skies," so-named due to the southern lights and the wondrous sunsets.

Eighty-five percent of this 172,000ha landmass forms Rakiura National Park. The entrance is marked by a chain sculpture that honors the Maori legend. Nearly 300km of walking tracks snake through this enormous bird sanctuary that is home to rare and native birds like the kaka, weka, tui, and fantail. The healthy population of birds massively outnumbers the 400 people in the town of Oban.

SIGHTS

Rakiura Museum

You'll leave the quaint volunteer-run **Rakiura Museum** (9 Ayr St., 03/219-1221, 10am-1:30pm Mon.-Sat., noon-2pm Sun. Oct.-May, 10am-noon Mon.-Fri., 10am-1:30pm Sat., noon-2pm Sun. June-Sept., $2) with an appreciation of island life and its history. Exhibits include Maori weapons, tools, and jewelry; shells and whale teeth; and an abundance of photos documenting the fishing, boatbuilding, and timber-milling industries.

★ Ulva Island

Just 11km of coastline surrounds **Ulva Island,** an area of 270ha that pulses with birdlife, just off the shore of the Paterson Inlet. Part of Rakiura National Park, this is one of New Zealand's most treasured lands. Its pest-free podocarp rainforest comprises mainly rimu, southern rata, and kamahi trees that shelter the kiwi, the Stewart Island robin, saddleback, yellowhead, weka, kaka, tui, parakeet, and fantail. Shags and oystercatchers frequent beaches where leopard seals, fur seals, elephant seals, and sea lions laze.

This open wildlife sanctuary can be easily explored via a network of well-formed tracks that leave the terminus at Post Office Bay. Download the DoC's *Ulva Island/Te Wharawhara Walking Tracks* booklet (www.doc.govt.nz) and book a water taxi to reach the island.

RECREATION

Walks

For the **Evening Cove** (90 minutes round-trip), turn right at the waterfront and follow the coast road to Leask Bay, which is littered with rusted whaling relics. Swing a right onto Evening Cove and follow it until the route ends. A short track leads to an isolated beach that you'll likely have to yourself.

Fern Gully (2 hours round-trip) leads through native bush along an old sawmill track next to a meandering stream. Get there from the visitors center (12 Elgin Terrace) by taking a left along Main Road. Turn right onto Kaipipi Road and look for a signpost. There is a clearing with some seating to sit and enjoy the birdlife.

For a comprehensive list of the numerous short walks departing from Oban, grab a copy of the DoC's *Stewart Island Short Walks* booklet (www.doc.govt.nz).

RAKIURA TRACK

What New Zealand's southernmost Great Walk lacks in climbs and mountain views it makes up for with wildlife and diversity. The **Rakiura Track** (32km loop, 3 days/2 nights) can be walked in either direction, any time of year; though it's cold during the winter months, the weather tends to be less volatile. Great chunks of the beginning and end points of the route are coastal, with some beach walking and a swing bridge. The middle day will be spent among ferns and rimu in a kamahi forest alive with birdsong; you may even spot a kiwi (you'll certainly hear one).

DoC operates two **huts** (adults $24, under age 17 free) and three **campsites** (adults $6, children free) along the track. Book in advance online or at the visitors center.

Guided Tours and Cruises

Being on the water is a big part of life for Stewart Islanders and their guests. **Phil's Sea Kayak** (03/219-1444, philskayak@observationrocklodge.co.nz) runs half-day ($145) or full-day ($219) guided paddles that can take in sights such as Ulva Marine reserve and Paterson Inlet, with much birdlife and the odd marine creature along the way. Savor at least one beach landing with a hot drink and sweet baked treat. At least four guests are required for the evening sunset tour ($90).

Rakiura Charters (10 Main Rd., 03/219-1487, www.rakiuracharters.co.nz, adults $100-240, children $70-135) runs guided and unguided fishing, hiking, bird-watching, and sailing packages. All include complimentary cake and hot drinks. Most popular is the Classic (adults $125, children $80), a personal setup that includes a four-hour cruise, fishing, and bush-walk tour plus a visit to Ulva Island and a historic whaling base. You may even spot some dolphins. The firm also operates a water taxi.

Stewart Island Experience (03/212-7660, www.stewartislandexperience.co.nz) is the island's major tour operator. They organize several cruises and walking expeditions,

Ulva Island

such as the four-hour Wild Kiwi Encounter ($160), which ferries guests across Paterson Inlet to Little Glory Cove at dusk. Following a short bush walk, visitors reach a secluded sandy beach where sightings of the southern brown kiwi are a given.

FOOD

Voluptuous burgers are served alongside revolving daily catches (gurnard, lemon sole, mussels, and blue cod) at ★ **Kai Kart** (Ayr St., 03/219-1225, 11:30am-2pm and 5pm-8pm daily, $6-20), a fixed food truck with a well-priced menu and million-dollar sea view.

Church Hill (36 Kamahi Rd., 03/219-1123, www.churchhill.co.nz, 5pm-close daily, $37-50) is the island's most stylish—and most secluded—eatery, its spire protruding from a cluster of hilltop trees. Snag an outside table to enjoy the ocean views as you dine on pasta, lamb, steak, and fish drizzled in delectable sauces, or order ahead for crayfish ($85).

For coffee and crepes, stop at **Kiwi-French Café** (6 Main Rd., 03/219-1422, 8am-8pm daily), an intimate timber-clad space with an open fire and indoor and outdoor seating.

ACCOMMODATIONS

Hilltop Backpackers (15 Whipp Place, 027/725-6665, hilltop@siss.co.nz, dorm $30, $50 s, $70 d) offers sea views surrounded by bush teeming with birdlife; come nightfall, you may even glimpse a kiwi. Rooms have private baths. Enjoy free tea and coffee, or make use of the bookshelves and an acoustic guitar in the communal lounge.

A colorful kitchen and vibrant rooms will put a smile on your face at **Stewart Island Backpackers** (18 Ayr St., 03/219-1114, www.stewartislandbackpackers.co.nz, dorm $36, $56 s, $76 d). Dorms are capped at four people, with single beds and no bunks. All rooms are equipped with central heating. The communal kitchen is well-stocked and accompanied by a barbecue, board games, billiards, and laundry facilities. The well-kept grounds, fringed by palms and ferns, cater to campers with tent sites ($20 pp).

Well-appointed units at **Bay Motel** (9 Dundee St., 03/219-1119, www.baymotel.co.nz) open onto a deck with views of bush and Oban and Half Moon Bays. Nine studio units ($175) accompany a spa unit ($200), a two-bedroom unit ($215), and a three-bedroom apartment ($325). Rooms have heating, cooking facilities, a fridge, complimentary tea and coffee, Wi-Fi, and Sky TV. Make use of guest laundry and a barbecue area.

The terra-cotta tones of idyllic ★ **Stewart Island Lodge** (14 Nichol Rd., 03/219-0085, www.stewartislandlodge.co.nz, $283 s or d) blend beautifully with its bush-carpeted hillside facing the Foveaux Strait. Six en suite rooms come with TVs, toiletries, and baths that open onto a shared sprawling balcony. Shady gardens bristle with birdlife, including a native parrot, the kaka. It's a five-minute stroll to the village.

TRANSPORTATION AND SERVICES

Air

Stewart Island Flights (03/218-9129, www.stewartislandflights.co.nz, round-trip adults $213, children $128, seniors $193, one-way adults $122.50, children $80, seniors $112.50) operate three flights daily to Stewart Island from Invercargill. Flights take 20 minutes.

Ferries and Water Taxis

Stewart Island Experience (03/212-7660, www.stewartislandexperience.co.nz) runs daily ferries ($77 one-way) across the Foveaux Strait, with coach transfers from Invercargill ($102), Te Anau ($152), and Queenstown ($152). The one-hour crossing is spectacular, if rough.

Water taxi operators include **Rakiura Charters** (10 Main Rd., 03/219-1487, www.rakiuracharters.co.nz), **Aihe Charters** (03/219-1066, www.aihe.co.nz), and **Ulva Island Ferry** (03/219-1013). Oban is easily walkable, but if you want to travel farther, you can rent cars, bicycles, and scooters through **Real Journeys** (03/249-6000, www.realjourneys.co.nz).

Services

To book tours and ferry services, contact the **Tourist Visitor Centre** (12 Elgin Terrace, 03/219-0056, www.stewartislandexperience.co.nz, 7:30am-6:30pm daily Nov.-Apr., 8am-5pm daily May-Oct.). For more information, visit the **DoC Rakiura National Park Visitor Centre** (Main Rd., 03/219-0009, www.doc.govt.nz, 8am-5pm daily Dec. 26-Apr., 8:30am-4:30pm Mon.-Fri., 10am-2pm Sat.-Sun. May-Oct., 8am-5pm Mon.-Fri., 9am-4pm Sat.-Sun. Nov.-Dec.)

There are no banks on Stewart Island. The only ATM machine is inside the Four-Square supermarket, and it only accepts New Zealand debit cards. There is a Wi-Fi hot spot outside the community center (Ayr St.), where there is also a **library** (8:30am-noon Mon.-Fri., 2pm-4pm Wed., 11am-noon Sat.). There is a **post office** (40 Elgin Terrace, 0800/501-501, 7:30am-6pm Mon.-Fri., 9:30am-5pm Sat.-Sun.) and a **medical center** (Argyle St., 03/219-1098, 10am-noon daily).

Background

The Landscape 493
Plants and Animals 495
History 498
Economy and Government 502
People and Culture 503

The Landscape

GEOGRAPHY

New Zealand's long, narrow shape is an above-sea-level section of the ancient supercontinent Gondwana, which broke up 85 million years ago. The country comprises around 700 islands but is mostly spread across three land masses—the substantial North Island and South Island, which are comparable in size, and the significantly smaller Stewart Island, off the southernmost coast—usually referred to as the "deep south" (likewise, the top end of North Island is known as the "far north"). New Zealand's land mass is equivalent to the United Kingdom's, but with a population under 5 million (compared to the United Kingdom's 66 million), there is considerably more room. Framing New Zealand's windswept coastlines are beaches of white, golden, and iron-rich volcanic dark sands.

Though separated only by the Cook Strait, just 22km wide at its narrowest point, North and South Islands differ wildly. Rolling verdant farmlands and geothermal landscapes around Auckland, Rotorua, and Lake Taupo—Australasia's largest freshwater lake, formed in an ancient volcanic crater—defines much of North Island, home to boiling mud pools, geysers, and iconic volcanic peaks like Mount Ngauruhoe, which *Lord of the Rings* fans will recognize as Mount Doom. To the east, smoldering White Island—New Zealand's only active marine volcano—protrudes from the sea 50km off the Bay of Plenty.

Other than some long extinct domes that form beautiful Banks Peninsula, southeast of Christchurch, little on South Island betrays a volcanic past. Rather, this is a landscape defined by the Southern Alps, a glorious mountain range that runs along the island's spine, cradling numerous lakes and glaciers, including a pair of the world's most accessible ice masses—Franz Josef and Fox glaciers—along with New Zealand's tallest peak: Aoraki, or Mount Cook, which rises to 3,724m, one of 18 Southern Alps mountains that tower over 3,000m. The southern end of the range gives way to dramatic Fiordland, an unforgiving national park of forested black monoliths that burst through equally black waters, its 215-km coastline punctuated by 14 fiords, such as the moody Milford Sound, often described as the eighth wonder of the world.

New Zealand sits on the Pacific Ring of Fire, straddling the colliding Pacific and Australian tectonic plates responsible for both the volcanic activity in the north (as the Pacific plate is forced down) and the formation of the alpine ranges to the south (as the Pacific plate rides over Australia), not to mention regular tremors and the occasional sizeable earthquake—hence New Zealand's nickname of "the Shaky Isles." Consistent throughout the country is an abundance of rich soils and fertile plains serviced by a wealth of waterways (and a favorable climate), resulting in lots of forests and thriving wine and farming industries.

CLIMATE

Thanks to its long narrow shape, meaning the coast is never too far away, New Zealand's climate is mainly temperate—but like its geological makeup, it can vary greatly for its relatively compact size (and often, frustratingly, in a day). Visitors from the northern hemisphere need to remember the rules are reversed Down Under, and that the farther south one heads, the chiller it often gets. Of course there are opposite seasons, with

Previous: keas, the world's only alpine parrot; bush-clad Southern Alps with snowy peaks.

summer coinciding with Christmas time and winter beginning in June.

But fear not; most of New Zealand receives at least 2,000 hours of sunshine annually, with some areas such as the Bay of Plenty and Marlborough getting around 350 hours more. The hottest months are usually January and February, when the average maximum temperature ranges 20-30°C, falling to 10-15°C in winter. Rainfall is also generally high (a fair tradeoff for the lush fields and forests) and can occur at any time, but falls more heavily on North Island in winter, and outside winter on South Island, averaging 640-1,500mm per year. Snow rarely troubles areas outside of the mountainous central plateau on North Island, but blankets the length of the South Island along the Southern Alps, and some inland regions of Otago and Canterbury. During winter, temperatures in inland alpine areas can fall to -10°C.

ENVIRONMENTAL ISSUES

New Zealand positions itself as the cleanest and greenest of nations, often with good reason. Having had a history of protesting nuclear testing in the Pacific that resulted in the sinking of a Greenpeace ship in Auckland by French spies, in 1987 parliament passed an act making New Zealand the world's first country to become a nuclear-free zone. The country is fortunate to have an abundance of renewable energy resources, including hydro, geothermal, and wind, and 75 percent of New Zealand's energy is generated from these sources—the fourth highest among OECD nations. There are aims to increase that to 90 percent by 2025.

Around a third of the country is listed as protected or as national parks, with all national parks and many reserves and forest parks managed by the Department of Conservation (www.doc.govt.nz), referred to as DoC. Established in 1991, the New Zealand Forest Accord put a stop to decades of dispute between the forestry industry and various environmental organizations by recognizing the need to protect native forests and their inhabitants while encouraging the likes of responsible logging. But though a strong green philosophy is an inherent part of the Kiwi psyche, the nation is certainly not without its eco-problems.

Uninhabited for millennia, New Zealand had flora and fauna that was ill-equipped to deal with human arrival and the introduction of new plants and animals. Early Maori came with rats and dogs that had a devastating effect on native bird populations (and, in the case of rats, still do—dogs are generally forbidden from entering DoC-maintained land), many of which had evolved to be flightless on these previously predator-free lands. Several larger bird species, such as the moa, were hunted to extinction within just a few hundred years of the Polynesian migration, while up to 40 percent of the nation's forests were burned to allow settlement building and crop growth.

Europeans compounded the environmental devastation, bringing more predatory species such as cats, stoats, and ferrets, while grazing animals like goats and deer further damaged forests. Along the coasts, sealers and whalers decimated marine mammal populations, while the introduction of more than 30,000 foreign plant species such as gorse and contorta pine impacted many native blooms. Around half of all native birds are extinct, and many remaining species endangered. An estimated 90 percent of swamps and wetlands have been drained for farming, while the

Pest-Free New Zealand

In 2016, the New Zealand government announced that it would aim to make the country predator-free by 2050. This means the elimination of rats, stoats, and possums, which kill 25 million native birds per year. It's known as the **Predator Free NZ Project** (www.predatorfreenz.org).

massive dairy industry especially has come under intense scrutiny in recent years for its land degradation and pollution of fresh waterways—many of which carry the microscopic giardia parasite. Per capita, New Zealand also ranks among the Western world's worst producers of carbon emissions.

Oil Exploration

In 1865 the Alpha well in Taranaki became one of the world's first oil wells, and the region remains New Zealand's main producer of gas and oil (there are also sizeable reserves around Canterbury). New Zealand is self-sufficient in natural gas and produces around 40 percent of its own oil, with the combined industries contributing $2.5 billion to the economy, employing 11,000 people, and raising $500 million in income tax and royalties. Extraction takes the form of fracking and deep-sea drilling, and there is significant opposition to both controversial practices, led not only by groups such as Greenpeace but also local councils, including Auckland, Dunedin, Kaikoura, Christchurch, and Gisborne. Since 2011 they have voted to ban offshore oil drilling and fracking. In 2018, Prime Minister Jacinda Ardern announced a ban on all new offshore oil and gas permits, effective immediately.

Plants and Animals

New Zealand's isolation allowed the evolution of a slew of endemic flora and fauna, much of which has unfortunately been threatened—or even wiped out—by the arrival of humans and introduced species. Eighty percent of New Zealand's native trees, ferns, and flowering plants cannot be found anywhere else.

TREES

Native forest covers less than a quarter of New Zealand, two-thirds of which contains some beech trees and half of which is almost entirely beech, of which there are five species: hard and black beech, found in lowland areas; red beech, which grows on foothills and inland valley floors; silver beech, which likes elevated wet conditions and is therefore especially prevalent in Fiordland; and mountain beech, which can grow on mountains with less nutritious soils than silver beech, usually forming the bush line. The kauri tree is among New Zealand's most majestic and revered residents, capable of growing to more than 50m, with a 16m girth and living for more than 2,000 years. The gorgeous pohutukawa glows with spectacular red flowers in summer—leading to its nickname, "the Christmas tree." The nikau palm is the southernmost-growing palm and New Zealand's only native palm. Podocarp forests have been around since New Zealand was still attached to supercontinent Gondwana and comprise hardwood conifers such as the rimu, miro, and totara. Flax is another ancient plant species, of which there are two endemic species: common and mountain. Perhaps the most iconic Kiwi flora is the silver fern, named because of its metallic-sheened underside—there are around 200 species of fern in New Zealand, 40 percent of which grow nowhere else on earth.

FLOWERS

The unofficial national flower of New Zealand is the kowhai, a bright-yellow bloom that grows on its eponymous trees, whose image has appeared on Kiwi coins and postage stamps. Previously known as the Mount Cook lily, the Mount Cook buttercup is the world's biggest buttercup and can grow larger than a hand. It is found in alpine regions throughout South Island. The ngutukaka, which translates as "beak of the kaka" (a native parrot), was named because of the shape of its red flowers, which hang in groups of up to 20. Pikao is a golden sand sedge found only in, and throughout, New Zealand, and serves an important role in binding dunes, each spring producing foot-long dark-brown flower heads. The most spectacular floral display, alas, comes courtesy of the introduced lupine that, though seen as a pest, erupts each summer to carpet vast expanses of the Mackenzie region in vibrant blues, yellows, and purples.

SEALIFE

Whales

Though it's known that a population of **blue whales**—the largest creature ever to have lived—inhabits the Kiwi coast for part of the year, it is not known for how long. They have been sighted around Taranaki and the Hauraki Gulf, but it's unlikely you'll see one of these very rare creatures.

Humpback whales are easily spotted owing to the arch of their backs, topped by a tiny dorsal fin. Famed for their incredible breaches, the endangered migratory species can be sighted through the Cook Strait to the southeast coast of South Island in winter, and along the west coast during spring as they make their way between their tropical breeding grounds and food stocks in Antarctica.

The **sperm whale** is your best bet of encountering a marine giant thanks to the resident 80-strong population that lives off the coast of Kaikoura. They are known for their enormous heads, which account for a third of their body length, as well as a stubby dorsal fin and a slit-like single blowhole.

Dolphins

Orcas—the largest member of the dolphin family—do patrol the entire coastline of New Zealand, but the nomadic hunters regularly visit the Hauraki Gulf, Wellington, the Kapiti Coast, and Marlborough. The common dolphin is especially fond of the waters around Auckland and Northland—but also surface pretty much everywhere, while the **bottlenose dolphin** mainly converges in the waters around the Bay of Islands, Fiordland, and Marlborough. The **Hector's dolphin,** one of the world's smallest at just 1.5m, gray with black and white markings and a rounded dorsal fin, is a native species found only in the waters around South Island, while the **maui dolphin,** a subspecies of the Hector's, inhabit only the waters off the west coast—and are among the rarest in the world, thought to number less than 100.

Seals and Sea Lions

The New Zealand **sea lion** is one of the world's rarest, found only on Aotearoa, mostly off the coasts of Otago and Southland. Populations of the New Zealand **fur seal** are on the rise—numbering well above 200,000—and can be found basking on rocky outcrops along most of New Zealand's coasts. **Leopard seals** generally inhabit Antarctic coasts and waters but come winter and fall regularly make their way to New Zealand—sometimes as far north as Auckland. They can grow up to 3.6m and boast dark gray or black spots. Though they may look cute and often slovenly, both seals and sea lions can bite without warning and should be given a wide berth; leopard seals are especially aggressive. Stay at least 10m away on land.

Sharks

Around 70 species of sharks, including the great white, occupy New Zealand's waters, but fatal attacks on humans are almost unheard of. The well-stocked waters keep the sharks well fed.

Fish

There are nearly 40 species of native freshwater fish in New Zealand, including bullies, eels, lampreys, and mudfish, while some of the most abundant saltwater swimmers include the snapper, kingfish, and blue cod. In the warmer months, the seas are visited by oceanic giants such as the marlin, sunfish, swordfish, and tuna. The *paua* (abalone) is important to Maori art—its iridescent shell is often used for the eyes in their carvings.

BIRDS

New Zealand is a bird-watching heaven, home to some of the rarest and distinctive species.

Extinct Giants

There were nine species of **moa**—the largest of which stood 3.6m tall. These flightless birds resembled muscular emus with thick trunk-like necks and lived across both islands. Although it is widely accepted that they were hunted to extinction around 500 years ago, there were unconfirmed sightings of them in the 18th and 19th centuries. Maori ate their flesh and used their skin and plumage for clothing and their bones to make fish hooks. The moa wasn't only hunted by Maori, however. It also had to contend with the **Haast's eagle,** history's largest-ever eagle, with a wingspan of up to 3m and claws comparable to a tiger's. It, too, died out once its main food source was depleted.

The flightless **kiwi** is the nation's unofficial mascot and a Maori *taonga* (treasure). The five species—brown, great spotted, little spotted, rowi, and totoeka—inhabit protected reserves and national parks around the country but due to their nocturnal nature and low populations, they're not the easiest bird to spot. But fear not; there are several guided expeditions and a slew of wildlife centers that enable visitors to encounter the cute quirky creature.

Tui are famed for their beautiful metallic blue, white tufts beneath their chins, and melodic calls, and can be found in native forests all over the country. The friendly **fantail** has a cheeky nature that loves to show off its aerial acrobatic skills—you'll recognize the tiny birds thanks to their loud call, pied markings, and lengthy tail that opens up into a—you guessed it—fan.

The **variable oystercatcher** can be found on coasts all around New Zealand, where it breeds on beaches and in dunes—and will soon let you know through loud calling if you near its nest. The black bird sports an almost comically long orange bill and pink legs.

The world's only alpine parrot, the handsome **kea** possesses supreme intelligence and an inquisitive nature that has seen it steal the laces of hikers' boots left outside huts. You'll find it in alpine areas around South Island—especially if it sees you take food out (don't feed them). The kea was voted New Zealand's Bird of the Year in 2017.

The flightless **weka** is around the size of a chicken and is a curious species that's relatively unafraid of humans—again, especially humans bearing food. Another cheeky character, they're expert burglars who have been known to raid the pantries of rural dwellings. The Otago Peninsula is home to the world's only mainland breeding colony of **royal albatross,** the world's largest seabird, which spends up to 85 percent of its life at sea.

New Zealand is home to three species of penguin: the **little blue penguin,** viewed when they come ashore at night—Oamaru is the best location to see them; the **yellow-eyed penguin,** most likely spotted along the Otago Peninsula; and the **Fiordland Crested Penguin,** one of the world's rarest, which inhabits the coasts of Fiordland and Stewart Island.

Kiwi skies are patrolled by three **birds of prey:** the New Zealand falcon, the swamp harrier, and the morepork—a native owl.

History

Aotearoa is among the world's youngest countries and was one of the last places to be colonized. It has been home to two populations: Maori and Pakeha (the Maori term for early European—usually British—settlers) during its history.

INDIGENOUS PEOPLES

There is no concrete evidence that pinpoints the exact date of human arrival on New Zealand's shores, but there is archaeological indications that it may have been as early as AD 700. According to Maori legend, Kupe was the first to find New Zealand, landing at Hokianga Harbor in Northland. He used the stars and ocean currents to cross the Pacific in his *waka* (canoe) from the ancestral island of Hawaiki. The navigator's wife, Kuramarotini, named the place Aotearoa: "the land of the long white cloud."

Modern Maori trace their ancestry to the Polynesian population that arrived here in AD 1200-1300, an era known as the Archaic Period. These legendary voyagers arrived in double-hulled canoes with crops such as the *kumara* (a sweet potato that remains a Kiwi staple) and domesticated dogs. These phenomenal ocean navigators were also highly skilled farmers, hunters, and anglers, weaving nets from native flax and carving hooks from bone and stone. They stored their quarry in stone units built on raised stilts. Early Polynesians initially settled on South Island in order to hunt the giant moa bird, but as their numbers dwindled, those Maori headed north and began settling the coasts.

Around AD 1350, a fresh wave of territorial Polynesians arrived in Aotearoa, bringing with them a disciplined warrior code. This new Classical Period saw the development of weaponry and fortified villages known as *pa,* built on raised ground surrounded by protective trenches and terraces. The remains of many *pa* can be visited around the country today.

ARRIVAL OF THE EUROPEANS

The first known European to sight (though not land on) New Zealand was Dutchman Abel Tasman. He was also the first European known to have made contact with Maori, but that did not end well. In 1642, under orders of the Dutch East India Company, the explorer sailed the South Pacific in search of the new trading lands of the almost mystical terra australis. There was no proof of its existence, rather a belief that there must be a southern continent to counterbalance those of the north. He happened upon Golden Bay at the top of South Island. Upon anchoring, some of the Dutch sailors in a rowing boat were met by Maori in a canoe and killed. Tasman fled up the west coast of what he named "Nieuw Zeeland" (after the Dutch island province), later plotting maps of both Tonga and Fiji.

In 1769, British navigator Lieutenant (later Captain) James Cook sailed into these South Pacific islands in a converted coal ship called the *Endeavour,* becoming the first European to step foot in New Zealand. (Upon his departure, he also became the first to sight Australia's east coast.) French explorers soon followed en masse. Cook circumnavigated North and South Islands charting extensive maps; he controversially claimed the country without Maori consent, although that claim was not recognized on imperial maps for some time. Following initial misunderstandings that resulted in a small number of deaths, Cook struck a working rapport with Maori chiefs and returned twice more, in 1773 and 1777, spending nearly a year in New Zealand in total. The captain was impressed by the complexity of Maori life and the sophistication of their weaponry, villages, and canoes. It was around this time that the indigenous population began referring to themselves as Maori, which means "ordinary," and their British visitors as Pakeha, meaning

Hawaiki: A Place on Earth?

According to legend, Hawaiki is the place from where all Maori originate and where they will return after death. In reality, the island doesn't exist, but given its ubiquity among Polynesian cultures, some scholars have argued that it may be an island of Hawaii, Samoa, or Indonesia. Others believe that it should be viewed in a strictly metaphorical sense.

"stranger"—a term still widely used by both Maori and European Kiwis to describe those of European descent.

For the next few decades, a substantial influx of whaling and sealing gangs hunted New Zealand's marine mammals to near extinction offshore. Stations peppered New Zealand's coast, and with them came transient communities. The logging industry also boomed as the British navy and traders chopped kauri for themselves and to sell to shipbuilders in Sydney.

By the end of the 1820s, the first permanent European settlement had been established in present-day Russell (then Kororareka). In 1840, New Zealand's first capital was founded 7km south at Okiato. It retained that title for a year until Auckland, and then Wellington, claimed the capital in 1865. It was near Russell that the first Christian mission was founded in 1814, with the purpose not only of saving Maori souls but saving them from other forms of exploitation by newly arrived Europeans. Missions soon sprung up all around North Island.

Seemingly symbiotic relations formed between Maori and Europeans, though in the long run at Maori expense. Intertribal warfare was rife, and so the settlers looked to local tribes for protection, as well as food and labor. Flax and timber were traded. Maori were introduced to the likes of European livestock, and to their detriment, alcohol and tobacco, but it was the musket that was to impart the most immediate and widespread harm.

With the European population mainly concentrated in Northland, Hongi Hika, chief of the resident Ngapuhi *iwi*, was the first to attain firearms, giving his warriors absolute advantage over their rivals. Intertribal fighting broke out throughout the land. Over time, munitions ownership rippled south, the bloodshed only halting, ironically, once all the tribes had guns and the power equilibrium was somewhat restored. The Musket Wars of 1818-1836 wiped out an estimated 20 percent of the 100,000 Maori. Human losses aside, many tribes had forsaken their finest crops and treasures to quench their musket thirst. It also intensified the grim trade of preserved Maori trophy heads *(toi moko)* taken from the bodies of defeated warriors.

COLONIZATION

Although there was a semblance of order to New Zealand society as the 19th century began, there was no formal organization to uphold any laws. In 1833, civil servant James Busby, under the title "British Resident," was sent from Australia to cement good relations with Maori and the missionaries, and to keep track of trade. In 1840, Busby was replaced by New Zealand's first governor, Captain William Hobson, who, on February 6, along with Maori leaders from around the country, signed the Treaty of Waitangi, the founding document of modern-day New Zealand, which gave sovereignty to the Crown but was supposed to pit Maori and Pakeha as equal partners in terms of trade and land and bring peace among the tribes. But confusion over the interpretation of the Maori translation centered around land use, with Maori believing they had agreed to let Britain lease the land, whereas the Crown claimed full sovereignty over the estates and all their resources. As more British arrived, so more land was confiscated, and soon British settlers outnumbered the Maori population. Disagreements regarding land use continue to this day.

NEW ZEALAND WARS

The 1840s saw tensions rise between Maori and Pakeha. The first revolt came in 1845, when Northland chief Hone Heke repeatedly felled a hilltop flagstaff at Russell in protest against British colonialism, and fighting broke out. In 1852, the New Zealand Constitution Act excluded some Maori from voting, further inflaming the volatile environment. In an attempt to peacefully strengthen their political hand, Waikato tribes formed an alliance, and in 1858, Tainui chief Te Wherowhero became the first Maori king, but the alienated British saw this as a challenge. In 1860, fighting broke out in Taranaki over a suspicious land sale, and the violence soon spread across North Island, lasting until the end of the decade. Maori fought valiantly, prevailing in a succession of bloody battles, but the New Zealand Wars were ultimately won by the heavily armed Crown, who, in turn, helped themselves to more land, or forced Maori to sell in order to settle impossible debts. By 1880 the Pakeha population had swelled to nearly 500,000 (up from 60,000 in 1860), and the colonization of New Zealand—along with Maori marginalization—was well and truly complete.

Perversely, while the war consumed North Island, South Island was consumed by gold fever, with the discovery of gold in Otago in 1861, and soon the precious metal was to become the nation's largest export, attracting prospectors from Australia, China, Europe, and the United States.

THE 20TH CENTURY

Following the signing of the Treaty of Waitangi, the country became the Colony of New Zealand led by a Crown-appointed governor (or, after 1917, governor-general). The first general election was held in 1853, with no political parties, rather with candidates standing as independents. New Zealand's elected leaders were known as "premiers," but with limited power, serving alongside the governor. In 1867, Maori were allocated four seats in Parliament with the aim of ensuring their fair political representation.

The rise of trade unionism in the late 19th century eroded the colonial elite's governmental power, and in 1890 the Liberal and Labour Parties formed an alliance known as the Liberal Pact, marking the start of social reform and attempts at an egalitarian society. Three years later, New Zealand became the world's first country to give women the vote (in 2017, Labour leader Jacinda Ardern became the nation's third female prime minister—and the first pregnant one), and in 1898 the Old-age Pensions Act meant that the state would provide for seniors with little savings as long as they were of "good moral character." Other socially progressive policies, such as the Industrial Conciliation and Arbitration Act 1894, another world first that legally recognized labor unions, meant that come the 20th century, living standards for the working classes were among the world's best (though mainly for Pakeha—even today, on average, Maori have lower incomes, worse health, worse housing, and are a wildly disproportionately higher portion of the prison population), and New Zealand gained a reputation as the "social laboratory of the world."

William Hall-Jones was bestowed the title of New Zealand's first official prime minister, sworn in on June 21, 1906, and the following year the country became the Dominion of New Zealand, which gave greater powers to the prime minister while reducing

Moriori

A group of early Maori known as Moriori immigrated to the Chatham Islands, 800km east of South Island, in the early 15th century. They lived there peacefully for around 400 years before they were attacked by mainland Maori tribes. Today, around 600 people on the islands claim Moriori descent.

Ten-Pound Poms

Between 1947 and 1966, there followed a second mass wave of British migrants to New Zealand and Australia who were lured by the dream of a new life Down Under to escape the drudgery, devastation, and rationing that followed World War II. The antipodeans were also in desperate need of labor, and so the governments agreed to subsidize the journey that enabled the "poms" (a colloquial term for the British, meaning "prisoners of Mother England") to sail south for just ten pounds sterling. The project was officially called the Assisted Passage Migration Scheme, and those who took part have since been known as the "ten-pound poms."

the governor-general's political role. Still, a first New Zealand-born governor-general would not be appointed until 1967. Today the governor-general is recommended by the prime minister, but the British monarch also remains the official head of state of New Zealand—but the two sovereign roles are entirely separate.

Having aided the United Kingdom during the Boer War at the turn of the 20th century, New Zealand came to Britain's aid during World War I with 100,000 troops—around 10 percent of the population—and suffering massive losses, with 17,000 dead and 45,000 wounded at battles such as Gallipoli. Following the country's involvement in World War II, New Zealand began to further cut the apron strings of the "mother country," the final step of independence arriving in 1947 with the passage of the State of Westminster Act. New Zealand remains part of the Commonwealth of Nations, a collection of self-governing countries of the former British Empire, including Australia, Canada, and India.

FLAG VOTE

In 2016, nearly 57 percent of the population voted against changing the national flag, which comprises a solid blue block with the stars of the Southern Cross constellation in red and the British Union Flag in the top corner. Reasons for the controversial vote included annoyance at the constant confusion with the Australian flag (the designs are practically identical, except the Australian version has a couple of extra stars, and they're white); lack of Maori insignia; and the colonial implications of the Union Flag. The result was largely seen less as a victory for the status quo and more a protest of the dull design alternatives that mainly centered around the clichéd silver fern (New Zealand's national sporting emblem), while the National party-led government was widely criticized for the referendum's $26 million cost. The five alternatives were whittled down from more than 10,000 entrants mostly designed by the public, the coolest of which was a cartoon kiwi bird firing laser beams from its eyes that, alas, didn't make the final cut.

Economy and Government

ECONOMY

New Zealand's free-market economy saw the country placed third on Forbes's 2014 "Best Country for Business" report, and the following year named by the World Bank as the easiest place in the world to start a business, and the second easiest country in which to do business. Exports account for around a third of New Zealand's GDP, with tourism and dairy leading the way, its main trading partners being North America, the European Union, East Asia, and Australia.

The New Zealand dairy industry accounts for a staggering one-third of international dairy trade, contributing $13 billion to the country's coffers and employing 40,000 workers. It was hailed as the main buffer against the global economic crash of 2008, which meant Kiwis fared better than most. However, in 2016 tourism overtook dairy as the country's biggest earner, and in 2017 it generated nearly $15 billion while providing more than 230,000 jobs—8.4 percent of the New Zealand workforce.

Primary industries—which include dairy—account for around a fifth of New Zealand's export value, and the country is the world's largest exporter of sheep meat and cross-bred wool. Forestry accounts for 9 percent of export earnings, and in 2016, horticulture—including the thriving wine, kiwifruit, and honey industries—brought in nearly $600 million, while the seafood industry raised $390 million.

GOVERNMENT

New Zealand is a constitutional monarchy with a parliamentary system of government like that of the United Kingdom, but with different voting and representational structures. The head of state, currently Queen Elizabeth II, is represented by the governor-general (who is recommended by the prime minister, and usually serves for five years), with parliament comprising the sovereign and the House of Representatives (which is parliament's only chamber—there is no upper house like a senate or House of Lords). Acting on behalf of the sovereign, the governor-general opens and dissolves parliament and signs off on bills passed by the house, enabling them to become law.

New Zealand's elected politicians are known as members of parliament (MPs), and there are usually 120 of them (the number can vary under certain circumstances), with each one designated a "seat." Most MPs are part of political parties, though some stand independently.

Elections are held every three years, with New Zealand citizens and permanent residents who have lived in the country for at least a year continuously entitled to vote, providing they are at least age 18. New Zealand operates mixed member proportional representation (MMP), which means the number of seats allocated to each party is proportional to their share of won votes. So a party with 25 percent of the vote would get 30 of the 120 seats. If a party does not have enough seats for an overall majority, then they will invite a smaller party or parties with any shared political philosophies to form a coalition government. The leader of the largest party in government serves as prime minister.

POLITICAL PARTIES

New Zealand's two main parties are Labour, in the center-left, and the center-right National Party. The Green Party usually does well in elections, often placing third, while populists New Zealand First are the other party of note—usually slapped with the right-wing label even though some of their policies on social welfare and state ownership take them a little left (they have sided with both National and Labour in previous coalition governments). The Maori Party's policies mainly concern the rights of New Zealand's indigenous people and their land claims, but it lost its only seat to Labour in the 2017 election.

The 2017 election was a fascinating and controversial one: National received the highest share of the vote, but not enough for a majority, so following weeks of negotiations, Labour was able to form a coalition government supported by the Greens, their natural ally, and New Zealand First, with Labour chief Jacinda Ardern as prime minister and Winston Peters of New Zealand First as her deputy.

People and Culture

DEMOGRAPHY

As of 2017, New Zealand's population was just shy of 4.8 million, and it's estimated that as many as 800,000 New Zealanders are living overseas—mostly in Australia (a reciprocal agreement means that Kiwis and Aussies can work and travel freely between the two countries). Three-quarters of New Zealand's population is on North Island, and around one-third live in Auckland.

A 2014 census revealed that the number of New Zealanders born overseas had topped one million. In the 1960s, two-thirds of foreign-born residents and citizens came from Ireland and the United Kingdom, but by 2013 that figure had dropped to just over one-quarter, while in the 12 years prior, New Zealand's Asian population had nearly doubled. However, those of European descent still account for more than 70 percent of the Kiwi population, followed by Maori at 15 percent, Asians at 11 percent, and Pacific peoples at 8 percent.

Auckland remains the most popular immigration destination, and Statistics New Zealand projects its population could double to more than three million within the next 25 years, while the national population may hit six million within a decade. Auckland is the most populous Polynesian city on earth, with 15 percent of its population identifying as Pacific, and a staggering total overseas-born population of 40 percent (compared with an 18 percent average elsewhere). The city also has by far the highest Asian population, at 23 percent, and nearly 30 percent of Aucklanders speak more than one language.

MAORI

As of June 2017, New Zealand's Maori population was estimated at 734,200, up 1.5 percent from the previous year. Though Maori and Pakeha generally live, work, and socialize side-by-side, with Maori also well represented across the social spectrum, even having served as governors-general, they are still statistically more likely than Pakeha to suffer a raw deal in terms of health care, housing, income, and legal justice.

Political groups and organizations such as the Maori Party have been founded in recent years to fight from the indigenous corner, while there has also been a genuine movement by a significant proportion of the Pakeha and Maori population to embrace and learn more of Maoritanga—the embodiment of Maori traditions, arts, and language. Even on non-Maori channels, newsreaders and television presenters will, for example, usually welcome and say farewell to their audiences in the Maori language, Te Reo.

LANGUAGE

There are three official languages: English, Te Reo Maori, and New Zealand Sign Language. English is by far the most used language, and all Maori are fluent in it.

For centuries, Te Reo was an oral

language, until European missionaries arrived in the 19th century and transcribed it, generally phonetically, making it relatively easy to pronounce. It is spoken in a melodic fashion, with five vowels being the same as English: *a* is pronounced as in "bar"; *e* as in "jest"; *i* as in "flee"; *o* as "awe," not "oh"; and *u* as in "due." Vowel sounds are sometimes lengthened, signified in writing by a macron or occasionally with a pair of the letters instead of just one.

There are eight regular consonants—*h, k, m, n, p, r, t, w*—and no letter *s*, meaning, for example, the plural of Maori is still Maori. The letter *r* should not be rolled, but rather pronounced closer to an *l*, with the tongue pushed toward the front of the mouth, and the *t* is closer in sound to a *d*. The grouping *ng* counts as a consonant, pronounced like the sound in "singer," and the consonant grouping *wh* is pronounced as *f*—this is an important one for visitors, as many places retain their Maori monikers and also begin with *wh*. But don't worry if you do mispronounce place names; people will not take offense, and will certainly know what, or where, you mean.

As Pakeha society became more embedded in New Zealand in the late 19th and early 20th centuries, Te Reo suffered, and was often suppressed. Even many Maori elders encouraged their youngsters to concentrate more on the English language, fearing they would otherwise be held back. In 1974, Te Reo was recognized as an official New Zealand language, and in 2016, an organization called Te Matawai was established under the Maori Language Act 2016 to promote the language on behalf of indigenous peoples. There are Maori television and radio stations, but numbers of Te Reo speakers are worryingly low, and there are genuine concerns for the future of the language. Current figures put the number of fluent Te Reo speakers at less than 130,000—just 3 percent of the population—but there are more than 300,000 kids studying at schools, and a further 10,000 in higher education.

Both Maori and Pakeha regularly drop the occasional Te Reo word or expression into everyday conversation, such as *kia ora* for "hello," or *whanau* when discussing family.

VISUAL ARTS

The most significant Maori *toi* (artform) are *whakairo* (carvings) mainly of wood, but also *pounamu* (greenstone), bone, and stones. Traditionally, creations should serve either a functional or symbolic purpose, with the most obvious examples being in the intricate designs of *whare whakairo* (meeting houses) and *waka* (canoes), forged from native woods. Each one tells stories passed down through the generations, while carved bones and greenstone are often worn for protection, or as a sign of prestige, as well as being incorporated in weaponry and tools. Historically, only men could train as carvers, while women honed their skills using *harakeke* (native flax) to weave *kete* (baskets) and *whariki* (mats), and natural fibers for the highly prized *whatu kakahu* (cloak-weaving), considered to among the most important of Maori *taonga* (treasures).

Ta moko or Maori tattooing—often of the face, considered the most scared part of the body—is a highly personalized tradition that reflects its wearer's ancestry, standing, and wisdom. It's traditionally done using a tapping hand tool known as an *ihu* that cuts into the skin, allowing ink to be rubbed into the wounds. Nowadays, most opt for a typical tattoo gun.

MUSIC AND DANCE

The *haka* tribal dance is among the best-known of Kiwi traditions, made famous by its performance by the All Blacks at the start of each rugby match. There are many forms of the *haka,* accompanied by chanting and involving the twirling of weaponry, created to display ferocity and instill fear in opposing tribes before battle (or, nowadays, minus the weapons, before sporting events). Today *haka* is used as a celebration of Maori culture during public shows. The *poi* is a dance usually performed by women in which spears are swapped for balls attached to cords that are struck against the body to create a rhythm. Traditional Maori song is known as *waiata-a-ringa* and involves hand movements that symbolize the movement of water, often accompanied by a guitar. Historically, storytelling was also a vital part of Maori culture—as for centuries it was only an oral language.

Essentials

Transportation 507
Visas and Officialdom 511
Recreation 512
Accommodations 513
Health and Safety 515
Travel Tips 516

Transportation

GETTING THERE

Air

Most travelers reach New Zealand by air. As New Zealand's popularity as a holiday destination increases, airfares become more competitive. When booking air travel, remember that the seasons are reversed in the southern hemisphere: The northern hemisphere's winter (November-March) is New Zealand's summer, when fares are at their peak.

New Zealand has four international airports: Auckland and Wellington on the North Island and Christchurch and Queenstown on the South Island.

Auckland Airport (AKL, Ray Emery Dr., 09/275-0789, www.aucklandairport.co.nz) has an international and domestic terminal, and a free terminal transfer bus that operates daily. **Air New Zealand** (09/357-3000, www.airnewzealand.co.nz) is the nation's flagship carrier, serving local and international routes. Check out Air New Zealand's **Grab A Seat** (www.grabaseat.co.nz) for regular discounts on domestic journeys. Low-priced domestic flights can also be consistently secured with **Jetstar** (09/975-9426, www.jetstar.com).

Wellington Airport (WLG, Stewart Duff Dr., 04/385-5100, www.wellingtonairport.co.nz) has domestic flights throughout New Zealand, primarily through Air New Zealand, with connections to Auckland, Christchurch, Taupo, Westport, Picton, Blenheim, and Nelson.

Christchurch Airport (CHC, Durey Rd., 03/353-7777, www.christchurchairport.co.nz) is New Zealand's second-largest airport. It hosts international flights and domestic routes to 15 North Island and South Island destinations through Air New Zealand or Jetstar.

Queenstown Airport (ZQN, Sir Henry Wigley Dr., Frankton, 03/450-9031, www.queenstownairport.co.nz) near downtown Queenstown, has international and domestic flights from Air New Zealand and Jetstar.

From North America

Air New Zealand (www.airnewzealand.co.nz) is the national carrier, connecting New Zealand to airports in Australia, the Pacific Islands, Asia, and North America, as well as Buenos Aires and London. Flights from North America are also operated by **Air Canada** (www.aircanada.com), **American Airlines** (www.americanairlines.com), **Hawaiian Airlines** (www.hawaiianairlines.com), and **United Airlines** (www.united.com).

From South America

Airlines that connect to New Zealand from South America include **Aerolíneas Argentinas** (www.aerolineas.com) and **LATAM** (www.latam.com).

From Europe and Australia

From Europe, **British Airways** (www.britishairways.com), **KLM** (www.klm.com), and **Lufthansa** (www.lufthansa.com) serve New Zealand. Visitors arriving from Australia should consider **Jetstar** (www.jetstar.com), **Qantas** (www.qantas.com), or **Virgin Australia** (www.virginaustralia.com).

From Asia and South Africa

The following airlines offer service to New Zealand from Asia: **Air Asia** (www.airasia.com), **Air China** (www.airchina.com), **ANA** (www.ana.co.jp), **Asiana** (www.flyasiana.com), **Cathay Pacific** (www.cathaypacific.com), **China Airlines** (www.china-airlines.

Previous: a Christchurch tram car; the shuttle to Kelly Tarlton's Sea Life Aquarium.

com), **China Eastern** (www.nz.ceair.com), **China Southern** (www.csair.com), **Emirates** (www.emirates.com), **Etihad** (www.etihad.com), **Hong Kong Airlines** (www.hongkongairlines.com), **Japan Airlines** (www.jal.com), **Korean Air** (www.koreanair.com), **Malaysia Airlines** (www.malaysiaairlines.com), **Philippine Airlines** (www.philippine-airlines.com), **Singapore Airlines** (www.singaporeair.com), and **Thai Airways** (www.thaiairways.com).

South African Airways (www.flysaa.com) serves Auckland, while **Air Calin** (www.nz.aircalin.com), **Air Tahiti Nui** (www.air-tahitinui.com), and **Fiji Airways** (www.fiji-airways.com) link New Zealand to the Pacific Islands.

GETTING AROUND

While navigating the nation is a cinch, there are still corners of New Zealand that are difficult (but not impossible) to reach without a private vehicle. A car is the way to go, however. Road tripping doesn't get much more spectacular than in New Zealand.

Air

Air New Zealand (0800/737-000, www.airnewzealand.co.nz) is the main domestic airline; their sister site, **Grab A Seat** (www.grabaseat.co.nz), offers regular discounts. Low-priced domestic flights can be consistently secured with **Jetstar** (09/975-9426, www.jetstar.com), though they don't serve as many destinations and can be prone to last-minute cancellations.

Other regional airlines with limited routes include **Air Nelson** (03/547-8700, www.airnelson.co.nz), **Golden Bay Air** (03/525-8725, www.goldenbayair.co.nz), and **Stewart Island Air** (03/218-9129, www.stewartislandflights.co.nz).

In addition to the four international airports, **Dunedin Airport** (DUD, Airport Rd., Momona, 03/486-2879, www.dunedinairport.co.nz) offers domestic travel via **Jetstar** (09/975-9426, www.jetstar.com) and **Air New Zealand** (09/357-3000, www.airnewzealand.co.nz).

Train

While the train network is neither vast nor cheap, it is offset by incredibly scenic routes. New Zealand's national train network is operated by the **Great Journeys of New Zealand** (www.greatjourneysofnz.co.nz). The three routes are limited and do not always run daily in both directions. However, the journeys are breathtaking—connecting Auckland to Greymouth via Wellington, Picton, and Christchurch, with numerous stops in between.

From the north, the ***Northern Explorer*** departs Auckland for Wellington, stopping at hot spots such as Otorohanga (near Waitomo Caves) and Tongariro National Park. Trains leave Auckland at 7:45am Monday, Thursday, and Saturday, and depart Wellington at 7:55am (Tuesday, Friday, and Sunday), arriving in Auckland at 6:50pm.

The ***Coastal Pacific*** is bookended by Picton and Christchurch via Kaikoura, with Marlborough Sounds and the Kaikoura Ranges as highlights. Along the way, the Pacific Ocean is rarely far from view. Trains run daily in both directions October-April, leaving Picton at 1:25pm and arriving in Christchurch at 6:45pm. Trains then leave Christchurch at 7am, terminating in Picton at 12:22pm. (The *Coastal Pacific* closed due to damage from the 2016 Kaikoura earthquake. The route is expected to open in 2019.)

The ***TranzAlpine*** is a cinematic trip across the Canterbury Plains and the Southern Alps through Arthur's Pass. Trains depart Christchurch daily, arriving in Greymouth.

Bus

Bus travel is the most flexible form of public transport throughout New Zealand. The national bus networks are superb and well-priced, with plenty of backpacker deals. The reliable **Intercity** (www.intercity.co.nz) operates the country's largest bus network, stopping at the main visitor hot spots on both the North and South Islands, with free Wi-Fi on all buses.

The **Intercity Tiki Tour** ($775 for 8 days) starts in Auckland and ends in Queenstown, stopping en route at the Waitomo Caves, Napier, Wellington, Franz Josef, Mount Cook, and Milford Sound. Shorter journeys include the **Big Fish** ($219, 2 days minimum), which links Auckland and Wellington via Hobbiton and the Geothermal Heartland. The **Alps and Fiords** ($485, 3 days minimum) travels from Christchurch to Queenstown, taking in Milford Sound and Franz Josef with a ride on the *TranzAlpine* train included.

Intercity's FlexiPass ($125 for 15 hours, $459 for 60 hours) enables you to book hours on Intercity buses and pick your destinations at will. You can add to your ticket's hours online. Should there be some leftover hours at the end of your vacation, you can simply sell them. Intercity also offers one-way tickets.

Stray Travel (09/526-2140, www.straytravel.com) is an excellent hop-on, hop-off backpacker bus service with a nationwide network. Buses are driven by knowledgeable (and often humorous) drivers who can also arrange activities and accommodations. Passes are valid for one year and range from the popular **Everywhere** ($1,995 for 31-32 days) ticket, which allows for every stop en route, to shorter options such as **Short Willy** ($675, 12-14 days), which starts in Picton and ends in Christchurch. The **Jack** ($105, 2 days) starts and ends in Auckland. It's a great way to see the country and meet like-minded souls. All buses offer Wi-Fi.

Kiwi Experience (09/336-4286, www.kiwiexperience.com) is the original New Zealand hop-on, hop-off backpacker bus. While the Kiwi services most corners of the country, it doesn't cover Hawke's Bay or Raglan. Passes are valid for 12 months and range from unlimited travel on the **Whole Kit & Caboodle** ($1,522, 30 days) to the **Bay of Islands** ($99, 2 days), a package deal between Auckland and Paihia. Bus drivers can also book tours and accommodations for passengers.

Other backpacker buses with hop-on, hop-off options include **Naked Bus** (09/979-1616, www.nakedbus.com), whose nationwide network includes an overnight sleeper between Auckland and Wellington—saving you one night's lodging. The well-priced **Mana Bus** (09/367-9140, www.manabus.com) only covers the North Island. Its high-end vehicles offer reclining leather seats and free Wi-Fi. They also run a sleeper between Wellington and Auckland, with ticket deals for as low as $1.

Ferry

Crossing the Cook Strait between Picton and Wellington and through the wondrous Marlborough Sounds is one of the country's great voyages. The trip is made by two ferry companies: **Interislander** (www.greatjourneysofnz.co.nz) and **Blue Ridge** (www.blueridge.co.nz). Both offer vehicle and passenger transport.

Car

Compact roads, winding paths, and little traffic (once you leave Auckland) make car travel through New Zealand the ultimate drive. Drivers must possess a current valid driving license, either an International Driving Permit or one from your country of origin. Most car rental companies only rent to drivers who are at least 21 years of age. Roads in New Zealand are generally paved and very well-maintained. Even backcountry gravel roads can be easily navigable, though some may require an SUV or 4WD vehicle. When renting a car, check the terms of the vehicle rental agreement, as many forbid driving on unpaved roads. Some contracts also include a cap on kilometers and charge for each kilometer that exceeds it. Insurance is always included.

The **New Zealand Automobile Association** (AA, www.aa.co.nz) has reciprocal agreements with motoring organizations around the world. The company offers deals on insurance, free maps, tourist guides, and emergency break-down coverage. Consider signing up for an AA Smartfuel card either online or at a BP or Caltex gas station to accumulate points for future fuel savings. The fuel price in New Zealand generally hovers around $2-2.20 per liter.

CAR AND CAMPER VAN RENTAL

Car and camper van hire are popular options. Most car rental companies have offices in main towns and cities, at airports, and at major ferry terminals. International car rental companies include **Budget** (www.budget.co.nz), **Thrifty** (www.thrifty.co.nz), and **Hertz** (www.hertz.co.nz) as well as local firms like **Apex** (www.apexrentals.co.nz), **Omega** (www.omegarentalcars.com), and **Bargain Rental Cars** (www.bargainrentalcars.co.nz). Some companies, such as **Jucy** (www.jucy.co.nz), **Britz** (www.britz.co.nz), and **eCampers** (www.ecampers.co.nz), specialize in camper vans and RVs. Prices vary widely depending on the vehicle size, age, and the season of travel.

In the peak summer season, expect to pay $50-80 per day for a small car and at least $100 per day for a medium-size vehicle. Off-season, rental rates are about half that cost. Camper van rates in summer usually start at around $100 per day for basic (and sometimes older) models. Large RVs or motor home rentals begin around $150 per day. The longer the rental period, the better the price. The website **Compare New Zealand Rental Cars** (www.comparenewzealandrentalcars.com) can help secure the best deals.

For something high-end, **Luxury Rentals** (022/436-5288, www.luxuryrentals.nz) has a fleet of Porsches, Range Rovers, BMWs, Rolls-Royces, and Lamborghinis.

When renting a car, ask about **relocation deals**—you can deliver a rental vehicle from one office to another for a reduced rate. Check the website **Transfercar** (www.transfercar.co.nz) for daily offers.

ROAD RULES

New Zealanders drive *on the left side of the road*. While there's always a divided line, highways often have no center barrier, and with little traffic, it can be easy to absent-mindedly drift into the wrong lane on a long journey. Winding roads mean that distances (given in kilometers) can be deceptive; always allow for extra time. When navigating winding one-lane roads, move over into a slow-vehicle bay to allow drivers to pass. Never cross a solid yellow line when overtaking another vehicle. When approaching a single-lane bridge, look for the small red arrow—this means that you yield to oncoming traffic. Always yield to the right at traffic circles and junctions.

The national speed limit for cars, vans, and motorcycles is 100km/h, and 110km/h for the Tauranga Eastern Link Toll Road and the Cambridge section of the Waikato Expressway. The speed limit is often reduced to 50km/h in urban areas. Cars towing a trailer cannot exceed 90km/h.

For most travelers, it's a *long* flight to New Zealand. You don't want to step straight off the plane and into an unfamiliar vehicle to drive on unfamiliar roads—especially if you live in a country that drives on the right. Upon arrival in New Zealand, plan to spend at least one night in town to get a good rest before hitting the road. Check out **DriveSafe** (www.drivesafe.org.nz) to familiarize yourself with road rules, signs, and etiquette.

Visas and Officialdom

PASSPORTS AND VISAS

A valid passport is required to enter New Zealand. New Zealand has a visa waiver agreement with several nations, including the United States and Canada, which means that tourists may stay for three months. Visitors from the United Kingdom and Australia don't need a visa; British visitors may remain for six months, and Australians indefinitely.

In 2018, the New Zealand government announced that, as of late 2019, visitors would be charged a $25-35 levy, paid through a proposed Electronic Travel Authority (ETA) system, to fund conservation and tourism infrastructure. Australians, Pacific Islanders, and children under age 2 will be exempt from the charge.

Australian, British, American, and Canadian citizens age 12 and older may use e-passports to avoid lengthy customs lines. Use the SmartGates at Auckland, Wellington, Queenstown, and Christchurch airports.

All visitors must provide a return ticket and proof of sufficient funds ($1,000 per month of stay). Extended visas, such as working holidays, should be secured online (www.immigration.govt.nz) prior to arrival.

No vaccinations are required to visit New Zealand.

EMBASSIES AND CONSULATES

Foreign embassies are located in Wellington; consulates are in Auckland.

- U.S. Embassy (29 Fitzherbert Terrace, Wellington, 04/462-6000, www.nz.usembassy.gov)
- U.S. Consulate General (23 Customs St. E., 3rd Fl., Auckland, 09/303-2724)
- Canadian High Commission (125 The Terrace, Level 11, Wellington, 04/473-9577, www.canadainternational.gc.ca)
- Canadian Consulate (48 Emily Place, Level 9, Auckland, 09/309-3690)
- British High Commission (44 Hill St., Wellington, 04/924-2888, www.gov.uk)
- British Consulate General (151 Queen St., Level 17, Auckland, 09/303-2973)
- Australian High Commission (72-76 Hobson St., Wellington, 04/473-6411, www.newzealand.embassy.gov.au)
- Australian Consulate General (186-194 Quay St., Level 7, Auckland, 09/921-8800)

CUSTOMS

New Zealand's **Biosecurity** (www.mpi.govt.nz) is strict. Visitors must declare all food, plants, and animals as well as any tools or equipment. Outdoors and sporting equipment, such as poles and boots, will be checked and cleaned if necessary.

The duty-free allowance is three 1,125ml bottles of spirits or liquor, 4.5 liters of wine, 50 cigarettes or 50g of tobacco or cigars, and $700 worth of goods. Fines are dished out freely when rules are broken.

Recreation

New Zealand's national parks and protected areas account for an astonishing one-third of the country's area. The 13 national parks incorporate diverse landscapes of mountains, forest, glaciers, fiords, and volcanoes and harbor nearly 3,000 species of threatened plants and animals.

HIKING AND BACKPACKING

The main "tramping" (Kiwi for hiking and backpacking) season is October-May. A multitude of hikes can be tackled year-round; however, as altitude and remoteness increase, the walks become more dangerous and are often impassible outside the summer months.

There are approximately 14,000km of public tracks managed by the DoC. These walks fall into five categories:

- **Short Walks** are well-formed, easy walks.
- **Walking Tracks** are longer walks but are still well-formed.
- **Easy Tramping Tracks** are less well-formed but are easily navigable and can be completed in multiple days.
- **Tramping Tracks** are unformed multiday walks. The tracks are lined with directional markers, poles, or cairns.
- **Routes** are strenuous, unformed, multi-day walks with few navigation aids. These should only be tackled by those with excellent backcountry skills.

In addition, there are nine **Great Walks** in New Zealand. These are premier multi-day hikes spread throughout the country (the Whanganui Journey is mainly a river voyage). The construction of a 10th Great Walk is planned through Paparoa National Park on the West Coast.

BIKING

Nga Haerenga—**The New Zealand Cycle Trail** (www.nzcycletrail.com)—is a 2,500km nationwide network of leisurely Great Rides. Nga Haerenga translates as "the journeys," and these scenic off-road trails do just that, following pioneer mining trails and abandoned rail tracks across viaducts, through tunnels, and past swing bridges. Rides range from Grades 1 to 4 across multiple days, or sections of the tracks can be tackled individually. There are also traditional mountain bike rides and downhill tracks in Queenstown and Rotorua.

WATER SPORTS

This island nation is laced with spectacular rivers and mystical lakes where **fishing** is an integral part of life. When renting a kayak or embarking on a coastal cruise, many operators also offer fishing options. You won't have to go far to find a specialized deep-sea fishing charter operating out of most ports, affording the chance to catch big game fish such as tuna, shark, or marlin.

New Zealand's lakes and rivers offer some of the world's finest trout and salmon fishing. The waters around Lake Taupo are especially known for stocks of rainbow trout. Rent equipment and buy fishing licenses from local sports stores. Licenses can also be ordered from Fish and Game New Zealand (www.fishandgame.org.nz); a separate license is required for Lake Taupo.

The **jet-boat** was invented by New Zealander Bill Hamilton at the beginning of the 1960s, so where better to try this exhilarating sport? There's a wealth of options around the country, but the **Shotover Jet** (Shotover Jet Beach, Gorge Rd., Queenstown, 03/442-8570, www.shotoverjet.com), which

Bringing Bungee to the Masses

For centuries, land-diving on Vanuatu's Pentecost Island—involving jumping from raised platforms with vines strapped around the ankles—has been used to test men's mettle, but the first bungee jump to use modern-day materials took place in Britain in 1979 when Oxford University's Dangerous Sports Club, dressed in top hats and tails, jumped from a bridge—and were duly arrested by the police. Inspired by their antics, nine years later Kiwi A. J. Hackett along with Henry van Asch and Chris Allum, founded the world's first commercial bungee jump at Queenstown's Kawarau Bridge. To promote the project, Hackett performed a jump from the Eiffel Tower, and was also arrested, but secured headlines around the globe. The launch of the Kawarau Bridge Bungy is credited with spawning New Zealand's adventure tourism.

reaches speeds of up to 80km/h, is one of the best.

Canoeing and **kayaking** are some of the most fun and popular ways to explore New Zealand's backyard. The Wanganui River is one of the best places on North Island; on South Island, make for the marine reserve of Abel Tasman National Park. New Zealand's most famous **surfing** spot is Raglan, on Waikato's west coast. Ample year-round breaks are also found off New Plymouth, the Bay of Plenty, and Gisborne.

Crystal-clear marine reserves are alive with curious fish and colorful coral. This, coupled with some fascinating wrecks, make the Kiwi coastal waters a **snorkeling** and **scuba diving** paradise. Don't miss the easily accessible Goat Island Marine Reserve or Poor Knights Islands. If you're feeling especially daring, dive the black waters of Milford Sound.

BUNGEE JUMPING

Queenstown is the site of the very first commercial jump at the 43m Kawerau Suspension Bridge, You can also test your mettle on the Nevis Bungy, New Zealand's highest bungee jump at 143m.

SPECTATOR SPORTS

Kiwis are crazy about watching sports. During the winter months, the national **rugby** (www.nzrugby.co.nz) team, the **All Blacks,** dominate the headlines. **Cricket** (www.nzcricket.co.nz) fills in over the summer months. Matches take place at stadiums around the country; tickets are available through **Ticketek** (www.ticketek.co.nz).

Accommodations

New Zealand offers an excellent range of accommodations for any budget—from quirky boutiques to farm stays. Many campgrounds come with million-dollar views, and some are even free. Travelers arriving outside the peak tourist season can expect better deals on lodging. When booking accommodations, look for the **Qualmark logo** (New Zealand Tourism's mark of quality) on hotel websites or in lodging windows to ensure they've received an official stamp of approval.

HOSTELS

New Zealand hostels (known as "backpackers") are of an exceptionally high standard. Dorm stays range $20-35 per night, single rooms are $50-80, and double rooms are $70-100.

Some of the best hostels are affiliated with charitable organization **YHA New Zealand** (0800/278-299, www.yha.co.nz). Sign up online for a 10 percent discount on hostel rooms, plus deals on DoC huts and other travel savings. A YHA memberships start at $25 for one year (for those age 18 and under, membership is free).

BBH (03/379-3014, www.bbh.co.nz, membership $45) is a network of individual hostels around the country. Order their BBH Club Card online, or pick one up at the Auckland Airport, i-SITE Visitor Centres, or at any BBH hostel. BBH members receive discounted stays at BBH hostels, plus discounts on activities, services, and transport, including Auckland ferries and the Cook Strait crossing. To find a BBH hostel, check online or look for the blue BBH sign in hostel windows across the country.

HOTELS AND MOTELS

Hotels range from quirky accommodations above historic pubs to modern, national, or international chains and independent boutiques. Prices run the gamut from budget to high-end, but most begin around $150 per night.

Slightly more affordable, motels can be secured for as little as $100 for a studio room and up to $300 for a two- or three-bedroom apartment. Motels are always fully self-contained and often include Sky TV and communal facilities such as a gym and a swimming pool.

B&BS AND FARM STAYS

Bed-and-breakfasts across the country are often housed in comfortable and charming historic villas where amiable owners create a home-away-from-home feel. Most are usually priced $100-300 per night. The term "B&B," however, may also apply to exclusive lodges in discreet stunning locations where the overnight cost may run into the thousands.

Farm stays are essentially rural B&Bs, idyllic settings where visitors can experience authentic Kiwi country life. These offer an excellent value at around $100-200 per night.

CAMPSITES AND HOLIDAY PARKS

New Zealand appeals to campers. High-quality private holiday parks (or motor camps) are positioned throughout the country and offer an abundance of amenities, such as games rooms, kayak rentals, pools, barbecues, and lounges. There are five levels of DoC campsites:

- **Basic** sites (free) come with a toilet. Drinking water must be treated or boiled.
- **Backcountry** campsites (adults $6, children $3) come with picnic tables, cooking shelters, and trash bins.
- **Standard** campsites (adults $8, children $4) have picnic tables, cooking shelters, trash bins, cold showers, and barbecues.
- **Scenic** campsites (adults $13, children $6.50) have amenities similar to standard campsites, but feature better locations and may have powered sites (adults $3, children $1.50).
- **Serviced** sites (adults $18, children $9) have flush toilets, fireplaces, laundry facilities, and hot showers.

Freedom campsites (designated public camping areas) sometimes have public sewage disposal, trash bins, and toilets; however, you could wind up with a $200 fine for parking or pitching somewhere illegally.

For tips on where to camp and how to camp responsibly, visit two useful websites: **Freedom Camping** (http://freedomcamping.org) and **Camper Mate** (www.campermate.co.nz), which also has an excellent mobile app.

TRAIL HUTS

There are nearly 1,000 backcountry trail huts maintained by DoC. Trail huts are raised wooden cabins strung along hiking trails and are generally only accessible to backpackers. Size and standards vary depending on the trail. Standard huts may have bunks with mattresses (no bedding), wood burners, running water, and toilets; posher offerings may have hot showers, flush toilets, solar lighting, and electric stoves. Some huts must be booked in advance, while others are first-come, first-served.

Trail huts fall into four categories:

- **Basic** huts (free) provide shelter but have little in the way of facilities, if any.
- **Standard** huts are equipped with bunk beds and mattresses, a toilet, drinking water, and wood-burners if the hut is below the bush line.
- **Serviced** huts may have cooking facilities (with no utensils) and a warden.
- **Great Walk** huts have cooking facilities and a warden and may be equipped with solar lighting.

Prices for the Standard, Serviced, and Great Walk huts vary according to the popularity of the walk and the season. Book ahead (www.doc.govt.nz) for Great Walk huts. Bring your own sleeping bag for all overnight stays.

Health and Safety

Ozone and **pollution levels** are low in New Zealand, which means harmful UV rays get through. Skin cancer rates in New Zealand are among the world's highest. Bring and use sunscreen.

MEDICAL SERVICES

There is a high standard of medical care in New Zealand. Visitors are covered for accidents by the **Accident Compensation Corporation** (www.acc.co.nz), but it is recommended that you have your own health insurance. New Zealand provider **Southern Cross** (www.scti.co.nz) offers insurance for overseas visitors. Over-the-counter medicines can be bought throughout the country, but antibiotics and birth control pills require a doctor's prescription. If bringing medications into New Zealand, leave them in the original packaging and bring a doctor's note.

For more details about New Zealand's health care system, consult **Healthline** (0800/611-116, www.health.govt.nz).

WILDERNESS SAFETY

Although the New Zealand waterways may look pristine enough to drink, do not drink water without boiling or filtering it first. Tap water is safe throughout the country.

When venturing into the bush, plan your route and check the weather; conditions change quickly, especially at high altitude. Carry extra layers, a hat, and a waterproof shell and pants. Other essentials include sunscreen, a first-aid kit, a flashlight (bring spare batteries), a whistle, food, and 2-3 liters of water. If you've never worn crampons or used an ice ax, avoid solo alpine hikes during winter. Depending on the length of your excursion, other essentials may include a portable stove and fuel, a survival kit, a sleeping bag, a tent, and a map and compass. Always tell someone of your plans, and when you intend to return.

Cell phone coverage can be nonexistent in the backcountry; consider buying a personal locator beacon. These can rented for as little as $15 per day. For a nationwide list of rental places, visit www.locatorbeacons.co.nz. **AdventureSmart** (www.adventuresmart.org.nz) can provide tips on navigating New Zealand's adventure activities safely—you can also leave your itinerary on the site. Those doing multiday hikes should fill in the DoC hut books en route; if you become lost, it will help speed up the search and rescue.

Travel Tips

WHAT TO PACK

Even in the height of summer, rainfall in New Zealand can reach biblical proportions. Pack a decent waterproof shell or jacket and warm layers (fleece and thermals) in case the notoriously capricious climate takes a turn for the worse. Sturdy footwear is a must if you plan on tackling any trails. While most dining and socializing is "dress casual," it's wise to pack a nice shirt or dress should you venture somewhere upscale. Dress codes rarely run much stricter than "no shorts."

MONEY

New Zealand currency is the dollar, available at exchange kiosks, international airports, and banks. Most banks are open 9am-4:30pm Monday-Friday; in some cities, bank hours extend to late at night or on weekends. ATMs are available throughout the country and are usually accessible 24 hours daily. Most stores, bars, and restaurants accept international debit and credit cards, referred to as EFTPOS (Electronic Funds Transfer at Point Of Sale). Tips, while not expected, are always welcome. New Zealand's goods and services tax (GST) is 15 percent and is always included in the price.

COMMUNICATIONS

New Zealand's country code is 64. To make an international call from New Zealand, dial 00 followed by the country code (without the national 0 prefix). To call within New Zealand, dial the full area code with the 0 prefix. Calls within New Zealand that begin 0800 are toll-free, but won't work with overseas SIM cards.

For emergencies, dial 111. For the local operator, dial 010, and for the international operator, dial 0170. New Zealand's directory assistance is available at 018; international directory assistance is at 0172. Public pay phones accept phone cards and credit cards and, occasionally, coins.

New Zealanders refer to cell phones as mobiles or mobile phones. Two of the main cell phone network operators are **2degrees** (www.2degreesmobile.co.nz) and **Vodafone** (www.vodafone.co.nz). Most international visitors will find it cheaper to invest in a prepaid New Zealand SIM card during their stay. Vodafone stores sell Travel SIMs preloaded with local and international minutes as well as data, or opt for a data-only SIM; 2degrees dishes out free traveler SIMs at 300 locations around the country, including their stores, hostels, and visitors centers.

Most Internet in the country is broadband, and many accommodations include free Wi-Fi, as do cafés, bars, and restaurants. Public libraries and i-SITE Visitor Information Centres provide free Internet access. Most cities, and some towns, have wireless hot spots with a complimentary connection, though a time cap may apply. Internet access can be slow to nonexistent in remote locations—even in urban areas, access is not as fast as many international visitors are accustomed to.

TOURISM OFFICES

New Zealand's 80-plus network of superb tourist offices are called **i-SITE Visitor Centres** (www.newzealand.com), scattered throughout the country. Any i-SITE can help book tours and accommodations locally and nationwide, as well as offer advice on weather and safety. Visitors also have access to free Wi-Fi as well as phone and laptop charging stations.

You may find a **Department of Conservation** (DoC, www.doc.govt.nz) incorporated within an i-SITE, but DoC usually has its own visitors center, staffed by rangers. DoC centers offer a wealth of information on hikes, weather, and track conditions. Some offices double as small museum and nature centers, where you can also book trail huts and campsites.

MAPS

The i-SITE Visitor Centres and DoC offices provide an extensive range of maps for a nominal cost. The **AA** (www.aa.co.nz) also provides free maps in booklets, brochures, and online.

WEIGHTS AND MEASURES

New Zealand adheres to the metric system. The power supply is 230-240 volts, 50 hertz AC via a three-prong flat-pin plug. Australian appliances may be used, but British ones will require a socket adapter (available from airports, online, and travel stores). North American appliances will require an adapter and sometimes a transformer.

New Zealand's time zone is GMT plus 13 hours. From the last Sunday in September to the first Sunday in April, the country switches to daylight savings time (GMT plus 12 hours).

ACCESS FOR TRAVELERS WITH DISABILITIES

A vast number of accommodations, sights, bars, restaurants, and transport services are wheelchair-accessible. Many of the walking tracks also offer wheelchair access.

Oyster (www.oysternz.co.nz) and **First Port** (www.firstport.co.nz) offer detailed information on accommodations, activities, equipment hire, and transport for travelers with disabilities or impairment issues. They also offer a booking service for disabled travelers. Other resources include **Disabled Snowsports NZ** (www.disabledsnowsports.org.nz); the **Blind Foundation** (www.blindfoundation.org.nz); **Accessible New Zealand** Tours (www.accessiblenz.com); and the **National Foundation for the Deaf** (www.nfd.org.nz).

TRAVELING WITH CHILDREN

Volcanoes, mud pools, theme parks, wildlife, water sports, beaches, parks, and bike tracks—there's plenty to keep the kids entertained in New Zealand. Most attractions offer discounted tickets for children and families; children under age five are often admitted for free. Accommodations that cater to families tend to include motels and holiday parks, which usually have pools and play areas. B&Bs are often adults-only.

For family-friendly trip-planning tips and resources, visit any i-SITE center or the following websites: www.kidsnewzealand.com, www.kidsfriendlytravel.com, and www.kidspot.co.nz.

LGBT TRAVELERS

Much of New Zealand—especially the sizeable communities of Wellington and Auckland—is welcoming to gay, lesbian, bisexual, and transgender visitors and residents. Smaller towns and rural villages may be less liberal but are unlikely to manifest open hostility.

In 2013, New Zealand became one of the first countries to legalize same-sex marriage; the age of consent is 16. Notable LGBT events include the **Auckland Pride Festival** (www.aucklandpridefestival.org.nz, Feb.) and Queenstown's **Gay Ski Week** (www.gayskiweekqt.com, Sept.). For LGBY-friendly venues and attractions, pick up a free issue of the ***Gay Express*** (www.gayexpress.co.nz). Useful websites include: www.gaytourismnewzealand.com, www.gaynz.net.nz, and www.lesbian.net.nz.

Resources

Glossary

COMMON WORDS AND PHRASES

abseiling: rappelling

All Blacks: New Zealand's legendary rugby union

Anzac: The combined Australia and New Zealand Army Corps that fought together. Anzac Day (April 25) is an important public holidays honoring of the countries' military personnel.

bach: a holiday home by the sea; pronounced "batch"

barbie: barbecue

beehive: nickname for New Zealand's oddly shaped Parliament House

bloke: a man

bogan: a derogatory term for an undesirable bloke

boozer: a bar

bludger: a lazy or untrustworthy person

bonnet: car hood

boot: car trunk

bro/bru: term of endearment like pal, mate, or brother

bush: the backcountry

BYO: eateries that allow you to "bring your own" wine (or beer) for a fee

chilly bin: an ice box for keeping food chilled

chocka: full, as in "that bar is chocka"

choice: great or awesome, as in "that car is choice"

chook: chicken

chur: thanks (informal)

crib: a holiday home by the sea; sometimes used instead of "bach" and more common on South Island

crook: ill

cuppa: cup of tea or coffee

cuz: used in lieu of "bro;" can also mean "cousin"

dairy: small, local grocery or convenience store

Domain: public park or grassy reserve

dorkland: South Islanders' nickname for Auckland

ditch: nickname for the Tasman Sea, which separates New Zealand and Australia (i.e., "across the ditch")

DoC: Department of Conservation

dunny: toilet

dustbin: trash can or rubbish bin

duvet: quilt or comforter

entrée: starter or appetizer; never the main meal

Eftpos: credit or debit card payment option in stores, bars and eateries

feijoa: a sweet, fragrant fruit

fizzy drink: soda or pop

flat white: similar to a latte, but stronger and with less milk

footie: used as a reference to rugby rather than soccer

footpath: sidewalk or pavement

fridge: refrigerator

Godzone: short for "God's own country;" used to denote the majesty of New Zealand

glad wrap: a brand of plastic cling wrap; used as a verb, as in "glad-wrap the sandwiches"

greenstone: a type of jade

gumboots: rubber boots for rain and mud

hoon: *see* bogan

JAFA: "just another f***ing Aucklander"

jandals: flip-flops

kiwi: New Zealand's iconic bird
Kiwi: a New Zealander
kiwifruit: a type of sweet, delicious gooseberry (never abbreviate to "kiwi")
laughing gear: mouth
lollies: candy
long drop: an outdoor pit toilet often found at basic campsites
OE: overseas experience (Many Kiwis in their late teens or early 20s take a year off to travel abroad.)
pavlova: a meringue-based dessert
piss: beer
pissed: drunk
pissed off: annoyed
Poms: Brits
post code: zip code
post shop: post office
sealed road: paved or tarmacked road
serviette: napkin
she'll be right: "don't worry about it"
skint: broke, no money
skull: drink quickly, as in a shot or beer
snag/snarler: sausage
sweet: often, "sweet as;" used to express agreement or describe something cool
tea: the drink or an evening meal
togs: swimwear
tramping: hiking
trundler: shopping cart
ute: pick-up truck
wop-wops: middle of nowhere
yeah, nah: Sometimes "yes", sometimes "no", sometimes "maybe." You'll figure it out. Maybe.

COMMON MAORI WORDS AND PHRASES

Aoraki: Maori name for New Zealand's tallest peak, Mount Cook (translates as "cloud piercer")
Aotearoa: Maori name for New Zealand, "the land of the long white cloud"
Ariki: chief
aroha: compassion
hāngī: a traditional Maori feast cooked in the earth
haka: war dance
hapū: sub-tribe or clan
Haere mai!: welcome or enter
Hei konā rā: goodbye
iwi: tribe
kai: food
Karanga: the calling ceremony that welcomes guests to the marae
Ka kite anō: see you later or see you soon
Kia ora: hello, hi, cheers
kūmara: sweet potato
mana: authority, reputation, or power
manuhiri: guests
Marae: a communal or sacred place for meetings
Mōrena: good morning
Pākehā: used to denote New Zealanders of European origin
pounamu: a type of jade or greenstone
tamariki: children
tāne: man
tangata whenua: local people or hosts
tapu: sacred
taonga: treasured or precious goods
Tēnā koe/kōrua/koutou: formal greeting
wāhine: woman
waka: canoe
whānau: extended, or non-nuclear family
wharepaku: toilet
whenua: homeland, or country

The following words are often used as place names. A good example is *Aotearoa,* which roughly translates as "the land of the long white cloud."

Ao: cloud
Arā: road or path
Awa: river
Iti: small
Kai: used to signify a plentiful food source (for example, crayfish-rich Kaikoura uses *koura,* which is crayfish)
Manga: stream
Mania: plain
Maunga: mountain
Moana: sea
Motu: island
Nui: big
O: when a place begins with an O, it means "the place of ..."

One: sand, or earth
Pā: a fortified village
Pae: ridge or range
Papa: flat
Poto: short
Puke: hill
Roa: long
Rōtō: lake
Te: the
Tai: coast or tide
Wai: water
Whanga: harbor or bay

Suggested Reading

HISTORY AND CULTURE

Belich, James. *The New Zealand Wars.* New York, NY: Penguin, 1998. An account of the 19th century conflicts between Maori and the British Crown.

Braunia, Steve. *Civilisation: Twenty Places on the Edge of the World.* Wellington: Awa Press, 2013. A collection of true-life tales of New Zealanders living in some of the nation's most remote regions.

Druett, Joan. *Tupaia.* Santa Barbara, CA: Praeger, 2010. The story of Tupaia, Captain Cook's Polynesian navigator who facilitated meetings with Maori.

King, Michael. *The Penguin History of New Zealand.* New York, NY: Penguin, 2012. A fabulous collection of everything from Maori oral tales to colonization and the modern age by one of New Zealand's most revered historians.

King, Michael. *Wrestling with the Angel: A life of Janet Frame.* Berkeley, CA: Counterpoint, 2002. A biography of one of New Zealand's most beloved authors and the subject of the Jane Campion film, *An Angel at My Table.*

Orange, Claudia. *The Treaty of Waitangi.* Crows Nest, AU: Allen & Unwin, 1996. The definitive guide to New Zealand's founding document.

Salmond, Anne. *Two Worlds: First Meetings Between Maori and Europeans, 1642–1772.* Honolulu, HI: University of Hawaii Press, 1992. An examination of early encounters between Maori and Western explorers.

Tindale, Jonathan. *Squashed Possums: Off the Beaten Track in New Zealand.* North Charleston, SC: CreateSpace, 2015. A narrative of Tindale's time living in a lone caravan in the New Zealand bush.

Tunney, Susan C. *Do they Speak English Down There?* North Charleston, SC: CreateSpace, 2016. A comical and insightful account of a California family's move Down Under.

NATURE

Crowe, Andrew. *Which Native Tree?* New York, NY: Penguin, 2009. A beginner's guide to New Zealand's native trees, with illustrations, maps, and the origins of Maori names.

Eagle, Audrey. *Eagle's Complete Trees and Shrubs of New Zealand.* Wellington: Te Papa Press, 2006. A beautifully illustrated and wonderfully personal account of the nation's plantlife.

Fitter, Julian. *Bateman Field Guide to Wild New Zealand.* Auckland: David Bateman Limited, 2010. An overview of New Zealand's flora, fauna, and geothermal landscape.

Heather, Barrie, Robertson, Hugh, and Onley, Derek. Princeton, NJ: Princeton University, 2012. *The Field Guide to the Birds of New*

Zealand. An informative classic with intricate color paintings.

Hunt, Janet. *Wetlands of New Zealand: A Bittersweet Story.* New York, NY: Random House, 2007. Everything you need to know about the nation's wetland areas and the flora and fauna that inhabitant them.

Roxburgh, Gus. *Wild About New Zealand.* New York, NY: Random House, 2013. A stunning photography collection of New Zealand's national and marine parks, with accompanying text.

RECREATION

Barnett, Shaun. *Tramping in New Zealand.* Nelson: Potton & Burton, 2015. A detailed guide to 40 of New Zealand's most popular treks, with maps and photos.

Hillary, Edmund. *View from the Summit.* New York, NY: Gallery Books, 2000. A memoir by Sir Edmund Hillary, the first man (along with Nepali Sherpa Tenzig Norgay) to climb Mount Everest.

Kennett Brothers. *Classic New Zealand Cycle Trails.* Wellington: Kennett Brothers, 2012. A comprehensive list of New Zealand's Great Rides and scenic cycle trails, with maps and suggested accommodations.

Morse, Peter B. *Wavetrack New Zealand Surfing Guide.* Wavetrack, 2004. A guide to New Zealand's best surf spots, with maps, access details, and gorgeous photos.

Romanos, Joseph. *New Zealand's Top 100 Sports History-Makers.* Wellington: Trio Books, 2016. An introduction to the country's finest athletes since the 20th century.

FICTION

Catton, Eleanor: *The Luminaries.* New York, NY: Back Bay Books, 2014. This epic thriller, set in Hokitika in 1866 at the height of the gold-rush, won the Man Booker Prize.

Cross, Ian. *The God Boy.* New York, NY: Penguin, 2003. A haunting story set in rural New Zealand about a 13-year-old boy raised in a strict Catholic household.

Crump, Barry. *A Good Keen Man.* Wellington: Hodder Moa Beckett, 1997. An amusing Kiwi classic about a young lad's exploits in the bush, accompanied by loyal dogs and some rather peculiar hunters.

Gee, Maurice. *Plumb.* London, UK: Faber & Faber, 1978. A great of the Kiwi literary cannon, Plumb follows the life of a devout yet tortured and self-destructive clergyman.

Grace, Patricia. *Potiki.* Honolulu, HI: University of Hawaii Press, 1995. This tale pits a small coastal Maori community against a wealthy property developer who seeks to redevelop their land.

Hulme, Keri. *The Bone People.* New York, NY: Penguin, 1986. This Booker Prize-winning novel includes a collection of colorful West Coast characters of European and Maori descent.

Ihimaera, Witi. *Pounamu Pounamu.* New York, NY: Penguin, 2008. A collection of short stories from a leading indigenous author about Maori life and culture in the 1960s.

Jones, Lloyd. *Mister Pip.* New York, NY: Penguin, 2008. A teacher on a war-ravaged Pacific Island reads Dickens' *Great Expectations* to his students.

Mansfield, Katherine. *The Garden Party and Other Stories.* New York, NY: Ecco, 2016. A collection of short stories with an unrivaled perception for the human condition.

Internet Resources

ACCOMMODATIONS

Budget Backpacker Hostels New Zealand
www.bbh.co.nz
A collection of hostels around the country, with travel and booking information. App available.

Camper Mate
www.campermate.co.nz
A free app with a comprehensive list of campgrounds, plus road maps and directions.

Holiday Parks New Zealand
www.holidayparks.co.nz
A collection campgrounds and holiday parks. The free app includes local visitor centers, gas stations, and more.

New Zealand Bed & Breakfast
www.bnb.co.nz
A comprehensive list of the nation's B&Bs, including current deals.

Top 10 Holiday Parks
www.top10.co.nz
A nationwide network of holiday parks with member discounts for camping, accommodations, and the Interislander ferry.

YHA New Zealand
www.yha.co.nz
The New Zealand branch of Hostelling International, with budget accommodations, travel and transport advice, maps, and booking services. App available.

ENTERTAINMENT

Eventfinder
www.eventfinda.co.nz
A guide to concerts, plays, festivals and other performances with a ticket booking service.

Neat Places
www.neatplaces.co.nz
An updated list of the coolest places to eat, drink, dance, or shop. App available.

TRANSPORTATION

AA Travel
www.aatravel.co.nz
The website of the New Zealand Automobile Association (AA).

Air New Zealand
www.airnewzealand.com
The website of New Zealand's national airline.

Blue Ridge
www.blueridge.co.nz
Vehicle and passenger ferry service between Wellington and Picton.

Fullers
www.fullers.co.nz
Fullers operates ferry, coach, and guided tours in North Island.

Grab A Seat
www.grabaseat.co.nz
Check for daily deals on discounted Air New Zealand flights.

Great Journeys of New Zealand
www.greatjourneysofnz.co.nz
The tourism division of national train operator Kiwi Rail (includes the TranzAlpine, Northern Explorer and Coastal Pacific routes, as well as the Interislander Ferry).

InterCity Coachlines
www.intercity.co.nz
The most expansive coach network across the country.

Interislander
www.greatjourneysofnz.co.nz/interislander
Vehicle and passenger ferry service across the Cook Strait between Wellington and Picton.

Jet Star
www.jetstar.com/nz
The New Zealand arm of the Australian budget airline, with regular deals on domestic flights.

Real Journeys
www.realjourneys.co.nz
Real Journeys operates bus, coach, and ferry services along with scenic flights and guided tours on South Island.

Cars and Campervans

Backpacker Car World
www.backpackercarworld.com
Backpacker Car World has some of the best deals around to buy or rent a vehicle.

Trade Me
www.trademe.co.nz
Use Trade Me to buy, sell, or trade items direct person-to-person. It's especially useful for used cars and campervans.

VTNZ
www.vtnz.co.nz
VTNZ offer pre-purchase vehicle inspections with branches all over the country.

RECREATION

100% Pure New Zealand
www.newzealand.com
New Zealand's official tourist website.

Adventure Smart
www.adventuresmart.org.nz
An online forum where backcountry visitors can leave information about their trip and expected return time.

Bookme
www.bookme.co.nz
The place to go for last minute deals on sights and activities.

Fish and Game New Zealand
www.fishandgame.org.nz
Learn about fishing and hunting regulations and about the various fish species and their habitat.

MetService
www.metservice.co.nz
Up-to-date, reliable weather forecasts including tides and snow reports. App available.

Mountain Safety
www.mountainsafety.org.nz
Advice on how to stay safe in the backcountry.

Sherpa Surf Guide
www.sherpasurfguide.com
A must-have app for surfers to find the best waves anywhere at any given time.

GOVERNMENT

Department of Conservation
www.doc.govt.nz
The Department of Conservation (DoC) manages all national parks and a wealth of public spaces. Book huts or campsites online, check trail and weather conditions, and download maps and brochures.

New Zealand Government
www.govt.nz
The official government website for visas and customs regulations.

Te Ara Encyclopedia of New Zealand
www.teara.govt.nz
A comprehensive guide to New Zealand.

Index

A

Abbey Caves: 97-98
Abel Tasman Coast Track: 26, 331-333
Abel Tasman National Park: 331-334; map 332
Academy Cinema: 58
Academy Gold Cinema: 356
accessibility: 517
accommodations: 513-515
Agrodome: 177
Agroventures: 181
Ahipara: 116, 119-120
Ah Reed Memorial Park: 97
Aigantighe Art Gallery: 381-382
Air Force Museum: 354
air travel: 507-508
Akaroa: 27, 364-367; map 365
Akaroa Lighthouse: 364-365
Akaroa Museum: 365
Albert Park: 38
Alexandra: 444
Alex Knob Track: 404
All Blacks (rugby): 52, 262, 513
Alps2Ocean Cycle Trail: 27, 379
Ambury Monument Walk: 251
America's Cup: 49
amusement/theme parks: 52, 181
animals: 496-497
Aniwaniwa Falls Track: 225
Antrim House: 272
Aoraki Mackenzie International Dark Sky Reserve: 372
Aoraki/Mount Cook National Park: 27, 376-380; map 377
Aoraki/Mount Cook Village: 376-377
Aotea Square: 24, 38
aquariums: 44, 45, 228
Aranui Cave: 145
Araroa Walkway: 102
Arataki Honey Visitor Centre: 235
Aratoi-Wairarapa Museum of Art and History: 296
Army Bay: 85
Arrowtown: 432-434
art deco architecture: 226, 228, 229
Arthur's Pass National Park: 367-371; map 368
Arthur's Pass Road: 367-368
Arts Centre: 349
ASB Waterfront Theatre: 57
Astro Café: 27, 372, 373
ATMs: 516
Auckland: 24, 34-78; maps 37, 39, 41
Auckland Art Gallery: 38
Auckland Blues (rugby): 52
Auckland Botanic Gardens: 47
Auckland Museum: 31, 41-42, 45
Auckland Philharmonic Orchestra: 57
Auckland Rugby: 52
Auckland Theatre Company: 57
Auckland Town Hall: 38
Auckland Zoo: 45
aurora australis: 479
Avalanche Peak: 368
Awanui: 120
Awaroa Beach: 333

B

ballooning: 363
Banks Peninsula: 27, 364-367; map 367
Banks Track: 365
Basement Theatre: 57
Bats Theatre: 281
Bay of Islands: 25, 103-116; map 104
Bay of Islands Vintage Railway: 103
Bay of Plenty: 160-170; map 161
beer/breweries: 18, 26, 280
Ben Lomond Track: 421
Bethells Beach: 83
bicycling: 27, 311, 328-329, 379, 445-446, 512
Big Totara Walk: 478
Bill Richardson Transport World: 480
birds/bird-watching: 496-497
Birdwoods: 235
Blackball: 397
Black Beach Walk: 225
Black Caps (cricket): 52
Blaketown Beach: 395
Blenheim: 316-318
Blokart Recreation Park: 166
Blue Lake: 341
Blue Lakes and Tasman Glacier View Walk: 377
Blue Lake Track: 183
Blue Pools: 412
Bluff: 484-485
Bluff Maritime Museum: 484
Bluff Oyster Festival: 485
Bonz 'n Stonz: 399
botanical gardens/arboretums: 47, 95, 218, 276, 349, 382
Botanical Hill: 324
Botanica Whangarei: 95
Botanic Garden (Wellington): 26, 276

Box Car Cave: 391
Brancott Estate: 318
Bream Head Scenic Reserve: 98
Bridal Veil Falls: 142
Bridge to Nowhere: 260
Britomart: 24, 45, 54
Brod Bay: 467
Buller Gorge: 342-343
bungee jumping: 27, 28, 50, 196, 419, 421, 513
Bushy Beach: 446
bus travel: 508-509
Butterfly Garden (Thames): 151
BYO service: 64

C

Cable Car Museum: 275
Cambridge: 139-140
camper vans: 510
camping: 514
Canterbury: 29, 344-382; map 346-347
Canterbury Museum: 349
canyoneering: 29; see also caves/caverns
Cape Egmont: 254
Cape Foulwind: 386
Cape Kidnappers: 236-237
Cape Palliser: 299
Cape Reinga: 121-123
Cardrona Alpine Resort: 436-437
car travel: 509-510
Cathedral Caves: 487
Cathedral Cove: 157
Catlins Coast: 486-488
Catlins River-Wisp Loop Track: 486
caves/caverns: 14, 25, 29, 144-147, 388
Central Otago: 443-446
Chapman-Taylor house: 245
Charming Creek Walkway: 391
Chasm, the: 473
Cheltenham Beach: 47
children, traveling with: 517
Chinese Community: 433
Christchurch: 26-27, 349-361; maps 350-351, 353
Christ Church (Russell): 106
Christchurch and Canterbury: 344-382; map 346-347
Christchurch Art Gallery: 349
Christchurch Botanic Gardens: 27, 349
Christ Church Cathedral: 324
Christchurch Gondola: 352, 354
churches/temples: 43, 106, 245, 260, 274, 324, 352, 372, 452
Church of the Good Shepherd: 372
Circa Theatre: 281
Circle Loop Walk: 314
Civic Theater: 57
Clapham's National Clock Museum: 95
Clarence St. Theatre: 136
Classic Comedy Club: 58
Clay Cliffs Scenic Reserve: 375
Clendon House: 125
Cleopatra's Pool: 333
Clevedon Village: 84
Clifden: 477
climate: 493-494
Coaltown Museum: 387
Coca Cola Lake: 117
Collingwood: 337-338
Collingwood Museum: 337
Colonial Cottage Museum: 272
Colville: 155
communications: 516
Cook Monument: 218
Cooks Cove Walkway: 217
Copland Track: 409-410
Cornwall Park: 46
Coromandel Coastal Walkway: 155
Coromandel Peninsula: 151-160; map 152
Coromandel Town: 153-155
Coronet Peak: 424
Court Theatre: 356
Crater Lake: 204
Craters of the Moon: 193
Crazy Paving Cave: 391
Creek Mangrove Forest Boardwalk: 109
Cromwell: 443-444
Cromwell Heritage Precinct: 443
Croydon Aviation Heritage Centre: 483
culture, local: 503-505
Curio Bay: 487-488
Curly Tree Whitebait Company: 410-411
currency: 516
Curtis Falls Track: 252
customs regulations: 511

D

Daily Telegraph Building: 226
dance: 504-505
Dargaville: 127-128
demographics: 503
Denniston: 390-391
Devils Punchbowl Waterfall: 368
Devonport: 45, 47
Diamond Harbour: 361
Divide, The: 472
dolphin encounters: 109-110, 161, 320, 365-366
Domain, The: 41-42,
Donut Island: 158-159
Doubtful Sound: 476
Doubtless Bay: 117-118
Dove-Myer Robinson Park: 43-44
Dowse Art Museum: 294
Driving Creek Railway & Pottery: 153-154

Dunedin: 449-457; maps 450, 452
Dunedin Chinese Garden: 453
Dunedin Public Art Gallery: 450-451
Dunedin Railway Station: 451
Dunedin Study: 454
Dunes Trail: 213
Dune Walk: 410
Durie Hill Elevator: 256
Dust and Rust: 342

E

Earnslaw Burn: 431-432
East Cape: 213, 216-217; map 214-215
East Cape Lighthouse: 217
East Coast Museum of Technology: 218
East Egmont: 252-253
Eastern Southland Art Gallery: 483
Eastwoodhill Arboretum: 218
economy: 502
Eco World: 307
Eden Garden: 46
Eden Park: 52
Edwin Fox Ship and Visitor Centre: 307
Eglington Valley: 472
Egmont National Park: 251-253
E. Hayes and Sons: 480-481
Elms Mission House and Gardens: 161
Elvy Waterfalls Track: 314
embassies and consulates: 511
environmental issues: 494-495
Evening Cove: 488
Ewelme Cottage: 43

F

Farewell Spit: 338-339
Far North Regional Museum: 118
fauna: 496-497
Fenton Library building: 444
Fern Gully: 488
Ferry Building: 40, 44
ferry travel: 509
festivals: *see specific place*
Fiordland and Southland: 460-491; map 462-463
Fiordland National Park: 28, 470-476
First Church of Otago: 452
fish/fishing: 512; *see specific place*
Fitzroy Seaside Park: 247
Flagstaff Hill: 106
flightseeing: 111, 185-186, 196, 205, 378-379, 404-405, 408, 424, 442, 465-466, 475
flora: 495-496
Footwhistle Cave: 146
Forgotten World Highway: 253
Fortune Theatre: 454
Founders Heritage Park: 324
Four Sisters Loop: 126
Foveaux Walkway: 485
Fox Glacier: 27, 405, 407-409
Fox Glacier/Te Moeka O Tuawe Valley Walk: 408
Fox River Cave Walk: 393
Fox Village: 409
Franz Josef Glacier: 27, 403-407
Frasers Beach Track: 475
Frying Pan Lake: 179
Fyffe House: 319

G

Gates of Haast: 412
Gemstone Beach: 479
geography: 493
Giant Circuit: 235
Gillespie Pass: 442
Gisborne: 218-222; map 219
Glencoe Walk: 378
Glenorchy: 430-432
Glenorchy Lagoon Walkway: 431
Globe, The (Dunedin): 454
Globe Theatrette: 230
Glowworm Dell: 398
glowworms: 93, 103, 144-146, 147, 398, 465, 477
Goat Island Marine Reserve: 86
Golden Bay: 335-339
Golden Bay Machinery & Early Settlers Museum: 337
Golden Bay Museum: 335
Goldfields Mining Centre: 443
Gore: 483
government: 502
Governors Bush Walk: 378
Govett-Brewster Art Gallery: 243, 245
Great Barrier Island: 81-82
Great Walks: 19, 32, 204, 224, 259, 331, 339, 431, 466, 470, 489, 512
Great War Exhibition: 272
greenstone: 396
Greymouth: 395-398; map 395
Gumdiggers Park: 120
Gunn, Davey: 472

H

Haast: 411-413
Haast Pass: 411-412
Haast Pass Highway: 443
Haast Pass Lookout Track: 412
Hahei: 157-158
Hakarimata Reserve: 136
Hamilton: 134-140; map 135
Hamilton City River Walk: 136
Hamilton Gardens: 134, 136
Hamurana Springs Recreation Reserve: 183

hang gliding: 375, 423-424
Hanmer Forest: 362
Hanmer Springs: 362-364
Haruru Falls: 109
Harwoods Hole: 335
Hastings: 233-234
Hatea Loop Walk: 97
Hauraki Gulf: 16, 38, 78-82
Hauraki Rail Trail: 151
Havelock: 313-315
Havelock North: 234-236
Hawera: 255
Hawera Water Tower: 255
Hawke's Bay: 18, 226-237; map 214-215
health and safety: 515
Heaphy Track: 339
Hell's Gate: 180-181
Heritage Trail: 481
Hibiscus Coast Highway: 92
hiking/backpacking: 29, 152, 202-203, 377, 436, 441, 512; see also Great Walks
Hillary Trail: 83
Hinau Track: 321
Hinerau Walk: 225
history: 498-501
History House Museum: 395
Hobbiton: 30, 149-150
Hobbit, The: 30-31, 149-150, 277, 430
Hokianga Harbour: 124
Hokitika: 398-401; map 399
Hokitika Beach: 398-399
Hokitika Gorge: 399-400
Hokitika Museum: 398
Hokonui Moonshine Museum: 483
holiday parks: see camping
Hollyford Track: 472
Homer Tunnel: 473
Honeycomb Hill Caves: 391
Hooker Valley Track: 378
Horeke: 124-125
horseback riding: 102, 290, 339, 372-373, 393, 422, 431
hot springs: 143, 177-181, 372
Hot Water Beach: 157, 181
Huka Falls: 192
Hump Ridge Track: 478-479
Hurworth Cottage: 245
Hutt River Trail: 294
Hutt Valley: 293-295

IJ

Inland Scenic Route 72: 370-371
Inland Track: 333
International Antarctic Centre: 354
Invercargill: 480-482, 484; map 481
Invincible Gold Mine Track: 431
Isaac Theatre Royal: 356
itineraries: 24-28
Jackson Bay: 413
jade: 396
Jens Hansen: 31, 325
jet-boating: 27, 29, 49, 194-195, 363, 422-423, 431, 442, 512
Judges Bay: 44, 47

K

Kahikatea Forest Loop Walk: 410
Kahurangi National Park: 339
Kai Iwi Lakes: 127
Kaikoura: 26, 319-323
Kaikoura Canyon: 322
Kaikoura Coast Track: 321
Kaikoura Museum: 319
Kaikoura Peninsula Walkway: 321
Kaikoura Quake: 321
Kaitaia: 116, 118-119
Kaiteriteri: 330
Kaitoke Regional Park: 30-31, 295
Kaka Point: 486
Kamahi Loop Track: 252
Kapiti Coast: 289-293
Kapiti Coast Museum: 292
Kapiti Island: 291-292
Kapuni Loop Track: 253
Karamea: 339, 391-392
Karangahake Gorge: 160
Karikari Peninsula: 117-118
Ka Roimata o Hine Hukatere Walk: 404
Katherine Mansfield House and Garden: 272
Kauri Coast: 124-128
Kauri Loop Track: 136
Kauri Museum: 128
Kawakawa: 103, 105
Kawarau Bridge: 421
Kawhia: 143-144
Kawiti Caves: 103
kayaking/canoeing: Auckland 49, 86, 513; Bay of Plenty 162, 164; Christchurch and Canterbury 366, 378; Marlborough and Nelson 312, 320, 322; Northland 110, 117; Queenstown and Otago 431; Rotorua 182-183, 195
Kelly Tariton's Sea Life Aquarium: 44
Kenepuru Sound: 313
Kepler Track: 466-467
Kerikeri: 114-116
Kerikeri Mission Station: 114
Kerr Bay: 340
Key Summit Track: 472
Kinder House: 43
King Domain Walk: 395
Kingsland: 45
Kiritehere Beach: 143-144

Kitekite Falls: 83
Kiwi Birdlife Park: 419
Kiwi North: 95, 97
Knight's Point: 410
Knoll Ridge: 205
Kohimaramara: 47
Kohukohu: 124
Kororipo Pa: 115
K' Road (Karangahape Road): 25, 38, 55
Kuirau Park: 177

L

Lake Crucible: 442
Lake Ferry: 299
Lake Hanlon: 391
Lake Hauroko: 477-478
Lake Hauroko Track: 478
Lake Kaniere Scenic Preserve: 400
Lake Manapouri: 474
Lake Matheson: 409
Lake Moeraki: 410
Lake Rotomahana: 180
Lake Rotopounamu: 199
Lake Rotoroa: 340
Lakes District Museum: 433
Lake Tarawera Hot Springs: 181
Lake Taupo: 25, 28, 29, 191-196
Lake Taupo Museum: 191
Lake Tekapo: 27, 372-374
Lake Waikaremoana: 224-226
Lake Waikaremoana Great Walk: 224
Lake Wainamu: 83
Landis Pass: 374
language: 503-504
Larnach Castle: 457
Leigh: 86
LGBT travelers: 517
lighthouses: 122, 217, 254, 294, 299, 364-365, 387, 486
Lion Rock: 83
Lord of the Rings, The (film sites): 30-31, 149-150, 202, 277, 294, 295, 299, 325, 430, 440, 465, 493
Lost Gypsy Gallery: 487
Lost Spring: 156
Lou's Lookout: 225
Lower Hollyford Road: 471-473
Lower Hutt: 294
Lye, Len: 246
Lyttelton: 361-362

M

Makarora: 442-443
Manapouri: 474-476
Mangapurua Track: 260
Mangarongapu Cave: 145-146
Mangawhai: 92
Mangawhai Heads: 92
Mangawhero Forest Walk: 208
Mangonui: 116, 117
Manu Bay: 141
Maori Cultural Performance: 42
Maori culture: 14, 31, 503
Maori Rock Carvings: 31
maps: 517
Mapua: 26, 329
Mapua Wharf: 328
Maraetai: 84
Marahau: 330-331
Marlborough: 18, 315-319
Marlborough and Nelson: 302-343; map 304-305
Marlborough Museum: 316
Marlborough Sounds: 26, 310-315
Martinborough: 297-298
Masterton: 295-297
Mataatua Wharenui: 31, 167-168
Matakana: 85-86
Matakohe: 128
Matamata: 149-150
Matapouri: 102
Matauri Bay: 117
Matiu/Somes Island: 278
Maukituki Valley: 440-442
Maungawhau: 45
Mavora Lakes: 469-470
McKenzie District: 27, 372-375
McLaren Falls Park: 162
measurements: 517
medical services: 515
Mercury Bay Museum: 156
Mermaid Pools: 102
Meteor: 136
Michael Fowler Centre: 280
Middle-Earth (Tolkien sights): 30-31, 149-150, 202, 277, 288, 294, 295, 299, 325, 430, 440, 465, 493
Milford Sound: 13, 28, 473-474
Milford Track: 470-471
Mine Bay: 25, 191
Mirror Lakes: 472
Mission Bay: 45
Mission Bay Beach: 47
Mitre Peak: 473
Moa Brewery: 316-317
Moeraki Boulders: 449
money: 516
Monro Beach Walk: 410
Monument Track: 475
Motorcycle Mecca: 480
Motuara Island: 311-312
Motueka: 329-330, 339
Motuihe Island: 82
Motutapu Island: 80-81

INDEX

Motu Trails: 213
Mountains to Sea Great Ride: 208, 260
Mount Aspiring National Park: 440-443; map 441
Mount Cook Village: 27
Mount Eden: 38, 45, 45-47
Mount Hot Pools: 164
Mount Hutt: 370-371
Mount Iron: 436
Mount John: 27, 372
Mount Karioi: 141-142
Mount Manaia: 98
Mount Maunganui: 164-166; map 165
Mount Parihaka: 97
Mount Taranaki: 29, 253
Mount, The: 164
Mount Victoria: 26, 30, 274-275
Moutohora Island: 170
Mt. Fyffe: 321
MTG Hawke's Bay Museum: 228
Mt. Isobel Track: 362
Murawai Beach: 83
Murchison: 339, 342
Murchison Museum: 342
Museum of Aviation: 290
Museum of New Zealand Te Papa Tongarewa: 22, 26, 270-271
Museum of Transport and Technology: 45
music and dance: 504-505

N

Napier: 226-233; map 227
Napier Municipal Theatre: 230
Napier Prison: 228-229
National Aquarium of New Zealand: 228
National Kiwi Centre: 399
national parks: Abel Tasman 331-334; Aoraki/Mount Cook 376-380; Arthur's Pass 367-371; Egmont 251-253; Fiordland 470-476; Kahurangi 339; Mount Aspiring 440-443; Nelson Lakes 340-342; Paparoa 392-394; Tongariro 202-209; Westland Tai Poutini 403-411; Whanganui 259-261
National Park Village: 207
National Tobacco Company Building: 226
National Transport Toy Museum: 435
Natural Flames: 342
Nature Walk (Egmont): 251
Nelson: 31, 324-328; maps 325, 326
Nelson Lakes National Park: 340-342; map 340
Nelson Provincial Museum: 324
Nevis Bungee: 28, 421
New Brighton: 354
New Chums Beach: 155
New Plymouth: 243-250; map 244
New Plymouth Coastal Walkway: 246
New Zealand Cycle Trail: 27, 512
New Zealand Maritime Museum: 40-41
New Zealand Opera: 57, 280
New Zealand Portrait Gallery: 272
New Zealand Royal Ballet: 280
New Zealand Rugby Museum: 262
New Zealand Sports Hall of Fame: 451
New Zealand Symphony Orchestra: 57, 280
Ngarua Caves: 335
Ngarunui (Ocean) Beach: 140
Ngatoro Loop: 251
Nga Tupuwae o Toi: 168
Ngauruhoe Peak: 202
Ngawi: 299
Ngu Manu Nature Reserve: 292
Ninety Mile Beach: 120-121
North Egmont: 251-252
Northern Walkway: 278
North Head Historic Military Site: 47
North Island: 33-299; map 2-3
Northland: 28, 87-128; map 90-91
Nugget Point: 486

O

Oakura: 254
Oamaru: 446-449
Oamaru Blue Penguin Colony: 446
Octagon, The: 449
Ogo: 184
Ohakune: 207-209
Okarito: 402
Old Coach Road: 208
Old Ghost Road: 388
Old St. Paul's: 274
Olveston House: 451
Omaka Aviation Heritage Centre: 316
Omapere: 125-126
Omarama: 374-375
Omorehu waterfall: 260
One Tree Hill: 46
Oparara Basin: 391
Opera House: 280
Opononi: 125-126
Opotiki: 213
Opua: 105
Opunake: 254-255
Opunake Mural Trail: 254
Orakei: 44
Orakei Korako: 193-194
Orana Wildlife Park: 354
Orewa: 85
Oriental Bay: 277
Otago: 29, 414-459; map 416-417
Otago Central Rail Trail: 27, 445-446
Otago Museum: 449-450
Otago Peninsula: 457-459; map 457
Otaki: 293

Otari-Wilton's Bush: 276
Otorohanga Kiwi House: 147
Otumuheke Stream: 193
Owaka: 486
Oyster Cliffs: 260

P

packing tips: 516
Paekakariki: 289-290
Paekakariki Escarpment Trail: 289
Paekakariki Railway Museum: 289
Paeroa: 160
Paiha: 107-114
Paihia: 25
Palmerston North: 262-264; map 263
Pancake Rocks: 392-393
Papakorito Falls: 225
Papamoa: 166-167
Paparoa National Park: 392-394; map 394
Papatowai: 487
Paradise Valley Springs: 177
paragliding: 423-424
Paraparaumu: 290-291
parasailing: 111, 182
Paritutu Rock: 246
parks and gardens: Auckland 38, 41-42, 43-45, 46, 85; Fiordland and Southland 480; Rotorua 177; Taranaki and Whanganui 245; Wellington and Wairarapa 295
Parliament buildings: 274
Parnell: 38, 42-44
Parnell Baths: 49
Parnell Rose Gardens: 44
Parry Kauri Park: 85
passports: 23, 511
Pataka Art + Museum: 289
Patuaua South Track: 98
Patuna Chasm: 298-299
Patuna Farm: 298
Pauranui: 158
Pearl Harbour-Circle Track: 475
Pearl Harbour to Hope Arm Track: 475
Peel Forest: 371
Pelorus Bridge Scenic Reserve: 313-314
Pelorus Sound: 313
Pencarrow Lighthouse: 294-295
Penguin Place: 458
Petone: 293-294
Petone Settlers Museum: 293
Picton: 307-310
Picton Heritage Museum: 307
Piha: 83
Pihea Beach: 45
Pinnacles, The: 29, 152
Pipiriki: 259, 261
Piwakawaka Loop: 234
planning tips: 20-23
plants: 495-496
Pohara: 337
Pohutukawa Coast: 84
political parties: 502-503
Polynesian Spa: 184-185
Pompallier Mission: 106
Ponsonby: 25, 38, 44, 45
Poor Knights Islands: 101-102
Porirua: 289
Porpoise Bay: 487-488
Port Jackson: 155
Promenade, The: 51
Pukaka Mount Bruce National Wildlife Centre: 296
Puke Ariki: 243
Pukeiti: 245
Pukekura Park and Brooklands: 245
Punting on the River Avon: 354-355
Purakaunui Falls: 487
Putangirua Pinnacles: 299
Puzzling World: 435-436

Q

Q Theatre: 57
Quail Island: 361
Quake City: 352
Queen Charlotte Sound: 311-313
Queen Charlotte Track: 26, 27, 311
Queen Elizabeth Park (Masterton): 295
Queen Elizabeth Park (Paekakariki): 289
Queens Park: 480
Queenstown: 16, 27-28, 28, 29, 419-430; maps 420, 422
Queenstown and Otago: 414-459; map 416-417
Queenstown Bike Park: 422
Queenstown Hill Walkway: 421
Queenstown Trail: 421
Queen Street: 24, 38, 40

R

Rabbit Island: 328
rafting: 29, 146, 182, 200, 343, 371, 423
Raglan: 25, 29, 140-143
Raglan Museum: 140
Raglan Old School Arts Centre: 140
Rainbow Springs Nature Park: 175, 177
Rakiura Museum: 488
Rakiura Track: 489
Ranfurly: 444-445
Rangitata Gorge: 371
Rangitoto: 47
Rangitoto Island: 80
Rawene: 125
recreation: 28-29, 512-513
Red Rocks Reserve: 278
Regent Theatre: 454

Remarkables, the: 424
rental cars: 510
Renwick: 318-319
Rere Rockslide: 218
resources: 518-523
Rewa's Village: 115
Riccarton House: 352
Ride the Golden Mile: 318
Ridge Track: 203
Rimutaka Cycle Trail: 294
Rimutaka Forest Park: 295
Ripiro Beach: 128
Rippon Vineyard: 436
Riverlea: 137
Riverton: 479
Roakuri Walk: 147
Roaring Billy Falls: 412
Roberts Point Track: 404
Rob Roy Glacier: 29, 441
Ross: 401
Rotoroa Island: 82
Rotorua: 25, 28, 29, 175-191; maps 176, 186
Rotorua and the Volcanic Heartland: 171-209; map 174
Rotorua Museum: 175
Round the Mountain Track: 204
Routeburn Track: 432
Royal Albatross Centre: 457-458
Royal New Zealand Ballet: 57
Roy's Peak Track: 29, 436
Ruakuri Cave: 145
Ruapehu Peak: 29, 202, 204
Ruapekapeka Pa: 102
Ruapuke Beach: 140
Rum Races: 48
Russell: 105-107
Russell Museum: 105-106
Rutherford's Den: 349

S

safety: 515
sandboarding: 120
Sandfly Bay: 458
Sarjeant Gallery Te Whare o Rehua: 256
scenic drives: 154, 367-368, 370-371, 411, 477-479
Scorching Bay: 277
scuba diving/snorkeling: 513
Sentinel Beach: 47
Sentinel Rock: 404
Shag Point: 449
Shakespear Regional Park: 85
Shantytown: 395
Ship Creek: 410
Sir Edmund Hillary Alpine Centre: 376
Skipper's Canyon: 423
Sky City: 40
skydiving: 28, 196, 405, 408, 423
Sky Jump: 40
Skyline Gondola: 419
Skyline Rotorua: 175
Sky Tower: 25, 38, 40, 45, 50
Sky Walk: 40
Slope Point: 488
Smoothwater Bay Track: 413
Snow Farm: 437
Soul Bar & Bistro: 24, 45, 63
South Canterbury Museum: 381
South Coast Track: 478
South Egmont: 253
Southern Scenic Route: 477-479
Southern Walkway: 278
South Island: 29, 301-491; map 4-5
Southward Car Museum: 290
Space Place: 275-276
spas: 247
spectator sports: 52, 513
Speights Brewery: 453
Split Apple Rock: 330
Staglands Wildlife Reserve: 295
Stardome Observatory and Planetarium: 46-47
St. Arnaud: 340
St. Bathans: 444
St. Benedict's Caverns: 147
Steampunk HQ: 447
Stewart Island: 488-491
St. Heliers: 47
Stirling Point: 484-485
St. James Theatre: 280
St. Mary's Church (Auckland): 43
St. Mary's Church of Upokongaro: 260
St. Paul's Rock: 117
Stratford: 252-253
Sugar Club: 25, 40, 45
Sugar Loaf Islands: 246
Summit Track: 251
Sumner: 354
Sunset Point: 399
Surf Highway: 254
surfing: 29, 513; Auckland 49; Bay of Plenty 140-141, 159, 164; Christchurch and Canterbury 354; East Cape and Hawke's Bay 220; Taranaki and Whanganui 247, 254; West Coast 388
Suter Art Gallery: 324-325
Sutherland Falls: 470
Swingbridge Adventure and Heritage Park: 343

TU

Taharoa Lake: 127
Taieri Gorge Rail Journey: 451-452
Tairawhiti Museum: 218
Tairua: 158
Takaka: 335-337, 339

Takaka Hill: 335
Takapuna: 47
Tamaki Maori Village: 25, 31, 177-178
Tane Mahuta: 126
Tapeka Point Reserve: 106
Ta Puia Hot Springs: 143
Taranaki: 29, 253
Taranaki and Whanganui: 238-264; map 240-241
Taranaki Cathedral Church of St. Mary: 245
Taranaki Falls Trail: 203
Tarawera Trail: 181
Tasman Glacier: 29, 377
Tasman's Great Taste Trail: 27, 328-329
Taumarunui: 259, 261
Taupo: 191-199; maps 192, 194
Tauranga: 160-164; map 165
Tauranga Art Gallery: 160
Tauranga Bay: 386-387
Tawa Walk: 314
Tawhiti Museum: 255
Tawhitokino Beach: 84
Te Aha Ari Cycle Trail: 184
Te Ana Maori Rock Art Centre: 31, 380-381
Te Anau: 28, 465-469; map 466
Te Anau Bird Sanctuary: 465
Te Anau Glowworm Caves: 465
Te Araroa: 217
Te Araroa Trail: 123, 289
Te Hana: 92
Te Hana Te Ao Marama Cultural Centre: 92
Te Hikoi: Southern Journey: 479
Te Kaha: 216
Tekapo Springs: 372
Te Kongahu Museum: 25, 108
Te Koputu a te whanga a Toi: 168
Te Manawa: 262
Te Mata Peak: 234-235, 236
Te Matua Ngahere Walk: 126
Te Papa Museum: 22, 26, 270-271
Te Rewa Rewa Bridge: 245
Te Urewera: 223-226
Te Waikoropupu Springs: 335
Te Waimate Mission: 115
Te Wairoa Buried Village: 181
Te Waka Huia O Mohua: 335
Te Weheka Walkway/Cycleway: 408
Thames: 151-153
That Tanaka Tree: 434-435
309 Road: 154
Thunder Creek Falls: 412
Tiki Trail: 421
Timaru: 380-382; map 381
Timaru Botanic Gardens: 382
Timber Trail: 195
Tiritiri Matangi Island: 81
Titahi Bay: 289
Toitu Otago Settlers Museum: 450
Tokaanu Thermal Pools: 199
Tokomaru Bay: 217
Tolaga Bay: 217
Tolkien, J. R. R.: see *Hobbit, The; Lord of the Rings, The;* Middle-Earth
Tongariro Alpine Crossing: 25, 29, 30, 202-203
Tongariro National Park: 25, 30, 202-209; map 204
Tongariro National Trout Centre: 199
Tongariro Northern Circuit: 203-204
Tongariro Peak: 202
Tongariro River Track: 200
Tongariro River Trail: 199
Totara Walk: 314
tourism offices: 516
train travel: 508
Transitional Cathedral: 352
transportation: 507-510
TranzAlpine: 18, 360
Travers-Sabine Circuit: 340-341
Treaty House: 108
Treaty of Waitangi: 108
Treble Cone: 437
Tree Trunk Gorge: 200
Trounson Kauri Park: 127
Truman Track: 393
TSB Arena: 281
TSS *Earnslaw* Steamship: 425
Tuatapere: 478-479
Tui Brewery: 296-297
Tupare: 245-246
Turangi: 199-202
Turoa: 205
Tutukaka: 100-101
Tutukaka Coast: 100-103
Tutukaka Headland Walkway: 100
Twin Coast Cycle Trail: 105
Twizel: 374

VWXYZ

Ulva Island: 488
University of Canterbury Mount John University Observatory: 372
Upper Hutt: 295
Vic, The: 58
Victorian Precinct: 447
Virgin Mary statue: 290
visas: 23, 511
visual arts: 504
Waiatoto River Safari: 411
Waiau River: 467
Waihau Bay: 216
Waiheke Island: 24-25, 45, 79-80
Waihi: 159-160
Waihi Beach: 159-160
Waikanae: 292-293

Waikato: 30, 134-150; map 139
Waikato, Bay of Plenty, and The Coromandel: 129-170; map 132-133
Waikato Museum: 134
Waikere Lake: 127
Waikite Valley Thermal Pools: 185
Waimangu Volcanic Valley: 179-180
Waimarie, the: 257
Waioeka Gorge: 216
Wai-O-Tapu: 17, 25, 180
Waipoua Forest: 126-127
Waipu: 92-94
Waipu Caves: 93-94
Waipu Museum: 93
Wairakei Terraces: 193
Wairarapa: 295-299
Wairere Boulders: 124-125
Wairere Falls: 150, 181
Wairoa: 223-224
Wairoa Museum: 223
Waitakere Ranges: 38, 45, 82-84
Waitaki Valley: 374
Waitangi Treaty Grounds: 25, 31, 107-109
Waitemata Harbour: 40
Waiti Bay: 84
Waitomo: 144-148
Waitomo Caves: 14, 25, 29, 144-147
Waitomo Discovery Centre: 144
Waitomo Glowworm Cave: 144-145
Waitomo Walkway: 147
walks: 32, 512, *see also* hiking and backpacking; Great Walks; *specific place*
Wanaka: 29, 434-440; map 435
Warbirds and Wheels: 435
Warkworth: 85
War Memorial Tower: 257
waterfalls: 97, 142, 150, 192, 487
Waterfall Track: 162, 362
Waterfront Cycle Path: 51
Water Race Walkway: 401
water sports: 29, 512-513
Waterworks, The: 154
weather: 493-494
weights and measures: 517
Wellington: 18, 25-26, 30-31, 270-288; maps 271, 273
Wellington and Wairarapa: 265-299; map 268-269
Wellington Cable Car: 26, 275
Wellington City Gallery: 272
Wellington Museum: 271-272
Wellington Tramway Museum: 289
West Coast: 29, 383-413; map 386-387
West Coast Treetop Walkway and Café: 399
West Coast Wilderness Trail: 395
West Coast Wildlife Centre: 403
Western Park: 44
Western Springs: 44-45, 52
Western Springs Park: 44-45
Westland Tai Poutini National Park: 403-411
Westpac Stadium: 281
Westport: 386-390
Weta Cave and Workshop: 31, 277
Whakapapa: 205
Whakapapa Village: 205-207
Whakarewarewa Forest: 183-184
Whakarewarewa Thermal Reserve: 178-179
Whakarewarewa Thermal Village: 179
Whakatane: 167-169
Whale Bay: 102, 140
Whananaki: 102-103
Whanarua Bay: 216
Whangamata: 158-159
Whanganui: 256-259; map 257
Whanganui A Hei Marine Reserve: 157
Whanganui Journey: 259-260
Whanganui National Park: 259-261
Whanganui Regional Museum: 256
Whanganui River: 258, 261
Whanganui River Road: 260
Whangapoua: 155
Whangarei: 95-100; map 96
Whangarei Art Museum: 95
Whangarei Falls: 97
Whangarei Heads: 98
Whangarei Quarry Gardens: 95
Whangaroa: 116
Whangaroa Harbour: 117
Whare Runanga: 108
Wharkai-Te Koua Walk: 413
Whataroa: 401-402
Whenuakura (Donut) Island: 158-159
whitebait: 410-411
White Heron Sanctuary: 401-402
White Island: 169-170
Whitianga: 156-157
wildlife refuges: 44, 170, 488
wildlife/wildlife-watching: 15, 25, 496-497
Wildwoods Festival: 401
Wilkies Pools Loop Track: 253
wine/wineries: 18, 26, 229, 315-316
Wingspan National Bird of Prey Centre: 177
Wintergarden: 41, 45
winter sports: 204-205, 363, 369, 370-371, 424, 436, 445
Wither Hills Farm Park: 317
Wool Shed Museum: 296
World of Wearable Art and Classic Car Museum: 324
Writers Walk: 278
Zealandia: 26, 276-277
Zealong: 136
zip lining: 28, 175, 182, 343, 419, 421
zoos/animal parks: 177, 354
zorbing: 29, 184

List of Maps

Front Maps
North Island: 2–3
South Island: 4–5

Discover New Zealand
chapter divisions map: 21

Auckland
Auckland: 37
Downtown Auckland: 39
Auckland Suburbs: 41

Northland
Northland: 90–91
Whangarei: 96
Bay of Islands: 104

Waikato, Bay of Plenty, and The Coromandel
Waikato, Bay of Plenty, and The Coromandel: 132–133
Hamilton: 135
Raglan and Vicinity: 141
Coromandel Peninsula: 152
Bay of Plenty: 161
Tauranga and Mount Maunganui: 165

Rotorua and the Volcanic Heartland
Rotorua and the Volcanic Heartland: 174
Rotorua: 176
Vicinity of Rotorua: 186
Taupo: 192
Taupo and Vicinity: 194
Tongariro National Park: 204

East Cape and Hawke's Bay
East Cape and Hawke's Bay: 214–215
Gisborne: 219
Napier: 227

Taranaki and Whanganui
Taranaki and Whanganui: 240–241
New Plymouth: 244
Whanganui: 257
Downtown Palmerston North: 263

Wellington and Wairarapa
Wellington and Wairarapa: 268–269
Wellington: 271
Downtown Wellington: 273

Marlborough and Nelson
Marlborough and Nelson: 304–305
Nelson: 325
Downtown Nelson: 326
Abel Tasman National Park: 332
Nelson Lakes National Park: 340

Christchurch and Canterbury
Christchurch and Canterbury: 346–347
Christchurch: 350–351
Downtown Christchurch: 353
Akaroa and the Banks Peninsula: 365
Arthur's Pass National Park: 368
Aoraki/Mount Cook Village: 377
Timaru: 381

West Coast
West Coast: 386–387
Paparoa National Park: 394
Greymouth: 395
Hokitika: 399

Queenstown and Otago
Queenstown and Otago: 416–417
Queenstown: 420
Vicinity of Queenstown: 422
Wanaka: 435
Mount Aspiring National Park: 441
Dunedin: 450
Downtown Dunedin: 452
Otago Peninsula: 457

Fiordland and Southland
Fiordland and Southland: 462–463
Te Anau: 466
Invercargill: 481

Photo Credits

All photos © Jamie Christian Desplaces except: page 8 © Filedimage | Dreamstime.com; Rusel1981 | Dreamstime.com; Tulipmix | Dreamstime.com; page 9 © Lucidwaters | Dreamstime.com; Dmitryp | Dreamstime.com; Lucidwaters | Dreamstime.com; page 10 © Minyun9260 | Dreamstime.com; page 11 © Haslinda | Dreamstime.com; Lucidwaters | Dreamstime.com; Hellen8 | Dreamstime.com; page 12 © Hellen8 | Dreamstime.com; page 14 © mkoenen/123RF; Kyrien | Dreamstime.com; page 15 © JoshDaniels | Dreamstime.com; page 16 © Dmitryserbin | Dreamstime.com; page 17 © Soranz | Dreamstime.com; page 18 © Hellen8 | Dreamstime.com; Hofmeester | Dreamstime.com; page 19 © Naruedom | Dreamstime.com; page 24 © Lucidwaters | Dreamstime.com; page 28 © Skydive Auckland; page 40 © Mrcmos | Dreamstime.com; page 46 © Totoglenn | Dreamstime.com; page 50 © Lucidwaters | Dreamstime.com; page 53 © Lucidwaters | Dreamstime.com; page 58 © Daiviet | Dreamstime.com; page 61 © Lucidwaters | Dreamstime.com; page 97 © Tomkli | Dreamstime.com; page 101 © Blagov58 | Dreamstime.com; page 105 © Curiosopl | Dreamstime.com; page 114 © Ruthie44 | Dreamstime.com; page 145 © www.waitomo.co.nz; page 146 © Thomaswong1990 | Dreamstime.com; page 149 © Weltreisendertj | Dreamstime.com; page 151 © Rickychung10 | Dreamstime.com; page 157 © Naruedom | Dreamstime.com; page 167 © Lucidwaters | Dreamstime.com; page 170 © Mlw450 | Dreamstime.com; page 180 © Waiotapu Thermal Wonderland; page 182 © Mauriehill | Dreamstime.com; page 184 © Mail2355 | Dreamstime.com; page 185 © Adwo | Dreamstime.com; page 200 © Steveprorak | Dreamstime.com; page 203 © Protonyzhao | Dreamstime.com; page 210 © Mead Norton Photography; page 224 © Blagov58 | Dreamstime.com; page 235 © Blagov58 | Dreamstime.com; page 237 © Travelling-light | Dreamstime.com; page 252 © Pstedrak | Dreamstime.com; page 256 © Brackishnewzealand | Dreamstime.com; page 260 © Blagov58 | Dreamstime.com; page 262 © Lucidwaters | Dreamstime.com; page 270 © Lucidwaters | Dreamstime.com; page 291 © Creativenature1 | Dreamstime.com; page 297 © Simonharrycollins | Dreamstime.com; page 331 © Jlazouphoto | Dreamstime.com; page 336 © Nigelspiers | Dreamstime.com; page 344 © Lucidwaters | Dreamstime.com; page 352 © Lucidwaters | Dreamstime.com; page 366 © Karlosxii | Dreamstime.com; page 369 © Tbures | Dreamstime.com; page 375 © Kovgabor79 | Dreamstime.com; page 376 © Hdamke | Dreamstime.com; page 379 © Pausethescene | Dreamstime.com; page 396 © Creativefire | Dreamstime.com; page 402 © Bobhilscher | Dreamstime.com; page 404 © Aiaikawa | Dreamstime.com; page 407 © Thomaslusth | Dreamstime.com; page 411 © Mkojot | Dreamstime.com; page 431 © Marconicouto | Dreamstime.com; page 434 © Maonakub | Dreamstime.com; page 440 © Kjwells86 | Dreamstime.com; page 445 © Jessicaknaupe | Dreamstime.com; page 446 © Oamaru Blue Penguin Colony; page 451 © Grace5648 | Dreamstime.com; page 453 © Grace5648 | Dreamstime.com; page 458 © Kiravolkov | Dreamstime.com; page 460 © Fyletto | Dreamstime.com; page 467 © Naruedom | Dreamstime.com; page 471 © Rue Flaherty; page 473 © Danielaphotography | Dreamstime.com; page 476 © Adwo | Dreamstime.com; page 480 © Yoavsinai | Dreamstime.com; page 489 © Lizcoughlan | Dreamstime.com.

MOON NEW ZEALAND

Avalon Travel
Hachette Book Group
1700 Fourth Street
Berkeley, CA 94710, USA
www.moon.com

Editor: Sabrina Young
Series Manager: Kathryn Ettinger
Copy Editor: Christopher Church
Production and Graphics Coordinator: Rue Flaherty
Cover Design: Faceout Studios, Charles Brock
Interior Design: Domini Dragoone
Moon Logo: Tim McGrath
Map Editor: Kat Bennett
Cartographers: Karin Dahl, Kat Bennett
Proofreader: Caroline Trefler
Indexer: Greg Jewett

ISBN-13: 978-1-63121-709-8

Printing History
1st Edition — December 2018
5 4 3 2 1

Front cover photo: Hooker Valley Track © Patrick Imrutai Photography/Getty Images

Back cover photo: Routeburn Track © Naruedom Yaempongsa | Dreamstime.com

Printed in China by RR Donnelley